rtisement   i

 The Church of Scotland

Our Stewardship Consultants are here to help your congregation increase

GIVING and
INVOLV

D1407258

Contact the Stewardship and Fina
The Church of Scotland, 121 George Street, Edinburgh, EH2 4YN
Tel: 0131 225 5722 ext 273   **Email:** sfadmin@cofscotland

 The Church of Scotland   www.churchofscotland.org.uk
Stewardship and Finance Department   Scottish National Charity Number: SC011353

Stained Glass Artists
Contemporary windows
Conservation of glass
Church, Historic Public

We have moved!!!

This has been an exciting year for Rainbow Glass Studio. We have expanded into new premises and welcomed 4 new members of staff.

New website to follow later in year.

14 Shaw Road | Prestwick | KA9 2LN | 01292 474279
info@rainbowglass.biz www.rainbowglass.biz

Accredited Artists of Church of Scotland. ICON Accredited Director

Christian Aid/Karen Lobo-Morell

CHRISTIAN AID BELIEVES ITS VISION – AN END TO POVERTY – CAN BECOME A REALITY

We are the agency of the churches. Our role in Scotland is to support and enable local congregations to give, act and pray on issues of global justice.

Christian Aid Scotland is here to help support and resource you. We can:

- provide information about our work with partners overseas
- speak at a Sunday morning service or lead a Bible study
- offer opportunities to get involved with our campaigns in Scotland
- run an event for local churches or help with ideas for local events
- run a youth workshop or youth leader training session
- point you to our wide range of worship, campaigning and fundraising resources.

Stay in touch with Christian Aid Scotland:

- Sign up to to our ezine to receive news and events about what's happening in Scotland, around the UK, and with our partners overseas (to register, email glasgow@christian-aid.org)
- visit our website: christianaid.org.uk/scotland
- like us on Facebook: facebook.com/ChristianAidScotland and follow us on Twitter: @christianaidsco
- call us on **0141 221 7475** or write to Christian Aid, Sycamore House, 290 Bath Street, Glasgow G2 4JR.

Together, we can bring about big change.

Honour the ones who didn't come home.
Help Erskine care for the ones who did.

Erskine has been providing care, accommodation and employment for ex-Service men and women in Scotland since 1916. We depend heavily on the generosity of people like you to continue our valuable work.

To donate, visit www.erskine.org.uk or call free on 0300 123 1203. Or text ERSKINE to 70707 to donate £3.

Texts cost £3 plus network charge. Erskine receives 100% of your donation. Obtain bill payers permission. Customer Care 0844 847 9800. Scottish Charity No. SC006609

CHILDREN OF THE MANSE

A fascinating account of the early years of William Robertson Smith, probably the greatest biblical scholar of 19th century Scotland, these memoirs were written late in life by his sister Alice and remain a classic of their kind.

A new and revised edition:
price £9.99 post free from
The Bellfield Press, 4 Bellfield
Terrace, Edinburgh EH15 2BJ
or email Gordon@gkbenterprises.fsnet.co.uk
www.gkbenterprises.org.uk

The Right Reverend E. Lorna Hood MA BD

MODERATOR

The Church of Scotland
YEAR BOOK
2013/2014

Editor
Douglas Galbraith

Production Editor
Ivor Normand

Published on behalf of
THE CHURCH OF SCOTLAND
by SAINT ANDREW PRESS
121 George Street, Edinburgh EH2 4YN

THE OFFICES OF THE CHURCH

121 George Street
Edinburgh EH2 4YN

Tel: 0131-225 5722
Fax: 0131-220 3113
Website: www.churchofscotland.org.uk/

Office Hours:
Facilities Manager:

Monday–Friday 9:00am–5:00pm
Carole Tait 0131-240 2214

THE COUNCILS OF THE CHURCH

The following five Councils of the Church operate from the Church Offices, 121 George Street, Edinburgh EH2 4YN (Tel: 0131-225 5722):

- The Council of Assembly
- The Church and Society Council
- The Ministries Council
- The Mission and Discipleship Council
- The World Mission Council

E-mail: churchandsociety@cofscotland.org.uk
E-mail: ministries@cofscotland.org.uk
E-mail: mandd@cofscotland.org.uk
Fax: 0131-226 6121
E-mail: world@cofscotland.org.uk

The Social Care Council (CrossReach) operates from Charis House, 47 Milton Road East, Edinburgh EH15 2SR

Tel: 0131-657 2000
Fax: 0131-657 5000
E-mail: info@crossreach.org.uk
Website: www.crossreach.org.uk

SCOTTISH CHARITY NUMBERS

The Church of Scotland: unincorporated Councils and Committees	SC011353
The Church of Scotland General Trustees	SC014574
The Church of Scotland Investors Trust	SC022884
The Church of Scotland Trust	SC020269

(For the Scottish Charity Numbers of congregations, see Section 7)

First published in 2013 by SAINT ANDREW PRESS, 121 George Street, Edinburgh EH2 4YN on behalf of THE CHURCH of SCOTLAND

Copyright © THE CHURCH of SCOTLAND, 2013

ISBN 978 0 86153 801 0

It is the Publisher's policy only to use papers that are natural and recyclable and that have been manufactured from timber grown in renewable, properly managed forests. All of the manufacturing processes of the papers are expected to conform to the environmental regulations of the country of origin.

Acceptance of advertisements for inclusion in the *Church of Scotland Year Book* does not imply endorsement of the goods or services or of any views expressed within the advertisements.

British Library Cataloguing in Publication Data
A catalogue record for this book is available from the British Library.

Printed and bound by Bell and Bain Ltd, Glasgow

QUICK DIRECTORY

A.C.T.S. 01259 216980
Christian Aid London 020 7620 4444
Christian Aid Scotland 0141-221 7475
Church and Society Council 0131-240 2275
Church of Scotland Insurance Co. Ltd 0131-220 4119
Council of Assembly 0131-240 2229
CrossReach 0131-657 2000
Eco-Congregation Scotland 0131-240 2274
Ecumenical Officer 0131-240 2208
Gartmore House 01877 382991
Glasgow Lodging House Mission 0141-552 0285
Iona Community 0141-332 6343
Media Relations Team (Press Office) 0131-240 2204/2268
Old Churches House, Dunblane (Scottish Churches House) 01786 823663
Pension Trustees (E-mail: pensions@cofscotland.org.uk) 0131-240 2255
Place for Hope 07884 580361
Principal Clerk (E-mail: pcoffice@cofscotland.org.uk) 0131-240 2240
Priority Areas Office 0141-248 2905
Safeguarding Service (item 32 in Assembly Committee list) 0131-240 2256
Scottish Churches Parliamentary Office 0131-220 0246
Scottish Storytelling Centre/John Knox House/Netherbow 0131-556 9579
Trust Housing Association Ltd (formerly Kirk Care) 0131-444 4949
Year Book Editor 01592 752403

Pulpit Supply: Fee and Expenses
Details of the current fee and related expenses in respect of Pulpit Supply will be found as the last item in
number 3 (the Ministries Council) on page 12.

**All correspondence regarding the *Year Book* should be sent to
The Editor, *Church of Scotland Year Book*,
Saint Andrew Press, 121 George Street, Edinburgh EH2 4YN
Fax: 0131-220 3113
[E-mail: yearbookeditor@cofscotland.org.uk]**

GENERAL ASSEMBLY OF 2014
The General Assembly of 2014 will convene on
Saturday, 17 May 2014

CONTENTS

FROM THE MODERATOR

As someone who likes numbers and statistics and who enjoys doing Sudoku and other number puzzles, I find the *Year Book* a fascinating book and a wonderful source of information. Every fact and figure you could ever want concerning the Church of Scotland can be found within its pages. Next to the Bible, it is probably the one book that is universally used most days by most ministers and deacons.

However, it is so much more than facts and figures, as behind each statistic is a story of a worshipping congregation and a serving minister and deacon. It is interesting to compare one year's story to the next, seeing how congregations have developed and changed. When the *Year Book* arrives, there is a constant flicking-through of the pages to see the movement of colleagues and friends, accepting a call from where they are on to the next part of their journey. Opening the *Year Book* helps us all to realise just how connected we are to one another, part of the one Church, serving Scotland and beyond.

It is also a quick reference guide for all sorts of information about Procedure in a Vacancy and details of Committees and Conveners, along with whom to contact within the Church Offices.

The importance of keeping the details up to date came home to me last year when my e-mail address changed just too late to be included – and, no matter how often I informed colleagues, the answer was always 'Oh, I just looked up the *Year Book*'.

Checking over the data and statistics is a painstaking task, and our gratitude must go the editor, Douglas Galbraith, and production editor, Ivor Normand.

I am happy to commend the *Year Book 2013/2014* to you and hope that, as you use it, you realise what an indispensable tool it is.

E. Lorna Hood

ON MHODERATOR

Mar thè aig a bheil ùidh ann an àireamhan agus toimhsean agus a tha a' gabhail tlachd ann a bhith a' dèanamh Sudoko agus tòimhseachain eile le figearan, tha an *Leabhar Bliadhnail* dhòmhsa 'na leabhar tarraingeach agus 'na dhòigh mhìorbhaileach air fiosrachadh fhaighinn. Air a dhuilleagan gheibhear a h-uile fiosrachadh agus figear a dh'iarradh tu mu Eaglais na h-Alba. A bharrachd air a' Bhìoball 's e seo an t-aon leabhar a tha a h-uile ministear agus deucon a' cur gu feum a' chuid mhòr den ùine.

Ach tha cus a bharrachd air fiosrachadh agus figearan an seo oir air cùl gach àireamh tha sgeulachd mu adhradh coitheanail agus obair ministeir agus deucoin. Tha e inntinneach a bhith a' coimeas aon bhliadhna ri bliadhna eile, a' coimhead mar a tha coitheanalan a' tighinn air adhart agus ag atharrachadh. Nuair a thig an *Leabhar Bliadhnail* bidh na duilleagan gan tionndadh a dh'fhaicinn mar tha co-obraichean agus càirdean air gluasad, a' gabhail ri gairm on àite anns a bheil iad chun an ath cheum air an turas. Tha a' fosgladh an *Leabhair Bhliadhnail* gar cuideachadh air fad gu bhith a' tuigsinn cho ceangailte agus a tha sinn ri chèile, mar phàirt den aon eaglais, a' dèanamh seirbheis do dh'Alba agus do dh'àiteachan eile.

Tha e cuideachd 'na leabhar-iùil a bheir dhut anns a' mhionaid a h-uile seòrsa fiosrachaidh air na tha ri dhèanamh nuair a tha coitheanal bàn le mion-chunntas air Comataidhean agus Luchd-gairm, agus mar an ceudna cò a bu chòir dhut fios a chur thuca aig Oifis na h-Eaglais.

An-uiridh thuig mi cho cudthromach agus a tha e am fiosrachadh a bhith ceart nuair a dh'atharraich mi seòladh mo phost-dealain dìreach ro-fhadalach airson a chur anns an *Leabhar Bhliadhnail* agus cha robh e gu diofar dè cho tric agus a dh'fhàg mi fios aig co-obraichean, 's e am freagairt a bha aca an còmhnaidh, 'O, cha do rinn mi ach a lorg anns an *Leabhar Bhliadhnail*'.

'S e obair throm a tha ann a bhith a' sgrùdadh dàta agus àireamhan agus tha sinn fo fhiachan mòra don fhear-deasachaidh, Dùbhghlas Mac a' Bhreatnaich, agus an deasaiche-dealbha-chaidh, Iamhar Normand.

Tha mi toilichte *Leabhar Bliadhnail 2013/2014* a mholadh dhuibh agus tha mi an dòchas mar a tha sibh ga chleachdadh gun tuig sibh cho do-sheachainte feumail agus a tha e.

E. Lorna Hood

FROM THE EDITOR

One of my secret hobbies is browsing through late nineteenth- and earlier twentieth-century editions of the *Church of Scotland Year Book*. How sad is that?

This, I should say, was not known to Saint Andrew Press when I was invited to take up the task of editorship. It was sheer coincidence – or should I say comeuppance?

But … what you learn! That at least by 1938 there existed a society whose aim was to campaign for women in eldership and ministry; that Glasgow Royal Infirmary was supported by voluntary contributions; that the largest congregation had 4,546 members and the smallest three; that lantern lectures on the Itu Leper Colony or 'Up the Yangtze to Ichang' cost two shillings to hire (carriage payable both ways); and no local choir association or society-with-a-cause was complete without at least one member of the aristocracy on its notepaper.

And then of course there are the adverts. I am not sure what the manufacturer promising 'safety at the Communion Table' was offering, but there is no mistaking the call to 'let your deaf members hear'. The system involved ten individual 'listening points' round the church with receivers you put to your ear. Not exactly discreet, and definitely not for those who refused to admit they were hard of hearing!

For many years, it was the custom to print articles, historical and practical: a history of the Reformed church; the ins and outs of teinds; the relationship of chapels of ease to *quoad omnia* and *quoad sacra* parishes; how to conduct a Bible class; who was St Kentigern?; sketches of particular parishes; sacramental fast days; non-churchgoing; the educational missions of India; the Church in the mining community. Maybe this is a feature that might be restored. In preparing this edition, it was clear we were still getting to grips with the concept of Ordained Local Ministry, and there were as many ways of dealing with Practising Certificates as there are of skinning the cat.

The first editor (1886) was one J. A. Graham, later Dr Graham of Kalimpong, and Moderator in 1931. Today's editions deviate little from his original design for the book: Assembly, committees, presbyteries and parishes, societies, statistics of communicants and members of organisations. It's striking the way old editions present you not just with facts but also with the *feel* of the Church at a particular time. Lists plus numbers plus turns of phrase combine to open up pictures both of Church and of world, and of how commitment to the Gospel was being played out in different times and circumstances.

And places. One feature, present until the mid-twentieth century, was the sheer space taken up by the listings of the foreign mission 'stations' and their numerous personnel. The roll-call of these now familiar places and Scottish family names year by year brought them as near as the next village. Many names are famous, and a few are still notable in our parishes and universities.

Home or overseas, the Church swims into view in the *Year Books*; but they do far more than show who we *are*. Looked at from another perspective, they show what we *offer*, as does this new volume. In the new age in which we live and witness, it is dawning on us that, out of necessity (or the Spirit's prompting), the future is with the churches together. The *Year Book* proves just how rich the Church of Scotland's offering continues to be, and indeed how valued in the wider Church.

This has been underlined for me recently. In the same week as I took up my prefatory pen, I laid down the convenership of ACTS (Action of Churches Together in Scotland). A rather enjoyable perk had been the invitations to high and holy occasions like the bicentenary of the birth of David Livingstone, the Queen's Diamond Jubilee, and the 400th anniversary of the Authorised Version of the Bible. A feature of these journeys was always to encounter, in crypt, cloister and choir vestry, the Moderator of the day, be it a David Arnott or an Albert Bogle; and it was salutary to be reminded in what respect that office and the Church which its holders represented was held by other churches and bodies.

Mind you, the new convener, the Scottish Episcopal Church nominee Helen Hood, has at the time of writing just attended the service in Westminster Abbey to mark the 60th anniversary of the coronation of Her Majesty the Queen. There also was the Moderator, so recently elected – also a Hood. And thus amid the archbishops, archimandrites, chief rabbis, monseigneurs and other eminences, the Scottish churches this time were represented, as they themselves observed, by a couple of Hoods.

A reminder there, perhaps, that there can be no assumption of strength and superiority in our offering, and that the charisms given to other denominations are now also, particularly in these times, being offered to us, for the good of Church and nation.

Acknowledgements

This *Year Book* would lack much without the considerable contributions made by Dr Roddy MacLeod, the Gaelic editor; Roy Pinkerton for the list of discontinued parish and congregational names; Sandy Gemmill for the congregational statistics; the Rev. Douglas Aitken for letting me raid his webcast of the 2013 Assembly; the Mission and Discipleship Council and the Communications Department; Ann Crawford of Saint Andrew Press; the many who contributed material; the former editor the Rev. Ronald Blakey, always willing to be consulted; and those who made it all into a book – Lawrie Law, and in particular the indefatigable Ivor Normand, production editor.

Douglas Galbraith
July 2013

SECTION 1

Assembly Councils, Committees, Departments and Agencies

[Note: Years, where given, indicate the year of appointment]

1. THE COUNCIL OF ASSEMBLY

The voting members of the Council of Assembly act as the Charity Trustees for the Unincorporated Councils and Committees of the General Assembly: Scottish Charity No. SC011353.

Remit (as amended May 2013)

Introduction
1. The Council of Assembly's main function is to support the Councils and Committees of the Church in seeking to inspire the people of Scotland and beyond with the Good News of Jesus Christ through enthusiastic, worshipping, witnessing, nurturing and serving communities.
2. The Council helps the General Assembly to determine strategy for the Church of Scotland, ensures that the strategic priorities, policies and decisions of the Assembly are implemented effectively and efficiently and supports, resources and nurtures the people of the Church in their work of mission, witness, worship and service.
3. The Council of Assembly is a standing committee of the General Assembly, to which it is directly accountable and to which it reports annually. The General Assembly-appointed members of the Council and the Conveners of the six major Councils are designated as the Charity Trustees of the Unincorporated Councils and Committees of the Church of Scotland (Scottish Charity Number SC011353). The Trustees have 'general control and management of the administration' of the Unincorporated Councils and Committees.
4. The Council has been given authority by the General Assembly to take necessary administrative decisions between General Assemblies and to coordinate, monitor and evaluate the work done by the Councils, Committees and central administrative offices of the Church. The General Assembly has also authorised it to attend to the general interests of the Church in matters which are not covered by the remit of any other Agency.
5. The Senior Management Team exists to support the coordinating and decision-making work of the Council of Assembly and to ensure the efficient implementation of the decisions of it and the General Assembly. The Senior Management Team is accountable to the Council of Assembly, and its minutes are submitted to the Council for information.
6. The Council has committed to displaying in its work and in the behaviour of its members and staff:
    * confidence in God
    * trust in each other
    * servant leadership
    * collaborative working
    * enthusiasm.
7. The Council, while exercising a supervisory role, nonetheless commits to working cooperatively and inclusively with Councils, Committees, Presbyteries, Kirk Sessions and all others in the Church, consulting widely where possible. Having regard to the international, evangelical and catholic nature of the Church, the Council of Assembly is committed to working with other churches, at home and overseas, and to encouraging all Agencies to work ecumenically where possible.

Strategy
1. To encourage vision among the members and the Councils and Committees of the Church.

2. To monitor, evaluate and coordinate the work of the Agencies of the General Assembly within the context of policy determined by the Assembly, encouraging the achievement of objectives and the wise use of resources.
3. To oversee the implementation of the Strategic Framework as from time to time agreed by the General Assembly.
4. To advise the General Assembly on the relative priority of work being undertaken by its various Agencies.
5. To keep under review the central administration of the Church, with particular regard to resolving issues of duplication of resources.
6. To advise the General Assembly on matters of reorganisation and structural change, including adjustments to the membership and remits of relevant Agencies of the General Assembly.
7. To advise and work with the Panel on Review and Reform on its priorities and also on the resourcing and implementation of policy decisions arising from its work.
8. To deal with urgent issues arising between meetings of the General Assembly, provided that (a) these do not fall within the jurisdiction of the Commission of Assembly or of any Presbytery or Kirk Session, (b) they are not of a legislative or judicial nature and (c) any action taken in terms of this clause shall be reported to the next General Assembly.
9. To attend to the general interests of the Church in matters which are not covered by the remit of any other Agency.

Governance
10. To exercise the supervisory function required by the Church's Designated Religious Charity status.
11. To ensure adherence to an approved Code of Conduct by the Charity Trustees of the Unincorporated Councils and Committees and to encourage and supervise compliance with such a Code of all other members of Councils and Committees.
12. To advise, support and oversee compliance by Councils, Committees and Presbyteries in the proper discharge of their duties and responsibilities under charity and accounting legislation.

Finance and Stewardship
13. To oversee the management of the finances of the Unincorporated Councils and Committees, ensuring that Church resources are used wisely and effectively and in accordance with the policies, priorities and strategic objectives of the General Assembly.
14. To set appropriate standards of financial management for the Unincorporated Councils and Committees, and to oversee compliance.
15. To supervise and assist Presbyteries and congregations in adhering to financial standards required by charity law and by Regulations of the General Assembly, and to oversee compliance.
16. To oversee the provision of financial services for the Councils and Committees, Statutory Corporations and other Agencies of the General Assembly.
17. To determine policy in relation to the teaching and promotion of Christian stewardship throughout the Church.
18. To provide support to Presbyteries and congregations in the promotion of stewardship with a view to generating sufficient income to resource the worship, mission, nurture and service of the Church.
19. To determine policy in relation to Ministries and Mission Contributions from congregations, subject to the approval of Regulations by the General Assembly and to determine with Presbyteries the Ministries and Mission Contributions required annually from congregations.

20. To determine annually the stipend rate, having regard to the recommendation of the Ministries Council, the determination to be made by the voting members of the Council of Assembly with the exception of those members in receipt of either a salary or stipend from the Parish Ministries Fund.

21. To determine the types and rates of expenses which may be claimed by members serving on Councils, Committees and Statutory Corporations.

22. To bring recommendations to the General Assembly concerning the total amount of the Church's Coordinated Budget for the Parish Ministries Fund and the Mission and Renewal Fund for the following financial year, and to determine the allocation of the budget for the Mission and Renewal Fund among the relevant Agencies of the General Assembly and Ecumenical Bodies.

23. To prepare and present to the General Assembly an indicative Rolling Budget and outline Financial Plan for the following five years.

24. To receive and distribute unrestricted legacies and donations among the Agencies of the General Assembly with power to specify the use to which these funds are to be applied.

25. To reallocate, following upon consultation with the Agency or Agencies affected, unrestricted funds held by or on behalf of any of the Agencies of the General Assembly to another Agency or Agencies with power to specify the use to which the same are to be applied.

26. To prepare, approve and submit annually to the General Assembly the audited Annual Report and Financial Statements of the Unincorporated Councils and Committees of the General Assembly.

Property and Contracts

27. To facilitate strategic property planning across the Unincorporated Councils and Committees to ensure that the best use is made of the property portfolio.

28. To consider and decide on proposals from Agencies of the General Assembly to purchase heritable property or any other asset (except investments) valued in excess of £50,000 or to lease any heritable property where the annual rental is greater than £25,000 per annum. No Agency except those referred to in section 31 of this remit shall purchase or lease such property without prior approval from the Council of Assembly.

29. To consider and decide on proposals from Agencies of the General Assembly, except for those referred to in section 31 of this remit, to sell or lease for a period in excess of five years or otherwise dispose of any heritable property, or to sell or otherwise dispose of any asset (except investments) valued above £50,000, held by or on behalf of that Agency. The Council of Assembly shall have power to allocate all or part of the sale or lease proceeds to another Agency or Agencies in terms of sections 22 and 25 of this remit.

30. To consider and decide on proposals from Agencies of the General Assembly to enter into an agreement or contract for receipt of goods or services (with the exception of contracts of employment or those relating to property transactions) with a total actual or potential financial commitment in excess of £50,000. No Agency shall proceed to enter into such an agreement or contract without prior approval from the Council.

31. For the avoidance of doubt, sections 28, 29 and 30 shall not apply to the Church of Scotland General Trustees and the Church of Scotland Housing and Loan Fund for Retired Ministers and Widows and Widowers of Ministers, both of which may deal with heritable property and other assets without the approval of the Council.

Staffing and Management

32. To receive reports from, offer guidance to and issue instructions to Agencies of the General Assembly as required from time to time on matters of management, resourcing, organisation, governance and administration.

33.   To determine staffing and resourcing requirements of Agencies of the General Assembly, including inter-Departmental sharing or transfer of staff, in accordance with policies drawn up by the Council of Assembly in line with priorities approved by the General Assembly, it being declared that the term 'staffing' shall not include those directly employed by the Ministries Council, the Social Care Council or the World Mission Council.
34.   To consult with the relative Councils and Agencies in their appointment of Council Secretaries to the Church and Society, Ministries, Mission and Discipleship, Social Care and World Mission Councils, to appoint the Ecumenical Officer, the Head of Stewardship, the Head of Communications and the Head of Human Resources and Information Technology and to nominate individuals to the General Assembly for appointment to the offices of Principal Clerk of the General Assembly, Depute Clerk of the General Assembly, Secretary to the Council of Assembly, General Treasurer of the Church and Solicitor of the Church.

Communication
35.   To oversee the development and implementation of the General Assembly's Communication Strategy across the Church.
36.   To oversee and manage any major reputational opportunities and risks for the Church, working with other Agencies as appropriate.
37.   To oversee effective communication with members and courts of the Church, encouraging good practice.

For the purposes only of this remit, the term 'Agencies' shall mean the following bodies being Standing Committees of the General Assembly, namely:
*   *The following Councils: Church and Society, Ministries, Mission and Discipleship, Social Care, World Mission.*
*   *The following Committees: Assembly Arrangements, Central Services, Chaplains to Her Majesty's Forces, Ecumenical Relations, Legal Questions, Panel on Review and Reform, Safeguarding, Theological Forum.*

Membership
The Council shall comprise the following:
1.   Convener, Vice-Convener and ten members appointed by the General Assembly on the Report of the Nomination Committee.
2.   The Conveners of the Councils, namely Church and Society, Ministries, Mission and Discipleship, Social Care and World Mission together with the Convener of the Panel on Review and Reform.
3.   The Secretaries of the following Councils, namely Church and Society, Ministries, Mission and Discipleship, Social Care and World Mission, all with a right to speak on matters affecting the interest of their Council, but not to vote or make a motion.
4.   The Principal Clerk, the General Treasurer and the Solicitor of the Church without a right to vote or make a motion.
5.   The Secretary to the Council of Assembly without a right to vote or make a motion.
6.   Other officials, as required by the Council, to be in attendance from time to time without a right to vote or make a motion.

Powers and Framework (Trusteeship)
1.   The General Assembly of 2011 approved a Strategic Framework to be used to help to identify priorities and to assist with the process of budgeting and resource allocation. The framework identifies the context in which we work and sets out core strategic priorities for the Church of Scotland, in particular for its Councils and Committees. It also sets

out the core values. The Framework makes it clear both what the Church's Councils and Committees should be doing and how they should be doing it. The Council of Assembly uses the Framework to help it to monitor and evaluate progress and commends it to other Councils and Committees and to the wider Church.

2. The General Assembly of 2010 appointed the voting members of the Council of Assembly to act as charity trustees for the Unincorporated Councils and Committees of the General Assembly (the Church of Scotland, Scottish Charity Number SC011353). 'Charity trustees' means the persons having the general control and management of the administration of a charity. A charity trustee must act in the interests of the charity and must, in particular, seek in good faith to ensure that the charity acts in a manner which is consistent with its purposes. All trustees must act with the care and diligence that it is reasonable to expect of a person who is managing the affairs of another person. The Conveners of the Church and Society Council, Ministries Council, Mission and Discipleship Council, Social Care Council and World Mission Council, and of the Panel on Review and Reform, are voting members of the Council and therefore charity trustees. Their first duty is to the interests of the Church of Scotland as a whole and not to their individual Councils.

3. The General Assembly decided that all trustees should:
   - possess an understanding of the life and culture of the Church of Scotland; and
   - be committed to developing and implementing the vision and mission of the General Assembly; and
   - possess an understanding of Scotland's contemporary culture.

   In addition, the Assembly requires that the Council has the following specific areas of expertise among its trustees:
   - communication
   - finance
   - governance
   - law (civil and church)
   - management
   - strategic planning
   - theology
   - training.

4. The Assembly recommended that trustees in receipt of a salary or stipend from the Church ought not to be in a majority; and the Nomination Committee takes account of this as it seeks to fill vacancies. The Council maintains a register of trustees' interests; this helps to ensure public confidence and also acts as a protection for individual trustees should there ever be allegations of impropriety. A Code of Conduct is in place. It sets out the key principles of trusteeship, advises on confidentiality and declaration of interests, provides a framework for expenses and contains provision for dealing with breaches of the Code.

5. Regular opportunities are given for voting members of the Council of Assembly to meet alone as charity trustees. This applies, for example, when significant staffing matters are under consideration.

6. Trustees may be personally liable in law for the actions of the Unincorporated Councils and Committees. The Council of Assembly, aided by the Audit Committee, has established a framework of realistic and robust risk assessments for all areas of Council and Committee work, across the Church. This helps trustees to exercise their duties under charity law and would also help to protect them against unexpected liabilities.

7. The Council has drawn up a Scheme of Delegation. This details the extent of and limits to the decision-making powers of the Council of Assembly, its groups and subcommittees, other Councils and Committees and senior staff. The Scheme is based on the formal remit

of the Council of Assembly but sets out more clearly how those broad powers operate in practice.

Convener: Rev. S. Grant Barclay LLB DipLP BD MSc PhD (2012)
Vice-Convener: Iain Johnston BA (2012)
Secretary: Mrs Pauline Weibye MA DPA Chartered FCIPD

2. THE CHURCH AND SOCIETY COUNCIL

Remit
The remit of the Church and Society Council is to facilitate the Church of Scotland's engagement with, and comment upon, national, political and social issues through:
* the development of theological, ethical and spiritual perspectives in the formulation of policy on such issues;
* the effective representation of the Church of Scotland in offering on its behalf appropriate and informed comment on political and social issues;
* the building, establishing and maintaining of a series of networks and relationships with leaders and influence-shapers in civic society, and engaging long-term in dialogue and the exchange of ideas with them;
* the support of the local church in its mission and engagement by offering professional and accessible resources on contemporary issues;
* the conducting of an annual review of progress made in discharging the remit and the provision of a written report to the Council of Assembly.
    The Church and Society Council also has oversight of a number of other specialised parts of the Church's work:
* **Education**: the oldest standing committee of the Church, working to ensure that chaplains to schools and further-education colleges are appropriately supported and resourced, and to encourage both religious education and religious observance in schools.
* **Responding to Climate Change Project (RCCP)**: helping the Church locally, nationally and internationally to respond to the challenge of climate change. The Project also works with partner organisations to engage in debate with government and other decision-makers. (See also Eco-Congregation Scotland, p. 59.)
                    Project Officer: Adrian Shaw (E-mail: ashaw@cofscotland.org.uk)
* **Society, Religion and Technology Project (SRTP)**: helping the Church to engage with ethical issues in relation to science, and seeking to bring a Christian ethical reflection on the impact of technology on society.
                    Policy Officer: Dr Murdo Macdonald (E-mail: mmacdonald@cofscotland.org.uk)

Membership
Convener, Vice-Convener, 28 members appointed by the General Assembly, one of whom will also be appointed to the Ecumenical Relations Committee, and one member appointed from and by the Social Care Council and the Guild. The Nomination Committee will ensure that the Council membership contains at least five individuals with specific expertise in each of the areas of Education, Societal/Political, Science and Technology and Social/Ethical. This number may include the Convener and Vice-Convener of the Council.

Convener:	Rev. Sally Foster-Fulton BA BD (2012)
Vice-Convener:	Rev. J. Christopher Wigglesworth MBE BSc PhD BD (2012)
Secretary:	Rev. Ewan R. Aitken BA BD

3. THE MINISTRIES COUNCIL
Tel: 0131-225 5722; Fax: 0131-240 2201
E-mail: ministries@cofscotland.org.uk

Ministries Council Remit

The remit of the Ministries Council is the enabling of ministries in every part of Scotland, giving special priority to the poorest and most marginalised, through the recruitment, training and support of recognised ministries of the Church and the assessment and monitoring of patterns of deployment of those ministries.

In the fulfilment of this remit, the Council offers strategic leadership in the development of patterns of collaborative ministry which enable the Church of Scotland to be effective in its missionary calling and faithful in its participation in the one ministry of Jesus Christ, and operates within the following spheres of work:

Priority Areas – following the Gospel imperative of priority to the poor
- Working directly in support of the poorest parishes in Scotland to enable and resource ministries and to build communities of hope;
- Assisting the whole Church in fulfilling its responsibility to the Gospel imperative of giving priority to the poorest and most marginalised in society;
- Enabling and supporting work in partnership with ecumenical, inter-faith and statutory agencies to achieve the goal of alleviating poverty in Scotland.

Education and Support – recruitment, training and support of ministries personnel
- Developing and implementing patterns of enquiry and assessment and vocational guidance which enable the identification of appropriately called and gifted people to train for recognised ministries;
- Developing and implementing training patterns for those accepted into training for the recognised ministries of the Church;
- Enabling the transfer of people from other denominations into the ministries of the Church;
- Delivering pastoral support to those involved in the recognised ministries of the Church through the development and resourcing of local pastoral networks, direct one-to-one engagement and the provision of occupational health support, counselling, mediation and conflict-resolution services;
- Promoting and providing vocational guidance and lifelong learning opportunities for ministries personnel through in-service events, self-appraisal processes and a study-leave programme.

Partnership Development – working with Presbyteries and other partners in planning and resourcing ministries
- Working with Presbyteries for effective deployment of ministries to meet the needs of the parishes of Scotland and charges in the Presbytery of England, including consulting with congregations and other denominations where appropriate;
- Working in partnership with other agencies of the Church and ecumenical partners, to enable the emergence of ministries to meet the needs of the people of Scotland in every part;

- Supporting those engaged in chaplaincy services both directly employed by the Council and employed by other agencies;
- Ensuring best practice in the employment, care and support of staff, including setting appropriate terms and conditions, offering developmental training to staff and those responsible for their management.

Finance – ensuring good management of funds and monitoring budgets
- Planning strategically for the future funding of the recognised ministries of the Church;
- Managing the funds and overseeing the budgeting processes of the Council to ensure that maximum benefit is derived for the Church's ministries through the use of income and capital;
- Preparing recommendations on the level of stipends and salaries and liaising with Pension Trustees on matters relating to the setting of the Standard Annuity and discretionary increases in pension, and negotiating and reaching agreement with Pension Trustees on funding rates.

Membership
Convener, four Vice-Conveners, 38 members appointed by the General Assembly, one of whom will also be appointed to the Ecumenical Relations Committee, and one member appointed from and by the General Trustees, the Housing and Loan Fund, the Committee on Chaplains to Her Majesty's Forces and the Diaconate Council. For the avoidance of doubt, where a representative of these other bodies is a member of staff, he or she will have no right to vote.

Convener:	Rev. Neil J. Dougall BD
Vice-Conveners:	Rev. Neil M. Glover
	Rev. Anne S. Paton BA BD
	Mr David A. Stewart MA DipEd
	Rev. Derek H.N. Pope BD

Staff

Council Secretary:	Rev. Martin Scott DipMusEd RSAM BD PhD
	(Tel: ext. 2389; E-mail: mscott@cofscotland.org.uk)
Education and Support Secretary:	Rev. Marjory McPherson LLB BD
	(Tel: ext. 2315; E-mail: mmcpherson@cofscotland.org.uk)
Partnership Development Secretary:	Rev. Angus R. Mathieson MA BD
	(Tel: ext. 2312; E-mail: amathieson@cofscotland.org.uk)
Priority Areas Secretary:	Rev. H. Martin J. Johnstone MA BD MTh PhD
	(Tel: 0141-248 2905; E-mail: mjohnstone@cofscotland.org.uk)
Strategic Projects Manager:	Ms Catherine Skinner BA MA
	(Tel: ext. 2274; cskinner@cofscotland.org.uk)
Ministries Support Officers:	Rev. Jane Denniston MA BD
	(Tel: ext. 2204; E-mail: jdenniston@cofscotland.org.uk)
	Rev. Gavin J. Elliott MA BD
	(Tel: ext. 2255; E-mail: gelliott@cofscotland.org.uk)
	Mrs Anne Law MA
	(Tel: ext. 2379; E-mail: alaw@cofscotland.org.uk)
	Mr Noel Mathias BA BTh MA
	(Tel: 0141-248 2905; E-mail: nmathias@cofscotland.org.uk)

Mr John Thomson
(Tel: ext. 2248; E-mail: jthomson@cofscotland.org.uk)
Mrs Joyce Watkinson CQSW COSCA, Accredited Counsellor
(Tel: ext. 2225; E-mail: jwatkinson@cofscotland.org.uk)
Mrs Moira Whyte MA
(Tel: ext. 2266; E-mail: mwhyte@cofscotland.org.uk)

Go For It Fund
Co-ordinator:

Ms Shirley Grieve
(Tel: ext. 2357; E-mail: sgrieve@cofscotland.org.uk)

Training and Development
Worker:

Miss Catherine McIntosh
(Tel: ext. 2319; E-mail: cmcintosh@cofscotland.org.uk)

The Chance to Thrive
Project Co-ordinator:

Rev. Russell McLarty MA BD
(Tel: 01875 614496)

Ministries Council

Further information about the Council's work and services is obtainable through the Ministries Council at the Church Offices. Information is available on a wide range of matters including the Consolidated Stipend Fund, National Stipend Fund, endowment grants, travelling and other expenses, pulpit supply, study leave, ministries development conferences, pastoral care services (including occupational health), Enquiry and Assessment, Education and Training, Presbytery Planning, Priority Areas, New Charge Development, Area Team Ministry, Interim Ministry, Readership, Chaplaincies, the Diaconate, Ministries Development Staff (MDS), the *Go For It* Fund, Emerging Church, and all aspects of work connected with ministers and the ministry of word and sacrament.

Committees

The policy development and implementation of the work of the Ministries Council is managed under the following committees:

1. Strategic Planning Group

Convener: Rev. Neil J. Dougall BD

The Strategic Planning Group comprises the Convener, Vice-Conveners and senior staff of all four areas (including Finance) of the Council and is empowered by the Council to engage in broad-ranging thinking regarding the future outlook and plans of the Council. It reports directly to Council and brings forward to it ideas and consultation papers offering options as to the future strategic direction of the Council's work. Though a key part of the Council's work, it is a consultative and advisory group rather than a decision-making one.

2. Priority Areas Committee

Convener: Rev. Derek H.N. Pope BD

The Priority Areas Committee implements the policy of the Council in developing, encouraging and overseeing strategy within Priority Area parishes. It is empowered to develop resources to enable congregations to make appropriate responses to the needs of people living in poverty in their parishes, and to raise awareness of the effects of poverty on people's lives in Scotland. It also co-ordinates the strategy of the wider Church in its priority to Scotland's poorest parishes.

3. Education and Support Committee

Convener: Rev. Anne S. Paton BA BD

The Education and Support Committee is responsible for the development and oversight of policy in relation to the enquiry and assessment process for ministers of Word and Sacrament (full-time and ordained local ministry), Deacons and Readers, together with the admission and readmission of ministers. It is further responsible for the supervision of those in training for those recognised ministries of the Church and operates with powers in relation to both of these areas of work to make recommendations on suitability for training and readiness to engage in ministries at the end of a training period. It also implements Council policies on pastoral care for all recognised ministries, the integration of Occupational Health with ministries support services, and the oversight of the working of those Acts relating to long-term illness of ministers in charges. It promotes development opportunities for those engaged in recognised ministries, including study leave and accompanied reviews.

4.   Partnership Development Committee
Convener: Mr David A. Stewart MA DipEd
The Partnership Development Committee is responsible for maintaining and developing relationships with Presbyteries and other agencies and partners in the planning and resourcing of ministries. This includes the overall planning of the deployment of the Church's ministries, primarily through the ongoing monitoring of the development of Presbytery Plans. The Committee also oversees work on emerging ministries (including New Charge Development work). It deals further with the work of Interim Ministry and Area Team Ministry, and with all aspects of chaplaincy work. The Committee also oversees the Church of Scotland *Go For It* Fund.

5.   Finance Committee
Convener: Rev. Neil M. Glover
The Finance Committee operates with powers to deal with the Parish Ministries Fund, the National Stipend Scheme, Vacancy Schedules, Maintenance Allowances, Hardship Grants and Bursaries, Stipend Advances, management of investments, writing-off shortfalls and the granting of further endowments. It also maintains an oversight of the budgets for all recognised ministries.

The Council also has several *ad hoc* Groups, which report to the Committees and implement specific policies of the Council, as follows:

The Chance to Thrive Steering Group
Leader: Mr Raymond K. Young CBE BArch FRIAS

Recruitment Task Group
Leader: Rev. Andrea E. Price

Training Task Group
Leader: Rev. A. Leslie Milton MA BD PhD

Pastoral and Vocational Care Task Group
Leader: Rev. Mhorag Macdonald MA BD

Go For It Fund Committee (see below)
Convener: Rev. Rolf H. Billes BD

Presbytery Planning Task Group
Leader: Rev. Alison A. Meikle BD

Interim Ministries Task Group
Leader: Rev. Scott Raby LTh

Joint Emerging Church Group (with Mission and Discipleship Council)
Leader: Rev. Colin M. Brough BSc BD

Chaplaincies Forum
Leader: Rev. C. Graham Taylor BSc BD FIAB

Other related bodies:
Chaplains to HM Forces
See separate entry at number 10.

The Church of Scotland Housing and Loan Fund
See separate entry at number 12.

Go For It: **funding change in church and community**
The Committee comprises members appointed by the Nominations Committee to the Ministries
Council, as well as a number of co-opted members with appropriate skills and knowledge. The
Mission and Discipleship Council and the Church and Society Council are also represented.
Convener: Rev. Rolf H. Billes BD
Co-ordinator: Shirley Grieve
Training and Development: Catherine McIntosh
The purpose of the Church of Scotland's *Go For It* Fund is to encourage and support creative
initiatives which address needs in local communities and/or encourage new ways of being the
Church in Scotland today.
    There are five criteria for receiving funding. To be able to apply, a proposal needs to meet at
least two of these criteria. These are:
• meeting identified needs in a community
• nurturing Christian faith within and beyond the Church
• tackling poverty and/or social injustice
• developing new ecclesial/Christian communities
• creating work which is genuinely innovative, developing good practice that can be shared.
The Fund gives grants totalling in the region of £1 million per annum. Awards of up to £45,000
(over a three-year period) are available to part-fund locally based work. Additional support
is available for schemes which can clearly demonstrate that they are engaged with the very
poorest members of Scottish society.
    Successful applications will be either from Church of Scotland congregations or from
organisations very closely associated with them. They will need to show how they are actively
working with other partners, including other churches, to bring about change.
    We want to encourage local Christians to have creative ideas and then, with the support and
help of the Fund, to turn these ideas into practice – to really *Go For It*.
    Additional information is available at www.churchofscotland.org.uk/serve/go_for_it. You
can contact the *Go For It* Team on 0131-225 5722 or by e-mailing goforit@cofscotland.org.uk

Pulpit Supply: Fee and Expenses
The General Assembly of 2011 approved new regulations governing the amount of Supply Fee
and Expenses. These were effective from 1 April 2012 and are as follows:
1.   In Charges where there is only one diet of worship, the Pulpit Supply Fee shall be a
      Standard Fee of £55 (or as from time to time agreed by the Ministries Council).

2.   In Charges where there are additional diets of worship on a Sunday, the person fulfilling the Supply shall be paid £15 for each additional Service (or as from time to time agreed by the Ministries Council).

3.   Where the person is unwilling to conduct more than one diet of worship on a given Sunday, he or she shall receive a pro-rata payment based on the total available Fee shared on the basis of the number of Services conducted.

4.   The Fee thus calculated shall be payable in the case of all persons permitted to conduct Services under Act II 1986.

5.   In all cases, Travelling Expenses shall be paid. Where there is no convenient public conveyance, the use of a private car shall be paid for at the Committee rate of Travelling Expenses. In exceptional circumstances, to be approved in advance, the cost of hiring a car may be met.

6.   Where weekend board and lodging are agreed as necessary, these may be claimed for the weekend at a maximum rate of that allowed when attending the General Assembly. The Fee and Expenses should be paid to the person providing the Supply before he or she leaves on the Sunday.

---

4.   THE MISSION AND DISCIPLESHIP COUNCIL
E-mail: mandd@cofscotland.org.uk; Website: www.resourcingmission.org.uk

Remit
The remit of the Mission and Discipleship Council is:

•   to take a lead role in developing and maintaining an overall focus for mission in Scotland, and to highlight its fundamental relationships with worship, service, doctrine, education and nurture;

•   to take a lead role in developing strategies, resources and services in Christian education and nurture, recognising these as central to both mission and discipleship;

•   to offer appropriate servicing and support nationally, regionally and locally in the promotion of nurturing, worshipping and witnessing communities of faith;

•   to introduce policy on behalf of the Church in the following areas: adult education and elder training, church art and architecture, congregational mission and development, doctrine, resourcing youth and children's work, worship;

•   to establish and support the Mission Forum with representatives of relevant Councils;

•   to encourage appropriate awareness of, and response to, the requirements of people with particular needs including physical, sensory and/or learning disabilities;

•   to conduct an annual review of progress made in discharging the remit and provide a written report to the Council of Assembly.

Statement of Purpose
Resourcing Christ's Mission: to enable and empower people to engage in Christ's mission through resourcing worship, witness and discipleship in the context of the changing contemporary culture of Scotland and beyond.
Specifically, we will:

•   stimulate critical reflection and development of places and practice of worship = WORSHIP

•   communicate Christ's message lovingly, effectively and relevantly = WITNESS

•   nurture and develop learning and growth within congregations and communities = DISCIPLESHIP.

Membership
Convener, three Vice-Conveners and 24 members appointed by the General Assembly, one of whom will also be appointed to the Ecumenical Relations Committee, the Director of Stewardship, one member appointed from and by the General Trustees, the Guild and the Scottish Community Trust, and the Convener or Vice-Convener of the Committee on Church Art and Architecture as that Committee shall determine. The Nomination Committee will ensure that the Council membership contains individuals with specific expertise in the areas of Mission, Education, Worship, Doctrine and Publishing.

Convener:	Rev. Colin A.M. Sinclair BA BD
Vice-Conveners:	Rev. Roderick G. Hamilton MA BD
	Rev. Norman A. Smith MA BD
	Mr John Hawthorn BSc

Staff

Council Secretary:	Rev. Dr Alister W. Bull BD DipMin MTh
	(E-mail: abull@cofscotland.org.uk)
Faith Expressions Team Leader:	Rev. Nigel Robb FCP MA BD ThM MTh
	(E-mail: nrobb@cofscotland.org.uk)
Church Without Walls Team Leader:	Mrs Lesley Hamilton-Messer MA
	(E-mail: lhamilton-messer@cofscotland.org.uk)
Congregational Learning Team Leader:	Mr Ronald H. Clarke BEng MSc PGCE
	(E-mail: rhclarke@cofscotland.org.uk)

Mission Development Workers
Mission Development Workers are tasked with supporting local congregations to help them become more resourceful so that they can engage effectively with their communities. They are:

Mr Steve Aisthorpe BA	(E-mail: saisthorpe@cofscotland.org.uk)
Mr Robert Rawson BA	(E-mail: rrawson@cofscotland.org.uk)
Mr Iain Campbell BA PGDE	(E-mail: icampbell@cofscotland.org.uk)

Specialist Development Workers
The following staff members provide specialist advice and support to congregations on key areas of work:

Mr Graham Fender-Allison BA	Worship Development Worker
	(E-mail: gfender-allison@cofscotland.org.uk)
Ms Suzi Farrant BSc BA	Children and Young People Development Worker
	(E-mail: sfarrant@cofscotland.org.uk)
Mr David Plews MA	Learning Development Worker
	(E-mail: dplews@cofscotland.org.uk)

The Netherbow: Scottish Storytelling Centre: The integrated facilities of the **Netherbow Theatre** and the **John Knox House Museum**, together with the outstanding new conference and reception areas, are an important cultural and visitor centre on the Royal Mile in Edinburgh and provide advice and assistance nationally in the use of the arts in mission, education and worship. 'Story Source', 'Scriptaid' and other resources are available. Contact the Director, The Netherbow: Scottish Storytelling Centre, 43–45 High Street, Edinburgh EH1 1SR (Tel: 0131-556 9579; E-mail; donald@scottishstorytellingcentre.com; Website: www.scottishstorytellingcentre.co.uk).

Life and Work
(Tel: 0131-225 5722; Fax: 0131-240 2207; E-mail: magazine@lifeandwork.org)
Life and Work is the Church of Scotland's monthly magazine. Its purpose is to keep the Church informed about events in church life at home and abroad and to provide a forum for Christian opinion and debate on a variety of topics. It has an independent editorial policy. Contributions which are relevant to any aspect of the Christian faith are welcome.

The price of *Life and Work* this year is £2.00. With a circulation of around 25,000, it also offers advertisers a first-class opportunity to reach a discerning readership in all parts of Scotland.

Saint Andrew Press
Saint Andrew Press is managed on behalf of the Church of Scotland by Hymns Ancient and Modern. New titles include the highly acclaimed *Looking for Mrs Livingstone, George Mackay Brown, Barclay on the Lectionary, Scots Worship – Lent, Holy Week and Easter* and *Revealing Love – Pray Now Daily Devotions and Monthly Prayers*. All books, CDs and Church of Scotland stationery can be ordered by telephoning 01603 785925 or by e-mail to orders@norwichbooksandmusic.co.uk

Saint Andrew Press invites readers to visit its website at www.standrewpress.com for a full list of publications, news of helpful new resources, competitions, special events, author news, exclusive offers and information on how to submit proposals for publication. Please contact Ann Crawford (ann@hymnsam.co.uk) with any queries about proposals. Saint Andrew Press is also on Twitter @standrewpress.

Committee on Church Art and Architecture
Convener: Dr J.G. Roberts MA

Membership
The Committee shall comprise a Convener, Vice-Convener and 15 members appointed by the General Assembly.

Remit
This Committee replaced the Committee on Artistic Matters and will take forward that Committee's remit, which is in the following terms:

The Committee advises congregations and Presbyteries regarding the most appropriate way of carrying out renovations, alterations and reordering of interiors, having regard to the architectural quality of Church buildings. It also advises on the installation of stained glass, tapestries, memorials, furniture and furnishings, and keeps a list of accredited artists and craftsworkers.

Any alteration to the exterior or interior of a Church building which affects its appearance must be referred to the Committee for approval, which is given through the General Trustees. Congregations contemplating alterations are urged to consult the Committee at an early stage.

Members of the Committee are prepared, when necessary, to visit churches and meet office-bearers. The Committee's services are given free.

The Committee seeks the conservation of the nation's heritage as expressed in its Church buildings, while at the same time helping to ensure that these buildings continue to serve the worship and witness of the Church in the present day.

In recent years, the General Assembly has conferred these additional duties on the Committee:
1.   preparation of reports on the architectural, historical and aesthetic merit of the buildings of congregations involved in questions of readjustment

2. verification of the propriety of repair and renovation work forming the basis of grant applications to public bodies
3. the offering of advice on the maintenance and installation of organs
4. facilitating the transfer of unwanted furnishings from one church to another through *Exchange and Transfer*
5. the processing of applications from congregations for permission to dispose of surplus communion plate, and the carrying out of an inventory of sacramental vessels held by congregations.

Work with Rural Churches

The Council aims to affirm, support and resource rural churches and is responsible for planning for a Church presence at the Royal Highland Show. It seeks to reflect the full extent of rural experience, encompassing farming, fishing, tourism, forestry and other professions/industries that have a bearing on rural life. This will involve collaboration with ecumenical partners and responding periodically to requests for submissions to government consultations.

---

5. THE SOCIAL CARE COUNCIL
SOCIAL CARE (CrossReach)
Charis House, 47 Milton Road East, Edinburgh EH15 2SR
Tel: 0131-657 2000; Fax: 0131-657 5000
E-mail: info@crossreach.org.uk; Website: www.crossreach.org.uk

The Social Care Council, known as CrossReach, provides social-care services as part of the Christian witness of the Church to the people of Scotland.

Remit

The remit of the Social Care Council is:
*   as part of the Church's mission, to offer services in Christ's name to people in need;
*   to provide specialist resources to further the caring work of the Church;
*   to identify existing and emerging areas of need, to guide the Church in pioneering new approaches to relevant problems and to make responses on issues arising within the area of the Council's concern through appropriate channels such as the Church's Church and Society Council, the Scottish Government and the like;
*   to conduct an annual review of progress made in discharging the remit and provide an annual written report to the General Assembly;
*   to oversee an appropriate corporate management and support service to deliver the above and be responsible for funding all salaries and related costs;
*   to set and review terms and conditions of staff and establish appropriate internal governance systems.

Membership

Convener, two Vice-Conveners and 28 members appointed by the General Assembly, one of whom will also be appointed to the Ecumenical Relations Committee. The Council shall have power to appoint such Committees and Groups as it may from time to time determine to be appropriate to ensure that the Council's Remit is fulfilled.

Convener: Dr Sally E. Bonnar (2013)
Vice-Conveners: Ian Huggan (2011)
                                         Rev. Dr Richard E. Frazer (2011)

Staff
Chief Executive Officer: Peter Bailey (peter.bailey@crossreach.org.uk)

Management Structure
The management structure is service-based. There are three Operational Directors, each with a specialist area of responsibility. They are supported by Heads of Service, who have lead roles for particular types of service and client groups.

Director of Services to Older People:	Allan Logan (allan.logan@crossreach.org.uk)
Heads of Service:	Brenda Fraser (East)
	Post vacant (West)
	Annie McDonald (North)
Director of Adult Care Services:	Calum Murray (calum.murray@crossreach.org.uk)
Heads of Service:	George McNeilly, Ronnie Black, Andy Cashman
Director of Children and Families:	Viv Dickenson (viv.dickenson@crossreach.org.uk)
Head of Service Residential Schools:	Paul Gilroy
Director of Finance and Resources:	Ian Wauchope (ian.wauchope@crossreach.org.uk)
Business Partners:	Arthur Akugbo, Eoin McDunphy, Iwona Lesniak
Director of Human Resources and Organisational Development:	Mari Rennie (mari.rennie@crossreach.org.uk)
Business Partners:	Jane Allan, Corinne Gillies
Head of Estates and Health and Safety:	David Reid (david.reid@crossreach.org.uk)
Health and Safety Manager:	Richard Park
Business, Compliance and Improvement Head of Service:	Claire Hay (claire.hay@crossreach.org.uk)
Business Development Head of Service:	Elizabeth Hay (elizabeth.hay@crossreach.org.uk)

List of Services
CrossReach operates 75 services across Scotland, and a list of these can be obtained from Charis House on 0131-657 2000, or from the CrossReach website: www.crossreach.org.uk

---

6.   THE WORLD MISSION COUNCIL
Tel: 0131-225 5722; Fax: 0131-226 6121
E-mail: world@cofscotland.org.uk

Remit
The remit of the World Mission Council is:
• to enable the Church of Scotland, as part of the holy catholic or universal Church, to participate effectively in the Mission of God in the world, following the example of Jesus Christ;

- to initiate, develop and maintain mutually enriching relationships with churches and church-related organisations internationally;
- to recruit, train and support paid staff and volunteers to work abroad, alone or in collaboration with other churches or church-related organisations;
- to inform, encourage and enable members of the Church of Scotland at local, Presbytery and national levels to become engaged in the life of the world church;
- to encourage and support local partnerships between congregations, Presbyteries and church-related organisations with those in other parts of the world;
- to discern priorities and establish policies enabling the Church of Scotland to express God's love for the world through the gospel of Jesus Christ;
- to be informed, and to keep the Church of Scotland informed, about the cultural, political, social, economic, religious and ecclesiastical issues of relevance to worldwide mission;
- to help the people of Scotland to appreciate the worldwide nature of the Christian faith;
- to conduct an annual review of progress made in discharging the remit and report to the Council of Assembly.

Membership
Convener, two Vice-Conveners and 28 members appointed by the General Assembly, one of whom will also be appointed to the Ecumenical Relations Committee, and one member appointed by the Presbytery of Europe (32 in total). In addition, the Church of Scotland Guild sends a representative.

Convener:	Very Rev. Andrew R.C. McLellan CBE MA BD STM DD (2010)
Vice-Conveners:	Rev. Iain D. Cunningham MA BD (2011)
	Rev. Christine Sime BSc BD (2012)

Departmental Staff

Council Secretary:	Rev. Ian W. Alexander BA BD STM
Secretaries:	Jennie Chinembiri (Africa and Caribbean)
	Carol Finlay (Twinning and Local Development)
	Sandy Sneddon (Asia)
Administration:	Donna Maclean
Finance Manager:	Catriona Scrimgeour (Assistant Treasurer)
Human Resources:	Angela Ocak
	Sarah-Jayne McVeigh

Vacancies Overseas
The Council welcomes enquiries from men and women interested in serving in the Church overseas. Vacancies for mission partner appointments in the volunteer programme and opportunities with other organisations can all be considered. Those interested in more information are invited to contact the Human Resources Department at the Church Offices (E-mail: hr@ cofscotland.org.uk).

HIV Programme
The Programme aims to raise awareness in congregations about the impact of HIV and AIDS and seeks to channel support to partner churches. For further information, contact Marjorie Clark, Co-ordinator, HIV Programme (E-mail: mclark@cofscotland.org.uk).

Christian Aid Scotland
Christian Aid is the official relief and development agency of 41 Churches in Britain and Ireland. Christian Aid's mandate is to challenge and enable us to fulfil our responsibilities to the poor of the world. Half a million volunteers and collectors make this possible, with money given by millions of supporters. The Church of Scotland marks its commitment as a Church to this part of its mission through an annual grant from the Mission and Renewal Fund, transmitted through the World Mission Council, which keeps in close touch with Christian Aid and its work. Up-to-date information about projects and current emergency relief work can be obtained from:
• The Head of Christian Aid Scotland, Rev. Dr Kathy Galloway: Christian Aid Scotland, Sycamore House, 290 Bath Street, Glasgow G2 4JR (Tel: 0141-221 7475)
• The Director: Loretta Minghella, Christian Aid Office, PO Box 100, London SE1 7RT (Tel: 020 7620 4444)

Pilgrimage
The Church of Scotland encourages visitors and pilgrims to visit the Christian Community of Israel and Palestine, to walk with them in fellowship and build relationships to help understand their life, witness and situation.
There are two Church of Scotland Residential Centres in Israel which provide comfortable accommodation for pilgrims and visitors to the Holy Land. Further information on planning a pilgrimage experience which includes meetings with the local Christian community and others is available from the ministers: George Shand (E-mail: stachjer@netvision.net.il) and Colin Johnston (E-mail: revcdj60@gmail.com).
(a)   St Andrew's Guest House, 1 David Remez Street, PO Box 8619, Jerusalem 91086, Israel (Tel: 00 972 2 6732401; Fax: 00 972 2 6731711; E-mail: standjer@netvision.net.il)
(b)   The Scots Hotel, St Andrew's, Galilee: 1 Gdud Barak Street, PO Box 104, Tiberias 14100, Israel (Tel: 00 972 4 671 0759; Fax: 00 972 4 672 5282; E-mail: scottie@netvision.net.il)

A list of Overseas Appointments will be found in List K in Section 6.
A list of Retired Missionaries will be found in List L in Section 6.

---

7.   Assembly Arrangements Committee

Membership
Convener, Vice-Convener and ten members appointed by the General Assembly on the Report of the Nomination Committee; the Convener and Vice-Convener also to serve as Convener and Vice-Convener of the General Assembly's Business Committee.
The Clerks are non-voting members of the Assembly Arrangements Committee, and the Moderator and Moderator Designate are members of the Committee.
Convener: Rev. Janet S. Mathieson MA BD
Vice-Convener: Rev. Derek Browning MA BD DMin
Secretary: The Principal Clerk

Remit
The Committee's remit is:
• to make all necessary arrangements for the General Assembly;
• to advise the Moderator on his or her official duties if so required;

- to be responsible to the General Assembly for the care and maintenance of the Assembly Hall and the Moderator's flat;
- to be responsible to the General Assembly for all arrangements in connection with the letting of the General Assembly Hall;
- to conduct an annual review of progress made in discharging the remit and provide a written report to the Council of Assembly.

8. Central Properties Department

Staff
Property, Health and Safety Manager: Colin Wallace
Property, Health and Safety Officer: Jacqueline Collins
Property Officer: Eunice Hessell
Support Assistant: Joyce McMurdo

Remit
The Central Properties Department has the remit to provide Property, Facilities and Health and Safety services to the Councils and Departments of the central administration of the Church. This includes:
- management of properties owned by the Councils and Departments
- procurement of land for new-build projects
- delivery of new-build projects including new church buildings
- delivery of major refurbishment programmes
- management of the furlough housing estate for World Mission
- management of facilities and procurement of work equipment
- development and ongoing review of the Health and Safety policy
- provision of Health and Safety management for employing agencies of the Church
- provision of Health and Safety training
- administration of the Health and Safety Committee
- support for arbitrations in the case of parish readjustment.
     Contact: Central Properties Department, 121 George Street, Edinburgh EH2 4YN (Tel: 0131-240 2254; E-mail: cpd@cofscotland.org.uk).

9. Central Services Committee

Membership
(13 members: nine appointed by the General Assembly, and four *ex officiis* and non-voting, namely the Secretary to the Council of Assembly, the Solicitor of the Church, the General Treasurer and the Head of Human Resources and Information Technology)
Convener: Mr Angus Macpherson MA BSc DPSA (2010)
Vice-Conveners: Mr Bill Steele (2010)
                         Mr Philip Craig MA MEd MSc DipRE (2010)

Staff
Administrative Secretary: Mrs Pauline Wilson
(E-mail: pwilson@cofscotland.org.uk)

Remit
- To be responsible for the proper maintenance and insurance of the Church Offices at 117–123 George Street and 21 Young Street, Edinburgh ('the Church Offices');
- To be responsible for matters relating to Health and Safety within the Church Offices;
- To be responsible for matters relating to Data Protection within the Church Offices and with respect to the General Assembly Councils based elsewhere;
- To be responsible for the allocation of accommodation within the Church Offices and the annual determination of rental charges to the Councils and other parties accommodated therein;
- To oversee the delivery of central services to departments within the Church Offices, to Councils of the General Assembly and, where appropriate, to the Statutory Corporations, Presbyteries and Congregations, namely:
  1. Those facilities directly managed by the Facilities Manager;
  2. Information Technology (including the provision of support services to Presbytery Clerks);
  3. Human Resources;
  4. Legal Services (as delivered by the Law Department and subject to such oversight not infringing principles of 'client/solicitor' confidentiality);
  5. Property Services (as delivered by the Central Properties Department).
- The Committee shall act as one of the employing agencies of the Church and shall, except in so far as specifically herein provided, assume and exercise the whole rights, functions and responsibilities of the former Personnel Committee;
- While the Committee shall *inter alia* have responsibility for determining the terms and conditions of the staff for whom it is the employing agency, any staff who are members of the Committee or who are appointed directly by the General Assembly shall not be present when matters solely relating to their own personal terms and conditions of employment/ office are under consideration;
- To conduct an annual review of progress made in discharging this remit and provide a written report to the Council of Assembly.

---

10.   Chaplains to HM Forces

Convener: Rev. Neil N. Gardner MA BD
Vice-Convener: Rev. Jackie G. Petrie
Secretary: Mr John K. Thomson, Ministries Council, 121 George Street, Edinburgh EH2 4YN

Recruitment
The Chaplains' Committee is entrusted with the task of recruitment of Chaplains for the Regular, Reserve and Auxiliary Forces. Vacancies occur periodically, and the Committee is happy to receive enquiries from all interested ministers.

Forces Registers
The Committee maintains a Register of all those who have been baptised and/or admitted to Communicant Membership by Service Chaplains.

Parish Ministers are asked to take advantage of the facilities by applying for Certificates, where appropriate, from the Secretary of the Committee.

Full information may be obtained from the Secretary, Mr John K. Thomson (Tel: 0131-225 5722; E-mail: jthomson@cofscotland.org.uk).

A list of Chaplains will be found in List B in Section 6.

---

11. The Church of Scotland Guild

National Office-bearers and Executive Staff

Convener:	Marjorie Paton MA
Vice-Convener:	Kay Keith MA
General Secretary:	Iain W. Whyte BA DCE DMS
Associate Secretary:	Fiona J. Punton MCIPR
	(E-mail: fpunton@cofscotland.org.uk)
	(Tel: 0131-225 5722 ext. 2317 or 0131-240 2217)

The Church of Scotland Guild is a movement within the Church of Scotland whose aim is '**to invite and encourage both women and men to commit their lives to Jesus Christ and to enable them to express their faith in worship, prayer and action**'. Membership of the Guild is open to all who subscribe to that aim.

Groups at congregational level are free to organise themselves under the authority of the Kirk Session, as best suits their own local needs and circumstances. Large groups with frequent meetings and activities continue to operate with a committee or leadership team, while other, smaller groups simply share whatever tasks need to be done among the membership as a whole. Similarly, at Presbyterial Council level, frequency and style of meetings vary according to local needs, as do leadership patterns. Each Council may nominate one person to serve at national level, where five committees take forward the work of the Guild in accordance with the stated Aim.

These committees are:

- National Executive
- Finance and General Purposes
- Projects and Topics
- Programmes and Resources
- Marketing and Publicity.

There has always been a close relationship between the Guild and other Departments of the Church, and members welcome the opportunity to contribute to the Church's wider mission through the Project Partnership Scheme and other joint ventures. The Guild is represented on both the Church and Society Council and the Mission and Discipleship Council.

The project scheme affords groups at congregational level the opportunity to select a project, or projects, from a range of up to six, selected from proposals submitted by a wide range of Church Departments and other Church-related bodies. A project partner in each group seeks ways of promoting the project locally, increasing awareness of the issues raised by it, and encouraging support of a financial and practical nature. Support is available from the Project Co-ordinator at Council level and the Associate Secretary based at the Guild Office.

The Guild is very aware of the importance of good communication in any large organisation, and regularly sends mailings to its groups to pass on information and resources to the members.

In addition, the Newsletter, sent to members three times per session, is a useful communication tool, as is the website (www.cos-guild.org.uk). These are a means of sharing experiences and of communicating something of the wider interest and influence of the Guild, which participates in other national bodies such as the Network of Ecumenical Women in Scotland and the Scottish Women's Convention.

Each year, the Guild follows a Theme and produces a resources pack covering worship and study material. There is also a related Discussion Topic with supporting material and background information. The theme, topic and projects all relate to a common three-year strategy which, for 2012–15, is **'Whose we are and Whom we Serve'**, the Guild's motto being chosen to reflect the fact that the Guild marked its 125th anniversary in 2012–13. Under this strategy, the first annual theme was **'A Faith to Proclaim'**. The one for 2013–14 is **'A Fellowship to Build'**, and the final year will be **'A World to Serve'**. At the same time, the Guild is supporting six partnership projects, each chosen to reflect something of the strategy and themes for the triennium. The related discussion topic for 2013–14 is **'Let's talk about … finding the right way'**.

Further information is available from the Guild Office (Tel: 0131-225 5722 ext. 2317, or 0131-240 2217) or from the website (www.cos-guild.org.uk).

---

12.   The Church of Scotland Housing and Loan Fund for Retired Ministers and Widows and Widowers of Ministers

Membership
The Trustees shall be a maximum of 11 in number, being:
1.   four appointed by the General Assembly on the nomination of the Trustees, who, having served a term of four years, shall be eligible for reappointment;
2.   three ministers and one member appointed by the Ministries Council;
3.   three appointed by the Baird Trust.

Chairman: Mr J.G. Grahame Lees MA LLB NP
Deputy Chairman: Rev. Ian Taylor BD ThM
Secretary: Miss Lin J. Macmillan MA

Staff
Property Manager: Miss Hilary J. Hardy
Property Assistant: Mr John Lunn

Remit
The Fund, as established by the General Assembly, facilitates the provision of housing accommodation for retired ministers and widows, widowers and separated or divorced spouses of Church of Scotland ministers. When provided, help may take the form of either a house to rent or a house-purchase loan.

The Trustees may grant tenancy of one of their existing houses or they may agree to purchase for rental occupation an appropriate house of an applicant's choosing. Leases are normally on very advantageous terms as regards rental levels. Alternatively, the Trustees may grant a housing loan of up to 70 per cent of a house-purchase price but with an upper limit. Favourable rates of interest are charged.

The Trustees are also prepared to consider assisting those who have managed to house themselves but are seeking to move to more suitable accommodation. Those with a mortgaged home on retirement may be granted a loan to enable them to repay such a mortgage and thereafter to enjoy the favourable rates of interest charged by the Fund.

Ministers making application within five years of retirement, upon their application being approved, will be given a fairly firm commitment that, in due course, either a house will be made available for renting or a house-purchase loan will be offered. Only within nine months of a minister's intended retiral date will the Trustees initiate steps to find a suitable house; only within one year of that date will a loan be advanced. Applications submitted about ten years prior to retirement have the benefit of initial review and, if approved, a place on the preliminary applications list for appropriate decision in due time.

Donations and legacies over the years have been significant in building up this Fund. Congregational contributions have been, and will continue to be, an essential backbone.

The Board of Trustees is a completely independent body answerable to the General Assembly, and enquiries and applications are dealt with in the strictest confidence.

Further information can be obtained from the Secretary, Miss Lin J. Macmillan MA, at the Church of Scotland Offices, 121 George Street, Edinburgh EH2 4YN (Tel: 0131-225 5722 ext. 2310; E-mail: lmacmillan@cofscotland.org.uk; Website: www.churchofscotland.org.uk).

13.   Church of Scotland Investors Trust

Membership
(Trustees are appointed by the General Assembly, on the nomination of the Investors Trust)
Chairman: Mr A.W.T. Gibb BA
Vice-Chairman: Ms C.Y. Alexander
Treasurer: Mr I.W. Grimmond BAcc CA
Deputy Treasurer: Mrs A.F. Macintosh BA CA
Secretary: Miss Nicola Laing

Remit
The Church of Scotland Investors Trust was established by the Church of Scotland (Properties and Investments) Order Confirmation Act 1994 – Scottish Charity Number SC022884 – and offers investment services to the Church of Scotland and to bodies and trusts within or connected with the Church. It offers simple and economical facilities for investment in its three Funds, and investors receive the benefits of professional management, continuous portfolio supervision, spread of investment risk and economies of scale.

The three Funds are:

1.   Deposit Fund
The Deposit Fund is intended for short-term investment and seeks to provide a competitive rate of interest while preserving nominal capital value. It is invested mainly in short-term loans to banks and building societies. Interest is calculated quarterly in arrears and paid gross on 15 May and 15 November. Withdrawals are on demand. The Fund is managed by Thomas Miller Investments Limited, Edinburgh and London.

2.   Growth Fund
The Growth Fund is a unitised fund, largely equity-based, intended to provide a growing annual income sufficient to meet the Trustees' target distributions and to provide an increase in the value of capital long term. Units can only be purchased or sold on a monthly dealing date, and income

is distributed gross on 15 May and 15 November. The Fund is managed by Newton Investment Management Limited, London.

3. Income Fund

The Income Fund is a unitised fund, invested predominantly in fixed-interest securities, intended to provide a high and sustainable income at a level as agreed between the Trustees and the manager from time to time and to protect the long-term nominal value of capital. Units can only be purchased or sold on a monthly dealing date, and income is distributed gross on 4 April and 4 October. The Fund is managed by Royal London Asset Management, London.

Further information and application forms for investment are available on the Church of Scotland website or by writing to the Secretary, The Church of Scotland Investors Trust, 121 George Street, Edinburgh EH2 4YN (E-mail: nlaing@cofscotland.org.uk).

14. The Church of Scotland Pension Trustees

Chairman: Mr W.J. McCafferty ACII APFS TEP
Vice-Chairman: Mr Graeme Caughey BSc FFIA
Secretary: Mr S.D. Kaney BSc MPMI

Staff
Pensions Manager: Mr Steve D. Kaney BSc MPMI
Pensions Administrators: Miss Fiona McCulloch
                            Mr Andrew McKenna
                            Mrs Mary Mackenzie
                            Miss Marshall Paterson
Team Secretary: Mrs Nancy Harper

Remit
The body acts as Trustees for the Church of Scotland's three Pension Schemes:
1.   The Church of Scotland Pension Scheme for Ministers and Overseas Missionaries
2.   The Church of Scotland Pension Scheme for Staff
3.   The Church of Scotland Pension Scheme for Presbytery and Parish Workers.
The Trustees have wide-ranging duties and powers detailed in the Trust Law, Pension Acts and other regulations, but in short the Trustees are responsible for the administration of the Pension Schemes and for the investment of the Scheme Funds. Six Trustees are appointed by the General Assembly, and members nominate up to three Trustees for each Scheme.

The investment of the Funds is delegated to external Investment Managers under the guidelines and investment principles set by the Trustees: Baillie Gifford & Co., Newton Investment Management Ltd, Aviva, BlackRock, Kames, Rogge and Legal & General.

The benefits provided by the three Pension Schemes differ in detail, but all provide a pension to the Scheme member and dependants on death of the member, and a lump-sum death benefit on death in service. Scheme members also have the option to improve their benefits by paying additional voluntary contributions (AVCs) to arrangements set up by the Trustees with leading Insurance Companies.

Further information on any of the Church of Scotland Pension Schemes or on individual benefits can be obtained from the Pensions Manager, Church of Scotland Offices, 121 George Street, Edinburgh EH2 4YN (Tel: 0131-240 2255; Fax: 0131-240 2220; E-mail: pensions@cofscotland.org.uk).

15. The Church of Scotland Trust

Membership
(Members are appointed by the General Assembly, on the nomination of the Trust)
Chairman: Mr Robert Brodie CB WS
Vice-Chairman: Mr Christopher N. Mackay WS
Treasurer: Mr Iain W. Grimmond BAcc CA
Secretary and Clerk: Mrs Jennifer M. Hamilton BA

Remit
The Church of Scotland Trust was established by Act of Parliament in 1932 and has Scottish Charity Number SC020269. The Trust's function since 1 January 1995 has been to hold properties outwith Scotland and to act as Trustee in a number of third-party trusts.
 Further information can be obtained from the Secretary and Clerk of The Church of Scotland Trust, 121 George Street, Edinburgh EH2 4YN (Tel: 0131-240 2222; E-mail: jhamilton@cofscotland.org.uk).

---

16. Committee on Church Art and Architecture

See entry in full under **The Mission and Discipleship Council** (number 4).

---

17. Communications Department

Communications Department
Head of Communications: Seonag Mackinnon

Communications and Media Relations Team
Senior Media Relations Officer: Nick Jury
Communications Officer: Fiona Lang

Programmes Co-ordinator: Virginia Cano

Web Team
Web Editor: Narelle McGowan
Web Developer: Alan Murray

Design Services
Senior Graphic Designer: Claire Bewsey
Senior Graphic Designer: Chris Flexen

The Communications Department has responsibility for providing and promoting effective internal and external communications across the Church of Scotland.
 The Media Relations Team services local, regional, national, UK and international media. News releases are issued on a regular basis to a large network of media contacts, and staff

provide advice and information on media matters within the Church. Media Relations staff can be contacted on 0131-240 2204/2268 during office hours, or on 07854 783539 after hours, at weekends and on public holidays.

The Web Team is responsible for developing and updating the Church's website (www.churchofscotland.org.uk) and managing the Church's social-media channels. The Design Team creates printed and online material for the Church.

18. The Department of the General Assembly

The Department of the General Assembly supports the General Assembly and the Moderator, the Council of Assembly and the Ecumenical Relations Committee. In addition, Departmental staff service the following Committees: Assembly Arrangements, Legal Questions, the Committee to Nominate the Moderator, the Nomination Committee, the Committee on Overtures and Cases, the Committee on Classifying Returns to Overtures and the Central Services Committee. The Clerks of Assembly are available for consultation on matters of Church Law, Practice and Procedure.

Staff

Principal Clerk of the General Assembly:	Rev. John P. Chalmers BD CPS
Depute Clerk of the General Assembly*:	Rev. George J. Whyte BSc BD DMin
Secretary to the Council of Assembly:	Mrs Pauline Weibye MA DPA Chartered FCIPD
Ecumenical Officer:	Very Rev. Sheilagh M. Kesting BA BD DD
Personal Assistant to the Principal Clerk:	Mrs Linda Jamieson
Legal and Learning Resources Officer:	Ms Christine Paterson LLB DipLP
Senior Administration Officer: (Assembly Arrangements and Moderatorial Support)	Mrs Alison Murray MA
Senior Administration Officer: (Council of Assembly, Central Services Committee and Nomination Committee)	Mrs Pauline Wilson
Senior Administrator: (Ecumenical Relations)	Miss Rosalind Milne

Contact Details:

Principal Clerk:	0131-240 2240
Secretary to the Council of Assembly:	0131-240 2229
Ecumenical Officer:	0131-240 2208
Linda Jamieson:	0131-240 2240
Rosalind Milne:	0131-225 5722 ext. 2370
Alison Murray:	0131-225 5722 ext. 2250
Christine Paterson:	0131-225 5722 ext. 2263
Pauline Wilson:	0131-240 2229
Office Fax number:	0131-240 2239
Office E-mail address:	pcoffice@cofscotland.org.uk

Note: the office of Depute Clerk is part-time, and the office-holder is not based in the Church Offices. Contact should be made through the Principal Clerk.

19. Design Services

For further details, see Communications Department at number 17.

20. Ecumenical Relations Committee

Remit
- to advise the General Assembly on matters of policy affecting ecumenical relations;
- to ensure that the members on the Committee serving on the other Councils are appropriately informed and resourced so as to be able to represent the ecumenical viewpoint on the Council on which they serve;
- to ensure appropriate support for the Ecumenical Officer's representative function in the event of his or her absence, whether through illness, holidays or other commitments;
- to nominate people from across the work of the Church of Scotland to represent the Church in Assemblies and Synods of other churches, ecumenical consultations and delegations to ecumenical assemblies and so on;
- to call for and receive reports from representatives of the Church of Scotland attending Assemblies and Synods of other churches and those ecumenical conferences and gatherings which are held from time to time;
- to ensure that appropriate parts of such reports are made available to relevant Councils;
- to ensure that information is channelled from and to ecumenical bodies of which the Church of Scotland is a member;
- to ensure that information is channelled from and to other churches in Scotland and beyond;
- to ensure the continued development of ecumenical relations by means of the Web and other publications;
- to ensure personal support for the Ecumenical Officer;
- to approve guidelines for the setting up and oversight of Local Ecumenical Partnerships.

Membership
a) Five members appointed by the General Assembly, each to serve as a member of one of the five Councils of the Church.
b) A Convener who is not a member of any of the other Councils and who will act as a personal support for the Ecumenical Officer, and a Vice-Convener, appointed by the General Assembly.
c) A representative of the United Free Church of Scotland appointed by that Church.
d) A representative of the Roman Catholic Church in Scotland appointed by the Bishops' Conference and one representative from each of three churches drawn from among the member churches of ACTS and the Baptist Union of Scotland, each to serve for a period of four years.
e) The Committee shall co-opt Church of Scotland members elected to the central bodies of Churches Together in Britain and Ireland (CTBI), the Conference of European Churches (CEC), the World Council of Churches (WCC), the World Communion of Reformed Churches (WCRC) and the Community of Protestant Churches in Europe (CPCE, formerly the Leuenberg Fellowship of Churches).
f) The General Secretary of ACTS shall be invited to attend as a corresponding member.

g) For the avoidance of doubt, while, for reasons of corporate governance, only Church of Scotland members of the Committee shall be entitled to vote, before any vote is taken the views of members representing other churches shall be ascertained.

Convener:	Rev. Alison P. McDonald MA BD (2013)
Vice-Convener:	Rev. Peter H. Donald MA PhD BD (2013)
Secretary and Ecumenical	
Officer:	Very Rev. Sheilagh M. Kesting BA BD DD
Senior Administrator:	Miss Rosalind Milne

INTER-CHURCH ORGANISATIONS

World Council of Churches
The Church of Scotland is a founder member of the World Council of Churches, formed in 1948. As its basis declares, it is 'a fellowship of Churches which confess the Lord Jesus Christ as God and Saviour according to the Scriptures, and therefore seek to fulfil their common calling to the glory of the one God, Father, Son and Holy Spirit'. Its member Churches, which number over 300, are drawn from all continents and include all the major traditions – Eastern and Oriental Orthodox, Reformed, Lutheran, Anglican, Baptist, Disciples, Methodist, Moravian, Friends, Pentecostalist and others. Although the Roman Catholic Church is not a member, there is very close co-operation with the departments in the Vatican.

The World Council holds its Assemblies every seven years. Its tenth Assembly will take place in Busan, Republic of Korea, from 30 October to 8 November 2013. The theme of the Assembly, 'God of life, lead us to justice and peace', was inspired by the diversity of Asian contexts and by a growing sense of urgency to care for life and seek justice. It is both a prayer and a statement of faith, calling Christians to engage with God's vision of justice and peace, so that all may have life in fullness.

The WCC is divided into six programme areas:
* WCC and the Ecumenical Movement in the 21st Century
* Unity, Mission, Evangelism and Spirituality
* Public Witness: Addressing Power, Affirming Peace
* Justice, Diakonia and Responsibility for Creation
* Education and Ecumenical Formation
* Inter-Religious Dialogue and Co-operation.

The General Secretary is Rev. Dr Olav Fykse Tveit, PO Box 2100, 150 route de Ferney, CH-1211 Geneva 2, Switzerland (Tel: 00 41 22 791 61 11; Fax: 00 41 22 791 03 61; E-mail: infowcc@wcc-coe.org; Website: www.oikumene.org).

World Communion of Reformed Churches
The Church of Scotland was a founder member of 'The Alliance of the Reformed Churches Throughout the World Holding the Presbyterian System', which began in 1875. As the World Alliance of Reformed Churches, it included also Churches of the Congregational tradition. In June 2010, WARC merged with the Reformed Ecumenical Council and became the World Communion of Reformed Churches.

The World Communion of Reformed Churches (WCRC) brings together 80 million Reformed Christians in 108 countries around the world – united in their commitment to mission, church unity and justice. WCRC links Presbyterian, Reformed, Congregational, Waldensian, United and Uniting Churches.

The WCRC works in four main areas:
* Communication (fostering church unity and interfaith dialogue)
* Justice (helping churches to act for social and economic rights and care of the environment)
* Mission (facilitating mission renewal and empowerment)

•   Partnership (providing funds for church unity, mission and justice projects).
The Uniting General Council was held in Grand Rapids, Michigan, USA from 18–28 June 2010. The theme was 'Unity of the Spirit in the Bond of Peace'.
The General Secretary is Rev. Dr Setri Nyomi, PO Box 2100, 150 route de Ferney, CH-1211 Geneva 2, Switzerland (Tel: 00 41 22 791 62 40; Fax: 00 41 22 791 65 05; E-mail: wcrc@wcrc.ch; Website: www.wcrc.ch).

Conference of European Churches
The Church of Scotland is a founder member of the Conference of European Churches, formed in 1959 and until recently the only body which involved in common membership representatives of every European country (except Albania) from the Atlantic to the Urals. More than 100 Churches, Orthodox and Protestant, are members. Although the Roman Catholic Church is not a member, there is very close co-operation with the Council of European Catholic Bishops' Conferences. With the removal of the long-standing political barriers in Europe, the Conference has now opportunities and responsibilities to assist the Church throughout the continent to offer united witness and service.
CEC held its fourteenth Assembly from 3–8 July 2013 in Budapest, Hungary. Its theme was 'And now what are you waiting for? CEC and its mission in a changing Europe'.
The General Secretary is Rev. Dr Guy Liagre, PO Box 2100, 150 route de Ferney, CH-1211 Geneva 2, Switzerland (Tel: 00 41 22 791 61 11; Fax: 00 41 22 791 62 27; E-mail: cec@cec-kek.org; Website: www.ceceurope.org).

CEC: Church and Society Commission
The Church of Scotland was a founder member of the European Ecumenical Commission for Church and Society (EECCS). The Commission owed its origins to the Christian concern and vision of a group of ministers and European civil servants about the future of Europe. It was established in 1973 by Churches recognising the importance of this venture. Membership included Churches and ecumenical bodies from the European Union. The process of integration with CEC was completed in 2000, and the name, Church and Society Commission (CSC), established. In Brussels, CSC monitors Community activity, maintains contact with MEPs and promotes dialogue between the Churches and the institutions. It plays an educational role and encourages the Churches' social and ethical responsibility in European affairs. It has a Director, a study secretary and an executive secretary in Brussels and a small office in Strasbourg.
The Director is Rev. Rüdiger Noll, Ecumenical Centre, 174 rue Joseph II, B-1000 Brussels, Belgium (Tel: 00 32 2 230 17 32; Fax: 00 32 2 231 14 13; E-mail: ved@cec-kek.be).

Community of Protestant Churches in Europe
The Church of Scotland is a founder member of the Community of Protestant Churches in Europe (CPCE), which was formerly known as the Leuenberg Church Fellowship. The Fellowship came into being in 1973 on the basis of the Leuenberg Agreement between the Reformation churches in Europe; the name was changed to the CPCE in 2003. The Leuenberg Agreement stipulates that a common understanding of the Gospel based on the doctrine of Justification by Faith, and interpreted with reference to the proclamation of the Word of God, Baptism and the Lord's Supper, is sufficient to overcome the Lutheran–Reformed church division.
Over 100 Protestant churches in Europe, and a number of South American churches with European origin, have been signatories to the Leuenberg Agreement, including Lutheran, Reformed, United and Methodist Churches, as well as pre-Reformation Waldensian, Hussite and Czech Brethren, and they grant each other pulpit and table fellowship. Most of the CPCE member churches are minority churches, and this imparts a particular character to their life and witness. A General Assembly is held

every six years – the seventh General Assembly was held in September 2012 in Florence, Italy – and a thirteen-member Council carries on the work of the CPCE in the intervening period.

The General Secretary is Bishop Professor Dr Michael Bunker, Severin-Schreiber-Gasse 3, A-1180 Vienna, Austria (Tel: 00 43 1 4791523 900; Fax: 00 43 1 4791523 110; E-mail: geke@leuenberg.eu; Website: www.leuenberg.eu).

Churches Together in Britain and Ireland (CTBI)

In September 1990, Churches throughout Britain and Ireland solemnly committed themselves to one another, promising to one another to do everything possible together. To provide frameworks for this commitment to joint action, the Churches established CTBI for the United Kingdom and Ireland, and, for Scotland, ACTS, with sister organisations for Wales and for England.

Churches Together in Britain and Ireland works with member churches to co-ordinate responses, share resources and learn from each other's experiences.

There are currently eight subject-based work areas:
- Church and Public Issues
- Theology and Unity
- Mission
- China Desk
- Inter-Religious
- International Students
- Racial Justice
- Action on Asylum and Refugees.

There are also three theme-based work areas:
- Environment and Climate Change
- Culture, Identity and the Public Square
- Migration and Movements of People.

The General Secretary is Rev. Bob Fyffe, 39 Eccleston Square, London SW1V 1BX (Tel: 0845 680 6851; Fax: 0845 680 6852; E-mail: info@ctbi.org.uk; Website: www.ctbi.org.uk).

Action of Churches Together in Scotland (ACTS)

ACTS is governed by a Board of Trustees which consults with the Members' Meeting. The Members' Meeting is composed of representatives from the nine trustee member Churches. There are four Networks: Church Life, Faith Studies, Mission, and Church and Society. Contributing to the life of the Networks are associated ecumenical groups. Such groups are expressions of the Churches' commitment to work together and to bring together key people in a defined field of interest or expertise. ACTS is an expression of the commitment of the Churches to one another.

ACTS is staffed by a General Secretary, an Assistant General Secretary and two Network Officers. Their offices are based in Alloa.

These structures facilitate regular consultation and intensive co-operation among those who frame the policies and deploy the resources of the Churches in Scotland and throughout Britain and Ireland. At the same time, they afford greater opportunity for a wide range of members of different Churches to meet in common prayer and study.

The General Secretary is Brother Stephen Smyth fms, 7 Forrester Lodge, Inglewood House, Alloa FK10 2HU (Tel: 01259 216980; Fax: 01259 215964; E-mail: ecumenical@acts-scotland. org; Website: www.acts-scotland.org).

21. Facilities Management Department

Staff
Facilities Manager: Carole Tait
                             (Tel: 0131-240 2214)

The responsibilities of the Facilities Manager's Department include:
* management of a maintenance budget for the upkeep of the Church Offices at 121 George Street, Edinburgh;
* responsibility for all aspects of health and safety for staff, visitors and contractors working in the building;
* managing a team of staff providing the Offices with security, reception, mail room, print room, switchboard, day-to-day maintenance services and Committee room bookings;
* overseeing all sub-contracted services to include catering, cleaning, boiler-room maintenance, intruder alarm, fire alarms, lifts and water management;
* maintaining building records in accordance with the requirements of statutory legislation;
* overseeing all alterations to the building and ensuring, where applicable, that they meet DDR, Planning and Building Control regulations.

22. General Treasurer's Department

The General Treasurer's Department and the Stewardship Department have merged to form the Stewardship and Finance Department. See number 31.

23. General Trustees

Membership
(New Trustees are appointed, as required, by the General Assembly, on the recommendation of the General Trustees)

Chairman: Rev. James A.P. Jack BSc BArch BD DMin RIBA ARIAS
                             (2010)
Vice-Chairman: Mr Iain C. Douglas RD BArch FRIAS RIBA (2010)
Secretary and Clerk: Mr David D. Robertson LLB NP
Depute Secretary and Clerk: Mr Keith S. Mason LLB NP

Committees:
Fabric Committee
Convener: Mr Roger G.G. Dodd DipBldgCons(RICS) FRICS (2010)

Chairman's Committee
Convener: Rev. James A.P. Jack BSc BArch BD DMin RIBA ARIAS
                             (2010)

Glebes Committee
Convener: Mr William M. Lawrie (2012)

Finance Committee
Convener: Mr Peter F. King LLB MCIBS (2010)

Audit Committee
Convener: Dr J. Kenneth Macaldowie LLD CA (2005)

Law Committee
Convener:

Staff
Secretary and Clerk: Mr David D. Robertson LLB NP
Depute Secretary and Clerk: Mr Keith S. Mason LLB NP
Assistant Secretaries: Mr Keith J. Fairweather LLB (Glebes)
                                   Mrs Morag J. Menneer BSc MRICS (Glebes)
                                   Mr Brian D. Waller LLB (Ecclesiastical Buildings)
Treasurer: Mr Iain W. Grimmond BAcc CA
Deputy Treasurer: Mrs Anne F. Macintosh BA CA
Assistant Treasurer: Ms Yvonne Winchester BAcc CA

Remit
The General Trustees are a Property Corporation created and incorporated under the Church of Scotland (General Trustees) Order Confirmation Act 1921. They have Scottish Charity Number SC014574. Their duties, powers and responsibilities were greatly extended by the Church of Scotland (Property & Endowments) Acts and Orders 1925 to 1995, and they are also charged with the administration of the Central Fabric Fund (see below) and the Consolidated Fabric Fund and the Consolidated Stipend Fund in which monies held centrally for the benefit of individual congregations are lodged.

The scope of the work of the Trustees is broad, covering all facets of property administration, but particular reference is made to the following matters:

1.   **ECCLESIASTICAL BUILDINGS.** The Trustees' Fabric Committee considers proposals for work at buildings, regardless of how they are vested, and plans of new buildings. Details of all such projects should be submitted to the Committee before work is commenced. The Committee also deals with applications for the release of fabric monies held by the General Trustees for individual congregations, and considers applications for assistance from the Central Fabric Fund from which grants and/or loans may be given to assist congregations faced with expenditure on fabric. Application forms relating to consents for work and possible financial assistance from the Central Fabric Fund are available from the Secretary of the Trustees and require to be submitted through Presbytery with its approval. The Committee normally meets on the first or second Tuesday of each month, apart from July, when it meets on the second last Tuesday, and August, when there is no meeting.

2.   **SALE, PURCHASE AND LETTING OF PROPERTIES.** All sales or lets of properties vested in the General Trustees fall to be carried out by them in consultation with the Financial Board of the congregation concerned, and no steps should be taken towards any sale or let without prior consultation with the Secretary of the Trustees. Where property

to be purchased is to be vested in the General Trustees, it is essential that contact be made at the earliest possible stage with the Solicitor to the Trustees, who is responsible for the lodging of offers for such properties and all subsequent legal procedure.

3.   **GLEBES.** The Trustees are responsible for the administration of Glebes vested in their ownership. All lets fall to be granted by them in consultation with the minister concerned. It should be noted that neither ministers nor Kirk Sessions may grant lets of Glebe land vested in the General Trustees. As part of their Glebe administration, the Trustees review regularly all Glebe rents.

4.   **INSURANCE.** Properties vested in the General Trustees must be insured with the Church of Scotland Insurance Co. Ltd, a company wholly owned by the Church of Scotland whose profits are applied for Church purposes. Insurance enquiries should be sent directly to the Company at 67 George Street, Edinburgh EH2 2JG (Tel: 0131-220 4119; Fax: 0131-220 4120; E-mail: enquiries@cosic.co.uk).

---

24. *Go For It* Fund

See entry in full under **The Ministries Council** (number 3).

---

25. Human Resources Department

Staff

Head of Human Resources and Information Technology:	Mike O'Donnell Chartered FCIPD
Human Resources Manager:	Karen Tait Chartered CIPD

Remit

The Human Resources Department has responsibility for Recruitment and Selection, Learning and Development, and producing and updating HR Policies and Procedures to ensure that the Central Services Committee, the Ministries Council and the World Mission Council, as employing agencies, are in line with current employment-law legislation. The Department produces contracts of employment and advises on any changes to an individual employee's terms and conditions of employment. It also provides professional Human Resources advice to the organisation on Employee Relations matters, Performance Management and Diversity and Equality.

Our main aim is to work closely with Councils within the organisation to influence strategy so that each Council is making best use of its people and its people opportunities. We take a consultancy role that facilitates and supports each Council's own initiatives and help each other share and work together in consultation with Unite.

26.   Information Technology Department

Staff
Head of Human Resources and Information Technology: Mike O'Donnell
Information Technology Manager: David Malcolm

The Department provides computer facilities to Councils and Departments within 121 George Street and to Presbytery Clerks and other groups within the Councils. It is also responsible for the telephone service within 121 George Street and the provision of assistance and advice on this to other groups.
    The facilities provided include:
* the provision and maintenance of data and voice networks
* the purchase and installation of hardware and software
* support for problems and guidance on the use of hardware and software
* development of in-house software
* maintenance of data within some central systems.

27.   Law Department

Staff
Solicitor of the Church
    and of the General Trustees: Mrs Janette Wilson LLB NP
Depute Solicitor: Miss Mary Macleod LLB NP
Solicitors: Mrs Jennifer Hamilton BA NP
    Mrs Elspeth Annan LLB NP
    Miss Susan Killean LLB NP
    Mrs Anne Steele LLB NP
    Miss Lesa Burns LLB NP
    Miss Jennifer Sharp LLB NP
    Mr Gregor Buick LLB WS NP

The Department's team of experienced solicitors is available to provide legal advice and assistance to all congregations, Presbyteries, Councils, Committees and Courts of the Church. It also represents the Church of Scotland General Trustees, the Church of Scotland Trust and the Church of Scotland Investors Trust. The solicitors in the Department act exclusively on behalf of Church of Scotland bodies and therefore have an understanding and experience of the law as it relates to the Church which cannot be equalled elsewhere. They also have an awareness of wider policy and financial issues affecting both congregations and central Church bodies.
    The Department is committed to meeting the particular needs of the Church. It provides a large number of free resources for congregations, which are available to download from the Church website (www.churchofscotland.org.uk/resources/subjects/law_circulars). These include style documents and circulars covering matters such as contracts of employment; guidance on the Bribery Act 2010 as it affects congregations; guidance on the Data Protection Act; charity law; licensing matters and the letting of church halls.
    The solicitors in the Department can offer tailored advice on most areas of the law, including:
* marketing properties for sale
* commercial and residential conveyancing

- commercial and residential leasing
- employment issues
- trusts and executries
- charity law
- litigation and dispute resolution
- data protection
- contract law
- planning law
- agricultural law
- licensing and regulatory matters
- mobile-phone installations.

Contact details: E-mail: lawdept@cofscotland.org.uk; Tel: 0131-225 5722 ext. 2230; Fax: 0131-240 2246.

---

28.   Legal Questions Committee

Membership
Convener, Vice-Convener and ten members appointed by the General Assembly on the Report of the Nomination Committee.

Convener:	Rev. Alan J. Hamilton LLB BD
Vice-Convener:	Rev. Sheila M. Kirk BA LLB BD
Secretary:	The Principal Clerk

The Assembly Clerks, Procurator and Solicitor of the Church are non-voting members of the Legal Questions Committee.

Remit
- to advise the General Assembly on questions of Church Law and of Constitutional Law affecting the relationship between Church and State;
- to advise and assist Agencies of the General Assembly in the preparation of proposed legislation and on questions of interpretation, including interpretation of and proposed changes to remits;
- to compile the statistics of the Church, except Youth and Finance; and to supervise on behalf of the General Assembly all arrangements for care of Church Records and for Presbytery visits;
- to conduct an annual review of progress made in discharging the remit and provide a written report to the Council of Assembly.

---

29.   Nomination Committee

Membership
(Convener, Vice-Convener and 24 members)
Convener: Rev. James Dewar MA BD (2011)

Vice-Convener: Rev. Kenneth Stott MA BD (2013)
Secretary: Mrs Pauline Weibye MA DPA Chartered FCIPD

Remit
1. To bring before the General Assembly names of persons to serve on the Councils and Standing Committees of the General Assembly.
2. To identify and interview suitable candidates for membership of the Council of Assembly, bringing before the General Assembly the names of persons to serve as charity trustees of the Unincorporated Councils and Committees.
3. To work with the main Councils of the General Assembly to ensure an open, fair and robust process for identifying suitable persons to serve as Conveners of such Councils, engaging with those so identified to ensure their suitability to serve as charity trustees of the Unincorporated Councils and Committees.

30. Panel on Review and Reform

Membership
(10 members appointed by the General Assembly)
Convener: Rev. Donald Campbell (2011)
Vice-Convener: Rev. Jack Holt (2011)
(The Ecumenical Officer attends but without the right to vote or make a motion.)

Staff
Senior Administrator: Mrs Valerie A. Cox
                            (Tel: 0131-225 5722 ext. 2336;
                            E-mail: vcox@cofscotland.org.uk)

Remit
- to listen to the voices of congregations, Presbyteries, Agencies, and those beyond the Church of Scotland;
- through such interaction, consultation and discussion with congregations, Presbyteries, Councils and Agencies of the Church as may be decided upon by the Panel, to formulate and bring before successive General Assemblies:
  (a) a clear statement of the long-term vision of the Church, and
  (b) paths and developments which might be followed by congregations, Presbyteries, Councils and Agencies of the Church to make such a vision a reality;
- to consider the changing needs, challenges and responsibilities of the Church;
- to have particular regard to the gospel imperative of priority for the poor, needy and marginalised.

31. Stewardship and Finance Department

The General Treasurer's Department and the Stewardship Department merged to form the Stewardship and Finance Department on 1 June 2009. This Department is accountable to the Council of Assembly through its Finance Group.
The Departmental e-mail address is: sfadmin@cofscotland.org.uk

Staff based at the Church Offices

General Treasurer:	Mr Iain W. Grimmond BAcc CA
Deputy Treasurer:	Mrs Anne F. Macintosh BA CA
Head of Stewardship:	Rev. Alan W. Gibson BA BD
Finance Managers:	
Congregational Finance	Mr Archie McDowall BA CA
General Trustees	Ms Yvonne Winchester BAcc CA
Ministries	Mrs Elaine Macadie BA CA
World Mission	Mrs Catriona M. Scrimgeour BSc ACA
Management and Pensions Accountant:	Mrs Kay C. Hastie BSc CA

Regional Staff
Stewardship Consultants:
*   Mrs Margot R. Robertson BA (Tel: 01620 893459) for the Presbyteries of:
    Edinburgh, West Lothian, Lothian, Melrose and Peebles, Duns, Jedburgh
*   Mrs Edith Scott (Tel: 01357 520503) for the Presbyteries of:
    Annandale and Eskdale, Dumfries and Kirkcudbright, Wigtown and Stranraer, Ayr, Irvine and Kilmarnock, Ardrossan, Lanark, Greenock and Paisley, Hamilton
*   Mr Stuart G. Sangster (Tel: 01360 622302) for the Presbyteries of:
    Glasgow, Dumbarton, Argyll, Stirling, Lochaber
*   Mrs Sandra Holt BSc for the Presbyteries of:
    Falkirk, Dunfermline, Kirkcaldy, St Andrews, Dunkeld and Meigle, Perth, Dundee
*   Mrs Fiona Penny (Tel: 01771 653442) for the Presbyteries of:
    Aberdeen, Kincardine and Deeside, Gordon, Buchan, Moray, Abernethy, Inverness

Stewardship requests from congregations in the Presbyteries of Angus, Ross, Sutherland, Caithness, Lochcarron – Skye, Uist, Lewis, Orkney, Shetland, England and Europe should be addressed to the Head of Stewardship at the Church Offices in the first instance.

Main Responsibilities of the Stewardship and Finance Department
*   Teaching and promoting Christian stewardship throughout the Church;
*   Planning and delivery of stewardship programmes in congregations;
*   Calculating the annual Ministries and Mission Contribution for each congregation, and processing payments;
*   Providing support, training and advice on financial and accounting matters to Congregational Treasurers;
*   Providing management and financial accounting support for the Councils, Committees and Statutory Corporations;
*   Providing banking arrangements and operating a central banking system for the Councils, Committees and Statutory Corporations;
*   Receiving and discharging legacies and bequests on behalf of the Councils, Committees and Statutory Corporations;

- Making VAT returns and tax recoveries on behalf of the Councils, Committees and Statutory Corporations;
- Payroll processing for the Ministries Council, Central Services Committee and the Pension Schemes.

32.   The Church of Scotland Safeguarding Service
Tel: 0131-240 2256; Fax: 0131-220 3113
E-mail: safeguarding@cofscotland.org.uk

Convener:	Ranald Mair (2010)
Vice-Convener:	Rev. Karen K. Campbell BD MTh DMin (2010)

Staff

Head of Safeguarding:	Richard Crosse MA MSW CQSW
Assistant Head of Safeguarding:	Jennifer Milligan CQSW DipSW

The Church of Scotland Safeguarding Service:
What we aim to do and how we provide the service

Introduction

Harm or abuse of children **and** 'adults at risk' can happen anywhere – even in church communities. We have a duty 'to ensure a safe church for all'. The Church of Scotland has a zero-tolerance approach to harm or abuse of people: any type or level is unacceptable.

The possibility of harm or abuse cannot be eliminated, but the safeguarding structures in the Church and the work of the Safeguarding Service seek to minimise the risk of harm occurring or not being responded to appropriately. The Safeguarding Committee, with representation from across the Church, ensures accountability back to the General Assembly, and also provides a forum for shaping policy and direction.

Remit

The Church of Scotland Safeguarding Service aims to:

- ensure best practice in preventing harm or abuse, and
- ensure that the Church makes a timely and appropriate response when harm or abuse is witnessed, suspected or reported.

Preventing harm and abuse

The Safeguarding Service aims to prevent harm or abuse through ensuring that there is good recognition and reporting. It does this by providing:

- information, support and advice on everyday safeguarding matters where there is not an incident of suspected or reported harm or abuse
- advice and support for the **safe recruitment and selection** of all paid staff and volunteers
- the process of applying for membership of the Protection of Vulnerable Groups (Scotland) Act 2007 Scheme for those working with children or 'protected adults'.

Safe recruitment
Safe recruitment is about ensuring that only people suitable to work with children and 'adults at risk' are employed. There is a comprehensive range of safeguarding training programmes to meet the particular learning needs of different groups of people in the Church, including, for example, volunteers, Kirk Sessions, Safeguarding Co-ordinators, Ministries Council, Parish Development Fund and CrossReach services.

Responding to disclosures of harm or abuse or risk of abuse
The Safeguarding Service provides:
*   verbal and written advice in situations where harm or abuse is suspected, witnessed or reported to members of the Church. This service is also provided for CrossReach Social Care Council services
*   support for Safeguarding Panels working with **convicted sex offenders** to ensure their safe inclusion in worship.

In summary, harm or abuse in the Church is rare, and thankfully the vast majority of people will have no knowledge or experience of it, but even one case is one too many. Our key message is:
'if you suspect or witness harm or abuse, or it is reported to you, you must immediately report it to your Safeguarding Co-ordinator or line manager'.
Contact can be made with the Safeguarding Office at the address, telephone number, e-mail address and website shown at the head of this article.

---

33. Scottish Churches Parliamentary Office
Tel: 0131-220 0246
E-mail: chloe@actsparl.org

The Scottish Churches Parliamentary Officer is Chloe Clemmons MA MA. The office is at 44 Hanover Street, Edinburgh EH2 2DR.

The Church of Scotland and the Gaelic Language

Duilleagan Gàidhlig
Ro-ràdh
Ann an 2008, airson a' chiad turais riamh, bha duilleagan air leth againn ann an Gàidhlig anns an *Leabhar Bhliadhnail*, agus a rèir iomraidh rinn mòran toileachadh ris a' ghluasad ùr seo. Tha sinn fo fhiachan am bliadhna a-rithist don Fhear-dheasachaidh airson a bhith cho deònach cuibhreann Ghàidhlig a bhith an lùib na Beurla. An deidh a bhith a' crìonadh fad ghrunn ghinealach, tha a' Ghàidhlig a-nis a' dèanamh adhartais. Tha e cudthromach gum bi Eaglais na h-Alba a' toirt cùl-taic don leasachadh seo, agus gu dearbha tha i aig teis-meadhan a' ghluasaid seo. Ma bheir sinn sùil air eachdraidh, chì sinn nuair a bha a' Ghàidhlig a' fulang làmhachais-làidir anns na linntean a dh'fhalbh, gu robh an Eaglais glè shoirbheachail ann a bhith a' gabhail ceum-tòisich airson an cànan a dhìon.

Eachdraidh

Bha na thachair an dèidh Blàr Chùil Lodair 'na bhuille chruaidh don Ghàidhlig. Cha do chuidich Achd an Fhòghlaim ann an 1872 le cùisean, Achd nach tug fiù 's iomradh air a' Ghàidhlig. Mar thoradh air seo bha a' Ghàidhlig air a fuadach à sgoiltean na h-Alba. Ach bha a' Ghàidhlig air a cleachdadh anns an Eaglais agus bha sin na mheadhan air a cumail o bhith a' dol à sealladh mar chainnt làitheil.

Poileataics

Tha Pàrlamaid na h-Eòrpa a' toirt inbhe don Ghàidhlig mar aon de na mion-chànanan Eòrpach a tha i a' smaoineachadh a bu chòir a cuideachadh agus a h-altram. Beagan bhliadhnachan air ais chuir iad lagh an gnìomh a bha a' cur mar dhleasdanas air Pàrlamaid Bhreatainn àite a thoirt don Ghàidhlig. Ann an 2005, thug Pàrlamaid na h-Alba Achd Gàidhlig na h-Alba air adhart a' cur na Gàidhlig air stèidh mar chainnt nàiseanta, leis an aon spèis ris a' Bheurla.

Cultar

Tha An Comunn Gàidhealach agus buidhnean eile air obair ionmholta a dhèanamh bho chionn fada ann a bhith a' cur na Gàidhlig air adhart mar nì cudthromach nar cultar. Bho chionn ghoirid chuir An Comunn air bhonn co-chruinneachadh de riochdairean o na h-Eaglaisean airson dòighean a lorg air a bhith a' cleachdadh na Gàidhlig ann an adhradh follaiseach. Fad còrr is fichead bliadhna chaidh adhartas mòr a dhèanamh ann am fòghlam tro mheadhan na Gàidhlig, an toiseach tro chròileagain, bun-sgoiltean, agus a-nis ann an àrd-sgoiltean. Thàinig seo gu ìre nuair a stèidhicheadh Sabhal Mòr Ostaig ann am fòghlam àrd-ìre. Bidh an Sabhal Mòr mar phàirt chudthromach de dh'Oilthigh ùr na Gàidhealtachd agus nan Eilean. Tha Comann Albannach a' Bhìobaill glè dhealasach ann a bhith a' sìor thoirt taic don Ghàidhlig le bhith a' foillseachadh nan Sgriobtar anns a' chànan. Rinn Gàidheil toileachadh mòr ris an eadar-theangachadh ùr de Shoigeul Eòin ann an Gàidhlig an latha an-diugh a thàinig a-mach bho chaidh an *Leabhar Bliadhnail* mu dheireadh fhoillseachadh.

Eaglais na h-Alba

1.   Air feadh na dùthcha, tha adhradh air a chumail ann an Gàidhlig, air Ghàidhealtachd agus air Ghalldachd. (Mar eisimpleir, anns na bailtean mòra tha seirbheis Ghàidhlig air a cumail gach Sàbaid ann an Eaglais Ghàidhealach nam Manach Liatha ann an Dùn Eideann, agus ann an Eaglais Chaluim Chille agus Eaglais Sràid a' Ghàradair ann an Glaschu.) Tha còir gum biodh fios aig Clèireach na Clèire air eaglaisean far a bheil seirbheisean Gàidhlig air a cumail. Thug an t-Àrd-sheanadh ann an 2008 misneachadh do Chlèirean coitheanalan freagarrach ainmeachadh far am bu chòir a' Ghàidhlig a bhith air a cleachdadh ann an adhradh nuair a bha iad a' cur phlànaichean-clèire air bhonn. A bharrachd air sin, tha goireasan ann a bheir cuideachadh don fheadhainn a tha airson Gàidhlig a chleachdadh ann an adhradh.

2.   Cha mhòr bho stèidhicheadh *Life and Work* tha *Na Duilleagan Gàidhlig* air a bhith rim faotainn as-asgaidh do neach sam bith a tha gan iarraidh.

3.   Tha Eaglais na h-Alba, mar phàirt de dh'Iomairt Chonaltraidh na h-Eaglais, airson a bhith a' brosnachadh cleachdadh na Gàidhlig. Tha duilleagan Gàidhlig air leth air an làraich-lìn.

4.   Bho chionn beagan bhliadhnachan tha an t-Àrd-sheanadh air na nithean cudthromach seo a mholadh co-cheangailte ris a' Ghàidhlig.

   (i)   Tha an t-Àrd-sheanadh a' cur mealadh-naidheachd air Pàrlamaid na h-Alba airson Achd a' Chànain Ghàidhlig (Alba) a stèidheachadh; tha e a' brosnachadh a' BhBC ach an toir iad cùl-taic do OFCOM a tha ag iarraidh craoladh na Gàidhlig a leudachadh; tha e duilich gu bheil chleachdadh na Gàidhlig a' dol an lughad anns an Eaglais, agus tha e a' toirt cuiridh do Chomhairlean na h-Eaglais, far a bheil sin freagarrach, rannsachadh a dhèanamh air dòighean a lorg a bheir don Ghàidhlig an t-àite sònraichte a chleachd a bhith aice ann am beatha spioradail na h-Alba.

(ii)   Tha an t-Àrd-sheanadh a' cur ìmpidh air Comhairle a' Mhisein agus na
       Deisciobalachd, ann an co-bhoinn ri Comhairle na Ministrealachd, rannsachadh a
       dhèanamh air inbhe na Gàidhlig ann an Eaglais na h-Alba ann an dùil ri aithisg a thoirt
       air beulaibh an Àrd-sheanaidh ann an 2008 air mar a ghabhas leasachadh a dhèanamh
       air cleachdadh na Gàidhlig anns an Eaglais.
(iii) Tha an t-Àrd-sheanadh a' gabhail beachd air àireamh nan sgìrean Gàidhlig, agus
       tha e a' cur ìmpidh Comhairle na Ministrealachd slatan-tomhais a thoirt chun an
       Ard-sheanaidh ann an 2008 airson gun tèid na sgìrean seo a chomharrachadh anns na
       bliadhnachan air thoiseach.
(iv)   Tha an t-Àrd-sheanadh a' cur ìmpidh air Comhairle an Àrd-sheanaidh cumail romhpa
       a bhith a' toirt cùl-taic don Ghàidhlig an taobh a-staigh na h-Eaglais, am measg rudan
       eile a bhith a' còmhradh ri buidhnean maoineachaidh freagarrach.
(v)   Tha an t-Àrd-sheanadh a' dèanamh toileachaidh ris an Aithisg air Leasachadh ann
       an Cleachdadh na Gàidhlig, agus tha e a' brosnachadh Comhairle a' Mhisein agus na
       Deisciobalachd na plànaichean a tha aca airson an ama air thoiseach a chur an gnìomh.
(vi)   Tha an t-Àrd-sheanadh a' dèanamh toileachaidh ris an naidheachd gu bheil Seanal
       Digiteach Gàidhlig ga chur air bhog, agus tha e a' cur ìmpidh air Comhaire na
       h-Eaglais agus na Coimhearsnachd, ann an co-bhoinn ri Comhairle an Àrd-sheanaidh,
       a bhith a' còmhradh ri Comhairle nam Meadhanan Gàidhlig mun àite shònraichte a bu
       chòir a bhith aig prògraman spioradail anns na prògraman a bhios iad a' cur a-mach.

'S e àm air leth inntinneach a tha seo don Ghàidhlig, agus tha an Eaglais airson a bhith a' gabhail
a h-àite anns an iomairt as leth ar cànain. 'S iad na duilleagan seo aon de na dòighean anns a
bheil sinn a' dèanamh sin.

An t-Àrd-sheanadh 2013
Am bliadhna bha an t-Urr. Dòmhnall MacSuain, ministear Chill Tighearna, air ceann seirbheis
Ghàidhlig an Àrd-sheanaidh ann an Eaglais nam Manach Liath. Air ceann na h-ùrnaigh
bha an t-Urr. Coinneach D. MacLeòid, ministear Inbhir Ghòrdain. Leugh fear de bhuill a'
choitheanail, Dòmhnall Iain Dòmhnallach, na Sgriobtaran, agus bha Alasdair MacLeòid air
ceann na seinn. Sheinn Còisir Ghàidhlig Lodainn aig toiseach agus aig deireadh na seirbheis.
Rinn am Moderàtor, an t-Urr. Lorna Hood, am Beannachadh, agus bhruidhinn i ris an luchd-
adhraidh aig an tì an dèidh na seirbheis.
   Cha robh Coinneamh Ghàidhealach aig Àrd-sheanadh na bliadhna seo, ach tha sinn an
dòchas gun tèid a' choinneamh seo a stèidheachadh as-ùr.

Anns an dealachadh
Tha *Na Duilleagan Gàidhlig* aig *Life and Work* air an leughadh le Gàidheil agus luchd-
ionnsachaidh air feadh an t-saoghail. Gheibhear iad an-asgaidh an lùib na h-iris Beurla ma
chuirear sibh fios gu oifis *Life and Work.*

Introduction
The *Year Book 2008/2009*, for the first time ever, featured dedicated pages in Gaelic; and
this innovation was very well received. Again, appreciation is expressed to the Editor for
his willing co-operation. After many generations of decline, Gaelic is once more moving
forward. It is important that the Church of Scotland is seen to be encouraging this progress
and indeed is part of it. History teaches that, in the past, when the Gaelic language has been
under political oppression, the Church has stood successfully in the vanguard of the defence
of the language.

History

The events of Culloden in 1746, as part of the Jacobite rebellion, dealt a cruel blow to the Gaelic language. This was compounded by the Education (Scotland) Act of 1872, which made no mention of the Gaelic language and, indeed, resulted in the outlawing of Gaelic in Scottish schools. The continued use of Gaelic in the Church proved to be the only formal antidote to the disappearance of Gaelic as a viable language.

Politics

The European Parliament recognises Gaelic as one of the minority European languages it sees as important to support and nurture. Some years ago, it passed appropriate legislation laying some responsibility on the United Kingdom Parliament. In 2005, the Scottish Parliament delivered the Gaelic (Scotland) Act, establishing Gaelic as a national language given the same respect as English.

Culture

Traditionally, An Comunn Gaidhealach has done an excellent job in promoting the cultural importance of Gaelic. In recent years, it convened a gathering of representatives from Churches to research how they could help promote the use of Gaelic in public worship. For over twenty years now, there has been substantial growth in Gaelic-medium education, first of all through nurseries, then primary schools and now secondary schools. This has moved on to the establishing of Sabhal Mòr Ostaig in the tertiary sector. The Church of Scotland welcomes the granting of a charter to the University of the Highlands and Islands, and looks forward to the Sabhal Mòr being a vital part of the University. The Scottish Bible Society is also eager to continue its support of Gaelic through the provision of Scriptures. Since the last *Year Book* appeared, Gaelic-speakers and learners have warmly welcomed the publication of John's Gospel in modern Gaelic.

The Church of Scotland and its ongoing support for Gaelic

1.   Across the nation, public worship continues to be conducted in Gaelic. The General Assembly of 2008 encouraged Presbyteries, as part of their planning, to identify appropriate congregations in which Gaelic must be used regularly in public worship. Furthermore, resources are available to encourage the use of Gaelic in worship in all congregations.

2.   Almost since its inception, *Na Duilleagan Gàidhlig*, as part of *Life and Work*, has been available free of charge to any who request it with their *Life and Work* subscription. This is still very much alive.

3.   The Church of Scotland, as part of its Communication Strategy, is concerned to promote the use of Gaelic. There are dedicated Gaelic pages on the website.

4.   Recent years have seen the General Assembly approve a number of important Deliverances relating to Gaelic. For example:

     (i)   The General Assembly congratulate the Scottish Parliament on its passing of the Gaelic Language (Scotland) Bill, encourage the BBC to support OFCOM in its desire for the extension of Gaelic broadcasting, express regret at the substantial decrease in the use of Gaelic in the Church and invite Councils of the Church, where appropriate, to explore ways in which Gaelic can resume its distinctive place within the religious life of Scotland.

     (ii) The General Assembly instructed the Mission and Discipleship Council, in collaboration with the Ministries Council, to undertake an investigation into the present status of Gaelic in the Church of Scotland with a view to reporting to the 2008 General Assembly on the strategic development of the use of the language in the Kirk.

(iii)   The General Assembly note the statistics regarding Gaelic-speaking charges and instructed the Ministries Council to bring to the General Assembly of 2008 an agreed set of criteria for future determination of such designations.

(iv)   The General Assembly instruct the Council of Assembly to continue to support the development of Gaelic within the Church, including discussions with appropriate funding bodies.

(v)   The General Assembly welcome the Report on the Strategic Development of the Use of Gaelic and encourage the Mission and Discipleship Council to develop its future plans.

(vi)   The General Assembly welcome the launch of the Gaelic Digital Broadcasting channel and instruct the Church and Society Council, in co-operation with the Council of Assembly, to discuss with the Gaelic Media Council the significant place of religious programmes in its output.

These are exciting times for the Gaelic language, and the Church is responding to the challenge of our day.

The General Assembly 2013
Conducting worship and preaching the sermon at this year's Gaelic service in Greyfriars Tolbooth and Highland Church was Rev. Donald MacSween (Kiltearn). Prayers were led by Rev. Kenneth D. MacLeod (Invergordon). A member of the Greyfriars Gaelic congregation, Donald John MacDonald, read the Scriptures, and the precentor was Alasdair MacLeod. Lothian Gaelic Choir sang at the beginning and end of the service. The Moderator, the Right Rev. Lorna Hood, pronounced the Benediction, and addressed the congregation at the tea which followed the service.

There was no Highland Meeting during the 2013 Assembly week, but it is hoped that this gathering may be revived.

In conclusion
The Gaelic Supplement of *Life and Work* is read by Gaels and learners of Gaelic all over the world. The monthly Supplement is available on request free of charge along with the main *Life and Work*.

SECTION 2

General Information

(1) OTHER CHURCHES IN THE UNITED KINGDOM

THE UNITED FREE CHURCH OF SCOTLAND
General Secretary: Rev. John Fulton BSc BD, United Free Church Offices, 11 Newton Place, Glasgow G3 7PR (Tel: 0141-332 3435; E-mail: office@ufcos.org.uk).

THE FREE CHURCH OF SCOTLAND
Principal Clerk: Rev. James MacIver, 15 North Bank Street, The Mound, Edinburgh EH1 2LS (Tel: 0131-226 5286; E-mail: principal.clerk@freechurch.org).

FREE CHURCH OF SCOTLAND (CONTINUING)
Clerk of Assembly: Rev. John MacLeod, Free Church Manse, Portmahomack, Tain IV20 1YL (Tel: 01862 871467; E-mail: principalclerk@fccontinuing.org).

THE FREE PRESBYTERIAN CHURCH OF SCOTLAND
Clerk of Synod: Rev. John MacLeod, 6 Church Avenue, Sidcup, Kent DA14 6BU (E-mail: jmacl265@aol.com).

ASSOCIATED PRESBYTERIAN CHURCHES
Clerk of Presbytery: Rev. Archibald N. McPhail, APC Manse, Polvinister Road, Oban PA34 5TN (Tel: 01631 567076; E-mail: archibald.mcphail@virgin.net).

THE REFORMED PRESBYTERIAN CHURCH OF SCOTLAND
Clerk of Presbytery: Rev. Andrew Quigley, Church Offices, 48 North Bridge Street, Airdrie ML6 6NE (Tel: 01236 620107; E-mail: sandrewq@aol.com).

THE PRESBYTERIAN CHURCH IN IRELAND
Clerk of the General Assembly and General Secretary: Rev. Dr Donald J. Watts, Church House, Fisherwick Place, Belfast BT1 6DW (Tel: 02890 322284; E-mail: clerk@presbyterianireland.org).

THE PRESBYTERIAN CHURCH OF WALES
General Secretary: Rev. Meiron Morris, Tabernacle Chapel, 81 Merthyr Road, Whitchurch, Cardiff CF14 1DD (Tel: 02920 627465; E-mail: swyddfa.office@ebcpcw.org.uk).

THE UNITED REFORMED CHURCH
General Secretary: Rev. Roberta Rominger, 86 Tavistock Place, London WC1H 9RT (Tel: 020 7916 8646; Fax: 020 7916 2021; E-mail: roberta.rominger@urc.org.uk).

UNITED REFORMED CHURCH SYNOD OF SCOTLAND
Synod Clerk: Mr Patrick Smyth, 113 West Regent Street, Glasgow G1 2RU (Tel: 0141-248 5382; E-mail: psmyth@urcscotland.org.uk).

BAPTIST UNION OF SCOTLAND
General Director: Rev. Alan Donaldson, 48 Speirs Wharf, Glasgow G4 9TH (Tel: 0141-423 6169; E-mail: director@scottishbaptist.org.uk).

CONGREGATIONAL FEDERATION IN SCOTLAND
Secretary: Rev. May-Kane Logan, 93 Cartside Road, Busby, Glasgow G76 8QD (Tel: 0141-237 1349; E-mail: maycita@talktalk.net).

RELIGIOUS SOCIETY OF FRIENDS (QUAKERS)
Robin Waterston, Clerk to the General Meeting for Scotland, 128 North Street, St Andrews KY16
9AF (Tel: 01334 474129; E-mail: robin.waterston128@gmail.com).

ROMAN CATHOLIC CHURCH
Mgr Hugh Bradley, General Secretary, Bishops' Conference of Scotland, 64 Aitken Street, Airdrie
ML6 6LT (Tel: 01236 764061; E-mail: gensec@bpsconfscot.com).

THE SALVATION ARMY
Lt-Col. Carol Bailey, Secretary for Scotland and Divisional Commander East Scotland
Division, Headquarters and Scotland Secretariat, 12A Dryden Road, Loanhead EH20
9LZ (Tel: 0131-440 9101; E-mail: carol.bailey@salvationarmy.org.uk).

SCOTTISH EPISCOPAL CHURCH
Secretary General: Mr John F. Stuart, 21 Grosvenor Crescent, Edinburgh EH12 5EL (Tel: 0131-
225 6357; E-mail: secgen@scotland.anglican.org).

THE SYNOD OF THE METHODIST CHURCH IN SCOTLAND
District Administrator: Mrs Fiona Inglis, Methodist Church Office, Scottish Churches House,
Kirk Street, Dunblane FK15 0AJ (Tel/Fax: 01786 820295; E-mail: meth@
scottishchurcheshouse.org).

GENERAL SYNOD OF THE CHURCH OF ENGLAND
Secretary General: Mr William Fittall, Church House, Great Smith Street, London SW1P 3NZ
(Tel: 020 7898 1360; E-mail: william.fittall@churchofengland.org).

---

(2) OVERSEAS CHURCHES

PRESBYTERIAN CHURCH IN CANADA
Clerk of Assembly: 50 Wynford Drive, Toronto, Ontario M3C 1J7, Canada (E-mail:
pccadmin@presbyterian.ca; Website: www.presbyterian.ca).

UNITED CHURCH OF CANADA
General Secretary: Suite 300, 3250 Bloor Street West, Toronto, Ontario M8X 2Y4, Canada
(E-mail: info@united-church.ca; Website: www.united-church.ca).

PRESBYTERIAN CHURCH (USA)
Stated Clerk: 100 Witherspoon Street, Louisville, KY 40202-1396, USA (E-mail:
presbytel@pcusa.org; Website: www.pcusa.org).

UNITING CHURCH IN AUSTRALIA
General Secretary: PO Box A2266, Sydney South, New South Wales 1235, Australia (E-mail:
enquiries@nat.uca.org.au; Website: www.uca.org.au).

PRESBYTERIAN CHURCH OF AUSTRALIA
Clerk of Assembly: PO Box 2196, Strawberry Hills, NSW 2012; 168 Chalmers Street,
Surry Hills, NSW 2010, Australia (E-mail: general@pcnsw.org.au; Website:
www.presbyterian.org.au).

PRESBYTERIAN CHURCH OF AOTEAROA, NEW ZEALAND
Executive Secretary: PO Box 9049, Te Aro, Wellington, Aotearoa/New Zealand (E-mail: info@presbyterian.org.nz; Website: www.presbyterian.org.nz).

EVANGELICAL PRESBYTERIAN CHURCH, GHANA
Synod Clerk: PO Box 18, Ho, Volta Region, Ghana (E-mail: epcgenassembly@hotmail.com).

PRESBYTERIAN CHURCH OF GHANA
Synod Clerk: PO Box 1800, Accra, Ghana (E-mail: pcghq@yahoo.com).

PRESBYTERIAN CHURCH OF EAST AFRICA
Secretary General: PO Box 27573, 00506 Nairobi, Kenya (E-mail: info@pcea.or.ke; Website: http://pceaheadoffice.org).

CHURCH OF CENTRAL AFRICA PRESBYTERIAN
Secretary General, General Synod: PO Box 30398, Lilongwe 3, Malawi (E-mail: ccapgeneral@africa-online.net).

IGREJA EVANGELICA DE CRISTO EM MOÇAMBIQUE (EVANGELICAL CHURCH OF CHRIST IN MOZAMBIQUE)
General Secretary: Cx. Postale 284, Nampula 70100, Mozambique (E-mail: mugema@tdm.co.mz).

PRESBYTERIAN CHURCH OF NIGERIA
Principal Clerk: 26–29 Ehere Road, Ogbor Hill, PO Box 2635, Aba, Abia State, Nigeria (E-mail: eme.ndukwe@yahoo.com).

UNITING PRESBYTERIAN CHURCH IN SOUTHERN AFRICA (SOUTH AFRICA)
General Secretary: PO Box 96188, Brixton, Johannesburg 2019, South Africa (E-mail: jpillay@presbyterian.org.za).

UNITING PRESBYTERIAN CHURCH IN SOUTHERN AFRICA (ZIMBABWE)
Presbytery Clerk: PO Box CY224, Causeway, Harare, Zimbabwe (E-mail: mpresby@mweb.co.zw).

PRESBYTERIAN CHURCH OF THE SUDAN
Head Office: PO Box 40, Malakal, Sudan (E-mail: pcosgassembly@yahoo.com).

UNITED CHURCH OF ZAMBIA
General Secretary: Nationalist Road at Burma Road, PO Box 50122, 15101 Ridgeway, Lusaka, Zambia (E-mail: uczsynod@gmail.com).

CHURCH OF BANGLADESH
Moderator: Synod Office, Church of Bangladesh, 54/1 Barobag, Mirpur-2, Dhaka 1216, Bangladesh (E-mail: sarkerps@gmail.com).

BURMA: PRESBYTERIAN CHURCH OF MYANMAR
Tahan, Kalaymyo, Myanmar (E-mail: pcm@myanmar.com.mm).

CHINA
• Amity Foundation, 71 Hankou Road, Nanjing, JS 210008, China.
• China Christian Council, 219 Jiujiang Road, Shanghai 200002, China.
• Nanjing Union Theological Seminary, 100 Qiaoge Lu, Jiangning, Nanjing 211112, China.

CHURCH OF NORTH INDIA
General Secretary: Synod Office, PO Box 311, 16 Pandit Pant Marg., New Delhi 110 001, India
(E-mail: enos@cnisynod.org).

CHURCH OF SOUTH INDIA
General Secretary: Synod Office, 5 White's Road, Royapettah, Chennai 600 014, India (E-mail:
csi@vsnl.com).

PRESBYTERIAN CHURCH OF KOREA
General Secretary: 135 Yunji Dong, Chongro-Gu, Seoul 110 470, Korea (E-mail: plan@pck.
or.kr).

PRESBYTERIAN CHURCH IN THE REPUBLIC OF KOREA
General Secretary: Academy House San 76, Suyu 6-dong, Kangbuk-Ku, Seoul 142070, Korea
(E-mail: prokshin@hanmail.net).

THE UNITED MISSION TO NEPAL
Executive Director: PO Box 126, Kathmandu, Nepal (E-mail: umn@umn.org.np).

CHURCH OF PAKISTAN
Moderator: Rt Rev. Samuel Azariah, Diocese of Raiwind, 17 Warris Road, Lahore 54000, Pakistan
(E-mail: sammyazariah@yahoo.com).

PRESBYTERY OF LANKA
Moderator: 127/1 D S Senanayake Veedyan, Kandy 2000, Sri Lanka (E-mail: scotskirksaman@
sltnet.lk).

PRESBYTERIAN CHURCH IN TAIWAN
General Secretary: 3 Lane 269 Roosevelt Road, Sec. 3, Taipei, Taiwan 10763, ROC (E-mail:
gs@mail.pct.org.tw).

CHURCH OF CHRIST IN THAILAND
General Secretary: 109 CCT Building, 328 Payathai Road, Ratchathevi, Bangkok 10400,
Thailand (E-mail: cctecume@loxinfo.co.th).

PRESBYTERIAN CHURCH IN SINGAPORE
Synod Office: 132 Sophia Road, Singapore (E-mail: office@presbysing.org.sg).

UNITED CHURCH IN JAMAICA AND THE CAYMAN ISLANDS
General Secretary: 12 Carlton Crescent, PO Box 359, Kingston 10, Jamaica (E-mail:
generalsecretary@ucjci.com).

PRESBYTERIAN CHURCH IN TRINIDAD AND TOBAGO
General Secretary: Box 187, Paradise Hill, San Fernando, Trinidad (E-mail: pctt@tstt.net.tt).

PRESBYTERIAN REFORMED CHURCH IN CUBA
General Secretary: Evangelical Theological Seminary of Matanzas, Apartada 149, Dos de Mayofinal, Matanzas, Cuba (E-mail: publiset@enet.cu).

EVANGELICAL CHURCH OF THE CZECH BRETHREN
Moderator: Jungmannova 9, PO Box 466, CZ-11121 Praha 1, Czech Republic (E-mail: ekumena@srcce.cz; Website: www.srcce.cz).

REFORMED CHURCH IN HUNGARY
General Secretary: Abonyi utca 21, H-1146 Budapest, Hungary (E-mail: oikumene@reformatus. hu; Website: www.reformatus.hu).

WALDENSIAN CHURCH
Moderator: Via Firenze 38, 00184 Rome, Italy (E-mail: moderatore@chiesavaldese.org; Website: www.chiesavaldese.org).

PROTESTANT CHURCH IN THE NETHERLANDS
Joseph Haydnlaan 2A, Postbus 8504, NL-3503 RM Utrecht (Tel/Fax: +31 30 880 1880; E-mail: servicedesk@pkn.nl; Website: www.pkn.nl).

SYNOD OF THE NILE OF THE EVANGELICAL CHURCH OF EGYPT
General Secretary: Synod of the Nile of the Evangelical Church, PO Box 1248, Cairo, Egypt (E-mail: epcegypt@yahoo.com).

DIOCESE OF THE EPISCOPAL CHURCH IN JERUSALEM AND THE MIDDLE EAST
Bishop's Office: PO Box 19122, Jerusalem 91191, Israel (E-mail: perexecassistant@j-diocese.org; Website: www.j.diocese.org).

NATIONAL EVANGELICAL SYNOD OF SYRIA AND LEBANON
General Secretary: PO Box 70890, Antelias, Lebanon (E-mail: nessl@synod-sl.org).

MIDDLE EAST COUNCIL OF CHURCHES
General Secretary: PO Box 5376, Deeb Building, Makhoul Street, Beirut, Lebanon (E-mail: mecc@cyberia.net.lb).

[Full information on Churches overseas may be obtained from the World Mission Council.]

---

(3) SCOTTISH DIVINITY FACULTIES
[* denotes a Minister of the Church of Scotland]
[(R) Reader   (SL) Senior Lecturer   (L) Lecturer]

ABERDEEN
(School of Divinity, History and Philosophy)
King's College, Old Aberdeen AB24 3UB
(Tel: 01224 272380; Fax: 01224 273750; E-mail: divinity@abdn.ac.uk)

Master of Christ's College:	Rev. John Swinton* BD PhD RNM RNMD (E-mail: christs-college@abdn.ac.uk)
Head of School:	John Morrison MA PhD
Deputy Head of School:	Lukas Pokorny MA PhD

Professors:

Tom Greggs MA(Oxon) PhD(Cantab) (Historical and Doctrinal Theology)
Steve Mason BA MA PhD (New Testament Exegesis)
Robert Segal BA MA PhD (Religious Studies)
Rev. Joachim Schaper DipTheol PhD (Old Testament)
Rev. John Swinton* BD PhD RNM RNMD (Practical Theology and Pastoral Care)
Rev. Bernd Wannenwetsch MA DrTheol DrTheolHabil (Theological Ethics)
Paul T. Nimmo MA DipIA BD ThM PhD (Systematic Theology)

Senior Lecturers:

Andrew Clarke BA MA PhD (New Testament)
Martin Mills MA PhD (Religious Studies)
Rev. Philip Ziegler BA MA MDiv ThD (Systematic Theology)

Lecturers:

Kenneth Aitken BD PhD (Hebrew Bible)
Thomas Bokedal ThD MTh (New Testament)
Rev. Christopher Brittain BA MDiv PhD (Practical Theology)
Brian Brock BS MA DipTheol DPhil (Moral and Practical Theology)
Marie-Luise Ehrenschwendtner DrTheol PhD (Church History)
Zohar Hadromi-Allouche BA PhD (Religious Studies)
Jutta Leonhardt-Balzer DipTheol PhD (New Testament)
Michael Mawson BA MA PhD (Theological Ethics)
Lukas Pokorny MA PhD (Religious Studies)
Lena-Sofia Tiemeyer BA MA MPhil (Old Testament/Hebrew Bible)
Will Tuladhar-Douglas BA MA MPhil DPhil (Religious Studies)
Donald Wood BA MA MPhil DPhil (Systematic Theology)

ST ANDREWS
(University College of St Mary)
St Mary's College, St Andrews, Fife KY16 9JU
(Tel: 01334 462850/1; Fax: 01334 462852)

Principal:	Rev. Dr Ian C. Bradley*
Head of School:	Dr Mark W. Elliott
Dean:	

Chairs:	M.I. Aguilar OSB Cam Obl BA MA STB PhD FRSA FRAS FRAI FIAI (Religion and Politics)

D.W. Brown MA PhD DLitt FBA FRSE (Theology, Aesthetics and
Culture and Wardlaw Professor)
I.J. Davidson MA PhD MTh (Systematic and Historical Theology)
J.R. Davila BA MA PhD (Early Jewish Studies)
K. De Troyer STB MA STL PhD (Old Testament/Hebrew Bible)
R.A. Piper BA BD PhD (Christian Origins)
A.J. Torrance* MA BD DrTheol (Systematic Theology)
J.B. Webster MA PhD DD FRSE (Divinity)
N.T. Wright MA DPhil DD (New Testament and Early Christianity)

Readers: I.C. Bradley* BA MA BD DPhil (Practical Theology)
                        M.W. Elliott BA BD PhD (Church History)
                        S.R. Hafemann BA MA DrTheol (New Testament)

Senior Lecturers: S.R. Holmes BA MA MTh PGDip PhD (Theology)
                        G. Macaskill BSc DipTh PhD (New Testament)
                        W.A. Tooman BA MA MA PhD (Old Testament/Hebrew Bible)

Lecturers: G.R. Hopps BA MPhil PhD (Literature and Theology)
                        W. Hyland BA MA PhD (Teaching Fellow – Church History)
                        J. Perry BA MDiv PhD (Theological Ethics)
                        E. Shively BA MDiv ThM PhD (New Testament)
                        E. Stoddart BD PhD (Practical Theology)

EDINBURGH
(School of Divinity and New College)
New College, Mound Place, Edinburgh EH1 2LX
(Tel: 0131-650 8900; Fax: 0131-650 7952; E-mail: divinity.faculty@ed.ac.uk)

Head of School: Graham Paul Foster BD MSt PhD
Principal of New College: Rev. Professor David A.S. Fergusson* MA BD DPhil FRSE
Assistant Principal of
New College: Rev. Alison M. Jack* MA BD PhD
Chairs: Professor Hans Barstad DrTheol (Hebrew and Old Testament)
                              Professor Stewart J. Brown BA MA PhD FRHistS FRSE
                              (Ecclesiastical History)
                              Professor Jane E.A. Dawson BA PhD DipEd
                              (John Laing Professor of Reformation History)
                              Rev. Professor David A.S. Fergusson* MA BD DPhil FRSE
                              (Divinity)
                              Professor Susan Hardman Moore* BA PGCE MA PhD (Early
                              Modern Religion)
                              Professor Timothy Lim BA MPhil DPhil (Biblical Studies)
                              Professor Jolyon Mitchell BA MA PhD (Communications, Arts
                              and Religion)

Professor Michael S. Northcott MA PhD (Ethics)
Professor Mona Siddiqui OBE FRSE FRSA DCivil Laws (hon)
DLitt (hon) (Islamic and Interreligious Studies)
Professor Brian Stanley MA PhD (World Christianity)

Readers, Senior Lecturers and Lecturers:

Biblical Studies:
David J. Reimer BTh BA MA DPhil (SL)
Graham Paul Foster BD MSt PhD (SL)
Helen K. Bond MTheol PhD (SL)
Matthew Novenson BA MDiv ThM PhD (L)

Theology and Ethics:
Nicholas Adams MA PhD (SL)
Cecelia Clegg BD MSc PhD (SL)
Rev. Ewan Kelly* MB ChB BD PhD (SL) (part-time)
Michael Purcell MA PhD PhL PhB (SL)
Mark Harris MA PhD MA (L)
David Grumett BA MPhil PhD (L)

History of Christianity:
Sara Parvis BA PhD (L)

Religious Studies:
Elizabeth Koepping MA PhD (SL)
Steven Sutcliffe BA MPhil PhD (SL)
Hannah Holtschneider MPhil PhD (SL)
Afeosemime U. Adogame BA MA PhD (SL)
Naomi Appleton BA MPhil DPhil (L)

Fulton Lecturer in Speech and Communication:
Richard Ellis BSc MEd LGSM

GLASGOW
School of Critical Studies
Theology and Religious Studies Subject Area
4 The Square, University of Glasgow, Glasgow G12 8QQ
(Tel: 0141-330 6526; Fax: 0141-330 4943;
Website: www.gla.ac.uk/departments/theology)

Head of Subject:
Dr Lloyd Ridgeon

Trinity College
Principal of Trinity College: Rev. Dr Doug Gay*
Clerk to Trinity College:

Chairs:
Rev. Prof. David Jasper (Theology and Literature)
Rev. Prof. David Pattison (Divinity)

Readers, Senior Lecturers, Lecturers and Fellows etc.

Biblical Studies:	Dr Sarah Nicholson (L)
Church History:	Rev. Canon Dr Charlotte Methuen
	Rev. Prof.-Emer. W. Ian P. Hazlett* (Hon. Professorial
	Research Fellow)
Catholic Theology:	Ms Julie Clague (L)
Practical Theology:	Rev. Dr Doug Gay* (L)
	Dr Heather Walton (SL)
Religious Studies:	Dr Lloyd Ridgeon (SL) (Islamic Studies)
	Dr Saeko Yazaki (Research Fellow: Islamic Studies)
	Dr Scott Spurlock (L) (Religion in Scotland)

Associate Staff (Free Church of Scotland College, Edinburgh)

Rev. Donald M. MacDonald
Rev. Prof. John R. McIntosh
Rev. Prof. John L. Mackay
Rev. Alasdair I. MacLeod
Rev. Prof. Donald Macleod
Rev. John A. MacLeod
Rev. Neil MacMillan
Rev. Duncan Peters

HIGHLAND THEOLOGICAL COLLEGE UHI
High Street, Dingwall IV15 9HA
(Tel: 01349 780000; Fax: 01349 780201;
E-mail: htc@uhi.ac.uk)

Principal of HTC:	Rev. Hector Morrison* BSc BD MTh
Vice-Principal of HTC:	Jamie Grant PhD MA LLB

Lecturers:	Hector Morrison* BSc BD MTh (Old Testament and Hebrew)
	Jamie Grant PhD MA LLB (Biblical Studies)
	Jason Maston BA MA PhD (New Testament)
	Innes Visagie MA BTh BA PhD (Pastoral Theology)
	Nick Needham BD PhD (Church History)
	Robert Shillaker BSc BA PhD (Systematic Theology)
	Bruce Ritchie BSc BD PhD (Church History)

---

(4) SOCIETIES AND ASSOCIATIONS

The undernoted list shows the name of the Association, along with the name and address of the Secretary.

1. INTER-CHURCH ASSOCIATIONS

The FELLOWSHIP OF ST ANDREW: The fellowship promotes dialogue between Churches of the east and the west in Scotland. Further information available from the Secretary, Rev. John G. Pickles, 1 Annerley Road, Annan DG12 6HE (Tel: 01461 202626; E-mail: jgpickles@hotmail.com).

The FELLOWSHIP OF ST THOMAS: An ecumenical association formed to promote informed interest in and to learn from the experience of Churches in South Asia (India, Pakistan, Bangladesh, Nepal, Sri Lanka and Burma (Myanmar)). Secretary: Miss Janet H. Brown, 6 Baxter Park Terrace, Dundee DD4 6NL (Tel: 01382 453066; E-mail: j.herries.brown@blueyonder.co.uk).

FRONTIER YOUTH TRUST: Encourages, resources and supports churches, organisations and individuals working with young people (in particular, disadvantaged young people). Through the StreetSpace initiative, the Trust is able to help churches to explore new ways of engaging young people in the community around mission and fresh expressions of church. All correspondence to: Frontier Youth Trust, Office S15b, St George's Community Hub, Great Hampton Row, Newtown, Birmingham B19 3JG (Tel: 0121-687 3505; E-mail: frontier@fyt.org.uk; Website: www.fyt.org.uk). For information on StreetSpace, contact Richard Passmore (07830 197160).

INTERSERVE SCOTLAND: We are part of Interserve, an international, evangelical and interdenominational organisation with 160 years of Christian service. The purpose of Interserve is 'to make Jesus Christ known through *wholistic* ministry in partnership with the global church, among the neediest peoples of Asia and the Arab world', and our vision is 'Lives and communities transformed through encounter with Jesus Christ'. Interserve supports over 800 people in cross-cultural ministry in a wide range of work including children and youth, the environment, evangelism, Bible training, engineering, agriculture, business development and health. We rely on supporters in Scotland and Ireland to join us. Director: Grace Penney, 4 Blairtummock Place, Panorama Business Village, Queenslie, Glasgow G33 4EN (Tel: 0141-781 1982; Fax: 0141-781 1572; E-mail: info@issi.org.uk; Website: www.interservescotlandandireland.org).

IONA COMMUNITY: An ecumenical Christian community of men and women from different walks of life and different traditions in the Church, committed to the gospel of Jesus Christ and to following where that leads, even into the unknown; engaged together, and with people of goodwill across the world, in acting, reflecting and praying for justice, peace and the integrity of creation; convinced that the inclusive community we seek must be embodied in the community we practise. The Iona Community's work with young people, Wild Goose Resource Group and Wild Goose Publications, is based in the Glasgow office. The Community also runs residential centres at the Abbey and MacLeod Centre, Iona and Camas, Mull. Leader: Rev. Peter Macdonald, 4th Floor, Savoy House, 140 Sauchiehall Street, Glasgow G2 3DH (Tel: 0141-332 6343; Fax: 0141-332 1090; E-mail: admin@iona.org.uk; Website: www.iona.org.uk). Centres Director: Rev. Joanna Anderson, Iona Abbey, Isle of Iona, Argyll PA76 6SN (Tel: 01681 700404).

PLACE FOR HOPE: An initiative with its roots in the Church of Scotland, offering a different way of addressing our differences. It is a network of professionally trained individuals, equipped to facilitate some of our more difficult conversations, offering the means of restoring broken relationships. To Kirk Sessions, Presbyteries and any other groups, we provide training in the skills which can lead to more effective conversations with one another, recognising and valuing our differences. We encourage and enable dialogue – rather than debate – and a means of enabling all voices to be heard. We seek to work across denominations and offer our skills and resources into the community. We operate on a confidential basis, and would be pleased to have a conversation at any time on how we might be of help. Visit www.placeforhope.org.uk or contact Natalie Barrett on 07884 580361.

The ST COLM'S FELLOWSHIP: An association for all from any denomination who have trained, studied or been resident at St Colm's, either when it was a college or later as International House. There is an annual retreat and annual lecture; and some local groups meet on a regular basis. Hon. Secretary: Margaret Nutter, 'Kilmorich', 14 Balloch Road, Balloch G83 8SR (Tel: 01389 754505; E-mail: mnutter@blueyonder.co.uk).

SCOTTISH CHURCHES HOUSING ACTION: Unites the Scottish Churches in tackling homelessness; supports local volunteering to assist homeless people; advises on using property for affordable housing. Chief Executive: Alastair Cameron, 44 Hanover Street, Edinburgh EH2 2DR (Tel: 0131-477 4500; E-mail: info@churches-housing.org; Website: www.churches-housing.org).

SCOTTISH JOINT COMMITTEE ON RELIGIOUS AND MORAL EDUCATION: This is an interfaith body that began as a joint partnership between the Educational Institute of Scotland and the Church of Scotland to provide resources, training and support for the work of religious and moral education in schools. Rev. Ewan R. Aitken, 121 George Street, Edinburgh EH2 4YN (Tel: 0131-225 5722), and Mr Lachlan Bradley, 6 Clairmont Gardens, Glasgow G3 7LW (Tel: 0141-353 3595).

SCRIPTURE UNION SCOTLAND: 70 Milton Street, Glasgow G4 0HR (Tel: 0141-332 1162; Fax: 0141-352 7600; E-mail: info@suscotland.org.uk; Website: www.suscotland.org.uk). Scripture Union Scotland's vision is to see the children and young people of Scotland exploring the Bible and responding to the significance of Jesus. SU Scotland works in schools running Christian Focus Weeks, taking part in assemblies and supporting extra-curricular groups. It also offers 'Classroom Outdoors', an outdoor education programme for school groups that is based around Curriculum for Excellence. These events take place at its two activity centres, Lendrick Muir (near Kinross) and Alltnacriche (near Aviemore), which also cater for church or school groups throughout the year. During the school holidays and at weekends, it runs an extensive programme of events for school-age children – including residential holidays (some focused on disadvantaged children and young people), missions and church-based holiday clubs. In addition, it runs discipleship and training programmes for young people and is committed to promoting prayer for, and by, the young people of Scotland through a range of national prayer events and the *Pray for Schools Scotland* initiative. The *SU Scotland Lounge* is our private, invitation-only Facebook group and public blog, providing a safe space for young people to explore the Bible, discuss issues of faith and encourage each other to follow Jesus.

STUDENT CHRISTIAN MOVEMENT: National Co-ordinator: Hilary Topp, SCM, 504F The Big Peg, 120 Vyse Street, Hockley, Birmingham B18 6NE (Tel: 0121-200 3355; E-mail: scm@movement.org.uk; Website: www.movement.org.uk). The Student Christian Movement (SCM) is a student-led community passionate about living out our faith in the real world. We have a network of groups around the country and organise national events.

UCCF: THE CHRISTIAN UNIONS: Blue Boar House, 5 Blue Boar Street, Oxford OX1 4EE (Tel: 01865 253678; E-mail: email@uccf.org.uk). UCCF is a family of students, staff and supporters. Christian Unions are mission teams operating in universities and colleges, supported by the local church, and resourced by UCCF staff. This family exists to proclaim the gospel of Jesus Christ in the student world.

WORLD DAY OF PRAYER: SCOTTISH COMMITTEE: Convener: Christian Williams, 61 McCallum Gardens, Strathview Estate, Bellshill ML4 2SR. Secretary: Marjorie Paton, Muldoanich, Stirling Street, Blackford, Auchterarder PH4 1QG (Tel: 01764 682234; E-mail: marjoriepaton.wdp@btinternet.com; Website: www.wdpscotland.org.uk).

YMCA SCOTLAND: Offers support, training and guidance to churches seeking to reach out to love and serve community needs. National General Secretary: Mr Peter Crory, James Love House, 11 Rutland Street, Edinburgh EH1 2DQ (Tel: 0131-228 1464; E-mail: ian@ymcascotland.org; Website: www.ymcascotland.org).

2. CHURCH OF SCOTLAND SOCIETIES

CHURCH OF SCOTLAND ABSTAINER'S ASSOCIATION: Recognising that alcohol is a major – indeed a growing – problem within Scotland, the aim of the Church of Scotland Abstainer's Association, with its motto 'Abstinence makes sense', is to encourage more people to choose a healthy alcohol-free lifestyle. Further details are available from 'Blochairn', 17A Culduthel Road, Inverness IV24 4AG (Website: www.kirkabstainers.org.uk).

The CHURCH OF SCOTLAND CHAPLAINS' ASSOCIATION: The Association consists of serving and retired chaplains to HM Forces. It holds an annual meeting and lunch, and organises the annual Service of Remembrance in St Giles' Cathedral on Chaplains' Day of the General Assembly. Hon. Secretary: Rev. Neil N. Gardner MA BD, The Manse of Canongate, Edinburgh EH8 8BR (Tel: 0131-556 3515).

The CHURCH OF SCOTLAND RETIRED MINISTERS' ASSOCIATION: Hon. Secretary: Rev. Murray Chalmers, 8 Easter Warriston, Edinburgh EH7 4QX (Tel: 0131-552 4211; E-mail: murr46mers@btopenworld.com).

CHURCH OF SCOTLAND WORLD MISSION COUNCIL OVERSEAS ASSOCIATION (previously AROS): Secretary: Mr Walter Dunlop, 50 Oxgangs Road North, Edinburgh EH13 9DR (Tel: 07854 487376).

The CHURCH SERVICE SOCIETY: Founded in 1865 to study the development of Christian worship through the ages and in the Reformed tradition, and to work towards renewal in contemporary worship. Secretary: Rev. Dr Douglas Galbraith (Tel: 01592 752403; E-mail: dgalbraith@hotmail.com; Website: www.churchservicesociety.org).

FORUM OF GENERAL ASSEMBLY AND PRESBYTERY CLERKS: Secretary: Rev. Rosemary Frew, 83 Milton Road, Kirkcaldy KY1 1TP (Tel: 01592 260315; E-mail: kirkcaldy@cofscotland.org.uk).

FORWARD TOGETHER: An organisation for evangelicals within the Church of Scotland. Contact Rev. Dr Norman Maciver MA BD DMin, 4 Mundi Crescent, Newmachar, Aberdeen AB21 0LY (Tel: 01651 869434; E-mail: director@forwardtogether.org.uk; Website: www.forwardtogether.org.uk).

The FRIENDS OF TABEETHA SCHOOL, JAFFA: President: Miss Eileen Robertson. Hon. Secretary: Rev. Iain F. Paton, Muldoanich, Stirling Street, Blackford, Auchterarder PH4 1QG (Tel: 01764 682234).

The IRISH GATHERING: Secretary: Rev. Eric G. McKimmon BA BD MTh PhD, The Manse, Manse Road, Woodside, Blairgowrie PH13 9NQ (Tel: 01828 670744; E-mail: ericmckimmon@gmail.com).

SCOTTISH CHURCH SOCIETY: Founded in 1892 to 'defend and advance Catholic doctrine as set forth in the Ancient Creeds and embodied in the Standards of the Church of Scotland'. Secretary: Rev. W. Gerald Jones MA BD MTh, The Manse, Patna Road, Kirkmichael, Maybole KA19 7PJ (Tel: 01655 750286; E-mail: revgerald@jonesg99.freeserve.co.uk).

SCOTTISH CHURCH THEOLOGY SOCIETY: Rev. Mary M. Cranfield MA BD DMin, The Manse, Daviot, Inverurie AB51 0HY (Tel: 01467 671241; E-mail: marymc@ukgateway. net). The Society encourages theological exploration and discussion of the main issues confronting the Church in the twenty-first century.

SOCIETY OF FRIENDS OF ST ANDREW'S JERUSALEM: Hon. Secretary: Major J.M.K. Erskine MBE, World Mission Council, 121 George Street, Edinburgh EH2 4YN. Hon. Treasurer: Mrs Catriona M. Scrimgeour BSc ACA, Finance Manager, The Church of Scotland, 121 George Street, Edinburgh EH2 4YN (Tel: 0131-225 5722).

3. BIBLE SOCIETIES

The SCOTTISH BIBLE SOCIETY: Chief Executive: Elaine Duncan, 7 Hampton Terrace, Edinburgh EH12 5XU (Tel: 0131-337 9701; E-mail: info@scottishbiblesociety.org).

WEST OF SCOTLAND BIBLE SOCIETY: Secretary: Rev. Finlay Mackenzie, Flat 3/2, 634 Alexandra Parade, Glasgow G31 3BT (Tel: 0141-554 0387; E-mail: f.c.mack51@ntlworld. com; Website: www.westofscotlandbiblesociety.com).

4. GENERAL

The BOYS' BRIGADE: Scottish Headquarters, Carronvale House, Carronvale Road, Larbert FK5 3LH (Tel: 01324 562008; Fax: 01324 552323; E-mail: scottishhq@ boys-brigade.org.uk).

BROKEN RITES: Support group for divorced and separated clergy spouses (Tel: 01896 759254 or 01257 423893; Website: www.brokenrites.org).

CHRISTIAN AID SCOTLAND: Kathy Galloway, Head of Christian Aid Scotland, Sycamore House, 290 Bath Street, Glasgow G2 4JR (Tel: 0141-221 7475; E-mail: glasgow@ christian-aid.org). Edinburgh Office: Tel: 0131-220 1254. Perth Office: Tel: 01738 643982.

CHRISTIAN ENDEAVOUR IN SCOTLAND: Challenging and encouraging children and young people in the service of Christ and the Church, especially through the CE Award Scheme: 16 Queen Street, Alloa FK10 2AR (Tel: 01259 215101; E-mail: admin@cescotland.org; Website: www.cescotland.org).

DAYONE CHRISTIAN MINISTRIES (THE LORD'S DAY OBSERVANCE SOCIETY): Ryelands Road, Leominster, Herefordshire HR6 8NZ. Contact Mark Roberts for further information (Tel: 01568 613740; E-mail: info@dayone.co.uk).

ECO-CONGREGATION SCOTLAND: 121 George Street, Edinburgh EH2 4YN (Tel: 0131-240 2274; E-mail: manager@ecocongregationscotland.org; Website: www.ecocongregationscotland.org). Eco-Congregation Scotland is the largest movement of community-based environment groups in Scotland. We offer a programme to help congregations reduce their impact on climate change and live sustainably in a world of limited resources.

FEED THE MINDS: Park Place, 12 Lawn Lane, London SW8 1UD (Tel: 020 7582 3535; E-mail: asach@feedtheminds.org; Website: www.feedtheminds.org).

GIRLGUIDING SCOTLAND: 16 Coates Crescent, Edinburgh EH3 7AH (Tel: 0131-226 4511; Fax: 0131-220 4828; E-mail: administrator@girlguiding-scot.org.uk; Website: www.girlguidingscotland.org.uk).

The GIRLS' BRIGADE IN SCOTLAND: 11A Woodside Crescent, Glasgow G3 7UL (Tel: 0141-332 1765; E-mail: enquiries@girls-brigade-scotland.org.uk; Website: www.girls-brigade-scotland.org.uk).

The LEPROSY MISSION SCOTLAND: Suite 2, Earlsgate Lodge, Livilands Lane, Stirling FK8 2BG (Tel: 01786 449266; E-mail: contactus@tlmscotland.org.uk; Website: www.tlmscotland.org.uk). National Director: Linda Todd. Communications Manager: Stuart McAra.

RELATIONSHIPS SCOTLAND: Chief Executive: Mr Stuart Valentine, 18 York Place, Edinburgh EH1 3EP (Tel: 0845 119 2020; Fax: 0845 119 6089; E-mail: enquiries@relationships-scotland.org.uk; Website: www.relationships-scotland.org.uk).

SCOTTISH CHURCH HISTORY SOCIETY: Hon. Secretary: Christine Lumsden BA MA PhD, 80/3 Slateford Road, Edinburgh EH11 1QU (Tel: 0131-337 3644; E-mail: christinaclumsden@gmail.com).

SCOTTISH EVANGELICAL THEOLOGY SOCIETY: Secretary: Rosemary Dowsett, 4 Borden Road, Glasgow G13 1QX (Tel: 0141-959 4976; E-mail: dickandrosedowsett@googlemail.com; Website: www.s-e-t-s.org.uk).

The SCOTTISH REFORMATION SOCIETY: Chairman: Rev. Dr S. James Millar. Vice-Chairman: Rev. John J. Murray. Secretary: Rev. Dr Douglas Somerset. Treasurer: Rev. Andrew W.F. Coghill, The Magdalen Chapel, 41 Cowgate, Edinburgh EH1 1JR (Tel: 0131-220 1450; E-mail: info@scottishreformationsociety.org; Website: www.scottishreformationsociety.org).

The SCOUT ASSOCIATION: Scottish Headquarters, Fordell Firs, Hillend, Dunfermline KY11 7HQ (Tel: 01383 419073; E-mail: shq@scouts-scotland.org.uk; Website: www.scouts-scotland.org.uk).

The SOCIETY IN SCOTLAND FOR PROPAGATING CHRISTIAN KNOWLEDGE: Chairman: Rev. Scott McKenna; Honorary Secretary: Philip Halford-MacLeod. Address:

SSPCK, c/o Tods Murray LLP, Edinburgh Quay, 133 Fountainbridge, Edinburgh EH3 9AG (Tel: 0131-656 2000; Website: www.sspck.co.uk; E-mail: philip_h@madasafish.com).

TEARFUND: 100 Church Road, Teddington TW11 8QE (Tel: 0845 355 8355). Director: Lynne Paterson, Tearfund Scotland, Challenge House, 29 Canal Street, Glasgow G4 0AD (Tel: 0141-332 3621; E-mail: scotland@tearfund.org; Website: www.tearfund.org).

THEATRE CHAPLAINCY UK (formerly the Actor's Church Union) is an ecumenical scheme providing a Church contact and support to staff and travelling theatre groups in theatres and concert halls throughout the UK. Area Chaplain Scotland: Rev. Thomas Coupar (Tel: 07814 588904; E-mail: chaplain@robinchapel.org.uk).

The WALDENSIAN MISSIONS AID SOCIETY FOR WORK IN ITALY: David A. Lamb SSC, 36 Liberton Drive, Edinburgh EH16 6NN (Tel: 0131-664 3059; E-mail: david@dlamb.co.uk).

YOUTH SCOTLAND: Balfour House, 19 Bonnington Grove, Edinburgh EH6 4BL (Tel: 0131-554 2561; Fax: 0131-454 3438; E-mail: office@youthscotland.org.uk).

YWCA SCOTLAND: National Co-ordinator: Kim Smith, 4B Gayfield Place, Edinburgh EH7 4AB (Tel: 0131-558 8000; E-mail: reception@ywcascotland.org; Website: www.ywcascotland.org).

---

(5) TRUSTS AND FUNDS

The ABERNETHY TRUST: Offers residential accommodation and outdoor activities for Youth Fellowships, Church family weekends and Bible Classes at four outdoor centres in Scotland. Further details from the Executive Director, Abernethy Trust, Nethy Bridge PH25 3ED (Tel: 01479 821279; Website: www.abernethy.org.uk).

The ARROL TRUST: The Arrol Trust gives small grants to young people between the ages of 16 and 25 for the purposes of travel which will provide education or work experience. Potential recipients would be young people with disabilities or who would for financial reasons be otherwise unable to undertake projects. It is expected that projects would be beneficial not only to applicants but also to the wider community. Application forms are available from Callum S. Kennedy WS, Lindsays WS, Caledonian Exchange, 19A Canning Street, Edinburgh EH3 8HE (Tel: 0131-229 1212).

The BAIRD TRUST: Assists in the building and repair of churches and halls, and generally assists the work of the Church of Scotland. Apply to Iain A.T. Mowat CA, 182 Bath Street, Glasgow G2 4HG (Tel: 0141-332 0476; E-mail: info@bairdtrust.org.uk; Website: www.bairdtrust.org.uk).

The Rev. Alexander BARCLAY BEQUEST: Assists a mother, daughter, sister or niece of a deceased minister of the Church of Scotland who at the time of his/her death was acting as his/her housekeeper and who is in needy circumstances. Applications should be made to the Secretary and Clerk, The Church of Scotland Trust, 121 George Street, Edinburgh EH2 4YN (Tel: 0131-240 2222; E-mail: jhamilton@cofscotland.org.uk).

BELLAHOUSTON BEQUEST FUND: Gives grants to Protestant evangelical denominations in the City of Glasgow and certain areas within five miles of the city boundary for building and repairing churches and halls and the promotion of religion. Apply to Mr Donald B. Reid, Mitchells Roberton, 36 North Hanover Street, Glasgow G1 2AD (Tel: 0141-552 3422; E-mail: info@mitchells-roberton.co.uk).

BEQUEST FUND FOR MINISTERS: Assists ministers in outlying districts with manse furnishings, pastoral efficiency aids, and their own and family medical or educational costs, including university. Apply to A. Linda Parkhill CA, 60 Wellington Street, Glasgow G2 6HJ (Tel: 0141-226 4994; E-mail: mail@parkhillmackie.co.uk).

CARNEGIE TRUST FOR THE UNIVERSITIES OF SCOTLAND: In cases of hardship, the Carnegie Trust is prepared to consider applications by students of Scottish birth or extraction (at least one parent born in Scotland), or who have had at least two years' education at a secondary school in Scotland, for financial assistance with the payment of their fees for a first degree at a Scottish university. For further details, students should apply to the Secretary, Carnegie Trust for the Universities of Scotland, Andrew Carnegie House, Pittencrieff Street, Dunfermline KY12 8AW (Tel: 01383 724990; Fax: 01383 749799; E-mail: admin@carnegie-trust.org; Website: www.carnegie-trust.org).

CHURCH OF SCOTLAND INSURANCE CO. LTD: Undertakes insurance of Church property and pays all its distributable profits to the Church of Scotland by way of Gift Aid. It is authorised and regulated by the Financial Services Authority. The company is also an intermediary and can arrange other classes of business including household insurance for members and adherents of the Church of Scotland. At 67 George Street, Edinburgh EH2 2JG (Tel: 0131-220 4119; Fax: 0131-220 4120; E-mail: enquiries@cosic.co.uk; Website: www.cosic.co.uk).

CHURCH OF SCOTLAND MINISTRY BENEVOLENT FUND: Makes grants to retired men and women who have been ordained or commissioned for the ministry of the Church of Scotland and to widows, widowers, orphans, spouses or children of such, who are in need. Apply to the Assistant Treasurer (Ministries), 121 George Street, Edinburgh EH2 4YN (Tel: 0131-225 5722).

The CINTRA BEQUEST: The Trust provides financial assistance towards the cost of accommodation in Scotland for missionaries on leave, or for ministers on temporary holiday, or on rest. In addition, due to additional funds generously donated by the Tod Endowment Trust (q.v.), grants can be given to defray the cost of obtaining rest and recuperation in Scotland. In appropriate cases, therefore, the cost of travel within Scotland may also be met. Applications should be made to Mrs J.S. Wilson, Solicitor, 121 George Street, Edinburgh EH2 4YN.

CLARK BURSARY: Awarded to accepted candidate(s) for the ministry of the Church of Scotland whose studies for the ministry are pursued at the University of Aberdeen. Applications or recommendations for the Bursary to the Clerk to the Presbytery of Aberdeen, Mastrick Church, Greenfern Road, Aberdeen AB16 6TR by 16 October annually.

CRAIGCROOK MORTIFICATION: Pensions are paid to poor men and women over 60 years old, born in Scotland or who have resided in Scotland for not less than ten years. At present, pensions amount to £1,000–£1,500 p.a.

Ministers are invited to notify the Clerk and Factor, Mrs Fiona M.M. Watson CA, Exchange Place 3, Semple Street, Edinburgh EH3 8BL (Tel: 0131-473 3500; E-mail: charity@scott-moncrieff. com) of deserving persons and should be prepared to act as a referee on the application form.

CROMBIE SCHOLARSHIP: Provides grants annually on the nomination of the Deans of Faculty of Divinity of the Universities of St Andrews, Glasgow, Aberdeen and Edinburgh, who each nominate one matriculated student who has taken a University course in Greek (Classical or Hellenistic) and Hebrew. Award by recommendation only.

The DRUMMOND TRUST: Makes grants towards the cost of publication of books of 'sound Christian doctrine and outreach'. The Trustees are also willing to receive grant requests towards the cost of audio-visual programme material, but not equipment. Requests for application forms should be made to the Secretaries, Hill and Robb, 3 Pitt Terrace, Stirling FK8 2EY (Tel: 01786 450985; E-mail: douglaswhyte@hillandrobb.co.uk). Manuscripts should *not* be sent.

The DUNCAN TRUST: Makes grants annually to students for the ministry in the Faculties of Arts and Divinity. Preference is given to those born or educated within the bounds of the former Presbytery of Arbroath. Applications not later than 31 October to Thorntons Law LLP, Brothockbank House, Arbroath DD11 1NE (reference: G.J.M. Dunlop; Tel: 01241 872683; E-mail: gdunlop@thorntons-law.co.uk).

ERSKINE CUNNINGHAM HILL TRUST: Donates 50% of its annual income to the central funds of the Church of Scotland and 50% to other charities. Individual donations are in the region of £1,000. Priority is given to charities administered by voluntary or honorary officials, in particular charities registered and operating in Scotland and relating to the elderly, young people, ex-service personnel or seafarers. Application forms from the Secretary, Nicola Laing, 121 George Street, Edinburgh EH2 4YN (Tel: 0131-225 5722; E-mail: nlaing@cofscotland. org.uk).

ESDAILE TRUST: Assists the education and advancement of daughters of ministers, missionaries and widowed deaconesses of the Church of Scotland between 12 and 25 years of age. Applications are to be lodged by 31 May in each year with the Clerk and Treasurer, Mrs Fiona M.M. Watson CA, Exchange Place 3, Semple Street, Edinburgh EH3 8BL (Tel: 0131-473 3500; E-mail: charity@scott-moncrieff.com).

FERGUSON BEQUEST FUND: Assists with the building and repair of churches and halls and, more generally, with the work of the Church of Scotland. Priority is given to the Counties of Ayr, Kirkcudbright, Wigtown, Lanark, Dunbarton and Renfrew, and to Greenock, Glasgow, Falkirk and Ardrossan; applications are, however, accepted from across Scotland. Apply to Iain A.T. Mowat CA, 182 Bath Street, Glasgow G2 4HG (Tel: 0141-332 0476; E-mail: info@ fergusonbequestfund.org.uk; Website: www.fergusonbequestfund.org.uk).

GEIKIE BEQUEST: Makes small grants to students for the ministry, including students studying for entry to the University, preference being given to those not eligible for SAAS awards. Apply to the Assistant Treasurer (Ministries), 121 George Street, Edinburgh EH2 4YN by September for distribution in November each year.

James GILLAN'S BURSARY FUND: Bursaries are available for male or female students for the ministry who were born or whose parents or parent have resided and had their home for not less than three years continually in the old counties (not Districts) of Moray or Nairn. Apply to R. and R. Urquhart LLP, 117–121 High Street, Forres IV36 1AB.

The GLASGOW SOCIETY OF THE SONS AND DAUGHTERS OF MINISTERS OF THE CHURCH OF SCOTLAND: The Society's primary purpose is to grant financial assistance to children (no matter what age) of deceased ministers of the Church of Scotland. Applications are to be submitted by 1 February in each year. To the extent that funds are available, grants are also given for the children of ministers or retired ministers, although such grants are normally restricted to university and college students. These latter grants are considered in conjunction with the Edinburgh-based Society. Limited funds are also available for individual application for special needs or projects. Applications are to be submitted by 31 May in each year. Emergency applications can be dealt with at any time when need arises. Application forms may be obtained from the Secretary and Treasurer, Mrs Fiona M.M. Watson CA, Exchange Place 3, Semple Street, Edinburgh EH3 8BL (Tel: 0131-473 3500; E-mail: charity@scott-moncrieff.com).

HAMILTON BURSARY TRUST: Awarded, subject to the intention to serve overseas under the Church of Scotland World Mission Council or to serve with some other Overseas Mission Agency approved by the Council, to a student at the University of Aberdeen. Preference is given to a student born or residing in (1) Parish of Skene, (2) Parish of Echt, (3) the Presbytery of Aberdeen, Kincardine and Deeside, or Gordon; failing which to Accepted Candidate(s) for the Ministry of the Church of Scotland whose studies for the Ministry are pursued at Aberdeen University. Applications or recommendations for the Bursary to the Clerk to the Presbytery of Aberdeen by 16 October annually.

Martin HARCUS BEQUEST: Makes annual grants to candidates for the ministry resident within the City of Edinburgh. Applications to the Clerk to the Presbytery of Edinburgh, 10/1 Palmerston Place, Edinburgh EH12 5AA by 15 October (E-mail: edinburgh@cofscotland.org.uk).

The HOPE TRUST: Gives some support to organisations involved in combating drink and drugs, and has as its main purpose the promotion of the Reformed tradition throughout the world. There is also a Scholarship programme for Postgraduate Theology Study in Scotland. Apply to Robert P. Miller SSC LLB, 31 Moray Place, Edinburgh EH3 6BY (Tel: 0131-226 5151).

KEAY THOM TRUST: The principal purposes of the Keay Thom Trust are:
1.   To benefit the widows, daughters or other dependent female relatives of deceased ministers, or wives of ministers who are now divorced or separated, all of whom have supported the minister in the fulfilment of his duties and who, by reason of death, divorce or separation, have been required to leave the manse. The Trust can assist them in the purchase of a house or by providing financial or material assistance whether it be for the provision of accommodation or not.
2.   To assist in the education or training of the above female relatives or any other children of deceased ministers.
Further information and application forms are available from Miller Hendry, Solicitors, 10 Blackfriars Street, Perth PH1 5NS (Tel: 01738 637311).

LADIES' GAELIC SCHOOLS AND HIGHLAND BURSARY ASSOCIATION: Distributes money to students, preferably with a Highland/Gaelic background, who are training to be ministers in the Church of Scotland. Apply by 15 October in each year to the Secretary, Donald J. Macdonald, 35 Durham Avenue, Edinburgh EH15 1RZ (E-mail: djandanne@btinternet.com).

The LYALL BEQUEST (Scottish Charity Number SC005542): Offers grants to ministers:
1. Grants to individual ministers and to couples for a holiday for a minimum of one week. No reapplication within a three-year period; and thereafter a 50 per cent grant to those reapplying.
2. Grants towards sickness and convalescence costs so far as not covered by the National Health Service. Applications should be made to the Secretary and Clerk, The Church of Scotland Trust, 121 George Street, Edinburgh EH2 4YN (Tel: 0131-240 2222; E-mail: jhamilton@cofscotland.org.uk).

Gillian MACLAINE BURSARY FUND: Open to candidates for the ministry of the Church of Scotland of Scottish or Canadian nationality. Preference is given to Gaelic-speakers. Application forms available from Dr Christopher T. Brett MA PhD, Clerk to the Presbytery of Argyll, Minahey Cottage, Kames, Tighnabruaich PA21 2AD (Tel: 01700 811142; E-mail: argyll@cofscotland.org.uk). Closing date for receipt of applications is 31 October.

The E. McLAREN FUND: The persons intended to be benefited are widows and unmarried ladies, preference being given to ladies above 40 years of age in the following order:
(a) Widows and daughters of Officers in the Highland Regiment, and
(b) Widows and daughters of Scotsmen.
Further details from the Secretary, The E. McLaren Fund, Messrs BMK Wilson, Solicitors, 90 St Vincent Street, Glasgow G2 5UB (Tel: 0141-221 8004; Fax: 0141-221 8088; E-mail: rrs@bmkwilson.co.uk).

MORGAN BURSARY FUND: Makes grants to candidates for the Church of Scotland ministry studying at the University of Glasgow. Apply to the Clerk to the Presbytery of Glasgow, 260 Bath Street, Glasgow G2 4JP (Tel: 0141-332 6606).

NOVUM TRUST: Provides small short-term grants – typically between £200 and £2,500 – to initiate projects in Christian action and research which cannot readily be financed from other sources. Trustees welcome applications from projects that are essentially Scottish, are distinctively new, and are focused on the welfare of young people, on the training of lay people or on new ways of communicating the Christian faith. The Trust cannot support large building projects, staff salaries or individuals applying for maintenance during courses or training. Application forms and guidance notes from novumt@cofscotland.org.uk or Mrs Susan Masterton, Blair Cadell WS, The Bond House, 5 Breadalbane Street, Edinburgh EH6 5JH (Tel: 0131-555 5800).

PARK MEMORIAL BURSARY FUND: Provides grants for the benefit of candidates for the ministry of the Church of Scotland from the Presbytery of Glasgow under full-time training. Apply to the Clerk to the Presbytery of Glasgow, 260 Bath Street, Glasgow G2 4JP (Tel: 0141-332 6606).

PATON TRUST: Assists ministers in ill health to have a recuperative holiday outwith, and free from the cares of, their parishes. Apply to Alan S. Cunningham CA, Alexander Sloan, Chartered Accountants, 38 Cadogan Street, Glasgow G2 7HF (Tel: 0141-204 8989; Fax: 0141-248 9931; E-mail: alan.cunningham@alexandersloan.co.uk).

PRESBYTERY OF ARGYLL BURSARY FUND: Open to students who have been accepted as candidates for the ministry and the readership of the Church of Scotland. Preference is given to applicants who are natives of the bounds of the Presbytery, or are resident within the bounds of the Presbytery, or who have a strong connection with the bounds of the Presbytery. Application forms available from Dr Christopher T. Brett MA PhD, Clerk to the Presbytery of Argyll, Minahey Cottage, Kames, Tighnabruaich PA21 2AD (Tel: 01700 811142; E-mail: argyll@cofscotland.org.uk). Closing date for receipt of applications is 31 October.

Margaret and John ROSS TRAVELLING FUND: Offers grants to ministers and their spouses for travelling and other expenses for trips to the Holy Land where the purpose is recuperation or relaxation. Applications should be made to the Secretary and Clerk, The Church of Scotland Trust, 121 George Street, Edinburgh EH2 4YN (Tel: 0131-240 2222; E-mail: jhamilton@cofscotland.org.uk).

SCOTLAND'S CHURCHES TRUST (formerly Scottish Churches Architectural Heritage Trust): Assists congregations of any denomination in the preservation of the fabric of buildings in use for public worship. Also supports the playing of church organs. Criteria and how to apply at www.scotlandschurchestrust.org.uk. Scotland's Churches Trust, 15 North Bank Street, Edinburgh EH1 2LP (E-mail: info@scotlandschurchestrust.org.uk).

SMIETON FUND: Makes small holiday grants to ministers. Administered at the discretion of the pastoral staff, who will give priority in cases of need. Applications to the Education and Support Secretary, Ministries Council, 121 George Street, Edinburgh EH2 4YN.

Mary Davidson SMITH CLERICAL AND EDUCATIONAL FUND FOR ABERDEENSHIRE: Assists ministers who have been ordained for five years or over and are in full charge of a congregation in Aberdeen, Aberdeenshire and the north, to purchase books, or to travel for educational purposes, and assists their children with scholarships for further education or vocational training. Apply to Alan J. Innes MA LLB, 100 Union Street, Aberdeen AB10 1QR (Tel: 01224 428000).

The SOCIETY FOR THE BENEFIT OF THE SONS AND DAUGHTERS OF THE CLERGY OF THE CHURCH OF SCOTLAND: Annual grants are made to assist in the education of the children (normally between the ages of 12 and 25 years) of ministers of the Church of Scotland. The Society also gives grants to aged and infirm daughters of ministers and ministers' unmarried daughters and sisters who are in need. Applications are to be lodged by 31 May in each year with the Secretary and Treasurer, Mrs Fiona M.M. Watson CA, Exchange Place 3, Semple Street, Edinburgh EH3 8BL (Tel: 0131-473 3500; E-mail: charity@scott-moncrieff.com).

The Nan STEVENSON CHARITABLE TRUST FOR RETIRED MINISTERS: Provides houses, or loans to purchase houses, for retired ministers or missionaries on similar terms to the Housing and Loan Fund, with preference given to those with a North Ayrshire connection. Secretary and Treasurer: Mrs Ann Turner, 42 Keir Hardie Drive, Ardrossan KA22 8PA (Tel: 01294 462834; E-mail: annturner62@btopenworld.com).

Miss M.E. SWINTON PATERSON'S CHARITABLE TRUST: The Trust can give modest grants to support smaller congregations in urban or rural areas who require to fund essential maintenance or improvement works at their buildings. Apply to Mr Callum S. Kennedy WS, Messrs Lindsays WS, Caledonian Exchange, 19A Canning Street, Edinburgh EH3 8HE (Tel: 0131-229 1212).

SYNOD OF GRAMPIAN CHILDREN OF THE CLERGY FUND: Makes annual grants to children of deceased ministers. Apply to Rev. Iain U. Thomson, Clerk and Treasurer, 4 Keirhill Gardens, Westhill AB32 6AZ (Tel: 01224 746743).

SYNOD OF GRAMPIAN WIDOWS' FUND: Makes annual grants (currently £240 p.a.) to widows or widowers of deceased ministers who have served in a charge in the former Synod. Apply to Rev. Iain U. Thomson, Clerk and Treasurer, 4 Keirhill Gardens, Westhill AB32 6AZ (Tel: 01224 746743).

TOD ENDOWMENT TRUST: CINTRA BEQUEST: MINISTRY BENEVOLENT FUND: The Trustees of the Cintra Bequest and of the Church of Scotland Ministry Benevolent Fund can consider an application for a grant from the Tod Endowment funds from any ordained or commissioned minister or deacon in Scotland of at least two years' standing before the date of application, to assist with the cost of the beneficiary and his or her spouse or partner and dependants obtaining rest and recuperation in Scotland. The Trustees of the Church of Scotland Ministry Benevolent Fund can also consider an application from an ordained or commissioned minister or deacon who has retired. Application forms are available from Mrs J.S. Wilson, Solicitor (for the Cintra Bequest), and from the Assistant Treasurer (Ministries) (for the Ministry Benevolent Fund). The address in both cases is 121 George Street, Edinburgh EH2 4YN (Tel: 0131-225 5722). (Attention is drawn to separate individual entries for both the Cintra Bequest and the Church of Scotland Ministry Benevolent Fund.)

YOUNG MINISTERS' FURNISHING LOAN FUND: Makes loans (of £1,000) to ministers in their first charge to assist with furnishing the manse. Apply to the Assistant Treasurer (Ministries), 121 George Street, Edinburgh EH2 4YN.

The undernoted hotels provide special terms as described. Fuller information may be obtained from the establishments:

CRIEFF HYDRO Ltd and MURRAYPARK HOTEL: The William Meikle Trust Fund and Paton Fund make provision whereby active ministers and their spouses and members of the Diaconate may enjoy the hotel and self-catering accommodation all year round at a supplemented rate, subject to availability and a maximum number of stays per year. Crieff Hydro offers a wide range of inclusive leisure facilities including leisure pool, gym, cinema and entertainment programme. BIG Country also provides free daily childcare for Crieff Hydro guests only. Over-60 on-site activities and five places to eat are also available at great prices.
    To book, please call Accommodation Sales on 01764 651670 between 8am and 9pm daily. Please quote your *Church of Scotland Year Book* page number. You must ask the Church of Scotland's Human Resources Department to e-mail Crieff Hydro verifying your eligibility. Only e-mails originated from the Church of Scotland address will be accepted.

(6) RECENT LORD HIGH COMMISSIONERS
TO THE GENERAL ASSEMBLY

1969	Her Majesty the Queen attended in person
1970	The Rt Hon. Margaret Herbison PC
1971/72	The Rt Hon. Lord Clydesmuir of Braidwood CB MBE TD
1973/74	The Rt Hon. Lord Ballantrae of Auchairne and the Bay of Islands GCMG GCVO DSO OBE
1975/76	Sir Hector MacLennan Kt FRCPGLAS FRCOG
1977	Francis David Charteris, Earl of Wemyss and March KT LLD
1978/79	The Rt Hon. William Ross MBE LLD
1980/81	Andrew Douglas Alexander Thomas Bruce, Earl of Elgin and Kincardine KT DL JP
1982/83	Colonel Sir John Edward Gilmour BT DSO TD
1984/85	Charles Hector Fitzroy Maclean, Baron Maclean of Duart and Morvern KT GCVO KBE
1986/87	John Campbell Arbuthnott, Viscount of Arbuthnott KT CBE DSC FRSE FRSA
1988/89	Sir Iain Mark Tennant KT FRSA
1990/91	The Rt Hon. Donald MacArthur Ross FRSE
1992/93	The Rt Hon. Lord Macfarlane of Bearsden KT FRSE
1994/95	Lady Marion Fraser LT
1996	Her Royal Highness the Princess Royal LT LG GCVO
1997	The Rt Hon. Lord Macfarlane of Bearsden KT FRSE
1998/99	The Rt Hon. Lord Hogg of Cumbernauld
2000	His Royal Highness the Prince Charles, Duke of Rothesay KG KT GCB OM
2001/02	The Rt Hon. Viscount Younger of Leckie
	Her Majesty the Queen attended the opening of the General Assembly of 2002
2003/04	The Rt Hon. Lord Steel of Aikwood KT KBE
2005/06	The Rt Hon. Lord Mackay of Clashfern KT
2007	His Royal Highness the Prince Andrew, Duke of York KG KCVO
2008/09	The Rt Hon. George Reid KT MA
2010/11	Lord Wilson of Tillyorn KT GCMG PRSE
2012/13	The Rt Hon. Lord Selkirk of Douglas QC MA LLB

(7) RECENT MODERATORS
OF THE GENERAL ASSEMBLY

1969	T.M. Murchison MA DD, Glasgow: St Columba Summertown
1970	Hugh O. Douglas CBE LLD DD, Dundee: St Mary's
1971	Andrew Herron MA BD LLB LLD DD, Clerk to the Presbytery of Glasgow
1972	R.W.V. Selby Wright CVO TD DD FRSE JP, Edinburgh: Canongate
1973	George T.H. Reid MC MA BD DD, Aberdeen: Langstane
1974	David Steel MA BD LLD DD, Linlithgow: St Michael's
1975	James G. Matheson MA BD DD, Portree
1976	Thomas F. Torrance MBE DLitt DD FRSE, University of Edinburgh
1977	John R. Gray VRD MA BD ThM DD, Dunblane: Cathedral

1978	Peter P. Brodie MA BD LLB DD, Alloa: St Mungo's
1979	Robert A.S. Barbour KCVO MC MA BD STM DD, University of Aberdeen
1980	William B. Johnston MA BD DLitt DD, Edinburgh: Colinton
1981	Andrew B. Doig BD STM DD, National Bible Society of Scotland
1982	John McIntyre CVO DLitt DD FRSE, University of Edinburgh
1983	J. Fraser McLuskey MC DD, London: St Columba's
1984	John M.K. Paterson MA BD DD ACII, Milngavie: St Paul's
1985	David M.B.A. Smith MA BD DUniv, Logie
1986	Robert Craig CBE DLitt LLD DD, Emeritus of Jerusalem
1987	Duncan Shaw of Chapelverna *Bundesverdienstkreuz* PhD ThDr Drhc, Edinburgh: Craigentinny St Christopher's
1988	James A. Whyte MA LLD DD DUniv, University of St Andrews
1989	William J.G. McDonald MA BD DD, Edinburgh: Mayfield
1990	Robert Davidson MA BD DD FRSE, University of Glasgow
1991	William B.R. Macmillan MA BD LLD DD, Dundee: St Mary's
1992	Hugh R. Wyllie MA DD FCIBS, Hamilton: Old Parish Church
1993	James L. Weatherhead CBE MA LLB DD, Principal Clerk of Assembly
1994	James A. Simpson BSc BD STM DD, Dornoch Cathedral
1995	James Harkness KCVO CB OBE MA DD, Chaplain General (Emeritus)
1996	John H. McIndoe MA BD STM DD, London: St Columba's linked with Newcastle: St Andrew's
1997	Alexander McDonald BA DUniv CMIWSc, General Secretary, Department of Ministry
1998	Alan Main TD MA BD STM PhD DD, University of Aberdeen
1999	John B. Cairns KCVO LTh LLB LLD DD, Dumbarton: Riverside
2000	Andrew R.C. McLellan CBE MA BD STM DD, Edinburgh: St Andrew's and St George's
2001	John D. Miller BA BD DD, Glasgow: Castlemilk East
2002	Finlay A.J. Macdonald MA BD PhD DD, Principal Clerk of Assembly
2003	Iain R. Torrance TD DPhil DD DTheol LHD FRSE, University of Aberdeen
2004	Alison Elliot OBE MA MSc PhD LLD DD FRSE, Associate Director CTPI
2005	David W. Lacy BA BD DLitt DL, Kilmarnock: Henderson
2006	Alan D. McDonald LLB BD MTh DLitt DD, Cameron linked with St Andrews: St Leonard's
2007	Sheilagh M. Kesting BA BD DD, Secretary of Ecumenical Relations Committee
2008	David W. Lunan MA BD DUniv DLitt DD, Clerk to the Presbytery of Glasgow
2009	William C. Hewitt BD DipPS, Greenock: Westburn
2010	John C. Christie BSc BD MSB CBiol, Interim Minister
2011	A. David K. Arnott MA BD, St Andrews: Hope Park with Strathkinness
2012	Albert O. Bogle BD MTh, Bo'ness: St Andrew's
2013	E. Lorna Hood MA BD, Renfrew: North

MATTER OF PRECEDENCE

The Lord High Commissioner to the General Assembly of the Church of Scotland (while the Assembly is sitting) ranks next to the Sovereign and the Duke of Edinburgh and before the rest of the Royal Family.

The Moderator of the General Assembly of the Church of Scotland ranks next to the Lord Chancellor of Great Britain and before the Keeper of the Great Seal of Scotland (the First Minister) and the Dukes.

(8) HER MAJESTY'S HOUSEHOLD IN SCOTLAND
ECCLESIASTICAL

Dean of the Chapel Royal:	Very Rev. Prof. Iain R. Torrance
	TD DPhil DD DTheol LHD FRSE
Dean of the Order of the Thistle:	Very Rev. Gilleasbuig Macmillan
	CVO MA BD Drhc DD FRSE

Domestic Chaplains:	Rev. Kenneth I. Mackenzie BD CPS
	Rev. Neil N. Gardner MA BD

Chaplains in Ordinary:	Very Rev. Gilleasbuig Macmillan
	CVO MA BD Drhc DD FRSE
	Rev. Norman W. Drummond MA BD FRSE DUniv
	Rev. Alastair H. Symington MA BD
	Very Rev. Finlay A.J. Macdonald MA BD PhD DD
	Rev. James M. Gibson TD LTh LRAM
	Rev. Angus Morrison MA BD PhD
	Rev. E. Lorna Hood MA BD
	Rev. Alastair G. Bennett BSc BD
	Rev. Susan M. Brown BD DipMin
	Rev. John P. Chalmers BD CPS

Extra Chaplains:	Rev. Kenneth MacVicar MBE DFC TD MA
	Very Rev. Prof. Robert A.S. Barbour
	KCVO MC BD STM DD
	Rev. Alwyn Macfarlane MA
	Very Rev. William J. Morris KCVO PhD LLD DD JP
	Rev. John MacLeod MA
	Very Rev. James L. Weatherhead CBE MA LLB DD
	Very Rev. James A. Simpson BSc BD STM DD
	Very Rev. James Harkness KCVO CB OBE MA DD
	Rev. John L. Paterson MA BD STM
	Rev. Charles Robertson LVO MA
	Very Rev. John B. Cairns KCVO LTh LLB LLD DD

---

(9) LONG SERVICE CERTIFICATES

Long Service Certificates, signed by the Moderator, are available for presentation to elders and others in respect of not less than thirty years of service. It should be noted that the period is years of *service*, not (for example) years of ordination in the case of an elder.

In the case of Sunday School teachers and Bible Class leaders, the qualifying period is twenty-one years of service.

Certificates are not issued posthumously, nor is it possible to make exceptions to the rules, for example by recognising quality of service in order to reduce the qualifying period, or by reducing the qualifying period on compassionate grounds, such as serious illness.

A Certificate will be issued only once to any particular individual.

Applications for Long Service Certificates should be made in writing to the Principal Clerk at 121 George Street, Edinburgh EH2 4YN by the parish minister, or by the session clerk on behalf of the Kirk Session. Certificates are not issued from this office to the individual recipients, nor should individuals make application themselves.

(10) LIBRARIES OF THE CHURCH

GENERAL ASSEMBLY LIBRARY AND RECORD ROOM
Most of the books contained in the General Assembly Library have been transferred to the New College Library. Records of the General Assembly, Synods, Presbyteries and Kirk Sessions are now in HM Register House, Edinburgh.

CHURCH MUSIC
The Library of New College contains a selection of works on Church music.

(11) RECORDS OF THE CHURCH OF SCOTLAND

Church records more than fifty years old, unless still in use, should be sent or delivered to the Principal Clerk for onward transmission to the National Records of Scotland. Where ministers or session clerks are approached by a local repository seeking a transfer of their records, they should inform the Principal Clerk, who will take the matter up with the National Records of Scotland.

Where a temporary retransmission of records is sought, it is extremely helpful if notice can be given three months in advance so that appropriate procedures can be carried out satisfactorily.

SECTION 3

Church Procedure

(1) THE MINISTER AND BAPTISM

The administration of Baptism to infants is governed by Act V 2000 as amended by Act IX 2003. A Statement and Exposition of the Doctrine of Baptism may be found at page 13/8 in the published volume of Reports to the General Assembly of 2003.

The Act itself is as follows:

3. Baptism signifies the action and love of God in Christ, through the Holy Spirit, and is a seal upon the gift of grace and the response of faith.
    (a)   Baptism shall be administered in the name of the Father and of the Son and of the Holy Spirit, with water, by sprinkling, pouring, or immersion.
    (b)   Baptism shall be administered to a person only once.
4. Baptism may be administered to a person upon profession of faith.
    (a)   The minister and Kirk Session shall judge whether the person is of sufficient maturity to make personal profession of faith, where necessary in consultation with the parent(s) or legal guardian(s).
    (b)   Baptism may be administered only after the person has received such instruction in its meaning as the minister and Kirk Session consider necessary, according to such basis of instruction as may be authorised by the General Assembly.
    (c)   In cases of uncertainty as to whether a person has been baptised or validly baptised, baptism shall be administered conditionally.
5. Baptism may be administered to a person with learning difficulties who makes an appropriate profession of faith, where the minister and Kirk Session are satisfied that the person shall be nurtured within the life and worship of the Church.
6. Baptism may be administered to a child:
    (a)   where at least one parent, or other family member (with parental consent), having been baptised and being on the communion roll of the congregation, will undertake the Christian upbringing of the child;
    (b)   where at least one parent, or other family member (with parental consent), having been baptised but not on the communion roll of the congregation, satisfies the minister and Kirk Session that he or she is an adherent of the congregation and will undertake the Christian upbringing of the child;
    (c)   where at least one parent, or other family member (with parental consent), having been baptised, professes the Christian faith, undertakes to ensure that the child grows up in the life and worship of the Church and expresses the desire to seek admission to the communion roll of the congregation;
    (d)   where the child is under legal guardianship, and the minister and Kirk Session are satisfied that the child shall be nurtured within the life and worship of the congregation;
    and, in each of the above cases, only after the parent(s), or other family member, has received such instruction in its meaning as the minister and Kirk Session consider necessary, according to such basis of instruction as may be authorised by the General Assembly.
7. Baptism shall normally be administered during the public worship of the congregation in which the person makes profession of faith, or of which the parent or other family member is on the communion roll, or is an adherent. In exceptional circumstances, baptism may be administered elsewhere (e.g. at home or in hospital). Further, a minister may administer baptism to a person resident outwith the minister's parish, and who is not otherwise

connected with the congregation, only with the consent of the minister of the parish in which the person would normally reside, or of the Presbytery.

8. In all cases, an entry shall be made in the Kirk Session's Baptismal Register and a Certificate of Baptism given by the minister. Where baptism is administered in a chaplaincy context, it shall be recorded in the Baptismal Register there, and, where possible, reported to the minister of the parish in which the person resides.

9. Baptism shall normally be administered by an ordained minister. In situations of emergency,
    (a) a minister may, exceptionally, notwithstanding the preceding provisions of the Act, respond to a request for baptism in accordance with his or her pastoral judgement, and
    (b) baptism may be validly administered by a person who is not ordained, always providing that it is administered in the name of the Father and of the Son and of the Holy Spirit, with water.
    In every occurrence of the latter case, of which a minister or chaplain becomes aware, an entry shall be made in the appropriate Baptismal Register and where possible reported to the Clerk of the Presbytery within which the baptism was administered.

10. Each Presbytery shall form, or designate, a committee to which reference may be made in cases where there is a dispute as to the interpretation of this Act. Without the consent of the Presbytery, no minister may administer baptism in a case where to his or her knowledge another minister has declined to do so.

11. The Church of Scotland, as part of the Universal Church, affirms the validity of the sacrament of baptism administered in the name of the Father and of the Son and of the Holy Spirit, with water, in accordance with the discipline of other members of the Universal Church.

---

(2) THE MINISTER AND MARRIAGE

1. BACKGROUND

Prior to 1939, every marriage in Scotland fell into one or other of two classes: regular or irregular. The former was marriage by a minister of religion after due notice of intention had been given; the latter could be effected in one of three ways: (1) declaration *de presenti*, (2) by promise *subsequente copula*, or (3) by co-habitation with habit and repute.

The Marriage (Scotland) Act of 1939 put an end to (1) and (2) and provided for a new classification of marriage as either religious or civil. Marriage by co-habitation with habit and repute was abolished by the Family Law (Scotland) Act 2006.

The law of marriage as it was thus established in 1939 had two important limitations to the celebration of marriage: (1) certain preliminaries had to be observed; and (2) in respect of religious marriage, the service had to be conducted according to the forms of either the Christian or the Jewish faith.

2. THE MARRIAGE (SCOTLAND) ACT 1977

These two conditions were radically altered by the Marriage (Scotland) Act 1977.

Since 1 January 1978, in conformity with the demands of a multi-racial society, the benefits of religious marriage have been extended to adherents of other faiths, the only requirements being the observance of monogamy and the satisfaction of the authorities with the forms of the vows imposed.

Since 1978, the calling of banns has also been discontinued. The couple themselves must each complete a Marriage Notice form and return this to the District Registrar for the area in which they are to be married, irrespective of where they live, at least fifteen days before the ceremony is due to take place. The form details the documents which require to be produced with it.

If everything is in order, the District Registrar will issue, not more than seven days before the date of the ceremony, a Marriage Schedule. This must be in the hands of the minister officiating at the marriage ceremony before the service begins. Under no circumstances must the minister deviate from this rule. To do so is an offence under the Act.

Ministers should note the advice given by the Procurator of the Church in 1962, that they should not officiate at any marriage until at least one day after the 16th birthday of the younger party.

Furthermore, a marriage involving someone who is not an EU citizen involves extra registration requirements, and initial contact should be made with the local Registrar several months before the intended date of marriage.

3. THE MARRIAGE (SCOTLAND) ACT 2002

Although there have never been any limitations as to the place where a religious marriage can be celebrated, civil marriage originally could take place only in the Office of a Registrar. The Marriage (Scotland) Act 2002 permits the solemnisation of civil marriages at places approved by Local Authorities. Regulations have been made to specify the kinds of place which may be 'approved' with a view to ensuring that the places approved will not compromise the solemnity and dignity of civil marriage and will have no recent or continuing connection with any religion so as to undermine the distinction between religious and civil ceremonies.

4. PROCLAMATION OF BANNS

Proclamation of banns is no longer required in Scotland; but, in the Church of England, marriage is governed by the provisions of the Marriage Act 1949, which requires that the parties' intention to marry has to have been proclaimed and which provides that in the case of a party residing in Scotland a Certificate of Proclamation given according to the law or custom prevailing in Scotland shall be sufficient for the purpose. In the event that a minister is asked to call banns for a person resident within the registration district where his or her church is situated, the proclamation needs only to be made on one Sunday if the parties are known to the minister. If they are not, it should be made on two Sundays. In all cases, the Minister should, of course, have no reason to believe that there is any impediment to the marriage.

Proclamation should be made at the principal service of worship in this form:

There is a purpose of marriage between AB (Bachelor/Widower/Divorced), residing at .... in this Registration District, and CD (Spinster/Widow/Divorced), residing at .... in the Registration District of ...., of which proclamation is hereby made for the first and only (second and last) time.

Immediately after the second reading, or not less than forty-eight hours after the first and only reading, a Certificate of Proclamation signed by either the minister or the Session Clerk should be issued in the following terms:

At .... the ...... day of ...... 20 ....
It is hereby certified that AB, residing at ...., and CD, residing at ...., have been duly proclaimed in order to marriage in the Church of .... according to the custom of the Church of Scotland, and that no objections have been offered.
Signed .... minister or
Signed .... Session Clerk

5. MARRIAGE OF FOREIGNERS

Marriages in Scotland of foreigners, or of foreigners with British subjects, are, if they satisfy the requirements of Scots Law, valid within the United Kingdom and the various British overseas territories; but they will not necessarily be valid in the country to which the foreigner belongs. This will be so only if the requirements of the law of his or her country have also been complied with. It is therefore most important that, before the marriage, steps should be taken to obtain from the Consul, or other diplomatic representative of the country concerned, a satisfactory assurance that the marriage will be accepted as valid in the country concerned.

6. REMARRIAGE OF DIVORCED PERSONS

By virtue of Act XXVI 1959, a minister of the Church of Scotland may lawfully solemnise the marriage of a person whose former marriage has been dissolved by divorce and whose former spouse is still alive. The minister, however, must carefully adhere to the requirements of the Act which, as slightly altered in 1985, are briefly as follows:

1. The minister should not accede as a matter of routine to a request to solemnise such a marriage. To enable a decision to be made, he or she should take all reasonable steps to obtain relevant information, which should normally include the following:
    (a) Adequate information concerning the life and character of the parties. The Act enjoins the greatest caution in cases where no pastoral relationship exists between the minister and either or both of the parties concerned.
    (b) The grounds and circumstances of the divorce case.
    (c) Facts bearing upon the future well-being of any children concerned.
    (d) Whether any other minister has declined to solemnise the proposed marriage.
    (e) The denomination to which the parties belong. The Act enjoins that special care should be taken where one or more parties belong to a denomination whose discipline in this matter may differ from that of the Church of Scotland.
2. The minister should consider whether there is danger of scandal arising if he or she should solemnise the remarriage, at the same time taking into careful consideration before refusing to do so the moral and spiritual effect of a refusal on the parties concerned.
3. As a determinative factor, the minister should do all he or she can to be assured that there has been sincere repentance where guilt has existed on the part of any divorced person seeking remarriage. He or she should also give instruction, where needed, in the nature and requirements of a Christian marriage.
4. A minister is not required to solemnise a remarriage against his or her conscience. Every Presbytery is required to appoint certain individuals with one of whom ministers in doubt as to the correct course of action may consult if they so desire. The final decision, however, rests with the minister who has been asked to officiate.

---

(3) CONDUCT OF MARRIAGE SERVICES
(CODE OF GOOD PRACTICE)

The code which follows was submitted to the General Assembly in 1997. It appears, on page 1/10, in the Volume of Assembly Reports for that year within the Report of the Board of Practice and Procedure.

1. *Marriage in the Church of Scotland is solemnised by an ordained minister in a religious ceremony wherein, before God, and in the presence of the minister and at least two competent witnesses, the parties covenant together to take each other as husband and wife as long as they both shall live, and the minister declares the parties to be husband and wife. Before solemnising a marriage, a minister must be assured that the necessary legal requirements are being complied with and that the parties know of no legal impediment to their marriage, and he or she must afterwards ensure that the Marriage Schedule is duly completed.* (Act I 1977)

2. Any ordained minister of the Church of Scotland who is a member of Presbytery or who holds a current Ministerial Certificate may officiate at a marriage service (see Act II 1987).

3. While the marriage service should normally take place in church, a minister may, at his or her discretion, officiate at a marriage service outwith church premises. Wherever conducted, the ceremony will be such as to reflect appropriately both the joy and the solemnity of the occasion. In particular, a minister shall ensure that nothing is done which would bring the Church and its teaching into disrepute.

4. A minister agreeing to conduct a wedding should endeavour to establish a pastoral relationship with the couple within which adequate pre-marriage preparation and subsequent pastoral care may be given.

5. 'A minister should not refuse to perform ministerial functions for a person who is resident in his or her parish without sufficient reason' (Cox, *Practice and Procedure in the Church of Scotland*, sixth edition, page 55). Where either party to the proposed marriage has been divorced and the former spouse is still alive, the minister invited to officiate may solemnise such a marriage, having regard to the guidelines in the Act anent the Remarriage of Divorced Persons (Act XXVI 1959 as amended by Act II 1985).

6. A minister is acting as an agent of the National Church which is committed to bringing the ordinances of religion to the people of Scotland through a territorial ministry. As such, he or she shall not be entitled to charge a fee or allow a fee to be charged for conducting a marriage service. When a gift is spontaneously offered to a minister as a token of appreciation, the above consideration should not be taken to mean that he or she should not accept such an unsolicited gift. The Financial Board of a congregation is at liberty to set fees to cover such costs as heat and light, and in addition Organists and Church Officers are entitled to a fee in respect of their services at weddings.

7. A minister should not allow his or her name to be associated with any commercial enterprise that provides facilities for weddings.

8. A minister is not at liberty to enter the bounds of another minister's parish to perform ministerial functions without the previous consent of the minister of that parish. In terms of Act VIII 1933, a minister may 'officiate at a marriage or funeral by private invitation', but, for the avoidance of doubt, an invitation conveyed through a commercial enterprise shall not be regarded as a 'private invitation' within the meaning of that Act.

9. A minister invited to officiate at a Marriage Service where neither party is a member of his or her congregation or is resident within his or her own parish or has any connection with the parish within which the service is to take place should observe the following courtesies:
   (a) he or she should ascertain from the parties whether either of them has a Church of Scotland connection or has approached the appropriate parish minister(s);
   (b) if it transpires that a ministerial colleague has declined to officiate, then he or she (the invited minister) should ascertain the reasons therefor and shall take these and all other relevant factors into account in deciding whether or not to officiate.

(4) CONDUCT OF FUNERAL SERVICES: FEES

The General Assembly of 2007 received the Report of the Legal Questions Committee which included a statement regarding fees for funerals. That statement had been prepared in the light of approaches from two Presbyteries seeking guidance on the question of the charging of fees (on behalf of ministers) for the conduct of funerals. It had seemed to the Presbyteries that expectations and practice were unacceptably varied across the country, and that the question was complicated by the fact that, quite naturally and legitimately, ministers other than parish ministers occasionally conduct funeral services.

The full text of that statement was engrossed in the Minutes of the General Assembly, and it was felt that it would be helpful to include it also in the *Year Book*.

The statement
The (Legal Questions) Committee believes that the question is two-fold, relating firstly to parish ministers (including associate and assistant ministers, deacons and the like) within their regular ministry, and secondly to ministers and others taking an occasional funeral, for instance by private invitation or in the course of pastoral cover of another parish.

Ministers in receipt of a living
The Committee believes that the position of the minister of a parish, and of other paid staff on the ministry team of a parish, is clear. The Third Declaratory Article affirms the responsibility of the Church of Scotland to provide the ordinances of religion through its territorial ministry, while the stipend system (and, for other staff members, the salary) provides a living that enables that ministry to be exercised without charging fees for services conducted. The implication of this principle is that no family in Scotland should ever be charged for the services of a Church of Scotland minister at the time of bereavement. Clearly, therefore, no minister in receipt of a living should be charging separately (effectively being paid doubly) for any such service. The Committee is conscious that the position of congregations outside Scotland may be different, and is aware that the relevant Presbyteries will offer appropriate superintendence of these matters.

A related question is raised about the highly varied culture of gift-giving in different parts of the country. The Committee believes it would be unwise to seek to regulate this. In some places, an attempt to quash a universal and long-established practice would seem ungracious, while in other places there is no such practice, and encouragement in that direction would seem indelicate.

A second related question was raised about Funeral Directors charging for the services of the minister. The Committee believes that Presbyteries should make it clear to Funeral Directors that, in the case of Church of Scotland funerals, such a charge should not be made.

Ministers conducting occasional services
Turning to the position of ministers who do not receive a living that enables them to conduct funerals without charge, the Committee's starting point is the principle articulated above that no bereaved person should have to pay for the services of a minister. The territorial ministry and the parish system of this Church mean that a bereaved family should not find itself being contingently charged because the parish minister happens to be unavailable, or because the parish is vacant.

Where a funeral is being conducted as part of the ministry of the local parish, but where for any reason another minister is taking it and not otherwise being paid, it is the responsibility of the congregation (through its financial body) to ensure that appropriate fees and expenses are met.

Where that imposes a financial burden upon a congregation because of the weight of pastoral need, the need should be taken into account in calculating the resource-needs of that parish in the course of updating the Presbytery Plan.

It is beyond the remit of the Legal Questions Committee to make judgements about the appropriate level of payment. The Committee suggests that the Ministries Council should give the relevant advice on this aspect of the issue.

The Committee believes that these principles could be applied to the conduct of weddings and are perfectly compatible with the Guidelines on that subject which are reproduced in the *Year Book* at item 3 of section 3 dealing with Church Procedure.

(5) THE MINISTER AND WILLS

The Requirements of Writing (Scotland) Act 1995, which came into force on 1 August 1995, has removed the power of a minister to execute wills notarially. Further clarification, if required, may be obtained from the Solicitor of the Church.

(6) PROCEDURE IN A VACANCY

Procedure in a vacancy is regulated by Act VIII 2003 as amended by Acts IX and X 2004, II 2005, V 2006, I, IV and VI 2008 and II and V 2009. The text of the most immediately relevant sections is given here for general information. Schedules of Intimation referred to are also included. The full text of the Act and subsequent amendments can be obtained from the Principal Clerk.

1. Vacancy Procedure Committee
(1)   Each Presbytery shall appoint a number of its members to be available to serve on Vacancy Procedure Committees and shall provide information and training as required for those so appointed.
(2)   As soon as the Presbytery Clerk is aware that a vacancy has arisen or is anticipated, he or she shall consult the Moderator of the Presbytery and they shall appoint a Vacancy Procedure Committee of five persons from among those appointed in terms of subsection (1), which Committee shall (a) include at least one minister and at least one elder and (b) exclude any communicant member or former minister of the vacant charge or of any constituent congregation thereof. The Vacancy Procedure Committee shall include a Convener and Clerk, the latter of whom need not be a member of the Committee but may be the Presbytery Clerk. The same Vacancy Procedure Committee may serve for more than one vacancy at a time.
(3)   The Vacancy Procedure Committee shall have a quorum of three for its meetings.
(4)   The Convener of the Vacancy Procedure Committee may, where he or she reasonably believes a matter to be non-contentious, consult members individually, provided that reasonable efforts are made to consult all members of the Committee. A meeting shall be held at the request of any member of the Committee.

(5)   Every decision made by the Vacancy Procedure Committee shall be reported to the next meeting of Presbytery, but may not be recalled by Presbytery where the decision was subject to the provisions of section 2 below.

2. Request for Consideration by Presbytery

Where in this Act any decision by the Vacancy Procedure Committee is subject to the provisions of this section, the following rules shall apply:

(1)   The Presbytery Clerk shall intimate to all members of the Presbytery by mailing or at a Presbytery meeting the course of action or permission proposed, and shall arrange for one Sunday's pulpit intimation of the same to be made to the congregation or congregations concerned, in terms of Schedule A. The intimation having been made, it shall be displayed as prominently as possible at the church building for seven days.

(2)   Any four individuals, being communicant members of the congregation or full members of the Presbytery, may give written notice requesting that action be taken in terms of subsection (3) below, giving reasons for the request, within seven days after the pulpit intimation.

(3)   Upon receiving notice in terms of subsection (2), the Presbytery Clerk shall sist the process or permission referred to in subsection (1), which shall then require the approval of the Presbytery.

(4)   The Moderator of the Presbytery shall in such circumstances consider whether a meeting *pro re nata* of the Presbytery should be called in order to avoid prejudicial delay in the vacancy process.

(5)   The Presbytery Clerk shall cause to have served upon the congregation or congregations an edict in terms of Schedule B citing them to attend the meeting of Presbytery for their interest.

(6)   The consideration by Presbytery of any matter under this section shall not constitute an appeal or a Petition, and the decision of Presbytery shall be deemed to be a decision at first instance subject to the normal rights of appeal or dissent-and-complaint.

3. Causes of Vacancy

The causes of vacancy shall normally include:

(a)   the death of the minister of the charge;

(b)   the removal of status of the minister of the charge or the suspension of the minister in terms of section 20(2) of Act III 2001;

(c)   the dissolution of the pastoral tie in terms of Act I 1988 or Act XV 2002;

(d)   the demission of the charge and/or status of the minister of the charge;

(e)   the translation of the minister of the charge to another charge;

(f)   the termination of the tenure of the minister of the charge in terms of Act VI 1984.

4. Release of Departing Minister

The Presbytery Clerk shall be informed as soon as circumstances have occurred that cause a vacancy to arise or make it likely that a vacancy shall arise. Where the circumstances pertain to section 3(d) or (e) above, the Vacancy Procedure Committee shall

(1)   except in cases governed by subsection (2) below, decide whether to release the minister from his or her charge and, in any case involving translation to another charge or introduction to an appointment, instruct him or her to await the instructions of the Presbytery or another Presbytery;

(2)   in the case of a minister in the first five years of his or her first charge, decide whether there are exceptional circumstances to justify releasing him or her from his or her charge and proceeding in terms of subsection (1) above;

(3)　determine whether a vacancy has arisen or is anticipated and, as soon as possible, determine the date upon which the charge becomes actually vacant, and

(4)　inform the congregation or congregations by one Sunday's pulpit intimation as soon as convenient.

(5)　The provisions of section 2 above shall apply to the decisions of the Vacancy Procedure Committee in terms of subsections (1) and (2) above.

5. Demission of Charge

(1)　Subject to the provisions of subsection (2) below, when a vacancy has occurred in terms of section 3(c), (d) or (f) above, the Presbytery shall determine whether the minister is, in the circumstances, entitled to a seat in the Presbytery in terms of section 16 of Act III 2000 (as amended).

(2)　In the case where it is a condition of any basis of adjustment that a minister shall demit his or her charge to facilitate union or linking, and the minister has agreed in writing in terms of the appropriate regulations governing adjustments, formal application shall not be made to the Presbytery for permission to demit. The minister concerned shall be regarded as retiring in the interest of adjustment, and he or she shall retain a seat in Presbytery unless in terms of Act III 2000 (as amended) he or she elects to resign it.

(3)　A minister who demits his or her charge without retaining a seat in the Presbytery shall, if he or she retains status as a minister, be subject to the provisions of sections 5 to 15 of Act II 2000 (as amended).

6. Appointment of Interim Moderator

(1)　At the same time as the Vacancy Procedure Committee makes a decision in terms of section 4 above, or where circumstances pertain to section 3(a), (b), (c) or (f) above, the Vacancy Procedure Committee shall appoint an Interim Moderator for the charge and make intimation thereof to the congregation subject to the provisions of section 2 above. The Interim Moderator shall be either a ministerial member of the Presbytery in terms of Act III 2000 or Act V 2001 or a member of the Presbytery selected from a list of those who have received such preparation for the task as the Ministries Council shall from time to time recommend or provide, and he or she shall not be a member in the vacant charge nor a member of the Vacancy Procedure Committee. The name of the Interim Moderator shall be forwarded to the Ministries Council.

(2)　If the Interim Moderator appointed is a ministerial member of Presbytery, it is understood that, in accepting the appointment, he or she is thereby disqualified from becoming an applicant or accepting an invitation to be considered in the current vacancy.

7. Duties of Interim Moderator

(1)　It shall be the duty of the Interim Moderator to preside at all meetings of the Kirk Session (or of the Kirk Sessions in the case of a linked charge) and to preside at all congregational meetings in connection with the vacancy, or at which the minister would have presided had the charge been full. In the case of a congregational meeting called by the Presbytery in connection with adjustment, the Interim Moderator, having constituted the meeting, shall relinquish the chair in favour of the representative of the Presbytery, but he or she shall be at liberty to speak at such a meeting. In consultation with the Kirk Session and the Financial Court, he or she shall make arrangements for the supply of the vacant pulpit.

(2)　The Interim Moderator appointed in a prospective vacancy may call and preside at meetings of the Kirk Session and of the congregation for the transaction of business relating to the

said prospective vacancy. He or she shall be associated with the minister until the date of the actual vacancy; after that date, he or she shall take full charge.
(3)   The Interim Moderator shall act as an assessor to the Nominating Committee, being available to offer guidance and advice. If the Committee so desire, he or she may act as their Convener, but in no case shall he or she have a vote.
(4)   In the event of the absence of the Interim Moderator, the Vacancy Procedure Committee shall appoint a member of the Presbytery who is not a member of the vacant congregation to fulfil any of the rights and duties of the Interim Moderator.
(5)   The Interim Moderator shall have the same duties and responsibilities towards all members of ministry teams referred to in section 16 of Act VII 2003 as if he or she were the parish minister, both in terms of this Act and in respect of the terms and conditions of such individuals.

8. Permission to Call

When the decision to release the minister from the charge has been made and the Interim Moderator appointed, the Vacancy Procedure Committee shall consider whether it may give permission to call a minister in terms of Act VII 2003, and may proceed subject to the provisions of section 2 above. The Vacancy Procedure Committee must refer the question of permission to call to the Presbytery if:
(a)   shortfalls exist which in the opinion of the Committee require consideration in terms of section 9 hereunder;
(b)   the Committee has reason to believe that the vacancy schedule referred to in section 10 below will not be approved;
(c)   the Committee has reason to believe that the Presbytery will, in terms of section 11 below, instruct work to be carried out on the manse before a call can be sustained, and judges that the likely extent of such work warrants a delay in the granting of permission to call, or
(d)   the Committee has reason to believe that the Presbytery may wish to delay or refuse the granting of permission for any reason.
Any decision by Presbytery to refuse permission to call shall be subject to appeal or dissent-and-complaint.

9. Shortfalls

(1)   As soon as possible after intimation of a vacancy or anticipated vacancy reaches the Presbytery Clerk, the Presbytery shall ascertain whether the charge has current or accumulated shortfalls in contributions to central funds, and shall determine whether and to what extent any shortfalls that exist are justified.
(2)   If the vacancy is in a charge in which the Presbytery has determined that shortfalls are to any extent unjustified, it shall not resolve to allow a call of any kind until:
(a)   the shortfalls have been met to the extent to which the Presbytery determined that they were unjustified, or
(b)   a scheme for the payment of the unjustified shortfall has been agreed between the congregation and the Presbytery and receives the concurrence of the Ministries Council and/or the Stewardship and Finance Committee for their respective interests, or
(c)   a fresh appraisal of the charge in terms of Act VII 2003 has been carried out, regardless of the status of the charge in the current Presbytery plan:
    (i)   During such appraisal, no further steps may be taken in respect of filling the vacancy, and the Presbytery shall make final determination of what constitutes such steps.
    (ii) Following such appraisal and any consequent adjustment or deferred adjustment,

the shortfalls shall be met or declared justifiable or a scheme shall be agreed in terms of subsection (b) above; the Presbytery shall inform the Ministries Council and the Stewardship and Finance Committee of its decisions in terms of this section; and the Presbytery shall remove the suspension-of-vacancy process referred to in sub-paragraph (i).

10. Vacancy Schedule
(1)   When in terms of sections 4 and 6 above the decision to release the minister from the charge has been made and the Interim Moderator appointed, there shall be issued by the Ministries Council a Schedule or Schedules for completion by the responsible Financial Board(s) of the vacant congregation(s) in consultation with representatives of the Presbytery, setting forth the proposed arrangements for payment of ministerial expenses and for provision of a manse, showing the ministry requirements and details of any endowment income. The Schedule, along with an Extract Minute from each relevant Kirk Session containing a commitment fully and adequately to support the ministry, shall be forwarded to the Presbytery Clerk.
(2)   The Schedule shall be considered by the Vacancy Procedure Committee and, if approved, transmitted to the Ministries Council by the Presbytery Clerk. The Vacancy Procedure Committee or Presbytery must not sustain an appointment and call until the Schedule has been approved by them and by the Ministries Council, which shall intimate its decision within six weeks of receiving the schedule from the Presbytery.
(3)   The accuracy of the Vacancy Schedule shall be kept under review by the Vacancy Procedure Committee.
(4)   The provisions of section 2 above shall apply to the decisions of the Vacancy Procedure Committee.

11. Manse
As soon as possible after the manse becomes vacant, the Presbytery Property Committee shall inspect the manse and come to a view on what work, if any, must be carried out to render it suitable for a new incumbent. The views of the Property Committee should then be communicated to the Presbytery, which should, subject to any modifications which might be agreed by that Court, instruct the Financial Board of the congregation to have the work carried out. No induction date shall be fixed until the Presbytery Property Committee has again inspected the manse and confirmed that the work has been undertaken satisfactorily.

12. Advisory Committee
(1)   As soon as possible after intimation of a vacancy or anticipated vacancy reaches the Presbytery Clerk, the Vacancy Procedure Committee shall appoint an Advisory Committee of three, subject to the following conditions:
(a)   at least one member shall be an elder and at least one shall be a minister;
(b)   the Advisory Committee may comprise members of the Vacancy Procedure Committee and act as a support committee to congregations in a vacancy;
(c)   the Advisory Committee may contain individuals who are not members of the Presbytery;
(d)   the appointment shall be subject to section 2 above.
(2)   The Advisory Committee shall meet:
(a)   before the election of the Nominating Committee, with the Kirk Session (or Kirk Sessions both separately and together) of the vacant charge, to consider together in the light of the whole circumstances of the parish or parishes (i) what kind of ministry would be best suited to their needs and (ii) which system of election of

the Nominating Committee described in paragraph 14(2)(d) hereunder shall be used;
(b)   with the Nominating Committee before it has taken any steps to fill the vacancy, to consider how it should proceed;
(c)   with the Nominating Committee before it reports to the Kirk Session and Presbytery the identity of the nominee, to review the process followed and give any further advice it deems necessary;
(d)   with the Kirk Session(s) as soon as an application is made for permission to proceed in terms of section 25A of this Act, to ensure that the requirements of that section are fulfilled;
(e)   with the Nominating Committee at any other time by request of either the Nominating Committee or the Advisory Committee.

In the case of charges which are in the opinion of the Presbytery remote, it will be adequate if the Interim Moderator (accompanied if possible by a member of the Nominating Committee) meets with the Advisory Committee for the purposes listed in paragraphs (a) to (c) above.

13. Electoral Register

(1)   It shall be the duty of the Kirk Session of a vacant congregation to proceed to make up the Electoral Register of the congregation. This shall contain (1) as communicants the names of those persons (a) whose names are on the communion roll of the congregation as at the date on which it is made up and who are not under Church discipline, (b) whose names have been added or restored to the communion roll on revision by the Kirk Session subsequently to the occurrence of the vacancy, and (c) who have given in valid Certificates of Transference by the date specified in terms of Schedule C hereto; and (2) as adherents the names of those persons who, being parishioners or regular worshippers in the congregation at the date when the vacancy occurred, and not being members of any other congregation, have claimed (in writing in the form prescribed in Schedule D and within the time specified in Schedule C) to be placed on the Electoral Register, the Kirk Session being satisfied that they desire to be permanently connected with the congregation and knowing of no adequate reasons why they should not be admitted as communicants should they so apply.

(2)   At a meeting to be held not later than fourteen days after intimation has been made in terms of Schedule C hereto, the Kirk Session shall decide on the claims of persons to be placed on the Electoral Register, such claims to be sent to the Session Clerk before the meeting. At this meeting, the Kirk Session may hear parties claiming to have an interest. The Kirk Session shall thereupon prepare the lists of names and addresses of communicants and of adherents which it is proposed shall be the Electoral Register of the congregation, the names being arranged in alphabetical order and numbered consecutively throughout. The decision of the Kirk Session in respect of any matter affecting the preparation of the Electoral Register shall be final.

(3)   The proposed Electoral Register having been prepared, the Interim Moderator shall cause intimation to be made on the first convenient Sunday in terms of Schedule E hereto that on that day an opportunity will be given for inspecting the Register after service, and that it will lie for inspection at such times and such places as the Kirk Session shall have determined; and further shall specify a day when the Kirk Session will meet to hear parties claiming an interest and will finally revise and adjust the Register. At this meeting, the list, having been revised, numbered and adjusted, shall on the authority of the court be attested by the Interim Moderator and the Clerk as the Electoral Register of the congregation.

(4)   This Register, along with a duplicate copy, shall without delay be transmitted to the Presbytery Clerk, who, in name of the Presbytery, shall attest and return the principal copy, retaining the duplicate copy in his or her own possession. For all purposes connected with this Act, the congregation shall be deemed to be those persons whose names are on the Electoral Register, and no other.

(5)   If after the attestation of the Register any communicant is given a Certificate of Transference, the Session Clerk shall delete that person's name from the Register and initial the deletion. Such a Certificate shall be granted only when application for it has been made in writing, and the said written application shall be retained until the vacancy is ended.

(6)   When a period of more than six months has elapsed between the Electoral Register being attested and the congregation being given permission to call, the Kirk Session shall have power, if it so desires, to revise and update the Electoral Register. Intimation of this intention shall be given in terms of Schedule F hereto. Additional names shall be added to the Register in the form of an Addendum which shall also contain authority for the deletions which have been made; two copies of this Addendum, duly attested, shall be lodged with the Presbytery Clerk, who, in name of the Presbytery, shall attest and return the principal copy, retaining the duplicate copy in his or her own possession.

14. Appointment of Nominating Committee

(1)   When permission to call has been given and the Electoral Register has been attested, intimation in terms of Schedule G shall be made that a meeting of the congregation is to be held to appoint a Committee of its own number for the purpose of nominating one person to the congregation with a view to the appointment of a minister.

(2)   (a)   The Interim Moderator shall preside at this meeting, and the Session Clerk, or in his or her absence a person appointed by the meeting, shall act as Clerk.

(b)   The Interim Moderator shall remind the congregation of the number of members it is required to appoint in terms of this section and shall call for Nominations. To constitute a valid Nomination, the name of a person on the Electoral Register has to be proposed and seconded, and assurance given by the proposer that the person is prepared to act on the Committee. The Clerk shall take a note of all Nominations in the order in which they are made.

(c)   For the avoidance of doubt, a member of a vacant charge shall not be eligible for nomination to serve on a Nominating Committee, if he or she is:
(i)   a minister (including a retired minister) of the Church of Scotland,
(ii)   a member of the diaconate of the Church of Scotland,
(iii)   an employee of the vacant charge,
(iv)   an employee of the Ministries Council who works in the vacant charge, or
(v)   the spouse of any former minister of the charge.

(d)   When it appears to the Interim Moderator that the Nominations are complete, they shall be read to the congregation and an opportunity given for any withdrawals. If the number of persons nominated does not exceed the maximum fixed in terms of subsection (4) below, there is no need for a vote, and the Interim Moderator shall declare that these persons constitute a Nominating Committee.

(e)   If the number exceeds the maximum, the election shall proceed by one of the following means, chosen in advance by the Kirk Session, and being either (i) the submission of the names by the Interim Moderator, one by one as they appear on the list, to the vote of the congregation, each member having the right to vote for up to the maximum number fixed for the Committee, and voting being by standing up, or (ii) a system of written ballot devised by the Kirk Session to suit the size of the congregation and approved by the Vacancy Procedure Committee or the Presbytery. In either case, in the event of a tie for the last place, a further vote shall be taken between or among those tying.

(f) The Interim Moderator shall, at the same meeting or as soon thereafter as the result of any ballot has been determined, announce the names of those thus elected to serve on the Nominating Committee, and intimate to them the time and place of their first meeting, which may be immediately after the congregational meeting provided that has been intimated along with the intimation of the congregational meeting.

(3) Where there is an agreement between the Presbytery and the congregation or congregations that the minister to be inducted shall serve either in a team ministry involving another congregation or congregations, or in a designated post such as a chaplaincy, it shall be competent for the agreement to specify that the Presbytery shall appoint up to two representatives to serve on the Nominating Committee.

(4) The Vacancy Procedure Committee shall, subject to the provisions of section 2 above, determine the number who will act on the Nominating Committee, being an odd number up to a maximum of thirteen.

(5) When the vacancy is in a linked charge, or when a union or linking of congregations has been agreed but not yet effected, or when there is agreement to a deferred union or a deferred linking, or where the appointment is to more than one post, the Vacancy Procedure Committee shall, subject to the provisions of section 2 above, determine how the number who will act on the Nominating Committee will be allocated among the congregations involved, unless provision for this has already been made in the Basis of Union or Basis of Linking as the case may be.

(6) The Nominating Committee shall not have power to co-opt additional members, but the relevant Kirk Session shall have power when necessary to appoint a replacement for any of its appointees who ceases, by death or resignation, to be a member of the Nominating Committee, or who, by falling ill or by moving away from the area, is unable to serve as a member of it.

15. Constitution of the Nominating Committee

It shall be the duty of the Interim Moderator to summon and preside at the first meeting of the Nominating Committee, which may be held at the close of the congregational meeting at which it is appointed and at which the Committee shall appoint a Convener and a Clerk. The Clerk, who need not be a member of the Committee, shall keep regular minutes of all proceedings. The Convener shall have a deliberative vote (if he or she is not the Interim Moderator) but shall in no case have a casting vote. If the Clerk is not a member of the Committee, he or she shall have no vote. At all meetings of the Committee, only those present shall be entitled to vote.

16. Task of the Nominating Committee

(1) The Nominating Committee shall have the duty of nominating one person to the congregation with a view to the election and appointment of a minister. It shall proceed by a process of announcement in a monthly vacancy list, application and interview, and may also advertise, receive recommendations and pursue enquiries in other ways.

(2) The Committee shall give due weight to any guidelines which may from time to time be issued by the Ministries Council or the General Assembly.

(3) The Committee shall make themselves aware of the roles of the other members of any ministry team as described in section 16 of Act VII 2003 and may meet with them for this purpose, but shall not acquire responsibility or authority for the negotiation or alteration of their terms and conditions.

17. Eligibility for Election
The following categories of persons, and no others, are eligible to be nominated, elected and called as ministers of parishes in the Church of Scotland, but always subject, where appropriate, to the provisions of Act IX 2002:
(1)   A minister of a parish of the Church, a minister holding some other appointment that entitles him or her to a seat in Presbytery or a minister holding a current Practising Certificate in terms of Section 5 of Act II 2000 (as amended).
(2)   A minister of the Church of Scotland who has retired from a parish or appointment as above, provided he or she has not reached his or her 65th birthday (or, subject to the provisions of Regulations II 2004, his or her 70th birthday).
(3)   (a)   A licentiate of the Church of Scotland who has satisfactorily completed, or has been granted exemption from, his or her period of probationary service.
       (b)   A graduate candidate in terms of section 22 of Act X 2004.
(4)   A minister, licentiate or graduate candidate of the Church of Scotland who, with the approval of the World Mission Council, has entered the courts of an overseas Church as a full member, provided he or she has ceased to be such a member.
(5)   A minister, licentiate or graduate candidate of the Church of Scotland who has neither relinquished nor been judicially deprived of the status he or she possessed and who has served, or is serving, furth of Scotland in any Church which is a member of the World Alliance of Reformed Churches.
(6)   The holder of a Certificate of Eligibility in terms of Act IX 2002. The holder of a Certificate of Eligibility who is a national outside the European Economic Area and Switzerland shall be eligible to apply for charges only in terms of section 25A of this Act.
(7)   For the avoidance of doubt, anyone who has served as an Interim Moderator in the current vacancy shall not be eligible to apply or to be considered as an applicant.

18. Ministers of a Team
Ministers occupying positions within a team ministry in the charge, or larger area including the charge, and former holders of such positions, shall be eligible to apply and shall not by virtue of office be deemed to have exercised undue influence in securing the call. A *locum tenens* in the vacant charge shall not by virtue of office be deemed to have exercised undue influence in securing the call. Any Interim Moderator in the current vacancy shall not be eligible to apply.

19. Ministers of Other Churches
(1)   Where a minister of a church furth of Scotland, who holds a certificate of eligibility in ˙ terms of Act IX 2002, is nominated, the nominee, Kirk Session and Presbytery may agree that he or she shall be inducted for a period of three years only and shall retain status as a minister of his or her denomination of origin.
(2)   Upon induction, such a minister shall be accountable to the Presbytery for the exercise of his or her ministry and to his or her own church for matters of life and doctrine. He or she shall be awarded corresponding membership of the Presbytery.
(3)   With the concurrence of the Presbytery and the Ministries Council, and at the request of the congregation, the period may be extended for one further period of not more than three years.
(4)   The provisions of this section shall apply in the case of an appointment as a member of a ministry team as defined in section 16(2)(a) of Act VII 2003 (as amended), provided that the appointment is one which the Presbytery deems must be held by a Ministry of Word and Sacrament.

20. Nomination
(1)   Before the candidate is asked to accept Nomination, the Interim Moderator shall ensure that the candidate is given an adequate opportunity to see the whole ecclesiastical buildings

(including the manse) pertaining to the congregation, and to meet privately with all members of staff of the charge or of any wider ministry team, and shall be provided with a copy of the constitution of the congregation, a copy of the current Presbytery Plan and of any current Basis of Adjustment or Basis of Reviewable Tenure, and the most recent audited accounts and statement of funds, and the candidate shall acknowledge receipt in writing to the Interim Moderator.

(2)   Before any Nomination is intimated to the Kirk Session and Presbytery Clerk, the Clerk to the Nominating Committee shall secure the written consent thereto of the nominee.

(3)   Before reporting the Nomination to the Vacancy Procedure Committee, the Presbytery Clerk shall obtain from the nominee or Interim Moderator evidence of the eligibility of the nominee to be appointed to the charge.

    (a)   In the case of a minister not being a member of any Presbytery of the Church of Scotland, this shall normally constitute an Exit Certificate in terms of Act X 2004, or evidence of status from the Ministries Council, or a current practising certificate, or certification from the Ministries Council of eligibility in terms of Act IX 2002.

    (b)   In the case of a minister in the first five years of his or her first charge, this shall consist of an extract minute either from the Vacancy Procedure Committee of his or her current Presbytery, or from that Presbytery, exceptionally releasing the minister.

21. Preaching by Nominee

(1)   The Interim Moderator, on receiving notice of the Committee's Nomination, shall arrange that the nominee conduct public worship in the vacant church or churches, normally within four Sundays, and that the ballot take place immediately after each such service.

(2)   The Interim Moderator shall thereupon cause intimation to be made on two Sundays regarding the arrangements made in connection with the preaching by the nominee and the ballot thereafter, all in terms of Schedule H hereto.

22. Election of Minister

(1)   The Interim Moderator shall normally preside at all congregational meetings connected with the election which shall be in all cases by ballot and shall normally be in charge of the ballot.

(2)   The Interim Moderator may invite one or more persons (not being persons whose names are on the Electoral Register of the vacant congregation) to assist him or her in the conduct of a ballot vote when he or she judges this desirable.

(3)   When a linking or a deferred union or deferred linking is involved, the Interim Moderator shall consult and reach agreement with the minister or Interim Moderator of the other congregation regarding the arrangements for the conduct of public worship in these congregations by the nominee as in section 21(1) above. The Interim Moderator shall in writing appoint a member of Presbytery to take full charge of the ballot vote for the other congregation. In the case of a deferred union or deferred linking, the minister already inducted shall not be so appointed, nor shall he or she be in any way involved in the conduct of the election.

23. Ballot Procedure

(1)   The Kirk Session shall arrange to have available at the time of election a sufficient supply of voting-papers printed in the form of Schedule I hereto, and these shall be put into the custody of the Interim Moderator who shall preside at the election, assisted as in section 22 above. He or she shall issue on request to any person whose name is on the Electoral Register a voting-paper, noting on the Register that this has been done. Facilities shall be provided whereby the voter may mark the paper in secrecy, and a ballot-box shall be available wherein the paper is to be deposited when marked. The Interim Moderator may

assist any person who asks for help in respect of completing the voting-paper, but no other person whatever shall communicate with the voter at this stage. The Interim Moderator, or the deputy appointed by him or her, shall be responsible for the safe custody of ballot-box, papers and Electoral Register.

(2)   As soon as practicable, and at latest within twenty-four hours after the close of the voting, the Interim Moderator shall constitute the Kirk Session, or the joint Kirk Sessions when more than one congregation is involved, and in presence of the Kirk Session shall proceed with the counting of the votes, in which he or she may be assisted as provided in section 22 above. When more than one ballot-box has been used and when the votes of more than one congregation are involved, all ballot-boxes shall be emptied and the voting-papers shall be mixed together before counting begins so that the preponderance of votes in one area or in one congregation shall not be disclosed.

(3)   A voting-paper shall only be considered as spoilt and the vote not counted where the intention of the voter is unclear, and in no other circumstances. It shall be for the Kirk Session, on the recommendation of the Interim Moderator, to determine whether the intention of the voter is clear.

(4)   If the number voting For exceeds the number voting Against, the nominee shall be declared elected and the Nominating Committee shall be deemed to be discharged.

(5)   If the number voting For is equal to or less than the number voting Against, the Interim Moderator shall declare that there has been failure to elect and that the Nominating Committee is deemed to have been discharged. He or she shall proceed in terms of section 26(b) without further reference to the Presbytery.

(6)   After the counting has been completed, the Interim Moderator shall sign a declaration in one of the forms of Schedule J hereto, and this shall be recorded in the minute of the Kirk Session or of the Kirk Sessions. An extract shall be affixed to the notice-board of the church, or of each of the churches, concerned. In presence of the Kirk Session, the Interim Moderator shall then seal up the voting-papers along with the marked copy of the Electoral Register, and these shall be transmitted to the Presbytery Clerk in due course along with the other documents specified in section 27 below.

24. Withdrawal of Nominee

(1)   Should a nominee intimate withdrawal before he or she has preached as nominee, the Nominating Committee shall continue its task and seek to nominate another nominee.

(2)   Should a nominee intimate withdrawal after he or she has been elected, the Interim Moderator shall proceed in terms of sections 23(4) above and 26(b) below without further reference to the Presbytery.

25. The Call

(1)   The Interim Moderator shall, along with the intimation regarding the result of the voting, intimate the arrangements made for members of the congregation over a period of not less than eight days to subscribe the Call (Schedule K). Intimation shall be in the form of Schedule L hereto.

(2)   The Call may be subscribed on behalf of a member not present to sign in person, provided a mandate authorising such subscription is produced as in Schedule M. All such entries shall be initialled by the Interim Moderator or by the member of the Kirk Session appending them.

(3)   Those eligible to sign the call shall be all those whose names appear on the Electoral Register. A paper of concurrence in the Call may be signed by regular worshippers in the congregation and by adherents whose names have not been entered on the Electoral Register.

25A. Ministers from Non-EEA Countries excluding Switzerland
(1)   Six months after the vacancy has first appeared in a monthly vacancy list, and provided
      there are no applications currently under the consideration of the Nominating Committee,
      the Kirk Session (or in the case of a linkage the Kirk Sessions in agreement) may apply to
      the Presbytery to have the charge listed for the purposes of this section.
(2)   Such applications shall be considered by the whole Presbytery, and shall not form part of
      the remit of the Vacancy Procedure Committee.
(3)   The Presbytery must be satisfied that there are no outstanding issues of superintendence,
      or other factors that would make such listing inappropriate, and must consult with
      the Ministries Council before deciding whether to permit the listing. The Presbytery
      Clerk shall within seven days send an extract minute of the decision to the Ministries Council.
(4)   Upon receiving notification of the listing from the Presbytery, the Nominating Committee
      shall proceed again from section 16 of this Act, and holders of Certificates of Eligibility who
      are nationals of countries outwith the EEA and Switzerland shall now be eligible to apply.
(5)   For the avoidance of doubt, the Nominating Committee (a) must always dispose of any
      competent applications received in terms of section 17 of this Act before considering those
      made in terms of this section, but (b) shall not be obliged to make a nomination from any
      particular group of applicants.
(6)   When a Presbytery withdraws permission to call, or the permission lapses in terms of
      section 26 of this Act, the Presbytery shall decide whether permission to proceed in terms
      of this section remains in force during the ensuing process to make a nomination.

26. Failure to Nominate
The exercise by a congregation of its right to call a minister shall be subject to a time-limit of
one year; this period shall be calculated from the date when intimation is given of the agreement
to grant leave to call. If it appears that an appointment is not to be made within the allotted time
(allowing one further calendar month for intimation to the Presbytery), the congregation may
make application to the Presbytery for an extension, which will normally be for a further six
months. For clear cause shown, a further extension of six months may be granted. If no election
has been made and intimated to the Presbytery by the expiry of that time, the permission to call
shall be regarded as having lapsed. The Presbytery may thereupon look afresh at the question of
adjustment. If the Presbytery is still satisfied that a minister should be appointed, it shall itself
take steps to make such an appointment, proceeding in one of the following ways:
      (a)   (i)   The Presbytery may discharge the Nominating Committee, strengthen the
                   Advisory Committee which had been involved in the case by the appointment
                   of an additional minister and elder, instruct that Committee to bring forward
                   to a subsequent meeting the name of an eligible individual for appointment to
                   the charge and intimate this instruction to the congregation. If satisfied with
                   the recommendation brought by the Advisory Committee, the Presbytery shall
                   thereupon make the appointment.
            (ii)   The Presbytery Clerk shall thereupon intimate to the person concerned the
                   fact of his or her appointment, shall request him or her to forward a letter of
                   acceptance along with appropriate Certificates if these are required in terms of
                   section 27 below, and shall arrange with him or her to conduct public worship
                   in the vacant church or churches on an early Sunday.
            (iii) The Presbytery Clerk shall cause intimation to be made in the form of Schedule
                   N that the person appointed will conduct public worship on the day specified and
                   that a Call in the usual form will lie with the Session Clerk or other suitable person
                   for not less than eight free days to receive the signatures of the congregation. The
                   conditions governing the signing of the Call shall be as in section 25 above.

(iv) At the expiry of the time allowed, the Call shall be transmitted by the Session Clerk to the Presbytery Clerk who shall lay it, along with the documents referred to in sub-paragraph (ii) above, before the Presbytery at its first ordinary meeting or at a meeting *in hunc effectum*.

(b) Otherwise, the Presbytery shall instruct that a fresh Nominating Committee be elected in terms of section 14 above. The process shall then be followed in terms of this Act from the point of the election of the Nominating Committee.

27. Transmission of Documents

(1) After an election has been made, the Interim Moderator shall secure from the person appointed a letter of acceptance of the appointment.

(2) The Interim Moderator shall then without delay transmit the relevant documents to the Presbytery Clerk. These are: the minute of Nomination by the Nominating Committee, all intimations made to the congregation thereafter, the declaration of the election and appointment, the voting-papers, the marked copy of the Register and the letter of acceptance. He or she shall also inform the Clerk of the steps taken in connection with the signing of the Call, and shall arrange that, at the expiry of the period allowed for subscription, the Call shall be transmitted by the Session Clerk to the Presbytery Clerk.

(3) After the person elected has been inducted to the charge, the Presbytery Clerk shall:

(a) deliver to him or her the approved copy of the Vacancy Schedule referred to in section 10(2) above, and

(b) destroy the intimations and voting-papers lodged with him or her in terms of subsection (2) above and ensure that confidential documents and correspondence held locally are destroyed.

28. Sustaining the Call

(1) All of the documents listed in section 27 above shall be laid before the Vacancy Procedure Committee, which may resolve to sustain the call and determine arrangements for the induction of the new minister, subject to (a) a request for the release, if appropriate, of the minister from his or her current charge in terms of this Act and (b) the provisions of section 2 above. The Moderator of the Presbytery shall, if no ordinary meeting of the Presbytery falls before the proposed induction date, call a meeting *pro re nata* for the induction.

(2) In the event that the matter comes before the Presbytery in terms of section 2 above, the procedure shall be as follows:

(a) The Call and other relevant documents having been laid on the table, the Presbytery shall hear any person whom it considers to have an interest. In particular, the Advisory Committee shall be entitled to be heard if it so desires, or the Presbytery may ask for a report from it. The Presbytery shall then decide whether to sustain the appointment in terms of subsection (1) above, and in doing so shall give consideration to the number of signatures on the Call. It may delay reaching a decision and return the Call to the Kirk Session to give further opportunity for it to be subscribed.

(b) If the Presbytery sustain an appointment and Call to a Graduate Candidate, and there be no appeal tendered in due form against its judgement, it shall appoint the day and hour and place at which the ordination and induction will take place.

(c) If the Presbytery sustain an appointment and Call to a minister of the Church of Scotland not being a minister of a parish, or to a minister of another denomination, and there be no ecclesiastical impediment, the Presbytery shall appoint the day and hour and place at which the induction will take place.

(3)   In the event that the Call is not sustained, the Presbytery shall determine either (a) to give more time for it to be signed in terms of section 25 above or (b) to proceed in terms of subsection (a) or (b) of section 26 above.

29. Admission to a Charge

(1)   When the Presbytery has appointed a day for the ordination and induction of a Graduate Candidate, or for the induction of a minister already ordained, the Clerk shall arrange for an edict in the form of Schedule O to be read to the congregation on the two Sundays preceding the day appointed.

(2)   At the time and place named in the edict, the Presbytery having been constituted, the Moderator shall call for the return of the edict attested as having been duly served. If the minister is being translated from another Presbytery, the relevant minute of that Presbytery or of its Vacancy Procedure Committee agreeing to translation shall also be laid on the table. Any objection, to be valid at this stage, must have been intimated to the Presbytery Clerk at the objector's earliest opportunity, must be strictly directed to life or doctrine and must be substantiated immediately to the satisfaction of the Presbytery, in which case procedure shall be sisted and the Presbytery shall take appropriate steps to deal with the situation that has arisen. Otherwise, the Presbytery shall proceed with the ordination and induction, or with the induction, as hereunder.

(3)   The Presbytery shall proceed to the church where public worship shall be conducted by those appointed for the purpose. The Clerk shall read a brief narrative of the cause of the vacancy and of the steps taken for the settlement. The Moderator, having read the Preamble, shall, addressing him or her by name, put to the person to be inducted the questions prescribed (*see the Ordinal of the Church as authorised from time to time by the General Assembly*). Satisfactory answers having been given, the person to be inducted shall sign the Formula. If he or she has not already been ordained, the person to be inducted shall then kneel, and the Moderator by prayer and the imposition of hands, in which members of the Presbytery, appointed by the Presbytery for the purpose, and other ordained persons associated with it, if invited to share in such imposition of hands, shall join, shall ordain him or her to the office of the Holy Ministry. Prayer being ended, the Moderator shall say: 'I now declare you to have been ordained to the office of the Holy Ministry, and in name of the Lord Jesus Christ, the King and Head of the Church, and by authority of this Presbytery, I induct you to this charge, and in token thereof we give you the right hand of fellowship'. The Moderator with all other members of Presbytery present and those associated with it shall then give the right hand of fellowship. The Moderator shall then put the prescribed question to the members of the congregation. Suitable charges to the new minister and to the congregation shall then be given by the Moderator or by a minister appointed for the purpose.

(4)   *[This subsection is to be construed in conformity with Act III 2004.]* When an ordained minister is being inducted to a charge, the act of ordination shall not be repeated, and the relevant words shall be omitted from the declaration. In other respects, the procedure shall be as in subsection (3) above.

(5)   When the appointment is for a limited or potentially limited period (including Reviewable Tenure, or an appointment in terms of section 19 above), the service shall proceed as in subsections (3) or (4) above, except that in the declaration the Moderator shall say: 'I induct you to this charge on the Basis of [specific Act and Section] and in terms of Minute of Presbytery of date . . .'.

(6)   After the service, the Presbytery shall resume its session, when the name of the new minister shall be added to the Roll of Presbytery, and the Clerk shall be instructed to send certified intimation of the induction to the Session Clerk to be engrossed in the minutes of

the first meeting of Kirk Session thereafter, and, in the case of a translation from another Presbytery or where the minister was prior to the induction subject to the supervision of another Presbytery, to the Clerk of that Presbytery.

30. Service of Introduction
(1)   When a minister has been appointed to a linked charge, the Presbytery shall determine in which of the churches of the linking the induction is to take place. This shall be a service of induction to the charge, in consequence of which the person inducted shall become minister of each of the congregations embraced in the linking. The edict regarding the induction, which shall be in terms of Schedule O, shall be read in all of the churches concerned. There shall be no other service of induction; but, if the churches are far distant from one another, or for other good reason, the Presbytery may appoint a service of introduction to be held in the other church or churches. Intimation shall be given of such service, but not in edictal form.

(2)   In any case of deferred union or deferred linking, the minister elected and appointed shall be inducted 'to the vacant congregation of A in deferred union (or linking) with the congregation of B' and there shall be no need for any further act to establish his or her position as minister of the united congregation or of the linked congregation as the case may be. The Presbytery, however, shall in such a case arrange a service of introduction to the newly united congregation of AB or the newly linked congregation of B. Intimation shall be given of such service, but not in edictal form.

(3)   When an appointment has been made to an extra-parochial office wholly or mainly under control of the Church (community ministry, full-time chaplaincy in hospital, industry, prison or university, full-time clerkship and so on), the Presbytery may deem it appropriate to arrange a service of introduction to take place in a church or chapel suitable to the occasion.

(4)   When an appointment has been made to a parochial appointment other than that of an inducted minister, the Presbytery may arrange a service of introduction to take place within the parish. If ordination is involved, suitable arrangements shall be made and edictal intimation shall be given in terms of Schedule P.

(5)   A service of introduction not involving ordination shall follow the lines of an induction except that, instead of putting the normal questions to the minister, the Moderator shall ask him or her to affirm the vows taken at his or her ordination. Where the service, in terms of subsection (3) or (4) above, includes the ordination of the minister, the vows shall be put in full. In either case, in the declaration, the Moderator in place of 'I induct you to . . .' shall say: 'I welcome you as . . .'.

31. Demission of Status
If a minister seeks to demit his or her status as a minister of the Church of Scotland, any accompanying demission of a charge will be dealt with by the Vacancy Procedure Committee in terms of section 4 of this Act without further delay, but the question of demission of status shall be considered by the Presbytery itself. The Moderator of Presbytery, or a deputy appointed by him or her, shall first confer with the minister regarding his or her reasons and shall report to the Presbytery if there appears to be any reason not to grant permission to demit status. Any decision to grant permission to demit status shall be immediately reported to the Ministries Council.

32. Miscellaneous
For the purposes of this Act, intimations to congregations may be made (a) verbally during every act of worship or (b) in written intimations distributed to the whole congregation provided that the congregation's attention is specifically drawn to the presence of an intimation there in terms of this Act.

For the purposes of this Act, attestation of all intimations to congregations shall consist of certification thereof by the Session Clerk as follows:

(a)   Certification that all intimations received have been duly made on the correct number of Sundays shall be sent to the Presbytery Clerk before the service of induction or introduction.

(b)   Certification that any particular intimation received has been duly made on the correct number of Sundays shall be furnished on demand to the Vacancy Procedure Committee or the Presbytery Clerk.

(c)   Intimation shall be made immediately to the Presbytery Clerk in the event that intimation has not been duly made on the appropriate Sunday.

33. Repeals and Amendments

(1)   Act V 1984 (as amended) is hereby repealed; it is hereby provided that all other legislation prior to this Act shall be construed in conformity with this Act.

(2)   Earlier Acts and Regulations are amended as follows:

(a)   In sections 2 and 7 of Act XVIII 1932, delete the latter sentence of section 2 and all of subsection 7(b).

(b)   In Act IV 1999, delete 'Act V 1984 section 25(3)' and substitute 'section 29(3) of Act VIII 2003'.

(c)   In section 19(2) of Act II 2000, delete 'section 2(3) of Act V 1984' and substitute 'section 7 of Act VIII 2003'.

(d)   In section 9 of Act XV 2002, delete 'in terms of section 27 of Act V 1984'.

(e)   In section 12(i) of Act XIII 2000 and in section 2(i) of Regulations V 2000, delete 'sections 6-8 of Act V 1984' and substitute section 13 of Act VIII 2003'.

(f)   In section 2(2) of Act IV 2001, delete 'in terms of Act V 1984 section 27' and 'in terms of the said Act V 1984'.

(g)   In paragraph 1 of Schedule 3 to Act V 2002, delete 'section 13 of Act V 1984' and substitute 'section 17 of Act VIII 2003'.

(h)   In paragraph 2(ii) of Schedule 3 to Act V 2002, delete 'Sections 6 to 8 of Act V 1984' and substitute 'section 13 of Act VIII 2003'.

(i)   In section 2 of Act VII 2002, delete 'Act V 1984 section 25' and substitute 'section 29 of Act VIII 2003'.

(j)   In section 9 of Act XV 2002, delete 'in terms of section 27 of Act V 1984'.

(k)   In Regulations II 1996, delete reference to Act V 1984 (as amended) and substitute Act VIII 2003.

(3)   Notwithstanding subsection (1) above, the repeal of Act V 1984 as amended shall not affect the operation of the said Act (or Deliverances of the General Assembly in pursuance thereof) prior to the repeal of the said Act, or anything done or suffered under the said Act or Deliverances; and any rights or obligations acquired or incurred thereunder shall have effect as if the said Act had not been repealed.

34. Interpretation

For the purposes of this Act, the Interpretation section (section 1) of Act VII 2003 will apply.

SCHEDULES

A INTIMATION OF ACTION OR DECISION OF VACANCY PROCEDURE COMMITTEE – Section 2(1)

To be read on one Sunday

The Vacancy Procedure Committee of the Presbytery of .... proposes [here insert action or permission proposed]....... Any communicant member of the congregation(s) of A [and B] may submit to the Presbytery Clerk a request for this proposal to be considered at the next meeting of the Presbytery: where such requests are received from four individuals, being communicant members of the congregation(s) or full members of the Presbytery, the request shall be met. Such request should be submitted in writing to [name and postal address of Presbytery Clerk] by [date seven days after intimation].

A .... B ....   Presbytery Clerk

B EDICT CITING A CONGREGATION TO ATTEND – Section 2(5)

To be read on one Sunday

Intimation is hereby given that, in connection with the [anticipated] vacancy in this congregation, a valid request has been made for the matter of [here insert action or permission which had been proposed] to be considered by the Presbytery. [The proposed course of action] is in the meantime sisted.

Intimation is hereby further given that the Presbytery will meet to consider this matter at .... on .... the .... day of .... at .... o'clock and that the congregation are hereby cited to attend for their interests.

A .... B ....   Presbytery Clerk

C PREPARATION OF ELECTORAL REGISTER – Section 13(1) and (2)

To be read on two Sundays

Intimation is hereby given that in view of the [1]anticipated vacancy, the Kirk Session is about to make up an Electoral Register of this congregation. Any communicant whose name is not already on the Communion Roll as a member should hand in to the Session Clerk a Certificate of Transference, and anyone wishing his or her name added to the Register as an adherent should obtain from the Session Clerk, and complete and return to him or her, a Form of Adherent's Claim. All such papers should be in the hands of the Session Clerk not later than .... The Kirk Session will meet in .... on .... at .... to make up the Electoral Register, when anyone wishing to support his or her claim in person should attend.

C .... D ....   Interim Moderator

[1] This word to be included where appropriate – otherwise to be deleted

D FORM OF ADHERENT'S CLAIM – Section 13(1)

I, [1] .... of [2] ...., being a parishioner or regular worshipper in the Church of .... and not being a member of any other congregation in Scotland, claim to have my name put on the Electoral Register of the parish of .... as an adherent.

Date ....   (Signed).......................

[1] Here enter full name in block capitals
[2] Here enter address in full

E INSPECTION OF ELECTORAL REGISTER – Section 13(3)

To be read on one Sunday

Intimation is hereby given that the proposed Electoral Register of this congregation has now been prepared and that an opportunity of inspecting it will be given today in .... at the close of this service, and that it will be open for inspection at .... on .... between the hours of .... and .... each day. Any questions regarding entries in the Register should be brought to the notice of the Kirk Session which is to meet in .... on .... at .... o'clock, when it will finally make up the Electoral Register.

C .... D ....   Interim Moderator

F REVISION OF ELECTORAL REGISTER – Section 13(6)

To be read on two Sundays

Intimation is hereby given that, more than six months having elapsed since the Electoral Register of this congregation was finally made up, it is now proposed that it should be revised. An opportunity of inspecting the Register will be given in .... at the close of this service, and also at .... on .... between the hours of .... and .... each day. Anyone wishing his or her name added to the Electoral Register as a member should give in a Transference Certificate, or as an adherent should give in a Form of Adherent's Claim (copies of which may be had from the Session Clerk) not later than .... The Kirk Session will meet in .... on .... at .... o'clock, when it will finally make up the Revised Register.

C .... D ....   Interim Moderator

G INTIMATION OF ELECTION OF NOMINATING COMMITTEE – Section 14(1)

To be read on two Sundays

Intimation is hereby given that a meeting of this congregation will be held in the Church [or other arrangement may be given here] on Sunday .... at the close of morning worship for the purpose of appointing a Nominating Committee which will nominate one person to the congregation with a view to the appointment of a minister.

C .... D ....   Interim Moderator

H MINUTE OF NOMINATION BY NOMINATING COMMITTEE – Section 21

To be read on two Sundays

(1)   The Committee chosen by this congregation to nominate a person with a view to the election and appointment of a minister, at a meeting held at .... on ...., resolved to name and propose [1] ...., and they accordingly do name and propose the said ....

Date ....

E .... F ....   Convener of Committee

[1] The name and designation of the person should at this point be entered in full

(2)   Intimation is therefore hereby given that the Nominating Committee having, as by minute now read, named and proposed [Name], arrangements have been made whereby public worship will be conducted in this Church by him or her on Sunday the .... day of .... at .... o'clock; and that a vote will be taken by voting-papers immediately thereafter; and that electors may vote For or Against electing and appointing the said [Name] as minister of this vacant charge.

C .... D ....   Interim Moderator

I VOTING-PAPER – Section 23

FOR Electing [Name]	
AGAINST Electing [Name]	

Directions to Voters: If you are in favour of electing [Name], put a cross (x) on the upper right-hand space. If you are not in favour of electing [Name], put a cross (x) in the lower right-hand space. Mark your voting-paper in this way with a cross and put no other mark on your voting-paper, or your vote may not be counted.

Note: The Directions to Voters must be printed prominently on the face of the voting-paper.

J DECLARATION OF ELECTION RESULT – Section 23(5)

First Form (Successful Election)

I hereby declare that the following are the results of the voting for the election and appointment of a minister to the vacant charge of [1] .... and that the said [Name] has accordingly been elected and appointed subject to the judgement of the courts of the Church.

Date ....   C .... D ....   Interim Moderator

[1] Here enter details

FOR Electing [Name]
AGAINST Electing [Name]

Second Form (Failure to Elect)

I hereby declare that the following are the results of the voting for the election and appointment of a minister to the vacant charge of [1] .... and that in consequence of this vote there has been a failure to elect, and the Nominating Committee is deemed to have been discharged. [Continue in terms of Schedule G if appropriate.]

Date .... C .... D .... Interim Moderator

¹ Here enter details

FOR Electing [*Name*]
AGAINST Electing [*Name*]

K THE CALL – Section 25(1)

Form of Call

We, members of the Church of Scotland and of the congregation known as ...., being without a minister, address this Call to be our minister to you, ..., of whose gifts and qualities we have been assured, and we warmly invite you to accept this Call, promising that we shall devote ourselves with you to worship, witness, mission and service in this parish, and also to the furtherance of these in the world, to the glory of God and for the advancement of His Kingdom.

Paper of Concurrence

We, regular worshippers in the congregation of the Church of Scotland known as ...., concur in the Call addressed by that congregation to .... to be their minister.

Note: The Call and Paper of Concurrence should be dated and attested by the Interim Moderator before they are transmitted to the Clerk of the Presbytery.

L SUBSCRIBING THE CALL – Section 25(1)

To be read on at least one Sunday

Intimation is hereby given that this congregation having elected [*Name*] to be their minister, a Call to the said [*Name*] has been prepared and will lie in .... on .... the .... day of .... between the hours of .... and ...., when those whose names are on the Electoral Register of the congregation may sign in person or by means of mandates. Forms of mandate may be obtained from the Session Clerk.

A Paper of Concurrence will also be available for signature by persons who are connected with the congregation but whose names are not on the Electoral Register of the congregation.

C .... D ....   Interim Moderator

M MANDATE TO SIGN CALL – Section 25(2)

I, ... of ...., being a person whose name is on the Electoral Register of the congregation, hereby authorise the Session Clerk, or other member of Session, to add my name to the Call addressed to [*Name*] to be our minister.

(Signed) ....

N CITATION IN CASE OF NOMINATION BY PRESBYTERY – Section 26(a)(iii)

To be read on one Sunday

Intimation is hereby given that [Name], whom the Presbytery has appointed to be minister of this congregation, will conduct public worship in the Church on Sunday the ………. day of ………. at ………. o'clock.

Intimation is hereby further given that a Call addressed to the said [Name] will lie in ………. on ………. the ………. day of ………. between the hours of ………. and ………. during the day and between the hours of ………. and ………. in the evening, when members may sign in person or by means of mandates, forms of which may be had from the Session Clerk.

Intimation is hereby further given that the Presbytery will meet to deal with the appointment and Call at ………. on ………. the ………. day of ………. at ………. o'clock and that the congregation are hereby cited to attend for their interests.

A ………. B ……….   Presbytery Clerk

O EDICTAL INTIMATION OF ADMISSION – Section 29

To be read on two Sundays

*   The Presbytery of ………. has received a Call from this congregation addressed to [Name] to be their minister, and the Call has been sustained as a regular Call, and has been accepted by him/her[1];
*   The Presbytery, having judged the said [Name] qualified[2] for the ministry of the Gospel and for this charge, has resolved to proceed to his or her[3] ordination and induction on ………. the ……… day of ………. at ………. o'clock unless something occur which may reasonably impede it:

Notice is hereby given to all concerned that if they, or any of them, have anything to object to in the life or doctrine of the said [Name], they should intimate their objection at their earliest opportunity to the Presbytery Clerk, with evidence of substantiation of the objection.
    The Presbytery is to meet at [time] on [date as above]. In accordance with section 29 of Act VIII 2003, an objection first brought at that time must be immediately substantiated, and the objector must satisfy the Presbytery that there was no earlier opportunity to bring the objection to the attention of the Presbytery Clerk. Otherwise the Presbytery shall proceed without further delay.

By order of the Presbytery

A ………. B ………. Presbytery Clerk

[1] add, where appropriate, 'and his or her translation has been agreed to by the Presbytery of ……….'
[2] omit 'for the ministry of the Gospel and' if the minister to be inducted has been ordained previously
[3] omit, where appropriate, 'ordination and'

P EDICTAL INTIMATION OF ORDINATION IN CASE OF INTRODUCTION – Section 30(1)

To be read on two Sundays

- Whereas [narrate circumstances requiring service of introduction]
- And whereas the Presbytery, having found the said [*Name*] to have been regularly appointed and to be qualified for the ministry of the Gospel and for the said appointment, has resolved to proceed to his or her ordination to the Holy Ministry and to his or her introduction as [specify appointment] on .... the .... day of .... at .... o'clock unless something occur which may reasonably impede it:

Notice is hereby given to all concerned that if they, or any of them, have anything to object to in the life or doctrine of the said [*Name*], they may appear at the Presbytery which is to meet at .... on .... the .... day of .... at .... o'clock; with certification that if no relevant objection be then made and immediately substantiated, the Presbytery will proceed without further delay.

By order of the Presbytery

A .... B ....   Presbytery Clerk

BARCLAY ON THE LECTIONARY

Matthew: Year A

William Barclay
Edited by Linda Foster

978-0-7152-0972-1 (paperback)

See our website for details of this and many
other wonderful books by William Barclay
www.standrewpress.com

SAINT ANDREW PRESS

SECTION 4

The
General Assembly
of 2013

(1) THE GENERAL ASSEMBLY

The Lord High Commissioner:	The Rt Hon. Lord Selkirk of Douglas QC MA LLB
Moderator:	Right Rev. E. Lorna Hood MA BD
Chaplains to the Moderator:	Rev. Eleanor J. McMahon BEd BD Rev. Arthur Sherratt BD
Principal Clerk:	Rev. John P. Chalmers BD CPS
Depute Clerk:	Rev. George J. Whyte BSc BD DMin
Procurator:	Ms Laura Dunlop QC
Law Agent:	Mrs Janette S. Wilson LLB NP
Convener of the Business Committee:	Rev. Janet S. Mathieson MA BD
Vice-Convener of the Business Committee:	Rev. Derek Browning MA BD DMin
Precentor:	Rev. Douglas Galbraith MA BD BMus MPhil ARSCM PhD
Assembly Officer:	Mr David McColl
Assistant Assembly Officer:	Mr Craig Marshall

(2) THE MODERATOR

The Right Reverend E. Lorna Hood MA BD

Lorna Hood is the essence of a parish minister. One week she was inducted into the charge (Renfrew North) she was to serve for thirty-three years, the next week she was married.

Born in 1953 and raised in Kilmarnock, she attended Kilmarnock Academy and thereafter the University of Glasgow, graduating MA in 1974 and BD (Honours) in 1977. It was during her time as probationer assistant at St Ninian's, Corstorphine, in Edinburgh, that she was to meet her husband Peter, who has been a constant companion and support throughout her ministry.

While not in the first wave of women ordained to the ministry of Word and Sacrament, Lorna was to know some of the issues that faced them. 'Was there nobody else?' had been the remark of one of her new flock when the announcement was made that Lorna was to be the sole nominee – and, in the early days as a young minister in the Presbytery of Paisley, she had to engage at times with older and more socially conservative colleagues, who in the 1970s and 1980s were finding it difficult to adjust to the changing times both within and outwith the Church. Yet Lorna had some 'firsts' of her own: she was the first Church of Scotland minister to take maternity leave – as she was to become mum to Laura and then to Michael; the first female Moderator of the Presbytery of Paisley; and of course the first female parish minister to become Moderator of the General Assembly.

Despite such achievements, Lorna is and will remain primarily a parish minister. The traditional aspects of pastoral visiting, the conduct of the Sacraments and the engagement with her parish have been of primary importance to her. While the Church at large has seen her ably conduct the business of the General Assembly, Lorna is equally at ease at the local coffee morning or school assembly, with many an hour spent visiting the elderly, the bereaved or the sick, building relationships with those both within the Church and on the fringes of the Church, allowing Renfrew North to minister to its wider community.

It is also in that wider community that Lorna's ministry was to have an impact. For twenty-two years, she served as chaplain in the Royal Alexandra Hospital in Paisley, where she was responsible for the Women's and Children's Directorate and was part of a team which pioneered the care plan for those who had suffered loss during pregnancy or shortly after, instigating an annual memorial service. For this work, the team was awarded the Association of British Insurers Medical Community Award in 1992. Lorna has also been actively involved with the local ACCORD hospice, speaking at fund-raising events and dinners and supporting staff and patients. Further engagement came with the Argyll and Clyde Health Board, which saw Lorna serving for ten years on the management committee of the Genesis Project, a mental-health project which used a Paisley church and Renfrew North as the bases which cared for those living within the community with mental-health needs, at a time when such work still faced intolerance and prejudice.

Lorna has served on various committees in the Church of Scotland. She was appointed a General Trustee in 2001, and prior to the 2013 General Assembly has been Vice-Convener of the Assembly Arrangements Committee and Vice-Convener of the Business Committee. She held various roles within the Presbytery of Paisley and brought great stability as Convener of the Business Committee of the fledgling Presbytery of Greenock and Paisley.

In 2011, she completed her training for the Church of Scotland's mediation project, 'A Place for Hope', and has served in various capacities, including at present in a group set up to consider the theology of mediation and reconciliation. In 2008, Lorna was appointed as a Chaplain to Her Majesty the Queen.

The ability to contribute at all levels of the Church is perhaps one of Lorna's greatest attributes. Very much a people person, she is able to relate across the social strata, bringing the same passion and perception to each matter or situation. With an energy for worship, a commitment to care, a loyalty to friends and a love for her family, Lorna has served the Church faithfully both locally and nationally.

It has been a great honour for us to have been asked to act as Lorna's Chaplains during her term of office. Lorna will bring much to her moderatorial year, not least a natural spontaneity of response which is grounded in her faith, together with the wisdom that her years in ministry have given her, which will ensure that the Church will be well served by her and can only gain from her commitment, her compassion and her care.

Eleanor McMahon and Arthur Sherratt
Chaplains

(3) GENERAL ASSEMBLY 2013

Same-sex relationships and the ministry
The General Assembly of 2013 was dominated by the issue of same-sex relationships and the ministry. The Report of the Theological Commission, which ran to ninety-four pages, ensured that the topic was framed broadly within recent consensus on the nature of the Church, Scripture, Sacraments, Marriage and Ministry and placed in the succession of other recent

studies on sexuality by the Assembly. The broad spectrum in the Commission had issued in two overtures, respectively from a 'revisionist' and a 'traditionalist' standpoint. The skilful presentation and guidance of the debate by Convener (Dr McPake) and Moderator, plus a focus on a desire for unity, ensured that the debate was pursued with calmness and grace. In the end, neither position was adopted but, at the prompting of a counter-motion by the retiring Moderator, Albert Bogle, the Church opted not to close the conversation, by not altering the currently held position while enabling Kirk Sessions to depart from it. The Legal Questions Committee was instructed to prepare an overture for the next Assembly.

Anniversaries

The Assembly recognised five significant anniversaries. The Guild was celebrating 125 remarkable years of service – a record, from its Report, being continued and indeed expanded. The six projects for the 2012–15 period range from the use of art therapy for individuals living with dementia to the building of homes for victims of the Rwanda genocide, the continuing participation in the Inter-faith Group on Domestic Abuse and the Guild's own work on Human Trafficking. For their projects in the years 2009–12, the Guild had raised a total of £790,555.54. New Guild groups for younger people were being planned.

Another was the 125th anniversary of the Diaconate, a pioneering ministry whose variety and flexibility might be said to have opened up space for the growing number of special ministries which are being explored and established by the Ministries Council, as evidenced by their report, in the present day. These took place in the wider context of the 1,450th anniversary of the arrival of St Columba on Iona, an anniversary marked both at the Heart and Soul event on the Sunday and in a major celebration by the Iona Community, whose seventy-fifth anniversary also falls this year. Finally, noted in the World Mission Council Report was the bicentenary of the birth of David Livingstone (see below).

Church and world

Once again, the sheer scope of the Church's engagement and influence in national and international contexts was evident, as expressed in the reports of the major Councils and in the ensuing debates. Under the Church and Society Council, there was discussion about the referendum of 2014 and issues surrounding Scottish independence (in a joint report), and about climate change, education, Israel and Palestine, world hunger, and poverty. These last two found echo in the World Mission Council report, which focused particularly on Africa; and the debate extended to encompass garment workers in Bangladesh, support for the new country of South Sudan, and the lifting of US sanctions against Cuba. More than once during these discussions, authoritative contributions were made by those with first-hand experience, including several of the ecumenical and overseas representatives whose presence is always valued by the Assembly.

There was plenty of evidence also in the Mission and Discipleship Council's report of innovative engagement with local communities and of the enrichment of the witness of the Church, national and local, through programmes and courses, publishing in print and online, and the Scottish Storytelling Centre, itself at the heart of the nation's cultural life. There was also ample evidence of engagement with the world church and other churches in Scotland through the Ecumenical Relations Committee report, in the demanding work of Forces Chaplaincy, and in the comprehensive programmes of CrossReach, whose work was declared by a Care Commission report as of the very highest standard – work nevertheless being threatened by rising costs. And there was engagement in a different mode in the re-establishment of a permanent theological forum to measure and assess the Church's practice over against Scripture and the still-unfolding tradition of Christian witness.

All in all, the Assembly revealed a Church continuing to wrestle with the needs of the world and the claims of Christ, evidenced also in the diligence reported by the several other committees, the scope and detail of whose work there is not room to give proper account of. All are important to the whole – not least the matter of pensions, which appeared in more than one guise during the proceedings, a sombre scenario lightened only by the statistic shared by one commissioner that ministers of the Church of Scotland are allegedly the longest-living group, second only to stockbrokers from Islington.

Enhancing the life of the Assembly

The Assembly, as always, had its 'moments', including (during the report on World Mission) the surprise visit of descendants of David Livingstone, who were greeted by the Moderator, and – to the acclaim of the Assembly – a steel band from Trinidad (COSTOS – Church of Scotland Trinidad on Steel) who prefaced the retiring Moderator's stirring address and participated in the worship on Tuesday morning before the World Mission Council report. There was also the point when welcome was given to the workshop manager of GRoW (Greyfriars Recycling of Wood Project, in which unemployed young people make furnishings from redundant pews), which previously had fashioned the Moderator's desk and now had added a plinth on which to mount the chair.

The Assembly was distinguished not only by the grace and firmness of the Moderator, Lorna Hood, but also by the undergirding efficiency and good humour of the Principal Clerk and his colleagues, supported by the friendliness of the stewards, and by the endlessly 'can do' approach of the Assembly Office.

For a detailed account, go to www.churchofscotland.org.uk. On the 'About Us' page, select 'General Assembly 2013' from the sidebar. Also, 'General Assembly Highlights' in the same list leads to the daily webcast from the Rev. Douglas Aitken.

Douglas Galbraith
Editor

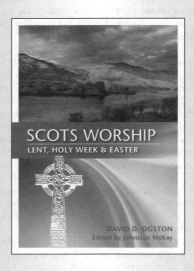

SCOTS WORSHIP
Lent, Holy Week & Easter

David D. Ogston
Edited by Johnston McKay

978-0-86153-787-7 (paperback)

See our website for details of this (out late November 2013)
and further titles in the *Scots Worship* series
www.standrewpress.com

SAINT ANDREW PRESS

SECTION 5

Presbytery Lists

See overleaf for an explanation of the two parts of each list; a Key to Abbreviations; and a list of the Presbyteries in their numerical order.

SECTION 5 – PRESBYTERY LISTS

In each Presbytery list, the congregations are listed in alphabetical order. In a linked charge, the names appear under the first named congregation. Under the name of the congregation will be found the name of the minister and, where applicable, that of an associate minister, auxiliary minister and member of the Diaconate. The years indicated after a minister's name in the congregational section of each Presbytery list are the year of ordination (column 1) and the year of current appointment (column 2). Where only one date is given, it is both the year of ordination and the year of appointment.

In the second part of each Presbytery list, those named are listed alphabetically. The first date is the year of ordination, and the following date is the year of appointment or retirement. If the person concerned is retired, then the appointment last held will be shown in brackets.

KEY TO ABBREVIATIONS

(E)　Indicates a Church Extension charge. New Charge Developments are separately indicated.
(GD)　Indicates a charge where it is desirable that the minister should have a knowledge of Gaelic.
(GE)　Indicates a charge where public worship must be regularly conducted in Gaelic.
(H)　Indicates that a Hearing Aid Loop system has been installed. In Linked charges, the (H) is placed beside the appropriate building as far as possible.
(L)　Indicates that a Chair Lift has been installed.
(T)　Indicates that the minister has been appointed on the basis of Terminable Tenure.

PRESBYTERY NUMBERS

1	Edinburgh	18	Dumbarton
2	West Lothian	19	Argyll
3	Lothian	20	
4	Melrose and Peebles	21	
5	Duns	22	Falkirk
6	Jedburgh	23	Stirling
7	Annandale and Eskdale	24	Dunfermline
8	Dumfries and Kirkcudbright	25	Kirkcaldy
9	Wigtown and Stranraer	26	St Andrews
10	Ayr	27	Dunkeld and Meigle
11	Irvine and Kilmarnock	28	Perth
12	Ardrossan	29	Dundee
13	Lanark	30	Angus
14	Greenock and Paisley	31	Aberdeen
15		32	Kincardine and Deeside
16	Glasgow	33	Gordon
17	Hamilton	34	Buchan

35	Moray
36	Abernethy
37	Inverness
38	Lochaber
39	Ross
40	Sutherland
41	Caithness
42	Lochcarron – Skye
43	Uist
44	Lewis
45	Orkney
46	Shetland
47	England
48	Europe
49	Jerusalem

(1) EDINBURGH

The Presbytery meets:
- at Palmerston Place Church, Edinburgh, on 6 November and 11 December 2012, and on 5 February, 12 March, 30 April and 18 June 2013;
- in the church of the Moderator on 11 September 2012.

Clerk:	REV. GEORGE J. WHYTE BSc BD DMin		10/1 Palmerston Place, Edinburgh EH12 5AA [E-mail: edinburgh@cofscotland.org.uk]	0131-225 9137
1	**Edinburgh: Albany Deaf Church of Edinburgh (H) (0131-444 2054)**			
	Alistair F. Kelly BL (Locum)	1961	19 Avon Place, Edinburgh EH4 6RE [E-mail: alistair_kelly@hotmail.co.uk]	0131-317 9877
2	**Edinburgh: Balerno (H)**			
	Louise J. Duncan (Mrs) BD	2005 2010	3 Johnsburn Road, Balerno EH14 7DN [E-mail: bpc-minister@btconnect.com]	0131-449 3830
3	**Edinburgh: Barclay Viewforth (0131-229 6810) (E-mail: admin@barclaychurch.org.uk)**			
	Samuel A.R. Torrens BD	1995 2005	113 Meadowspot, Edinburgh EH10 5UY [E-mail: minister@barclayviewforth.org.uk]	0131-478 2376
	Howard Espie (Mission Facilitator and Enabler)	2011	Barclay Viewforth Parish Church, 1 Barclay Place, Edinburgh EH10 4HW	0131-229 6810
4	**Edinburgh: Blackhall St Columba's (0131-332 4431) (E-mail: secretary@blackhallstcolumba.org.uk)**			
	Alexander B. Douglas BD	1979 1991	5 Blinkbonny Crescent, Edinburgh EH4 3NB [E-mail: alexandjill@douglas.net]	0131-343 3708
5	**Edinburgh: Bristo Memorial Craigmillar**			
	Vacant		72 Blackchapel Close, Edinburgh EH15 3SL	0131-657 3266
6	**Edinburgh: Broughton St Mary's (H) (0131-556 4786)**			
	Graham G. McGeoch MA BTh MTh	2009 2013	103 East Claremont Street, Edinburgh EH7 4JA [E-mail: minister@bstmchurch.org.uk]	0131-556 7313
7	**Edinburgh: Canongate (H)**			
	Neil N. Gardner MA BD	1991 2006	The Manse of Canongate, Edinburgh EH8 8BR [E-mail: nng22@btinternet.com]	0131-556 3515

8   **Edinburgh: Carrick Knowe (H) (0131-334 1505) (E-mail: ckchurch@talktalk.net)**
Fiona M. Mathieson (Mrs)   1988   2001   21 Traquair Park West, Edinburgh EH12 7AN
BEd BD PGCommEd MTh   [E-mail: fiona.mathieson@ukgateway.net]   0131-334 9774

9   **Edinburgh: Colinton (H) (0131-441 2232) (E-mail: church.office@colinton-parish.com)**
Rolf H. Billes BD   1996   2009   The Manse, Colinton, Edinburgh EH13 0JR
                                                  [E-mail: rolf.billes@colinton-parish.com]   0131-466 8384
Gayle J.A. Taylor (Mrs) MA BD (Assoc) 1999 2009 Colinton Parish Church, Dell Road, Edinburgh EH13 0JR
                                                  [E-mail: gayle.taylor@colinton-parish.com]   0131-441 2232

10 **Edinburgh: Colinton Mains (H)**
Iain M. Goring BSc BD (Interim Minister) 1976 2013 c/o Presbytery Office, 10/1 Palmerston Place, Edinburgh EH12 5AA   0131-225 9137
                                                  [E-mail: imgoring@tiscali.co.uk]   07762 254140 (Mbl)

11 **Edinburgh: Corstorphine Craigsbank (H) (0131-334 6365)**
Stewart M. McPherson BD CertMin   1991   2003   17 Craigs Bank, Edinburgh EH12 8HD   0131-467 6826
                                                  [E-mail: smcpherson@blueyonder.co.uk]   07814 901429 (Mbl)

12 **Edinburgh: Corstorphine Old (H) (0131-334 7864) (E-mail: corold@aol.com)**
Moira McDonald MA BD   1997   2005   23 Manse Road, Edinburgh EH12 7SW   0131-476 5893
                                                  [E-mail: moira-mc@live.co.uk]

13 **Edinburgh: Corstorphine St Anne's (0131-316 4740) (E-mail: office@stannes.corstorphine.org.uk)**
James J. Griggs BD MTh   2011   2013   23 Belgrave Road, Edinburgh EH12 6NG   0131-334 3188
                                                  [E-mail: cstannesminister@gmail.com]

14 **Edinburgh: Corstorphine St Ninian's (H) (0131-539 6204) (E-mail: office@st-ninians.co.uk)**
Alexander T. Stewart MA BD FSAScot 1975 1995   17 Templeland Road, Edinburgh EH12 8RZ   0131-334 2978
                                                  [E-mail: alextstewart@blueyonder.co.uk]

15 **Edinburgh: Craigentinny St Christopher's (0131-258 2759)**
Vacant   61 Milton Crescent, Edinburgh EH15 3PQ   0131-258 2759

16 **Edinburgh: Craiglockhart (H) (E-mail: office@craiglockhartchurch.org.uk)**
Gordon Kennedy BSc BD MTh   1993   2012   20 Craiglockhart Quadrant, Edinburgh EH14 1HD   0131-444 1615
                                                  [E-mail: gordonkennedy15@gmail.com]

17 **Edinburgh: Craigmillar Park (H) (0131-667 5862) (E-mail: cpkirk@btinternet.com)**
John C.C. Urquhart MA MA BD   2010   14 Hallhead Road, Edinburgh EH16 5QJ   0131-667 1623
                                                  [E-mail: jccurquhart@gmail.com]

18   Edinburgh: Cramond (H) (E-mail: cramond.kirk@blueyonder.co.uk)
G. Russell Barr BA BD MTh DMin   1979   1993   Manse of Cramond, Edinburgh EH4 6NS
                                                          [E-mail: rev.r.barr@blueyonder.co.uk]   0131-336 2036

19   Edinburgh: Currie (H) (0131-451 5141) (E-mail: currie_kirk@btconnect.com)
Lezley J. Stewart BD ThM MTh   2000   2008   43 Lanark Road West, Currie EH14 5JX
                                                          [E-mail: lezleystewart@btinternet.com]   0131-449 4719

20   Edinburgh: Dalmeny linked with Edinburgh: Queensferry
David C. Cameron BD CertMin   1993   2009   1 Station Road, South Queensferry EH30 9HY
                                                          [E-mail: minister@qpcweb.org]   0131-331 1100

21   Edinburgh: Davidson's Mains (H) (0131-312 6282) (E-mail: life@dmainschurch.plus.com)
Jeremy R.H. Middleton LLB BD   1981   1988   1 Hillpark Terrace, Edinburgh EH4 7SX
                                                          [E-mail: life@dmainschurch.plus.com]   0131-336 3078

22   Edinburgh: Dean (H)
Mark M. Foster BSc BD   1998   1 Ravelston Terrace, Edinburgh EH4 3EF
                                                          [E-mail: markmfoster@mac.com]   0131-332 5736

23   Edinburgh: Drylaw (0131-343 6643)
Vacant   15 House o' Hill Gardens, Edinburgh EH4 2AR   0131-343 1441

24   Edinburgh: Duddingston (H) (E-mail: dodinskirk@aol.com)
James A.P. Jack   1989   2001   Manse of Duddingston, Old Church Lane, Edinburgh EH15 3PX
  BSc BArch BD DMin RIBA ARIAS   [E-mail: jamesjack2829@aol.com]   0131-661 4240

25   Edinburgh: Fairmilehead (H) (0131-445 2374) (E-mail: fairmilehead.p.c@btconnect.com)
John R. Munro BD   1976   1992   6 Braid Crescent, Edinburgh EH10 6AU
                                                          [E-mail: revjohnmunro@hotmail.com]   0131-446 9363
Hayley O'Connor BS MDiv (Assist)   2009   19 Caiystane Terrace, Edinburgh EH10 6SR
                                                          [E-mail: oconnorhe@gmail.com]   0131-629 1610

26   Edinburgh: Gorgie Dalry (H) (0131-337 7936)
Peter I. Barber MA BD   1984   90 Myreside Road, Edinburgh EH10 5BZ
                                                          [E-mail: pibarber@toucansurf.com]   0131-337 2284

27 Edinburgh: Granton (H) (0131-552 3033)
Norman A. Smith MA BD   1997   2005   8 Wardie Crescent, Edinburgh EH5 1AG   0131-551 2159
[E-mail: norm@familysmith.biz]

28 Edinburgh: Greenbank (H) (0131-447 9969) (E-mail: greenbankchurch@btconnect.com; Website: www.greenbankchurch.org)
Alison I. Swindells (Mrs) LLB BD   1998   2007   112 Greenbank Crescent, Edinburgh EH10 5SZ   0131-447 4032
[E-mail: alisonswindells@blueyonder.co.uk]
William H. Stone BA MDiv ThM   2012   19 Caiystane Terrace, Edinburgh EH10 6SR   0131-629 1610
(Youth Minister)   [E-mail: billstoneiii@gmail.com]   07883 815598   (Mbl)

29 Edinburgh: Greenside (H) (0131-556 5588)
Vacant   80 Pilrig Street, Edinburgh EH6 5AS   0131-554 3277   (Tel/Fax)

30 Edinburgh: Greyfriars Tolbooth and Highland Kirk (GE) (H) (0131-225 1900) (E-mail: enquiries@greyfriarskirk.com)
Richard E. Frazer BA BD DMin   1986   2003   12 Tantallon Place, Edinburgh EH9 1NZ   0131-667 6610
[E-mail: minister@greyfriarskirk.com]

31 Edinburgh: High (St Giles') (0131-225 4363) (E-mail: info@stgilescathedral.org.uk)
Vacant   St Giles' Cathedral, Edinburgh EH1 1RE   0131-225 4363
Helen J.R. Alexander BD DipSW (Assist)   1981   2012   7 Polwarth Place, Edinburgh EH11 1LG   0131-346 0685
[E-mail: st_giles_cathedral@btconnect.com]

32 Edinburgh: Holyrood Abbey (H) (0131-661 6002)
Philip R. Hair BD   1980   1998   100 Willowbrae Avenue, Edinburgh EH8 7HU   0131-652 0640
[E-mail: phil@holyroodabbey.f2s.com]

33 Edinburgh: Holy Trinity (H) (0131-442 3304)
Kenneth S. Borthwick MA BD   1983   2005   16 Thorburn Road, Edinburgh EH13 0BQ   0131-441 1403
[E-mail: kennysamuel@aol.com]
Ian MacDonald (Assoc)   2005   12 Sighthill Crescent, Edinburgh EH11 4QE   0131-453 6279
[E-mail: ianafrica@hotmail.com]
Oliver M.H. Clegg BD (Youth Minister)   2003   4 Blinkbonny Steading, Blinkbonny Road, Currie EH14 6AE   0131-478 5341
[E-mail: ollieclegg@btinternet.com]

34 Edinburgh: Inverleith St Serf's (H)
Joanne G. Finlay (Mrs)
DipTMus BD AdvDipCouns   1996   2012   24 East Lillypot, Edinburgh EH5 3BH   0131-552 3874
[E-mail: minister@inverleithsaintserfs.org.uk]

35 **Edinburgh: Juniper Green (H)**
    James S. Dewar MA BD   1983   2000   476 Lanark Road, Juniper Green, Edinburgh EH14 5BQ
    [E-mail: jim.dewar@blueyonder.co.uk]   0131-453 3494

36 **Edinburgh: Kaimes Lockhart Memorial linked with Edinburgh: Liberton**
    John N. Young MA BD PhD   1996   7 Kirk Park, Edinburgh EH16 6HZ
    [E-mail: LLLjyoung@btinternet.com]   0131-664 3067
    David Rankin (Assoc)   2009   Office: 76 Lasswade Road, Edinburgh EH16 6SF
    [E-mail: davebobrankin@gmail.com]   07827 815599 (Mbl)

37 **Edinburgh: Kirkliston**
    Margaret R. Lane (Mrs) BA BD MTh   2009   43 Main Street, Kirkliston EH29 9AF
    [E-mail: margaretlane@btinternet.com]   0131-333 3298
                                            07795 481441 (Mbl)

38 **Edinburgh: Kirk o' Field (T) (H)**
    Vacant   31 Hatton Place, Edinburgh EH9 1UA   0131-667 7954

39 **Edinburgh: Leith North (H) (0131-553 7378) (E-mail: nlpc-office@btinternet.com)**
    Alexander T. McAspurren BD MTh   2002   2011   6 Craighall Gardens, Edinburgh EH6 4RJ
    [E-mail: alexander.mcaspurren@btinternet.com]   0131-551 5252

40 **Edinburgh: Leith St Andrew's (H)**
    Robert A. Mackenzie LLB BD   1993   2013   30 Lochend Road, Edinburgh EH6 8BS
    [E-mail: rob.anne@blueyonder.co.uk]   0131-554 7695

41 **Edinburgh: Leith South (H) (0131-554 2578) (E-mail: slpc@dial.pipex.com)**
    John S. (Iain) May   2012   37 Claremont Road, Edinburgh EH6 7NN
    [E-mail: johnsmay@blueyonder.co.uk]   0131-554 3062

42 **Edinburgh: Leith Wardie (H) (0131-551 3847) (E-mail: churchoffice@wardie.org.uk)**
    Brian C. Hilsley LLB BD   1990   35 Lomond Road, Edinburgh EH5 3JN
    [E-mail: minister@wardie.org.uk]   0131-552 3328

43 **Edinburgh: Liberton (H)** See Edinburgh: Kaimes Lockhart Memorial

44 **Edinburgh: Liberton Northfield (H) (0131-551 3847)**
    John M. McPake LTh   2000   9 Claverhouse Drive, Edinburgh EH16 6BR
    [E-mail: john_mcpake9@yahoo.co.uk]   0131-658 1754

45 Edinburgh: London Road (H) (0131-661 1149)
Sigrid Marten   1997   2006
26 Inchview Terrace, Edinburgh EH7 6TQ
[E-mail: minister@londonroadchurch.com]
                                                                                    0131-669 5311

46 Edinburgh: Marchmont St Giles' (H) (0131-447 4359)
Karen K. Campbell BD MTh DMin   1997   2002
2 Trotter Haugh, Edinburgh EH9 2GZ
[E-mail: karen@marchmontstgiles.org.uk]
                                                                                    0131-447 2834

47 Edinburgh: Mayfield Salisbury (0131-667 1522)
Scott S. McKenna BA BD MTh MPhil   1994   2000
26 Seton Place, Edinburgh EH9 2JT
[E-mail: ScottSMcKenna@aol.com]
                                                                                    0131-667 1286

48 Edinburgh: Morningside (H) (0131-447 6745) (E-mail: office@morningsideparishchurch.org.uk)
Derek Browning MA BD DMin   1987   2001
20 Braidburn Crescent, Edinburgh EH10 6EN
[E-mail: minister@morningsideparishchurch.org.uk]
                                                                                    0131-447 1617

49 Edinburgh: Morningside United (H) (0131-447 3152)
Vacant
1 Midmar Avenue, Edinburgh EH10 6BS
                                                                                    0131-447 8724

50 Edinburgh: Muirhouse St Andrew's (E) (Website: www.stampc.co.uk)
Vacant
35 Silverknowes Road, Edinburgh EH4 5LL
                                                                                    0131-312 7773

51 Edinburgh: Murrayfield (H) (0131-337 1091) (E-mail: mpchurch@btconnect.com)
Vacant
45 Murrayfield Gardens, Edinburgh EH12 6DH
                                                                                    0131-337 5431

52 Edinburgh: Newhaven (H)
Peter Bluett   2007
158 Granton Road, Edinburgh EH5 3RF
[E-mail: peterbluett@sky.com]
                                                                                    0131-476 5212

53 Edinburgh: New Restalrig (H) 0131-661 5676)
David L. Court BSc BD   1989   2000
19 Abercorn Road, Edinburgh EH8 7DP
[E-mail: david@dlc.org.uk]
                                                                                    0131-661 4045

54 Edinburgh: Old Kirk (H) (0131-332 4354) (E-mail: minister.oldkirk@btinternet.com)
Vacant
24 Pennywell Road, Edinburgh EH4 4HD
                                                                                    0131-332 4354

55 **Edinburgh: Palmerston Place (H) (0131-220 1690) (E-mail: admin@palmerstonplacechurch.com)**
Colin A.M. Sinclair BA BD   1981   1996
30B Cluny Gardens, Edinburgh EH10 6BJ
[E-mail: colins.ppc@virgin.net]
0131-447 9598
0131-225 3312 (Fax)

56 **Edinburgh: Pilrig St Paul's (0131-553 1876)**
Vacant
78 Pilrig Street, Edinburgh EH6 5AS
0131-554 1842

57 **Edinburgh: Polwarth (H) (0131-346 2711) (E-mail: polwarthchurch@tiscali.co.uk)**
Jack Holt BSc BD MTh   1985   2011
88 Craiglockhart Road, Edinburgh EH14 1EP
[E-mail: jack9holt@gmail.com]
0131-441 6105

58 **Edinburgh: Portobello Old (H)**
Vacant
6 Hamilton Terrace, Edinburgh EH15 1NB
0131-657 5545

59 **Edinburgh: Portobello St James' (H)**
Peter Webster BD   1977   2002
34 Brighton Place, Edinburgh EH15 1LT
[E-mail: peterwebster101@hotmail.com]
0131-669 1767

60 **Edinburgh: Portobello St Philip's Joppa (H) (0131-669 3641)**
Stewart G. Weaver BA BD PhD   2003
6 St Mary's Place, Edinburgh EH15 2QF
[E-mail: stewartweaver@btinternet.com]
0131-669 2410

61 **Edinburgh: Priestfield (H) (0131-667 5644)**
Jared W. Hay BA MTh DipMin DMin   1987   2009
13 Lady Road, Edinburgh EH16 5PA
[E-mail: jared.hay@blueyonder.co.uk]
0131-468 1254

62 **Edinburgh: Queensferry (H)** See Edinburgh: Dalmeny

63 **Edinburgh: Ratho**
Ian J. Wells BD   1999
2 Freelands Road, Ratho, Newbridge EH28 8NP
[E-mail: ianjwells@btinternet.com]
0131-333 1346

64 **Edinburgh: Reid Memorial (H) (0131-662 1203) (E-mail: reid.memorial@btinternet.com)**
Brian M. Embleton BD   1976   1985
20 Wilton Road, Edinburgh EH16 5NX
[E-mail: brianembleton@btinternet.com]
0131-667 3981

65 **Edinburgh: Richmond Craigmillar (H) (0131-661 6561)**
Elizabeth M. Henderson (Mrs) MA BD MTh   1985   1997   Manse of Duddingston, Old Church Lane, Edinburgh EH15 3PX   0131-661 4240
[E-mail: lizhende@tiscali.co.uk]

66 **Edinburgh: St Andrew's and St George's West (H) (0131-225 3847) (E-mail: info@standrewsandstgeorges.org.uk)**
Ian Y. Gilmour BD   1985   2011   25 Comely Bank, Edinburgh EH4 1AJ   0131-332 5848
[E-mail: ianyg2@gmail.com]

67 **Edinburgh: St Andrew's Clermiston**
Alistair H. Keil BD DipMin   1989   87 Drum Brae South, Edinburgh EH12 8TD   0131-339 4149
[E-mail: ahkeil@blueyonder.co.uk]

68 **Edinburgh: St Catherine's Argyle (H) (0131-667 7220)**
Robin S. Sydserff PhD   5 Palmerston Road, Edinburgh EH9 1TL   0131-667 9344
[E-mail: robin@stcaths.org]

69 **Edinburgh: St Cuthbert's (H) (0131-229 1142) (E-mail: office@st-cuthberts.net)**
David W. Denniston BD DipMin   1981   2008   34A Murrayfield Road, Edinburgh EH12 6ER   0131-337 6637
[E-mail: denniston.david@googlemail.com]   07903 926727 (Mbl)

70 **Edinburgh: St David's Broomhouse (H) (0131-443 9851)**
Vacant
Liz Crocker (Mrs) DipComEd DCS   33 Traquair Park West, Edinburgh EH12 7AN   0131-334 1730
77C Craigcrook Road, Edinburgh EH4 3PH   0131-332 0227

71 **Edinburgh: St John's Oxgangs**
Iain M. Goring BSc BD (Interim Minister) 1976   2013   c/o Presbytery Office, 10/1 Palmerston Place, Edinburgh EH12 5AA   0131-225 9137
[E-mail: imgoring@tiscali.co.uk]   07762 254140 (Mbl)

72 **Edinburgh: St Margaret's (H) (0131-554 7400) (E-mail: stm.parish@virgin.net)**
Carol H.M. Ford DSD RSAMD BD   2003   43 Moira Terrace, Edinburgh EH7 6TD   0131-669 7329
[E-mail: revcford@btinternet.com]
Pauline Rycroft (Mrs) DCS   6 Ashville Terrace, Edinburgh EH6 8DD   0131-554 6564
[E-mail: pauline70@rocketmail.com]   07759 436303 (Mbl)

73 **Edinburgh: St Martin's**
Russel Moffat BD MTh PhD   1986   2008   5 Duddingston Crescent, Edinburgh EH15 3AS   0131-657 9894
[E-mail: rbmoffat@tiscali.co.uk]

74 Edinburgh: St Michael's (H) (E-mail: office@stmichaels-kirk.co.uk)
James D. Aitken BD   2002   2005   9 Merchiston Gardens, Edinburgh EH10 5DD   0131-346 1970
[E-mail: james.aitken2@btinternet.com]

75 Edinburgh: St Nicholas' Sighthill
Vacant   122 Sighthill Loan, Edinburgh EH11 4NT   0131-442 2510

76 Edinburgh: St Stephen's Comely Bank (0131-315 4616)
Jonathan de Groot BD MTh CPS   2007   8 Blinkbonny Crescent, Edinburgh EH4 3NB   0131-332 3364
[E-mail: jonathan@comelybankchurch.com]

77 Edinburgh: Slateford Longstone
Michael W. Frew BSc BD   1978   2005   50 Kingsknowe Road South, Edinburgh EH14 2JW   0131-466 5308
[E-mail: minister@slatefordlongstone.org.uk]

78 Edinburgh: Stenhouse St Aidan's
Keith Edwin Graham MA PGDip BD   2008   65 Balgreen Road, Edinburgh EH12 5UA   0131-337 7711
[E-mail: minister@ssapc.org.uk]

79 Edinburgh: Stockbridge (H) (0131-552 8738) (E-mail: stockbridgechurch@btconnect.com)
John A. Cowie BSc BD   1983   2013   19 Eildon Street, Edinburgh EH3 5JU   0131-557 6052
[E-mail: jacowie54@gmail.com]   07506 104416 (Mbl)

80 Edinburgh: The Tron Kirk (Gilmerton and Moredun)
Cameron Mackenzie BD   1997   2010   467 Gilmerton Road, Edinburgh EH17 7JG   0131-664 7538
[E-mail: macken2550@aol.com]

Name			Charge/Position	Address	Phone
Abernethy, William LTh	1979	1993	(Glenrothes: St Margaret's)	120/1 Willowbrae Road, Edinburgh EH8 7HW	0131-661 0390
Aitken, Alexander R. MA	1965	1997	(Newhaven)	36 King's Meadow, Edinburgh EH16 5JW	0131-667 1404
Aitken, Ewan R. BA BD	1992	2002	Church and Society Council	159 Restalrig Avenue, Edinburgh EH7 6PJ	0131-467 1660
Alexander, Ian W. BA BD STM	1990	2010	World Mission Council	World Mission Council, 121 George Street, Edinburgh EH2 4YN	0131-225 5722
				[E-mail: iwalexander@gmail.com]	
Anderson, Andrew F. MA BD	1981	2011	(Edinburgh: Greenside)	58 Reliance Way, Oxford OX4 2FG	01865 778397
				[E-mail: andrew@pilrig.fsnet.co.uk]	
Anderson, Robert S. BD	1988	1997	(Scottish Churches World Exchange)		
Armitage, William L. BSc BD	1976	2006	(Edinburgh: London Road)	Flat 7, 4 Papermill Wynd, Edinburgh EH7 4GJ	0131-558 8534
				[E-mail: bill@billarm.plus.com]	
Baird, Kenneth S. MSc PhD BD MIMarEST	1998	2009	(Edinburgh: Leith North)	3 Maule Terrace, Gullane EH31 2DB	01620 843447
Barrington, Charles W.H. MA BD	1997	2007	(Associate: Edinburgh: Balerno)	502 Lanark Road, Edinburgh EH14 5DH	0131-453 4826

Name			Charge	Address	Tel.
Beckett, David M. BA BD	1964	2002	(Edinburgh: Greyfriars, Tolbooth and Highland Kirk)	1F1, 31 Sciennes Road, Edinburgh EH9 1NT [E-mail: davidbeckett3@aol.com]	0131-667 2672
Blakey, Ronald S. MA BD MTh	1962	2000	(Assembly Council)	5 Moss Side Road, Biggar ML12 6GF	01899 229226
Booth, Jenifer (Mrs) BD	1996	2004	(Associate: Leith South)	39 Lilyhill Terrace, Edinburgh EH8 7DR	0131-661 3813
Boyd, Kenneth M. MA BD PhD FRCPE	1970	1996	University of Edinburgh: Medical Ethics	1 Doune Terrace, Edinburgh EH3 6DY	0131-225 6485
Brady, Ian D. BSc ARCST BD	1967	2001	(Edinburgh: Corstorphine Old)	28 Frankfield Crescent, Dalgety Bay, Dunfermline KY11 9LW [E-mail: pidb@dbay28.fsnet.co.uk]	01383 825104
Brown, William D. MA	1963	1989	(Wishaw: Thornlie)	9/3 Craigend Park, Edinburgh EH16 5XY [E-mail: wdbrown@surefish.co.uk]	0131-672 2936
Brown, William D. BD CQSW	1987	2013	(Edinburgh: Murrayfield)	79 Carnbee Park, Edinburgh EH16 6GG [E-mail: wdb@talktalk.net]	0131-261 7297
Cameron, G. Gordon MA BD STM	1957	1997	(Juniper Green)	4 Ladywell Grove, Clackmannan FK10 4JQ	01259 723769
Cameron, John W.M. MA BD	1957	1996	(Liberton)	10 Plewlands Gardens, Edinburgh EH10 5JP	0131-447 1277
Chalmers, Murray MA	1965	2006	(Hospital Chaplain)	8 Easter Warriston, Edinburgh EH7 4QX	0131-552 4211
Clinkenbeard, William W. BSc BD STM	1966	2000	(Edinburgh: Carrick Knowe)	3/17 Western Harbour Breakwater, Edinburgh EH6 6PA [E-mail: bjclinks@compuserve.com]	
Cook, John MA BD	1967	2005	(Edinburgh: Leith St Andrew's)	26 Silverknowes Court, Edinburgh EH4 5NR	0131-312 8447
Cook, John Weir MA BD	1962	2002	(Edinburgh: Portobello St Philip's Joppa)	74 Pinkie Road, Musselburgh EH21 7QT [E-mail: johnweircook@gmail.com]	0131-653 0992
Curran, Elizabeth M. (Miss) BD	1995	2008	(Aberlour)	27 Captain's Road, Edinburgh EH17 8HR [E-mail: ecurran8@aol.com]	0131-664 1358
Cuthell, Tom C. MA BD MTh	1965	2007	(Edinburgh: St Cuthbert's)	Flat 10, 2 Kingsburgh Crescent, Waterfront, Edinburgh EH5 1JS	0131-476 3864
Davidson, D. Hugh MA	1965	2009	(Edinburgh: Inverleith)	Flat 1/2, 22 Summerside Place, Edinburgh EH6 4NZ [E-mail: dhd39@btinternet.com]	0131-554 8420
Davidson, Ian M.P. MBE MA BD	1957	1994	(Stirling: Allan Park South with Church of the Holy Rude)	13/8 Craigend Park, Edinburgh EH16 5XX	0131-664 0074
Dawson, Michael S. BTech BD	1979	2005	(Associate: Edinburgh: Holy Trinity)	9 The Broich, Alva FK12 5NR [E-mail: mixpen.dawson@btinternet.com]	01259 769309
Denniston, Jane M. MA BD		2002	Ministries Council	34A Murrayfield Road, Edinburgh EH12 6ER	0131-337 6637
Dilbey, Mary D. (Miss) BD	1997	2002	(West Kirk of Calder)	41 Bonaly Rise, Edinburgh EH13 0QU	0131-441 9092
Donald, Alistair P. MA PhD BD	1999	2009	Chaplain: Heriot-Watt University	The Chaplaincy, Heriot-Watt University, Edinburgh EH14 4AS [E-mail: a.p.donald@hw.ac.uk]	0131-451 4508
Dougall, Elspeth G. (Mrs) MA BD	1989	2001	(Edinburgh: Marchmont St Giles')	60B Craigmillar Park, Edinburgh EH16 5PU	0131-668 1342
Douglas, Colin R. MA BD STM	1969	2007	(Livingston Ecumenical Parish)	34 West Pilton Gardens, Edinburgh EH4 4EQ [E-mail: colinrdouglas@btinternet.com]	0131-551 3808
Doyle, Ian B. MA BD PhD	1946	1991	(Department of National Mission)	21 Lygon Road, Edinburgh EH16 5QD	0131-667 2697
Drummond, Rhoda (Miss) DCS	2000	2013	(Deaconess)		0131-668 3631
Dunbar, Linda J. BSc BA BD PhD FRHS	1983	1998	(Edinburgh: Muirhouse St Andrew's)	Flat K, 23 Grange Loan, Edinburgh EH9 2ER [E-mail: revljd@gmail.com]	(Mbl) 07801 969995
Dunn, W. Iain C. DA LTh	1976	2004	(Pilrig and Dalmeny Street)	10 Fox Covert Avenue, Edinburgh EH12 6UQ	0131-334 1665
Elliott, Gavin J. MA BD	1988	2010	Ministries Council	c/o 121 George Street, Edinburgh EH2 4YN	0131-225 5722
Embleton, Sara R. (Mrs) BA BD MTh			(Edinburgh: Leith St Serf's)	20 Wilton Road, Edinburgh EH16 5NX [E-mail: sara.embleton@blueyonder.co.uk]	0131-478 1624

Name	Years	Position	Address	Telephone
Evans, Mark BSc MSc DCS	2006	Chaplain: Queen Margaret Hospital, Dunfermline	13 Easter Drylaw Drive, Edinburgh EH4 2QA [E-mail: mark.evans59@nhs.net]	(Home) 0131-343 3089 (Office) 01383 674136
Farquharson, Gordon MA BD DipEd	1998 2007	(Stonehaven: Dunnottar)	26 Learmonth Court, Edinburgh EH4 1PB [E-mail: gfarqu@talktalk.net]	0131-343 1047
Faulds, Norman L. MA BD FSAScot	1968 2000	(Aberlady with Gullane)	10 West Fenton Court, West Fenton, North Berwick EH39 5AE	01620 842331
Fergusson, David A.S. (Prof.) MA BD DPhil FRSE	1984 2000	University of Edinburgh	23 Riselaw Crescent, Edinburgh EH10 6HN	0131-447 4022
Foggitt, Eric W. MA BSc BD	1991 2009	(Dunbar)	Christiaan de Wet Straat 19/2, 1091 NG Amsterdam, The Netherlands [E-mail: ericleric3@btinternet.com]	
Forrester, Duncan B. (Prof.) MA BD DPhil DD FRSE	1962 1978	(University of Edinburgh)	25 Kingsburgh Road, Edinburgh EH12 6DZ [E-mail: dbforrester@rosskeen.org.uk]	0131-337 5646
Forrester, Margaret R. (Mrs) MA BD	1974 2003	(Edinburgh: St Michael's)	25 Kingsburgh Road, Edinburgh EH12 6DZ [E-mail: margaret@rosskeen.org.uk]	0131-337 5646
Fraser, Shirley A. (Miss) MA BD	1992 2008	(Scottish Field Director: Friends International)	6/50 Roseburn Drive, Edinburgh EH12 5NS	0131-347 1400
Gardner, John V.	1997 2003	(Glamis, Inverarity and Kinnettles)	75/1 Lockharton Avenue, Edinburgh EH14 1BD [E-mail: jvg66@hotmail.com]	0131-443 7126
Gordon, Margaret (Mrs) DCS	1974 2009	(Edinburgh: Currie)	92 Lanark Road West, Currie EH14 5LA	0131-449 2554
Gordon, Tom MA BD	1967 2008	(Chaplain: Marie Curie Hospice, Edinburgh)	23 Gosford Road, Port Seton, Prestonpans EH32 0HF	01875 812262
Graham, W. Peter MA BD	2013	(Presbytery Clerk)	23/6 East Coniston, Edinburgh EH10 6RZ	0131-445 5763
Hardman Moore, Susan (Prof.) BA PGCE MA PhD		Ordained Local Minister	c/o New College, Mound Place, Edinburgh EH1 2LX [E-mail: s.hardmanmoore@ed.ac.uk]	0131-650 8908 (Mbl) 07811 345699
Harkness, James CB OBE QHC MA DD	1961 1995	(Chaplain General: Army)	13 Saxe Coburg Place, Edinburgh EH3 5BR	0131-343 1297
Hill, J. William BA BD	1967 2001	(Edinburgh: Corstorphine St Anne's)	33/9 Murrayfield Road, Edinburgh EH12 6EP	0131-441 3384
Irving, William D. LTh	1985 2005	(Golspie)	122 Swanston Muir, Edinburgh EH10 7HY	0131-229 7815
Jeffrey, Eric W.S. JP MA	1954 1994	(Edinburgh: Bristo Memorial)	18 Gillespie Crescent, Edinburgh EH10 4HT	0131-551 7706
Kelly, Ewan R. MB ChB BD PhD	1994 2006	NHS Education for Scotland	15 Boswall Road, Edinburgh EH5 3RW [E-mail: ewan.kelly@nes.scot.nhs.uk]	
Lawson, Kenneth C. MA BD	1963 1999	(Adviser in Adult Education)	56 Easter Drylaw View, Edinburgh EH4 2QP	0131-539 3311
Logan, Anne T. (Mrs) MA BD MTh DMin	1981 2012	(Edinburgh: Stockbridge)	Sunnyside Cottage, 18 Upper Broomieknowe, Lasswade EH18 1LP [E-mail: annetlogan@blueyonder.co.uk]	0131-663 9550
McCaskill, George I.L. MA BD	1953 1990	(Religious Education)	19 Tyler's Acre Road, Edinburgh EH12 7HY	0131-334 7451
Macdonald, Finlay A.J. MA BD PhD DD	1971 2010	(Principal Clerk)	8 St Ronan's Way, Innerleithen EH44 6RG [E-mail: finlay_macdonald@btinternet.com]	01896 831631
Macdonald, Peter J. BD	1986 2009	Leader of the Iona Community	63 Jim Bush Drive, Prestonpans EH32 9GB [E-mail: petermacdonald@iona.org.uk] [E-mail: petermacdonald166@btinternet.com]	(Office) 0141-332 6343 (Mbl) 07946 715166
Macdonald, William J. BD	1976 2002	(Board of National Mission: New Charge Development)	1/13 North Werber Park, Edinburgh EH4 1SY	01875 819655
McFadzean, Iain MA BD	1989 2010	National Director: Workplace Chaplaincy	2 Lowfield Crescent, Luncarty, Perth PH1 3FG [E-mail: iain.mcfadzean@wpcscotland.co.uk]	0131-332 0254
MacGregor, Margaret S. (Miss) MA BD DipEd	1985 1994	(Calcutta)	16 Learmonth Court, Edinburgh EH4 1PB	0131-332 1089
McGregor, Alistair G.C. QC BD	1987 2002	(Edinburgh: Leith North)	22 Primrose Bank Road, Edinburgh EH5 3JG	0131-551 2802

Name			Position	Address	Tel.
McGregor, T. Stewart MBE MA BD	1957	1998	(Chaplain: Edinburgh Royal Infirmary)	19 Lonsdale Terrace, Edinburgh EH3 9HL [E-mail: cetsm@uwclub.net]	0131-229 5332
MacKay, Stewart A.	2009		Chaplain: Army	2 Bn The Parachute Regiment, Merville Barracks, Colchester CO2 7UT	
Mackenzie, James G. BA BD	1980	2005	(Jersey: St Columba's)	26 Drylaw Crescent, Edinburgh EH4 2AU [E-mail: jgmackenzie@jerseymail.co.uk]	0131-332 3720
MacLaughlan, Grant BA BD	1998	2013	Workplace Chaplain	54 Crieff Road, Perth PH1 2RS [E-mail: grn6871@gmail.com]	
Maclean, Ailsa G. (Mrs) BD DipCE	1979	1988	Chaplain: George Heriot's School	28 Swan Spring Avenue, Edinburgh EH10 6NJ	0131-445 1320
Macmillan, Gilleasbuig CVO MA BD Drhc DD FRSE	1969	2013	(Edinburgh: High (St Giles'))	207 Dalkeith Road, Edinburgh EH16 5DS [E-mail: gmacmillan1@btinternet.com]	
MacMurchie, F. Lynne LLB BD	1998	2003	Healthcare Chaplain	Edinburgh Community Mental Health Chaplaincy, 41 George IV Bridge, Edinburgh EH1 1EL	0131-220 5150
McPheat, Elspeth DCS	1953	1993	Deaconess: CrossReach	11/5 New Orchardfield, Edinburgh EH6 5ET	0131-554 4143
McPhee, Duncan C. MA BD	1958	1996	(Department of National Mission)	8 Belvedere Park, Edinburgh EH6 4LR	0131-552 6784
Macpherson, Colin C.R. MA BD	1993	2012	(Dunfermline St Margaret's)	7 Eva Place, Edinburgh EH9 3ET	0131-667 1456
McQuarrie, Ian A. BD	1988	1998	(Edinburgh: Colinton Mains)	41 Lochnagar Road, Motherwell ML1 2PG [E-mail: ianmcquarrie1@btinternet.com]	01698 262000
Mathieson, Angus R. MA BD	1962	2000	Ministries Council	21 Traquair Park West, Edinburgh EH12 7AN	0131-334 9774
Moir, Ian A. MA BD	1974	1994	(Adviser for Urban Priority Areas)	28/6 Comely Bank Avenue, Edinburgh EH4 1EL	0131-332 2748
Monteith, W. Graham BD PhD	1957	1991	(Flotta and Fara with Hoy and Walls)	20/3 Grandfield, Edinburgh EH6 4TL	0131-552 2564
Morrice, William T. MA BD STM PhD	1978	2000	(St John's College Durham)	Flat 37, The Cedars, 2 Manse Road, Edinburgh EH12 7SN [E-mail: w.g.morrice@btinternet.com]	0131-316 4845
Morrison, Mary B. (Mrs) MA BD DipEd	1956	1994	(Edinburgh: Stenhouse St Aidan's)	14 Eildon Terrace, Edinburgh EH3 5LU	0131-556 1962
Morton, Andrew R. MA BD DD	1968	2000	(Board of World Mission and Unity)	7A Laverockbank Terrace, Edinburgh EH5 3DJ	0131-538 7049
Moyes, Sheila A. (Miss) DCS	1977	2007	(Deaconess)	158 Pilton Avenue, Edinburgh EH5 2JZ	0131-551 1731
Mulligan, Anne MA DCS	1953	1996	Deaconess: Hospital Chaplain	27A Craigour Avenue, Edinburgh EH17 1NH	0131-664 3426
Munro, George A.M.	1966	2006	(Edinburgh: Cluny)	108 Caiyside, Edinburgh EH10 7HR	0131-445 5829
Munro, John P.L. MA BD PhD	1976	2000	(Kinross)	5 Marchmont Crescent, Edinburgh EH9 1HN [E-mail: jplmunro@yahoo.co.uk]	0131-623 0198
Murrie, John BD	1976	2010	(Kirkliston)	31 Nicol Road, The Whins, Broxburn EH52 6JJ	01506 852464
Musgrave, Clarence W. BA BD ThM	1985	2013	(Jerusalem: St Andrew's)	4 Ravelston Heights, Edinburgh EH4 3LX [E-mail: clarencejoan@talktalk.net]	0131-332 6337
Page, Ruth MA BD DPhil	1983	2000	(University of Edinburgh)	22/5 West Mill Bank, West Mill Road, Edinburgh EH13 0QT	0131-441 3740
Paterson, Douglas S. MA BD	1982	2000	(Edinburgh: St Colm's)	4 Ards Place, High Street, Aberlady EH32 0DB	01875 870192
Paterson, Andrew R.M. MA BD	1965	2005	(Edinburgh: Portobello Old)	6 Hamilton Terrace, Edinburgh EH15 1NB [E-mail: apatt@tiscali.co.uk]	0131-657 5545
Plate, Maria A.G. (Miss) LTh BA	1993	2002	(South Ronaldsay and Burray)	Flat 29, 77 Barnton Park View, Edinburgh EH4 6EL	0131-339 8539
Rennie, Agnes M. (Miss) DCS			(Deaconess)	3/1 Craigmillar Court, Edinburgh EH16 4AD	0131-661 8475
Ridland, Alistair K. MA BD			Chaplain: Western General Hospital	13 Stewart Place, Kirkliston EH29 0BQ	0131-333 2711
Robertson, Charles LVO MA			(Edinburgh: Canongate)	3 Ross Gardens, Edinburgh EH9 3BS	0131-662 9025
Robertson, Norma P. (Miss) BD DMin MTh			(Kincardine O'Neil with Lumphanan)	Flat 5, 2 Burnbrae Drive, Grovewood Hill, Edinburgh EH12 8AS	0131-339 6701
Ronald, Norma A. (Miss) MBE DCS	1960	2000	(Deaconess)	2B Saughton Road North, Edinburgh EH12 7HG	0131-334 8736
Schofield, Melville F. MA			(Chaplain: Western General Hospitals)	25 Rowantree Grove, Currie EH14 5AT	0131-449 4745

Name			Position	Address	Phone
Scott, Ian G. BSc BD STM	1965	2006	(Edinburgh: Greenbank)	50 Forthview Walk, Tranent EH33 1FE [E-mail: igscott50@btinternet.com]	01875 612907
Scott, Martin DipMusEd RSAM BD PhD	1986	2000	Ministries Council	The Manse, Culross, Dunfermline KY12 8JD	01383 880231
Shewan, Frederick D. MA BD	1970	2005	(Edinburgh: Muirhouse St Andrew's)	38 Tremayne Place, Dunfermline KY12 9YH	01383 734354
Smith, Angus MA LTh	1965	2006	(Chaplain to the Oil Industry)	3/7 West Powburn, West Savile Gait, Edinburgh EH9 3EW	0131-667 1761
Stark, Suzie BD	2013		Assistant: Edinburgh: St Cuthbert's	St Cuthbert's Church, 5 Lothian Road, Edinburgh EH1 2EP [E-mail: sstark1962@btinternet.com]	0131-229 1142
Steele, Marilynn J. (Mrs) BD DCS			(Deaconess)	2 Northfield Gardens, Prestonpans EH32 9LQ [E-mail: marilynnsteele@aol.com]	01875 811497
Stephen, Donald M. TD MA BD ThM	1962	2001	(Edinburgh: Marchmont St Giles')	10 Hawkhead Crescent, Edinburgh EH16 6LR	0131-658 1216
Stevenson, John MA BD PhD	1963	2001	(Department of Education)	12 Swanston Gardens, Edinburgh EH10 7DL	0131-445 3960
Stirling, A. Douglas BSc	1956	1994	(Rhu and Shandon)	162 Avontoun Park, Linlithgow EH49 6QH	01506 845021
Tait, John M. BSc BD	1985	2012	(Edinburgh: Pilrig St Paul's)	82 Greenend Gardens, Edinburgh EH17 7QH [E-mail: j.m.tait@blueyonder.co.uk]	0131-258 9105
Taylor, William R. MA BD MTh	1983	2004	Chaplaincy Adviser (Church of Scotland): Scottish Prison Service	Calton House, 5 Redheughs Rigg, South Gyle, Edinburgh EH12 9DQ [E-mail: bill.taylor@sps.pnn.gov.uk]	0131-244 8640
Teague, Yvonne (Mrs) DCS			(Board of Ministry)	46 Craigcrook Avenue, Edinburgh EH4 3PX	0131-336 3113
Telfer, Iain J.M. BD DPS	1978	2001	Chaplain: Royal Infirmary	Royal Infirmary of Edinburgh, 51 Little France Crescent, Edinburgh EH16 4SA	0131-242 1997
Thom, Helen (Miss) DCS			(Deaconess)	84 Great King Street, Edinburgh EH3 6QU	0131-556 5687
Thomson, Donald M. BD	1975	2013	(Tullibody: St Serf's)	50 Sighthill Road, Edinburgh EH11 4NY [E-mail: donniethomson@tiscali.co.uk]	
Tweedie, Fiona PhD	2011		Ordained Local Minister; Presbytery Mission Facilitator	10/1 Palmerston Place, Edinburgh EH12 5AA [E-mail: fjtweedie@yahoo.co.uk]	0131-225 9137
Watson, Nigel G. MA	1998	2012	(Associate: East Kilbride: Old/Stewartfield/West)	7 St Catherine's Place, Edinburgh EH9 1NU [E-mail: nigel.g.watson@gmail.com]	0131-662 4191
Whyte, George J. BSc BD DMin	1981	2008	Presbytery Clerk	4 Baberton Mains Lea, Edinburgh EH14 3HB [E-mail: edinburgh@cofscotland.org.uk]	0131-466 1674
Whyte, Iain A. BA BD STM PhD	1968	2005	(Community Mental Health Chaplain)	14 Carlingnose Point, North Queensferry, Inverkeithing KY11 1ER [E-mail: iainisabel@whytes28.fsnet.co.uk]	01383 410732
Wigglesworth, J. Christopher MBE BSc PhD BD	1968	1999	(St Andrew's College, Selly Oak)	12 Leven Terrace, Edinburgh EH3 9LW	0131-228 6335
Wilkie, James L. MA BD	1959	1998	(Board of World Mission)	7 Comely Bank Avenue, Edinburgh EH4 1EW [E-mail: jl.wilkie@btinternet.com]	0131-343 1552
Wilkinson, John BD MD FRCP DTM&H	1946	1975	(Kikuyu)	70 Craigleith Hill Gardens, Edinburgh EH4 2JH	0131-332 2994
Williams, Jenny M. (Miss) BSc CQSW BD	1996	1997	Christian Fellowship of Healing	16 Blantyre Terrace, Edinburgh EH10 5AE	0131-447 0050
Wilson, John M. MA	1964	1995	(Adviser in Religious Education)	27 Bellfield Street, Edinburgh EH15 2BR	0131-669 5257
Wynne, Alistair T.E. BA BD	1982	2009	(Nicosia Community Church, Cyprus)	Flat 6, 14 Burnbrae Drive, Edinburgh EH12 8AS [E-mail: awynne2@googlemail.com]	0131-339 6462
Young, Alexander W. BD DipMin	1988	1999	Lead Chaplain: NHS Lothian	32 Lindsay Circus, The Hawthorns, Rosewell EH24 9EP	(Work) 0131-242 1997

EDINBURGH ADDRESSES

Church	Address
Albany	82 Montrose Terrace
Balerno	Johnsburn Road, Balerno
Barclay Viewforth	Barclay Place
Blackhall St Columba's	Queensferry Road
Bristo Memorial	Peffermill Road, Craigmillar
Broughton St Mary's	Bellevue Crescent
Canongate	Canongate
Carrick Knowe	North Saughton Road
Colinton	Dell Road
Colinton Mains	Oxgangs Road North
Corstorphine	
Craigsbank	Craig's Crescent
Old	Kirk Loan
St Anne's	Kaimes Road
St Ninian's	St John's Road
Craigentinny	
St Christopher's	Craigentinny Road
Craiglockhart	Craiglockhart Avenue
Craigmillar Park	Craigmillar Park
Cramond	Cramond Glebe Road
Currie	Kirkgate, Currie
Davidson's Mains	Quality Street
Dean	Dean Path
Drylaw	Groathill Road North
Duddingston	Old Church Lane, Duddingston
Fairmilehead	Frogston Road West, Fairmilehead
Gorgie Dalry	Gorgie Road
Granton	Boswell Parkway
Greenbank	Braidburn Terrace
Greenside	Royal Terrace
Greyfriars Tolbooth and Highland Kirk	Greyfriars Place
High (St Giles')	High Street
Holyrood Abbey	Dalziel Place x London Road
Holy Trinity	Hailesland Place, Wester Hailes
Inverleith St Serf's	Ferry Road
Juniper Green	Lanark Road, Juniper Green
Kaimes Lockhart Memorial	Gracemount Drive
Kirkliston	The Square, Kirkliston
Kirk o' Field	Pleasance
Leith	
North	Madeira Street off Ferry Road
St Andrew's	Easter Road
South	Kirkgate, Leith
Wardie	Primrosebank Road
Liberton	Kirkgate, Liberton
Northfield	Gilmerton Road, Liberton
London Road	London Road
Marchmont St Giles'	Kilgraston Road
Mayfield Salisbury	Mayfield Road x West Mayfield
Morningside	Cluny Gardens
Morningside United	Bruntsfield Place x Chamberlain Rd
Muirhouse St Andrew's	Pennywell Gardens
Murrayfield	Abinger Gardens
Newhaven	Craighall Road
New Restalrig	Willowbrae Road
Old Kirk	Pennywell Road
Palmerston Place	Palmerston Place
Pilrig St Paul's	Pilrig Street
Polwarth	Polwarth Terrace x Harrison Road
Portobello	
Old	Bellfield Street
St James'	Rosefield Place
St Philip's Joppa	Abercorn Terrace
Priestfield	Dalkeith Road x Marchhall Place
Queensferry	The Loan, South Queensferry
Ratho	Baird Road, Ratho
Reid Memorial	West Savile Terrace
Richmond Craigmillar	Niddrie Mains Road
St Andrew's and St George's West	George Street and Shandwick Place
St Andrew's Clermiston	Clermiston View
St Catherine's Argyle	Grange Road x Chalmers Crescent
St Cuthbert's	Lothian Road
St David's Broomhouse	Broomhouse Crescent
St John's Oxgangs	Oxgangs Road
St Margaret's	Restalrig Road South
St Martin's	Magdalene Drive
St Michael's	Slateford Road
St Nicholas' Sighthill	Calder Road
St Stephen's Comely Bank	Comely Bank
Slateford Longstone	Kingsknowe Road North
Stenhouse St Aidan's	Chesser Avenue
Stockbridge	Saxe Coburg Street
The Tron Kirk (Gilmerton and Moredun)	Craigour Gardens and Ravenscroft Street

(2) WEST LOTHIAN

Meets in the church of the incoming Moderator on the first Tuesday of September and in St John's Church Hall, Bathgate, on the first Tuesday of every other month, except December, when the meeting is on the second Tuesday, and January, July and August, when there is no meeting.

Clerk: REV. DUNCAN SHAW BD MTh   St John's Manse, Mid Street, Bathgate EH48 1QD   01506 653146
[E-mail: westlothian@cofscotland.org.uk]

Abercorn (H) linked with Pardovan, Kingscavil (H) and Winchburgh (H)
A. Scott Marshall DipComm BD   1984   1998   The Manse, Winchburgh, Broxburn EH52 6TT   01506 890919
[E-mail: pkwla@aol.com]

Armadale (H)
Julia C. Wiley (Ms) MA(CE) MDiv — 1998 2010 — 70 Mount Pleasant, Armadale, Bathgate EH48 3HB [E-mail: preachergrace@gmail.com] — 01501 730358

Brenda Robson PhD (Aux) — 2005 2012 — 2 Baird Road, Ratho, Newbridge EH28 8RA [E-mail: brendarobson@hotmail.co.uk] — 0131-333 2746

Avonbridge (H) linked with Torphichen (H)
Sandi McGill (Ms) BD — 2002 2012 — Manse Road, Torphichen, Bathgate EH48 4LT [E-mail: sandimac376@gmail.com] — 01506 676803

Bathgate: Boghall (H)
Christopher Galbraith BA LLB BD — 2012 — 1 Manse Place, Ash Grove, Bathgate EH48 1NJ [E-mail: chrisgalbraith@phonecoop.coop] — 01506 652715

Bathgate: High (H)
Murdo C. Macdonald MA BD — 2002 2011 — 19 Hunter Grove, Bathgate EH48 1NN [E-mail: murdocmacdonald@gmail.com] — 01506 652654

Bathgate: St John's (H)
Duncan Shaw BD MTh — 1975 1978 — St John's Manse, Mid Street, Bathgate EH48 1QD [E-mail: westlothian@cofscotland.org.uk] — 01506 653146

Blackburn and Seafield (H)
Robert A. Anderson MA BD DPhil — 1980 1998 — The Manse, 5 MacDonald Gardens, Blackburn, Bathgate EH47 7RE [E-mail: robertanderson307@btinternet.com] — 01506 652825

Blackridge (H) linked with Harthill: St Andrew's (H)
Vacant — East Main Street, Harthill, Shotts ML7 5QW — 01501 751239

Breich Valley (H)
Robert J. Malloch BD — 1987 2013 — Breich Valley Manse, Stoneyburn, Bathgate EH47 8AU [E-mail: rojama@live.com] — 01501 763142

Broxburn (H)
Terry Taylor BA MTh — 2005 — 2 Church Street, Broxburn EH52 5EL [E-mail: terryanntaylor@btinternet.com] — 01506 852825

Fauldhouse: St Andrew's (H)
Robert Sloan BD — 1997 2011 — 7 Glebe Court, Fauldhouse, Bathgate EH47 9DX [E-mail: robertsloan@scotnet.co.uk] — 01501 771190

Harthill: St Andrew's See Blackridge

Kirknewton (H) and East Calder (H)

Andre Groenewald BA BD MDiv DD	1995	2009	8 Manse Court, East Calder, Livingston EH53 0HF [E-mail: groenstes@yahoo.com]	01506 884585 / 07588 845814 (Mbl)

Kirk of Calder (H)

John M. Povey MA BD	1981	19 Maryfield Park, Mid Calder, Livingston EH53 0SB [E-mail: revjpovey@aol.com]	01506 882495

Linlithgow: St Michael's (H) (E-mail: info@stmichaels-parish.org.uk)

D. Stewart Gillan BSc MDiv PhD	1985	2004	St Michael's Manse, Kirkgate, Linlithgow EH49 7AL [E-mail: stewart@stmichaels-parish.org.uk]	01506 842195
Cheryl McKellar-Young (Mrs) BA BD (Assoc)	2013		c/o Cross House, The Cross, Linlithgow EH49 7AL [E-mail: cheryl@stmichaels-parish.org.uk]	01506 842188
Thomas S. Riddell BSc CEng FIChemE (Aux)	1993	1994	4 The Maltings, Linlithgow EH49 6DS [E-mail: tsriddell@blueyonder.co.uk]	01506 843251

Linlithgow: St Ninian's Craigmailen (H)

W. Richard Houston BSc BD	1998	2004	29 Philip Avenue, Linlithgow EH49 7BH [E-mail: wrichardhouston@blueyonder.co.uk]	01506 202246

Livingston Ecumenical Parish

Robin R. Hine MA (Team Leader)			21 Bankton Gardens, Livingston EH54 9DZ [E-mail: robin@hiner.com]	01506 207360
(*The United Reformed Church*)				
Ronald G. Greig MA BD	1987	2008	2 Eastcroft Court, Livingston EH54 7ET [E-mail: rgglep@gmail.com]	01506 467426
Helen Jenkins BSc MRES PhD BA MA			13 Eastcroft Court, Livingston EH54 7ET [E-mail: revhelen@chjenkins.plus.com]	01506 464567
(*The Methodist Church*)				
Darren Philip BSc			72 Pinebank, Ladywell, Livingston EH54 6EX [E-mail: darren@lepyouth.com]	01506 797712
(Youth and Children's Worker)				

Livingston: Old (H)

Graham W. Smith BA BD FSAScot	1995	Manse of Livingston, Charlesfield Lane, Livingston EH54 7AJ [E-mail: gwsmith2010@live.co.uk]	01506 420227

Pardovan, Kingscavil and Winchburgh See Abercorn

Polbeth Harwood linked with West Kirk of Calder (H)
Vacant — 27 Learmonth Crescent, West Calder EH55 8AF — 01506 870460

Strathbrock (H)
Marc B. Kenton BTh MTh — 1997 2009 — 1 Manse Park, Uphall, Broxburn EH52 6NX [E-mail: marc@kentonfamily.co.uk] — 01506 852550

Torphichen See Avonbridge

Uphall: South (H)
Ian D. Maxwell MA BD PhD — 1977 2013 — 8 Fernlea, Uphall, Broxburn EH52 6DF [E-mail: i.d.maxwell@quista.net] — 01506 852788

West Kirk of Calder (H) See Polbeth Harwood

Whitburn: Brucefield (H)
Vacant

Whitburn: South (H)
Angus Kerr BD CertMin ThM DMin — 1983 2013 — 5 Mansewood Crescent, Whitburn, Bathgate EH47 8HA [E-mail: revdrkerr@gmail.com] — 01501 740333

Name	Ord.	Ret.	(Charge / Position)	Address	Tel
Black, David W. BSc BD	1968	2008	(Strathbrock)	66 Bridge Street, Newbridge EH28 8SH [E-mail: dw.black66@yahoo.co.uk]	0131-333 2609
Cameron, Ian MA BD	1953	1981	(Kilbrandon and Kilchattan)	Craigellen, West George Street, Blairgowrie PH10 6DZ	01250 872087
Darroch, Richard J.G. BD MTh MA(CMS)	1993	2010	(Whitburn: Brucefield)	23 Barnes Green, Livingston EH54 8PP [E-mail: richdarr@aol.com]	01506 436648
Dundas, Thomas B.S. LTh	1969	1996	(West Kirk of Calder)	35 Coolkill, Sandyford, Dublin 18, Republic of Ireland	00353 12953061
Jamieson, Gordon D. MA BD	1974	2012	(Head of Stewardship)	41 Goldpark Place, Livingston EH54 6LW [E-mail: gdj1949@talktalk.net]	01506 412020
Kelly, Isobel J.M. (Miss) MA BD DipEd	1974	2010	(Greenock: St Margaret's) Part-time Parish Assistant	76 Bankton Park East, Livingston EH54 9BN	01506 438511
McIntosh, Kay (Mrs) DCS				4 Jacklin Green, Livingston EH54 8PZ [E-mail: kay@backedge.co.uk]	01506 440543
Mackay, Kenneth J. MA BD	1971	2007	(Edinburgh: St Nicholas' Sighthill)	46 Chuckethall Road, Livingston EH54 8FB [E-mail: kmnth_mackay@yahoo.co.uk]	01506 410884
MacRae, Norman I. LTh	1966	2003	(Inverness: Trinity)	144 Hope Park Gardens, Bathgate EH48 2QX [E-mail: normanmacrae@talktalk.com]	01506 635254
Merrilees, Ann (Miss) DCS			(Deaconess)	23 Cuthill Brae, West Calder EH55 8QE [E-mail: ann@merrilees.freeserve.co.uk]	01501 762909
Morrison, Iain C. BA BD	1990	2003	(Linlithgow: St Ninian's Craigmailen)	Whaligoe, 53 Eastcroft Drive, Polmont, Falkirk FK2 0SU [E-mail: iain@kirkweb.org]	01324 713249

Name			Role / Charge	Address	Tel
Nelson, Georgina (Mrs) MA BD PhD DipEd	1990	1995	Hospital Chaplain (Jersey: St Columba's)	63 Hawthorn Bank, Seafield, Bathgate EH47 7EB	01506 670391
Nicol, Robert M.	1984	1996		59 Kinloch View, Blackness Road, Linlithgow EH49 7HT [E-mail: revrob.nicol@tiscali.co.uk]	01506 840515
Orr, J. McMichael MA BD PhD	1949	1986	(Aberfoyle with Port of Menteith)	17a St Ninians Way, Linlithgow EH49 7HL [E-mail: mikeandmargorr@googlemail.com]	01506 883207
Thomson, Phyllis (Miss) DCS	2003	2010	(Deaconess)	63 Caroline Park, Mid Calder, Livingston EH53 0SJ	01506 412504
Trimble, Robert DCS			(Deacon)	5 Templar Rise, Dedridge, Livingston EH54 6PJ	
Walker, Ian BD MEd DipMS	1973	2007	(Rutherglen: Wardlawhill)	92 Carseknowe, Linlithgow EH49 7LG [E-mail: walk10822@aol.com]	01506 844412
Whitson, William S. MA	1959	1999	(Cumbernauld: St Mungo's)	2 Chapman's Brae, Bathgate EH48 4LH [E-mail: william_whitson@tiscali.co.uk]	01506 650027

(3) LOTHIAN

Meets at Musselburgh: St Andrew's High Parish Church at 7pm on the last Thursday in February, April, June and November, and in a different church on the last Thursday in September.

Clerk: MR JOHN D. McCULLOCH DL | 20 Tipperwell Way, Howgate, Penicuik EH26 8QP [E-mail: lothian@cofscotland.org.uk] | 01968 676300

Aberlady (H) linked with Gullane (H)
Christine M. Clark (Mrs) BA BD MTh | 2006 | 2009 | The Manse, Hummel Road, Gullane EH31 2BG [E-mail: minister@agpc.org.uk] | 01620 843192

Athelstaneford linked with Whitekirk and Tyninghame
Joanne H.G. Evans-Boiten BD | 2004 | 2009 | The Manse, Athelstaneford, North Berwick EH39 5BE [E-mail: joanne.evansboiten@gmail.com] | 01620 880378

Belhaven (H) linked with Spott
Laurence H. Twaddle MA BD MTh | 1977 | 1978 | The Manse, Belhaven Road, Dunbar EH42 1NH [E-mail: revtwaddle@aol.com] | 01368 863098

Bilston linked with Glencorse (H) linked with Roslin (H)
John R. Wells BD DipMin | 1991 | 2005 | 31A Manse Road, Roslin EH25 9LG [E-mail: wellsjr3@aol.com] | 0131-440 2012

Bolton and Saltoun linked with Humbie linked with Yester (H)
Malcolm Lyon BD   2007   The Manse, Tweeddale Avenue, Gifford, Haddington EH41 4QN   01620 810515
[E-mail: malcolmlyon2@hotmail.com]

Bonnyrigg (H)
John Mitchell LTh CMin   1991   9 Viewbank View, Bonnyrigg EH19 2HU   0131-663 8287 (Tel/Fax)
[E-mail: jmitchell19539@gmail.com]

Cockenzie and Port Seton: Chalmers Memorial (H)
Kristina M. Herbold Ross (Mrs)   2008   2011   2 Links Road, Port Seton, Prestonpans EH32 0HA   01875 819254
[E-mail: khross@btinternet.com]

Cockenzie and Port Seton: Old (H)
Guardianship of the Presbytery   1 Links Road, Port Seton, Prestonpans EH32 0HA   01875 812310

Cockpen and Carrington (H) linked with Lasswade (H) and Rosewell (H)
Matthew Z. Ross LLB BD MTh FSAScot   1998   2009   Braemar Villa, 2 Links Road, Port Seton, Prestonpans EH32 0HA   01875 819544
07711 706950 (Mbl)
[E-mail: mzross@btinternet.com]

Dalkeith: St John's and King's Park (H)
Keith L. Mack BD MTh DPS   2002   13 Weir Crescent, Dalkeith EH22 3JN   0131-454 0206
[E-mail: kthmacker@aol.com]

Dalkeith: St Nicholas' Buccleuch (H)
Alexander G. Horsburgh MA BD   1995   2004   116 Bonnyrigg Road, Dalkeith EH22 3HZ   0131-663 3036
[E-mail: alexanderhorsburgh@googlemail.com]

Dirleton (H) linked with North Berwick: Abbey (H) (Office: 01620 892800) (E-mail: abbeychurch@btconnect.com)
David J. Graham BSc BD PhD   1982   1998   Sydserff, Old Abbey Road, North Berwick EH39 4BP   01620 840878
[E-mail: dirletonkirk@btinternet.com]

Dunbar (H)
Gordon Stevenson BSc BD   2010   The Manse, 10 Bayswell Road, Dunbar EH42 1AB   01368 865482
[E-mail: gstev@btconnect.com]

Dunglass
Suzanne G. Fletcher (Mrs) BA MDiv MA   2001   2011   The Manse, Cockburnspath TD13 5XZ   01368 830713
[E-mail: revfletcher@btinternet.com]

Garvald and Morham linked with Haddington: West (H)
John Vischer | 1993 | 2011 | 15 West Road, Haddington EH41 3RD [E-mail: j_vischer@yahoo.co.uk] | 01620 822213

Gladsmuir linked with Longniddry (H)
Robin E. Hill LLB BD PhD | 2004 | The Manse, Elcho Road, Longniddry EH32 0LB [E-mail: robinailsa@btinternet.com] | 01875 853195

Glencorse (H) See Bilston

Gorebridge (H)
Mark S. Nicholas MA BD | 1999 | 100 Hunterfield Road, Gorebridge EH23 4TT [E-mail: mark@gorepc.com] | 01875 820387

Gullane See Aberlady

Haddington: St Mary's (H)
Jennifer Macrae (Mrs) MA BD | 1998 | 2007 | 1 Nungate Gardens, Haddington EH41 4EE [E-mail: minister@stmaryskirk.co.uk] | 01620 823109

Haddington: West See Garvald and Morham

Howgate (H) linked with Penicuik: South (H)
Ian A. Cathcart BSc BD | 1994 | 2007 | 15 Stevenson Road, Penicuik EH26 0LU [E-mail: reviac@yahoo.co.uk] | 01968 674692

Humbie See Bolton and Saltoun
Lasswade and Rosewell See Cockpen and Carrington

Loanhead
Graham L. Duffin BSc BD DipEd | 1989 | 2001 | 120 The Loan, Loanhead EH20 9AJ [E-mail: gduffin@talktalk.net] | 0131-448 2459

Longniddry See Gladsmuir

Musselburgh: Northesk (H)
Alison P. McDonald MA BD | 1991 | 1998 | 16 New Street, Musselburgh EH21 6JP [E-mail: alisonpmcdonald@btinternet.com] | 0131-665 2128

Musselburgh: St Andrew's High (H) (0131-665 7239)
Yvonne E.S. Atkins (Mrs) BD   1997   8 Ferguson Drive, Musselburgh EH21 6XA   0131-665 1124
[E-mail: yesatkins@hotmail.co.uk]

Musselburgh: St Clement's and St Ninian's
Vacant   The Manse, Wallyford Loan Road, Wallyford,   0131-653 6588
Musselburgh EH21 8BU

Musselburgh: St Michael's Inveresk
Andrew B. Dick BD DipMin   1986   1999   8 Hope Place, Musselburgh EH21 7QE   0131-665 0545
[E-mail: dixbit@aol.com]

Newbattle (H) (Website: http://freespace.virgin.net/newbattle.focus)
Sean Swindells BD DipMin MTh   1996   2011   112 Greenbank Crescent, Edinburgh EH10 5SZ   0131-447 4032
[E-mail: minister@newbattleparish.org]   07791 755976 (Mbl)
Michael D. Watson   2013   47 Crichton Terrace, Pathhead EH37 5QZ   01875 320043
(Ordained Local Minister)   [E-mail: mikewatson225@btinternet.com]

Newton
Vacant   The Manse, Newton, Dalkeith EH22 1SR   0131-663 3845
Andrew Don MBA   2006   5 Eskvale Court, Penicuik EH26 8HT   01968 675766
(Ordained Local Minister)   [E-mail: a.a.don@btinternet.com]

North Berwick: Abbey See Dirleton

North Berwick: St Andrew Blackadder (H) (E-mail: admin@standrewblackadder.org.uk) (Website: www.standrewblackadder.org.uk)
Neil J. Dougall BD   1991   2003   7 Marine Parade, North Berwick EH39 4LD   01620 892132
[E-mail: neil@neildougall.co.uk]

Ormiston linked with Pencaitland
David J. Torrance BD DipMin   1993   2009   The Manse, Pencaitland, Tranent EH34 5DL   01875 340963
[E-mail: torrance@talktalk.net]

Pencaitland See Ormiston

Penicuik: North (H)
Ruth D. Halley BA BEd   2012   93 John Street, Penicuik EH26 8AG   01968 675761
[E-mail: ruth.halley@googlemail.com]

Penicuik: St Mungo's (H)
Vacant   31A Kirkhill Road, Penicuik EH26 8JB   01968 677040

Penicuik: South See Howgate

Prestonpans: Prestongrange
Charles M. Cameron BA BD PhD   1980 2012   The Manse, East Loan, Prestonpans EH32 9ED   01875 571579
[E-mail: minister@prestongrange-church.org.uk]

Roslin See Bilston
Spott See Belhaven

Tranent
Jan Gillies BD   1998 2008   1 Toll House Gardens, Tranent EH33 2QQ   01875 824604
[E-mail: jan@tranentparishchurch.co.uk]

Traprain
David D. Scott BSc BD   1981 2010   The Manse, Preston Road, East Linton EH40 3DS   01620 860227 (Tel/Fax)
[E-mail: revdd.scott@gmail.com]

Tyne Valley Parish (H)
Alan R. Cobain BD   2000 2013   Cranstoun Cottage, Ford, Pathhead EH37 5RE   01875 320314
[E-mail: erinbro44@yahoo.co.uk]
June E. Johnston BSc MEd BD   2013   49 Braeside Road South, Gorebridge EH23 4DL   01875 823086 / 07754 448889 (Mbl)
(Ordained Local Minister)   [E-mail: johnston330@btinternet.com]

Whitekirk and Tyninghame See Athelstaneford
Yester See Bolton and Saltoun

Andrews, J. Edward MA BD DipCG FSAScot	1985	2005	(Armadale)	Dunnichen, 1B Cameron Road, Nairn IV12 5NS [E-mail: edward.andrews@btinternet.com]	01667 459466
Bayne, Angus L. LTh BEd MTh	1969	2005	(Edinburgh: Bristo Memorial Craigmillar)	14 Myredale, Bonnyrigg EH19 3NW [E-mail: angus@mccookies.com]	(Mbl) 07808 720708 0131-663 6871
Berry, Geoff T. BD BSc	2009	2011	Chaplain: Army	38 Muirfield Drive, Gullane EH31 2HJ [E-mail: geofftalk@yahoo.co.uk]	
Black, A. Graham MA	1964	2003	(Gladsmuir with Longniddry)	26 Hamilton Crescent, Gullane EH31 2HR [E-mail: grablack@btinternet.com]	01620 843899
Brown, Ronald H.	1974	1998	(Musselburgh: Northesk)	6 Monktonhall Farm Cottages, Musselburgh EH21 6RZ	0131-653 2531
Brown, William BD	1972	1997	(Edinburgh: Polwarth)	13 Thornyhall, Dalkeith EH22 2ND	0131-654 0929
Buchanan, John DCS			(Deacon)	19 Gillespie Crescent, Edinburgh EH10 4HZ	0131-229 0794
Cairns, John B. KCVO LTh LLB LLD DD	1974	2009	(Aberlady with Gullane)	Bell House, Roxburghe Park, Dunbar EH42 1LR [E-mail: johncairns@mail.com]	01368 862501
Coltart, Ian O. CA BD	1988	2010	(Arbirlot with Carmyllie)	25 Bothwell Gardens, Dunbar EH42 1PZ	01368 860064
Forbes, Iain M. BSc BD	1964	2005	(Aberdeen: Beechgrove)	69 Dobbie's Road, Bonnyrigg EH19 2AY [E-mail: panama.forbes@tiscali.co.uk]	0131-454 0717

Name	Years	Charge	Address	Telephone
Fraser, John W. MA BD	1974 2011	(Penicuik: North)	66 Camus Avenue, Edinburgh EH10 6QX [E-mail: jjjj2005@hotmail.co.uk]	0131-623 0647
Glover, Robert L. BMus BD MTh ARCO	1971 2010	(Cockenzie and Port Seton: Chalmers Memorial)	27 Winton Park, Cockenzie, Prestonpans EH32 0JN [E-mail: rlglover@btinternet.com]	01875 818759
Hutchison, Alan E.W.		(Deacon)	132 Lochbridge Road, North Berwick EH39 4DR	01620 894077
Jones, Anne M. (Mrs) BD	1998 2002	(Hospital Chaplain)	7 North Elphinstone Farm, Tranent EH33 2ND [E-mail: revamjones@aol.com]	01875 614442
Kellock, Chris N. MA BD	1998 2012	Army Chaplain	7 Para RHA, Merville Barracks, Colchester CO2 7UT	
Lithgow, Anne R. (Mrs) MA BD	1992 2009	(Dunglass)	14 Thorntonloch Holdings, Dunbar EH42 1QT [E-mail: anne.lithgow@btinternet.com]	01620 810341
Macdonell, Alasdair W. MA BD	1955 1992	(Haddington: St Mary's)	St Andrews Cottage, Duns Road, Gifford, Haddington EH41 4QW [E-mail: alasdair.macdonell@btinternet.com]	
Manson, James A. LTh	1981 2004	(Glencorse with Roslin)	31 Nursery Gardens, Kilmarnock KA1 3JA [E-mail: james.manson@virgin.net]	01563 535430
Pirie, Donald LTh	1975 2006	(Bolton and Saltoun with Humbie with Yester)	46 Caiystane Avenue, Edinburgh EH10 6SH	0131-445 2654
Ritchie, James McL. MA BD MPhil	1950 1985	(Coalsnaughton)	Flat 2/25, Croft-an-Righ, Edinburgh EH8 8EG [E-mail: jasritch_77@msn.com]	0131-557 1084
Stein, Jock MA BD	1973 2008	(Tulliallan and Kincardine)	35 Dunbar Road, Haddington EH41 3PJ [E-mail: jstein@handselpress.org.uk]	01620 824896
Stein, Margaret E. (Mrs) DA BD DipRE	1984 2008	(Tulliallan and Kincardine)	35 Dunbar Road, Haddington EH41 3PJ [E-mail: margaretestein@hotmail.com]	01620 824896
Swan, Andrew F. BD	1983 2000	(Loanhead)	Park View, 2 Park Place, Lanark ML11 9HH	
Torrance, David W. MA BD	1955 1991	(Earlston)	38 Forth Street, North Berwick EH39 4JQ [E-mail: torrance103@btinternet.com]	(Tel/Fax) 01620 895109
Underwood, Florence A. (Mrs) BD	1992 2006	(Assistant: Gladsmuir with Longniddry)	18 Covenanters Rise, Pitreavie Castle, Dunfermline KY11 8SQ [E-mail: geoffrey.underwood@homecall.co.uk]	01383 740745
Underwood, Geoffrey H. BD DipTh FPhS	1964 1992	(Cockenzie and Port Seton: Chalmers Memorial)	18 Covenanters Rise, Pitreavie Castle, Dunfermline KY11 8SQ [E-mail: geoffrey.underwood@homecall.co.uk]	01383 740745

(4) MELROSE AND PEEBLES

Meets at Innerleithen on the first Tuesday of February, March, May, October, November and December, and on the fourth Tuesday of June, and in places to be appointed on the first Tuesday of September.

Clerk: **REV. VICTORIA LINFORD LLB BD** **The Manse, 209 Galashiels Road, Stow, Galashiels TD1 2RE** **01578 730237**
[E-mail: melrosepeebles@cofscotland.org.uk]

Ashkirk linked with Selkirk (H)

Margaret D.J. Steele (Miss) BSc BD	2000	2011	1 Loanside, Selkirk TD7 4DJ [E-mail: mdjsteele@gmail.com]	01750 23308

Bowden (H) and Melrose (H)
Alistair G. Bennett BSc BD — 1978 1984 — Tweedmount Road, Melrose TD6 9ST [E-mail: agbennettmelrose@aol.com] — 01896 822217

Broughton, Glenholm and Kilbucho (H) linked with Skirling linked with Stobo and Drumelzier linked with Tweedsmuir (H)
Robert B. Milne BTh — 1999 2009 — The Manse, Broughton, Biggar ML12 6HQ [E-mail: rbmilne@aol.com] — 01899 830331

Caddonfoot (H) linked with Galashiels: Trinity (H)
Vacant — 8 Mossilee Road, Galashiels TD1 1NF — 01896 752420

Carlops linked with Kirkurd and Newlands (H) linked with West Linton: St Andrew's (H)
Vacant — The Manse, West Linton EH46 7EN — 01968 660221

Channelkirk and Lauder
Vacant — The Manse, Brownsmuir Park, Lauder TD2 6QD — 01578 722616

Earlston
Julie M. Woods (Ms) BTh — 2005 2011 — The Manse, High Street, Earlston TD4 6DE [E-mail: missjulie@btinternet.com] — 01896 849236

Eddleston (H) linked with Peebles: Old (H)
Malcolm M. Macdougall BD MTh DipCE — 1981 2001 — The Old Manse, Innerleithen Road, Peebles EH45 8BD [E-mail: calum.macdougall@btopenworld.com] — 01721 720568

Ettrick and Yarrow
Samuel Siroky BA MTh — 2003 — Yarrow Manse, Yarrow, Selkirk TD7 5LA [E-mail: sesiroky@tiscali.co.uk] — 01750 82336

Galashiels: Old and St Paul's (H) (Website: www.oldparishandstpauls.org.uk)
Vacant — Woodlea, Abbotsview Drive, Galashiels TD1 3SL — 01896 752320

Galashiels: St John's (H)
Jane M. Howitt (Miss) MA BD — 1996 2006 — St John's Manse, Hawthorn Road, Galashiels TD1 2JZ [E-mail: jane@sfjohnsgalashiels.co.uk] — 01896 752573

Galashiels: Trinity (H) See Caddonfoot

Innerleithen (H), Traquair and Walkerburn
Janice M. Faris (Mrs) BSc BD   1991 2001   The Manse, 1 Millwell Park, Innerleithen, Peebles EH44 6JF   01896 830309
[E-mail: revjfaris@hotmail.com]

Kirkurd and Newlands See Carlops

Lyne and Manor linked with Peebles: St Andrew's Leckie (H) (01721 723121)
Malcolm S. Jefferson   2012   Mansefield, Innerleithen Road, Peebles   EH45 8BE   01721 721148
[E-mail: jeffersons02@btinternet.com]

Maxton and Mertoun linked with Newtown linked with St Boswells
Sheila W. Moir (Ms) MTheol   2008   7 Strae Brigs, St Boswells, Melrose TD6 0DH   01835 822255
[E-mail: sheila377@btinternet.com]

Newtown See Maxton and Mertoun
Peebles: Old See Eddleston
Peebles: St Andrew's Leckie See Lyne and Manor
St Boswells See Maxton and Mertoun
Selkirk See Ashkirk
Skirling See Broughton, Glenholm and Kilbucho
Stobo and Drumelzier See Broughton, Glenholm and Kilbucho

Stow: St Mary of Wedale and Heriot
Victoria J. Linford (Mrs) LLB BD   2010   The Manse, 209 Galashiels Road, Stow, Galashiels TD1 2RE   01578 730237
[E-mail: victorialinford@yahoo.co.uk]

Tweedsmuir See Broughton, Glenholm and Kilbucho
West Linton: St Andrew's See Carlops

Name			Charge	Address	Phone
Arnott, A. David K. MA BD	1971	2010	(St Andrews: Hope Park with Strathkinness)	53 Whitehaugh Park, Peebles EH45 9DB [E-mail: adka53@btinternet.com]	01721 725979 (Mbl) 07759 709205
Bowie, Adam McC.	1976	1996	(Cavers and Kirkton with Hobkirk and Southdean)	Glenbield, Redpath, Earlston TD4 6AD	01896 848173
Brown, Robert BSc	1962	1997	(Kilbrandon and Kilchattan)	11 Thornfield Terrace, Selkirk TD7 4DU [E-mail: ruwcb@tiscali.co.uk]	01750 20311
Burt, Thomas W. BD	1982	2013	(Carlops with Kirkurd and Newlands with West Linton: St Andrew's)	7 Arkwright Court, North Berwick EH39 4RT [E-mail: tomburt@westlinton.com]	01620 895494
Cashman, P. Hamilton BSc	1985	1998	(Dirleton with North Berwick: Abbey)	38 Abbotsford Road, Galashiels TD1 3HR [E-mail: mcashman@tiscali.co.uk]	01896 752711

Name			Charge / Role	Address	Phone
Cutler, James S.H. BD CEng MIStructE	1986	2011	(Black Mount with Culter with Libberton and Quothquan)	12 Kittlegairy Place, Peebles EH45 9LW [E-mail: revjc@btinternet.com]	01721 723950
Devenny, Robert P.	2002		Hospital Chaplain	Blakeburn Cottage, Wester Housebyres, Melrose TD6 9BW	01896 822350
Dick, J. Ronald BD	1973	1996	(Hospital Chaplain)	5 Georgefield Farm Cottages, Earlston TD4 6BH	01896 848956
Dobie, Rachel J.W. (Mrs) LTh	1991	2008	(Broughton, Glenholm and Kilbucho with Skirling with Stobo and Drumelzier with Tweedsmuir)	20 Moss Side Crescent, Biggar ML12 6GE [E-mail: revracheldobie@talktalk.net]	01899 229244
Dodd, Marion E. (Miss) MA BD LRAM	1988	2010	(Kelso: Old and Sprouston)	Esdaile, Tweedmount Road, Melrose TD6 9ST [E-mail: mariondodd@btinternet.com]	01896 822446
Duncan, Charles A. MA	1956	1992	(Heriot with Stow: St Mary of Wedale)	10 Elm Grove, Galashiels TD1 3JA	01896 753261
Hardie, H. Warner BD	1979	2005	(Blackridge with Harthill: St Andrew's)	Keswick Cottage, Kingsmuir Drive, Peebles EH45 9AA [E-mail: hardies@bigfoot.com]	01721 724003
Hogg, Thomas M. BD	1986	2007	(Tranent)	22 Douglas Place, Galashiels TD1 3BT	01896 759381
Hughes, Barry MA	2011		Ordained Local Minister	Dunslair, Cardrona Way, Cardrona, Peebles EH45 9LD [E-mail: gill_baz@hotmail.com]	01896 831197
Kellet, John M. MA	1962	1995	(Leith: South)	4 High Cottages, Walkerburn EH43 6AZ	01896 870351
Kennon, Stanley BA BD RN	1992	2000	Chaplain: Royal Navy	Britannia Royal Naval College, Dartmouth, Devon TQ6 0HJ [E-mail: bmc-csf@fleetfost.mod.uk]	
Laing, William F. DSC VRD MA	1952	1986	(Selkirk: St Mary's West)	10 The Glebe, Selkirk TD7 5AB	01750 21210
Lawrie, Bruce B. BD	1974	2012	(Duffus, Spynie and Hopeman)	5 Thorncroft, Scotts Place, Selkirk TD7 4LN [E-mail: bruce@brucelawrie.plus.com]	
MacFarlane, David C. MA	1957	1997	(Eddleston with Peebles: Old)	Lorimer House Nursing Home, 491 Lanark Road, Edinburgh EH14 5DQ	
Milloy, A. Miller DPE LTh DipTrMan	1979	2012	(General Secretary: United Bible Societies)	18 Kittlegairy Crescent, Peebles EH45 9NJ [E-mail: ammilloy@aol.com]	01721 723380
Moore, W. Haisley MA	1966	1996	(Secretary: The Boys' Brigade)	26 Tweedbank Avenue, Tweedbank, Galashiels TD1 3SP	01896 668577
Munson, Winnie (Ms) BD	1996	2006	(Delting with Northmavine)	6 St Cuthbert's Drive, St Boswells, Melrose TD6 0DF	01835 823375
Norman, Nancy M. (Miss) BA MDiv MTh	1988	2012	(Lyne and Manor)	25 March Street, Peebles EH45 8EP [E-mail: nancy.norman1@googlemail.com]	01721 721699
Rae, Andrew W.	1951	1987	(Annan: St Andrew's Greenknowe Erskine)	Roseneuk, Tweedside Road, Newtown St Boswells TD6 0PQ	01835 823783
Rennie, John D. MA	1962	1996	(Broughton, Glenholm and Kilbucho with Skirling with Stobo and Drumelzier with Tweedsmuir)	29/1 Rosetta Road, Peebles EH45 8HJ [E-mail: tworennies@talktalk.net]	01721 720963
Riddell, John A. MA BD	1967	2006	(Jedburgh: Trinity)	Orchid Cottage, Gingham Row, Earlston TD4 6ET	01896 848784
Steele, Leslie M. MA BD	1973	2013	(Galashiels: Old and St Paul's)	c/o 57 Speedwell Road, Colchester CO2 8DN [E-mail: lms@hotmail.co.uk]	01206 619541 (Mbl) 07786 797974
Taverner, Glyn R. MA BD	1957	1995	(Maxton and Mertoun with St Boswells)	Woodcot Cottage, Waverley Road, Innerleithen EH44 6QW	01896 830156
Wallace, James H. MA BD	1973	2011	(Peebles: St Andrew's Leckie)	52 Waverley Mills, Innerleithen EH44 6RH [E-mail: jimwallace121@btinternet.com]	01896 831637

(5) DUNS

Meets at Duns, in the Parish Church hall, normally on the first Tuesday of February, March, April, May, October, November and December, on the last Tuesday in June, and in places to be appointed on the first Tuesday of September.

Clerk: MRS HELEN LONGMUIR   Viewfield, South Street, Gavinton, Duns TD11 3QT   01361 882728
[E-mail: duns@cofscotland.org.uk]

Ayton (H) and Burnmouth linked with Foulden and Mordington linked with Grantshouse and Houndwood and Reston
Norman R. Whyte BD MTh DipMin   1982   2006   The Manse, Beanburn, Ayton, Eyemouth TD14 5QY   01890 781333
[E-mail: burraman@msn.com]

Berwick-upon-Tweed: St Andrew's Wallace Green (H) and Lowick
Adam J.J. Hood MA BD DPhil   1989   2012   3 Meadow Grange, Berwick-upon-Tweed TD15 1NW   01289 332787
[E-mail: minister@sawg.org.uk]

Bonkyl and Preston linked with Duns (H) linked with Edrom Allanton (H)
Stephen A. Blakey BSc BD   1977   2012   The Manse, Castle Street, Duns TD11 3DG   01361 883755
[E-mail: stephenablakey@aol.com]

Chirnside linked with Hutton and Fishwick and Paxton
Vacant   Parish Church Manse, The Glebe, Chirnside, Duns TD11 3XL   01890 819109

Coldingham and St Abbs linked with Eyemouth
Andrew Haddow BEng BD   2012   The Manse, Victoria Road, Eyemouth TD14 5JD   01890 750327
[E-mail: andy@blakkie.co.uk]

Coldstream (H) linked with Eccles
David J. Taverner MCIBS ACIS BD   1996   2011   36 Bennecourt Drive, Coldstream TD12 4BY   01890 883887
[E-mail: rahereuk@hotmail.com]

Duns (H) See Bonkyl and Preston
Eccles See Coldstream
Edrom Allanton See Bonkyl and Preston
Eyemouth See Coldingham and St Abbs

Fogo and Swinton linked with Ladykirk and Whitsome linked with Leitholm (H)
Alan C.D. Cartwright BSc BD   1976   The Manse, Swinton, Duns TD11 3JJ   01890 860228
    [E-mail: alan@cartwright-family.co.uk]

Foulden and Mordington See Ayton and Burnmouth

Gordon: St Michael's linked with Greenlaw (H) linked with Legerwood linked with Westruther
Thomas S. Nicholson BD DPS   1982 1995   The Manse, Todholes, Greenlaw, Duns TD10 6XD   01361 810316
    [E-mail: nst54@hotmail.com]

Grantshouse and Houndwood and Reston See Ayton and Burnmouth
Greenlaw See Gordon: St Michael's
Hutton and Fishwick and Paxton See Chirnside
Ladykirk and Whitsome See Fogo and Swinton

(New charge formed by the union of Ladykirk and Whitsome)

Langton and Lammermuir Kirk
Ann Inglis (Mrs) LLB BD   1986   2003   The Manse, Cranshaws, Duns TD11 3SJ   01361 890289
    [E-mail: revainglis@btinternet.com]

Legerwood See Gordon: St Michael's
Leitholm See Fogo and Swinton
Westruther See Gordon: St Michael's

Gaddes, Donald R.	1961 1994	(Kelso: North and Ednam)	2 Teindhill Green, Duns TD11 3DX	01361 883172
			[E-mail: drgaddes@btinternet.com]	
Gale, Ronald A.A. LTh	1982 1995	(Dunoon: Old and St Cuthbert's)	55 Lennel Mount, Coldstream TD12 4NS	01890 883699
			[E-mail: rgale89@aol.com]	
Graham, Jennifer D. (Mrs) BA MDiv PhD	2000 2011	(Eday with Stronsay: Moncur Memorial)	18 Wheatriggs Avenue, Milfield, Wooler NE71 6HU	01668 216744
			[E-mail: jdgraham67@gmail.com]	
Hay, Bruce J.L.	1957 1997	(Makerstoun and Smailholm with Stichill, Hume and Nenthorn)	Tweedmouth House, 4 Main Street, Tweedmouth, Berwick-upon-Tweed TD15 2HD	
Higham, Robert D. BD	1985 2002	(Tiree)	36 Low Greens, Berwick-upon-Tweed TD15 1LZ	01289 302392
Hope, Geraldine H. (Mrs) MA BD	1986 2007	(Foulden and Mordington with Hutton and Fishwick and Paxton)	4 Well Court, Chirnside, Duns TD11 3UD	01890 818134
			[E-mail: geraldine.hope@virgin.net]	
Kerr, Andrew MA BLitt	1948 1991	(Kilbarchan: West)	4 Lairds Gate, Port Glasgow Road, Kilmacolm PA13 4EX	01505 874852
Landale, William S.	2005	Auxiliary Minister	Green Hope Guest House, Ellemford, Duns TD11 3SG	01361 890242
			[E-mail: bill@greenhope.co.uk]	

Name					
Ledgard, J. Christopher BA	1969	2004	(Ayton and Burnmouth with Grantshouse and Houndwood and Reston)	Streonshalh, 8 David Hume View, Chirnside, Duns TD11 3SX [E-mail: ledgard07@btinternet.com]	01890 819966
Lindsay, Daniel G. BD	1978	2011	(Coldingham and St Abbs with Eyemouth)		
Murray, Duncan E. BA BD	1970	2012	(Bonkyl and Preston with Chirnside with Edrom Allanton)	18 Hallidown Crescent, Eyemouth TD14 5TB Beech Cottage, York Road, Knaresborough HG5 0TT [E-mail: duncanemurray@tiscali.co.uk]	01890 751389 01423 313287
Neill, Bruce F. MA BD	1966	2007	(Maxton and Mertoun with St Boswells)	18 Brierydean, St Abbs, Eyemouth TD14 5PQ [E-mail: bneill@phonecoop.coop]	01890 771569
Paterson, William BD	1977	2001	(Bonkyl and Preston with Chirnside with Edrom Allanton)	Benachie, Gavinton, Duns TD11 3QT [E-mail: billdm.paterson@btinternet.com]	01361 882727
Walker, Kenneth D.F. MA BD PhD	1976	2008	(Athelstaneford with Whitekirk and Tyninghame)	Allanbank Kothi, Allanton, Duns TD11 3PY [E-mail: kenver.walker@btinternet.com]	01890 817102
Watson, James B. BSc	1968	2009	(Coldstream with Eccles)	49 Lennel Mount, Coldstream TD12 4NS [E-mail: revjamesbwatson@f2s.com]	01890 883149

(6) JEDBURGH

Meets at various venues on the first Wednesday of February, March, May, September, October, November and December and on the last Wednesday of June.

Clerk   REV. FRANK CAMPBELL   22 The Glebe, Ancrum, Jedburgh TD8 6UX   **01835 830318**
[E-mail: jedburgh@cofscotland.org.uk]

Ale and Teviot United (H) (Website: www.aleandteviot.org.uk)
Frank Campbell   1989 1991   22 The Glebe, Ancrum, Jedburgh TD8 6UX   01835 830318
[E-mail: jedburgh@cofscotland.org.uk]

Cavers and Kirkton linked with Hawick: Trinity
Michael D. Scouler MBE BSc BD   1988 2009   Kerrscroft, Howdenburn, Hawick TD9 8PH   01450 378248
[E-mail: michaelscouler@hotmail.co.uk]

Hawick: Burnfoot (Website: www.burnfootparishchurch.org.uk)
Charles J. Finnie LTh DPS   1991 1997   29 Wilton Hill, Hawick TD9 8BA   01450 373181
[E-mail: charles.finnie@gmail.com]

Hawick: St Mary's and Old (H)
Vacant   The Manse of St Mary's and Old, Braid Road, Hawick TD9 9LZ   01450 378163

Hawick: Teviot (H) and Roberton
Neil R. Combe BSc MSc BD | 1984 | Teviot Manse, Buccleuch Road, Hawick TD9 0EL | 01450 372150
[E-mail: neil.combe@btinternet.com]

Hawick: Trinity (H) See Cavers and Kirkton

Hawick: Wilton linked with Teviothead
Lisa-Jane Rankin (Miss) BD CPS | 2003 | 4 Wilton Hill Terrace, Hawick TD9 8BE | 01450 370744 (Tel/Fax)
[E-mail: revlj@talktalk.net]

Hobkirk and Southdean (Website: www.hobkirkruberslaw.org) linked with Ruberslaw (Website: www.hobkirkruberslaw.org)
Douglas A.O. Nicol MA BD | 1974 2009 | The Manse, Denholm, Hawick TD9 8NB | 01450 870268
[E-mail: daon@lineone.net]

Jedburgh: Old and Trinity (Website: www.jedburgh-parish.org.uk)
Graham D. Astles BD MSc | 2007 | The Manse, Honeyfield Drive, Jedburgh TD8 6LQ | 01835 863417 / 07906 290568 (Mbl)
[E-mail: minister@jedburgh-parish.org.uk]

Kelso Country Churches (Website: www.kelsolinkedchurchescofs.org) linked with Kelso: Old and Sprouston (Website: www.kelsolinkedchurchescofs.org)
Jenny Earl MA BD | 2007 | The Manse, 1 The Meadow, Stichill, Kelso TD5 7TG | 01573 470607
[E-mail: jennyearl@btinternet.com]

Kelso: North (H) and Ednam (H) (01573 224154) (E-mail: office@kelsonorthandednam.org.uk) (Website: www.kelsonorthandednam.org.uk)
Tom McDonald BD | 1994 | 20 Forestfield, Kelso TD5 7BX | 01573 224677
[E-mail: revtom@20thepearlygates.co.uk]

Kelso: Old (H) and Sprouston See Kelso Country Churches

Linton, Morebattle, Hownam and Yetholm (H) (Website: www.cheviotchurches.org)
Robin D. McHaffie BD | 1979 1991 | The Manse, Main Street, Kirk Yetholm, Kelso TD5 8PF | 01573 420308
[E-mail: robinmchaffie@btinternet.com]

Oxnam (Website: www.oxnamkirk.co.uk)
Guardianship of the Presbytery
Anna S. Rodwell (Mrs) BD DipMin (Locum) | 1998 2003 | The Old Mill House, Hownam Howgate, Kelso TD5 8AJ | 01573 440761
[E-mail: anna.rodwell@gmail.com]

Ruberslaw   See Hobkirk and Southdean
Teviothead   See Hawick: Wilton

Auld, A. Graeme (Prof.)	1973	2008	(University of Edinburgh)	Nether Swanshiel, Hobkirk, Bonchester Bridge, Hawick TD9 8JU [E-mail: a.g.auld@ed.ac.uk]	01450 860636
MA BD PhD DLitt FSAScot FRSE					
McNicol, Bruce	1967	2006	(Jedburgh: Old and Edgerston)	42 Dounehill, Jedburgh TD8 6LJ [E-mail: mcnicol95@btinternet.com]	01835 862991
Shields, John M. MBE LTh	1972	2007	(Channelkirk and Lauder)	12 Eden Park, Ednam, Kelso TD5 7RG [E-mail: john.shields118@btinternet.com]	01573 229015
Thomson, E.P. Lindsay MA	1964	2008	(Cavers and Kirkton with Hawick: Trinity)	4 Bourtree Bank, Hawick TD9 9HP [E-mail: eplindsayt@aol.com]	01450 374318

HAWICK ADDRESSES

Burnfoot	Fraser Avenue
St Mary's and Old	Kirk Wynd
Teviot	off Buccleuch Road
Trinity	Central Square
Wilton	Princes Street

(7) ANNANDALE AND ESKDALE

Meets on the first Tuesday of February, May, September and December, and the third Tuesday of March, June and October. The September meeting is held in the Moderator's charge. The other meetings are held in Dryfesdale Church Hall, Lockerbie, except for the June meeting, which is separately announced.

Clerk:	**REV. C. BRYAN HASTON LTh**	**The Manse, Gretna Green, Gretna DG16 5DU** **[E-mail: annandaleeskdale@cofscotland.org.uk]** **[E-mail: cbhaston@cofs.demon.co.uk]**	**01461 338313**

Annan: Old (H) linked with Dornock
Vacant   12 Plumdon Park Avenue, Annan DG12 6EY   01461 201405

Annan: St Andrew's (H) linked with Brydekirk
John G. Pickles BD MTh MSc   2011   1 Annerley Road, Annan DG12 6HE   01461 202626
[E-mail: jgpickles@hotmail.com]

Applegarth, Sibbaldbie (H) and Johnstone linked with Lochmaben (H)
Vacant   The Manse, Barrashead, Lochmaben, Lockerbie DG11 1QF   01387 810066

Brydekirk See Annan: St Andrew's

Canonbie United (H) linked with Liddesdale (H)
Vacant   23 Langholm Street, Newcastleton TD9 0QX   01387 375242

Dalton linked with Hightae linked with St Mungo
Morag A. Dawson BD MTh   1999   The Manse, Hightae, Lockerbie DG11 1JL   01387 811499
                                        [E-mail: moragdawson@yahoo.co.uk]

Dornock See Annan: Old

Gretna: Old (H), Gretna: St Andrew's (H), Half Morton and Kirkpatrick Fleming
C. Bryan Haston LTh   1975   The Manse, Gretna Green, Gretna DG16 5DU   01461 338313
                                        [E-mail: cbhaston@cofs.demon.co.uk]
                                        [E-mail: cbhaston@gretnagreen.eu]

Hightae See Dalton

Hoddom, Kirtle-Eaglesfield and Middlebie
Frances M. Henderson BA BD PhD 2006 2013 The Manse, Main Road, Ecclefechan, Lockerbie DG11 3BU   01576 300108
                                        [E-mail: f-henderson@hotmail.co.uk]

Kirkpatrick Juxta linked with Moffat: St Andrew's (H) linked with Wamphray
Adam J. Dillon BD ThM   2003 2008 The Manse, 1 Meadowbank, Moffat DG10 9LR   01683 220128
                                        [E-mail: adamdillon@btinternet.com]

Langholm Eskdalemuir Ewes and Westerkirk
I. Scott McCarthy BD   2010   The Manse, Langholm DG13 0BL   01387 380252
                                        [E-mail: iscottmccarthy@gmail.com]

Liddesdale (H) See Canonbie United
Lochmaben See Applegarth, Sibbaldbie and Johnstone

Lockerbie: Dryfesdale, Hutton and Corrie

| Alexander C. Stoddart BD | 2001 | 2008 | The Manse, 5 Carlisle Road, Lockerbie DG11 2DW [E-mail: sandystoddart@supanet.com] | 01576 202361 |

Moffat: St Andrew's (H) See Kirkpatrick Juxta
St Mungo See Dalton

The Border Kirk (Church office: Chapel Street, Carlisle CA1 1JA; Tel: 01228 591757)

| David G. Pitkeathly LLB BD | 1996 | 2007 | 95 Pinecroft, Carlisle CA3 0DB [E-mail: david.pitkeathly@btinternet.com] | 01228 593343 |

Tundergarth
Guardianship of the Presbytery

Wamphray See Kirkpatrick Juxta

Annand, James M. MA BD	1955	1995	(Lockerbie: Dryfesdale)	Dere Cottage, 48 Main Street, Newstead, Melrose TD6 9DX	0131-225 3393
Beveridge, S. Edwin P. BA	1959	2004	(Brydekirk with Hoddom)	19 Rothesay Terrace, Edinburgh EH3 7RY	01461 206512
Byers, Alan J.	1959	1992	(Gamrie with King Edward)	Meadowbank, Plumdon Road, Annan DG12 6SJ	01461 206512
Byers, Mairi C. (Mrs) BTh CPS	1992	1998	(Jura)	Meadowbank, Plumdon Road, Annan DG12 6SJ [E-mail: aljbyers@hotmail.com]	
Gibb, J. Daniel M. BA LTh	1994	2006	(Aberfoyle with Port of Menteith)	21 Victoria Gardens, Eastriggs, Annan DG12 6TW [E-mail: dannygibb@hotmail.co.uk]	01461 40560
Harvey, P. Ruth (Ms) MA BD	2009	2012	Place for Hope	Croslands, Beacon Street, Penrith CA11 7TZ [E-mail: ruth.harvey@placeforhope.org.uk]	01768 840749 (Mbl) 07403 638339
MacMillan, William M. LTh	1980	1998	(Kilmory with Lamlash)	Balskia, 61 Queen Street, Lochmaben, Lockerbie DG11 1PP	01387 811528
Macpherson, Duncan J. BSc BD	1993	2002	Chaplain: Army	HQ Hereford Garrison, Hereford HR4 7DD	
Ross, Alan C. CA BD	1988	2007	(Eskdalemuir with Hutton and Corrie with Tundergarth)	Yarra, Ettrickbridge, Selkirk TD7 5JN [E-mail: alkaross@aol.com]	01750 52324
Sanders, Martyn S. BA CertEd MA	2013		Ordained Local Minister: Parish Assistant	26 Wood Avenue, Annan DG12 6DA [E-mail: martyn.sanders@furtherministriesteam.com]	(Mbl) 07830 697976
Seaman, Ronald S. MA	1967	2007	(Dornock)	1 Springfield Farm Court, Springfield, Gretna DG16 5EH	01461 337228
Steenbergen, Pauline (Ms) MA BD	1996	2012	Hospice Chaplain	Eden Valley Hospice, Durdar Road, Carlisle CA2 4SD [E-mail: pauline.steenbergen@edenvalleyhospice.co.uk]	01228 817609
Swinburne, Norman BA	1960	1993	(Sauchie)	Dameroschay, Birch Hill Lane, Kirkbride, Wigton CA7 5HZ	01697 351497
Vivers, Katherine A.	2004		Auxiliary Minister	Blacket House, Eaglesfield, Lockerbie DG11 3AA [E-mail: katevivers@yahoo.co.uk]	01461 500412 (Mbl) 07748 233011
Williams, Trevor C. LTh	1990	2007	(Hoddom with Kirtle-Eaglesfield with Middlebie with Waterbeck)	c/o Presbytery Clerk [E-mail: revtrev@btinternet.com]	

(8) DUMFRIES AND KIRKCUDBRIGHT

Meets at Dumfries on the last Wednesday of February, June, September and November.

Clerk: REV. WILLIAM T. HOGG MA BD
St Bride's Manse, Glasgow Road, Sanquhar DG4 6BZ
[E-mail: dumfrieskirkcudbright@cofscotland.org.uk]   **01659 50247**

Auchencairn (H) and Rerrick linked with Buittle (H) and Kelton (H)
Vacant
Auchencairn, Castle Douglas DG7 1QS

Balmaclellan and Kells (H) linked with Carsphairn (H) linked with Dalry (H)
David S. Bartholomew BSc MSc PhD BD   1994
The Manse, Dalry, Castle Douglas DG7 3PJ   01644 430380
[E-mail: dhbart@care4free.net]

Balmaghie linked with Tarff and Twynholm (H)
Christopher Wallace BD DipMin   1988
The Manse, Manse Road, Twynholm, Kirkcudbright DG6 4NY   01557 860381
[E-mail: minister@twynholm.org.uk]

Borgue linked with Gatehouse of Fleet
Valerie J. Ott (Mrs) BA BD   2002
The Manse, Planetree Park, Gatehouse of Fleet,
Castle Douglas DG7 2EQ   01557 814233
[E-mail: valanddav98@btinternet.com]

Buittle and Kelton See Auchencairn and Rerrick

Caerlaverock linked with Dumfries: St Mary's-Greyfriars'
Vacant
4 Georgetown Crescent, Dumfries DG1 4EQ   01387 253877

Carsphairn See Balmaclellan and Kells

Castle Douglas (H)
Vacant
1 Castle View, Castle Douglas DG7 1BG   01556 502171

Closeburn
Guardianship of the Presbytery

Colvend, Southwick and Kirkbean
James F. Gatherer BD   1984   2003   The Manse, Colvend, Dalbeattie DG5 4QN   01556 630255
[E-mail: james@gatherer.net]

Corsock and Kirkpatrick Durham linked with Crossmichael and Parton
Sally Russell BTh MTh   2006   Knockdrocket, Clarebrand, Castle Douglas DG7 3AH   01556 503645
[E-mail: rev.sal@btinternet.com]

Crossmichael and Parton See Corsock and Kirkpatrick Durham

Cummertrees, Mouswald and Ruthwell (H)
Vacant   The Manse, Ruthwell, Dumfries DG1 4NP   01387 870217

Dalbeattie (H) linked with Urr (H)
Vacant   36 Mill Street, Dalbeattie DG5 4HE   01556 610029

Dalry See Balmaclellan and Kells

Dumfries: Maxwelltown West (H)
Vacant   Maxwelltown West Manse, 11 Laurieknowe, Dumfries DG2 7AH   01387 252929

Dumfries: Northwest
Neil G. Campbell BA BD   1988   2006   c/o Church Office, Dumfries Northwest Church, Lochside Road, Dumfries DG2 0DZ   01387 249964
[E-mail: neilcampbell@dumfriesnorthwest.org.uk]

Dumfries: St George's (H)
Donald Campbell BD   1997   9 Nunholm Park, Dumfries DG1 1JP   01387 252965
[E-mail: minister@saint-georges.org.uk]

Dumfries: St Mary's-Greyfriars' (H) See Caerlaverock

Dumfries: St Michael's and South
Maurice S. Bond MTh BA DipEd PhD   1981   1999   39 Cardoness Street, Dumfries DG1 3AL   01387 253849
[E-mail: mauricebond399@btinternet.com]

Dumfries: Troqueer (H)
William W. Kelly BSc BD   1994   Troqueer Manse, Troqueer Road, Dumfries DG2 7DF   01387 253043
[E-mail: wwkelly@yahoo.com]

Dunscore linked with Glencairn and Moniaive
Vacant — Wallaceton, Auldgirth, Dumfries DG2 0TJ — 01387 820245

Durisdeer linked with Penpont, Keir and Tynron linked with Thornhill (H)
J. Stuart Mill — 1976 2013 — The Manse, Manse Park, Thornhill DG3 5ER [E-mail: stuartmill1@hotmail.co.uk] — 01848 331191

Gatehouse of Fleet See Borgue
Glencairn and Moniaive See Dunscore

Irongray, Lochrutton and Terregles
Vacant — Shawhead Road, Dumfries DG2 9SJ — 01387 730287

Kirkconnel (H)
Alistair J. MacKichan MA BD — 1984 2009 — The Manse, 31 Kingsway, Kirkconnel, Sanquhar DG4 6PN [E-mail: alistairjmck@btinternet.com] — 01659 67241

Kirkcudbright (H)
Douglas R. Irving LLB BD WS — 1984 1998 — 6 Bourtree Avenue, Kirkcudbright DG6 4AU [E-mail: douglasirving05@tiscali.co.uk] — 01557 330489

Kirkgunzeon linked with Lochend and New Abbey
Vacant — The Manse, 28 Main Street, New Abbey, Dumfries DG2 8BY — 01387 850232

Kirkmahoe
David M. Almond BD — 1996 2008 — The Manse, Kirkmahoe, Dumfries DG1 1ST [E-mail: almond.david138@googlemail.com] — 01387 710572

Kirkmichael, Tinwald and Torthorwald
Willem J. Bezuidenhout BA BD MHEd MEd — 1977 2010 — Manse of Tinwald, Tinwald, Dumfries DG1 3PL [E-mail: willembezuidenhout@btinternet.com] — 01387 710246

Lochend and New Abbey See Kirkgunzeon
Penpont, Keir and Tynron See Durisdeer

Sanquhar: St Bride's (H)
William T. Hogg MA BD — 1979 2000 — St Bride's Manse, Glasgow Road, Sanquhar DG6 6BZ [E-mail: wthogg@yahoo.com] — 01659 50247

Tarff and Twynholm See Balmaghie
Thornhill (H) See Durisdeer
Urr See Dalbeattie

Bennett, David K.P. BA	1974	2000	(Kirkpatrick Irongray with Lochrutton with Terregles)	53 Anne Arundel Court, Heathhall, Dumfries DG1 3SL	01387 257755
Duncan, Maureen M. (Mrs) BD	1996	2008	(Dunlop)	Dunedin, Whitepark, Castle Douglas DG7 1QA [E-mail: revmo@talktalk.net]	01556 502867
Greer, A. David C. LLB DMin DipAdultEd	1956	1996	(Barra)	17 Duthac Wynd, Tain IV19 1LP [E-mail: greer2@talktalk.net]	01862 892065
Hamill, Robert BA	1956	1989	(Castle Douglas: St Ringan's)	11 St Andrew Drive, Castle Douglas DG7 1EW	01556 502962
Hammond, Richard J. BA BD	1993	2007	(Kirkmahoe)	3 Marchfield Mount, Marchfield, Dumfries DG1 1SE [E-mail: libby.hammond@virgin.net]	(Mbl) 07764 465783
Henig, Gordon BSc BD	1997	2003	(Bellie with Speymouth)	4 Galla Crescent, Dalbeattie DG5 4JY	01556 611183
Holland, William MA	1967	2009	(Lochend and New Abbey)	Ardshean, 55 Georgetown Road, Dumfries DG1 4DD [E-mail: billholland55@btinternet.com]	01387 256131 (Mbl) 07766 531732
Hutcheson, Norman M. MA BD	1973	2012	(Dalbeattie with Urr)	73 Gallo Road, Colpetty, Colombo 3, Sri Lanka [E-mail: norman.hutcheson@gmail.com]	0094 11 2386774
Kirk, W. Logan MA BD MTh	1988	2000	(Dalton with Hightae with St Mungo)	2 Raecroft Avenue, Collin, Dumfries DG1 4LP	01387 750489
Leishman, James S. LTh BD MA(Div)	1969	1999	(Kirkmichael with Tinwald with Torthorwald)	11 Hunter Avenue, Heathhall, Dumfries DG1 3UX	01387 249241
Mack, Elizabeth A. (Miss) DipEd	1994	2011	(Auxiliary Minister)	24 Roberts Crescent, Dumfries DG2 7RS [E-mail: mackliz@btinternet.com]	01387 264847
McKay, David M. MA BD	1979	2007	(Kirkpatrick Juxta with Moffat: St Andrew's with Wamphray)	20 Auld Brig View, Auldgirth, Dumfries DG2 0XE [E-mail: davidmckay20@tiscali.co.uk]	01387 740013
McKenzie, William M. DA	1958	1993	(Dumfries: Troqueer)	41 Kingholm Road, Dumfries DG1 4SR [E-mail: mckenzie.dumfries@btinternet.com]	01387 253688
McLauchlan, Mary C. (Mrs) LTh	1997	2013	(Mochrum)	3 Ayr Street, Moniaive, Thornhill DG3 4HP [E-mail: mary@revmother.co.uk]	01848 200786
Miller, John R. MA BD	1958	1992	(Carsphairn with Dalry)	4 Fairgreen Court, Rhonehouse, Castle Douglas DG7 1SA	01556 680428
Owen, John J.C. LTh	1967	2001	(Applegarth and Sibbaldbie with Lochmaben)	5 Galla Avenue, Dalbeattie DG5 4JZ [E-mail: jj.owen@onetel.net]	01556 612125
Robertson, Ian W. MA BD	1956	1995	(Colvend, Southwick and Kirkbean)	10 Marjoriebanks, Lochmaben, Lockerbie DG11 1QH	01387 810541
Smith, Richmond OBE MA BD	1952	1983	(World Alliance of Reformed Churches)	Aignish, Merse Way, Kippford, Dalbeattie DG5 4LH	01556 620624
Strachan, Alexander E. MA BD	1974	2012	(Healthcare Chaplain)	2 Leafield Road, Dumfries DG1 2DS [E-mail: aestrachan@aol.com]	01387 279460
Sutherland, Colin A. LTh	1995	2007	(Blantyre: Livingstone Memorial)	71 Caulstran Road, Dumfries DG2 9FJ [E-mail: colin.csutherland@btinternet.com]	01387 279954
Wallace, Mhairi (Mrs)	2013		Ordained Local Minister	The Manse, Manse Road, Twynholm, Kirkcudbright DG6 4NY [E-mail: tobythewestie@msn.com]	01557 860381 (Mbl) 07880 546743
Wilkie, James R. MA MTh	1957	1993	(Penpont, Keir and Tynron)	31 West Morton Street, Thornhill DG3 5NF	01848 331028

Williamson, James BA BD	1986 2009	(Cummertrees with Mouswald with Ruthwell)	12 Mulberry Drive, Dunfermline KY11 8BZ [E-mail: jimwill@rcmkirk.fsnet.co.uk]	01383 734872
Wotherspoon, Robert C. LTh	1976 1998	(Corsock and Kirkpatrick Durham with Crossmichael and Parton)	7 Hillowton Drive, Castle Douglas DG7 1LL [E-mail: robert.wotherspoon@tiscali.co.uk]	01556 502267
Young, John MTh DipMin	1963 1999	(Airdrie: Broomknoll)	Craigview, North Street, Moniaive, Thornhill DG3 4HR	01848 200318

DUMFRIES ADDRESSES

Maxwelltown West	Laurieknowe	
Northwest	St George's	Lochside Road
	St Mary's-Greyfriars	George Street
		St Mary's Street
St Michael's and South		St Michael's Street
Troqueer		Troqueer Road

(9) WIGTOWN AND STRANRAER

Meets at Glenluce, in the church hall, on the first Tuesday of March, October and December for ordinary business; on the first Tuesday of September for formal business followed by meetings of committees; on the first Tuesday of November, February and May for worship followed by meetings of committees; and at a church designated by the Moderator on the first Tuesday of June for Holy Communion followed by ordinary business.

Clerk:　MR SAM SCOBIE		40 Clenoch Parks Road, Stranraer DG9 7QT [E-mail: wigtownstranraer@cofscotland.org.uk]	01776 703975

Ervie Kirkcolm linked with Leswalt
Michael J. Sheppard BD	1997	Ervie Manse, Stranraer DG9 0QZ [E-mail: mjs@uwclub.net]	01776 854225

Glasserton and Isle of Whithorn linked with Whithorn: St Ninian's Priory
Alexander I. Currie BD CPS	1990	The Manse, Whithorn, Newton Stewart DG8 8PT	01988 500267

Inch linked with Portpatrick linked with Stranraer: Trinity (H)
John H. Burns BSc BD	1985 1988	Bayview Road, Stranraer DG9 8BE	01776 702383

Kirkcowan (H) linked with Wigtown (H)
Eric Boyle BA MTh	2006	Seaview Manse, Church Lane, Wigtown, Newton Stewart DG8 9HT [E-mail: ecthered@aol.com]	01988 402314

Kirkinner linked with Sorbie (H)
Jeffrey M. Mead BD   1978   1986   The Manse, Kirkinner, Newton Stewart DG8 9AL   01988 840643

Kirkmabreck linked with Monigaff (H)
Vacant   Creebridge, Newton Stewart DG8 6NR   01671 403361

Kirkmaiden (H) linked with Stoneykirk
Melvyn J. Griffiths BTh DipTheol DMin   1978   2011   Church Road, Sandhead, Stranraer DG9 9JJ
[E-mail: mel@thehavyn.wanadoo.co.uk]   01776 830548

Leswalt See Ervie Kirkcolm

Mochrum (H)
Vacant   Manse of Mochrum, Port William, Newton Stewart DG8 9QP   01988 700871

Monigaff (H) See Kirkmabreck

New Luce (H) linked with Old Luce (H)
Thomas M. McWhirter MA MSc BD   1992   1997   Glenluce, Newton Stewart DG8 0PU   01581 300319

Old Luce See New Luce

Penninghame (H)
Edward D. Lyons BD MTh   2007   The Manse, 1A Corvisel Road, Newton Stewart DG8 6LW
[E-mail: edwardlyons@hotmail.com]   01671 404425

Portpatrick See Inch
Sorbie See Kirkinner
Stoneykirk See Kirkmaiden

Stranraer: High Kirk (H)
Ian McIlroy BSS BD   1996   2009   Stoneleigh, Whitehouse Road, Stranraer DG9 0JB   01776 700616

Stranraer: Trinity See Inch

(New charge formed by the union of Stranraer: St Ninian's and Stranraer: Town Kirk)

Whithorn: St Ninian's Priory See Glasserton and Isle of Whithorn
Wigtown See Kirkcowan

Aiken, Peter W.I.	1996 2013	(Kirkmabreck with Monigaff)	Garroch, Viewhills Road, Newton Stewart DG8 6JA [E-mail: revpetevon@gmail.com]	01671 402201
Baker, Carolyn M. (Mrs) BD	1997 2008	(Ochiltree with Stair)	Clanary, 1 Maxwell Drive, Newton Stewart DG8 6EL [E-mail: cncbaker@btinternet.com]	
Binks, Mike	2007 2009	Auxiliary Minister	5 Maxwell Drive, Newton Stewart DG8 6EL [E-mail: mike@hollybank.net]	07590 507917 (Mbl)
Crawford, Joseph F. BA	1970 2006	(Bowden with Newtown)	21 South Street, Port William, Newton Stewart DG8 9SH	01988 700761
Harvey, Joyce (Mrs)	2013	Ordained Local Minister	4A Allanfield Place, Newton Stewart DG8 6BS [E-mail: joyceharvey01@btinternet.com]	01671 403693
Munro, Mary (Mrs) BA	1993 2004	(Auxiliary Minister)	14 Auchneel Crescent, Stranraer DG9 0JH	01776 702305

(10) AYR

Meets in Alloway Church Hall on the first Tuesday of every month from September to May, excluding January and April. The June meeting takes place on the third Tuesday of the month in the newly installed Moderator's church. The October meeting is held in a venue determined by the Business Committee.

Clerk:	REV. KENNETH C. ELLIOTT BD BA CertMin		68 St Quivox Road, Prestwick KA9 1JF [E-mail: ayr@cofscotland.org.uk]	01292 478788
Presbytery Office:			Prestwick South Parish Church, 50 Main Street, Prestwick KA9 1NX [E-mail: ayroffice@cofscotland.org.uk]	01292 678556

Alloway (H)
Neil A. McNaught BD MA | 1987 | 1999 | 1A Parkview, Alloway, Ayr KA7 4QG [E-mail: nandjmcnaught@btinternet.com] | 01292 441252

Annbank (H) linked with Tarbolton
Vacant | 1 Kirkport, Tarbolton, Mauchline KA5 5QJ | 01292 541236

Auchinleck (H) linked with Catrine
Stephen F. Clipston MA BD | 1982 | 2006 | 28 Mauchline Road, Auchinleck KA18 2BN [E-mail: steveclipston@btinternet.com] | 01290 424776

Ayr: Auld Kirk of Ayr (St John the Baptist) (H)
David R. Gemmell MA BD   1991   1999   58 Monument Road, Ayr KA7 2UB
[E-mail: drgemmell@hotmail.com]   0292 262580 (Tel/Fax)

Ayr: Castlehill (H)
Elizabeth A. Crumlish (Mrs) BD   1995   2008   3 Old Hillfoot Road, Ayr KA7 3LW
[E-mail: lizcrumlish@aol.com]   01292 263001

Ayr: Newton Wallacetown (H)
Vacant   9 Nursery Grove, Ayr KA7 3PH   01292 264251

Ayr: St Andrew's (H)
Morag Garrett (Mrs) BD   2011   2013   31 Bellevue Crescent, Ayr KA7 2DP
[E-mail: morag_garrett@yahoo.co.uk]   01292 261472

Ayr: St Columba (H)
Fraser R. Aitken MA BD   1978   1991   3 Upper Crofts, Alloway, Ayr KA7 4QX
[E-mail: frasercolumba@msn.com]   01292 443747

Ayr: St James' (H)
Robert McCrum BSc BD   1982   2005   1 Prestwick Road, Ayr KA8 8LD
[E-mail: robert@stjamesayr.org.uk]   01292 262420

Ayr: St Leonard's (H) linked with Dalrymple
Linda Godfrey BSc BD   2012   35 Roman Road, Ayr KA7 3SZ
[E-mail: godfreykayak@aol.com]   01292 283825

Ayr: St Quivox (H)
Rona M. Young (Mrs) BD DipEd   1991   2009   11 Springfield Avenue, Prestwick KA9 2HA
[E-mail: revronyoung@hotmail.com]   01292 478306
Douglas T. Moore (Aux)   2003   2012   9 Midton Avenue, Prestwick KA9 1PU
[E-mail: douglastmoore@hotmail.com]   01292 671352

Ballantrae (H) linked with St Colmon (Arnsheen Barrhill and Colmonell)
Stephen Ogston MPhys MSc BD   2009   The Manse, 1 The Vennel, Ballantrae, Girvan KA26 0NH
[E-mail: ogston@macfish.com]   01465 831252

Barr linked with Dailly linked with Girvan: South
Ian K. McLachlan MA BD   1999
30 Henrietta Street, Girvan KA26 9AL
[E-mail: iankmclachlan@yetiville.freeserve.co.uk]
01465 713370

Catrine See Auchinleck

Coylton linked with Drongan: The Schaw Kirk
David Whiteman BD   1998   2008
4 Hamilton Place, Coylton, Ayr KA6 6IQ
[E-mail: davesoo@sky.com]
01292 571442

Craigie linked with Symington
Glenda J. Keating (Mrs) MTh   1996   2008
16 Kerrix Road, Symington, Kilmarnock KA1 5QD
[E-mail: kirkglen@btinternet.com]
01563 830205

Crosshill (H) linked with Maybole
Brian Hendrie BD   1992   2010
The Manse, 16 McAdam Way, Maybole KA19 8FD
[E-mail: hendrie962@btinternet.com]
01655 883710

Dailly See Barr

Dalmellington linked with Patna Waterside
Fiona A. Wilson (Mrs) BD   2008   2012
4 Carsphairn Road, Dalmellington, Ayr KA6 7RE
[E-mail: weefi12b@hotmail.co.uk]
01292 551503

Dalrymple See Ayr: St Leonard's
Drongan: The Schaw Kirk See Coylton

Dundonald (H)
Robert Mayes BD   1982   1988
64 Main Street, Dundonald, Kilmarnock KA2 9HG
[E-mail: bobmayes@fsmail.net]
01563 850243

Fisherton (H) linked with Kirkoswald
Vacant
The Manse, Kirkoswald, Maybole KA19 8HZ
01655 760210

Girvan: North (Old and St Andrew's) (H)
Richard G. Moffat BD   1994   2013
38 The Avenue, Girvan KA26 9DS
[E-mail: moffatclan@me.com]
01465 713203

Girvan: South See Barr

Kirkmichael linked with Straiton: St Cuthbert's
W. Gerald Jones MA BD MTh   1984 1985   The Manse, Patna Road, Kirkmichael, Maybole KA19 7PJ   01655 750286
[E-mail: revgerald@jonesg99.freeserve.co.uk]

Kirkoswald (H) See Fisherton

Lugar linked with Old Cumnock: Old (H)
John W. Paterson BSc BD DipEd   1994   33 Barrhill Road, Cumnock KA18 1PJ   01290 420769
[E-mail: ocochurchwow@hotmail.com]

Mauchline (H) linked with Sorn
David A. Albon BA MCS   1991 2011   4 Westside Gardens, Mauchline KA5 5DJ   01290 518528
[E-mail: albon@onetel.com]

Maybole See Crosshill

Monkton and Prestwick: North (H)
David Clarkson BSc BA MTh   2010   40 Monkton Road, Prestwick KA9 1AR   01292 471379
[E-mail: revdavidclarkson@gmail.com]

Muirkirk (H) linked with Old Cumnock: Trinity
Scott M. Rae MBE BD CPS   1976 2008   46 Ayr Road, Cumnock KA18 1DW   01290 422145
[E-mail: scottrae1@btopenworld.com]

New Cumnock (H)
Helen E. Cuthbert MA MSc BD   2009   37 Castle, New Cumnock, Cumnock KA18 4AG   01290 338296
[E-mail: helencuthbert@mypostoffice.co.uk]

Ochiltree linked with Stair
William R. Johnston BD   1998 2009   10 Mauchline Road, Ochiltree, Cumnock KA18 2PZ   01290 700365

Old Cumnock: Old See Lugar
Old Cumnock: Trinity See Muirkirk
Patna Waterside See Dalmellington

Prestwick: Kingcase (H) (E-mail: office@kingcase.freeserve.co.uk)
T. David Watson BSc BD   1988   1997   15 Bellrock Avenue, Prestwick KA9 1SQ   01292 479571
                                                            [E-mail: tdavidwatson@btinternet.com]

Prestwick: St Nicholas' (H)
George R. Fiddes BD   1979   1985   3 Bellevue Road, Prestwick KA9 1NW   01292 477613
                                                            [E-mail: gfiddes@stnicholasprestwick.org.uk]

Prestwick: South (H) (E-mail: office@pwksouth.plus.com)
Kenneth C. Elliott BD BA CertMin   1989   68 St Quivox Road, Prestwick KA9 1JF   01292 478788
                                                            [E-mail: kcelliott@tiscali.co.uk]

St Colmon (Arnsheen Barrhill and Colmonell) See Ballantrae
Sorn See Mauchline
Stair See Ochiltree
Straiton: St Cuthbert's See Kirkmichael
Symington See Craigie
Tarbolton See Annbank

Troon: Old (H)
David B. Prentice-Hyers BA MDiv   2003   2013   85 Bentinck Drive, Troon KA10 6HZ   01292 313644
                                                            [E-mail: daveph@troonold.org.uk]

Troon: Portland (H)
Jamie Milliken BD   2005   2011   89 South Beach, Troon KA10 6EQ   01292 318929
                                                            [E-mail: minister@troonportlandchurch.org.uk]   07929 349045 (Mbl)

Troon: St Meddan's (H) (E-mail: st.meddan@virgin.net)
Derek Peat   2013   27 Bentinck Drive, Troon KA10 6HX   01292 311784

Birse, G. Stewart CA BD BSc   1980   2013   (Ayr: Newton Wallacetown)   43 Donald Wynd, Largs KA30 8TH   01475 329081
                                                            [E-mail: axhp44@dsl.pipex.com]
Blyth, James G.S. BSc BD   1963   1986   (Glenmuick)   40 Robsland Avenue, Ayr KA7 2RW   01292 261276
Bogle, Thomas C. BD   1983   2003   (Fisherton with Maybole: West) 38 McEwan Crescent, Mossblown, Ayr KA6 5DR   01292 521215
Boyd, Ronald M.H. BD DipTh   1995   2010   Chaplain and Teacher of RMPS:
                                                            Queen Victoria School, Dunblane   6 Victoria Green, Queen Victoria School, Dunblane FK15 0JY
Brown, Jack M. BSc BD   1977   2012   (Applegarth, Sibbaldbie and   69 Berelands Road, Prestwick KA9 1ER   01786 822288
                                                            Johnstone with Lochmaben)   [E-mail: jackm.brown@tiscali.co.uk]   01292 477151

Name			Charge / Position	Address	Tel
Cranston, George BD	1976	2001	(Rutherglen: Wardlawhill)	20 Capperview, Prestwick KA9 1BH	01292 476627
Crichton, James MA BD MTh	1969	2010	(Crosshill with Dalrymple)	4B Garden Court, Ayr KA8 0AT [E-mail: crichton.james@btinternet.com]	01292 288978
Dickie, Michael M. BSc	1955	1994	(Ayr: Castlehill)	8 Nolmire Road, Ayr KA8 9ES	01292 618512
Geddes, Alexander J. MA BD	1960	1998	(Stewarton: St Columba's)	2 Gregory Street, Mauchline KA5 6BY [E-mail: sandy270736@gmail.com]	01290 518597
Glencross, William M. LTh	1968	1999	(Bellshill: Macdonald Memorial)	1 Lochay Place, Troon KA10 7HH	01292 317097
Grant, J. Gordon MA BD PhD	1957	1997	(Edinburgh: Dean)	33 Fullarton Drive, Troon KA10 6LE	01292 311852
Guthrie, James A.	1969	2005	(Corsock and Kirkpatrick Durham with Crossmichael and Parton)	2 Barrhill Road, Pinwherry, Girvan KA26 0QE [E-mail: p.h.m.guthrie@btinternet.com]	01465 841236
Hannah, William BD MCAM MIPR	1987	2001	(Muirkirk)	8 Dovecote View, Kirkintilloch, Glasgow G66 3HY [E-mail: revbillnews@btinternet.com]	0141-776 1337
Harper, David L. BSc BD	1972	2012	(Troon: St Meddan's)	19 Calder Avenue, Troon KA10 7JT [E-mail: d.l.harper@btinternet.com]	01292 312626
Harris, Samuel McC. OStJ BA BD	1974	2010	(Rothesay: Trinity)	36 Adam Wood Court, Troon KA10 6BP	01292 319603
Helon, George G. BA BD	1984	2000	(Barr linked with Dailly)	9 Park Road, Maxwelltown, Dumfries DG2 7PW	01387 259255
Jackson, Nancy	2009	2013	Auxiliary Minister	35 Auchentrae Crescent, Ayr KA7 4BD	01292 262034
Kent, Arthur F.S.	1966	1999	(Monkton and Prestwick: North)	17 St David's Drive, Evesham, Worcs WR11 2AS [E-mail: afskent@onetel.com]	01386 421562
King, Chris (Mrs) MA BD DCS	1971	2009	Deaconess	28 Kilnford Drive, Dundonald, Kilmarnock KA2 9ET	01563 851197
Laing, Iain A. MA BD			(Bishopbriggs: Kenmuir)	9 Annfield Road, Prestwick KA9 1PP [E-mail: iandrlaing@yahoo.co.uk]	01292 471732
Lennox, Lawrie I. MA BD DipEd	1991	2006	(Cromar)	7 Carwinshoch View, Ayr KA7 4AY [E-mail: lennox127@btinternet.com]	
Lochrie, John S. BSc BD MTh PhD	1967	2008	(St Colmon)	Cosyglen, Kilkerran, Maybole KA19 8LS	01465 811262
Lynn, Robert MA BD	1984	2011	(Ayr: St Leonard's with Dalrymple)	8 Kirkbrae, Maybole KA19 7ER	(Mbl) 07771 481698
McCrorie, William	1965	1999	(Free Church Chaplain: Royal Brompton Hospital)	12 Shieling Park, Ayr KA7 2UR [E-mail: billevemcrorie@btinternet.com]	01292 288854
Macdonald, Ian U.	1960	1997	(Tarbolton)	18 Belmont Road, Ayr KA7 2PF	01292 283085
McGurk, Andrew F. BD	1983	2011	(Largs: St John's)	15 Fraser Avenue, Troon KA10 6XF [E-mail: afmcg.largs@talk21.com]	01292 676008
McNidder, Roderick H. BD	1987	1997	Chaplain: NHS Ayrshire and Arran Trust	6 Hollow Park, Alloway, Ayr KA7 4SR	01292 442554
McPhail, Andrew M. BA	1968	2002	(Ayr: Wallacetown)	25 Maybole Road, Ayr KA7 2QA	01292 282108
Matthews, John C. MA BD OBE	1992	2010	(Glasgow: Ruchill Kelvinside)	12 Arrol Drive, Ayr KA7 4AF [E-mail: mejohnmatthews@gmail.com]	01292 264382
Mealyea, Harry B. BArch BD	1984	2011	(Ayr: St Andrew's)	38 Rosamunde Pilcher Drive, Longforgan, Dundee DD2 5EF [E-mail: mealyea1@sky.com]	
Mitchell, Sheila M. (Miss) BD MTh	1995	2002	Chaplain: NHS Ayrshire and Arran Trust	Ailsa Hospital, Ayr KA6 6BQ	01292 513197
Morrison, Alistair H. BTh DipYCS	1985	2004	(Paisley: St Mark's Oldhall)	92 St Leonard's Road, Ayr KA7 2PU [E-mail: alistairmorrison@supanet.com]	01292 266021
Ness, David T. LTh	1972	2008	(Ayr: St Quivox)	17 Winston Avenue, Prestwick KA9 2EZ [E-mail: dtness@tiscali.co.uk]	
Russell, Paul R. MA BD	1984	2006	Chaplain: NHS Ayrshire and Arran Trust	23 Nursery Wynd, Ayr KA7 3NZ	01292 618020

Sanderson, Alastair M. BA LTh	1971	2007	(Craigie with Symington)	26 Main Street, Monkton, Prestwick KA9 2QL	01292 475819
				[E-mail: alel@sanderson29.fsnet.co.uk]	
Saunders, Campbell M. MA BD	1952	1989	(Ayr: St Leonard's)	27 St Vincent Crescent, Alloway, Ayr KA7 4QW	01292 441673
Simpson, Edward V. BSc BD	1972	2009	(Glasgow: Giffnock South)	8 Paddock View, Thorntoun, Crosshouse, Kilmarnock KA2 0BH	01563 522841
				[E-mail: eddie.simpson3@talktalk.net]	
Smith, Elizabeth (Mrs) BD	1996	2009	(Fauldhouse: St Andrew's)	16 McIntyre Road, Prestwick KA9 1BE	01292 471588
				[E-mail: smithrevb@btinternet.com]	
Stirling, Ian R. BSc BD	1990	2002	Chaplain: The Ayrshire Hospice	Ayrshire Hospice, 35–37 Racecourse Road, Ayr KA7 2TG	01292 269200
Symington, Alastair H. MA BD	1972	2012	(Troon: Old)	1 Cavendish Place, Troon KA10 6JG	01292 312556
				[E-mail: revdahs@btinternet.com]	
Wilkinson, Arrick D. BSc BD	2000	2013	(Fisherton with Kirkoswald)	Dunwhinny, Main Street, Ballantrae, Girvan KA26 0NB	01465 831704
				[E-mail: arrick@dunwhinny.plus.com]	
Yorke, Kenneth B.	1982	2009	(Dalmellington with Patna Waterside)	13 Annfield Terrace, Prestwick KA9 1PS	(Mbl) 07766 320525
				[E-mail: kenneth.yorke@googlemail.com]	

AYR ADDRESSES

Ayr
Auld Kirk	Kirkport (116 High Street)
Castlehill	Castlehill Road x Hillfoot Road
Newton Wallacetown	Main Street
St Andrew's	Park Circus
St Columba	Midton Road x Carrick Park
St James'	Prestwick Road x Falkland Park Road
St Leonard's	St Leonard's Road x Monument Road

Girvan
| North | Montgomerie Street |
| South | Stair Park |

Prestwick
Kingcase	Waterloo Road
Monkton and Prestwick North	Monkton Road
St Nicholas	Main Street
South	Main Street

Troon
Old	Ayr Street
Portland	St Meddan's Street
St Meddan's	St Meddan's Street

(11) IRVINE AND KILMARNOCK

The Presbytery meets ordinarily at 7:00pm in the Howard Centre, Portland Road, Kilmarnock, on the first Tuesday in September, December and March and on the fourth Tuesday in June for ordinary business and on the first Tuesday in October, November, February and May for mission. The October meeting commences with the celebration of Holy Communion.

Clerk:	MR I. STEUART DEY LLB	72 Dundonald Road, Kilmarnock KA1 1RZ	01563 521686 (Home)
			01563 526295 (Office)
		[E-mail: irvinekilmarnock@cofscotland.org.uk]	
		[E-mail: steuart.dey@btinternet.com]	
Depute Clerk:	REV. S. GRANT BARCLAY LLB DipLP BD MSc PhD	1 Thirdpart Place, Kilmarnock KA1 1UL	01563 571280
		[E-mail: minister@stkentigern.org.uk]	
Treasurer:	MR JAMES McINTOSH BA CA	15 Dundonald Road, Kilmarnock KA1 1RU	01563 523552

The Presbytery office is staffed each Tuesday, Wednesday and Thursday from 9am until 12:30pm. The office telephone number is 01563 526295.

Caldwell linked with Dunlop
David Donaldson MA BD DMin — 1969 — 2010 — 4 Dampark, Dunlop, Kilmarnock KA3 4BZ [E-mail: jd.donaldson@talktalk.net] — 01560 483268

Crosshouse (H)
T. Edward Marshall BD — 1987 — 2007 — 27 Kilmarnock Road, Crosshouse, Kilmarnock KA2 0EZ [E-mail: marshall1654@hotmail.com] — 01563 524089

Darvel (01560 322924)
Charles Lines BA — 2010 — 46 West Main Street, Darvel KA17 0AQ [E-mail: cmdlines@tiscali.co.uk] — 01560 322924

Dreghorn and Springside
Gary E. Horsburgh BA — 1976 — 1983 — 96A Townfoot, Dreghorn, Irvine KA11 4EZ [E-mail: garyhorsburgh@hotmail.co.uk] — 01294 217770

Dunlop See Caldwell

Fenwick (H)
Geoffrey Redmayne BSc BD MPhil — 2000 — 2 Kirkton Place, Fenwick, Kilmarnock KA3 6DW [E-mail: gnredmayne@googlemail.com] — 01560 600217

Galston (H) (01563 820136)
Vacant — 60 Brewland Street, Galston KA4 8DX

Hurlford (H)
James D. McCulloch BD MIOP MIP3 FSAScot 1996 — 12 Main Road, Crookedholm, Kilmarnock KA3 6JT [E-mail: mccullochmanse1@btinternet.com] — 01563 535673

Irvine: Fullarton (H) (Website: www.fullartonchurch.co.uk)
Neil Urquhart BD DipMin — 1989 — 48 Waterside, Irvine KA12 8QJ [E-mail: minister@fullartonchurch.co.uk] — 01294 279909

Irvine: Girdle Toll (H) (Website: www.girdletoll.fsbusiness.co.uk)
Vacant — 2 Littlestane Rise, Irvine KA11 2BJ — 01294 213565

Irvine: Mure (H)
Vacant   9 West Road, Irvine KA12 8RE   01294 279916

Irvine: Old (H) (01294 273503)
Robert Travers BA BD   1993   1999   22 Kirk Vennel, Irvine KA12 0DQ   01294 279265
[E-mail: robert.travers@live.co.uk]

Irvine: Relief Bourtreehill (H)
Andrew R. Black BD   1987   2003   4 Kames Court, Irvine KA11 1RT   01294 216939
[E-mail: andrewblack@tiscali.co.uk]

Irvine: St Andrew's (H) (01294 276051)
Ian W. Benzie BD   1999   2008   St Andrew's Manse, 206 Bank Street, Irvine KA12 0YD   01294 216139
[E-mail: revianb@gmail.com]

Fiona Blair (Miss) DCS   Mure Church Manse, 9 West Road, Irvine KA12 8RE   07977 235168 (Mbl)
[E-mail: fiobla12@aol.com]

Kilmarnock: Kay Park (H) (01563 541302) (Website: www.kayparkparishchurch.co.uk)
David W. Lacy BA BD DLitt DL   1976   2013   52 London Road, Kilmarnock KA3 7AJ   01563 523113 (Tel/Fax)
[E-mail: thelacys@tinyworld.co.uk]
(New charge formed by the union of Kilmarnock: Henderson and Kilmarnock: Old High Kirk)

Kilmarnock: New Laigh Kirk (H)
David S. Cameron BD   2001   2009   1 Holmes Farm Road, Kilmarnock KA1 1TP   01563 525416
[E-mail: dvdcam5@msn.com]

Barbara Urquhart (Mrs) DCS   9 Standalane, Kilmaurs, Kilmarnock KA3 2NB   01563 538289
[E-mail: barbaraurquhart1@gmail.com]

Colin Ogilvie DCS   32 Upper Bourtree Court, Rutherglen, Glasgow G73 4HT   0141-569 2725
[E-mail: colinogilvie2@gmail.com]   07837 287804 (Mbl)

Kilmarnock: Riccarton (H)
Colin A. Strong BSc BD   1989   2007   2 Jasmine Road, Kilmarnock KA1 2HD   01563 549490
[E-mail: colinastrong@aol.com]

Kilmarnock: St Andrew's and St Marnock's
James McNaughtan BD DipMin   1983   1989   35 South Gargieston Drive, Kilmarnock KA1 1TB   01563 521665
[E-mail: jmcnaughtan@gmail.com]

Kilmarnock: St John's Onthank (H)
Susan M. Anderson (Mrs) BD 1997 84 Wardneuk Drive, Kilmarnock KA3 2EX 01563 521815
[E-mail: stjohnthank@talktalk.net]

Colin Ogilvie DCS 32 Upper Bourtree Court, Rutherglen, Glasgow G73 4HT 0141-569 2725
[E-mail: colinogilvie2@gmail.com] 07837 287804 (Mbl)

Kilmarnock: St Kentigern's (Website: www.stkentigern.org.uk)
S. Grant Barclay LLB DipLP BD MSc PhD 1995 1 Thirdpart Place, Kilmarnock KA1 1UL 01563 571280
[E-mail: minister@stkentigern.org.uk]

Kilmarnock: South (01563 524705)
H. Taylor Brown BD CertMin 1997 2002 14 McLelland Drive, Kilmarnock KA1 1SE 01563 529920
[E-mail: kspc@live.co.uk]

Kilmaurs: St Maur's Glencairn (H) (Website: www.jimcorbett.freeserve.co.uk/page2.html)
John A. Urquhart BD 1993 9 Standalane, Kilmaurs, Kilmarnock KA3 2NB 01563 538289
[E-mail: john.urquhart@talktalk.net]

Newmilns: Loudoun (H)
Vacant Loudoun Manse, 116A Loudoun Road, Newmilns KA16 9HH 01560 320174

Stewarton: John Knox
Gavin A. Niven BSc MSc BD 2010 27 Avenue Street, Stewarton, Kilmarnock KA3 5AP 01560 482418
[E-mail: minister@johnknox.org.uk]

Stewarton: St Columba's (H)
George K. Lind BD MCIBS 1998 2010 1 Kirk Glebe, Stewarton, Kilmarnock KA3 5BJ 01560 485113
[E-mail: gklind@talktalk.net]

Ayrshire Mission to the Deaf
Richard C. Durno DSW CQSW 1989 2013 31 Springfield Road, Bishopbriggs, Glasgow G64 1PJ 0141-772 1052 (Voice/Text/Fax)
[E-mail: richard.durno@btinternet.com] (Voice/Text/Voicemail) (Mbl) 07748 607721

Brockie, Colin G.F. 1967 2007 (Presbytery Clerk) 36 Braehead Court, Kilmarnock KA3 7AB 01563 559960
BSc(Eng) BD SOSc [E-mail: revcol@revcol.demon.co.uk]
Campbell, George H. 1957 1992 (Stewarton: John Knox) 20 Woodlands Grove, Kilmarnock KA3 1TZ 01563 536365
[E-mail: george.campbell13@hotmail.co.uk]

Name			Charge	Address	Tel
Campbell, John A. JP FIEM	1984	1998	(Irvine: St Andrew's)	Flowerdale, Balmoral Lane, Blairgowrie PH10 7AF [E-mail: exrevjack@aol.com]	01250 872795
Cant, Thomas M. MA BD	1964	2004	(Paisley: Laigh Kirk)	3 Meikle Cutstraw Farm, Stewarton, Kilmarnock KA3 5HU [E-mail: revtmcant@aol.com]	01560 480566
Christie, Robert S. MA BD ThM	1964	2001	(Kilmarnock: West High)	24 Homeroyal House, 2 Chalmers Crescent, Edinburgh EH9 1TP	01294 312515
Davidson, James BD DipAFH	1989	2002	(Wishaw: Old)	13 Redburn Place, Irvine KA12 9BQ	01563 573994
Davidson Kelly, Thomas A. MA BD FSAScot	1975	2002	(Glasgow: Govan Old)	2 Springhill Stables, Portland Road, Kilmarnock KA1 2EJ [E-mail: dks33@btinternet.com]	
Gillon, C. Blair BD	1975	2007	(Glasgow: Ibrox)	East Muirshield Farmhouse, by Dunlop, Kilmarnock KA3 4EJ [E-mail: blair.gillon2@btinternet.com]	01560 483778
Hall, William M. BD	1972	2010	(Kilmarnock: Old High Kirk)	33 Cairns Terrace, Kilmarnock KA1 1JG [E-mail: revwillie@talktalk.net]	
Hare, Malcolm M.W. BA BD	1956	1994	(Kilmarnock: St Kentigern's)	21 Raith Road, Fenwick, Kilmarnock KA3 6DB	01560 600388
Hay, W.J.R. MA BD	1959	1995	(Buchanan with Drymen)	18 Jamieson Place, Stewarton, Kilmarnock KA3 3HX	01560 482799
Hosain Lamarti, Samuel BD MTh PhD	1979	2006	(Stewarton: John Knox)	7 Dalwhinnie Crescent, Kilmarnock KA3 1QS [E-mail: sam.hos@mypostoffice.co.uk]	01563 529632
Huggett, Judith A. (Miss) BA BD	1990	1998	Hospital Chaplain	4 Westmoor Crescent, Kilmarnock KA1 1TX [E-mail: judith.huggett@aaaht.scotnhs.uk]	01560 483191
McAllister, Anne C. (Mrs)	2013		Ordained Local Minister	39 Bowes Rigg, Stewarton, Kilmarnock KA3 5EN [E-mail: annecmcallister@btinternet.com]	
McAlpine, Richard H.M. BA FSAScot	1968	2000	(Lochgoilhead and Kilmorich)	7 Kingsford Place, Kilmarnock KA3 6FG	01563 572075
MacDonald, James M.	1964	1987	(Kilmarnock: St John's Onthank)	29 Carmel Place, Kilmaurs, Kilmarnock KA3 2QU	01563 525254
Scott, Thomas T.	1968	1989	(Kilmarnock: St Marnock's)	6 North Hamilton Place, Kilmarnock KA1 2QN [E-mail: tomtscott@btinternet.com]	01563 531415
Shaw, Catherine A.M. MA	1998	2006	(Auxiliary Minister)	40 Merrygreen Place, Stewarton, Kilmarnock KA3 5EP [E-mail: catherine.shaw@tesco.net]	01560 483352
Welsh, Alex M. MA BD	1979	2007	Hospital Chaplain	8 Greenside Avenue, Prestwick KA9 2HB [E-mail: alexandevelyn@hotmail.com]	01292 475341

IRVINE and KILMARNOCK ADDRESSES

Irvine

Dreghorn and Springside	Townfoot x Station Brae
Fullarton	Marress Road x Church Street
Girdle Toll	Bryce Knox Court
Mure	West Road
Old	Kirkgate
Relief Bourtreehill	Crofthead, Bourtreehill
St Andrew's	Caldon Road x Oaklands Ave

Kilmarnock

Ayrshire Mission to the Deaf	10 Clark Street
Kay Park	London Road
Kilmarnock South	Whatrigs Road
New Laigh Kirk	John Dickie Street
Riccarton	Old Street
St Andrew's and St Marnock's	St Marnock Street
St John's Onthank	84 Wardneuk Street

(12) ARDROSSAN

Meets at Saltcoats, New Trinity, on the first Tuesday of February, March, April, May, September, October, November and December, and on the second Tuesday of June.

| Clerk: | MR ALAN K. SAUNDERSON | 17 Union Street, Largs KA30 8DG
[E-mail: ak.dj.saunderson@hotmail.co.uk] | 01475 687217
07866 034355 (Mbl) |

Ardrossan: Barony St John's (H) (01294 465009) (E-mail: www.baronystjohns.co.uk)

Dorothy A. Granger BA BD	2009	10 Seafield Drive, Ardrossan KA22 8NU [E-mail: dorothygranger61@gmail.com]	01294 463571 07918 077877 (Mbl)

Ardrossan: Park (01294 463711)

Tanya Webster BCom DipAcc BD	2011	35 Ardneil Court, Ardrossan KA22 7NQ [E-mail: parkchurchminister@mail.com]	01294 538903
Mandy R. Hickman RGN (Ordained Local Minister)	2013	Lagnaleon, 4 Wilson Street, Largs KA30 9AQ [E-mail: mandyrhickman@gmail.com]	01475 675347

Beith (H) (01505 502686)

Roderick I.T. MacDonald BD CertMin	1992	2005	2 Glebe Court, Beith KA15 1ET [E-mail: rodanmmac@btinternet.com]	01505 503858

Brodick linked with Corrie linked with Lochranza and Pirnmill linked with Shiskine (H)

Angus Adamson BD	2006	4 Manse Crescent, Brodick, Isle of Arran KA27 8AS [E-mail: adamsonangus@btinternet.com]	01770 302334

Corrie See Brodick

Cumbrae

Vacant		Marine Parade, Millport, Isle of Cumbrae KA28 0ED	01475 530416

Dalry: St Margaret's

James R. Teasdale BA BD	2009	33 Templand Crescent, Dalry KA24 5EZ [E-mail: jamesrteasdale@hotmail.com]	01294 832747

Dalry: Trinity (H)

Martin Thomson BSc DipEd BD	1988	2004	Trinity Manse, West Kilbride Road, Dalry KA24 5DX [E-mail: martin.thomson40@btinternet.com]	01294 832363

Fairlie (H)
Vacant

14 Fairlieburne Gardens, Fairlie, Largs KA29 0ER

01475 568342

Kilbirnie: Auld Kirk (H)
Vacant

49 Holmhead, Kilbirnie KA25 6BS

01505 682348

Kilbirnie: St Columba's (H) (01505 685239)
Fiona C. Ross (Miss) BD DipMin   1996

Manse of St Columba's, Dipple Road, Kilbirnie KA25 7JU
[E-mail: fionaross@calvin78.freeserve.co.uk]

2004

01505 683342

Kilmory linked with Lamlash
Vacant

Lamlash, Isle of Arran KA27 8LE

01770 600318

Kilwinning: Mansefield Trinity (E) (01294 550746)
Alan H. Ward MA BD (Interim Minister)   1978

47 Meadowfoot Road, West Kilbride KA23 9BU
[E-mail: alanhward@hotmail.co.uk]

2013

01294 822224
07709 906130 (Mbl)

Kilwinning: Old
Jeanette Whitecross BD   2002

54 Dalry Road, Kilwinning KA13 7HE
[E-mail: jwx@hotmail.co.uk]

2011

01294 552606

Lamlash See Kilmory

Largs: Clark Memorial (H) (01475 675186)
Stephen J. Smith BSc BD   1993

31 Douglas Street, Largs KA30 8PT
[E-mail: stephenrevsteve@aol.com]

1998

01475 672370

Largs: St Columba's (01475 686212)
Vacant

17 Beachway, Largs KA30 8QH

Largs: St John's (H) (01475 674468)
Vacant

1 Newhaven Grove, Largs KA30 8NS

Lochranza and Pirnmill See Brodick

Saltcoats: New Trinity (H) (01294 472001)
Vacant

1 Montgomerie Crescent, Saltcoats KA21 5BX

01294 461143

Saltcoats: North (01294 464679)
Alexander B. Noble MA BD ThM   1982 2003   25 Longfield Avenue, Saltcoats KA21 6DR   01294 604923

Saltcoats: St Cuthbert's (H)
Vacant   10 Kennedy Road, Saltcoats KA21 5SF

Shiskine (H) See Brodick

Stevenston: Ardeer linked with Stevenston: Livingstone (H)
Vacant   32 High Road, Stevenston KA20 3DR   01294 464180

Stevenston: High (H) (Website: www.highkirk.com)
M. Scott Cameron MA BD   2002   Glencairn Street, Stevenston KA20 3DL   01294 463356
[E-mail: revhighkirk@btinternet.com]

Stevenston: Livingstone (H) See Stevenston: Ardeer

West Kilbride (H) (Website: www.westkilbrideparishchurch.org.uk)
James J. McNay MA BD   2008   The Manse, Goldenberry Avenue, West Kilbride KA23 9LJ   01294 823186
[E-mail: minister@westkilbrideparishchurch.org.uk]

Whiting Bay and Kildonan
Elizabeth R.L. Watson (Miss) BA BD   1981 1982   The Manse, Whiting Bay, Brodick, Isle of Arran KA27 8RE   01770 700289
[E-mail: revewatson@btinternet.com]

Cruickshank, Norman BA BD   1983 2006   (West Kilbride: Overton)   24D Faulds Wynd, Seamill, West Kilbride KA23 9FA   01294 822239
Currie, Ian S. MBE BD   1975 2010   (The United Church of Bute)   15 Northfield Park, Largs KA30 8NZ   (Mbl) 07764 254300
[E-mail: ianscurrie@tiscali.co.uk]

Dailly, John R. BD DipPS   1979 2007   (Chaplain: Army)   2 Curtis Close, Pound Street, Warminster, Wiltshire BA12 9NN
Drysdale, James H. LTh   1987 2006   (Blackbraes and Shieldhill)   10 John Clark Street, Largs KA30 9AH   01475 674870
Falconer, Alan D. MA BD DLitt   1972 2011   (Aberdeen: St Machar's Cathedral)   18 North Crescent Road, Ardrossan KA22 8NA   01294 472991
[E-mail: alanfalconer@gmx.com]

Forsyth, D. Stuart MA   1948 1992   (Belhelvie)   39 Homemount House, Gogoside Road, Largs KA30 9LS   01475 673379
Gordon, David C.   1953 1988   (Gigha and Cara)   South Beach House, South Crescent Road, Ardrossan KA22 8DU   01294 834092
Harbison, David J.H.   1958 1998   (Beith: High with Beith: Trinity)   42 Mill Park, Dalry KA24 5BB
[E-mail: djh@harbi.fsnet.co.uk]

Hebenton, David J. MA BD   1958 2002   (Ayton and Burnmouth with Grantshouse   22B Faulds Wynd, Seamill, West Kilbride KA23 9FA   01294 829228
and Houndwood and Reston)

Name	Dates	Position	Address	Phone
Howie, Marion L.K. (Mrs) MA ACRS	1992	Auxiliary Minister	51 High Road, Stevenston KA20 3DY [E-mail: marion@howiefamily.net]	01294 466571
Leask, Rebecca M. (Mrs)	1977 1985	(Callander: St Bride's)	20 Strathclyde House, 31 Shore Road, Skelmorlie PA17 5AN [E-mail: mleask@hotmail.com]	01475 520765
McCallum, Alexander D. BD	1987 2005	(Saltcoats: New Trinity)	59 Woodcroft Avenue, Largs KA30 9EW [E-mail: sandyandjose@madasafish.com]	01475 670133
McCance, Andrew M. BSc	1986 1995	(Coatbridge: Middle)	6A Douglas Place, Largs KA30 8PU	01475 673303
Mackay, Marjory H. (Mrs) BD DipEd CCE	1998 2008	(Cumbrae)	4 Golf Road, Millport, Isle of Cumbrae KA28 0HB [E-mail: mhmackay@tiscali.co.uk]	01475 530388
MacLeod, Ian L.Th BA MTh PhD	1969 2006	(Brodick with Corrie)	Cromla Cottage, Corrie, Isle of Arran KA27 8JB [E-mail: i.macleod829@btinternet.com]	01770 810237
Mitchell, D. Ross BA BD	1972 2007	(West Kilbride: St Andrew's)	11 Dunbar Gardens, Saltcoats KA21 6GJ [E-mail: ross.mitchell@virgin.net]	
Paterson, John H. BD	1977 2000	(Kirkintilloch: St David's Memorial Park)	Creag Bhan, Golf Course Road, Whiting Bay, Isle of Arran KA27 8QT	01770 700569
Roy, Iain M. MA BD	1960 1997	(Stevenston: Livingstone)	2 The Fieldings, Dunlop, Kilmarnock KA3 4AU	01560 483072
Taylor, Andrew S. BTh FPhS	1959 1992	(Greenock Union)	9 Raillies Avenue, Largs KA30 8QY [E-mail: andrew.taylor_123@btinternet.com]	01475 674709
Thomson, Margaret (Mrs)	1988 1993	(Saltcoats: Erskine)	7 Glen Farg, St Leonards, East Kilbride, Glasgow G74 2JW	

(13) LANARK

Meets on the first Tuesday of February, March, May, September, October, November and December, and on the third Tuesday of June.

Clerk:	**REV. MRS HELEN E. JAMIESON BD DipEd**	120 Clyde Street, Carluke ML8 5BG [E-mail: lanark@cofscotland.org.uk]	01555 771218
Depute Clerk:	**REV. BRYAN KERR BA BD**	Greyfriars Manse, 3 Bellefield Way, Lanark ML11 7NW	01555 663363

Biggar (H) linked with Black Mount
Mike Fucella BD MTh   1997   2013   'Candlemas', 6C Leafield Road, Biggar ML12 6AY   01899 229291
[E-mail: mike@fishwrapper.net]

Black Mount See Biggar

Cairngryffe linked with Libberton and Quothquan (H) linked with Symington (The Tinto Parishes)
Vacant

Carluke: Kirkton (H) (Church office: 01555 750778) (Website: www.kirktonchurch.co.uk)
Iain D. Cunningham MA BD   1979   1987   9 Station Road, Carluke ML8 5AA   01555 771262
[E-mail: iaindc@btconnect.com]

Carluke: St Andrew's (H)
Helen E. Jamieson (Mrs) BD DipEd 1989 120 Clyde Street, Carluke ML8 5BG 01555 771218
[E-mail: helenejamieson@o2.co.uk]

Carluke: St John's (H) (Website: www.carluke-stjohns.org.uk)
Vacant 18 Old Bridgend, Carluke ML8 4HN

Carnwath (H)
Vacant

Carstairs and Carstairs Junction, The United Church of
Vacant 11 Range View, Kames, Carstairs, Lanark ML11 8TF

Coalburn (H) linked with Lesmahagow: Old (H) (Church office: 01555 892425)
Vacant 9 Elm Bank, Lesmahagow, Lanark ML11 0EA

Crossford (H) linked with Kirkfieldbank
Steven Reid BAcc CA BD 1989 1997 74 Lanark Road, Crossford, Carluke ML8 5RE 01555 860415
[E-mail: steven.reid@sky.com]

Forth: St Paul's (H) (Website: www.forthstpauls.com)
Sarah L. Ross (Mrs) BD MTh PGDip 2004 22 Lea Rig, Forth, Lanark ML11 8EA 01555 812832
[E-mail: minister@forthstpauls.com]

Kirkfieldbank See Crossford

Kirkmuirhill (H)
Ian M. Watson LLB DipLP BD 1998 2003 The Manse, 2 Lanark Road, Kirkmuirhill, Lanark ML11 9RB 01555 892409
[E-mail: ian.watson21@btopenworld.com]

Lanark: Greyfriars (Church office: 01555 661510) (Website: www.lanarkgreyfriars.com)
Bryan Kerr BA BD 2002 2007 Greyfriars Manse, 3 Bellefield Way, Lanark ML11 7NW 01555 663363
[E-mail: bryan@lanarkgreyfriars.com]

Lanark: St Nicholas' (H)
Alison A. Meikle (Mrs) BD 1999 2002 2 Kaimhill Court, Lanark ML11 9HU 01555 662600
[E-mail: alison-meikle@sky.com]

Law

| Una B. Stewart (Ms) BD DipEd | 1995 | 2009 | 3 Shawgill Court, Law, Carluke ML8 5SJ | 01698 373180 |

[E-mail: rev.ubs@virgin.net]

Lesmahagow: Abbeygreen

| David S. Carmichael | | 1982 | Abbeygreen Manse, Lesmahagow, Lanark ML11 0DB | 01555 893384 |

[E-mail: david.carmichael@abbeygreen.org.uk]

Lesmahagow: Old (H) See Coalburn
Libberton and Quothquan (H) See Cairngryffe
Lowther See Glencaple
Symington See Cairngryffe

The Douglas Valley Church (Church office: 01555 850000) (Website: www.douglasvalleychurch.org)

| Robert Cleland | 1997 | 2009 | The Manse, Douglas, Lanark ML11 0RB | 01555 851213 |

[E-mail: cleland810@btinternet.com]

Upper Clyde

Vacant   66 Carlisle Road, Crawford, Biggar ML12 6TW

(New charge formed by the union of Glencaple and Lowther)

| Clelland, Elizabeth (Mrs) BD | 2002 | 2012 | Assistant Chaplain: Braehead House | Braehead House Christian Healing Centre, Braidwood Road, Crossford, Carluke ML8 5NQ | 01555 860716 |

[E-mail: liz_clelland@yahoo.co.uk]

Cowell, Susan G. (Miss) BA BD	1986	1998	(Budapest)	3 Gavel Lane, Regency Gardens, Lanark ML11 9FB	01555 665509
Craig, William BA LTh	1974	1997	(Cambusbarron: The Bruce Memorial)	31 Heathfield Drive, Blackwood, Lanark ML11 9SR	01555 893710
Easton, David J.C. MA BD	1965	2005	(Glasgow: Burnside-Blairbeth)	Rowanbank, Cormiston Road, Quothquan, Biggar ML12 6ND	01899 308459

[E-mail: deaston@btinternet.com]

| Findlay, Henry J.W. MA BD | 1965 | 2005 | (Wishaw: St Mark's) | 2 Alba Gardens, Carluke ML8 5US | 01555 759995 |
| Fox, George H. | 1959 | 1977 | (Coalsnaughton) | Braehead House Christian Healing Centre, Braidwood Road, Crossford, Carluke ML8 5NQ | 01555 860716 |

| Gauld, Beverly G.D.D. MA BD | 1972 | 2009 | (Carnwath) | 7 Rowan View, Lanark ML11 9FQ | 01555 665765 |
| Gibson, Alan W. BA BD | 2001 | 2012 | Head of Stewardship | c/o 121 George Street, Edinburgh EH2 4YN | 0131-225 5722 |

[E-mail: agibson@cofscotland.org.uk]

| Houston, Graham R. BSc BD MTh PhD | 1978 | 2011 | (Cairngryffe with Symington) | 3 Alder Lane, Beechtrees, Lanark ML11 9FT | 01555 678004 |

[E-mail: gandih6156@btinternet.com]

| Lyall, Ann (Miss) DCS | 1980 | 2011 | The Biggar Area | 17 Mercat Loan, Biggar ML12 6DG | 01899 229443 |

[E-mail: ann.lyall@btinternet.com]

| McLarty, R. Russell MA BD | 1985 | 2011 | The Chance to Thrive – Project Co-ordinator | 9 Sanderson's Wynd, Tranent EH33 1DA | 01875 614496 |

Name				Tel
Paciti, Stephen A. MA	1963 2003	(Black Mount with Culter with Libberton and Quothquan)	157 Nithsdale Road, Glasgow G41 5RD	0141-423 5972
Seath, Thomas J.G.	1980 1992	(Motherwell: Manse Road)	Flat 11, Wallace Court, South Vennel, Lanark ML11 7LL	01555 665399
Turnbull, John LTh	1994 2006	(Balfron with Fintry)	4 Rathmor Road, Biggar ML12 6QG	01899 221502
Young, David A.	1972 2003	(Kirkmuirhill)	15 Mannachie Rise, Forres IV36 2US [E-mail: youngdavid@aol.com]	01309 672849

(14) GREENOCK AND PAISLEY

Meets on the second Tuesday of September, October, November, December, February, March, April and May, and on the third Tuesday of June.

Clerk:	REV. PETER McENHILL BD PhD	
Presbytery Office:	The Presbytery Office as detailed below [E-mail: greenockpaisley@cofscotland.org.uk] 'Homelea', Faith Avenue, Quarrier's Village, Bridge of Weir PA11 3SX	01505 615033 (Tel) 01505 615088 (Fax)

Barrhead: Bourock (H) (0141-881 9813)
Vacant — 14 Maxton Avenue, Barrhead, Glasgow G78 1DY — 0141-881 1462

Barrhead: St Andrew's (H) (0141-881 8442)
James S.A. Cowan BD DipMin — 1986 1998 — 10 Arthurlie Avenue, Barrhead, Glasgow G78 2BU [E-mail: jim_cowan@ntlworld.com] — 0141-881 3457
(New charge formed by the union of Barrhead: Arthurlie and Barrhead: South and Levern)

Bishopton (H) (Office: 01505 862583)
Daniel Manastireanu BA MTh — 2010 — The Manse, Newton Road, Bishopton PA7 5JP [E-mail: daniel@bishoptonkirk.org.uk] — 01505 862161

Bridge of Weir: Freeland (H) (01505 612610)
Kenneth N. Gray BA BD — 1988 — 15 Lawmarnock Crescent, Bridge of Weir PA11 3AS [E-mail: aandkgray@btinternet.com] — 01505 690918

Bridge of Weir: St Machar's Ranfurly (01505 614364)
Suzanne Dunleavy (Miss) BD DipEd — 1990 1992 — 9 Glen Brae, Bridge of Weir PA11 3BH [E-mail: suzanne.dunleavy@btinternet.com] — 01505 612975

Elderslie Kirk (H) (01505 323348)
Robin N. Allison BD DipMin   1994   2005   282 Main Road, Elderslie, Johnstone PA5 9EF
[E-mail: revrobin@sky.com]   01505 321767

Erskine (0141-812 4620)
Jonathan Fleming MA BD   2012   The Manse, 7 Leven Place, Linburn, Erskine PA8 6AS
[E-mail: jonathancfleming@me.com]   0141-570 8103

Gourock: Old Gourock and Ashton (H)
Vacant   331 Eldon Street, Gourock PA16 7QN
[E-mail: minister@ogachurch.org.uk]   01475 635578

Gourock: St John's (H)
Glenn A. Chestnutt BA DASE MDiv ThM PhD   2009   6 Barrhill Road, Gourock PA19 1JX
[E-mail: glenn.chestnutt@gmail.com]   01475 632143

Greenock: East End (New Charge Development)
David J. McCarthy BSc BD   1985   2003   29 Denholm Street, Greenock PA16 8RH
[E-mail: greenockeastendparish@googlemail.com]   01475 722111

Greenock: Lyle Kirk
C. Ian W. Johnson MA BD   1997   39 Fox Street, Greenock PA16 8PD
[E-mail: ian.ciw.johnson@btinternet.com]   01475 888277

Greenock: Mount Kirk
Francis E. Murphy BEng DipDSE BD   2006   76 Finnart Street, Greenock PA16 8HJ
[E-mail: francis_e_murphy@hotmail.com]   01475 722338

Greenock: St Margaret's (01475 781953)
Vacant   105 Finnart Street, Greenock PA16 8HN   01475 786590
Eileen Manson (Mrs) DipCE (Aux: Locum)   1994   2010   1 Cambridge Avenue, Gourock PA19 1XT   01475 632401
[E-mail: rev.eileen@ntlworld.com]

Greenock: St Ninian's
Allan G. McIntyre BD   1985   5 Auchmead Road, Greenock PA16 0PY
[E-mail: agmcintyre@lineone.net]   01475 631878

Greenock: Wellpark Mid Kirk
Alan K. Sorensen BD MTh DipMin FSAScot — 1983 — 2000 — 101 Brisbane Street, Greenock PA16 8PA [E-mail: alan.sorensen@ntlworld.com] — 01475 721741

Greenock: Westburn
Vacant — 50 Ardgowan Street, Greenock PA16 8EP — 01475 721048

Houston and Killellan (H)
Donald Campbell BD — 1998 — 2007 — The Manse of Houston, Main Street, Houston, Johnstone PA6 7EL [E-mail: houstonmanse@btinternet.com] — 01505 612569

Howwood
Vacant — The Manse, Beith Road, Howwood, Johnstone PA9 1AS — 01505 703678

Inchinnan (H) (0141-812 1263)
Alison McBrier MA BD — 2011 — The Manse, Inchinnan, Renfrew PA4 9PH — 0141-812 1688

Inverkip (H) linked with Skelmorlie and Wemyss Bay
Vacant — The Manse, Langhouse Road, Inverkip, Greenock PA16 0BJ — 01475 521207

Johnstone: High (H) (01505 336303)
Ann C. McCool (Mrs) BD DSD IPA ALCM — 1989 — 2001 — 76 North Road, Johnstone PA5 8NF [E-mail: ann.mccool@ntlworld.com] — 01505 320006

Johnstone: St Andrew's Trinity
Vacant — 1 Swallow Brae, Inverkip, Greenock PA16 0LF — 01475 529312

Johnstone: St Paul's (H) (01505 321632)
Alistair N. Shaw MA BD MTh — 1982 — 2003 — 9 Stanley Drive, Brookfield, Johnstone PA5 8UF [E-mail: ans2006@talktalk.net] — 01505 320060

Kilbarchan: East
Vacant — East Manse, Church Street, Kilbarchan, Johnstone PA10 2JQ — 01505 702621

Kilbarchan: West
Arthur Sherratt BD — 1994 — West Manse, Shuttle Street, Kilbarchan, Johnstone PA10 2JR [E-mail: arthur.sherratt@ntlworld.com] — 01505 342930

Kilmacolm: Old (H) (01505 873911)				
Peter McEnhill BD PhD	1992	2007	The Old Kirk Manse, Glencairn Road, Kilmacolm PA13 4NJ [E-mail: petermcenhill@btinternet.com]	01505 873174
Kilmacolm: St Columba (H)				
R. Douglas Cranston MA BD	1986	1992	6 Churchill Road, Kilmacolm PA13 4LH [E-mail: robert.cranston@sccmanse.plus.com]	01505 873271
Langbank (T) linked with Port Glasgow: St Andrew's (H)				
Andrew T. MacLean BA BD	1980	1993	St Andrew's Manse, Barr's Brae, Port Glasgow PA14 5QA [E-mail: standrews.pg@me.com]	01475 741486
Linwood (H) (01505 328802)				
Eileen M. Ross (Mrs) BD MTh	2005	2008	1 John Neilson Avenue, Paisley PA1 2SX [E-mail: eileenmross@btinternet.com]	0141-887 2801
Lochwinnoch (T)				
Vacant			1 Station Rise, Lochwinnoch PA12 4NA	01505 843484
Neilston (0141-881 9445)				
Fiona E. Maxwell BA BD	2004	2013	The Manse, Neilston Road, Neilston, Glasgow G78 3NP [Email: fiona.maxwell@aol.co.uk]	0141-258 0805
Paisley: Abbey (H) (Tel: 0141-889 7654; Fax: 0141-887 3929)				
Alan D. Birss MA BD	1979	1988	15 Main Road, Castlehead, Paisley PA2 6AJ [E-mail: alan.birss@paisleyabbey.com]	0141-889 3587
Paisley: Glenburn (0141-884 2602)				
Vacant			10 Hawick Avenue, Paisley PA2 9LD	0141-884 4903
Paisley: Lylesland (H) (0141-561 7139)				
Alistair W. Cook BSc CA BD	2008		36 Potterhill Avenue, Paisley PA2 8BA [E-mail: alistaircook@ntlworld.com]	0141-561 9277
Greta Gray (Miss) DCS			67 Crags Avenue, Paisley PA3 6SG [E-mail: greta.gray@ntlworld.com]	0141-884 6178

Paisley: Martyrs' Sandyford (0141-889 6603)
Kenneth A.L. Mayne BA MSc CertEd   1976   2007   27 Acer Crescent, Paisley PA2 9LR   0141-884 7400

Paisley: Oakshaw Trinity (H) (Tel: 0141-889 4010; Fax: 0141-848 5139)
Gordon B. Armstrong BD FIAB BRC   2010   2012   The Manse, 16 Golf Drive, Paisley PA1 3LA   0141-887 0884
[E-mail: revgordon@ntlworld.com]

Paisley: St Columba Foxbar (H) (01505 812377)
Drausio Goncalves   2008   13 Corsebar Drive, Paisley PA2 9QD   0141-848 5826
[E-mail: drausiopg@gmail.com]

Paisley: St James' (0141-889 2422)
Ivan C. Warwick TD MA BD   1980   2012   38 Woodland Avenue, Paisley PA2 8BH   0141-884 7978
[E-mail: L70rev@btinternet.com]   07787 535083 (Mbl)

Paisley: St Luke's (H)
D. Ritchie M. Gillon BD DipMin   1994   31 Southfield Avenue, Paisley PA2 8BX   0141-884 6215
[E-mail: revgillon@hotmail.com]

Paisley: St Mark's Oldhall (H) (0141-882 2755)
Robert G. McFarlane BD   2001   2005   36 Newtyle Road, Paisley PA1 3JX   0141-889 4279
[E-mail: robertmcf@hotmail.com]

Paisley: St Ninian's Ferguslie (E) (0141-887 9436) (New Charge Development)
Vacant   10 Stanely Drive, Paisley PA2 6HE   0141-884 4177

Paisley: Sherwood Greenlaw (H) (0141-889 7060)
Vacant   5 Greenlaw Drive, Paisley PA1 3RX   0141-889 3057

Paisley: Stow Brae Kirk
Robert Craig BA BD DipRS   2008   2012   25 John Neilson Avenue, Paisley PA1 2SX   0141-328 6014
[E-mail: stowbraekirk@gmail.com]

Paisley: Wallneuk North (0141-889 9265)
Peter G. Gill MA BA   2008   5 Glenville Crescent, Paisley PA2 8TW   0141-884 4429
[E-mail: petergill18@hotmail.com]

Port Glasgow: Hamilton Bardrainney
Vacant
80 Bardrainney Avenue, Port Glasgow PA14 6HD
01475 701213

Port Glasgow: St Andrew's (H) See Langbank

Port Glasgow: St Martin's

Archibald Speirs BD	1995	2006	Clunebraehead, Clune Brae, Port Glasgow PA14 5SL [E-mail: archiespeirs1@aol.com]	01475 704115

Renfrew: North (0141-885 2154)

E. Lorna Hood (Mrs) MA BD	1978	1979	1 Alexandra Drive, Renfrew PA4 8UB [E-mail: revlornahood@gmail.com]	0141-886 2074
John C. Christie BSc BD MSB CBiol (Interim Moderator and Locum)	1990	2013	10 Cumberland Avenue, Helensburgh G84 8QG [E-mail: rev.jcc@btinternet.com]	01436 674078 07711 336392 (Mbl)

Renfrew: Trinity (H) (0141-885 2129)

Stuart C. Steell BD CertMin	1992	25 Paisley Road, Renfrew PA4 8JH [E-mail: ssren@tiscali.co.uk]	0141-886 2131

Skelmorlie and Wemyss Bay See Inverkip

Name				Address	Phone
Alexander, Douglas N. MA BD	1961	1999	(Bishopton)	West Morningside, Main Road, Langbank, Port Glasgow PA4 6XP	01475 540249
Armstrong, William R. BD	1979	2008	(Skelmorlie and Wemyss Bay)	25A The Lane, Skelmorlie PA17 5AR [E-mail: warmstrong17@tiscali.co.uk]	01475 520891
Bell, Ian W. LTh	1990	2011	(Erskine)	40 Brueacre Drive, Wemyss Bay PA18 6HA [E-mail: rviwbepc@ntlworld.com]	01475 529312
Bell, May (Mrs) LTh	1998	2012	(Johnstone: St Andrew's Trinity)	40 Brueacre Drive, Wemyss Bay PA18 6HA [E-mail: may.bell@ntlbusiness.com]	01475 529312
Black, Janette M.K. (Mrs) BD	1993	2006	(Assistant: Paisley: Oakshaw Trinity)	5 Craigiehall Avenue, Erskine PA8 7DB	0141-812 0794
Breingan, Mhairi		2011	Ordained Local Minister	6 Park Road, Inchinnan, Renfrew PA4 4QJ	0141-812 1425
Cameron, Margaret (Miss) DCS			(Deaconess)	2 Rowans Gate, Paisley PA2 6RD	0141-840 2479
Campbell, John MA BA BSc	1973	2009	(Caldwell)	96 Boghead Road, Lenzie, Glasgow G66 4EN [E-mail: johncampbell.lenzie@gmail.com]	0141-776 0874
Chestnut, Alexander MBE BA	1948	1987	(Greenock: St Mark's Greenbank)	5 Douglas Street, Largs KA30 8PS	01475 674168
Copland, Agnes M. (Mrs) MBE DCS			(Deacon)	3 Craigmuschat Road, Gourock PA19 1SE	01475 631870
Coull, Morris C. BD	1974	2011	(Skelmorlie and Wemyss Bay)	Flat 0/1 Toward, The Lighthouses, Greenock Road, Wemyss Bay PA18 6DT	01475 522677
Cubie, John P. MA BD	1961	1999	(Caldwell)	36 Winram Place, St Andrews KY16 8XH	01334 474708

Easton, Lilly C. (Mrs)	(Renfrew: Old)	1999 2012	Flat 0/2, 90 Beith Street, Glasgow G11 6DG [E-mail: revlillyeaston@hotmail.co.uk]	0141-586 7628
Erskine, Morag (Miss) DCS	(Deacon)	1979	111 Mains Drive, Park Mains, Erskine PA8 7JJ [E-mail: morag.erskine@ntlworld.com]	0141-812 6096
Forrest, Kenneth P. CBE BSc PhD	Auxiliary Minister	2006	5 Carruth Road, Bridge of Weir PA11 3HQ [E-mail: kenpforrest@hotmail.com]	01505 612651
Fraser, Ian C. BA BD	(Glasgow: St Luke's and St Andrew's)	1983 2008	62 Kingston Avenue, Neilston, Glasgow G78 3JG [E-mail: ianandlindafraser@gmail.com]	0141-563 6794
Gardner, Frank J. MA	(Gourock: Old Gourock and Ashton)	1966 2007	1 Levanne Place, Gourock PA16 1AX [E-mail: fjg@clyde-mail.co.uk]	(Tel/Fax) 01475 630187
Hamilton, W. Douglas BD	(Greenock: Westburn)	1975 2009	5 Corse Road, Penilee, Glasgow G52 4DG [E-mail: douglas.hamilton44@hotmail.co.uk]	0141-810 1194
Hetherington, Robert M. MA BD	(Barrhead South and Levern)	1966 2002	31 Brodie Park Crescent, Paisley PA2 6EU [E-mail: r-hetherington@sky.com]	0141-848 6560
Irvine, Euphemia H.C. (Mrs) BD	(Milton of Campsie)	1972 1988	32 Baird Drive, Bargarran, Erskine PA8 6BB	0141-812 2777
Johnston, Mary (Miss) DCS	(Deaconess)		19 Lounsdale Drive, Paisley PA2 9ED	0141-849 1615
Kay, David BA BD MTh	(Paisley: Sandyford: Thread Street)	1974 2008	36 Donaldswood Park, Paisley PA2 8RS [E-mail: david.kay500@o2.co.uk]	0141-884 2080
Leitch, Maureen (Mrs) BA BD	(Barrhead: Bourock)	1995 2011	Rockfield, 92 Paisley Road, Barrhead G78 1NW [E-mail: maureen.leitch@ntlworld.com]	0141-580 2927
Lodge, Bernard P. BD	(Glasgow: Govanhill Trinity)	1967 2004	6 Darluith Park, Brookfield, Johnstone PA5 8DD [E-mail: bernardlodge@yahoo.co.uk]	01505 320378
McBain, Margaret (Miss) DCS		1966 2002	33 Quarry Road, Paisley PA2 7RD	0141-884 2920
MacColl, James C. BSc BD	(Johnstone: St Andrew's Trinity)	1989 2001	Greenways, Winton, Kirkby Stephen, Cumbria CA17 4HL	01768 372290
MacColl, John BD DipMin	Teacher: Religious Education		1 Birch Avenue, Johnstone PA5 0DD	01505 326506
McCully, M. Isobel (Miss) DCS	(Deacon)		10 Broadstone Avenue, Port Glasgow PA14 5BB [E-mail: mi.mccully@btinternet.com]	01475 742240
Macdonald, Alexander MA BD	(Neilston)	1966 2006	35 Lochore Avenue, Paisley PA3 4BY [E-mail: alexmacdonald42@aol.com]	0141-889 0066
McDonald, Alexander BA CMIWSC DUniv	(Department of Ministry)	1968 2000	36 Alloway Grove, Paisley PA2 7DQ [E-mail: amcdonald1@ntlworld.com]	0141-560 1937
Macfarlane, Thomas G. BSc PhD BD	(Glasgow: South Shawlands)	1956 1992	12 Elphinstone Court, Lochwinnoch Road, Kilmacolm PA13 4DW	01505 874962
McKaig, William G. BD	(Langbank)	1979 2011	54 Brisbane Street, Greenock PA16 8NT [E-mail: bill.mckaig@virgin.net]	
MacLaine, Marilyn (Mrs) LTh	(Inchinnan)	1995 2009	37 Bankton Brae, Livingston EH54 9LA	01506 400619
Nicol, Joyce M. (Mrs) BA DCS	(Deacon)		93 Brisbane Street, Greenock PA16 8NY [E-mail: joycenicol@hotmail.co.uk]	01475 723235
Page, John R. BD DipMin	(Gibraltar)	1988 2003	1 The Walton Building, North Street, Mere, Warminster, Wiltshire BA12 6HU	
Palmer, S.W. BD	(Kilbarchan: East)	1980 1991	4 Bream Place, Houston PA6 7ZJ	01505 615280

Name			Charge	Address	Tel
Prentice, George BA BTh	1964	1997	(Paisley: Martyrs')	46 Victoria Gardens, Corsebar Road, Paisley PA2 9AQ [E-mail: g.prentice04@talktalk.net]	0141-842 1585
Simpson, James H. BD LLB	1964	2004	(Greenock: Mount Kirk)	82 Harbourside, Inverkip, Greenock PA16 0BF [E-mail: jameshsimpson@yahoo.co.uk]	01475 520582
Smillie, Andrew M. LTh	1990	2005	(Langbank)	7 Turnbull Avenue, West Freeland, Erskine PA8 7DL [E-mail: andrewsmillie@talktalk.net]	0141-812 7030
Stevenson, Stuart	2011		Ordained Local Minister	143 Springfield Park, Johnstone PA5 8JT	0141-886 2131
Stewart, David MA DipEd BD MTh	1977	2013	(Howwood)	72 Glen Avenue, Largs KA30 8QQ [E-mail: revdavidst@aol.com]	
Stone, W. Vernon MA BD	1949	1985	(Langbank)	36 Woodrow Court, Port Glasgow Road, Kilmacolm PA13 4QA [E-mail: stone@kilmacolm.fsnet.co.uk]	01505 872644
Whyte, John H. MA	1946	1986	(Gourock: Ashton)	6 Castle Levan Manor, Cloch Road, Gourock PA19 1AY	01475 636788
Whyte, Margaret A. (Mrs) BA BD	1988	2011	(Glasgow: Pollokshaws)	4 Springhill Road, Barrhead G78 2AA [E-mail: tdpwhyte@tiscali.co.uk]	0141-881 4942
Wishart, William DCS			(Deacon)	10 Stanely Drive, Paisley PA2 6HE	0141-884 4177 (Mbl) 07846 555654
Young, David T. BA BD	2007	2012	Chaplain: University of Strathclyde	51 Marchfield Avenue, Paisley PA3 2QE [E-mail: david.t.young@strath.ac.uk]	0141-237 5128 (Work) 0141-553 4144

GREENOCK ADDRESSES

Gourock

Old Gourock and Ashton	41 Royal Street
St John's	Bath Street x St John's Road

Greenock

Lyle Kirk	31 Union Street; Newark Street x Bentinck Street; Esplanade x Campbell Street

(Lyle Kirk is continuing meantime to retain all three buildings)

Mount Kirk	Dempster Street at Murdieston Park
St Margaret's	Finch Road x Kestrel Crescent
St Ninian's	Warwick Road, Larkfield
Wellpark Mid Kirk	Cathcart Square
Westburn	9 Nelson Street

Port Glasgow

Hamilton	Bardrainney Avenue x Auchenbothie Road
Bardrainney	
St Andrew's	Princes Street
St Martin's	Mansion Avenue

PAISLEY ADDRESSES

Abbey	Town Centre
Glenburn	Nethercraigs Drive off Glenburn Road
Lylesland	Rowan Street off Neilston Road
Martyrs'	King Street
Oakshaw Trinity	Churchill
St Columba Foxbar	Amochrie Road, Foxbar
St James'	Underwood Road
St Luke's	Neilston Road
St Mark's Oldhall	Glasgow Road, Ralston
St Ninian's Ferguslie	Blackstoun Road
Sandyford (Thread St)	Montgomery Road
Sherwood Greenlaw	Glasgow Road
Stow Brae Kirk	Causeyside Street
Wallneuk North	off Renfrew Road

(16) GLASGOW

Meets at Govan and Linthouse Parish Church, Govan Cross, Glasgow, on the following Tuesdays: 2013: 10 September, 8 October, 12 November, 10 December; 2014: 4 February, 4 March, 1 April, 13 May, 17 June.

Clerk (pro tem.):	VERY REV. WILLIAM C. HEWITT BD DipPS	260 Bath Street, Glasgow G2 4JP [E-mail: glasgow@cofscotland.org.uk] [Website: www.presbyteryofglasgow.org.uk] [E-mail: treasurer@presbyteryofglasgow.org.uk]	0141-332 6606 0141-352 6646 (Fax)
Treasurer:	DOUGLAS BLANEY		

1	**Banton** linked with **Twechar**			
	Vacant		Manse of Banton and Twechar, Banton, Glasgow G65 0QL	01236 826129
2	**Bishopbriggs: Kenmure**			
	James Gemmell BD MTh	1999 2010	5 Marchfield, Bishopbriggs, Glasgow G64 3PP [E-mail: revgemmell@hotmail.com]	0141-772 1468
3	**Bishopbriggs: Springfield Cambridge (0141-772 1596)**			
	Ian Taylor BD ThM	1995 2006	64 Miller Drive, Bishopbriggs, Glasgow G64 1FB [E-mail: taylorian@btinternet.com]	0141-772 1540
4	**Broom (0141-639 3528)**			
	James A.S. Boag BD CertMin	1992 2007	3 Laigh Road, Newton Mearns, Glasgow G77 5EX [E-mail: office@broomchurch.org.uk]	0141-639 2916 (Tel) 0141-639 3528 (Fax)
5	**Burnside Blairbeth (0141-634 4130)**			
	William T.S. Wilson BSc BD	1999 2006	59 Blairbeth Road, Burnside, Glasgow G73 4JD [E-mail: william.wilson@burnsideblairbethchurch.org.uk]	0141-583 6470
6	**Busby (0141-644 2073)**			
	Jeremy C. Eve BSc BD	1998	17A Carmunnock Road, Busby, Glasgow G76 8SZ [E-mail: j-eve@sky.com]	0141-644 3670
7	**Cadder (0141-772 7436)**			
	Graham S. Finch MA BD	1977 1999	231 Kirkintilloch Road, Bishopbriggs, Glasgow G64 2JB [E-mail: gsf1957@ntlworld.com]	0141-772 1363

#	Charge / Minister	Years	Address / E-mail	Telephone
8	**Cambuslang: Flemington Hallside** Neil M. Glover	2005	103 Overton Road, Halfway, Cambuslang, Glasgow G72 7XA [E-mail: neilmglover@gmail.com]	0141-641 1049 07779 280074 (Mbl)
9	**Cambuslang Parish Church** A. Leslie Milton MA BD PhD	1996 2008	74 Stewarton Drive, Cambuslang, Glasgow G72 8DG [E-mail: alesliemilton.milton@gmail.com]	0141-641 2028
10	**Campsie (01360 310939)** Alexandra Farrington LTh	2003 2011	19 Redhills View, Lennoxtown, Glasgow G66 7BL [E-mail: revsfarrington@aol.co.uk]	01360 238126
11	**Chryston (H) (0141-779 4188)** Mark Malcolm MA BD	1999 2008	The Manse, 109 Main Street, Chryston, Glasgow G69 9LA [E-mail: mark.minister@btinternet.com]	0141-779 1436 07731 737377 (Mbl)
12	**Eaglesham (01355 302047)** Lynn M. McChlery BA BD	2005	The Manse, Cheapside Street, Eaglesham, Glasgow G76 0NS [E-mail: lsmcchlery@btinternet.com]	01355 303495
13	**Fernhill and Cathkin** Margaret McArthur BD DipMin	1995 2002	82 Blairbeth Road, Rutherglen, Glasgow G73 4JA [E-mail: revmaggiemac@hotmail.co.uk]	0141-634 1508
14	**Gartcosh (H) (01236 873770) linked with Glenboig** David G. Slater BSc BA DipThRS	2011	26 Inchnock Avenue, Gartcosh, Glasgow G69 8EA [E-mail: minister@gartcoshchurch.co.uk] [E-mail: minister@glenboigchurch.co.uk]	01236 870331 01236 872274 (Office)
15	**Giffnock: Orchardhill (0141-638 3604)** Chris Vermeulen DipLT BTh MA	1986 2005	23 Huntly Avenue, Giffnock, Glasgow G46 6LW [E-mail: chris@orchardhill.org.uk]	0141-620 3734
16	**Giffnock: South (0141-638 2599)** Catherine J. Beattie (Mrs) BD	2008 2011	164 Ayr Road, Newton Mearns, Glasgow G77 6EE [E-mail: catherinejbeat@aol.com]	0141-258 7804

17	**Giffnock: The Park (0141-620 2204)**			
	Calum D. Macdonald BD	1993	2001	41 Rouken Glen Road, Thornliebank, Glasgow G46 7JD	0141-638 3023
				[E-mail: parkchurch@hotmail.co.uk]	
18	**Glenboig** See Gartcosh				
19	**Greenbank (H) (0141-644 1841)**				
	Jeanne Roddick BD		2003	Greenbank Manse, 38 Eaglesham Road, Clarkston, Glasgow G76 7DJ	0141-644 1395
				[E-mail: jeanne.roddick@ntlworld.com]	
20	**Kilsyth: Anderson**				
	Allan S. Vint BSc BD MTh	1989	2013	Anderson Manse, Kingston Road, Kilsyth, Glasgow G65 0HR	01236 822345
				[E-mail: allan@vint.co.uk]	07795 483070 (Mbl)
21	**Kilsyth: Burns and Old**				
	Vacant			The Grange, 17 Glasgow Road, Kilsyth, Glasgow G65 9AE	01236 823116
22	**Kirkintilloch: Hillhead**				
	Lily F. McKinnon MA BD PGCE	1993	2011	The Manse, 64 Waverley Park, Kensington Gate, Kirkintilloch, Glasgow G66 2BP	0141-776 4785
				[E-mail: lily.mckinnon@yahoo.co.uk]	
23	**Kirkintilloch: St Columba's (H) (0141-578 0016)**				
	David M. White BA BD DMin	1988	1992	14 Crossdykes, Kirkintilloch, Glasgow G66 3EU	0141-578 4357
				[E-mail: write.to.me@ntlworld.com]	
24	**Kirkintilloch: St David's Memorial Park (H) (0141-776 4989)**				
	Bryce Calder MA BD	1995	2001	2 Roman Road, Kirkintilloch, Glasgow G66 1EA	0141-776 1434
				[E-mail: ministry100@aol.com]	07986 144834 (Mbl)
25	**Kirkintilloch: St Mary's (0141-775 1166)**				
	Mark E. Johnstone MA BD	1993	2001	St Mary's Manse, 60 Union Street, Kirkintilloch, Glasgow G66 1DH	0141-776 1252
				[E-mail: markjohnstone@me.com]	
26	**Lenzie: Old (H)**				
	Douglas W. Clark LTh	1993	2000	41 Kirkintilloch Road, Lenzie, Glasgow G66 4LB	0141-776 2184
				[E-mail: douglaswclark@hotmail.com]	

27 **Lenzie: Union (H) (0141-776 1046)**
Daniel J.M. Carmichael MA BD   1994   2003
1 Larch Avenue, Lenzie, Glasgow G66 4HX
[E-mail: minister@lupc.org]
0141-776 3831

28 **Maxwell Mearns Castle (Tel/Fax: 0141-639 5169)**
Scott R.McL. Kirkland BD MAR   1996
122 Broomfield Avenue, Newton Mearns, Glasgow G77 5JR
[E-mail: scottkirkland@maxwellmearns.org.uk]
0141-560 5603   2011

29 **Mearns (H) (0141-639 6555)**
Joseph A. Kavanagh BD DipPTh MTh MTh 1992   1998
11 Belford Grove, Newton Mearns, Glasgow G77 5FB
[E-mail: revjoe@hotmail.co.uk]
0141-384 2218

30 **Milton of Campsie (H)**
Julie H.C. Moody BA BD PGCE   2006
Dunkeld, 33 Birdston Road, Milton of Campsie, Glasgow G66 8BX
[E-mail: jhcwilson@msn.com]
01360 310548
07787 184800 (Mbl)

31 **Netherlee (H) (0141-637 2503)**
Thomas Nelson BSc BD   1992   2002
25 Ormonde Avenue, Netherlee, Glasgow G44 3QY
[E-mail: tomnelson@ntlworld.com]
0141-585 7502 (Tel/Fax)

32 **Newton Mearns (H) (0141-639 7373)**
Esther J. Ninian (Miss) MA BD   1993   2009
28 Waterside Avenue, Newton Mearns, Glasgow G77 6TJ
[E-mail: estherninian5194@btinternet.com]
0141-616 2079

33 **Rutherglen: Old (H)**
Vacant
31 Highburgh Drive, Rutherglen, Glasgow G73 3RR
0141-647 6178

34 **Rutherglen: Stonelaw (0141-647 5113)**
Alistair S. May LLB BD PhD   2002
80 Blairbeth Road, Rutherglen, Glasgow G73 4JA
[E-mail: alistair.may@ntlworld.com]
0141-583 0157

35 **Rutherglen: West and Wardlawhill (0844 736 1470)**
Vacant
12 Albert Drive, Rutherglen, Glasgow G73 3RT
0141-569 8547

36 **Stamperland (0141-637 4999) (H)**
George C. MacKay
BD CertMin CertEd DipPc   1994   2004
109 Ormonde Avenue, Netherlee, Glasgow G44 3SN
[E-mail: g.mackay3@btinternet.com]
0141-637 4976 (Tel/Fax)

37 Stepps (H)
Vacant

38 Thornliebank (H)
Vacant
19 Arthurlie Drive, Giffnock, Glasgow G46 6UR

39 Torrance (T) (01360 620970)
Nigel L. Barge BSc BD   1991
1 Atholl Avenue, Torrance, Glasgow G64 4JA
[E-mail: nigel.barge@sky.com]
01360 622379

40 Twechar See Banton

41 Williamwood (0141-638 2091)
Iain M.A. Reid MA BD   1990 2007
125 Greenwood Road, Clarkston, Glasgow G76 7LL
[E-mail: reviain.reid@ntlworld.com]
0141-571 7949

42 Glasgow: Anderston Kelvingrove (0141-221 9408)
Vacant
16 Royal Terrace, Glasgow G3 7NY
0141-332 7704

43 Glasgow: Baillieston Mure Memorial (0141-773 1216) linked with Glasgow: Baillieston St Andrew's (0141-771 6629)
Malcolm Cuthbertson BA BD   1984 2010
28 Beech Avenue, Baillieston, Glasgow G69 6LF
[E-mail: malcuth@aol.com]
0141-771 1217

44 Glasgow: Baillieston St Andrew's See Glasgow: Baillieston Mure Memorial

45 Glasgow: Balshagray Victoria Park
Campbell Mackinnon BSc BD   1982 2001
20 St Kilda Drive, Glasgow G14 9JN
[E-mail: campbell54@btinternet.com]
0141-954 9780

46 Glasgow: Barlanark Greyfriars (0141-771 6477)
Vacant
4 Rhindmuir Grove, Glasgow G69 6NE
0141-771 1240

47 Glasgow: Blawarthill
G. Melvyn Wood MA BD   1982 2009
46 Earlbank Avenue, Glasgow G14 9HL
[E-mail: gmelvynwood@gmail.com]
0141-579 6521

48 Glasgow: Bridgeton St Francis in the East (H) (L) (0141-556 2830) (Church House: Tel: 0141-554 8045)
Howard R. Hudson MA BD   1982 1984   10 Albany Drive, Rutherglen, Glasgow G73 3QN   0141-587 8667
                                                [E-mail: howard.hudson@ntlworld.com]
                                                64 Gardenside Grove, Carmyle, Glasgow G32 8EZ   0141-646 2297
Margaret S. Beaton (Miss) DCS   [E-mail: margaret@churchhouse.plus.com]   07796 642382 (Mbl)
    (Deacon and Leader of Centre)

49 Glasgow: Broomhill (0141-334 2540)
Vacant   27 St Kilda Drive, Glasgow G14 9LN   0141-959 3204

50 Glasgow: Calton Parkhead (0141-554 3866)
Alison Davidge MA BD   1990 2008   98 Drumover Drive, Glasgow G31 5RP   07843   625059 (Mbl)
                                                [E-mail: adavidge@sky.com]

51 Glasgow: Cardonald (0141-882 6264)
Calum MacLeod BA BD   1979 2007   133 Newtyle Road, Paisley PA1 3LB   0141-887 2726
                                                [E-mail: pangur@sky.com]

52 Glasgow: Carmunnock (0141-644 0655)
G. Gray Fletcher BSc BD   1989 2001   The Manse, 161 Waterside Road, Carmunnock, Glasgow G76 9AJ   0141-644 1578 (Tel/Fax)
                                                [E-mail: gray.fletcher@virgin.net]

53 Glasgow: Carmyle linked with Glasgow: Kenmuir Mount Vernon
Murdo Maclean BD CertMin   1997 1999   3 Meryon Road, Glasgow G32 9NW   0141-778 2625
                                                [E-mail: murdo.maclean@ntlworld.com]

54 Glasgow: Carnwadric (E)
Graeme K. Bell BA BD   1983   62 Loganswell Road, Thornliebank, Glasgow G46 8AX   0141-638 5884
                                                [E-mail: graemekbell@googlemail.com]
Mary Gargrave (Mrs) DCS   1989   90 Mount Annan Drive, Glasgow G44 4RZ   0141-561 4681
                                                [E-mail: mary.gargrave@btinternet.com]

55 Glasgow: Castlemilk (H) (0141-634 1480)
Sarah Brown (Ms)   2012   156 Old Castle Road, Glasgow G44 5TW   0141-637 5451
    MA BD ThM DipYW/Theol PDCCE   [E-mail: ministercastlemilk@gmail.com]   07532 457245 (Mbl)
    (New charge formed by the union of Glasgow: Castlemilk East and Glasgow: Castlemilk West)

56 Glasgow: Cathcart Old (0141-637 4168)
Neil W. Galbraith BD CertMin   1987   21 Courthill Avenue, Cathcart, Glasgow G44 5AA   0141-633 5248 (Tel/Fax)
                                                [E-mail: revneilgalbraith@hotmail.com]

57 Glasgow: Cathcart Trinity (H) (0141-637 6658)
Vacant   82 Merrylee Road, Glasgow G43 2QZ
Wilma Pearson (Mrs) BD (Assoc)   2004   90 Newlands Road, Glasgow G43 2JR
 [E-mail: wilma.pearson@ntlworld.com]   0141-633 3744 / 0141-632 2491

58 Glasgow: Cathedral (High or St Mungo's) (0141-552 6891)
Laurence A.B. Whitley MA BD PhD   1975   2007   41 Springfield Road, Bishopbriggs, Glasgow G64 1PL
 [E-mail: labwhitley@btinternet.com]   0141-762 2719
Ada MacLeod MA BD PGCE (Assist)   2013   133 Newtyle Road, Paisley PA1 3LB
 [E-mail: ada@uk7.net]   0141-887 2726

59 Glasgow: Clincarthill (H) (0141-632 4206)
Mike R. Gargrave BD   2008   2010   90 Mount Annan Drive, Glasgow G44 4RZ
 [E-mail: mike.gargrave@btinternet.com]   0141-561 4681

60 Glasgow: Colston Milton (0141-772 1922)
Christopher J. Rowe BA BD   2008   118 Birsay Road, Milton, Glasgow G22 7QP
 [E-mail: ministercolstonmilton@yahoo.co.uk]   0141-564 1138

61 Glasgow: Colston Wellpark (H)
Vacant   16 Bishopsgate Gardens, Colston, Glasgow G21 1XS   0141-589 8866

62 Glasgow: Cranhill (H) (0141-774 3344)
Muriel B. Pearson (Ms) MA BD PGCE   2004   31 Lethamhill Crescent, Glasgow G33 2SH
 [E-mail: murielpearson@btinternet.com]   0141-770 6873 / 07951 888860 (Mbl)

63 Glasgow: Croftfoot (H) (0141-637 3913)
Robert M. Silver BA BD   1995   2011   4 Inchmurrin Gardens, High Burnside, Rutherglen, Glasgow G73 5RU
 [E-mail: rob.silver@talktalk.net]   0141-258 7268

64 Glasgow: Dennistoun New (H) (0141-550 2825)
Ian M.S. McInnes BD DipMin   1995   2008   31 Pencaitland Drive, Glasgow G32 8RL
 [E-mail: ian.liz1@ntlworld.com]   0141-564 6498

65 Glasgow: Drumchapel St Andrew's (0141-944 3758)
John S. Purves LLB BD   1983   1984   6 Firdon Crescent, Old Drumchapel, Glasgow G15 6QQ
 [E-mail: john.s.purves@talk21.com]   0141-944 4566

66 Glasgow: Drumchapel St Mark's
Audrey Jamieson BD MTh   2004   2007   146 Garscadden Road, Glasgow G15 6PR
 [E-mail: audrey.jamieson2@btinternet.com]   0141-944 5440

67	**Glasgow: Easterhouse St George's and St Peter's (E) (0141-771 8810)**				
	Vacant			3 Barony Gardens, Baillieston, Glasgow G69 6TS	0141-573 8200
68	**Glasgow: Eastwood**				
	Graham R.G. Cartlidge MA BD STM	1977	2010	54 Mansewood Road, Eastwood, Glasgow G43 1TL [E-mail: cartlidge262@btinternet.com]	0141-649 0463
69	**Glasgow: Gairbraid (H)**				
	Donald Michael MacInnes BD	2002	2011	4 Blackhill Gardens, Summerston, Glasgow G23 5NE [E-mail: revdmmi@gmail.com]	0141-946 0604
70	**Glasgow: Gallowgate**				
	Peter L.V. Davidge BD MTh	2003	2009	98 Drumover Drive, Glasgow G31 5RP [E-mail: rev_dav46@yahoo.co.uk]	07765 096599 (Mbl)
71	**Glasgow: Garthamlock and Craigend East (E)**				
	Valerie J. Duff (Miss) DMin	1993	1996	9 Craigievar Court, Glasgow G33 5DJ [E-mail: valduff@tiscali.co.uk]	0141-774 6364
	Marion Buchanan (Mrs) MA DCS			16 Almond Drive, East Kilbride, Glasgow G74 2HX [E-mail: marion.buchanan@btinternet.com]	01355 228776
72	**Glasgow: Gorbals**				
	Ian F. Galloway BA BD	1976	1996	44 Riverside Road, Glasgow G43 2EF [E-mail: ianfgalloway@msn.com]	0141-649 5250
73	**Glasgow: Govan and Linthouse**				
	Moyna McGlynn (Mrs) BD PhD	1999	2008	19 Dumbreck Road, Glasgow G41 5LJ [E-mail: moyna_mcglynn@hotmail.com]	0141-419 0308
	Paul Cathcart DCS			9 Glen More, East Kilbride, Glasgow G74 2AP [E-mail: paulcathcart@msn.com]	01355 243970 / 07708 396074 (Mbl)
74	**Glasgow: Govanhill Trinity**				
	Vacant			12 Carlton Gate, Giffnock, Glasgow G46 6NU	0141-637 8399

75 Glasgow: High Carntyne (0141-778 4186)
Joan Ross (Miss) BSc BD PhD   1999   2005   163 Lethamhill Road, Glasgow G33 2SQ   0141-770 9247
[E-mail: joan@highcarntyne.plus.com]

76 Glasgow: Hillington Park (H)
John B. MacGregor BD   1999   2004   61 Ralston Avenue, Glasgow G52 3NB   0141-882 7000
[E-mail: johnmacgregor61@hotmail.co.uk]

77 Glasgow: Hyndland (H) (Website: www.hyndlandparishchurch.org)
Vacant   24 Hughenden Gardens, Glasgow G12 9YH   0141-334 1002

78 Glasgow: Ibrox (H) (0141-427 0896)
Elisabeth G.B. Spence (Miss) BD DipEd   1995   2008   59 Langhaul Road, Glasgow G53 7SE   0141-883 7744
[E-mail: revelisabeth@spenceweb.net]

79 Glasgow: John Ross Memorial Church for Deaf People
(Voice Text: 0141-420 1391; Fax: 0141-420 3778)
Richard C. Durno DSW CQSW   1989   1998   31 Springfield Road, Bishopbriggs,   (Voice/Text/Fax) 0141-772 1052
Glasgow G64 1PJ   (Voice/Text/Voicemail) (Mbl) 07748 607721
[E-mail: richard.durno@btinternet.com]

80 Glasgow: Jordanhill (Tel: 0141-959 2496)
Colin C. Renwick BMus BD   1989   1996   96 Southbrae Drive, Glasgow G13 1TZ   0141-959 1310
[E-mail: c.renwick@btopenworld.com]

81 Glasgow: Kelvin Stevenson Memorial (0141-339 1750)
Gordon Kirkwood BSc BD PGCE MTh   1987   2003   Flat 2/2, 94 Hyndland Road, Glasgow G12 9PZ   0141-334 5352
[E-mail: gordonkirkwood@hotmail.co.uk]

82 Glasgow: Kelvinside Hillhead (0141-334 2788)
Vacant   39 Athole Gardens, Glasgow G12 9BQ   0141-339 2865

83 Glasgow: Kenmuir Mount Vernon See Carmyle

84 Glasgow: King's Park (H) (0141-636 8688)
Sandra Boyd (Mrs) BEd BD   2007   1101 Aikenhead Road, Glasgow G44 5SL   0141-637 2803
[E-mail: sandraboyd.bofa@btopenworld.com]

85	**Glasgow: Kinning Park (0141-427 3063)**				
	Margaret H. Johnston BD	1988	2000	168 Arbroath Avenue, Cardonald, Glasgow G52 3HH [E-mail: marniejohnston7@aol.com]	0141-810 3782
86	**Glasgow: Knightswood St Margaret's (H)**				
	Alexander M. Fraser BD DipMin	1985	2009	26 Airthrey Avenue, Glasgow G14 9LJ [E-mail: sandyfraser2@hotmail.com]	0141-959 7075
87	**Glasgow: Langside (0141-632 7520)**				
	David N. McLachlan BD	1985	2004	36 Madison Avenue, Glasgow G44 5AQ [E-mail: dmclachlan77@hotmail.com]	0141-637 0797
88	**Glasgow: Lansdowne**				
	Vacant				
89	**Glasgow: Lochwood (H) (0141-771 2649)**				
	Stuart M. Duff BA	1997		42 Rhindmuir Road, Swinton, Glasgow G69 6AZ [E-mail: stuart.duff@gmail.com]	0141-773 2756
90	**Glasgow: Maryhill (H) (0141-946 3512)**				
	Stuart C. Matthews BD MA	2006		251 Milngavie Road, Bearsden, Glasgow G61 3DQ [E-mail: stuart.maryhill@gmail.com]	0141-942 0804
	James Hamilton DCS			6 Beckfield Gate, Glasgow G33 1SW [E-mail: j.hamilton111@btinternet.com]	0141-558 3195
91	**Glasgow: Merrylea (0141-637 2009)**				
	David P. Hood BD CertMin DiplOB(Scot)	1997	2001	4 Pilmuir Avenue, Glasgow G44 3HX [E-mail: dphood3@ntlworld.com]	0141-637 6700
92	**Glasgow: Mosspark (H) (0141-882 2240)**				
	Vacant			396 Kilmarnock Road, Glasgow G43 2DJ	0141-632 1247
93	**Glasgow: Newlands South (H) (0141-632 3055)**				
	John D. Whiteford MA BD	1989	1997	24 Monreith Road, Glasgow G43 2NY [E-mail: jwhiteford@hotmail.com]	0141-632 2588

94 Glasgow: Partick South (H)
James Andrew McIntyre BD   2010   3 Branklyn Crescent, Glasgow G13 1GJ   0141-959 3732
[E-mail: revpartricksouth@hotmail.co.uk]

95 Glasgow: Partick Trinity (H)
Stuart J. Smith BEng BD MTh   1994   99 Balshagray Avenue, Glasgow G11 7EQ   0141-576 7149
[E-mail: ssmith99@ntlworld.com]

96 Glasgow: Penilee St Andrew (H) (0141-882 2691)
Lyn Peden (Mrs) BD   2010   80 Tweedsmuir Road, Glasgow G52 2RX   0141-883 9873
[E-mail: psa.minister@yahoo.co.uk]

97 Glasgow: Pollokshaws (0141-649 1879)
Roy J.M. Henderson MA BD DipMin   1987 2013   33 Mannering Road, Glasgow G41 3SW   0141-649 0458
[E-mail: roy.henderson7@ntlworld.com]

98 Glasgow: Pollokshields (H)
David R. Black MA BD   1986 1997   36 Glencairn Drive, Glasgow G41 4PW   0141-423 4000
[E-mail: davidrblack@btinternet.com]

99 Glasgow: Possilpark (0141-336 8028)
Vacant   108 Erradale Street, Lambhill, Glasgow G22 6PT   0141-336 6909

100 Glasgow: Queen's Park (0141-423 3654)
David S.M. Malcolm BD   2011   17 Linndale Drive, Carmunnock Grange, Glasgow G45 0QE   0141-634 1097
[E-mail: DavidSMMalcolm@aol.com]

101 Glasgow: Renfield St Stephen's (Tel: 0141-332 4293; Fax: 0141-332 8482)
Peter M. Gardner MA BD   1988 2002   101 Hill Street, Glasgow G3 6TY   0141-353 0349
[E-mail: peter@rsschurch.net]

102 Glasgow: Robroyston (New Charge Development) (0141-558 8414)
Jonathan A. Keefe BSc BD   2009   7 Beckfield Drive, Glasgow G33 1SR   0141-558 2952
[E-mail: jonathanakeefe@aol.com]

103 Glasgow: Ruchazie (0141-774 2759)
Vacant   18 Borthwick Street, Glasgow G33 3UU   0141-774 6860

104 Glasgow: Ruchill Kelvinside (0141-946 0466)
Vacant — 9 Kirklee Road, Glasgow G12 0RQ — 0141-357 3249

105 Glasgow: St Andrew's East (0141-554 1485)
Barbara D. Quigley (Mrs) MTheol ThM DPS — 1979 2011 — 43 Broompark Drive, Glasgow G31 2JB
[E-mail: bdquigley@aol.com] — 0141-237 7982

106 Glasgow: St Christopher's Priesthill and Nitshill (0141-881 6541)
Douglas M. Nicol BD CA — 1987 1996 — 36 Springkell Drive, Glasgow G41 4EZ
[E-mail: dougiemnicol@aol.com] — 0141-427 7877
(New charge formed by the union of Glasgow: Househillwood St Christopher's and Glasgow: Priesthill and Nitshill)

107 Glasgow: St Columba (GE) (0141-221 3305)
Vacant — 1 Reelick Avenue, Peterson Park, Glasgow G13 4NF — 0141-952 0948

108 Glasgow: St David's Knightswood (0141-954 1081)
Graham M. Thain LLB BD — 1988 1999 — 60 Southbrae Drive, Glasgow G13 1QD
[E-mail: graham_thain@btopenworld.com] — 0141-959 2904

109 Glasgow: St Enoch's Hogganfield (H) (Tel: 0141-770 5694; Fax: 0870 284 0084) (E-mail: church@st-enoch.org.uk)
(Website: www.stenochshogganfield.org.uk)
Graham K. Blount LLB BD PhD — 1976 2010 — 43 Smithycroft Road, Glasgow G33 2RH
[E-mail: graham.blount@yahoo.co.uk] — 0141-770 7593

110 Glasgow: St George's Tron (0141-221 2141)
Alastair S. Duncan MA BD — 1989 2013 — 27 Kelvindale Court, Glasgow G12 0JG
(Transition Minister) [E-mail: stgeorgestroncofs@gmail.com] — 07968 852083 (Mbl)

111 Glasgow: St James' (Pollok) (0141-882 4984)
John W. Mann BSc MDiv DMin — 2004 — 30 Ralston Avenue, Glasgow G52 3NA
[E-mail: drjohnmann@hotmail.com] — 0141-883 7405

112 Glasgow: St John's Renfield (0141-339 7021) (Website: www.stjohns-renfield.org.uk)
Fiona L. Lillie (Mrs) BA BD MLitt — 1995 2009 — 26 Leicester Avenue, Glasgow G12 0LU
[E-mail: fionalillie@btinternet.com] — 0141-339 4637

113 Glasgow: St Margaret's Tollcross Park
Vacant — 31 Kenmuir Avenue, Sandyhills, Glasgow G32 9LE — 0141-778 5060

114 Glasgow: St Nicholas' Cardonald
Eleanor J. McMahon BEd BD   1994   2013   81 Moorpark Square, Renfrew PA4 8DB   0141-886 1351
(Interim Minister)   [E-mail: e.mcmahon212@btinternet.com]

115 Glasgow: St Paul's (0141-770 8559)
Vacant

116 Glasgow: St Rollox (0141-558 1809)
Vacant   42 Melville Gardens, Bishopbriggs, Glasgow G64 3DE   0141-562 6296

117 Glasgow: Sandyford Henderson Memorial (H) (L)
Vacant   66 Woodend Drive, Glasgow G13 1TG   0141-954 9013

118 Glasgow: Sandyhills (0141-778 3415)
Graham T. Atkinson MA BD MTh   2006   60 Wester Road, Glasgow G32 9JJ   0141-778 2174
                                                    [E-mail: gtatkinson@o2.co.uk]

119 Glasgow: Scotstoun (T)
Richard Cameron BD DipMin   2000   15 Northland Drive, Glasgow G14 9BE   0141-959 4637
                                                    [E-mail: rev.rickycam@live.co.uk]

120 Glasgow: Shawlands (0141-649 1773)
Vacant   29 St Ronan's Drive, Glasgow G41 3SQ   0141-649 2034

121 Glasgow: Sherbrooke St Gilbert's (H) (0141-427 1968)
Thomas L. Pollock   1982   2003   114 Springkell Avenue, Glasgow G41 4EW   0141-427 2094
BA BD MTh FSAScot JP   [E-mail: tompollock06@aol.com]

122 Glasgow: Shettleston New (0141-778 0857)
Ronald A.S. Craig BAcc BD   1983   2007   211 Sandyhills Road, Glasgow G32 9NB   0141-778 1286
                                                    [E-mail: rascraig@ntlworld.com]

123 Glasgow: Shettleston Old (T) (H) (0141-778 2484)
Vacant   57 Mansionhouse Road, Mount Vernon, Glasgow G32 0RP   0141-778 8904

124 Glasgow: South Carntyne (H) (0141-778 1343)
Vacant   47 Broompark Drive, Glasgow G31 2JB   0141-554 3275

125 Glasgow: South Shawlands (T) (0141-649 4656)
Vacant
391 Kilmarnock Road, Glasgow G43 2NU
0141-632 0013

126 Glasgow: Springburn (H) (0141-557 2345)
Vacant
3 Tofthill Avenue, Bishopbriggs, Glasgow G64 3PA
0141-762 1844

127 Glasgow: Temple Anniesland (0141-959 1814)
Fiona Gardner (Mrs) BD MA MLitt   1997   2011
76 Victoria Park Drive North, Glasgow G14 9PJ
[E-mail: fionandcolin@hotmail.com]
0141-959 5647

128 Glasgow: Toryglen (H)
Vacant

129 Glasgow: Trinity Possil and Henry Drummond
Richard G. Buckley BD MTh   1990   1995
50 Highfield Drive, Glasgow G12 0HL
[E-mail: richardbuckleyis@hotmail.com]
0141-339 2870

130 Glasgow: Tron St Mary's (0141-558 1011)
P. Jill Clancy (Mrs) BD DipMin   2000   2008
6 Broomfield Drive, Glasgow G21 3HE
[E-mail: jgibson@totalise.co.uk]
0141-558 1011

Karen Hamilton (Mrs) DCS   1995   2009
6 Beckfield Gate, Glasgow G33 1SW
[E-mail: k.hamilton6@btinternet.com]
0141-558 3195
07970 872859 (Mbl)

131 Glasgow: Victoria Tollcross
Monica Michelin Salomon BD   1999   2007
228 Hamilton Road, Glasgow G32 9QU
[E-mail: monica@michelin-salomon.freeserve.co.uk]
0141-778 2413

132 Glasgow: Wallacewell (New Charge Development)
Daniel Frank BA MDiv DMin   1984   2011
8 Streamfield Gate, Glasgow G33 1SJ
[E-mail: daniellouis106@gmail.com]
0141-585 0283

133 Glasgow: Wellington (H) (0141-339 0454)
David I. Sinclair BSc BD PhD DipSW   1990   2008
31 Hughenden Gardens, Glasgow G12 9YH
[E-mail: davidsinclair@btinternet.com]
0141-334 2343

134 Glasgow: Whiteinch (Website: www.whiteinchcofs.co.uk)

| Alan McWilliam BD MTh | 1993 | 2000 | 65 Victoria Park Drive South, Glasgow G14 9NX | 0141-576 9020 |

[E-mail: alan@whiteinchchurch.org]

135 Glasgow: Yoker (T)

| Karen E. Hendry BSc BD | 2005 | 15 Coldingham Avenue, Glasgow G14 0PX | 0141-952 3620 |

[E-mail: karen@hendry-k.fsnet.co.uk]

Name			Position	Address	Phone
Alexander, Eric J. MA BD	1958	1997	(Glasgow: St George's Tron)	77 Norwood Park, Bearsden, Glasgow G61 2RZ	0141-942 4404
Allen, Martin A.W. MA BD ThM	1977	2007	(Chryston)	Lealenge, 85 High Barrwood Road, Kilsyth, Glasgow G65 0EE	01236 826616
Allison, May M. (Mrs) BD	1988	2012	(Glasgow: Househillwood St Christopher's)	12 Leverndale Court, Crookston, Glasgow G53 7SJ	0141-810 5953
				[E-mail: revmayallison@hotmail.com]	
Alston, William G.	1961	2009	(Glasgow: North Kelvinside)	Flat 0/2, 5 Knightswood Court, Glasgow G13 2XN	0141-959 3113
				[E-mail: williamalston@hotmail.com]	
Barr, Alexander C. MA BD	1950	1992	(Glasgow: St Nicholas' Cardonald)	25 Fisher Drive, Phoenix Park, Paisley PA1 2TP	0141-848 5941
Bayes, Muriel C. DCS	1963		(Deaconess)	Flat 6, Carlton Court, 10 Fenwick Road, Glasgow G46 6AN	0141-633 0865
Bell, John L. MA BD FRSCM DUniv	1978	1988	Iona Community	Flat 2/1, 31 Lansdowne Crescent, Glasgow G20 6NH	0141-334 0688
Bell, Sandra (Mrs) DCS			(Hospital Chaplain)	62 Loganswell Road, Glasgow G42 8AX	0141-638 5884
				[E-mail: slbellmrs@yahoo.co.uk]	
Birch, James PgDip FRSA FIOC	2001	2007	(Auxiliary Minister)	1 Kirkhill Grove, Cambuslang, Glasgow G72 8EH	0141-583 1722
Black, Sandra (Mrs) BSc BD	1988	2013	Interim Minister	36 Glencairn Drive, Glasgow G41 4PW	0141-423 4000
				[E-mail: revsblack@btinternet.com]	
Black, William B. MA BD	1972	2011	(Stornoway: High)	33 Tankerland Road, Glasgow G44 4EN	0141-637 4717
				[E-mail: revwillieblack@gmail.com]	
Blount, A. Sheila (Mrs) BD BA	1978	2010	(Cupar: St John's and Dairsie United)	43 Smithycroft Road, Glasgow G33 2RH	0141-770 7593
				[E-mail: asblount@orange.net]	
Brain, Isobel J. (Mrs) MA	1987	1997	(Ballantrae)	10/11 Maxwell Street, Edinburgh EH10 5GZ	0131-466 6115
Brice, Dennis G. BSc BD	1981		(Taiwan)	8 Parkwood Close, Broxbourne, Herts EN10 7PF	
				[E-mail: dbrice1@comcast.net]	
Bryden, William A. BD	1977	1984	(Yoker: Old with St Matthew's)	145 Bearsden Road, Glasgow G13 1BS	0141-959 5213
Bull, Alister W. BD DipMin MTh PhD	1994	2001	Mission and Discipleship Council	c/o 121 George Street, Edinburgh EH2 4YN	0131-225 5722
				[E-mail: abull@cofscotland.org.uk]	
Campbell, A. Iain MA DipEd	1961	1997	(Busby)	430 Clarkston Road, Glasgow G44 3QF	0141-637 7460
				[E-mail: bellmac@sagainternet.co.uk]	
Cunningham, Alexander MA BD	1961	2002	(Presbytery Clerk)	The Glen, 103 Glenmavis Road, Airdrie ML6 0PQ	01236 763012
Cunningham, James S.A. MA BD BLitt PhD	1992	2000	(Glasgow: Barlanark Greyfriars)	'Kirkland', 5 Inveresk Place, Coatbridge ML5 2DA	01236 421541
Dean, Roger A.F. LTh	1983	2004	(Mochrum)	0/2, 20 Ballogie Road, Glasgow G44 4TA	
				[E-mail: roger.dean4@btopenworld.com]	
Drummond, John W. MA BD	1971	2011	(Rutherglen: West and Wardlawhill)	25 Kingsburn Drive, Rutherglen, Glasgow G73 2AN	0141-571 6002
Duff, T. Malcolm F. MA BD	1985	2009	(Glasgow: Queen's Park)	54 Hawkhead Road, Paisley PA1 3NB	0141-570 0614
					(Mbl) 07846 926584

Name	Position			Address	Tel
Ferguson, James B. LTh	(Lenzie: Union)	1972	2002	3 Bridgeway Place, Kirkintilloch, Glasgow G66 3HW	0141-588 5868
Ferguson, William B. BA BD	(Glasgow: Broomhill)	1971	2012	20 Swift Crescent, Knightswood Gate, Glasgow G13 4QL [E-mail: revferg@btinternet.com]	0141-954 6655
Finlay, William P. MA BD	(Glasgow: Townhead Blochairn)	1969	2000	High Corrie, Brodick, Isle of Arran KA27 8JB	01770 810689
Fleming, Alexander F. MA BD	(Strathblane)	1966	1995	11 Bankwood Drive, Kilsyth, Glasgow G65 0GZ	01236 821461
Ford, Alan A. BD	(Glasgow: Springburn)	1977	2013	14 Corsankell Wynd, Saltcoats KA21 6HY [E-mail: alan.andy@btinternet.com]	01294 465740 (Mbl) 07710 455737
Forrest, Martin R. BA MA BD	Prison Chaplain	1988	2012	4/1, 7 Blochairn Place, Glasgow G21 2EB [E-mail: martinrforrest@gmail.com]	0141-552 1132
Forsyth, Sandy LLB BD DipLP PhD	(Associate: Kirkintilloch: St David's Memorial Park)	2009	2013	48 Kerr Street, Kirkintilloch, Glasgow G66 1JZ [E-mail: sandyforsyth67@hotmail.co.uk]	0141-777 8194 (Mbl) 07739 639037
Galloway, Kathy (Mrs) BD DD	(Leader: Iona Community)	1977	2002	20 Hamilton Park Avenue, Glasgow G12 8UU	0141-357 4079
Gay, Douglas C. MA BD PhD	University of Glasgow	1998	2005	1F, 16 Royal Terrace, Glasgow G3 7NY [E-mail: douggay@mac.com]	0141-332 4040 (Mbl) 07971 321452
Getliffe, Dot (Mrs) DCS BA BD DipEd	Families Worker, West Mearns	2006	2013	3 Woodview Terrace, Hamilton ML3 9DP [E-mail: dgetliffe@aol.co.uk]	01698 423504 (Mbl) 07766 910171
Gibson, H. Marshall MA BD	(Glasgow: St Thomas' Gallowgate)	1957	1996	39 Burnbroom Drive, Glasgow G69 7XG	0141-771 0749
Gibson, Michael BD STM	(Giffnock: The Park)	1974	2001	12 Mile End Park, Pocklington, York YO42 2TH	0141-770 7186
Grant, David I.M. MA BD	(Dalry: Trinity)	1969	2003	8 Mossbank Drive, Glasgow G33 1LS	0141-571 1008
Gray, Christine M. (Mrs)	(Deaconess)			11 Woodside Avenue, Thorniebank, Glasgow G46 7HR	01360 313001
Green, Alex H. MA BD	(Strathblane)	1986	2010	44 Laburnum Drive, Milton of Campsie, Glasgow G66 8HY [E-mail: lesvert@btinternet.com]	0141-563 1918
Gregson, Elizabeth M. (Mrs) BD	(Glasgow: Drumchapel St Andrew's)	1996	2001	17 Westfields, Bishopbriggs, Glasgow G64 3PL	0141-942 9281
Haley, Derek BD DPS	(Chaplain: Gartnavel Royal)	1960	1999	9 Kinnaird Crescent, Bearsden, Glasgow G61 2BN	0141-429 3774
Harvey, W. John BA BD DD	(Edinburgh: Corstorphine Craigsbank)	1965	2002	501 Shields Road, Glasgow G41 2RF	0141-423 7461
Hazlett, W. Ian P. (Prof.-Emer.) BA BD Dr theol DLitt DD	University of Glasgow		2009	587 Shields Road, Glasgow G41 2RW [E-mail: ian.hazlett@glasgow.ac.uk]	(Work) 0141-330 5155
Hewitt, William C. BD DipPS	Interim Minister	1977	2012	60 Woodlands Grove, Kilmarnock KA3 1TZ [E-mail: billhewitt@btinternet.com]	01563 533312
Hope, Evelyn P. (Miss) BA BD	(Wishaw: Thornlie)	1990	1998	Flat 0/1, 48 Moss Side Road, Glasgow G41 3UA	0141-649 1522
Houston, Thomas C. BA	(Glasgow: Priesthill and Nitshill)	1975	2004	63 Broomhouse Crescent, Uddingston, Glasgow G71 7RE	0141-771 0577
Hughes, Helen (Miss) DCS	(Deacon)			2/2, 43 Burnbank Terrace, Glasgow G20 6UQ	0141-333 9459
Hunter, Alastair G. MSc BD	(University of Glasgow)	1976	1980	487 Shields Road, Glasgow G41 2RG	0141-429 1687
Johnston, Robert W.M. MA BD STM	(Glasgow: Temple Anniesland)	1964	1999	13 Kilmardinny Crescent, Bearsden, Glasgow G61 3NP	0141-931 5862
Johnstone, H. Martin J. MA BD MTh PhD	Priority Areas Secretary	1989	2000	3/1, 952 Pollokshaws Road, Glasgow G41 2ET [E-mail: mjohnstone@cofscotland.org.uk]	0141-636 5819
Keddie, David A. MA BD	(Glasgow: Linthouse St Kenneth's)	1966	2005	21 Ilay Road, Bearsden, Glasgow G61 1QG [E-mail: revkeddie@gmail.com]	0141-942 5173
Lang, I. Pat (Miss) BSc	(Dunoon: The High Kirk)	1996	2003	37 Crawford Drive, Glasgow G15 6TW	0141-944 2240
Levison, Chris L. MA BD	(Health Care Chaplaincy Training and Development Officer)	1972	1998	Gardenfield, Nine Mile Burn, Penicuik EH26 9LT	
Lloyd, John M. BD CertMin	(Glasgow: Croftfoot)	1984	2009	17 Acacia Way, Cambuslang, Glasgow G72 7ZY	(Mbl) 07879 812816
Love, Joanna (Ms) BSc DCS	Iona Community: Wild Goose Resource Group	1992	2009	92 Everard Drive, Glasgow G21 1XQ	0141-772 0149

Name	Position	Ordained	Appointed	Address / E-mail	Telephone
Lunan, David W. MA BD DUniv DLitt DD	(Presbytery Clerk)	1970	2002	30 Mill Road, Banton, Glasgow G65 0RD	01236 824110
MacBain, Ian W. BD	(Coatbridge: Coatdyke)	1971	1993	24 Thornyburn Drive, Baillieston, Glasgow G69 7ER	0141-771 7030
MacDonald, Anne (Miss) BA DCS	Healthcare Chaplain: Leverndale Hospital			c/o Leverndale Hospital, Glasgow G53 7TU	0141-211 6695
MacDonald, Kenneth MA BA	(Auxiliary Minister)	2001	2006	5 Henderland Road, Bearsden, Glasgow G61 1AH	0141-943 1103
McDougall, Hilary N. (Mrs) MA PGCE BD (Assoc)	Congregational Facilitator: Presbytery of Glasgow	2002	2013	6 Inchmurrin Gardens, High Burnside, Glasgow G73 5RU [E-mail: hilary@presbyteryofglasgow.org.uk]	0141-384 4428 (Mbl) 07539 321832
MacFadyen, Anne M. (Mrs) BSc BD FSAScot	(Auxiliary Minister)	1995		295 Mearns Road, Glasgow G77 5LT	0141-639 3605
MacKay, Alan H. BD	(Glasgow: Mosspark)	1974	2010	Flat 1/1, 18 Newburgh Street, Glasgow G43 2XR [E-mail: alanhmackay@aol.com]	0141-632 0527
MacKinnon, Charles M. BD	(Kilsyth: Anderson)	1989	2009	36 Hilton Terrace, Bishopbriggs, Glasgow G64 3HB [E-mail: cm.ccmackinnon@tiscali.co.uk]	0141-772 3811
McLachlan, Eric BD MTh	(Glasgow: Cardonald)	1978	2005	16 Kinpurnie Road, Paisley PA1 3HH [E-mail: eric.janis@btinternet.com]	0141-810 5789
McLachlan, Fergus C. BD	(Hospital Chaplain)	1982	2009	46 Queen Square, Glasgow G41 2AZ	0141-423 3830
McLachlan, T. Alastair BSc	(Craignish with Kilbrandon and Kilchattan with Kilninver and Kilmelford)	1972	2009	9 Alder Road, Milton of Campsie, Glasgow G66 8HH [E-mail: talastair@btinternet.com]	01360 319861
McLaren, D. Muir MA BD MTh PhD	(Glasgow: Mosspark)	1971	2001	House 44, 145 Shawhill Road, Glasgow G43 1SX [E-mail: muir44@yahoo.co.uk]	(Mbl) 07931 155779
McLay, Alastair D. BSc BD	(Glasgow: Shawlands)	1989	2004	183 King's Park Avenue, Glasgow G44 4HZ	0141-569 5503
Macleod, Donald BD LRAM DRSAM	(Blairgowrie)	1987	2008	9 Millersneuk Avenue, Lenzie G66 5HJ [E-mail: donmac2@sky.com]	0141-776 6235
MacLeod, Iain A.	Ordained Local Minister: Renfield Centre	2012		6 Hallydown Drive, Glasgow G13 1UF [E-mail: iainamacleod@googlemail.com]	(Mbl) 07795 014889
MacLeod-Mair, Alisdair T. MEd DipTheol	(Glasgow: Baillieston St Andrew's)	2001	2012	2/2, 44 Leven Street, Pollokshields, Glasgow G41 2JE [E-mail: revalisdair@hotmail.com]	0141-423 9600
Macnaughton, J.A. MA BD	(Glasgow: Hyndland)	1949	1989	62 Lauderdale Gardens, Glasgow G12 9QW	0141-339 1294
MacPherson, James B. DCS	(Deacon)			0/1, 104 Cartside Street, Glasgow G42 9TQ	0141-616 6468
McPherson, Marjory (Mrs) LLB BD MTh	Ministries Council	1990	1998	1/3, 2 Wyndham Court, Glasgow G12 0TY [E-mail: mmcpherson@cofscotland.org.uk]	0141-357 6196
MacQuarrie, Stuart JP BD BSc MBA	Chaplain: Glasgow University	1984	2001	The Chaplaincy Centre, University of Glasgow, Glasgow G12 8QQ	(Home) 0131-225 5722 (Work) 0141-330 5419
MacQuien, Duncan DCS	(Deacon)	1988		35 Criffel Road, Mount Vernon, Glasgow G32 9JE	0141-575 1137
Martindale, John P.F. BD	(Glasgow: Sandyhills)	1994	2005	Flat 3/2, 25 Albert Avenue, Glasgow G42 8RB	0141-433 4367
Miller, John D. BA BD DD	(Glasgow: Castlemilk East)	1971	2007	98 Kirkcaldy Road, Glasgow G41 4LD [E-mail: rev.john.miller@zol.co.zw]	0141-423 0221
Moffat, Thomas BSc BD	(Culross and Torryburn)	1976	2008	Flat 8/1, 8 Cranston Street, Glasgow G3 8GG [E-mail: tom@gallus.org.uk]	0141-248 1886
Moore, William B.	(Prison Chaplain: Low Moss)	1968	2002	10 South Dumbreck Road, Kilsyth, Glasgow G65 9LX	01236 821918
Morrice, Alastair M. MA BD	(Rutherglen: Stonelaw)	1951	2005	5 Brechin Road, Kirriemuir DD8 4BX	
Morris, William J. KCVO PhD LLD DD JP	(Glasgow: Cathedral)			1 Whitehill Grove, Newton Mearns, Glasgow G77 5DH	0141-639 6327
Morrison, Iain BD	(Glasgow: Cathcart Trinity)	1991	2013	11 Ralston Path, Glasgow G52 3LW [E-mail: imorrison144@gmail.com]	(Mbl) 07812 435012

Name	Ord.	Ind./Ret.	Charge / Role	Address	Telephone
Muir, Fred C. MA BD ThM ARCM	1961	1997	(Stepps)	20 Alexandra Avenue, Stepps, Glasgow G33 6BP	0141-779 2504
Murray, George M. LTh	1995	2011	(Glasgow: St Margaret's Tollcross Park)	6 Mayfield, Lesmahagow ML11 0FH [E-mail: george.murray7@gmail.com]	
Philip, George M. MA	1953	1996	(Glasgow: Sandyford Henderson Memorial)		
Raeburn, Alan C. MA BD	1971	2010	(Glasgow: Battlefield East)	44 Beech Avenue, Bearsden, Glasgow G61 3EX	0141-942 1327
				3 Orchard Gardens, Strathaven ML10 6UN [E-mail: acraeburn@hotmail.com]	(Mbl) 07709 552161
Ramsay, W.G.	1967	1999	(Glasgow: Springburn)	53 Kelvinvale, Kirkintilloch, Glasgow G66 1RD [E-mail: billram@btopenworld.com]	0141-776 2915
Robertson, Archibald MA BD	1957	1999	(Glasgow: Eastwood)	19 Canberra Court, Braidpark Drive, Glasgow G46 6NS	0141-637 7572
Robertson, Blair MA BD ThM	1990	1998	Chaplain: Southern General Hospital	c/o Chaplain's Office, Southern General Hospital, 1345 Govan Road, Glasgow G51 4TF	0141-201 2357
Ross, Donald M. MA	1953	1994	(Industrial Mission Organiser)	14 Cartsbridge Road, Busby, Glasgow G76 8DH	0141-644 2220
Ross, James MA BD	1968	1998	(Kilsyth: Anderson)	53 Turnberry Gardens, Westerwood, Cumbernauld, Glasgow G68 0AY	01236 730501
Saunders, Keith BD	1983	1999	Hospital Chaplain	Western Infirmary, Dumbarton Road, Glasgow G11 6NT	0141-211 2000
Shackleton, William	1960	1996	(Greenock: Wellpark West)	3 Tynwald Avenue, Burnside, Glasgow G73 4RN	0141-569 9407
Shanks, Norman J. MA BD DD	1983	2007	(Glasgow: Govan Old)	1 Marchmont Terrace, Glasgow G12 9LT [E-mail: rufuski@btinternet.com]	0141-339 4421
Simpson, Neil A. BA BD PhD	1992	2001	(Glasgow: Yoker Old with Yoker St Matthew's)	c/o Glasgow Presbytery Office	
Smeed, Alex W. MA BD	2008	2013	(Glasgow: Whiteinch: Associate)	3/1, 24 Thornwood Road, Glasgow G11 7RB [E-mail: alexsmeed@yahoo.co.uk]	0141-337 3878 (Mbl) 07709 756495
Smith, G. Stewart MA BD STM	1966	2006	(Glasgow: King's Park)	33 Brent Road, Stewartfield, East Kilbride, Glasgow G74 4RA [E-mail: stewartandmary@googlemail.com]	(Tel/Fax) 01355 226718
Smith, James S.A.	1956	1991	(Drongan: The Schaw Kirk)	146 Aros Drive, Glasgow G52 1TJ	0141-883 9666
Spencer, John MA BD	1962	2001	(Dumfries: Lincluden with Holywood)	10 Kinkell Gardens, Kirkintilloch, Glasgow G66 2HJ	0141-777 8935
Spiers, John M. LTh MTh	1972	2004	(Giffnock: Orchardhill)	58 Woodlands Road, Thorniebank, Glasgow G46 7JQ	(Tel/Fax) 0141-638 0632
Stewart, Diane E. BD	1988	2006	(Milton of Campsie)	4 Miller Gardens, Bishopbriggs, Glasgow G64 1FG [E-mail: destewart@givemail.co.uk]	0141-762 1358
Stewart, Norma D. (Miss) MA MEd BD MTh	1977	2000	(Glasgow: Strathbungo Queen's Park)	127 Nether Auldhouse Road, Glasgow G43 2YS	0141-637 6956
Sutherland, David A.	2001		Auxiliary Minister	3/1, 145 Broomhill Drive, Glasgow G11 7ND [E-mail: dave.a.sutherland@gmail.com]	0141-357 2058
Sutherland, Denis I.	1963	1995	(Glasgow: Hutchesontown)	56 Lime Crescent, Cumbernauld, Glasgow G67 3PQ	01236 731723
Sutherland, Elizabeth W. (Miss) BD	1972	1996	(Balornock North with Barmulloch)	20 Kirkland Avenue, Blanefield, Glasgow G63 9BZ [E-mail: ewsutherland@aol.com]	01360 770154
Thomson, Alexander BSc BD MPhil PhD	1973	2012	(Rutherglen: Old)	[E-mail: alexander.thomson6@btopenworld.com]	
Thomson, Andrew BA	1976	2007	(Airdrie: Broomknoll)	3 Laurel Wynd, Drumsagard Village, Cambuslang, Glasgow G72 7BH [E-mail: andrewthomson@hotmail.com]	0141-641 2936
Turner, Angus BD	1976	1998	(Industrial Chaplain)	46 Keir Street, Pollokshields, Glasgow G41 2LA	0141-424 0493
Tuton, Robert M. MA	1957	1995	(Glasgow: Shettleston Old)	6 Holmwood Gardens, Uddingston, Glasgow G71 7BH	01698 321108
Walker, A.L.	1955	1988	(Glasgow: Trinity Possil and		

Name	Dates	Role	Address	Phone
Walker, Linda	2008 2013	Auxiliary Minister	18 Valeview Terrace, Glasgow G42 9LA [E-mail: walkerlinda@hotmail.com]	0141-649 1340
Walton, Ainslie MA MEd	1954 1995	(University of Aberdeen)	501 Shields Road, Glasgow G41 2RF [E-mail: revainslie@aol.com]	0141-420 3327
White, C. Peter BVMS BD MRCVS	1974 2011	(Glasgow: Sandyford Henderson Memorial)	2 Hawthorn Place, Torrance, Glasgow G64 4EA [E-mail: revcpw@gmail.com]	01360 622680
Whyte, James BD	1981 2011	(Fairlie)	32 Torburn Avenue, Giffnock, Glasgow G46 7RB [E-mail: jameswhyte89@btinternet.com]	
Wilson, John BD	1985 2010	(Glasgow: Temple Anniesland)	4 Carron Crescent, Bearsden, Glasgow G61 1HJ [E-mail: revjwilson@btinternet.com]	0141-931 5609
Younger, Adah (Mrs) BD	1978 2004	(Glasgow: Dennistoun Central)	Flat 0/1, 101 Greenhead Street, Glasgow G40 1HR	0141-550 0878

GLASGOW ADDRESSES

Congregation	Church	Address
Banton		Kelvinhead Road, Banton
Bishopbriggs	Kenmure	Viewfield Road, Bishopbriggs
	Springfield Cambridge	The Leys, off Springfield Road
Broom		Mearns Road, Newton Mearns
Burnside Blairbeth		Church Avenue, Burnside / Kirkriggs Avenue, Blairbeth
Busby		Church Road, Busby
Cadder		Cadder Road, Bishopbriggs
Cambuslang	Flemington Hallside	Hutchinson Place
	Parish	Arnot Way
Campsie		Main Street, Lennoxtown
Chryston		Main Street, Chryston
Eaglesham		Montgomery Street, Eaglesham
Fernhill and Cathkin		Neilvaig Drive
Gartcosh		113 Lochend Road, Gartcosh
Giffnock	Orchardhill	Church Road
	South	Eastwood Toll
	The Park	Ravenscliffe Drive
Glenboig		138 Main Street, Glenboig
Greenbank		Eaglesham Road, Clarkston
Kilsyth	Anderson	Kingston Road, Kilsyth
	Burns and Old	Church Street, Kilsyth
Kirkintilloch	Hillhead	Newdyke Road, Kirkintilloch
	St Columba's	Waterside Road nr Auld Aisle Road
	St David's Mem Pk	Alexandra Street
	St Mary's	Cowgate
Lenzie	Old	Kirkintilloch Road x Garngaber Ave
	Union	65 Kirkintilloch Road
Maxwell Mearns Castle		Waterfoot Road
Mearns		Mearns Road, Newton Mearns
Milton of Campsie		Antermony Road, Milton of Campsie
Netherlee		Ormonde Drive x Ormonde Avenue
Newton Mearns		Ayr Road, Newton Mearns
Rutherglen	Old	Main Street at Queen Street
	Stonelaw	Stonelaw Road x Dryburgh Avenue
	West and Wardlawhill	3 Western Avenue
Stamperland		Stamperland Gardens, Clarkston
Stepps		Whitehill Avenue
Thorniebank		61 Spiersbridge Road
Torrance		School Road, Torrance
Twechar		Main Street, Twechar
Williamwood		4 Vardar Avenue, Clarkston

Glasgow

Congregation	Church	Address
Anderston Kelvingrove		759 Argyle St x Elderslie St
Baillieston	Mure Memorial	Maxwell Drive, Garrowhill
	St Andrew's	Bredisholm Road
Balshagray Victoria Pk		218–230 Broomhill Drive
Barlanark Greyfriars		Edinburgh Rd x Hallhill Rd (365)
Blawarthill		Millbrix Avenue
Bridgeton St Francis in the East		26 Queen Mary Street
Broomhill		64–66 Randolph Rd (x Marlborough Ave)
Calton Parkhead		122 Helenvale Street
Cardonald		2155 Paisley Road West
Carmunnock		Kirk Road, Carmunnock
Carmyle		155 Carmyle Avenue
Carnwadric		556 Boydstone Road, Thornliebank
Castlemilk		Carmunnock Road
Cathcart	Old	119 Carmunnock Road
	Trinity	90 Clarkston Road
Cathedral		Cathedral Square, 2 Castle Street
Clincarthill		1216 Cathcart Road
Colston Milton		Egilsay Crescent
Colston Wellpark		1378 Springburn Road
Cranhill		109 Bellrock St (at Bellrock Cr)
Croftfoot		Croftpark Ave x Crofthill Road
Dennistoun New		9 Armadale Street
Drumchapel St Andrew's		153 Garscadden Road

Church	Address
St Mark's	281 Kinfauns Drive
Easterhouse St George's and St Peter's	Boyndie Street
Eastwood	Mansewood Road
Gairbraid	1517 Maryhill Road
Gallowgate	David Street
Garthamlock and Craigend East	46 Porchester Street
Gorbals	1 Errol Gardens
Govan and Linthouse	Govan Cross
Govanhill Trinity	28 Daisy Street nr Allison Street
High Carntyne	358 Carntynehall Road
Hillington Park	24 Berryknowes Road
Hyndland	79 Hyndland Rd, opp Novar Dr
Ibrox	Carillon Road x Clifford Street
John Ross Memorial	100 Norfolk Street
Jordanhill	28 Woodend Drive (x Munro Road)
Kelvin Stevenson Mem	Belmont Street at Belmont Bridge
Kelvinside Hillhead	Observatory Road
Kenmuir Mount Vernon	2405 London Road, Mount Vernon
King's Park	242 Castlemilk Road
Kinning Park	Eaglesham Place
Knightswood St Margaret's	2000 Great Western Road
Langside	167–169 Ledard Road (x Lochleven Road)
Lansdowne	416 Gt Western Rd at Kelvin Bridge
Lochwood	2A Liff Place, Easterhouse
Maryhill	1990 Maryhill Road
Merrylea	78 Merrylee Road
Mosspark	167 Ashkirk Drive
Newlands South	Riverside Road x Langside Drive
Partick South	259 Dumbarton Road
Trinity	20 Lawrence Street
Penilee St Andrew's	Bowfield Cres x Bowfield Avenue
Pollokshaws	223 Shawbridge Street
Pollokshields	Albert Drive x Shields Road
Possilpark	124 Saracen Street
Queen's Park	170 Queen's Drive
Renfield St Stephen's	260 Bath Street
Robroyston	34 Saughs Road
Ruchazie	4 Elibank Street (x Milncroft Road)
Ruchill Kelvinside	Shakespeare Street nr Maryhill Rd and 10 Kelbourne Street (two buildings)
St Andrew's East	681 Alexandra Parade
St Christopher's Priesthill and Nitshill	
Priesthill building	100 Priesthill Rd (x Muirshiel Cr)
Nitshill building	36 Dove Street
St Christopher's	Meikle Road
St Columba	300 St Vincent Street
St David's Knightswood	66 Boreland Drive (nr Lincoln Avenue)
St Enoch's Hogganfield	860 Cumbernauld Road
St George's Tron	163 Buchanan Street
St James' (Pollok)	Lyoncross Road x Byrebush Road
St John's Renfield	22 Beaconsfield Road
St Margaret's Tollcross Pk	179 Braidfauld Street
St Nicholas' Cardonald	Hartlaw Crescent nr Gladsmuir Road
St Paul's	30 Langdale St (x Greenrig St)
St Rollox	9 Fountainwell Road
Sandyford Henderson Memorial	Kelvinhaugh Street at Argyle Street
Sandyhills	28 Baillieston Rd nr Sandyhills Rd
Scotstoun	Earlbank Avenue x Ormiston Avenue
Shawlands	Shawlands Cross (1114 Pollokshaws Road)
Sherbrooke St Gilbert's	Nithsdale Rd x Sherbrooke Avenue
Shettleston New	679 Old Shettleston Road
Shettleston Old	99–111 Killin Street
South Carntyne	538 Carntyne Road
South Shawlands	Regwood Street x Deanston Drive
Springburn	180 Springburn Way
Temple Anniesland	869 Crow Road
Torgylen	Glenmore Ave nr Prospecthill Road
Trinity Possil and Henry Drummond	2 Crowhill Street (x Broadholm Street)
Tron St Mary's	128 Red Road
Victoria Tollcross	1134 Tollcross Road
Wallacewell New Charge Development	no building yet obtained
Wellington	University Ave x Southpark Avenue
Whiteinch	35 Inchlee Street
Yoker	10 Hawick Street

(17) HAMILTON

Meets at Motherwell: Dalziel St Andrew's Parish Church Halls, on the first Tuesday of February, March, May, September, October, November and December, and on the third Tuesday of June.

Presbytery Office:	353 Orbiston Street, Motherwell ML1 1QW	01698 259135
	[E-mail: hamilton@cofscotland.org.uk]	
	[E-mail: clerk@presbyteryofhamilton.co.uk]	
Clerk: REV. SHAW J. PATERSON BSc BD MSc	c/o The Presbytery Office	
Depute Clerk: REV. JOHN L. McPAKE BA BD PhD	c/o The Presbytery Office	
Presbytery Treasurer: MR ROBERT A. ALLAN	7 Graham Place, Ashgill, Larkhall ML9 3BA	01698 883246
	[E-mail: Fallan3246@aol.com]	

1	**Airdrie: Broomknoll (H)** (01236 762101) linked with Calderbank			
	Vacant		38 Commonhead Street, Airdrie ML6 6NS	01236 609584
2	**Airdrie: Clarkston**			
	F. Derek Gunn BD	1986 2009	Clarkston Manse, Forrest Street, Airdrie ML6 7BE	01236 769676
3	**Airdrie: Flowerhill (H)**			
	Gary J. Caldwell BSc BD	2007	31 Victoria Place, Airdrie ML6 9BU	01236 754430
			[E-mail: garyjcaldwell@btinternet.com]	
4	**Airdrie: High**			
	Ian R.W. McDonald BSc BD PhD	2007	17 Etive Drive, Airdrie ML6 9QL	01236 760023
			[E-mail: ian@spingetastic.freeserve.co.uk]	
5	**Airdrie: Jackson**			
	Kay Gilchrist (Miss) BD	1996 2008	48 Dunrobin Road, Airdrie ML6 8LR	01236 760154
			[E-mail: gilky61@yahoo.co.uk]	
6	**Airdrie: New Monkland (H)** linked with Greengairs			
	William Jackson BD CertMin	1994 2008	3 Dykehead Crescent, Airdrie ML6 6PU	01236 763554
			[E-mail: newmonkgreengair@aol.com]	

7 Airdrie: St Columba's
Margaret F. Currie BEd BD 1980 1987
52 Kennedy Drive, Airdrie ML6 9AW
[E-mail: margaret_currie250@o2.co.uk]
01236 763173

8 Airdrie: The New Wellwynd
Robert A. Hamilton BA BD 1995 2001
20 Arthur Avenue, Airdrie ML6 9EZ
[E-mail: revrob13@blueyonder.co.uk]
01236 763022

9 Bargeddie (H)
John Fairful BD 1994 2001
The Manse, Manse Road, Bargeddie, Baillieston, Glasgow G69 6UB
[E-mail: johnfairful@yahoo.co.uk]
0141-771 1322

10 Bellshill: Macdonald Memorial linked with Bellshill: Orbiston
Alan McKenzie BSc BD 1988 2001
32 Adamson Street, Bellshill ML4 1DT
[E-mail: rev.a.mckenzie@btopenworld.com]
01698 849114

11 Bellshill: Orbiston See Bellshill: Macdonald Memorial

12 Bellshill: West (H) (01698 747581)
Agnes A. Moore (Miss) BD 1987 2001
16 Croftpark Street, Bellshill ML4 1EY
[E-mail: revamoore2@tiscali.co.uk]
01698 842877

13 Blantyre: Livingstone Memorial
Vacant
286 Glasgow Road, Blantyre, Glasgow G72 9DB
01698 823794

14 Blantyre: Old (H)
Vacant
The Manse, Craigmuir Road, High Blantyre, Glasgow G72 9UA
01698 823130

15 Blantyre: St Andrew's
Vacant
332 Glasgow Road, Blantyre, Glasgow G72 9LQ
01698 828633

16 Bothwell (H)
James M. Gibson TD LTh LRAM 1978 1989
Manse Avenue, Bothwell, Glasgow G71 8PQ
[E-mail: jamesmgibson@msn.com]
01698 853189 (Tel)
01698 854903 (Fax)

17 Calderbank See Airdrie: Broomknoll

18	**Caldercruix and Longriggend (H)** George M. Donaldson MA BD	1984	2005	Main Street, Caldercruix, Airdrie ML6 7RF [E-mail: g.donaldson505@btinternet.com]	01236 842279
19	**Chapelhall (H)** Gordon R. Mackenzie BScAgr BD	1977	2009	The Manse, Russell Street, Chapelhall, Airdrie ML6 8SG [E-mail: rev.g.mackenzie@btopenworld.com]	01236 763439
20	**Chapelton linked with Strathaven: Rankin (H)** Shaw J. Paterson BSc BD MSc	1991		15 Lethame Road, Strathaven ML10 6AD [E-mail: s.paterson195@btinternet.com]	01357 520019 (Tel) 01357 529316 (Fax)
	Maxine Buck (Aux)	2007		Brownlee House, Mauldslie Road, Carluke ML8 5HW [E-mail: maxinebuck01@aol.com]	01555 759063
21	**Cleland (H)** John A. Jackson BD	1997		The Manse, Bellside Road, Cleland, Motherwell ML1 5NP [E-mail: johnajackson932@btinternet.com]	01698 860260
22	**Coatbridge: Blairhill Dundyvan (H)** Vacant			18 Blairhill Street, Coatbridge ML5 1PG	01236 432304
23	**Coatbridge: Calder (H) linked with Coatbridge: Old Monkland** Vacant			26 Bute Street, Coatbridge ML5 4HF	01236 421516
24	**Coatbridge: Middle** Alexander M. Roger BD PhD	1982	2009	47 Blair Road, Coatbridge ML5 1JQ [E-mail: s.roger@btinternet.com]	01236 432427
25	**Coatbridge: New St Andrew's** Fiona Nicolson BA BD	1996	2005	77 Eglinton Street, Coatbridge ML5 3JF	01236 437271
26	**Coatbridge: Old Monkland** See Coatbridge: Calder				
27	**Coatbridge: Townhead (H)** Ecilo Selemani LTh MTh	1993	2004	Crinan Crescent, Coatbridge ML5 2LH [E-mail: eciloselemani@msn.com]	01236 702914

28 **Dalserf**
D. Cameron McPherson BSc BD DMin 1982
Manse Brae, Dalserf, Larkhall ML9 3BN
[E-mail: revcam@talktalk.net]
01698 882195

29 **East Kilbride: Claremont (H) (01355 238088)**
Gordon R. Palmer MA BD STM 1986
17 Deveron Road, East Kilbride, Glasgow G74 2HR
[E-mail: gkrspalmer@blueyonder.co.uk]
01355 248526

30 **East Kilbride: Greenhills (E) (01355 221746)**
John Brewster MA BD DipEd 1988
21 Turnberry Place, East Kilbride, Glasgow G75 8TB
[E-mail: johnbrewster@blueyonder.co.uk]
01355 242564

31 **East Kilbride: Moncreiff (H) (01355 223328)**
Neil Buchanan BD 1991
16 Almond Drive, East Kilbride, Glasgow G74 2HX
[E-mail: neil.buchanan@talk21.com]
01355 238639

32 **East Kilbride: Mossneuk (E) (01355 260954)**
John L. McPake BA BD PhD 1987
30 Eden Grove, Mossneuk, East Kilbride, Glasgow G75 8XU
[E-mail: jlm1961@hotmail.co.uk]
01355 234196

33 **East Kilbride: Old (H) (01355 279004)**
Anne S. Paton BA BD 2001
40 Maxwell Drive, East Kilbride, Glasgow G74 4HJ
[E-mail: annepaton@fsmail.net]
01355 220732

34 **East Kilbride: South (H)**
Mark Lowey BD DipTh 2012
7 Clamps Wood, East Kilbride, Glasgow G74 2HB
01355 702681

35 **East Kilbride: Stewartfield (New Charge Development)**
Douglas W. Wallace MA BD 1981 2001
8 Thistle Place, Stewartfield, East Kilbride, Glasgow G74 4RH
01355 260879

36 **East Kilbride: West (H)**
Mahboob Masih BA MDiv MTh 1999 2008
4 East Milton Grove, East Kilbride, Glasgow G75 8FN
[E-mail: m_masih@sky.com]
01355 224469

37 **East Kilbride: Westwood (H) (01355 245657)**
Kevin Mackenzie BD DPS 1989 1996
16 Inglewood Crescent, East Kilbride, Glasgow G75 8QD
[E-mail: kevin@westwoodmanse.freeserve.co.uk]
01355 223992

No.	Congregation / Minister		Address	Tel
38	**Glasford linked with Strathaven: East** William T. Stewart BD	1980	68 Townhead Street, Strathaven ML10 6DJ	01357 521138
39	**Greengairs** See Airdrie: New Monkland			
40	**Hamilton: Cadzow (H) (01698 428695)** John Carswell BS MDiv	1996 2009	3 Carlisle Road, Hamilton ML3 7BZ [E-mail: revcarswell@gmail.com]	01698 426682
41	**Hamilton: Gilmour and Whitehill (H)** Vacant			
	(This congregation has united with the congregation of Hamilton: Burnbank)			
42	**Hamilton: Hillhouse** David W.G. Burt BD DipMin	1989 1998	66 Wellhall Road, Hamilton ML3 9BY [E-mail: dwgburt@blueyonder.co.uk]	01698 422300
43	**Hamilton: Old (H) (01698 281905)** John M.A. Thomson TD JP BD ThM	1978 2001	1 Chateau Grove, Hamilton ML3 7DS [E-mail: jt@john1949.plus.com]	01698 422511
	(This congregation has united with the congregation of Hamilton: North)			
44	**Hamilton: St Andrew's (T)** Vacant		15 Bent Road, Hamilton ML3 6QB	01698 283264
45	**Hamilton: St John's (H) (01698 283492)** Joanne C. Hood (Miss) MA BD	2003 2012	9 Shearer Avenue, Ferniegair, Hamilton ML3 7FX [E-mail: hood137@btinternet.com]	01698 425002
46	**Hamilton: South (H) (01698 281014) linked with Quarter** Donald R. Lawrie	2012	The Manse, Limekilnburn Road, Quarter, Hamilton ML3 7XA	01698 424511
47	**Hamilton: Trinity (01698 284254)** Karen E. Harbison (Mrs) MA BD	1991	69 Buchan Street, Hamilton ML3 8JY [E-mail: calumkaren@yahoo.co.uk]	01698 425326

48 Hamilton: West (H) (01698 284670)
Elizabeth A. Waddell (Mrs) BD — 1999 2005
43 Bothwell Road, Hamilton ML3 0BB
[E-mail: elizabethwaddell@tiscali.co.uk]
01698 458770

49 Holytown linked with New Stevenston: Wrangholm Kirk
Caryl A.E. Kyle (Mrs) BD DipEd — 2008
The Manse, 260 Edinburgh Road, Holytown, Motherwell ML1 5RU
[E-mail: caryl_kyle@hotmail.com]
01698 832622

50 Kirk o' Shotts (H)
Vacant
The Manse, Kirk o' Shotts, Salsburgh, Shotts ML7 4NS
01698 870208

51 Larkhall: Chalmers (H)
Andrea M. Boyes — 2013
Quarry Road, Larkhall ML9 1HH
01698 882238

52 Larkhall: St Machan's (H)
Alastair McKillop BD DipMin — 1995 2004
2 Orchard Gate, Larkhall ML9 1HG
[E-mail: revicar@blueyonder.co.uk]
01698 321976

53 Larkhall: Trinity
Lindsay Schluter ThE CertMin PhD — 1995
13 Machan Avenue, Larkhall ML9 2HE
[E-mail: lindsay.schluter@o2.co.uk]
01698 881401

54 Motherwell: Crosshill (H) linked with Motherwell: St Margaret's
Gavin W.G. Black BD — 2006
15 Orchard Street, Motherwell ML1 3JE
[E-mail: gavin.black12@blueyonder.co.uk]
01698 263410

55 Motherwell: Dalziel St Andrew's (H) (01698 264097)
Derek W. Hughes BSc BD DipEd — 1990 1996
4 Pollock Street, Motherwell ML1 1LP
[E-mail: derekthecleric@btinternet.com]
01698 263414

56 Motherwell: North
Derek H.N. Pope BD — 1987 1995
35 Birrens Road, Motherwell ML1 3NS
[E-mail: derekpopemotherwell@hotmail.com]
01698 266716

57 Motherwell: St Margaret's See Motherwell: Crosshill

58 Motherwell: St Mary's (H)
David W. Doyle MA BD — 1977 1987
19 Orchard Street, Motherwell ML1 3JE
01698 263472

59 Motherwell: South (H)

Georgina M. Baxendale (Mrs) BD	1981	2009	62 Manse Road, Motherwell ML1 2PT [E-mail: georgiebaxendale6@tiscali.co.uk]	01698 239245
Linda E. Pollock (Miss) BD ThM ThM (Assoc)	2001	2012	33 Catherine Street, Motherwell ML1 2RW [E-mail: fantazomi@yahoo.co.uk]	01698 591091

60 Newarthill and Carfin

Vacant	Church Street, Newarthill, Motherwell ML1 5HS	01698 860316

61 Newmains: Bonkle (H) linked with Newmains: Coltness Memorial (H)

Graham Raeburn MTh	2004	5 Kirkgate, Newmains, Wishaw ML2 9BT [E-mail: grahamraeburn@tiscali.co.uk]	01698 383858

62 Newmains: Coltness Memorial See Newmains: Bonkle
63 New Stevenston: Wrangholm Kirk See Holytown

64 Overtown

Bruce H. Sinclair BA BD	2009	The Manse, 146 Main Street, Overtown, Wishaw ML2 0QP [E-mail: brucehsinclair@btinternet.com]	01698 352090

65 Quarter See Hamilton: South

66 Shotts: Calderhead Erskine

Allan B. Brown BD MTh	1995	2010	The Manse, 9 Kirk Road, Shotts ML7 5ET	01501 823204 07578 448655 (Mbl)

67 Stonehouse: St Ninian's (H)

Paul G.R. Grant BD MTh	2003	4 Hamilton Way, Stonehouse, Larkhall ML9 3PU [E-mail: minister@st-ninians-stonehouse.org.uk]	01698 792587

68 Strathaven: Avendale Old and Drumclog (H) (01357 529748)

Alan B. Telfer BA BD	1983	2010	4 Fortrose Gardens, Strathaven ML10 6SH [E-mail: minister@avendale-drumclog.com]	01357 523031

69 Strathaven: East See Glasford
70 Strathaven: Rankin See Chapelton

71 Uddingston: Burnhead (H)				
Les Brunger BD	2010		90 Laburnum Road, Uddingston, Glasgow G71 5DB [E-mail: lesbrunger@hotmail.co.uk]	01698 813716
72 Uddingston: Old (H) (01698 814015)				
Fiona L.J. McKibbin (Mrs) MA BD	2011		1 Belmont Avenue, Uddingston, Glasgow G71 7AX [E-mail: fionamckibbin@sky.com]	01698 814757
73 Uddingston: Viewpark (H)				
Michael G. Lyall BD	1993	2001	14 Holmbrae Road, Uddingston, Glasgow G71 6AP [E-mail: michaellyall@blueyonder.co.uk]	01698 813113
74 Wishaw: Cambusnethan North (H)				
Mhorag Macdonald (Ms) MA BD	1989		350 Kirk Road, Wishaw ML2 8LH [E-mail: mhoragmacdonald@btinternet.com]	01698 381305
75 Wishaw: Cambusnethan Old and Morningside				
Iain C. Murdoch MA LLB DipEd BD	1995		22 Coronation Street, Wishaw ML2 8LF [E-mail: iaincmurdoch@btopenworld.com]	01698 384235
76 Wishaw: Craigneuk and Belhaven (H) linked with Wishaw: Old				
Alan Greig BSc BD (Interim Minister)	1977	2013	130 Glen Road, Wishaw ML2 7NP	01698 375134
77 Wishaw: Old (H) (01698 376080) See Wishaw: Craigneuk and Belhaven				
78 Wishaw: St Mark's				
Graham Austin BD	1997	2008	The Manse, 302 Coltness Road, Wishaw ML2 7EY [E-mail: graham.austin4@btinternet.com]	01698 384596
79 Wishaw: South Wishaw (H)				
Vacant			3 Walter Street, Wishaw ML2 8LQ	01698 387292

Barrie, Arthur P. LTh	1973 2007	(Hamilton: Cadzow)	30 Airbles Crescent, Motherwell ML1 3AR [E-mail: elizabethbarrie@ymail.com]	01698 261147

Name			Charge	Address	Phone
Carruth, Patricia A. (Mrs) BD	1998	2012	(Coatbridge: Blairhill Dundyvan)	38 Springhill Farm Road, Baillieston, Glasgow G69 6GW	0141-771 3758
Colvin, Sharon E.F. (Mrs) BD LRAM LTCL	1985	2007	(Airdrie: Jackson)	25 Balblair Road, Airdrie ML6 6GQ [E-mail: dibleycol@hotmail.com]	01236 590796
Cook, J. Stanley BD Dip PSS	1974	2001	(Hamilton: West)	Mansend, 137A Old Manse Road, Netherton, Wishaw ML2 0EW [E-mail: stancook@blueyonder.co.uk]	01698 299600
Cullen, William T. BA LTh	1984	1996	(Kilmarnock: St John's Onthank)	6 Laurel Wynd, Cambuslang, Glasgow G72 7BA	0141-641 4337
Currie, David E.P. BSc BD	1983	2012	(Congregational Development Consultant)		
Currie, R. David BSc BD	1984	2004	(Cambuslang: Flemington Hallside)	69 Kethers Street, Motherwell ML1 3HN	01698 323424
Davidson, Amelia (Mrs) BD	2004	2011	(Coatbridge: Calder)	11 St Mary's Place, Saltcoats KA21 5NY	01698 383453
Dick, Roddy S.	2010		Auxiliary Minister	27 Easter Crescent, Wishaw ML2 8XB [E-mail: roddy.dick@btopenworld.com]	
Dunn, W. Stuart LTh	1970	2006	(Motherwell: Crosshill)	10 Macrostie Gardens, Crieff PH7 4LP	01764 655178
Fraser, James P.	1951	1988	(Strathaven: Avendale Old and Drumclog)	26 Hamilton Road, Strathaven ML10 6JA	01357 522758
Gordon, Alasdair B. BD LLB EdD	1970	1980	(Aberdeen: Summerhill)	Flat 1, 13 Auchingramont Road, Hamilton ML3 6JP [E-mail: alasdairbgordon@hotmail.com]	01698 200561 (Mbl) 07768 897843
Grier, James BD	1991	2005	(Coatbridge: Middle)	14 Love Drive, Bellshill ML4 1BY	01698 742545
Hastie, James S.G. CA BD	1990	2009	(Larkhall: Chalmers)	29 Mornington Grove, Blackwood, Kirkmuirhill, Lanark ML11 9GQ [E-mail: jim@jimandros.co.uk]	01555 896965
Hunter, James E. LTh	1974	1997	(Blantyre: Livingstone Memorial)	57 Dalwhinnie Avenue, Blantyre, Glasgow G72 9NQ	01698 826177
Kent, Robert M. MA BD	1973	2011	(Hamilton: St John's)	48 Fyne Crescent, Larkhall ML9 2UX [E-mail: robertmkent@talktalk.net]	01698 769244
Lusk, Alastair S. BD	1974	2010	(East Kilbride: Moncreiff)	9 MacFie Place, Stewartfield, East Kilbride, Glasgow G74 4TY	
McAlpine, John BSc	1988	2004	(Auxiliary Minister)	Braeside, 201 Bonkle Road, Newmains, Wishaw ML2 9AA	01698 384610
McCabe, George	1963	1996	(Airdrie: High)	Flat 8, Park Court, 2 Craighouse Park, Edinburgh EH10 5LD	0131-447 9522
McDonald, John A. MA BD	1978	1997	(Cumbernauld: Condorrat)	17 Thomson Drive, Bellshill ML4 3ND	
McKee, Norman B. BD	1987	2010	(Uddingston: Old)	148 Station Road, Blantyre, Glasgow G72 9BW [E-mail: n.mckee@btinternet.com]	01698 827358
MacKenzie, Ian C. MA BD	1970	2011	(Interim Minister)	21 Wilson Street, Motherwell ML1 1NP [E-mail: iancmac@blueyonder.co.uk]	01698 301230
McKenzie, Raymond D. BD	1978	2012	(Hamilton: Burnbank with Hamilton: North)	25 Austine Drive, Hamilton ML3 7YE [E-mail: rdmackenzie@hotmail.co.uk]	
MacLeod, Norman BTh	1999	2013	(Hamilton: St Andrew's)	15 Bent Road, Hamilton ML3 6QB [E-mail: normanmacleod@blueyonder.co.uk]	01698 283264
Martin, James MA BD DD	1946	1987	(Glasgow: High Carntyne)	9 Magnolia Street, Wishaw ML2 7EQ	01698 385825
Melrose, J.H. Loudon MA BD MEd	1955	1996	(Gourock: Old Gourock and Ashton [Assoc])	1 Laverock Avenue, Hamilton ML3 7DD	01698 427958
Munton, James G. BA	1969	2002	(Coatbridge: Old Monkland)	2 Moorcroft Drive, Airdrie ML6 8ES [E-mail: jacjim@supanet.com]	01236 754848
Price, Peter O. CBE QHC BA FPhS	1960	1996	(Blantyre: Old)	22 Old Bothwell Road, Bothwell, Glasgow G71 8AW [E-mail: peteroprice@aol.com]	01698 854032
Rogerson, Stuart D. BSc BD	1980	2001	(Strathaven: West)	17 Westfield Park, Strathaven ML10 6XH [E-mail: srogerson@cnetwork.co.uk]	01357 523321
Ross, Keith W. MA BD	1984	2007	Congregational Development Officer for the Presbytery of Hamilton	Easter Bavelaw House, Pentland Hills Regional Park, Balerno EH14 7JS [E-mail: keithross.hamiltonpresbytery@googlemail.com]	(Mbl) 07855 163449

Name			Charge	Address	Tel
Salmond, James S. BA BD MTh ThD	1979	2003	(Holytown)	165 Torbothie Road, Shotts ML7 5NE	01555 892742
Sharp, John C. BSc BD PhD	1980	2011	(East Kilbride: South)	10 Rogerhill Gait, Kirkmuirhill, Lanark ML11 9XR	01698 870598
Spence, Sheila M. (Mrs) MA BD	1979	2010	(Kirk o' Shotts)	6 Drumbowie Crescent, Salsburgh, Shotts ML7 4NP	
Stevenson, John LTh	1998	2006	(Cambuslang: St. Andrew's)	20 Knowehead Gardens, Uddingston, Glasgow G71 7PY [E-mail therev20@sky.com]	01698 817582
Stitt, Ronald J. Maxwell LTh BA ThM BREd DMin FSAScot	1977	2012	(Hamilton: Gilmour and Whitehill)	413 Gilmerton Road, Edinburgh EH17 7JJ	
Thorne, Leslie W. BA LTh	1987	2001	(Coatbridge: Clifton)	'Hatherleigh', 9 Chatton Walk, Coatbridge ML5 4FH [E-mail: lesthorne@tiscali.co.uk]	01236 432241 (Mbl) 07963 199921
Wilson, James H. LTh	1970	1996	(Cleland)	21 Austine Drive, Hamilton ML3 7YE [E-mail: wilsonjh@blueyonder.co.uk]	01698 457042
Wyllie, Hugh R. MA DD FCIBS	1962	2000	(Hamilton: Old)	18 Chantinghall Road, Hamilton ML3 8NP	01698 420002
Zambonini, James LIADip	1997		Auxiliary Minister	100 Old Manse Road, Wishaw ML2 0EP	01698 350889

HAMILTON ADDRESSES

Airdrie
- Broomknoll — Broomknoll Street
- Clarkston — Forrest Street
- Flowerhill — 89 Graham Street
- High — North Bridge Street
- Jackson — Glen Road
- New Monkland — Glenmavis
- St Columba's — Thrashbush Road
- The New Wellwynd — Wellwynd

Coatbridge
- Blairhill Dundyvan — Blairhill Street
- Calder — Calder Street
- Middle — Bank Street
- New St Andrew's — Church Street
- Old Monkland — Woodside Street
- Townhead — Crinan Crescent

East Kilbride
- Claremont — High Common Road, St Leonard's
- Greenhills — Greenhills Centre
- Moncreiff — Calderwood Road
- Mossneuk — Eden Drive
- Old — Montgomery Street
- South — Baird Hill, Murray
- West — Kittoch Street
- Westwood — Belmont Drive, Westwood

Hamilton
- Burnbank — High Blantyre Road
- Cadzow — Woodside Walk
- Gilmour and Whitehill — Glasgow Road, Burnbank
- Hillhouse — Abbotsford Road, Whitehill
- North — Clerkwell Road
- Old — Windmill Road
- St Andrew's — Leechlee Road
- St John's — Avon Street
- South — Duke Street
- Trinity — Strathaven Road
- West — Neilsland Square off North Road
- Burnbank Road

Motherwell
- Crosshill — Windmillhill Street x Airbles Street
- Dalziel St Andrew's — Merry Street and Muir Street
- North — Chesters Crescent
- St Margaret's — Shields Road
- St Mary's — Avon Street
- South — Gavin Street

Uddingston
- Burnhead — Laburnum Road
- Old — Old Glasgow Road
- Viewpark — Old Edinburgh Road

Wishaw
- Cambusnethan
  - North — Kirk Road
  - Old — Kirk Road
- Craigneuk and Belhaven — Craigneuk Street
- Old — Main Street
- St Mark's — Coltness Road
- South Wishaw — East Academy Street

(18) DUMBARTON

Meets at Dumbarton, in Riverside Church Halls, on the first Tuesday of February, March, April (if required), May (if required), June, September, October (if required), November and December, and on the third Tuesday of June at the incoming Moderator's church for the installation of the Moderator.

Clerk:	REV. DAVID W. CLARK MA BD			37 Campbell Street, Helensburgh G84 9NH [E-mail: dumbarton@cofscotland.org.uk]	01436 674063
Alexandria Elizabeth W. Houston MA BD DipEd		1985	1995	32 Ledrish Avenue, Balloch, Alexandria G83 8JB	01389 751933
Arrochar linked with Luss H. Dane Sherrard BD DMin		1971	1998	The Manse, Luss, Alexandria G83 8NZ [E-mail: dane@lussonline.net]	01436 860240 07801 939138 (Mbl)
Baldernock (H) Andrew P. Lees BD		1984	2002	The Manse, Bardowie, Milngavie, Glasgow G62 6ES [E-mail: andrew.lees@yahoo.co.uk]	01360 620471
Bearsden: Baljaffray (H) Ian McEwan BSc PhD BD FRSE		2008		5 Fintry Gardens, Bearsden, Glasgow G61 4RJ [E-mail: mcewan7@btinternet.com]	0141-942 0366
Bearsden: Cross (H) Graeme R. Wilson MCIBS BD ThM		2006	2013	61 Drymen Road, Bearsden, Glasgow G61 2SU [E-mail: graeme.wilson@gmail.com]	0141-942 0507
Bearsden: Killermont (H) Alan J. Hamilton LLB BD		2003		8 Clathic Avenue, Bearsden, Glasgow G61 2HF [E-mail: ajh63@o2.co.uk]	0141-942 0021
Bearsden: New Kilpatrick (H) (0141-942 8827) (E-mail: mail@nkchurch.org.uk) Roderick G. Hamilton MA BD		1992	2011	51 Manse Road, Bearsden, Glasgow G61 3PN [E-mail: rghamilton@ntlworld.com]	0141-942 0035
Bearsden: Westerton Fairlie Memorial (H) (0141-942 6960) Christine M. Goldie LLB BD MTh DMin		1984	2008	3 Canniesburn Road, Bearsden, Glasgow G61 1PW [E-mail: christinegoldie@talktalk.net]	0141-942 2672

Bonhill (H) (01389 756516) linked with Renton: Trinity (H)
Vacant   1 Glebe Gardens, Bonhill, Alexandria G83 9NZ

Cardross (H) (01389 841322)
Vacant

Clydebank: Abbotsford (E-mail: abbotsford@lineone.net) (Website: www.abbotsford.org.uk) linked with Dalmuir: Barclay (0141-941 3988)
Vacant   16 Parkhall Road, Dalmuir, Clydebank G81 3RJ   0141-941 3317

Clydebank: Faifley
Gregor McIntyre BSc BD   1991   Kirklea, Cochno Road, Hardgate, Clydebank G81 6PT   01389 876836
[E-mail: mail@gregormcintyre.com]

Clydebank: Kilbowie St Andrew's linked with Clydebank: Radnor Park (H)
Margaret J.B. Yule BD   1992   11 Tiree Gardens, Old Kilpatrick, Glasgow G60 5AT   01389 875599
[E-mail: mjbyule@yahoo.co.uk]

Clydebank: Radnor Park See Clydebank: Kilbowie St Andrew's

Clydebank: St Cuthbert's linked with Duntocher (H)
Guardianship of the Presbytery

Craigrownie linked with Rosneath: St Modan's (H)
Vacant   Edenkiln, Argyll Road, Kilcreggan, Helensburgh G84 0JW   01436 842274

Dalmuir: Barclay See Clydebank: Abbotsford

Dumbarton: Riverside (H) (01389 742551)
Vacant   18 Castle Road, Dumbarton G82 1LF

Dumbarton: St Andrew's (H) linked with Old Kilpatrick Bowling
Vacant   17 Mansewood Drive, Dumbarton G82 3EU   01389 726715

Dumbarton: West Kirk (H)
Elaine W. McKinnon MA BD   1988   2010   3 Havoc Road, Dumbarton G82 4JW   01389 765234

Duntocher (H) See Clydebank: St Cuthbert's

Garelochhead (01436 810589)
Vacant
Old School Road, Garelochhead, Helensburgh G84 0AT
01436 810022

Helensburgh: Park (H) (01436 674825)
Vacant

Helensburgh: St Andrew's Kirk (H) (01436 676880) linked with Rhu and Shandon (H)
David W. Clark MA BD   1975   1986   37 Campbell Street, Helensburgh G84 9NH   01436 674063
[E-mail: clarkdw@talktalk.net]
George Vidits BD MTh   2000   2006   46 Suffolk Street, Helensburgh G84 9QZ   01436 672054
[E-mail: george.vidits@btinternet.com]

Jamestown (H)
Norma Moore MA BD   1995   2004   26 Kessog's Gardens, Balloch, Alexandria G83 8QJ   01389 756447
[E-mail: norma.moore5@btinternet.com]

Kilmaronock Gartocharn
Guardianship of the Presbytery

Luss See Arrochar

Milngavie: Cairns (H) (0141-956 4868)
Andrew Frater BA BD MTh   1987   1994   4 Cairns Drive, Milngavie, Glasgow G62 8AJ   0141-956 1717
[E-mail: office@cairnschurch.org.uk]

Milngavie: St Luke's (0141-956 4226)
Ramsay B. Shields BA BD   1990   1997   70 Hunter Road, Milngavie, Glasgow G62 7BY   0141-577 9171 (Tel)
[E-mail: rbs@minister.com]   0141-577 9181 (Fax)

Milngavie: St Paul's (H) (0141-956 4405)
Fergus C. Buchanan MA BD MTh   1982   1988   8 Buchanan Street, Milngavie, Glasgow G62 8DD   0141-956 1043
[E-mail: f.c.buchanan@ntlworld.com]

Old Kilpatrick Bowling See Dumbarton: St Andrew's
Renton: Trinity See Bonhill
Rhu and Shandon See Helensburgh: St Andrew's Kirk
Rosneath: St Modan's See Craigrownie

Name	Ord.	Ind.	Charge	Address	Tel
Booth, Frederick M. LTh	1970	2005	(Helensburgh: St Columba)	Achnashie Coach House, Clynder, Helensburgh G84 0QD [E-mail: boothef@btinternet.com]	01436 831858
Crombie, William D. MA BD	1947	1987	(Glasgow: Calton New with St Andrew's)	9 Fairview Court, 46 Main Street, Milngavie, Glasgow G62 6BU	0141-956 1898
Donaghy, Leslie G. BD DipMin PGCE FSAScot	1990	2004	(Dumbarton: St Andrew's)	53 Oak Avenue, East Kilbride, Glasgow G75 9ED [E-mail: leslie@donaghy.org.uk]	(Mbl) 07809 484812
Ferguson, Archibald M. MSc PhD CEng FRINA	1989	2004	(Auxiliary Minister)	The Whins, 2 Barrowfield, Station Road, Cardross, Dumbarton G82 5NL [E-mail: drarchieferguson@gmail.com]	01389 841517
Hamilton, David G. MA BD	1971	2004	(Braes of Rannoch with Foss and Rannoch)	79 Finlay Rise, Milngavie, Glasgow G62 6QL [E-mail: davidhamilton40@googlemail.com]	0141-956 4202
Harris, John W.F. MA	1967	2012	(Bearsden: Cross)	68 Mitre Road, Glasgow G14 9LL [E-mail: jwfh@sky.com]	0141-321 1061
Hudson, Eric V. LTh	1971	2007	(Bearsden: Westerton Fairlie Memorial)	2 Murrayfield Drive, Bearsden, Glasgow G61 1JE [E-mail: evhudson@hotmail.co.uk]	0141-942 6110
Inglis, Donald B.C. MA MEd BD	1975	2000	(Turriff: St Andrew's)	39 Thomson Drive, Bearsden, Glasgow G61 3PA	0141-942 1387
Kemp, Tina MA		2005	Auxiliary Minister	12 Oaktree Gardens, Dumbarton G82 1EU [E-mail: tinakemp@blueyonder.co.uk]	01389 730477
Lawson, Alexander H. ThM ThD FPhS	1950	1988	(Clydebank: Kilbowie)	Erskine Park Nursing Home, Bishopton PA7 5QA	
McIntyre, J. Ainslie MA BD	1963	1984	(University of Glasgow)	60 Bonnaughton Road, Bearsden, Glasgow G61 4DB [E-mail: jamcintyre@hotmail.com]	0141-942 5143 (Mbl) 07050 295103
MacMahon, Janet P.H. (Mrs) MSc BD	1992	2010	(Kilmaronock Gartocharn)	14 Hillfoot Drive, Bearsden, Glasgow G61 3QQ [E-mail: janetmacmahon@yahoo.co.uk]	0141-942 8611
Miller, Ian H. BA BD	1975	2012	(Bonhill)	Derand, Queen Street, Alexandria G83 0AS [E-mail: revianmiller@btinternet.com]	01389 753039
Munro, David P. MA BD STM	1953	1996	(Bearsden: North)	14 Birch Road, Killearn, Glasgow G63 9SQ [E-mail: david.munro1929@btinternet.com]	01360 550098
Murdoch, Christine	1999	2012	(Lochwinnoch)	Flat 2, The Ponderosa, Shore Road, Kilcreggan, Helensburgh G84 0HQ [E-mail: rev.christine@btinternet.com]	01436 842565 (Mbl) 07973 331890
O'Donnell, Barbara		2007	Auxiliary Minister	Ashbank, 258 Main Street, Alexandria G83 0NU	01389 752356
Ramage, Alastair E. MA BA ADB CertEd	1996	2004	Auxiliary Minister	16 Claremont Gardens, Milngavie, Glasgow G62 6PG [E-mail: sueandalastairramage@btinternet.com]	0141-956 2897
Speed, David K. LTh	1969	2004	(Glasgow: Shettleston Old)	153 West Princes Street, Helensburgh G84 8EZ [E-mail: dkspeed@btinternet.com]	01436 674493
Steven, Harold A.M. MStJ LTh FSA Scot	1970	2001	(Baldernock)	9 Cairnhill Road, Bearsden, Glasgow G61 1AT [E-mail: harold.allison.steven@gmail.com]	0141-942 1598
Stewart, Charles E. BSc BD MTh PhD	1976	2010	(Chaplain of the Fleet)	105 Sinclair Street, Helensburgh G84 9HY [E-mail: c.e.stewart@btinternet.com]	01436 678113
West, Richard B.	1994	2013	(Craigrownie with Rosneath: St Modan's)	Carriden, Shore Road, Kilcreggan, Helensburgh G84 0HG [E-mail: rickangelawest@yahoo.co.uk]	(Mbl) 07751 834832
Wright, Malcolm LTh	1970	2003	(Craigrownie with Rosneath: St Modan's)	30 Clairinsh, Drumkinnon Gate, Balloch, Alexandria G83 8SE [E-mail: malcolmcatherine@msn.com]	01389 720338

DUMBARTON ADDRESSES

Bearsden
Baljaffray — Grampian Way
Cross — Drymen Road
Killermont — Rannoch Drive
New Kilpatrick — Manse Road
Westerton — Crarae Avenue

Clydebank
Abbotsford — Town Centre
Faifley — Faifley Road

Kilbowie St Andrew's — Radnor Park
St Cuthbert's

Dumbarton
Riverside
St Andrew's — West Kirk

Kilbowie Road — Radnor Street
Linnvale

High Street
Aitkenbar Circle
West Bridgend

Helensburgh
Park — St Andrew's Kirk — Charlotte Street — Colquhoun Square

Milngavie
Cairns — St Luke's — Buchanan Street
St Paul's — Kirk Street — Strathblane Road

(19) ARGYLL

Meets in the Village Hall, Tarbert, Loch Fyne, Argyll on the first Tuesday or Wednesday of March, June, September and December. For details, contact the Presbytery Clerk.

Clerk:	**DR CHRISTOPHER T. BRETT MA PhD**		Minahey Cottage, Kames, Tighnabruaich PA21 2AD	**01700 811142**
			[E-mail: argyll@cofscotland.org.uk]	
Treasurer:	**MRS PAMELA A. GIBSON**		Allt Ban, Portsonachan, Dalmally PA33 1BJ	**01866 833344**
			[E-mail: justpam1@tesco.net]	

Appin linked with Lismore
Roderick D.M. Campbell
OStJ TD BD DMin FSAScot   1975   2008   The Manse, Appin PA38 4DD   01631 730143
[E-mail: rdmcampbell@aol.com]

Ardchattan (H)
Jeffrey A. McCormick BD   1984   Ardchattan Manse, North Connel, Oban PA37 1RG   01631 710364
[E-mail: jeff.mcc@virgin.net]

Ardrishaig (H) linked with South Knapdale
David Carruthers BD   1998   The Manse, Park Road, Ardrishaig, Lochgilphead PA30 8HE   01546 603269

Barra (GD)
Vacant   Cuithir, Castlebay, Isle of Barra HS9 5XD   01871 810230

Campbeltown: Highland (H)
Vacant — Highland Church Manse, Kirk Street, Campbeltown PA28 6BN — 01586 551146

Campbeltown: Lorne and Lowland (H)
Philip D. Burroughs BSc BTh DTS — 1998 2004 — Lorne and Lowland Manse, Castlehill, Campbeltown PA28 6AN
[E-mail: burroughs@btinternet.com] — 01586 552468

Kirsty-Ann Burroughs (Mrs) BA BD CertTheol DRM PhD (Aux) — 2007 — Lorne and Lowland Manse, Castlehill, Campbeltown PA28 6AN
[E-mail: burroughs@btinternet.com] — 01586 552468

Coll linked with Connel
George G. Cringles BD — 1981 2002 — St Oran's Manse, Connel, Oban PA37 1PJ
[E-mail: george.cringles@btinternet.com] — (Connel) 01631 710242 / (Coll) 01879 230366

Colonsay and Oronsay (Website: www.islandchurches.org.uk)
Vacant

Connel See Coll

Craignish linked with Kilbrandon and Kilchattan linked with Kilninver and Kilmelford (Netherlorn)
Kenneth R. Ross BA BD PhD — 1982 2010 — The Manse, Kilmelford, Oban PA34 4XA
[E-mail: kennethr.ross@btinternet.com] — 01852 200565

Cumlodden, Lochfyneside and Lochgair linked with Glenaray and Inveraray (West Lochfyneside)
Louis C. Bezuidenhout BA MA BD DD — 1978 2009 — The Manse, Inveraray PA32 8XT
[E-mail: macbez@btinternet.com] — 01499 302060

Dunoon: St John's linked with Kirn (H) linked with Sandbank (H) (Central Cowal)
Vacant — The Manse, 13 Dhailling Park, Hunter Street, Kirn, Dunoon PA23 8FB — 01369 702256

Glenda M. Wilson (Mrs) DCS — 1990 2006 — Ardlayne, 23 Bullwood Road, Dunoon PA23 7QJ
[E-mail: deacglendamwilson@gmail.com] — 01369 700848

Dunoon: The High Kirk (H) linked with Innellan linked with Toward (South-East Cowal)
Aileen M. Robson (Miss) BD — 2003 2011 — 7A Mathieson Lane, Innellan, Dunoon PA23 7SH
[E-mail: am65robson@ymail.com] — 01369 830276

Ruth I. Griffiths (Mrs) (Aux) — 2004 — Kirkwood, Mathieson Lane, Innellan, Dunoon PA23 7TA
[E-mail: ruthigriffiths@googlemail.com] — 01369 830145

Gigha and Cara (H) (GD) linked with Kilcalmonell linked with Killean and Kilchenzie
Vacant
The Manse, Isle of Gigha PA41 7AA
and/or The Manse, Muasdale, Tarbert, Argyll PA29 6XD
01583 505245
01583 421249

Glassary, Kilmartin and Ford linked with North Knapdale
Clifford R. Acklam BD MTh   1997   2010
The Manse, Kilmichael Glassary, Lochgilphead PA31 8QA
[E-mail: clifford.acklam@btinternet.com]
01546 606926

Glenaray and Inveraray See Cumlodden, Lochfyneside and Lochgair

Glenorchy and Innishael linked with Strathfillan
Elizabeth A. Gibson (Mrs) MA MLitt BD   2003   2008
The Manse, Dalmally PA33 1AA
[E-mail: lizgibson@phonecoop.coop]
01838 200207

Innellan (H) See Dunoon: The High Kirk

Iona linked with Kilfinichen and Kilvickeon and the Ross of Mull
John K. Collard MA BD (Interim Minister)   1986   2013
The Manse, Bunessan, Isle of Mull PA67 6DW
01681 700227

Jura (GD) linked with Kilarrow (H) linked with Kildalton and Oa (GD) (H)
Vacant
The Manse, Bowmore, Isle of Islay PA43 7LH
01496 810271

Kilarrow See Jura
Kilbrandon and Kilchattan See Craignish
Kilcalmonell See Gigha and Cara

Kilchoman (GD) linked with Kilmeny linked with Portnahaven (GD)
Valerie G.C. Watson MA BD STM   1987   2013
The Manse, Port Charlotte, Isle of Islay PA48 7TW
[E-mail: vgcwatson@btinternet.com]
01496 850241

Kilchrenan and Dalavich linked with Muckairn
Robert E. Brookes BD   2009
Muckairn Manse, Taynuilt PA35 1HW
[E-mail: eilanview@uwclub.net]
01866 822204

Kildalton and Oa (GD) (H) See Jura

Kilfinan linked with Kilmodan and Colintraive linked with Kyles (H) (West Cowal)
David Mitchell BD DipPTheol MSc   1988   2006
West Cowal Manse, Kames, Tighnabruaich PA21 2AD
[E-mail: revdmitchell@yahoo.co.uk]
01700 811045

Kilfinichen and Kilvickeon and the Ross of Mull See Iona
Killean and Kilchenzie (H) See Gigha and Cara
Kilmeny See Kilchoman
Kilmodan and Colintraive See Kilfinan

Kilmore (GD) and Oban (Website: www.obanchurch.com)
Dugald J.R. Cameron BD DipMin MTh   1990   2007   Kilmore and Oban Manse, Ganavan Road, Oban PA34 5TU   01631 566253
[E-mail: obancofs@btinternet.com]

Kilmun (St Munn's) (H) linked with Strone (H) and Ardentinny
David Mill KJSJ MA BD   1978   2010   The Manse, Blairmore, Dunoon PA23 8TE   01369 840313
[E-mail: revandevmill@aol.com]

Kilninian and Kilmore linked with Salen (H) and Ulva linked with Tobermory (GD) (H)
linked with Torosay (H) and Kinlochspelvie (North Mull)
John H. Paton BSc BD   1983   2013   The Manse, Gruline Road, Salen, Aros, Isle of Mull PA72 6XF   01680 300001
[E-mail: jpaton160@btinternet.com]
(Kilninian and Kilmore is the new name for the charge formerly known as Mull, Isle of, Kilninian and Kilmore)

Kilninver and Kilmelford See Craignish
Kirn (H) See Dunoon: St John's
Kyles See Kilfinan
Lismore See Appin

Lochgilphead
Hilda C. Smith (Miss) MA BD MSc   1992   2005   Parish Church Manse, Manse Brae, Lochgilphead PA31 8QZ   01546 602238
[E-mail: hilda.smith2@btinternet.com]

Lochgoilhead (H) and Kilmorich linked with Strachur and Strathlachlan (Upper Cowal)
Robert K. Mackenzie MA BD PhD   1976   1998   The Manse, Strachur, Cairndow PA27 8DG   01369 860246
[E-mail: rkmackenzie@strachurmanse.fsnet.co.uk]

Muckairn See Kilchrenan and Dalavich
North Knapdale See Glassary, Kilmartin and Ford
Portnahaven See Kilchoman

Rothesay: Trinity (H) (Website: www.rothesaytrinity.org)
Andrew Barrie BSc BD   1984   2010   12 Crichton Road, Rothesay, Isle of Bute PA20 9JR   0170 503010
[E-mail: drew.barrie@btinternet.com]

Saddell and Carradale (H) linked with Southend (H)
Stephen Fulcher BA MA   1993   2012   St Blaan's Manse, Southend, Campbeltown PA28 6RQ   01586 830504
[E-mail: steve@pcmanse.plus.com]

Salen and Ulva See Kilninian and Kilmore
Sandbank (H) See Dunoon: St John's

Skipness
Vacant

Southend (H) See Saddell and Carradale
South Knapdale See Ardrishaig

South Uist (GD)
Vacant   Daliburgh, Lochboisdale, Isle of South Uist HS8 5SS   01878 700265

Strachur and Strathlachlan See Lochgoilhead and Kilmorich
Strathfillan See Glenorchy and Innishael
Strone (H) and Ardentinny See Kilmun

Tarbert, Loch Fyne and Kilberry (H)
Thomas M. Bryson BD   1997   2011   The Manse, Campbeltown Road, Tarbert, Argyll PA29 6SX   01880 821012
[E-mail: thomas@bryson3.wanadoo.co.uk]
(New charge formed by the union of Tarbert (Loch Fyne) and Kilberry)

The United Church of Bute
John Owain Jones MA BD FSAScot   1981   2011   10 Bishop Terrace, Rothesay, Isle of Bute PA20 9HF   01700 504502
[E-mail: johnowainjones@ntlworld.com]

Tiree (GD)
Elspeth J. MacLean (Mrs) BVMS BD   2011   The Manse, Scarinish, Isle of Tiree PA77 6TN   01879 220377
[E-mail: ejmaclean@yahoo.co.uk]

Tobermory   See Kilninian and Kilmore
Torosay and Kinlochspelvie   See Kilninian and Kilmore
Toward (H)   See Dunoon: The High Kirk

Beautyman, Paul H. MA BD	1993	2009	Team Leader: Youth Education Ministries	59 Alexander Street, Dunoon PA23 7BB [E-mail: paul.beautyman@argyll-bute.gov.uk]	(Mbl) 07596 164112
Bell, Douglas W. MA LLB BD	1975	1993	(Alexandria: North)	3 Cairnbaan Lea, Cairnbaan, Lochgilphead PA31 8BA	01546 606815
Bristow, W.H.G. BEd HDipRE DipSpecEd	1951	2002	(Chaplain: Army)	Choc Ban, Southend, Campbeltown PA28 6RQ	01586 830667
Dunlop, Alistair J. MA	1965	2004	(Saddell and Carradale)	8 Pipers Road, Cairnbaan, Lochgilphead PA31 8UF [E-mail: dunrevn@btinternet.com]	01546 600316
Forrest, Alan B. MA	1956	1993	(Uphall: South)	126 Shore Road, Innellan, Dunoon PA23 7SX	01369 830424
Fulcher, Christine	2012	2013	Ordained Local Minister	St Blaan's Manse, Southend, Campbeltown PA28 6RQ [E-mail: chris@pcmanse.plus.com]	01586 830504
Gibson, Frank S. BL BD STM DSWA DD	1963	1995	(Kilarrow with Kilmeny)	163 Gilbertstoun, Edinburgh EH15 2RG	0131-657 5208
Goss, Alister J. BD DMin	1975	2009	(Industrial Chaplain)	24 Albert Place, Ardnadam, Sandbank, Dunoon PA23 8QF [E-mail: scimwest@hotmail.com]	01369 704495
Gray, William LTh	1971	2006	(Kilberry with Tarbert)	Lochnagar, Longsdale Road, Oban PA34 5DZ [E-mail: gray98@hotmail.com]	01631 567471
Henderson, Charles M.	1952	1989	(Campbeltown: Highland)	Springbank House, Askomill Walk, Campbeltown PA28 6EP	01586 552759
Henderson, Grahame McL. BD	1974	2008	(Kirn)	6 Gerthallow, Bullwood Road, Dunoon PA23 7QB [E-mail: ghende5884@aol.com]	01369 702433
Hood, Catriona A.		2006	Auxiliary Minister	'Elyside', Dalintober, Campbeltown PA28 6EB [E-mail: catriona.hood@argyll-bute.gov.uk]	01586 551490
Hood, H. Stanley C. MA BD	1966	2000	(London: Crown Court)	10 Dalriada Place, Kilmichael Glassary, Lochgilphead PA31 8QA	01546 606168
Lamont, Archibald	1952	1994	(Kilcalmonell with Skipness)	8 Achlonan, Taynuilt PA35 1JJ	01866 822385
Lind, Michael J. LLB BD	1984	2012	(Campbeltown: Highland)	Maybank, Station Road, Conon Bridge, Dingwall IV7 8BJ [E-mail: mijylind@btinternet.com]	
Macfarlane, James PhD	1991	2011	(Lochgoilhead and Kilmorich)	'Lindores', 11 Bullwood Road, Dunoon PA23 7QJ [E-mail: mac.farlane@btinternet.com]	01369 710626
McIvor, Anne (Miss) SRD BD	1996	2013	(Gigha and Cara)	20 Albyn Avenue, Campbeltown PA28 6LY [E-mail: annemcivor@btinternet.com]	
MacLeod, Roderick MA BD PhD(Edin) PhD(Open)	1966	2011	(Cumlodden, Lochfyneside and Lochgair)	Creag-nam-Barnach, Furnace, Inveraray PA32 8XU [E-mail: revroddy@btinternet.com]	01499 500629
Marshall, Freda (Mrs) BD FCII	1993	2005	(Colonsay and Oronsay with Kilbrandon and Kilchattan)	Allt Mhaluidh, Glenview, Dalmally PA33 1BE [E-mail: mail@freda.org.uk]	01838 200693
Millar, Margaret R.M. (Miss) BTh	1977	2008	(Kilchrenan and Dalavich with Muckairn)	Fearnoch Cottage, Fearnoch, Taynuilt PA35 1JB [E-mail: macoje@aol.com]	01866 822416
Morrison, Angus W. MA BD	1959	1999	(Kildalton and Oa)	1 Livingstone Way, Port Ellen, Isle of Islay PA42 7EP	01496 300043
Risby, Lesley P. (Mrs) BD	1994	2013	(Saline and Blairingone)	Tigh an Achaidh, 21 Fernoch Crescent, Lochgilphead PA31 8AE [E-mail: mrsrisby@hotmail.com]	01546 600464

Name			(Parish)	Address	Phone
Ritchie, Walter M.	1973	1999	(Uphall: South)		
Scott, Randolph MA BD	1991	2013	(Jersey: St Columba's)	Hazel Cottage, Barr Mor View, Kilmartin, Lochgilphead PA31 8UN	01546 510343
				18 Lochan Avenue, Kirn, Dunoon PA23 8HT	01369 703175
				[E-mail: rev.rs@hotmail.com]	
Shedden, John CBE BD DipPSS	1971	2008	(Fuengirola)	Orchy Cottage, Dalmally PA33 1AX	01838 200535
				[E-mail: shedden7@googlemail.com]	
Stewart, Joseph LTh	1979	2011	(Dunoon: St John's with Sandbank)	7 Glenmorag Avenue, Dunoon PA23 7LG	01369 703438
Taylor, Alan T. BD	1980	2005	(Isle of Mull Parishes)	Erray Road, Tobermory, Isle of Mull PA75 6PS	01688 302496
Watson, James LTh	1968	1994	(Bowden with Lilliesleaf)	7 Lochan Avenue, Kirn, Dunoon PA23 8HT	01369 702851
Wilkinson, W. Brian MA BD	1968	2007	(Glenaray and Inveraray)	3 Achlonan, Taynuilt PA35 1JJ	01866 822036
				[E-mail: brianwilkinson@f2s.com]	

ARGYLL Communion Sundays

Parish	Communion Sundays	Parish	Communion Sundays	Parish	Communion Sundays
Ardrishaig	4th Apr, 1st Nov	Kilarrow	1st Mar, Jun, Sep, Dec	Portnahaven	3rd Jul
Barra	2nd Mar, June, Sep, Easter, Advent	Kilcalmonell	1st Jul, 3rd Nov	Rothesay: Trinity	1st Feb, Jun, Nov
Campbeltown		Kilchoman	1st Jul, 2nd Dec, Easter	Saddell and Carradale	2nd May, 1st Nov
Highland	1st May, Nov	Kildalton and Oa	Last Jan, Jun, Oct, Easter	Sandbank	1st Jan, May, Nov
Lorne and Lowland	1st May, Nov	Kilfinan	Last Apr, Oct	Skipness	2nd May, Nov
Craignish	1st Jun, Nov	Killean and Kilchenzie	1st Mar, Jul, Oct	Southend	1st Jun, Dec
Cumlodden, Lochfyneside and Lochgair	1st May, 3rd Nov	Kilmeny	2nd May, 3rd Nov	South Knapdale	4th Apr, 1st Nov
Dunoon		Kilmodan and Colintraive	1st Apr, Sep	South Uist	
St John's	1st Mar, Jun, Nov	Kilmun	Last Jun, Nov	Howmore	1st Jun
The High Kirk	1st Feb, Jun, Oct	Kilninver and Kilmelford	Last Feb, Jun, Oct	Daliburgh	1st Sep
Gigha and Cara	1st May, Nov	Kirn	2nd Jun, Oct	Strachur and Strathlachlan	1st Mar, Jun, Nov
Glassary, Kilmartin and Ford	1st Apr, Sep	Kyles	1st May, Nov	Strone and Ardentinny	Last Feb, Jun, Oct
Glenaray and Inveraray	1st Apr, Jul, Oct, Dec	Lochgair	Last Apr, Oct	Tarbert and Kilberry	1st May, Oct
Innellan	1st Mar, Jun, Sep, Dec	Lochgilphead	2nd Oct (Gaelic)	Tayvallich	2nd May, Nov
Inverlussa and Bellanoch	2nd May, Nov	Lochgoilhead and Kilmorich	1st Apr, Nov	The United Church of Bute	1st Feb, Jun, Nov
Jura	Passion Sun., 2nd Jul, 3rd Nov	North Knapdale	2nd Mar, Jun, Sep, Nov	Toward	Last Feb, May, Aug, Nov

(22) FALKIRK

Meets at Falkirk Old and St Modan's Parish Church on the first Tuesday of September, December, March and May, on the fourth Tuesday of October and January and on the third Tuesday of June.

Clerk:	REV. ROBERT S.T. ALLAN LLB DipLP BD	9 Major's Loan, Falkirk FK1 5QF
		[E-mail: falkirk@cofscotland.org.uk]
		01324 625124
Treasurer:	MR ARTHUR PRIESTLY	32 Broomhill Avenue, Larbert FK5 3EH
		[E-mail: treasurer@falkirkpresbytery.org]
		01324 557142

Airth (H)
James F. Todd BD CPS | 1984 | The Manse, Airth, Falkirk FK2 8LS | 01324 831120

Blackbraes and Shieldhill linked with Muiravonside
Louise J.E. McClements RGN BD | 2008 | 81 Stevenson Avenue, Polmont, Falkirk FK2 0GU | 01324 717757
[E-mail: louise.mcclements@virgin.net]

Bo'ness: Old (H)
Douglas I. Campbell BD DPS | 2004 | 2009 | 10 Dundas Street, Bo'ness EH51 0DG | 01506 204585
[E-mail: douglas@bokonline.org.uk]

Bo'ness: St Andrew's (Website: www.standonline.org.uk) (01506 825803)
Albert O. Bogle BD MTh | 1981 | St Andrew's Manse, 11 Erngath Road, Bo'ness EH51 9DP | 01506 822195
[E-mail: albertbogle@mac.com]

Bonnybridge: St Helen's (H) (Website: www.bbshnc.com)
George MacDonald BTh | 2004 | 2009 | The Manse, 32 Reilly Gardens, High Bonnybridge FK4 2BB | 01324 874807
[E-mail: georgemacdonald1@virginmedia.com]

Bothkennar and Carronshore
Andrew J. Moore BSc BD | 2007 | 11 Hunter Place, Greenmount Park, Carronshore, Falkirk FK2 8QS | 01324 570525
[E-mail: theminister@themoores.me.uk]

Brightons (H)
Murdo M. Campbell BD DipMin | 1997 | 2007 | The Manse, Maddiston Road, Brightons, Falkirk FK2 0JP | 01324 712062
[E-mail: murdocampbell@hotmail.com]

Carriden (H)
Vacant | The Spires, Foredale Terrace, Carriden, Bo'ness EH51 9LW | 01506 822141

Cumbernauld: Abronhill (H)
Joyce A. Keyes (Mrs) BD | 1996 | 2003 | 26 Ash Road, Cumbernauld, Glasgow G67 3ED | 01236 723833

Cumbernauld: Condorrat (H)
Grace Saunders BSc BTh | 2007 | 2011 | 11 Rosehill Drive, Cumbernauld, Glasgow G67 4EQ | 01236 452090
[E-mail: rev.grace.saunders@btinternet.com]
Marion Perry (Mrs) (Aux) | 2009 | 2013 | 17a Tarbolton Road, Cumbernauld, Glasgow G67 2AJ | 01236 898519
[E-mail: perryask@hotmail.com] | 07563 180662 (Mbl)

Cumbernauld: Kildrum (H)
Elinor J. Gordon (Miss) BD   1988   2004   64 Southfield Road, Balloch, Cumbernauld, Glasgow G68 9DZ   01236 723204
                                                          [E-mail: elinorgordon@aol.com]
David Nicholson DCS   2D Doonside, Kildrum, Cumbernauld, Glasgow G67 2HX   01236 732260
                                                          [E-mail: deacdave@btinternet.com]

Cumbernauld: Old (H) (Website: www.cumbernauldold.org.uk)
Catriona Ogilvie (Mrs) MA BD   1999   The Manse, 23 Baronhill, Cumbernauld, Glasgow G67 2SD   01236 721912
Valerie Cuthbertson (Miss) DCS   105 Bellshill Road, Motherwell ML1 3SJ   01698 259001

Cumbernauld: St Mungo's
Vacant   18 Fergusson Road, Cumbernauld, Glasgow G67 1LS   01236 721513

Denny: Old
John Murning BD   1988   2002   31 Duke Street, Denny FK6 6NR   01324 824508
                                                          [E-mail: bridgebuilder@supanet.com]

Denny: Westpark (H) (Website: www.westparkchurch.org.uk)
Vacant   13 Baxter Crescent, Denny FK6 5EZ   01324 876224

Dunipace (H)
Jean W. Gallacher (Miss)   1989   The Manse, 239 Stirling Street, Dunipace, Denny FK6 6QJ   01324 824540
    BD CMin CTheol DMin

Falkirk: Bainsford
Michael R. Philip BD   1978   2001   1 Valleyview Place, Newcarron Village, Falkirk FK2 7JB   01324 621087
                                                          [E-mail: mrphilip@btinternet.com]

Falkirk: Camelon (Church office: 01324 870011)
Stuart Sharp MTheol DipPA   2001   30 Cotland Drive, Falkirk FK2 7GE   01324 623631
Margaret Corrie (Miss) DCS   44 Sunnyside Street, Falkirk FK1 4BH   01324 670656

Falkirk: Erskine (H)
Vacant   Burnbrae Road, Falkirk FK1 5SD   01324 623701

Falkirk: Grahamston United (H)
Ian Wilkie BD PGCE   2001   2007   16 Cromwell Road, Falkirk FK1 1SF   01324 624461
                                                          [E-mail: yanbluejeans@aol.com]   07877 803280 (Mbl)

Falkirk: Laurieston linked with Redding and Westquarter 1990 2009
J. Mary Henderson MA BD DipEd PhD
11 Polmont Road, Laurieston, Falkirk FK2 9QQ
[E-mail: jmary.henderson@tiscali.co.uk]
01324 621196

Falkirk: Old and St Modan's (H) 1991 2003
Robert S.T. Allan LLB DipLP BD
9 Major's Loan, Falkirk FK1 5QF
01324 625124

Falkirk: St Andrew's West (H) 1989 1997
Alastair M. Horne BSc BD
1 Maggiewood's Loan, Falkirk FK1 5SJ
01324 623308

Falkirk: St James'
Vacant
13 Wallace Place, Falkirk FK2 7EN
01324 632501

Grangemouth: Abbotsgrange 1995 2010
Aftab Gohar MA MDiv PgDip
8 Naismith Court, Grangemouth FK3 9BQ
[E-mail: abbotsgrange@aol.com]
01324 482109
07528 143784 (Mbl)

Grangemouth: Kirk of the Holy Rood 1992 2003
David J. Smith BD DipMin
The Manse, Bowhouse Road, Grangemouth FK3 0EX
[E-mail: davidkhrood@tiscali.co.uk]
01324 471595

Grangemouth: Zetland (H) 1976 1991
Ian W. Black MA BD
Ronaldshay Crescent, Grangemouth FK3 9JH
[E-mail: iwblack@hotmail.com]
01324 472868
Lorna I. MacDougall (Miss) MA DipGC (Aux) 2003
34 Millar Place, Carron, Falkirk FK2 8QB
01324 552739

Haggs (H) 1998
Helen F. Christie (Mrs) BD
5 Watson Place, Dennyloanhead, Bonnybridge FK4 2BG
01324 813786

Larbert: East 1984 1995
Melville D. Crosthwaite BD DipEd DipMin
1 Cortachy Avenue, Carron, Falkirk FK2 8DH
01324 562402

Larbert: Old (H)
Vacant
The Manse, 38 South Broomage Avenue, Larbert FK5 3ED
01324 872760

Larbert: West (H)
Vacant
11 Carronvale Road, Larbert FK5 3LZ
01324 562878

Muiravonside See Blackbraes and Shieldhill

Polmont: Old
Jerome O'Brien BA LLB MTh   2001 2005   3 Orchard Grove, Polmont, Falkirk FK2 0XE   01324 718677

Redding and Westquarter See Falkirk: Laurieston

Slamannan
Vacant   The Manse, Manse Place, Slamannan, Falkirk FK1 3EN   01324 851307

Stenhouse and Carron (H)
William Thomson BD   2001 2007   The Manse, 21 Tipperary Place, Stenhousemuir, Larbert FK5 4SX   01324 416628

Brown, James BA BD DipHSW DipPsychol	1973	2001	(Abercorn with Dalmeny)	6 Salmon Court, Schoolbrae, Bo'ness EH51 9HF	01506 822454
Brown, T. John MA BD	1995	2006	(Tullibody: St Serf's)	1 Callendar Park Walk, Callendar Grange, Falkirk FK1 1TA [E-mail: johnbrown1cpw@talktalk.net]	01324 617352
Campbell-Jack, W.C. BD MTh PhD	1979	2011	(Glasgow: Possilpark)	35 Castle Avenue, Airth, Falkirk FK2 8GA [E-mail: c.c-j@homecall.co.uk]	01324 832011
Chalmers, George A. MA BD MLitt	1962	2002	(Catrine with Sorn)	3 Cricket Place, Brightons, Falkirk FK2 0HZ	01324 712030
Hardie, Robert K. MA BD	1968	2005	(Stenhouse and Carron)	33 Palace Street, Berwick-upon-Tweed TD15 1HN	
Heriot, Charles R. JP BA	1962	1996	(Brightons)	Oakbank Nursing Home, Wilson Avenue, Polmont, Falkirk FK2 0QZ	
Hill, Stanley LTh	1967	1998	(Muiravonside)	The Erskine Home, Bishopton PA7 5PU	0141-812 1100
Holland, John C.	1976	1985	(Strone and Ardentinny)	7 Polmont Park, Polmont, Falkirk FK2 0XT	01324 880109
Job, Anne J. BSc BD	1993	2010	(Kirkcaldy: Viewforth with Thornton)	5 Carse View, Airth, Falkirk FK2 8NY [E-mail: aj@ajjob.co.uk]	01324 832094
Kesting, Sheilagh M. (Miss) BA BD DD	1980	1993	Ecumenical Relations	12 Glenview Drive, Falkirk FK1 5JU	01324 671489
Macaulay, Glendon BD	1999	2012	(Falkirk: Erskine)	43 Gavin's Lee, Tranent EH33 2AP [E-mail: gd.macaulay@blueyonder.co.uk]	
McCallum, John	1962	1998	(Falkirk: Irving Camelon)	11 Burnbrae Gardens, Falkirk FK1 5SB	01324 619766
McDonald, William G. MA BD	1959	1975	(Falkirk: Grahamston United)	4 Roome Bay Crescent, Crail, Anstruther KY10 3TT	
McDowall, Ronald J. BD	1980	2001	(Falkirk: Laurieston with Redding and Westquarter)	'Kailas', Windsor Road, Falkirk FK1 5EJ	01324 871947
MacKinnon, Ronald M. DCS			(Deacon)	12 Mossywood Court, McGregor Avenue, Airdrie ML6 7DY	01236 763389
Mathers, Daniel L. BD	1982	2001	(Grangemouth: Charing Cross and West)	10 Ercall Road, Brightons, Falkirk FK2 0RS	01324 872253
Maxton, Ronald M. MA	1955	1995	(Dollar: Associate)	5 Rulley View, Denny FK6 6QQ	01324 825441
Miller, Elsie M. (Miss) DCS			(Deaconess)	30 Swinton Avenue, Rowansbank, Baillieston, Glasgow G69 6JR	0141-771 0857
Munroe, Henry BA LTh LTI	1971	1988	(Denny: Dunipace North with Old)	Viewforth, High Road, Maddiston, Falkirk FK2 0BL	01324 712446

| Orr, Sheena BA MSc MBA BD | 2011 | Prison Ministry in Kenya | PO Box 2299-00621, Village Market, Nairobi, Kenya | 00254 (0)732630215 |

[E-mail: sheens59@gmail.com]

Ross, Evan J. LTh	1986 1998	(Cowdenbeath: West with Mossgreen and Crossgates)	5 Arneil Place, Brightons, Falkirk FK2 0NJ	01324 719936
Sarle, Andrew BSc BD	2013	Ordained Local Minister	114 High Station Road, Falkirk FK1 5LN	01324 621648
Scott, Donald H. BA BD	1983 2002	Chaplain: HMYOI Polmont	14 Gibsongray Street, Falkirk FK2 0AB	01324 722241

[E-mail: donaldhscott@hotmail.com]

| Smith, Richard BD | 1976 2002 | (Denny: Old) | Easter Wayside, 46 Kennedy Way, Airth, Falkirk FK2 8GB | 01324 831386 |

[E-mail: richards@uklinux.net]

| Smith, Ronald W. BA BEd BD | 1979 2011 | (Falkirk: St James') | 1F1, 2 Middlefield, Edinburgh EH7 4PF | 0131-553 1174 |

(Mbl) 07900 896954

| Thomson, Raymond BD DipMin | 1992 2013 | (Slamannan) | 5 Cawder View, Carrickstone Meadows, Cumbernauld, Glasgow G68 0BN | 01236 723288 |
| Wandrum, David | 1993 | Auxiliary Minister | | |

| Wilson, Phyllis M. (Mrs) DipCom DipRE | 1985 2006 | (Motherwell: South Dalziel) | 'Landemer', 17 Sneddon Place, Airth, Falkirk FK2 8GH | 01324 832257 |

[E-mail: thomas.wilson38@btinternet.com]

FALKIRK ADDRESSES

Blackbraes and Shieldhill	Main St x Anderson Cr
Bo'ness: Old	Panbrae Road
St Andrew's	Grahamsdyke Avenue
Carriden	Carriden Brae
Cumbernauld: Abronhill	Larch Road
Condorrat	Main Road
Kildrum	Clouden Road
Old	Baronhill
St Mungo's	St Mungo's Road

Denny: Old	Denny Cross
Westpark	Duke Street
Dunipace	Stirling Street
Falkirk: Bainsford	Hendry Street, Bainsford
Camelon	Dorrator Road
Erskine	Cockburn St x Hodge St
Grahamston	Bute Street
Laurieston	Main Falkirk Road
Old and St Modan's	Kirk Wynd
St Andrew's West	Newmarket Street
St James'	Thornhill Road x Firs Street

Grangemouth: Abbotsgrange	Abbot's Road
Kirk of the Holy Rood	Bowhouse Road
Zetland	Ronaldshay Crescent
Haggs	Glasgow Road
Larbert: East	Kirk Avenue
Old	Denny Road x Stirling Road
West	Main Street
Muiravonside	off Vellore Road
Polmont: Old	Kirk Entry/Bo'ness Road
Redding and Westquarter	Main Street
Slamannan	Manse Place
Stenhouse and Carron	Church Street

(23) STIRLING

Meets at the Moderator's church on the second Thursday of September, and at Bridge of Allan Parish Church on the second Thursday of February, March, April, May, June, October, November and December.

Clerk: REV. ALEXANDER M. MILLAR MA BD MBA MCMI   St Columba's Manse, 5 Clifford Road, Stirling FK8 2AQ   01786 469979
[E-mail: alexmillar0406@gmail.com]
Depute Clerk: MR ANDREW MUIRHEAD MA MLitt   Ythanglen, Copland Place, Alva FK12 5LN   01259 760143
[E-mail: andrew.muirhead1@btinternet.com]
Treasurer: MR GILMOUR CUTHBERTSON   'Denovan', 1 Doune Road, Dunblane FK15 9AR   01786 823487
[E-mail: gilmour.c@virgin.net]

Presbytery Office: Bridge of Allan Parish Church, 12 Keir Street, Bridge of Allan FK9 4NW
[E-mail: stirling@cofscotland.org.uk]

Aberfoyle (H) linked with Port of Menteith (H)
Vacant
The Manse, Lochard Road, Aberfoyle, Stirling FK8 3SZ   01877 382391

Alloa: Ludgate
Vacant
30 Claremont, Alloa FK10 2DF   01259 210403

Alloa: St Mungo's (H)
Sang Y. Cha BD   2011
37A Claremont, Alloa FK10 2DG   01259 213872
[E-mail: syc@cantab.net]

Alva
James N.R. McNeil BSc BD   1990   1997
34 Ochil Road, Alva FK12 5JT   01259 760262

Balfron linked with Fintry (H)
Vacant
7 Station Road, Balfron, Glasgow G63 0SX   01360 440285

Balquhidder linked with Killin and Ardeonaig (H)
John Lincoln MPhil BD   1986   1997
The Manse, Killin FK21 8TN   01567 820247
[E-mail: eoin22@gmail.com]

Bannockburn: Allan (H) (Website: www.allanchurch.org.uk)
Jim Landels BD CertMin   1990
The Manse, Bogend Road, Bannockburn, Stirling FK7 8NP   01786 814692
[E-mail: revjimlandels@btinternet.com]

Bannockburn: Ladywell (H)
Elizabeth M.D. Robertson (Miss) BD CertMin   1997
57 The Firs, Bannockburn FK7 0EG   01786 812467
[E-mail: lizrob@talktalk.net]

Bridge of Allan (H) (01786 834155)
Gillian Weighton (Mrs) BD STM   1992   2004
29 Keir Street, Bridge of Allan, Stirling FK9 4QJ   01786 832753
[E-mail: gillweighton@aol.com]

Buchanan linked with Drymen
Alexander J. MacPherson BD   1986   1997
Buchanan Manse, Drymen, Glasgow G63 0AQ   01360 870212
[E-mail: revalex1@gmail.com]

Buchlyvie (H) linked with Gartmore (H)
Elaine H. MacRae (Mrs) BD   1985   2004   The Manse, Kippen, Stirling FK8 3DN   01786 871170
[E-mail: ge.macrae@btopenworld.com]

Callander (H) (Tel/Fax: 01877 331409)
Robert R. Simpson BA BD   1994   2010   3 Aveland Park Road, Callander FK17 8FD   01877 330097
[E-mail: robert@pansmanse.co.uk]

Cambusbarron: The Bruce Memorial (H)
Graham Nash MA BD   2006   2012   14 Woodside Court, Cambusbarron, Stirling FK7 9PH   01786 442068
[E-mail: gpnash@btopenworld.com]

Clackmannan (H)
Scott Raby LTh   1991   2007   The Manse, Port Street, Clackmannan FK10 4JH   01259 211255
[E-mail: minister@clackmannankirk.org]

Cowie (H) and Plean linked with Fallin (Website: www.cowiepleanandfallinchurch.com)
Alan L. Dunnett LLB BD   1994   2008   5 Fincastle Place, Cowie, Stirling FK7 7DS   01786 818413
[E-mail: alan.dunnett@sky.com]
Linda Dunnett (Mrs) BA DCS   5 Fincastle Place, Cowie, Stirling FK7 7DS   01786 818413
[E-mail: lindadunnett@sky.com]

Dollar (H) linked with Glendevon linked with Muckhart (Website: www.dollarparishchurch.org.uk)
Vacant   2 Princes Crescent East, Dollar FK14 7BU

Drymen See Buchanan

Dunblane: Cathedral (H)
Vacant   Cathedral Manse, The Cross, Dunblane FK15 0AQ   01786 822205
Sally Foster-Fulton (Mrs) BA BD (Assoc)   1999   2007   21 Craiglea, Causewayhead, Stirling FK9 5EE   01786 463060
[E-mail: sallyfulton01@gmail.com]

Dunblane: St Blane's (H)
Alexander B. Mitchell BD   1981   2003   49 Roman Way, Dunblane FK15 9DJ   01786 822268
[E-mail: alex.mitchell6@btopenworld.com]

Fallin See Cowie and Plean
Fintry See Balfron

Gargunnock linked with Kilmadock linked with Kincardine-in-Menteith
Andrew B. Campbell BD DPS MTh   1979   2011   The Manse, Manse Brae, Gargunnock, Stirling FK8 3BQ   01786 860678
[E-mail: andycampbell53@btinternet.com]

Gartmore See Buchlyvie
Glendevon See Dollar

Killearn (H)
Lee Messeder BD PgDipMin   2003   2010   2 The Oaks, Killearn, Glasgow G63 9SF   01360 550045
[E-mail: minister@killearnkirk.org.uk]

Killin and Ardeonaig (H) See Balquhidder
Kilmadock See Gargunnock
Kincardine-in-Menteith See Gargunnock

Kippen (H) linked with Norrieston
Gordon MacRae BD MTh   1985   1998   The Manse, Main Street, Kippen, Stirling FK8 3DN   01786 870229
[E-mail: ge.macrae@btopenworld.com]

Lecropt (H)
Vacant   Braehead, 5 Henderson Street, Bridge of Allan, Stirling FK9 4NA   01786 832382

Logie (H)
R. Stuart M. Fulton BA BD   1991   2006   21 Craiglea, Causewayhead, Stirling FK9 5EE   01786 463060
[E-mail: stuart.fulton@btinternet.com]
Anne F. Shearer BA DipEd (Aux)   2010   10 Colsnaur, Menstrie FK11 7HG   01259 769176
[E-mail: annefshearer@btinternet.com]

Menstrie (H)
Vacant   The Manse, 7 Long Row, Menstrie FK11 7BA   01259 761461

Muckhart See Dollar
Norrieston See Kippen
Port of Menteith See Aberfoyle

Sauchie and Coalsnaughton
Margaret Shuttleworth MA BD — 2013 — 62 Toll Road, Kincardine, Alloa FK10 4QZ
[E-mail: revmshuttleworth@gmail.com] — 01259 731002

Stirling: Allan Park South (T) (H)
Alistair Cowper BSc BD — 2011 — 22 Laurelhill Place, Stirling FK8 2JH
[E-mail: alistaircowper@talktalk.net] — 01786 358872 / 07791 524504 (Mbl)

Stirling: Church of the Holy Rude (H) linked with Stirling: Viewfield Erskine
Alan F. Miller BA MA BD — 2000 2010 — 7 Windsor Place, Stirling FK8 2HY
[E-mail: revafmiller@gmail.com] — 01786 465166

Stirling: North (H) (01786 463376) (Website: www.northparishchurch.com)
Calum Jack BSc BD — 2004 — 18 Shirras Brae Road, Stirling FK7 0BA
[E-mail: calum@northparishchurch.com] — 01786 357428

Stirling: St Columba's (H) (01786 449516)
Alexander M. Millar MA BD MBA MCMI — 1980 2010 — St Columba's Manse, 5 Clifford Road, Stirling FK8 2AQ
[E-mail: alexmillar0406@gmail.com] — 01786 469979

Stirling: St Mark's (Website: www.stmarksstirling.org.uk)
Stuart Davidson BD — 2008 — 176 Drip Road, Stirling FK8 1RR
[E-mail: stuart_davidson1@sky.com] — 01786 473716
Jean Porter (Mrs) BD DCS — 2006 2008 — 3 Cochrie Road, Tullibody, Alloa FK10 2RR
[E-mail: JayteePorter@aol.com] — 07729 316321 (Mbl)

Stirling: St Ninians Old (H)
Gary J. McIntyre BD DipMin — 1993 1998 — 7 Randolph Road, Stirling FK8 2AJ
[E-mail: gary.mcintyre7@btinternet.com] — 01786 474421

Stirling: Viewfield Erskine (H) See Stirling: Church of the Holy Rude

Strathblane (H)
Richard Begg MA BD — 2008 2011 — 2 Campsie Road, Strathblane, Glasgow G63 9AB
[E-mail: RBEGG711@aol.com] — 01360 770226

Tillicoultry (H)
Alison E.P. Britchfield (Mrs) MA BD   1991 2013   The Manse, 17 Dollar Road, Tillicoultry FK13 6PD
[E-mail: alibritchfield@gmail.com]   01259 750340

Tullibody: St Serf's (H)
Vacant   16 Menstrie Road, Tullibody, Alloa FK10 2RG   01259 729804

Name	Years	Charge/Position	Address	Telephone
Abeledo, Benjamin J.A. BTh DipTh PTh	1991 2000	Chaplain: Army	15 Birch Grove, Menstrie FK11 7DW [E-mail: benjamin.abeledo@btinternet.com]	
Aitken, E. Douglas MA	1961 1998	(Clackmannan)	1 Dolan Grove, Saline, Dunfermline KY12 9UP [E-mail: douglasaitken14@btinternet.com]	01383 852730
Allen, Valerie L. (Ms) BMus MDiv DMin	1990 2013	(Arbroath: Old and Abbey)	16 Pine Court, Doune FK16 6JE [E-mail: VL2allen@aol.com]	01786 842577 (Mbl) 07801 291538
Barr, John BSc PhD BD	1958 1979	(Kilmalcolm: Old)	6 Ferry Court, Stirling FK9 5GJ [E-mail: kilbrandon@btinternet.com]	01786 472286
Brown, James H. BD	1977 2005	(Helensburgh: Park)	14 Gullipen View, Callander FK17 8HN [E-mail: revjimhbrown@yahoo.co.uk]	01877 339425
Cloggie, June (Mrs)	1997 2006	(Auxiliary Minister)	11A Tulipan Crescent, Callander FK17 8AR [E-mail: david.cloggie@hotmail.co.uk]	01877 331021
Cochrane, James P.N. LTh	1994 2012	(Tillicoultry)	12 Sandpiper Meadow, Alloa Park, Alloa FK10 1QU [E-mail: jcochrane1@btinternet.com]	01259 218883
Cook, Helen (Mrs) BD	1974 2012	Hospital Chaplain	60 Pelstream Avenue, Stirling FK7 0BG [E-mail: revhcook@btinternet.com]	01786 464128
Gaston, A. Ray C. MA BD	1969 2002	(Leuchars: St Athernase)	'Hamewith', 13 Manse Road, Dollar FK14 7AL [E-mail: raygaston@onetel.com]	01259 489969
Gillespie, Irene C. (Mrs) BD	1991 2007	(Tiree)	39 King O'Muirs Drive, Tullibody, Alloa FK10 3AY [E-mail: revicg@btinternet.com]	01259 723937
Gilmour, William M. MA BD	1969 2008	(Lecropt)	14 Pine Court, Doune FK16 6JE	01786 842928
Goodison, Michael J. BSc BA	2013	Chaplain: Army	82 Nevis Crescent, Alloa FK10 2BN	01259 724333
Izett, William A.F.	1968 2000	(Law)	1 Duke Street, Clackmannan FK10 4EF	01259 724203
Jack, Alison M. MA BD PhD	1998 2001	Assistant: Carse of Gowrie	5 Murdoch Terrace, Dunblane FK15 9JE [E-mail: alisonmjack809@btinternet.com]	01786 825116
MacCormick, Moira G. BA LTh	1986 2003	(Buchlyvie with Gartmore)	12 Rankine Wynd, Tullibody, Alloa FK10 2UW [E-mail: mgmaccormick@o2.co.uk]	01259 724619
McIntosh, Hamish N.M. MA	1949 1987	(Fintry)	9 Abbeyfield House, 17 Allan Park, Stirling FK8 2QG	01786 470294
Mack, Lynne (Mrs)	2013	Ordained Local Minister	36 Middleton, Menstrie FK11 7HD [E-mail: lynne.mack@aol.co.uk]	01259 761465
Malloch, Philip R.M. LLB BD	1970 2009	(Killearn)	8 Michael McParland Drive, Torrance, Glasgow G64 4EE [E-mail: pmalloch@mac.com]	01360 620089
Millar, Jennifer M. (Mrs) BD DipMin	1986 1995	Teacher: Religious and Moral Education	5 Clifford Road, Stirling FK8 2AQ [E-mail: ajrmillar@blueyonder.co.uk]	01786 469979
Ovens, Samuel B. BD	1982 1993	(Slamannan)	21 Bevan Drive, Alva FK12 5PD	01259 763456

Paterson, John L. MA BD STM	1964 2003	(Linlithgow: St Michael's)	'Kirkmichael', 22 Waterfront Way, Stirling FK9 5GH [E-mail: revianpaterson@hotmail.co.uk]	01786 447165
Roderick, Maggie R. BA BD FRSA FTSI	2010 2012	(Associate: Stirling: St Ninians Old)	34 Craiglea, Stirling FK9 5EE [E-mail: revmaggieroderick@btinternet.com]	(Mbl) 07984 604205
Sangster, Ernest G. MA BD ThM	1958 1997	(Alva)	6 Lawhill Road, Dollar FK14 7BG	01259 742344
Scott, James F.	1957 1997	(Dyce)	5 Gullipen View, Callander FK17 8HN	01877 330565
Scoular, J. Marshall	1954 1996	(Kippen)	6 Buccleuch Court, Dunblane FK15 0AR	01786 825976
Sewell, Paul M.N. MA BD	1970 2010	(Berwick-upon-Tweed: St Andrew's Wallace Green and Lowick)	7 Bohun Court, Stirling FK7 7UT [E-mail: paulmsewell@btinternet.com]	01786 489969
Sherry, George T. LTh	1977 2004	(Menstrie)	4 Woodburn Way, Alva FK12 5LB [E-mail: gandms@btinternet.com]	01259 763779
Sinclair, James H. MA BD DipMin	1966 2004	(Auchencairn and Rerrick with Buittle and Kelton)	16 Delaney Court, Alloa FK10 1RB	01259 729001
Wright, John P. BD FSA	1977 2000	(Glasgow: New Govan)	Plane Castle, Airth, Falkirk FK2 8SF	01786 480840

STIRLING ADDRESSES

Allan Park South	Dumbarton Road	St Columba's	Park Terrace	Viewfield Erskine	Barnton Street
Holy Rude	St John Street	St Mark's	Drip Road		
North	Springfield Road	St Ninians Old	Kirk Wynd, St Ninians		

(24) DUNFERMLINE

Meets at Dunfermline in St Andrew's Erskine Church, Robertson Road, on the first Thursday of each month, except January, July and August when there is no meeting, and June when it meets on the last Thursday.

Clerk:	**REV. ELIZABETH S.S. KENNY BD RGN SCM**	**5 Cobden Court, Crossgates, Cowdenbeath KY4 8AU** **[E-mail: dunfermline@cofscotland.org.uk]**	**01383 741495 (Office)** **07831 763494 (Mbl)**

Aberdour: St Fillan's (H) (Website: www.stfillans.presbytery.org)

Peter S. Gerbrandy-Baird MA BD MSc FRSA FRGS	2004	St Fillan's Manse, 36 Bellhouse Road, Aberdour, Fife KY3 0TL	01383 861522

Beath and Cowdenbeath: North (H)

David W. Redmayne BSc BD	2001	10 Stuart Place, Cowdenbeath KY4 9BN [E-mail: beathandnorth@dunfermlinepresbytery.org.uk]	01383 511033

Cairneyhill (H) (01383 882352) linked with Limekilns (H) (01383 873337)
Norman M. Grant BD   1990   The Manse, 10 Church Street, Limekilns, Dunfermline KY11 3HT   01383 872341
[E-mail: nmg57@live.com]

Carnock and Oakley (H)
Vacant   The Manse, Main Street, Carnock, Dunfermline KY12 9JG   01383 850327

Cowdenbeath: Trinity (H)
Gavin Boswell BTheol   1993   2013   66 Barclay Street, Cowdenbeath KY4 9LD   01383 515089
John Wyllie (Pastoral Assistant)   51 Seafar Street, Kelty KY4 0JX   01383 839200

Culross and Torryburn (H)
Jayne E. Scott (Mrs) BA MEd MBA   1988   2009   The Manse, Culross, Dunfermline KY12 8JD   01383 880231
[E-mail: jayne.scott5@btinternet.com]

Dalgety (H) (01383 824092) (E-mail: office@dalgety-church.co.uk) (Website: www.dalgety-church.co.uk)
Christine Sime (Miss) BSc BD   1994   2012   9 St Colne Drive, Dalgety Bay, Dunfermline KY11 9LQ   01383 822316
[E-mail: revsime@btinternet.com]

Dunfermline: Abbey (H) (Website: www.dunfabbey.freeserve.co.uk)
MaryAnn R. Rennie (Mrs) BD MTh   1998   2012   12 Garvock Hill, Dunfermline KY12 7UU   01383 721022
[E-mail: maryann.r.rennie@gmail.com]

Dunfermline: East (New Charge Development)
Andrew A. Morrice MA BD   1999   2010   9 Dover Drive, Dunfermline KY11 8HQ   01383 621050
[E-mail: andrew@dunfermlineeastchurch.org.uk]

Dunfermline: Gillespie Memorial (H) (01383 621253) (E-mail: gillespie.church@btopenworld.com)
Iain A. Sutherland BSc BD   1996   2009   4 Killin Court, Dunfermline KY12 7XF   01383 723329
[E-mail: RevISutherland@aol.com]

Dunfermline: North
Ian G. Thom BSc PhD BD   1990   2007   13 Barbour Grove, Dunfermline KY12 9YB   01383 733471
[E-mail: ianthom58@btinternet.com]

Dunfermline: St Andrew's Erskine (01383 841660)
Muriel F. Willoughby (Mrs) MA BD   2006   2013   71A Townhill Road, Dunfermline KY12 0BN   01383 734657
[E-mail: muriel.willoughby@btinternet.com]

Dunfermline: St Leonard's (01383 620106) (E-mail: office@stleonardsparishchurch.org.uk) (Website: www.stleonardsparishchurch.org.uk)
Vacant   12 Torvean Place, Dunfermline KY11 4YY   01383 721054

Dunfermline: St Margaret's
Iain M. Greenshields   1985   2007   38 Garvock Hill, Dunfermline KY12 7UU   01383 723955
BD DipRS ACMA MSc MTh   [E-mail: revimaclg@hotmail.co.uk]

Dunfermline: St Ninian's
Elizabeth A. Fisk (Mrs) BD   1996   51 St John's Drive, Dunfermline KY12 7TL   01383 722256

Dunfermline: Townhill and Kingseat (H)
Rosemary A. Smith BD   1997   2010   7 Lochwood Park, Kingseat, Dunfermline KY12 0UX   01383 626181
[E-mail: revrosieann@gmail.com]

Inverkeithing linked with North Queensferry (T)
Colin M. Alston BMus BD BN RN   1975   1 Dover Way, Dunfermline KY11 8HR   01383 621050
[E-mail: ca5884400@gmail.com]

Kelty (Website: www.keltykirk.org.uk)
Hugh D. Steele LTh DipMin   1994   2013   15 Arlick Road, Kelty KY4 0BH   01383 830291
[E-mail: hugdebra@aol.com]

Limekilns See Cairneyhill

Lochgelly and Benarty: St Serf's
Elisabeth M. Stenhouse (Ms) BD   2006   82 Main Street, Lochgelly KY5 9AA   01592 780435
[E-mail: lissten@sky.com]

North Queensferry See Inverkeithing

Rosyth
Violet C.C. McKay (Mrs) BD   1988   2002   42 Woodside Avenue, Rosyth KY11 2LA   01383 412776
[E-mail: v.mckay@btinternet.com]
Morag Crawford (Miss) MSc DCS   118 Wester Drylaw Place, Edinburgh EH4 2TG   0131-332 2253
[E-mail: morag.crawford.dcs@blueyonder.co.uk]   07970 982563   (Mbl)

Saline and Blairingone
Vacant

Tulliallan and Kincardine
Alexander Shuttleworth MA BD | 8 The Glebe, Saline, Dunfermline KY12 9UT | 01383 853062
62 Toll Road, Kincardine, Alloa FK10 4QZ | 01259 731002
[E-mail: revshuttleworth@aol.com]

Name			Role	Address	Contact
Adams, David G. BD	1991	2011	(Cowdenbeath: Trinity)	13 Fernhill Gardens, Windygates, Leven KY8 5DZ [E-mail: adams69@sky.com]	
Boyle, Robert P. LTh	1990	2010	(Saline and Blairingone)	43 Dunipace Crescent, Dunfermline KY12 7JE [E-mail: boab.boyle@btinternet.com]	01383 740980
Brown, Peter MA BD FRAScot	1953	1987	(Holm)	24 Inchmickery Avenue, Dalgety Bay, Dunfermline KY11 5NF	01383 822456
Chalmers, John P. BD CPS	1979	1995	Principal Clerk	10 Liggars Place, Dunfermline KY12 7XZ	01383 739130
Donald, Kenneth W. BA BD	1982	2011	Service of the Church	24 Fieldfare View, Dunfermline KY11 4FY [E-mail: kenneth@kdonald.freeserve.co.uk]	
Farquhar, William E. BA BD	1987	2006	(Dunfermline: Townhill and Kingseat)	29 Queens Drive, Middlewich, Cheshire CW10 0DG	01606 835097
Jenkins, Gordon F.C. MA BD PhD	1968	2006	(Dunfermline: North)	20 Lumsden Park, Cupar KY15 5YL [E-mail: jenkinsgordon1@sky.com]	01334 652548
Jessamine, Alistair L. MA BD	1979	2011	(Dunfermline: Abbey)	11 Gallowhill Farm Cottages, Strathaven ML10 6BZ [E-mail: chatty.1@talktalk.net]	01357 520934
Johnston, Thomas N. LTh	1972	2008	(Edinburgh: Priestfield)	71 Main Street, Newmills, Dunfermline KY12 8ST [E-mail: tomjohnston@blueyonder.co.uk]	01383 889240
Kenny, Elizabeth S.S. BD RGN SCM	1989	2010	(Carnock and Oakley)	5 Cobden Court, Crossgates, Cowdenbeath KY4 8AU [E-mail: esskenny@btinternet.com]	(Mbl) 07831 763494
Laidlaw, Victor W.N. BD	1975	2008	(Edinburgh: St Catherine's Argyle)	9 Tern Road, Dunfermline KY11 8GA	01383 620134
Leitch, D. Graham MA BD	1974	2012	(Tyne Valley Parish)	9 St Margaret Wynd, Dunfermline KY12 0UT [E-mail: dgrahamleitch@gmail.com]	01383 249245
McLellan, Andrew R.C. CBE MA BD STM DD	1970	2002	(HM Inspector of Prisons)	4 Liggars Place, Dunfermline KY12 7XZ	01383 725959
Reid, A. Gordon BSc BD	1982	2008	(Dunfermline: Gillespie Memorial)	7 Arkleston Crescent, Paisley PA3 4TG [E-mail: reid501@fsmail.net]	0141-842 1542 (Mbl) 07773 300989
Reid, David MSc LTh FSAScot	1961	1992	(St Monans with Largoward)	North Lethans, Saline, Dunfermline KY12 9TE	01383 733144
Shewan, Frederick D.F. MA BD	1970	2005	(Edinburgh: Muirhouse St Andrew's)	38 Tremayne Place, Dunfermline KY12 9YH	01383 734354
Stuart, Anne (Miss) DCS			(Deaconess)	1 Murrell Terrace, Aberdour, Burntisland KY3 0XH	01383 860049
Watt, Robert J. BD	1994	2009	(Dumbarton: Riverside)	101 Birrell Drive, Dunfermline KY11 8FA [E-mail: r.watt21@virginmedia.com]	01383 735417 (Mbl) 07753 683717
Whyte, Isabel H. (Mrs) BD	1993		(Chaplain: Queen Margaret Hospital, Dunfermline)	14 Carlingnose Point, North Queensferry, Inverkeithing KY11 1ER [E-mail: iainisabel@whytes28.fsnet.co.uk]	01383 410732

(25) KIRKCALDY

Meets at Kirkcaldy, in the St Bryce Kirk Centre, on the first Tuesday of February, March, April (when necessary), May, September, October, November and December, and on the fourth Tuesday of June.

Clerk:	REV. ROSEMARY FREW (Mrs) MA BD	83 Milton Road, Kirkcaldy KY1 1TP [E-mail: kirkcaldy@cofscotland.org.uk]	01592 260315
Depute Clerk:	MR DOUGLAS G. HAMILL BEM	41 Abbots Mill, Kirkcaldy KY2 5PE [E-mail: hamilldg@tiscali.co.uk]	01592 267500

Auchterderran: St Fothad's linked with Kinglassie
Ben Pieterse BA BTh LTh 2001 7 Woodend Road, Cardenden, Lochgelly KY5 0NE 01592 720202
[E-mail: benhp1@gmail.com]

Auchtertool linked with Kirkcaldy: Linktown (H) (01592 641080)
Catriona M. Morrison (Mrs) MA BD 1995 16 Raith Crescent, Kirkcaldy KY2 5NN 01592 265536
[E-mail: catriona@linktown.org.uk]
Marc Prowe 16 Raith Crescent, Kirkcaldy KY2 5NN 01592 265536
[E-mail: marc@linktown.org.uk]

Buckhaven (01592 715577) and Wemyss
Wilma Cairns (Miss) BD 1999 2004 33 Main Road, East Wemyss, Kirkcaldy KY1 4RE 01592 712870
[E-mail: wilcairns@blueyonder.co.uk]
Jacqueline Thomson (Mrs) MTh DCS 1 Barron Terrace, Leven KY8 4DL 01333 301115
[E-mail: churchdeacon@blueyonder.co.uk] 07806 776560 (Mbl)

Burntisland (H)
Alan Sharp BSc BD 1980 2001 21 Ramsay Crescent, Burntisland KY3 9JL 01592 874303
[E-mail: alansharp03@aol.com]

Dysart: St Clair (H)
Vacant

Glenrothes: Christ's Kirk (H)
Alexandra M. Rosener (Mrs) 2007 2010 12 The Limekilns, Glenrothes KY6 3QJ 01592 620536
[E-mail: alexandrarosener@gmx.de]

Glenrothes: St Columba's (01592 752539) (Rothes Trinity Parish Grouping)
Alan Kimmitt BSc BD   2013   40 Liberton Drive, Glenrothes KY6 3PB — 01592 742233
[E-mail: alan@kimmitt.org.uk]

Glenrothes: St Margaret's (H) (01592 328162)
Vacant   8 Alburne Park, Glenrothes KY7 5RB — 01592 752241

Glenrothes: St Ninian's (H) (01592 610560) (E-mail: office@stninians.co.uk) (Rothes Trinity Parish Grouping)
Allistair Roy BD DipSW PGDip   2007   1 Cawdor Drive, Glenrothes KY6 2HN — 01592 611963
[E-mail: alli@stninians.co.uk]

Kennoway, Windygates and Balgonie: St Kenneth's (01333 351372) (E-mail: stkennethsparish@gmail.com)
Richard Baxter MA BD   1997   2 Fernhill Gardens, Windygates, Leven KY8 5DZ — 01333 352329
[E-mail: richard-baxter@msn.com]

Kinghorn
James Reid BD   1985   1997   17 Myre Crescent, Kinghorn, Burntisland KY3 9UB — 01592 890269
[E-mail: jim17reid@aol.com]

Kinglassie See Auchterderran: St Fothad's

Kirkcaldy: Abbotshall (H)
Rosemary Frew (Mrs) MA BD   1988   2005   83 Milton Road, Kirkcaldy KY1 1TP — 01592 260315
[E-mail: rosiefrew@blueyonder.co.uk]

Kirkcaldy: Bennochy
Robin J. McAlpine BDS BD MTh   1988   2011   25 Bennochy Avenue, Kirkcaldy KY2 5QE — 01592 643518
[E-mail: robinmcalpine@blueyonder.co.uk]

Kirkcaldy: Linktown (01592 641080) See Auchtertool

Kirkcaldy: Pathhead (H) (Tel/Fax: 01592 204635) (E-mail: pathhead@btinternet.com) (Website: www.pathheadparishchurch.co.uk)
Andrew C. Donald BD DPS   1992   2005   73 Loughborough Road, Kirkcaldy KY1 3DD — 01592 652215
[E-mail: andrewcdonald@blueyonder.co.uk]

Kirkcaldy: St Bryce Kirk (H) (01592 640016) (E-mail: office@stbrycekirk.org.uk)

Ken Froude MA BD	1979		6 East Fergus Place, Kirkcaldy KY1 1XT [E-mail: kenfroude@blueyonder.co.uk]	01592 264480
Kirkcaldy: Templehall (H)				
Anthony J.R. Fowler BSc BD	1982	2004	35 Appin Crescent, Kirkcaldy KY2 6EJ [E-mail: ajrf@btinternet.com]	01592 260156
Kirkcaldy: Torbain				
Ian Elston BD MTh	1999		91 Sauchenbush Road, Kirkcaldy KY2 5RN [E-mail: elston667@btinternet.com]	01592 263015
Leslie: Trinity (Rothes Trinity Parish Grouping)				
Guardianship of the Presbytery				
Leven				
Gilbert C. Nisbet CA BD	1993	2007	5 Forman Road, Leven KY8 4HH [E-mail: gcn-leven@blueyonder.co.uk]	01333 303339
Markinch				
Alexander R. Forsyth TD BA MTh	1973	2002	7 Guthrie Crescent, Markinch, Glenrothes KY7 6AY [E-mail: alex@arforsyth.com]	01592 758264
Methil: Wellesley (H)				
Gillian Paterson (Mrs) BD	2010		10 Vettriano Vale, Leven KY8 4GD [E-mail: gillianpaterson10@hotmail.co.uk]	01333 423147
Methilhill and Denbeath				
Elisabeth F. Cranfield (Miss) MA BD	1988		9 Chemiss Road, Methilhill, Leven KY8 2BS [E-mail: ecranfield@btinternet.com]	01592 713142
Thornton				
Guardianship of the Presbytery				
Collins, Mitchell BD CPS	1996	2005	(Creich, Flisk and Kilmany with Monimail) 6 Netherby Park, Glenrothes KY6 3PL [E-mail: collinsmit@aol.com]	

Name			(Charge)	Address	Tel
Elston, Peter K.	1963	2000	(Dalgety)	6 Cairngorm Crescent, Kirkcaldy KY2 5RF [E-mail: peterkelston@btinternet.com]	01592 205622
Ferguson, David J.	1966	2001	(Bellie with Speymouth)	4 Russell Gardens, Ladybank, Cupar KY15 7LT	01337 831406
Forrester, Ian L. MA	1964	1996	(Friockheim Kinnell with Inverkeilor and Lunan)		
Galbraith, Douglas MA BD BMus MPhil ARSCM PhD	1965	2005	(Editor: *The Year Book*)	8 Bennochy Avenue, Kirkcaldy KY2 5QE	01592 260251
				34 Balbirnie Street, Markinch, Glenrothes KY7 6DA [E-mail: dgalbraith@hotmail.com]	01592 752403
Gatt, David W.	1981	1995	(Thornton)	15 Beech Avenue, Thornton, Kirkcaldy KY1 4AT	01592 774328
Gibson, Ivor MA	1957	1993	(Abercorn with Dalmeny)	15 McInnes Road, Glenrothes KY7 6BA	01592 759982
Gisbey, John E. MA BD MSc DipEd	1964	2002	(Thornhill)	Whitemyre House, 28 St Andrews Road, Largoward, Leven KY9 1HZ	01334 840540
Gordon, Ian D. LTh	1972	2001	(Markinch)	2 Somerville Way, Glenrothes KY7 5GE	01592 742487
Houghton, Christine (Mrs) BD	1997	2010	(Whitburn: South)	39 Cedar Crescent, Thornton, Kirkcaldy KY1 4BE [E-mail: c.houghton1@btinternet.com]	01592 772823
McLean, John P. BSc BPhil BD	1994	2013	(Glenrothes: St Margaret's)	72 Lawmill Gardens, St Andrews KY16 8QF [E-mail: john@mcleanmail.me.uk]	01592 744558
McLeod, Alistair G.	1988	2005	(Glenrothes: St Columba's)	13 Greenmantle Way, Glenrothes KY6 3QG [E-mail: aagm@btinternet.com]	01592 742352
McNaught, Samuel M. MA BD MTh	1968	2002	(Kirkcaldy: St John's)	6 Munro Court, Glenrothes KY7 5GD [E-mail: sjmcnaught@btinternet.com]	01592 566129
Munro, Andrew MA BD PhD	1972	2000	(Glencaple with Lowther)	7 Dunvegan Avenue, Kirkcaldy KY2 5SG [E-mail: am.smm@blueyonder.co.uk]	01592 873258
Nicol, George G. BD DPhil	1982	2013	(Falkland with Freuchie)	48 Fidra Avenue, Burntisland KY3 0AZ [E-mail: ggnicol@totalise.co.uk]	01592 262300
Paterson, Maureen (Mrs) BSc	1992	2010	(Auxiliary Minister)	91 Dalmahoy Crescent, Kirkcaldy KY2 6TA [E-mail: m.e.paterson@blueyonder.co.uk]	01333 427102
Templeton, James L. BSc BD	1975	2012	(Innerleven: East)	29 Coldstream Avenue, Leven KY8 5TN [E-mail: jamietempleton@btinternet.com]	01592 655313
Thomson, John D. BD	1985	2005	(Kirkcaldy: Pathhead)	3 Tottenham Court, Hill Street, Dysart, Kirkcaldy KY1 2XY [E-mail: j.thomson10@sky.com]	07885 414979 (Mbl)
Tomlinson, Bryan L. TD	1969	2003	(Kirkcaldy: Abbotshall)	2 Duddingston Drive, Kirkcaldy KY2 6JP [E-mail: abbkirk@blueyonder.co.uk]	01592 564843
Webster, Elspeth H. (Miss) DCS	1990	2012	(Deaconess)	82 Broomhill Avenue, Burntisland KY3 0BP	01592 873616
Wilson, Tilly (Miss) MTh			(Dysart)	6 Citron Glebe, Kirkcaldy KY1 2NF [E-mail: tillywilson@blueyonder.co.uk]	01592 263141

KIRKCALDY ADDRESSES

Abbotshall	Abbotshall Road	Linktown	Nicol Street x High Street
Bennochy	Elgin Street	Pathhead	Harriet Street x Church Street
		St Bryce Kirk	St Brycedale Avenue x Kirk Wynd
		Templehall	Beauly Place
Torbain	Lindores Drive		
Viewforth	Viewforth Street x Viewforth Terrace		

(26) ST ANDREWS

Meets at Cupar, in St John's Church Hall, on the first Wednesday of February, March, May, September, October, November and December, and on the last Wednesday of May and June.

Clerk:	REV. JAMES G. REDPATH BD DipPTh	**The Manse, Kirk Wynd, Strathmiglo, Cupar KY14 7QS** [E-mail: standrews@cofscotland.org.uk]	01337 860256
Depute Clerk:	MR WILLIAM IMLAY DipCE ACE CPSM BA	7 Castle Bank, Newport-on-Tay DD6 8JP [E-mail: imlay@btinternet.com] **Presbytery Office**	01382 543446 01337 858442

Abdie and Dunbog (H) linked with Newburgh (H)
Lynn Brady (Miss) BD DipMin   1996   2002   2 Guthrie Court, Cupar Road, Newburgh, Cupar KY14 6HA   01337 842228
[E-mail: revbrady1963@yahoo.co.uk]

Anstruther linked with Cellardyke linked with Kilrenny
Arthur A. Christie BD   1997   2009   16 Taeping Close, Cellardyke, Anstruther KY10 3YL   01333 313917
[E-mail: revaac@btinternet.com]

Auchtermuchty (H) linked with Edenshead and Strathmiglo
James G. Redpath BD DipPTh   1988   2006   The Manse, Kirk Wynd, Strathmiglo, Cupar KY14 7QS   01337 860256
[E-mail: james.redpath2@btopenworld.com]

Balmerino (H) linked with Wormit (H)
James Connolly   1982   2004   5 Westwater Place, Newport-on-Tay DD6 8NS   01382 542626
DipTh CertMin MA(Theol) DMin   [E-mail: revconnolly@btinternet.com]

Boarhills and Dunino
Guardianship of the Presbytery (in deferred linking with St Andrews: Holy Trinity)

Cameron linked with St Andrews: St Leonard's (01334 478702) (E-mail: stlencam@btconnect.com)
Alan D. McDonald LLB BD MTh DLitt DD   1979   1998   1 Cairnhill Gardens, St Andrews KY16 8QY   01334 472793
[E-mail: alan.d.mcdonald@talk21.com]

Carnbee linked with Pittenweem
Margaret E.S. Rose BD   2007   29 Milton Road, Pittenweem, Anstruther KY10 2LN   01333 312838
[E-mail: mgt.r@btopenworld.com]

Cellardyke (H) See Anstruther

Ceres, Kemback and Springfield				
James W. Campbell BD	1995	2010	The Manse, St Andrews Road, Ceres, Cupar KY15 5NQ [E-mail: revjimashkirk@aol.com]	01334 829350

Crail linked with Kingsbarns (H)

Ann Allison BSc PhD BD	2000	2011	The Manse, St Andrews Road, Crail, Anstruther KY10 3UH [E-mail: revann@sky.com]	01333 451986

Creich, Flisk and Kilmany linked with Monimail

Vacant			Creich Manse, Brunton, Cupar KY15 4PA	01337 870332

Cupar: Old (H) and St Michael of Tarvit

Kenneth S. Jeffrey BA BD PhD	2002		76 Hogarth Drive, Cupar KY15 5YH [E-mail: ksjeffrey@btopenworld.com]	01334 653196

Cupar: St John's and Dairsie United

Jan J. Steyn (Mr)	2011		The Manse, 23 Hogarth Drive, Cupar KY15 5YH [E-mail: jansteyn464@btinternet.com]	01334 650751

Edenshead and Strathmiglo See Auchtermuchty

Elie (H) Kilconquhar and Colinsburgh (H)

Emma McDonald	2013		30 Bank Street, Elie, Leven KY9 1BW	01333 330685

Falkland linked with Freuchie (H)

Vacant			1 Newton Road, Falkland, Cupar KY15 7AQ	01337 858557

Freuchie (H) See Falkland

Howe of Fife

William F. Hunter MA BD	1986	2011	The Manse, 83 Church Street, Ladybank, Cupar KY15 7ND [E-mail: mail@billhunter.plus.com]	01337 832717

Kilrenny See Anstruther

Kingsbarns See Crail

Largo and Newburn (H) linked with Largo: St David's
John A.H. Murdoch BA BD DPSS　1979　2006　The Manse, Church Place, Upper Largo, Leven KY8 6EH　01333 360286
[E-mail: jm.largo@btinternet.com]

Largo: St David's See Largo and Newburn

Largoward (H) linked with St Monans (H)
Peter W. Mills CB BD DD CPS　1984　2013　The Manse, St Monans, Anstruther KY10 2DD　01333 730258
[E-mail: pwmills@live.co.uk]

Leuchars: St Athernase
Caroline Taylor (Mrs) MA BD　1995　2003　7 David Wilson Park, Balmullo, St Andrews KY16 0NP　01334 870038
[E-mail: caro234@btinternet.com]

Monimail See Creich, Flisk and Kilmany
Newburgh See Abdie and Dunbog

Newport-on-Tay (H)
Stanley A. Brook BD MTh　1977　2009　8 Gowrie Street, Newport-on-Tay DD6 8ED　01382 540009
[E-mail: stan_brook@hotmail.com]

Pittenweem See Carnbee

St Andrews: Holy Trinity
Rory MacLeod BA MBA BD　1994　2004　5 Cupar Road, Guardbridge, St Andrews KY16 0UA　01334 838038
[E-mail: annicerory@gmail.com]

St Andrews: Hope Park and Martyrs' (H) linked with Strathkinness
Allan McCafferty BSc BD　1993　2011　20 Priory Gardens, St Andrews KY16 8XX　01334 478287 (Tel/Fax)
[E-mail: minister@hpmchurch.org.uk]

St Andrews: St Leonard's (H) See Cameron
St Monans See Largoward
Strathkinness See St Andrews: Hope Park and Martyrs'

Tayport
Brian H. Oxburgh BSc BD   1980 2011   27 Bell Street, Tayport DD6 9AP   01382 553879
[E-mail: b.oxburgh@btinternet.com]

Wormit See Balmerino

Name			Previous charge / post	Address	Telephone
Alexander, James S. MA BD BA PhD	1966	1973	(University of St Andrews)	5 Strathkinness High Road, St Andrews KY16 9RP	01334 472680
Bews, James MA	1942	1981	(Dundee: Craigiebank)	21 Balrymonth Court, St Andrews KY16 8XT	01334 476087
Bradley, Ian C. MA BD DPhil	1990	1990	University of St Andrews	4 Donaldson Gardens, St Andrews KY16 9DN	01334 475389
Brown, Harry J. LTh	1991	2009	(Dundee: Menzieshill)	6 Hall Street, Kettlebridge, Cupar KY15 7QF	01337 830088
				[E-mail: harrybrown@aol.com]	
Brown, Lawson R. MA	1960	1997	(Cameron with St Andrew's: St Leonard's)	10 Park Street, St Andrews KY16 8AQ	01334 473413
Cameron, John U.	1974	2008	(Dundee: Broughty Ferry St Stephen's		
BA BSc PhD BD ThD			and West)	10 Howard Place, St Andrews KY16 9HL	01334 474474
Casebow, Brian C. MA BD	1959	1993	(Edinburgh: Salisbury)	c/o 6 Lawhead Place, Penicuik EH26 9JU	
Douglas, Peter C. JP	1966	1993	(Boarhills linked with Dunino)	The Old Schoolhouse, Flisk, Newburgh, Cupar KY14 6HN	01337 870218
Earnshaw, Philip BA BSc BD	1986	1996	(Glasgow: Pollokshields)	22 Castle Street, St Monans, Anstruther KY10 2AP	01333 730640
Edington, George L.	1952	1989	(Tayport)	64B Burghmuir Road, Perth PH1 1LH	
Fairlie, George BD BVMS MRCVS	1971	2002	(Crail with Kingsbarns)	41 Warrack Street, St Andrews KY16 8DR	01334 475868
Fraser, Ann G. BD CertMin	1990	2007	(Auchtermuchty)	24 Irvine Crescent, St Andrews KY16 8LG (Tel/Fax)	01334 461329
				[E-mail: anngilfraser@btinternet.com]	
Galloway, Robert W.C. LTh	1970	1998	(Cromarty)	22 Haughgate, Leven KY8 4SG	01333 426223
Gibson, Henry M. MA BD PhD	1960	1999	(Dundee: The High Kirk)	4 Comerton Place, Drumoig, Leuchars, St Andrews KY16 0NQ	01382 542199
Gordon, Peter M. MA BD	1958	1995	(Airdrie: West)	3 Cupar Road, Cuparmuir, Cupar KY15 5RH	01334 652341
				[E-mail: machrie@madasafish.com]	
Hamilton, Ian W.F.	1978	2012	(Nairn: Old)	Mossneuk, 9 Windsor Gardens, St Andrews KY16 8XL	01334 477745
BD LTh, ALCM AVCM				[E-mail: reviwfh@btinternet.com]	
Harrison, Cameron	2006		(Auxiliary Minister)	Woodfield House, Priormuir, St Andrews KY16 8LP	01334 478067
Hegarty, John D. LTh ABSC	1988	2004	(Buckie: South and West with Enzie)	26 Montgomery Way, Kinross KY13 8FD	01577 863829
				[E-mail: john.hegarty@tesco.net]	
Lancaster, Craig MA BD	2004	2011	Chaplain: RAF	Station Chaplain, RAF Leuchars, St Andrews KY16 0JX	01334 857782
				[E-mail: craiglancaster@yahoo.co.uk]	(Mbl) 07968 270391
Learmonth, Walter LTh	1968	1997	(Ceres with Springfield)	14 Marionfield Place, Cupar KY15 5JN	01334 656290
MacEwan, Donald G. MA BD PhD	2001	2012	Chaplain: University of St Andrews	Chaplaincy Centre, 3A St Mary's Place, St Andrews KY16 9UY	01334 462865
				[E-mail: dgm21@st-andrews.ac.uk]	(Mbl) 07713 322036
McGregor, Duncan J. MIFM	1982	1996	(Channelkirk with Lauder: Old)	14 Mount Melville, St Andrews KY16 8NG	01334 478314
Mackenzie, A. Cameron MA	1955	1995	(Biggar)	Hedgerow, 5 Shiels Avenue, Freuchie, Cupar KY15 7JD	01337 857763
Meager, Peter					
MA BD CertMgmt(Open)	1971	1998	(Elie with Kilconquhar and Colinsburgh)	7 Lorraine Drive, Cupar KY15 5DY	01334 656991
Neilson, Peter MA BD MTh	1975	2006	Mission Consultant	Linne Bheag, 2 School Green, Anstruther KY10 3HF	01333 310477
				[E-mail: neilson.peter@btinternet.com]	(Mbl) 07818 418608

Petrie, Ian D. MA BD	1970	2008	(Dundee: St Andrew's)	27 High Street East, Anstruther KY10 3DQ [E-mail: idp-77@hotmail.com]	01333 310181
Reid, Alan A.S. MA BD STM	1962	1995	(Bridge of Allan: Chalmers)	Wayside Cottage, Bridgend, Ceres, Cupar KY15 5LS	01334 828509
Robb, Nigel J. FCP MA BD ThM MTh	1981	1998	Associate Secretary: Mission and Discipleship Council	c/o 121 George Street, Edinburgh EH2 4YN [E-mail: nrobb@cofscotland.org.uk]	0131-225 5722
Roy, Alan J. BSc BD	1960	1999	(Aberuthven with Dunning)	14 Comerton Place, Drumoig, Leuchars, St Andrews KY16 0NQ [E-mail: a.roy225@btinternet.com]	01382 542225
Salters, Robert B. MA BD PhD	1966	1971	(University of St Andrews)	Vine Cottage, 119 South Street, St Andrews KY16 9UH	01334 473198
Strong, Clifford LTh	1983	1995	(Creich, Flisk and Kilmany with Monimail)		
Taylor, Ian BSc MA LTh DipEd	1983	1997	(Abdie and Dunbog with Newburgh)	60 Maryknowe, Gauldry, Newport-on-Tay DD6 8SL	01382 330445
Thrower, Charles G. BSc	1965	2002	(Carnbee with Pittenweem)	Lundie Cottage, Arncroach, Anstruther KY10 2RN	01333 720222
				Grange House, Wester Grangemuir, Pittenweem, Anstruther KY10 2RB [E-mail: charlesandsteph@btinternet.com]	01333 312631
Torrance, Alan J. (Prof.) MA BD DrTheol	1984	1999	University of St Andrews	Kincaple House, Kincaple, St Andrews KY16 9SH	(Home) 01334 850755 (Office) 01334 462843
Walker, James B. MA BD DPhil	1975	2011	(Chaplain: University of St Andrews)	5 Priestden Park, St Andrews KY16 8DL	01334 472839
Wotherspoon, Ian G. BA LTh	1967	2004	(Coatbridge: St Andrew's)	12 Cherry Lane, Cupar KY15 5DA [E-mail: wotherspoonrig@aol.com]	01334 650710
Wright, Lynda (Miss) BEd DCS	1984	2003	Deacon: Retreat Leader, Key House	6 Key Cottage, High Street, Falkland, Cupar KY15 7BD	01337 857705
Young, Evelyn M. (Mrs) BSc BD			(Kilmun (St Munn's) with Strone and Ardentinny)	2 Priestden Place, St Andrews KY16 8DP	01334 479662

(27) DUNKELD AND MEIGLE

Meets at Pitlochry on the first Tuesday of September and December, on the third Tuesday of February, April and October, and at the Moderator's church on the third Tuesday of June.

| Clerk: | REV. JOHN RUSSELL MA | Kilblaan, Gladstone Terrace, Birnam, Dunkeld PH8 0DP [E-mail: dunkeldmeigle@cofscotland.org.uk] | 01350 728896 |

Aberfeldy (H) linked with Amulree (H) and Strathbraan linked with Dull and Weem (H)

| Mark Drane BD | 2007 | The Manse, Taybridge Terrace, Aberfeldy PH15 2BS [E-mail: mark_drane@hotmail.co.uk] | 01887 820656 |

Alyth (H)
Michael J. Erskine MA BD | 1985 | 2012 | The Manse, Cambridge Street, Alyth, Blairgowrie PH11 8AW
[E-mail: erskinemike@gmail.com] | 01828 632238

Amulree and Strathbraan See Aberfeldy

Ardler, Kettins and Meigle
Vacant | The Manse, Dundee Road, Meigle, Blairgowrie PH12 8SB | 01828 640074

Bendochy linked with Coupar Angus: Abbey
Bruce Dempsey BD | 1997 | Caddam Road, Coupar Angus, Blairgowrie PH13 9EF
[E-mail: revbruce.dempsey@btopenworld.com] | 01828 627331

Blair Atholl and Struan linked with Tenandry
Vacant | Blair Atholl, Pitlochry PH18 5SX | 01796 481213

Blairgowrie
Harry Mowbray BD CA | 2003 | 2008 | The Manse, Upper David Street, Blairgowrie PH10 6HB
[E-mail: hmowbray@viewlands.plus.com] | 01250 872146

Braes of Rannoch linked with Foss and Rannoch (H)
Vacant | The Manse, Kinloch Rannoch, Pitlochry PH16 5QA | 01882 632381

Caputh and Clunie (H) linked with Kinclaven (H)
Peggy Roberts BA BD | 2003 | 2011 | Caputh Manse, Caputh, Perth PH1 4JH
[E-mail: revpeggy.r@googlemail.com] | 01738 710520

Coupar Angus: Abbey See Bendochy
Dull and Weem See Aberfeldy

Dunkeld (H)
R. Fraser Penny BA BD | 1984 | 2001 | Cathedral Manse, Dunkeld PH8 0AW
[E-mail: fraserpenn@aol.com] | 01350 727249

Fortingall and Glenlyon linked with Kenmore and Lawers
Anne J. Brennan BSc BD MTh | 1999 | The Manse, Balnaskeag, Kenmore, Aberfeldy PH15 2HB
[E-mail: annebrennan@yahoo.co.uk] | 01887 830218

Foss and Rannoch See Braes of Rannoch

Grantully, Logierait and Strathtay
Vacant — The Manse, Strathtay, Pitlochry PH9 0PG — 01887 840251

Kenmore and Lawers (H) See Fortingall and Glenlyon
Kinclaven See Caputh and Clunie

Kirkmichael, Straloch and Glenshee linked with Rattray (H)
Linda Stewart (Mrs) BD 1996 2012 — The Manse, Alyth Road, Rattray, Blairgowrie PH10 7HF — 01250 872462
[E-mail: lindacstewart@tiscali.co.uk]

Pitlochry (H) (01796 472160)
Mary M. Haddow (Mrs) BD 2001 2012 — Manse Road, Moulin, Pitlochry PH16 5EP — 01796 472774
[E-mail: mary_haddow@btconnect.com]

Rattray See Kirkmichael, Straloch and Glenshee
Tenandry See Blair Atholl and Struan

Cassells, Alexander K. MA BD	1961	1997	(Leuchars: St Athernase and Guardbridge)	47 Burghmuir Road, Perth PH1 1JG	01738 637995
Creegan, Christine M. (Mrs) MTh	1993	2005	(Grantully, Logierait and Strathtay)	Lonaig, 28 Lettoch Terrace, Pitlochry PH16 5BA	01796 472422
Duncan, James BTh FSAScot	1980	1995	(Blair Atholl and Struan)	25 Knockard Avenue, Pitlochry PH16 5JE	01796 474096
Ewart, William BSc BD	1972	2010	(Caputh and Clunie with Kinclaven)	Cara Beag, Essendy Road, Blairgowrie PH10 6QU [E-mail: ewe1@btinternet.com]	01250 876897
Henderson, John D. MA BD	1953	1992	(Cluny with Monymusk)	Aldersyde, George Street, Blairgowrie PH10 6HP	01250 875181
Knox, John W. MTheol	1992	1997	(Lochgelly: Macainsh)	Heatherlea, Main Street, Ardler, Blairgowrie PH12 8SR	01828 640731
McAlister, D.J.B. MA BD PhD	1951	1989	(North Berwick: Blackadder)	2 Duff Avenue, Moulin, Pitlochry PH16 5EN	01796 473591
MacRae, Malcolm H. MA PhD	1971	2010	(Kirkmichael, Straloch and Glenshee with Rattray)	10B Victoria Place, Stirling FK8 2QU [E-mail: malcolm.macrae1@btopenworld.com]	01786 465547
MacVicar, Kenneth MBE DFC TD MA	1950	1990	(Kenmore with Lawers with Fortingall and Glenlyon)	Illeray, Kenmore, Aberfeldy PH15 2HE	01887 830514
Nelson, Robert C. BA BD	1980	2010	(Isle of Mull, Kilninian and Kilmore with Salen and Ulva with Tobermory with Torosay and Kinlochspelvie)	St Colme's, Perth Road, Birnam, Dunkeld PH8 0BH [E-mail: robertnelson@onetel.net]	01350 727455
Ormiston, Hugh C. BSc BD MPhil PhD	1969	2004	(Kirkmichael, Straloch and Glenshee with Rattray)	Cedar Lea, Main Road, Woodside, Blairgowrie PH13 9NP	01828 670539
Oswald, John BSc PhD BD	1997	2011	(Muthill with Trinity Gask and Kinkell)	1 Woodlands Meadow, Rosemount, Blairgowrie PH10 6GZ [E-mail: revdocoz@bigfoot.com]	01250 872598
Ramsay, Malcolm BA LLB DipMin	1986	2011	Overseas service in Nepal	c/o World Mission Council, 121 George Street, Edinburgh EH2 4YN [E-mail: amalcolmramsay@gmail.com]	0131-225 5722
Robertson, Matthew LTh	1968	2002	(Cawdor with Croy and Dalcross)	Inver, Strathtay, Pitlochry PH9 0PG	01887 840780

Russell, John MA	(Tillicoultry)	1959	2000	Kilblaan, Gladstone Terrace, Birnam, Dunkeld PH8 0DP	01350 728896
Shannon, W.G. MA BD	(Pitlochry)	1955	1998	19 Knockard Road, Pitlochry PH16 5HJ	01796 473533
Tait, Thomas W. BD	(Rattray)	1972	1997	3 Rosemount Park, Blairgowrie PH10 6TZ	01250 874833
White, Brock A. LTh	(Kirkcaldy: Templehall)	1971	2001	1 Littlewood Gardens, Blairgowrie PH10 6XZ	01250 870399
Whyte, William B. BD	(Nairn: St Ninian's)	1973	2003	The Old Inn, Park Hill Road, Rattray, Blairgowrie PH10 7DS	01250 874401
Wilson, John M. MA BD	(Altnaharra and Farr)	1965	2004	Berbice, The Terrace, Blair Atholl, Pitlochry PH18 5SZ	01796 481619
Wilson, Mary D. (Mrs) RGN SCM DTM	(Auxiliary Minister)	1990	2004	Berbice, The Terrace, Blair Atholl, Pitlochry PH18 5SZ	01796 481619

(28) PERTH

Meets at Riverside Church, Perth, at 7:00pm on the second Tuesday of February, March, May, June, November and December, and in the Moderator's church on the second Tuesday of September.

Clerk:	**REV. ALAN D. REID MA BD**		
Presbytery Office:	**209 High Street, Perth PH1 5PB**	**01738 451177**
	[E-mail: perth@cofscotland.org.uk]	

Abernethy and Dron and Arngask
Vacant — 3 Manse Road, Abernethy, Perth PH2 9JP — 01738 850607

Almondbank Tibbermore linked with Methven and Logiealmond
Philip W. Patterson BMus BD — 1999 2008 — The Manse, Pitcairngreen, Perth PH1 3EA — 01738 583217
[E-mail: philip.patterson@btinternet.com]

Ardoch (H) linked with Blackford (H)
Stuart D.B. Picken MA BD PhD — 1966 2005 — 3 Millhill Crescent, Greenloaning, Dunblane FK15 0LH — 01786 880217
[E-mail: picken@eikoku.demon.co.uk]

Auchterarder (H)
Robert D. Barlow — 2010 2013 — 22 Kirkfield Place, Auchterarder PH3 1FP — 01764 662210
BA BSc MSc PhD CChem MRSC — [E-mail: rob@miragemedia.co.uk]

Auchtergaven and Moneydie linked with Redgorton and Stanley
Adrian J. Lough BD — 2012 — 22 King Street, Stanley, Perth PH1 4ND — 01738 827952
[E-mail: revlough@btinternet.com]

Blackford See Ardoch

Cargill Burrelton linked with Collace
Eric G. McKimmon BA BD MTh PhD   1983   The Manse, Manse Road, Woodside, Blairgowrie PH13 9NQ   01828 670352
[E-mail: ericmckimmon@gmail.com]

Cleish (H) linked with Fossoway: St Serf's and Devonside
Vacant   The Manse, Cleish, Kinross KY13 7LR   01577 850231

Collace See Cargill Burrelton

Comrie (H) linked with Dundurn (H)
Graham McWilliams BSc BD   2005   The Manse, Strowan Road, Comrie, Crieff PH6 2ES   01764 670076
[E-mail: Themansefamily@aol.com]

Crieff (H)
Andrew J. Philip BSc BD   1996   8 Strathearn Terrace, Crieff PH7 3AQ   01764 653907
[E-mail: andrewphilip@minister.com]

Dunbarney (H) and Forgandenny
Allan J. Wilson BSc MEd BD   2007   Dunbarney Manse, Manse Road, Bridge of Earn, Perth PH2 9DY   01738 812211
[E-mail: allanjwilson@dfpchurch.org.uk]

Dundurn See Comrie

Errol (H) linked with Kilspindie and Rait
Douglas M. Main BD   1986   South Bank, Errol, Perth PH2 7PZ   01821 642279
[E-mail: revdmain@sky.com]

Fossoway: St Serf's and Devonside See Cleish

Fowlis Wester, Madderty and Monzie linked with Gask
Eleanor D. Muir (Miss) MTheol DipPTheol   1986   Beechview, Abercairney, Crieff PH7 3NF   01764 652116
[E-mail: eleanordmuir@tiscali.co.uk]

Gask (H) See Fowlis Wester, Madderty and Monzie
Kilspindie and Rait See Errol

Kinross (H) (Office: 01577 862570)
Alan D. Reid MA BD   1989   15 Green Wood, Kinross KY13 8FG   01577 862952
[E-mail: kinrossmanse@tiscali.co.uk]

Margaret Michie (Mrs)   2013   3 Loch Leven Court, Wester Balgedie, Kinross KY13 9NE   01592 840602
(Ordained Local Minister)   [E-mail: margaretmichie@btinternet.com]

Methven and Logiealmond See Almondbank Tibbermore

Muthill (H) linked with Trinity Gask and Kinkell

Klaus O.F. Buwert LLB BD DMin	1984	2013	The Manse, Station Road, Muthill, Crieff PH5 2AR [E-mail: klaus@buwert.co.uk]	01764 681205

Orwell (H) and Portmoak (H) (Office: 01577 862100)

Angus Morrison MA BD PhD	1979	2011	41 Auld Mart Road, Milnathort, Kinross KY13 9FR [E-mail: angusmorrison3@gmail.com]	01577 863461

Perth: Craigie and Moncreiffe

Carolann Erskine BD	2009	The Manse, 46 Abbot Street, Perth PH2 0EE [E-mail: erskine13@blueyonder.co.uk]	01738 623748
Robert Wilkie (Aux)	2011	24 Huntingtower Road, Perth PH1 2JS [E-mail: robert.wilkie.07@aberdeen.ac.uk]	01738 628301

Perth: Kinnoull (H)

David I. Souter BD	1996	2001	The Broch, 34 Monart Road, Perth PH1 5UQ [E-mail: d.souter@blueyonder.co.uk]	01738 626046

Perth: Letham St Mark's (H) (Office: 01738 446377)

James C. Stewart BD DipMin	1997	35 Rose Crescent, Perth PH1 1NT [E-mail: diamondboy09@yahoo.com]	01738 624167
Kenneth D. McKay DCS		11F Balgowan Road, Perth PH1 2JG [E-mail: deakendan@gmail.com]	01738 621169 / 07843 883042 (Mbl)

Perth: North (Office: 01738 622298)

Hugh O'Brien CSS MTheol	2001	2009	127 Glasgow Road, Perth PH2 0LU [E-mail: the.manse@btconnect.com]	01738 625728

Perth: Riverside (Office: 01738 622341)

Vacant	44 Hay Street, Perth PH1 5HS	01738 631148

Perth: St John's Kirk of Perth (H) (01738 626159) linked with Perth: St Leonard's-in-the-Fields

James K. Wallace MA BD STM	1988	2009	5 Strathearn Terrace, Perth PH2 0LS [E-mail: revjwspc@hotmail.com]	01738 621709

Perth: St Leonard's-in-the-Fields (H) (01738 632238) See Perth: St John's Kirk of Perth

Perth: St Matthew's (Office: 01738 636757; Vestry: 01738 630725)
Scott Burton BD DipMin   1999 2007   23 Kincarrathie Crescent, Perth PH2 7HH   01738 626828
[E-mail: minister@stmatts.org.uk]

Redgorton and Stanley See Auchtergaven and Moneydie

St Madoes and Kinfauns
Marc F. Bircham BD MTh   2000   Glencarse, Perth PH2 7NF   01738 860837
[E-mail: mark.bircham@btinternet.com]

Scone and St Martins
Gordon A. McCracken BD CertMin DMin   1988 2013   13 Haddon Road, Perth PH2 7JA   01738 451481
(Interim Minister)   [E-mail: gordonangus@btopenworld.com]

The Stewartry of Strathearn (H) (Office: 01738 621674)
Vacant   Aberdalgie, Perth PH2 0QD

Trinity Gask and Kinkell See Muthill

Ballentine, Ann M. (Miss) MA BD   1981 2007   (Kirknewton and East Calder)   17 Nellfield Road, Crieff PH7 3DU   01764 652567
[E-mail: annballentine@hotmail.com]

Barr, George K. ARIBA BD PhD   1967 1993   (Uddingston: Viewpark)   7 Tay Avenue, Comrie, Crieff PH6 2PE   01764 670454
[E-mail: gbarr2@compuserve.com]

Barr, T. Leslie LTh   1969 1997   (Kinross)   8 Fairfield Road, Kelty KY4 0BY   01383 839330
Bertram, Thomas A.   1972 1995   (Patna Waterside)   3 Scrimgeours Corner, 29 West High Street, Crieff PH7 4AP   01764 652066
Brown, Elizabeth (Mrs) JP RGN   1996 2007   (Auxiliary Minister)   8 Viewlands Place, Perth PH1 1BS   01738 552391
[E-mail: liz.brown@blueyonder.co.uk]

Brown, Marina D. (Mrs) MA BD MTh   2000 2012   (Hawick: St Mary's and Old)   Moneydie School Cottage, Luncarty, Perth PH1 3HZ   01738 582163
[E-mail: revmdb1711@btinternet.com]

Buchan, William DipTheol BD   1987 2001   (Kilwinning: Abbey)   34 Bridgewater Avenue, Auchterarder PH3 1DQ   01764 660306
[E-mail: wbuchan3@aol.com]

Cairns, Evelyn BD   2004 2012   (Chaplain: Rachel House)   15 Talla Park, Kinross KY13 8AB   01577 863990
[E-mail: revelyn@btinternet.com]

Caskie, J. Colin BA BD   1977 2012   (Rhu and Shandon)   13 Anderson Drive, Perth PH1 1JZ
[E-mail: colin@jcaskie.eclipse.co.uk]

Name			(Parish)	Address	Phone
Coleman, Sidney H. BA BD MTh	1961	2001	(Glasgow: Merrylea)	'Blaven', 11 Clyde Place, Perth PH2 0EZ [E-mail: sidney.coleman@blueyonder.co.uk]	01738 565072
Craig, Joan H. (Miss) MTheol	1986	2005	(Orkney: East Mainland)	7 Jedburgh Place, Perth PH1 1SJ [E-mail: joanhcraig@bigfoot.com]	01738 580180
Donaldson, Robert B. BSocSc	1953	1997	(Kilchoman with Portnahaven)	11 Strathearn Court, Crieff PH7 3DS	01764 654976
Drummond, Alfred G. BD DMin	1991	2006	Scottish General Secretary: Evangelical Alliance	10 Errochty Court, Perth PH1 2SU [E-mail: frddrmmnd@aol.com]	01738 621305
Fleming, Hamish K. MA	1966	2001	(Banchory Ternan: East)	36 Earnmuir Road, Comrie, Crieff PH6 2EY	01764 679178
Graham, Sydney S. DipYL MPhil BD	1987	2009	(Iona with Kilfinichen and Kilvickeon and the Ross of Mull)	'Aspen', Milton Road, Luncarty, Perth PH1 3ES [E-mail: sydgraham@btinternet.com]	01738 829350
Gregory, J.C. LTh	1968	1992	(Blantyre: St Andrew's)	2 Southlands Road, Auchterarder PH3 1BA	01764 664594
Gunn, Alexander M. MA BD	1967	2006	(Aberfeldy with Amulree and Strathbraan with Dull and Weem)	'Navarone', 12 Cornhill Road, Perth PH1 1LR [E-mail: sandygunn@btinternet.com]	01738 443216
Halliday, Archibald R. BD MTh	1964	1999	(Duffus, Spynie and Hopeman)	8 Turretbank Drive, Crieff PH7 4LW [E-mail halliday@pittenzie.wanadoo.co.uk]	01764 656464
Hughes, Clifford E. MA BD	1993	2001	(Haddington: St Mary's)	Pavilion Cottage, Briglands, Rumbling Bridge, Kinross KY13 0PS	01577 840506
Kelly, T. Clifford	1973	1995	(Ferintosh)	20 Whinfield Drive, Kinross KY13 8UB	01577 864946
Lawson, James B. MA BD	1961	2002	(South Uist)	4 Cowden Way, Comrie, Crieff PH6 2NW [E-mail: james.lawson7@btopenworld.com]	01764 679180
Lawson, Ronald G. MA BD	1964	1999	(Greenock: Wellpark Mid Kirk)	6 East Brougham Street, Stanley, Perth PH1 4NJ	01738 828871
Low, J.E. Stewart MA	1957	1997	(Tarbat)	15 Stormont Place, Scone, Perth PH2 6SR	01738 552023
McCormick, Alastair F.	1962	1998	(Creich with Rosehall)	14 Balmanno Park, Bridge of Earn, Perth PH2 9RJ	01738 813588
MacDonald, James W. BD	1976	2012	(Crieff)	'Mingulay', 29 Hebridean Gardens, Crieff PH7 3BP [E-mail: rev_up@btinternet.com]	01764 654500
McGregor, William LTh	1987	2003	(Auchtergaven and Moneydie)	'Ard Choille', 7 Taypark Road, Luncarty, Perth PH1 3FE [E-mail: bill.mcgregor7@btinternet.com]	01738 827866
McIntosh, Colin G. MA BD	1976	2013	(Dunblane: Cathedral)	Drumhead Cottage, Drum, Kinross KY13 0PR [E-mail: colinmcintosh4@btinternet.com]	01577 840012
MacKenzie, Donald W. MA	1941	1983	(Auchterarder: The Barony)	81 Kingswell Terrace, Perth PH1 2DA	01738 633716
MacMillan, Riada M. (Mrs) BD	1991	1998	(Perth: Craigend Moncreiffe with Rhynd)	73 Muirend Gardens, Perth PH1 1JR	01738 628867
McNaughton, David J.H. BA CA	1976	1995	(Killin and Ardeonaig)	30 Hollybush Road, Crieff PH7 3HB	01764 653028
Malcolm, Alistair BD DPS	1976	2012	(Inverness: Inshes)	11 Kinclaven Gardens, Murthly, Perth PH1 4EX [E-mail: amalcolm067@btinternet.com]	01738 710979
Millar, Archibald E. DipTh	1965	1991	(Perth: St Stephen's)	7 Maple Place, Perth PH1 1RT	01738 621813
Munro, Gillian (Miss) BSc BD	1989	2003	Head of Spiritual Care, NHS Tayside	Royal Victoria Hospital, Liff, Dundee DD2 5NF	01382 423116
Munro, Patricia (Ms) BSc DCS			Perth: St John's Kirk of Perth with Perth: St Leonard's-in-the-Fields	4 Hewat Place, Perth PH1 2UD	01738 443088
				[E-mail: pat.munrodcs@gmail.com]	07814 836314 (Mbl)
Paton, Iain F. BD FCIS	1980	2006	(Elie with Kilconquhar and Colinsburgh)	Muldoanich, Stirling Street, Blackford, Auchterarder PH4 1QG	01764 682234
Pattison, Kenneth J. MA BD STM	1967	2004	(Kilmuir and Logie Easter)	2 Castle Way, St Madoes, Glencarse, Perth PH2 7NY [E-mail: k_pattison@btinternet.com]	01738 860340
Reid, David T. BA BD	1954	1993	(Cleish with Fossoway: St Serf's and Devonside)	Benarty, Wester Balgedie, Kinross KY13 9HE	01592 840214
Robertson, Thomas G.M. LTh	1971	2004	(Edenshead and Strathmiglo)	23 Muirend Avenue, Perth PH1 1JL	01738 624432

Name			Address	Phone
Ross, William B. LTh CPS	1988	2011	(Muthill with Trinity Gask and Kinkell) [E-mail: williamross278@btinternet.com]	01764 681205
Russell, Kenneth G. BD CCE	1986	2013	Prison Chaplain 158 Bannockburn Road, Stirling FK7 0EW [E-mail: kenrussell1000@hotmail.com]	01786 812680
Searle, David C. MA DipTh	1965	2003	(Warden: Rutherford House) Stonefall Lodge, 30 Abbey Lane, Grange, Errol PH2 7GB [E-mail: des@davidsearle.plus.com]	01821 641004
Shirra, James MA	1945	1987	(St Martins with Scone: New) 17 Dunbarney Avenue, Bridge of Earn, Perth PH2 9BP	01738 812610
Simpson, James A. BSc BD STM DD	1960	2000	(Dornoch Cathedral) 'Dornoch', Perth Road, Bankfoot, Perth PH1 4ED [E-mail: ja@simpsondornoch.co.uk]	01738 787710
Sloan, Robert P. MA BD	1968	2007	(Braemar and Crathie) 1 Broomhill Avenue, Perth PH1 1EN [E-mail: sloans1@btinternet.com]	01738 443904
Stenhouse, W. Duncan MA BD	1989	2006	(Dunbarney and Forgandenny) 32 Sandport Gait, Kinross KY13 8FB [E-mail: duncan.stenhouse@btinternet.com]	01577 866992
Stewart, Anne E. (Mrs) BD CertMin	1998		Prison Chaplain 35 Rose Crescent, Perth PH1 1NT [E-mail: anne.stewart2@sps.pnn.gov.uk]	01738 624167
Stewart, Gordon G. MA	1961	2000	(Perth: St Leonard's-in-the-Fields and Trinity) 'Balnoe', South Street, Rattray, Blairgowrie PH10 7BZ	01250 870626
Stewart, Robin J. MA BD STM	1959	1995	(Orwell with Portmoak) 'Oakbrae', Perth Road, Murthly, Perth PH1 4HF	01738 710220
Thomson, J. Bruce MA BD	1972	2009	(Scone: Old) 47 Elm Street, Errol, Perth PH2 7SQ [E-mail: RevBruceThomson@aol.com]	01821 641039 07850 846404 (Mbl)
Thomson, Peter D. MA BD	1968	2004	(Comrie with Dundurn) 34 Queen Street, Perth PH2 0EJ [E-mail: peterthomson208@btinternet.com]	01738 622418

PERTH ADDRESSES

Craigie	Abbot Street
Kinnoull	Dundee Rd near Queen's Bridge
Letham St Mark's	Rannoch Road
Moncreiffe	Glenbruar Crescent
North	Mill Street near Kinnoull Street
Riverside	Bute Drive
St John's	St John's Street
St Leonard's-in-the-Fields	Marshall Place
St Matthew's	Tay Street

(29) DUNDEE

Meets at Dundee, Meadowside St Paul's Church Halls, Nethergate, on the second Wednesday of February, March, May, September, November and December, and on the fourth Wednesday of June.

Clerk:	REV. JAMES L. WILSON BD CPS	[E-mail: dundee@cofscotland.org.uk]	01382 459249 (Home) 07885 618659 (Mobile)
Depute Clerk:	REV. JANET P. FOGGIE MA BD PhD	[E-mail: r3vjw@aol.com]	01382 660152
Presbytery Office:		[E-mail: rev.foggie@btinternet.com] Whitfield Parish Church, Haddington Crescent, Dundee DD4 0NA	01382 503012

Abernyte linked with Inchture and Kinnaird linked with Longforgan (H)

Marjory A. MacLean (Miss) LLB BD PhD RNR	1991	2011	The Manse, Longforgan, Dundee DD2 5HB [E-mail: mrjrymcln@aol.com]	01382 360238

Auchterhouse (H) linked with Monikie and Newbigging and Murroes and Tealing (H)

David A. Collins BSc BD	1993	2006	New Kirk Manse, 25 Ballinard Gardens, Broughty Ferry, Dundee DD5 1BZ [E-mail: revdacollins@btinternet.com]	01382 778874

Dundee: Balgay (H)

Patricia Ramsay (Mrs) BD	2005	2013	150 City Road, Dundee DD2 2PW [E-mail: p.g.ramsay68@gmail.com]	01382 668806 07813 189776 (Mbl)

Dundee: Barnhill St Margaret's (H) (01382 737294) (E-mail: church.office@btconnect.com)

Susan Sutherland (Mrs) BD		2009	2 St Margaret's Lane, Barnhill, Dundee DD5 2PQ [E-mail: susan.sutherland@sky.com]	01382 779278

Dundee: Broughty Ferry New Kirk (H)

Catherine E.E. Collins (Mrs) MA BD	1993	2006	New Kirk Manse, 25 Ballinard Gardens, Broughty Ferry, Dundee DD5 1BZ [E-mail: revccollins@dsl.pipex.com]	01382 778874

Dundee: Broughty Ferry St James' (H)

Alberto A. de Paula BD MTh	1991	2005	2 Ferry Road, Monifieth, Dundee DD5 4NT [E-mail: albertodepaula@blueyonder.co.uk]	01382 534468

Dundee: Broughty Ferry St Luke's and Queen Street (01382 770329)

C. Graham Taylor BSc BD FIAB		2001	22 Albert Road, Broughty Ferry, Dundee DD5 1AZ [E-mail: cgdtaylor@tiscali.co.uk]	01382 779212

Dundee: Broughty Ferry St Stephen's and West (H) linked with Dundee (St Mary's) (H) (01382 226271)

Keith F. Hall MA BD	1980	1994	33 Strathern Road, West Ferry, Dundee DD5 1PP	01382 778808

Dundee: Camperdown (H) (01382 623958)

Vacant			Camperdown Manse, Myrekirk Road, Dundee DD2 4SF	01382 621383

Dundee: Chalmers Ardler (H)

Kenneth D. Stott MA BD	1989	1997	The Manse, Turnberry Avenue, Dundee DD2 3TP [E-mail: arkstotts@aol.com]	01382 827439

Dundee: Coldside
Anthony P. Thornthwaite MTh   1995   2011   9 Abercorn Street, Dundee DD4 7HY   01382 458314
[E-mail: tony.thornthwaite@sky.com]

Dundee: Craigiebank (H) (01382 731173) linked with Dundee: Douglas and Mid Craigie
Edith F. McMillan (Mrs) MA BD   1981   1999   19 Americanmuir Road, Dundee DD3 9AA   01382 812423

Dundee: Douglas and Mid Craigie See Dundee: Craigiebank

Dundee: Downfield Mains (H) (01382 810624/812166)
Vacant   9 Elgin Street, Dundee DD3 8NL   01382 827207

Dundee: Dundee (St Mary's) See Dundee: Broughty Ferry St Stephen's and West

Dundee: Fintry Parish Church (01382 508191)
Colin M. Brough BSc BD   1998   2002   4 Clive Street, Dundee DD4 7AW   01382 458629
[E-mail: colin.brough@blueyonder.co.uk]

Dundee: Lochee (H)
Hazel Wilson (Ms) MA BD DipEd DMS   1991   2006   32 Clayhills Drive, Dundee DD2 1SX   01382 561989
[E-mail: hwilson704@btinternet.com]
Willie Strachan MBA DipY&C   2013   Ladywell House, Lucky Slap, Monikie, Dundee DD5 3QG   01382 370286
(Ordained Local Minister)   [E-mail: luckyslapdees@btinternet.com]

Dundee: Logie and St John's Cross (H) (01382 668514)
Vacant   7 Hyndford Street, Dundee DD2 1HQ   01382 641572

Dundee: Meadowside St Paul's (H) (01382 202255)
Maudeen I. MacDougall (Miss) BA BD MTh   1978   1984   36 Blackness Avenue, Dundee DD2 1HH   01382 668828

Dundee: Menzieshill
Robert Mallinson BD   2010   The Manse, Charleston Drive, Dundee DD2 4ED   01382 667446
[E-mail: bobmalli1975@hotmail.co.uk]   07595 249089 (Mbl)

Dundee: St Andrew's (H) (01382 224860)
Janet P. Foggie MA BD PhD   2003   2009   39 Tullideph Road, Dundee DD2 2JD   01382 660152
[E-mail: rev.foggie@btinternet.com]

Dundee: St David's High Kirk (H) Marion J. Paton (Miss) MA BMus BD	1991	2007	6 Adelaide Place, Dundee DD3 6LF [E-mail: sdhkrev@googlemail.com]	01382 322955
Dundee: Steeple (H) (01382 200031) David M. Clark MA BD	1989	2000	128 Arbroath Road, Dundee DD4 7HR [E-mail: dmclark72@blueyonder.co.uk]	01382 455411
Dundee: Stobswell (H) (01382 461397) William McLaren MA BD	1990	2007	23 Shamrock Street, Dundee DD4 7AH [E-mail: williammclaren63@googlemail.com]	01382 459119
Dundee: Strathmartine (H) (01382 825817) Stewart McMillan BD	1983	1990	19 Americanmuir Road, Dundee DD3 9AA [E-mail: mcmillan_strath@btinternet.com]	01382 812423
Dundee: Trinity (H) David J.H. Laing BD DPS	1976	2008	65 Clepington Road, Dundee DD4 7BQ [E-mail: edlaing@tiscali.co.uk]	01382 458764
Dundee: West Andrew T. Greaves BD	1985	2000	Manse of Dundee West Church, Wards of Keithock, by Brechin DD9 7PZ [E-mail: andrewgreaves2@btinternet.com]	01356 624479
Dundee: Whitfield (H) (01382 503012) James L. Wilson BD CPS	1986	2001	53 Old Craigie Road, Dundee DD4 7JD [E-mail: r3vjw@aol.com]	01382 459249
Fowlis and Liff linked with Lundie and Muirhead (H) Donna M. Hays (Mrs) MTheol DipEd DipTMHA	2004		149 Coupar Angus Road, Muirhead of Liff, Dundee DD2 5QN [E-mail: dmhays32@aol.com]	01382 580210
Inchture and Kinnaird See Abernyte				
Invergowrie (H) Robert J. Ramsay LLB NP BD	1986	1997	2 Boniface Place, Invergowrie, Dundee DD2 5DW [E-mail: s3rjr@tiscali.co.uk]	01382 561118

Longforgan See Abernyte
Lundie and Muirhead See Fowlis and Liff

Monifieth (H)
Dorothy U. Anderson (Mrs) LLB DipLP BD 2006 2009 8 Church Street, Monifieth, Dundee DD5 4JP 01382 532607
[E-mail: dorothy@kirkyard.plus.com]

Monikie and Newbigging and Murroes and Tealing See Auchterhouse

Name / Qualifications			Charge / Position	Address	Telephone
Barrett, Leslie M. BD FRICS	1991	2001	Chaplain: University of Abertay, Dundee	Dunelm Cottage, Logie, Cupar KY15 4SJ	01334 870396
				[E-mail: l.barrett@abertay.ac.uk]	
Campbell, Gordon MA BD CDipAF DipHSM MCMI MIHM AFRIN ARSGS FRGS FSAScot		2001	Auxiliary Minister: Chaplain: University of Dundee (Dundee: Camperdown)	2 Falkland Place, Kingoodie, Invergowrie, Dundee DD2 5DY	01382 561383
				[E-mail: gordon.campbell@dundeepresbytery.org.uk]	
Craik, Sheila (Mrs) BD	1989	2001	(Industrial Mission Organiser)	35 Haldane Terrace, Dundee DD3 0HT	01382 802078
Cramb, Erik M. LTh	1973	1989		Flat 35, Braehead, Methven Walk, Dundee DD2 3FJ	01382 526196
				[E-mail: erikcramb@aol.com]	
Donald, Robert M. LTh BA	1969	2005	(Kilmodan and Colintraive)	2 Blacklaw Drive, Birkhill, Dundee DD2 5RJ	01382 581337
				[E-mail: robbie.donald@dundeepresbytery.org.uk]	
Douglas, Fiona C. (Ms) MBE MA BD PhD	1989	1997	Chaplain: University of Dundee	10 Springfield, Dundee DD1 4JE	01382 384157
Ferguson, John F. MA BD	1987	2001	(Perth: Kinmoull)	10 Glamis Crescent, Inchture, Perth PH14 9QU	01828 687881
Fraser, Donald W. MA	1958	2010	(Monifieth)	1 Blake Avenue, Broughty Ferry, Dundee DD5 3LH	01382 477491
				[E-mail: fraserdonald37@yahoo.co.uk]	(Mbl) 07531 863316
Galbraith, W. James L. BSc BD MICE	1973	1996	(Kilchrenan and Dalavich with Muckairn)	586 Brook Street, Broughty Ferry, Dundee DD5 2EA	01382 732110
Gammack, George BD	1985	1999	(Dundee: Whitfield)	13A Hill Street, Broughty Ferry, Dundee DD5 2JP	01382 778636
Hawdon, John E. BA MTh AICS	1961	1995	(Dundee: Clepington)	53 Hillside Road, Dundee DD2 1QT	01382 646212
				[E-mail: john.hawdon@dundeepresbytery.org.uk]	
Hudson, J. Harrison DipTh MA BD	1961	1999	(Dundee: St Peter's McCheyne)	22 Hamilton Avenue, Tayport DD6 9BW	01382 552052
Ingram, J.R.	1954	1978	(Chaplain: RAF)	48 Marlee Road, Broughty Ferry, Dundee DD5 3EX	01382 736400
Jamieson, David B. MA BD STM	1974	2011	(Monifieth)	8A Albert Street, Monifieth, Dundee DD5 4JS	01382 532772
Kay, Elizabeth (Miss) DipYCS	1993	2007	(Auxiliary Minister)	1 Kintail Walk, Inchture, Perth PH14 9RY	01828 686029
				[E-mail: liz.kay@dundeepresbytery.org.uk]	
Laidlaw, John J. MA	1964	1973	(Adviser in Religious Education)	14 Dalhousie Road, Barnhill, Dundee DD5 2SQ	01382 477458
Lynn, Joyce (Mrs) MIPM BD	1995	1999	(Shapinsay)	Flat 8, 131 St Vincent Street, Broughty Ferry, Dundee DD5 2DA	01382 690556
McLeod, David C. BSc MEng BD	1969	2001	(Dundee: Fairmuir)	6 Carseview Gardens, Dundee DD2 1NE	01382 641371
McMillan, Charles D. LTh	1979	2004	(Elgin: High)	11 Troon Terrace, The Orchard, Ardler, Dundee DD2 3FX	01382 831358
Mair, Michael V.A. MA BD	1967	2007	(Craigiebank with Dundee: Douglas and Mid Craigie)	48 Panmure Street, Monifieth DD5 4EH	01382 530538
				[E-mail: mvamair@gmail.com]	
Martin, Janie (Miss) DCS			(Deaconess)	16 Wentworth Road, Ardler, Dundee DD2 8SD	01382 813786

Name			Role	Address		
Mowat, Gilbert M. MA	1948	1986	(Dundee: Albany-Butterburn)	Abbeyfield House, 16 Grange Road, Bearsden, Glasgow G61 3PL	0141	572503
Powrie, James E. LTh	1969	1995	(Dundee: Chalmers Ardler)	3 Kirktonhill Road, Kirriemuir DD8 4HU	01575	
Rae, Robert LTh	1968	1983	(Chaplain: Dundee Acute Hospitals)	14 Neddertoun View, Liff, Dundee DD3 5RU	01382	581790
Reid, R. Gordon BSc BD MIET	1993	2010	(Carriden)	6 Bayview Place, Monifieth, Dundee DD5 4TN	01382	520519
				[E-mail: GordonReid@aol.com]	(Mbl) 07952	349884
Robson, George K. LTh DPS BA	1983	2011	(Dundee: Balgay)	11 Ceres Crescent, Broughty Ferry, Dundee DD5 3JN	01382	901212
				[E-mail: gkrobson@tiscali.co.uk]		
Rogers, James M. BA DB DCult	1955	1996	(Gibraltar)	24 Mansion Drive, Dalclaverhouse, Dundee DD4 9DD	01382	506162
Rose, Lewis (Mr) DCS	1993		(Deacon)	6 Gauldie Crescent, Dundee DD3 0RR	01382	622167
				[E-mail: scinnorth@uk.uumail.com]	(Mbl) 07899	790446
Roy, James A. MA BD	1965	2006	(Dundee: Lochee West)	'Beechwood', 7 Northview Terrace, Wormit, Newport-on-Tay DD6 8PP	01382	543578
				[E-mail: jim.roy@dundeepresbytery.org.uk]		
Scott, James MA BD	1973	2010	(Drumoak-Durris)	3 Blake Place, Broughty Ferry, Dundee DD5 3LQ	01382	739595
				[E-mail: jimscott73@yahoo.co.uk]		
Scoular, Stanley	1963	2000	(Rosyth)	31 Duns Crescent, Dundee DD4 0RY	01382	501653
Strickland, Alexander LTh	1971	2005	(Dairsie with Kemback with Strathkinness)	12 Ballumbie Braes, Dundee DD5 0UN	01382	685539

DUNDEE ADDRESSES

Balgay	200 Lochee Road	Coldside		Mains	Foot of Old Glamis Road
Barnhill St Margaret's	10 Invermark Terrace	Craigiebank	Isla Street	Meadowside St Paul's	114 Nethergate
Broughty Ferry		Douglas and Mid Craigie	Craigie Avenue at Greendykes Road	Menzieshill	Charleston Drive, Menzieshill
New Kirk	370 Queen Street	Downfield South	Balbeggie Place/ Longtown Terrace	St Andrew's	2 King Street
St James'	5 Fort Street		Haldane Street off Strathmartine Road	St David's High Kirk	119A Kinghorne Road and 273 Strathmore Avenue
St Luke's and Queen Street	5 West Queen Street	Dundee (St Mary's)	Nethergate	Steeple	Nethergate
St Stephen's and West	96 Dundee Road	Fintry	Fintry Road x Fintry Drive	Stobswell	170 Albert Street
Camperdown	22 Brownhill Road	Lochee	191 High Street, Lochee	Strathmartine	507 Strathmartine Road
Chalmers Ardler	Turnberry Avenue	Logie and		Trinity	73 Crescent Street
		St John's Cross	Shaftesbury Rd x Blackness Ave	West	130 Perth Road
				Whitfield	Haddington Crescent

(30) ANGUS

Meets at Forfar in St Margaret's Church Hall on the first Tuesday of February, March, May, September, November and December, and on the last Tuesday of June.

Clerk:	**REV. MICHAEL S. GOSS BD DPS**	[E-mail: michaelgoss@blueyonder.co.uk]		
Depute Clerk:	**REV. IAN A. McLEAN BSc BD DMin**	[E-mail: iamclean@lineone.net]		
Presbytery Office:	**St Margaret's Church, West High Street, Forfar DD8 1BJ**			01307 464224
	[E-mail: angus@cofscotland.org,uk]			

Aberlemno (H) linked with Guthrie and Rescobie

Brian Ramsay BD DPS MLitt	1980	1984	The Manse, Guthrie, Forfar DD8 2TP	01241 828243
			[E-mail: revdbrianr@hotmail.com]	

Arbirlot linked with Carmyllie
Stewart J. Lamont BSc BD   1972   2011

The Manse, Arbirlot, Arbroath DD11 2NX
[E-mail: lamontsj@gmail.com]

01241 879800

Arbroath: Knox's (H) linked with Arbroath: St Vigeans (H)
Nelu I. Balaj BD MA ThD   2010

The Manse, St Vigeans, Arbroath DD11 4RF
[E-mail: nelu@gmx.co.uk]

01241 873206
07954 436879 (Mbl)

Arbroath: Old and Abbey (H) (Church office: 01241 877068)
Vacant

51 Cliffburn Road, Arbroath DD11 5BA

01241 872196 (Tel/Fax)

Arbroath: St Andrew's (H) (E-mail: office@arbroathstandrews.org.uk)
W. Martin Fair BA BD DMin   1992

92 Grampian Gardens, Arbroath DD11 4AQ
[E-mail: martin.fair@sky.com]

01241 873238 (Tel/Fax)

Stuart D. Irvin BD (Assoc)   2013

67 Brechin Road, Arbroath DD11 1TA
[E-mail: stuart.d.irvin@googlemail.com]

01241 872339

Arbroath: St Vigeans See Arbroath: Knox's

Arbroath: West Kirk (H)
Alasdair G. Graham BD DipMin   1981   1986

1 Charles Avenue, Arbroath DD11 2EY
[E-mail: alasdairggraham@tiscali.co.uk]

01241 872244

Barry linked with Carnoustie
Michael S. Goss BD DPS   1991   2003

44 Terrace Road, Carnoustie DD7 7AR
[E-mail: michaelgoss@blueyonder.co.uk]

01241 410194
07787 141567 (Mbl)

Brechin: Cathedral (H) (Cathedral office: 01356 629360) (Website: www.brechincathedral.org.uk)
Roderick J. Grahame BD CPS   1991   2010

Chanonry Wynd, Brechin DD9 6JS
[E-mail: rjgrahame@talktalk.net]

01356 624980

Brechin: Gardner Memorial (H) linked with Farnell
Jane M. Blackley MA BD   2009

15 Caldhame Gardens, Brechin DD9 7JJ
[E-mail: jmblackley6@aol.com]

01356 622034

Carmyllie See Arbirlot
Carnoustie See Barry

Carnoustie: Panbride (H)
Matthew S. Bicket BD — 1989 — 8 Arbroath Road, Carnoustie DD7 6BL [E-mail: matthew@bicket.freeserve.co.uk] — 01241 854478 (Tel) / 01241 855088 (Fax)

Colliston linked with Friockheim Kinnell linked with Inverkeilor and Lunan (H)
Peter A. Phillips BA — 1995　2004 — The Manse, Inverkeilor, Arbroath DD11 5SA [E-mail: rev.p.phillips@gmail.com] — 01241 830464

Dun and Hillside
Linda J. Broadley (Mrs) LTh DipEd — 1996　2004 — 4 Manse Road, Hillside, Montrose DD10 9FB [E-mail: lindabroadley@btinternet.com] — 01674 830288

Dunnichen, Letham and Kirkden
Dale London BTh FSAScot — 2011　2013 — 7 Braehead Road, Letham, Forfar DD8 2PG [E-mail: dlondon@hotmail.com] — 01307 818025

Eassie, Nevay and Newtyle
Carleen Robertson (Miss) BD — 1992 — 2 Kirkton Road, Newtyle, Blairgowrie PH12 8TS [E-mail: carleen.robertson120@btinternet.com] — 01828 650461

Edzell Lethnot Glenesk (H) linked with Fern Careston Menmuir
David T. Gray BArch BD — 2010 — 19 Lethnot Road, Edzell, Brechin DD9 7TG [E-mail: davidgray64@sky.com] — 01356 647846 / 07789 718622 (Mbl)

Farnell See Brechin: Gardner Memorial
Fern Careston Menmuir See Edzell Lethnot Glenesk

Forfar: East and Old (H)
Barbara Ann Sweetin BD — 2011 — The Manse, Lour Road, Forfar DD8 2BB [E-mail: barbara.ann17@talktalk.net] — 01307 248228

Forfar: Lowson Memorial (H)
Karen Fenwick PhD MPhil BSc BD — 2006 — 1 Jamieson Street, Forfar DD8 2HY [E-mail: kmfenwick@talktalk.net] — 01307 468585

Forfar: St Margaret's (H) (Church office: 01307 464224)
David Logan BD MA FRSA — 2009 — St Margaret's Manse, 15 Potters Park Crescent, Forfar DD8 1HH [E-mail: minister@castleroy.org] — 01307 462044

Friockheim Kinnell See Colliston

Glamis (H), Inverarity and Kinnettles
Guardianship of the Presbytery   (See Eassie, Nevay and Newtyle)

Guthrie and Rescobie See Aberlemno

Inchbrayock linked with Montrose: Melville South
David S. Dixon MA BD   1976   1994   The Manse, Ferryden, Montrose DD10 9SD   01674 672108
[E-mail: david@inchbrayock.wanadoo.co.uk]

Inverkeilor and Lunan See Colliston

Kirriemuir: St Andrew's (H) linked with Oathlaw Tannadice
John K. Orr BD MTh   2012   26 Quarry Park, Kirriemuir DD8 4DR   01575 572610
[E-mail: minister@standrews-kirriemuir.org.uk]

Montrose: Melville South See Inchbrayock

Montrose: Old and St Andrew's
Ian A. McLean BSc BD DMin   1981   2008   2 Rosehill Road, Montrose DD10 8ST   01674 672447
[E-mail: iamclean@lineone.net]

Oathlaw Tannadice See Kirriemuir: St Andrew's

The Glens and Kirriemuir: Old (H) (Church office: 01575 572819) (Website: www.gkopc.co.uk)
Malcolm I.G. Rooney DPE BEd BD   1993   1999   20 Strathmore Avenue, Kirriemuir DD8 4DJ   01575 573724
[E-mail: malcolm@gkopc.co.uk]   07909 993233 (Mbl)
Linda Stevens (Mrs) BSc BD PgDip   2006   17 North Latch Road, Brechin DD9 6LE   01356 623415
(Team Minister)   [E-mail: linda@gkopc.co.uk]   07701 052552 (Mbl)

The Isla Parishes
Brian Ian Murray BD   2002   2010   Balduff House, Kilry, Blairgowrie PH11 8HS   01575 560268
[E-mail: bentleymurray@googlemail.com]

Anderson, John F. MA BD FSAScot   1966 2006   (Aberdeen: Mannofield)   8 Eider Close, Montrose DD10 9NE   01674 672029
[E-mail: jfa94l@aol.com]

Name			Charge	Address	Tel
Brodie, James BEM MA BD STM	1955	1974	(Hurlford)	25A Keptie Road, Arbroath DD11 3ED	01241 873298
Butters, David	1964	1998	(Turriff: St Ninian's and Forglen)	68A Millgate, Friockheim, Arbroath DD11 4TN	01241 828030
Dingwall, Brian BTh CQSW	1999	2013	(Upper Donside)	20 Woodend Drive, Kirriemuir DD8 4TF	01575 573918
				[E-mail: brian.d12@btinternet.com]	(Mbl) 07906 656847
Drysdale James P.R.	1967	1999	(Brechin: Gardner Memorial)	51 Airlie Street, Brechin DD9 6JX	01356 625201
Duncan, Robert F. MTheol	1986	2001	(Lochgelly: St Andrew's)	25 Rowan Avenue, Kirriemuir DD8 4TB	01575 573973
Gough, Ian G. MA BD MTh DMin	1974	2009	(Arbroath: Knox's with Arbroath: St Vigeans)	23 Keptie Road, Arbroath DD11 3ED	(Mbl) 07891 838379
				[E-mail: ianggough@btinternet.com]	
Hastie, George I. MA BD	1971	2009	(Mearns Coastal)	23 Borrowfield Crescent, Montrose DD10 9BR	01674 672290
Hodge, William N.T.	1966	1995	(Longside)	19 Craigengar Park, Craigshill, Livingston EH54 5NY	01506 435813
Milton, Eric G. RD	1963	1994	(Blairdaff)	16 Bruce Court, Links Parade, Carnoustie DD7 7JE	01241 854928
Morrice, Alastair M. MA BD	1968	2002	(Rutherglen: Stonelaw)	5 Brechin Road, Kirriemuir DD8 4BX	01575 574102
				[E-mail: ambishkek@swissmail.org]	
Norrie, Graham MA BD	1967	2007	(Forfar: East and Old)	'Novar', 14A Wyllie Street, Forfar DD8 3DN	01307 468152
				[E-mail: grahamnorrie@hotmail.com]	
Perry, Joseph B.	1955	1989	(Farnell)	19 Guthrie Street, Letham, Forfar DD8 2PS	01307 818741
Reid, Albert B. BD BSc	1996	2001	(Ardler, Kettins and Meigle)	1 Dundee Street, Letham, Forfar DD8 2PQ	01307 818416
				[E-mail: abreid@btinternet.com]	
Robertson, George R. LTh	1985	2004	(Udny and Pitmedden)	3 Slateford Gardens, Edzell, Brechin DD9 7SX	01356 647322
				[E-mail: geomag.robertson@btinternet.com]	
Smith, Hamish G.	1965	1993	(Auchterless with Rothienorman)	11A Guthrie Street, Letham, Forfar DD8 2PS	01307 818973
Thomas, Martyn R.H. CEng MIStructE	1987	2002	(Fowlis and Liff with Lundie and Muirhead of Liff)	14 Kirkgait, Letham, Forfar DD8 2XQ	01307 818084
				[E-mail: martyn.thomas@mypostoffice.co.uk]	
Thomas, Shirley A. (Mrs) DipSocSci AMIA (Aux)	2000	2006	(Auxiliary Minister)	14 Kirkgait, Letham, Forfar DD8 2XQ	01307 818084
				[E-mail: martyn.thomas@mypostoffice.co.uk]	
Watt, Alan G.N. MTh CQSW DipCommEd	1996	2009	(Edzell Lethnot Glenesk with Fern Careston Menmuir)	128 Restenneth Drive, Forfar DD8 2DH	01307 461686
				[E-mail: watt455@btinternet.com]	
Webster, Allan F. MA BD	1978	2008	(Workplace Chaplain)	42 McCulloch Drive, Forfar DD8 2EB	01307 464252
				[E-mail: allanfwebster@aol.com]	(Mbl) 07546 276725
Youngson, Peter	1961	1996	(Kirriemuir: St Andrew's)	'Coreen', Woodside, Northmuir, Kirriemuir DD8 4PG	01575 572832

ANGUS ADDRESSES

Arbroath: Knox's	Howard Street	Carnoustie:	Dundee Street
Old and Abbey	West Abbey Street	Panbride	Arbroath Road
St Andrew's	Hamilton Green		
West Kirk	Keptie Street	Forfar: East and Old	East High Street
		Lowson Memorial	Jamieson Street
Brechin: Cathedral	Bishops Close	St Margaret's	West High Street
Gardner Memorial	South Esk Street		

Kirriemuir: Old	High Street	Montrose: Melville South	Castle Street
St Andrew's	Glamis Road	Old and St Andrew's	High Street

(31) ABERDEEN

Meets on the first Tuesday of February, March, May, September, October, November and December, and on the fourth Tuesday of June. The venue varies.

Joint Clerks:	REV. GEORGE S. COWIE BSc BD REV. JOHN A. FERGUSON BD DipMin DMin	
Administrator and Depute Clerk:	MRS MOYRA CAMERON	
Presbytery Office:	Mastrick Church, Greenfern Road, Aberdeen AB16 6TR [E-mail: aberdeen@cofscotland.org.uk]	01224 698119

Aberdeen: Bridge of Don Oldmachar (01224 709299) (Website: www.oldmacharchurch.org)
David J. Stewart BD MTh DipMin   2000   2012   60 Newburgh Circle, Aberdeen AB22 8QZ   01224 701365
[E-mail: brigodon@clara.co.uk]

Aberdeen: Cove (E)
David Swan BVMS BD   2005   4 Charleston Way, Cove, Aberdeen AB12 3FA   01224 899933
[E-mail: david@covechurch.org.uk]

Aberdeen: Craigiebuckler (H) (01224 315649)
Kenneth L. Petrie MA BD   1984   1999   185 Springfield Road, Aberdeen AB15 8AA   01224 315125
[E-mail: patandkenneth@aol.com]

Aberdeen: Ferryhill (H) (01224 213093)
J. Peter N. Johnston BSc BD   2001   2013   54 Polmuir Road, Aberdeen AB11 7RT   01224 949192

Aberdeen: Garthdee (H) linked with Aberdeen: Ruthrieston West (H)
Benjamin D.W. Byun BS MDiv MTh PhD   1992   2008   53 Springfield Avenue, Aberdeen AB15 8JJ   01224 312706
[E-mail: benjamin@byun1.fsnet.co.uk]

Aberdeen: Gilcomston South (H) (01224 647144)
Vacant   37 Richmondhill Road, Aberdeen AB15 5EQ

Aberdeen: High Hilton (H) (01224 494717)
G. Hutton B. Steel MA BD   1982   2013   24 Rosehill Drive, Aberdeen AB24 4JJ   01224 493552
[E-mail: hsteel57@btinternet.com]

Aberdeen: Holburn West (H) (01224 571120)
Duncan C. Eddie MA BD   1992   1999   31 Cranford Road, Aberdeen AB10 7NJ   01224 325873
[E-mail: dceddies@tiscali.co.uk]

Aberdeen: Mannofield (H) (01224 310087) (E-mail: office@mannofieldchurch.org.uk)
Keith T. Blackwood BD DipMin   1997   2007   21 Forest Avenue, Aberdeen AB15 4TU   01224 315748
[E-mail: minister@mannofieldchurch.org.uk]

Aberdeen: Mastrick (H) (01224 694121)
Elizabeth J.B. Youngson BD   1996   2011   8 Corse Wynd, Kingswells, Aberdeen AB15 8TP   01224 749346
[E-mail: elizabeth.youngson@btinternet.com]

Aberdeen: Middlefield (H)
Vacant

Aberdeen: Midstocket
Sarah E.C. Nicol (Mrs) BSc BD MTh   1985   2013   182 Midstocket Road, Aberdeen AB15 5HS   01224 561358
[E-mail: sarahmidstocket@btinternet.com]

Aberdeen: Northfield
Scott C. Guy BD   1989   1999   28 Byron Crescent, Aberdeen AB16 7EX   01224 692332
[E-mail: scguy55@gmail.com]

Aberdeen: Queen Street (01224 643567)
Graham D.S. Deans MA BD MTh DMin   1978   2008   51 Osborne Place, Aberdeen AB25 2BX   01224 646429
[E-mail: graham.deans@btopenworld.com]

Aberdeen: Queen's Cross (H) (01224 644742)
Scott Rennie MA BD STM   1999   2009   1 St Swithin Street, Aberdeen AB10 6XH   01224 322549
[E-mail: minister@queenscrosschurch.org.uk]

Aberdeen: Rubislaw (H) (01224 645477)
Vacant   45 Rubislaw Den South, Aberdeen AB15 4BD   01224 314878

Aberdeen: Ruthrieston West (H) See Aberdeen: Garthdee

Aberdeen: St Columba's Bridge of Don (H) (01224 825653)
Louis Kinsey BD DipMin TD   1991   151 Jesmond Avenue, Aberdeen AB22 8UG   01224 705337
[E-mail: louis@stcolumbaschurch.org.uk]

Aberdeen: St George's Tillydrone (H) (01224 482204)
James Weir BD — 1991 — 2003 — 127 Clifton Road, Aberdeen AB24 4RH
[E-mail: rjimw@sky.com] — 01224 483976

Aberdeen: St John's Church for Deaf People (H) (01224 494566)
Vacant

Aberdeen: St Machar's Cathedral (H) (01224 485988)
Jane L. Barron (Mrs) BA DipEd BD — 1999 — 2011 — 18 The Chanonry, Old Aberdeen AB24 1RQ
[E-mail: janebarron23@hotmail.com] — 01224 483688

Aberdeen: St Mark's (H) (01224 640672)
Diane L. Hobson (Mrs) BA BD — 2002 — 2010 — 65 Mile-end Avenue, Aberdeen AB15 5PU
[E-mail: dianehobson.rev@btinternet.com] — 01224 622470

Aberdeen: St Mary's (H) (01224 487227)
Elsie J. Fortune (Mrs) BSc BD — 2003 — 456 King Street, Aberdeen AB24 3DE
[E-mail: eric.fortune@lineone.net] — 01224 633778

Aberdeen: St Nicholas Kincorth, South of
Edward C. McKenna BD DPS — 1989 — 2002 — The Manse, Kincorth Circle, Aberdeen AB12 5NX
[E-mail: eddiemckenna@uwclub.net] — 01224 872820
Daniel Robertson BA BD (Assoc) — 2009 — 2011 — 5 Bruce Walk, Nigg, Aberdeen AB12 3LX
[E-mail: dan@southstnicholas.org.uk] — 01224 878418 / 07909 840654 (Mbl)

Aberdeen: St Nicholas Uniting, Kirk of (H) (01224 643494)
B. Stephen C. Taylor BA BBS MA MDiv — 1984 — 2005 — 12 Louisville Avenue, Aberdeen AB15 4TX
[E-mail: minister@kirk-of-st-nicholas.org.uk] — 01224 314318 / 01224 649242 (Fax)

Aberdeen: St Stephen's (H) (01224 624443)
Maggie Whyte BD — 2010 — 6 Belvidere Street, Aberdeen AB25 2QS
[E-mail: maggiewhyte@aol.com] — 01224 635694

Aberdeen: South Holburn (H) (01224 211730)
George S. Cowie BSc BD — 1991 — 2006 — 54 Woodstock Road, Aberdeen AB15 5JF
[E-mail: gscowie@aol.com] — 01224 315042

Aberdeen: Stockethill (New Charge Development)
Ian M. Aitken MA BD   1999   52 Ashgrove Road West, Aberdeen AB16 5EE
                                             [E-mail: ncdstockethill@uk.uumail.com]   01224 686929

Aberdeen: Summerhill (H) (Website: www.summerhillchurch.org.uk)
Michael R.R. Shewan MA BD CPS   1985 2010   36 Stronsay Drive, Aberdeen AB15 6JL
                                             [E-mail: michaelshewan@btinternet.com]   01224 324669

Aberdeen: Torry St Fittick's (H) (01224 899183)
Edmond Gatima BEng BD MSc MPhil PhD   2013   11 Devanha Gardens East, Aberdeen AB11 7UH   01224 588245

Aberdeen: Woodside (H) (01224 277249)
Markus Auffermann DipTheol   1999 2006   322 Clifton Road, Aberdeen AB24 4HQ
                                             [E-mail: mauffermann@yahoo.com]   01224 484562

Bucksburn Stoneywood (H) (01224 712411)
Nigel Parker BD MTh DMin   1994   23 Polo Park, Stoneywood, Aberdeen AB21 9JW
                                             [E-mail: revdr.n.parker@btinternet.com]   01224 712635

Cults (H)
Ewen J. Gilchrist BD DipMin DipComm   1982 2005   1 Cairnlee Terrace, Bieldside, Aberdeen AB15 9AE
                                             [E-mail: ewengilchrist@btconnect.com]   01224 861692

Dyce (H) (01224 771295)
Manson C. Merchant BD CPS   1992 2008   100 Burnside Road, Dyce, Aberdeen AB21 7HA
                                             [E-mail: mc.merchant@btinternet.com]   01224 722380

Kingswells
Alisa McDonald BA MDiv   2008 2013   Kingswells Manse, Lang Stracht, Aberdeen AB15 8PL   01224 740229

Newhills (H) (Tel/Fax: 01224 716161)
Hugh M. Wallace MA BD   1980 2007   Newhills Manse, Bucksburn, Aberdeen AB21 9SS
                                             [E-mail: revhugh@hotmail.com]   01224 712655

Peterculter (H) (01224 735845)
John A. Ferguson BD DipMin DMin   1988 1999   7 Howie Lane, Peterculter AB14 0LJ
                                             [E-mail: john.ferguson525@btinternet.com]   01224 735041

Name			Role	Address	Tel
Aitchison, James W. BD	1993		Chaplain: Army	84 Wakefords Park, Church Crookham, Fleet, Hampshire GU52 8EZ	01224 329259
Beattie, Walter G. MA BD	1956	1995	(Arbroath: Old and Abbey)	126 Seafield Road, Aberdeen AB15 7YQ	07761 235815
Campbell, W.M.M. BD CPS	1970	2003	(Hospital Chaplain)	43 Murray Terrace, Aberdeen AB11 7SA	
Cowie, Marian (Mrs) MA BD MTh	1990	2012	(Aberdeen: Midstocket)	54 Woodstock Road, Aberdeen AB15 5JF [E-mail: mcowieou@aol.com]	01224 315042
Craig, Gordon T. BD DipMin	1998	2012	Chaplain to UK Oil and Gas Industry	c/o Total E and P (UK) plc, Altens Industrial Estate, Crawpeel Road, Aberdeen AB12 3FG [E-mail: gordon.craig@ukoilandgaschaplaincy.com]	01224 297532
Crawford, Michael S.M. LTh	1966	2002	(Aberdeen: St Mary's)	Brownside of Strichen, New Pitsligo, Fraserburgh AB43 6NY	
Dick, John H.A. MA MSc BD	1982	2012	(Aberdeen: Ferryhill)	18 Fairfield Road, Kelty KY4 0BY [E-mail: jhadick01@talktalk.net]	
Douglas, Andrew M. MA	1957	1995	(Aberdeen: High Hilton)	219 Countesswells Road, Aberdeen AB15 7RD	01224 311932
Falconer, James B. BD	1982	1991	Hospital Chaplain	3 Brimmond Walk, Westhill AB32 6XH	01224 744621
Garden, Margaret J. (Miss) BD	1993	2009	(Cushnie and Tough)	26 Earns Heugh Circle, Cove Bay, Aberdeen AB12 3PY [E-mail: mj.garden@btinternet.com]	
Goldie, George D. ALCM	1953	1995	(Aberdeen: Greyfriars)	27 Broomhill Avenue, Aberdeen AB10 6JL	01224 322503
Gordon, Laurie Y.	1960	1995	(Aberdeen: John Knox)	1 Alder Drive, Portlethen, Aberdeen AB12 4WA	01224 782703
Graham, A. David M. BA BD	1971	2005	(Aberdeen: Rosemount)	Elmhill House, 27 Shaw Crescent, Aberdeen AB25 3BT	01224 648041
Grainger, Harvey L. LTh	1975	2004	(Kingswells)	13 St Ronan's Crescent, Peterculter, Aberdeen AB14 0RL [E-mail: harveygrainger@tiscali.co.uk]	01224 739824 (Mbl) 07768 333216
Haddow, Angus H. BSc	1963	1999	(Methlick)	25 Lerwick Road, Aberdeen AB16 6RF	01224 696362
Hamilton, Helen (Miss) BD	1991	2003	(Glasgow: St James' Pollok)	The Cottage, West Tilbouries, Maryculter, Aberdeen AB12 5GD	01224 739632
Harley, Elspeth BA MTh	1991	2010	(Aberdeen: Middlefield)	8 Donmouth Road, Aberdeen AB23 8DT [E-mail: eharley@hotmail.com]	01224 703017
Hutchison, Alison M. (Mrs) BD DipMin	1988	1988	Hospital Chaplain	Ashfield, Drumoak, Banchory AB31 5AG [E-mail: amhutch62@aol.com]	01330 811309
Hutchison, David S. BSc BD ThM	1991	1999	(Aberdeen: Torry St Fittick's)	51 Don Street, Aberdeen AB24 1UH	01224 276122
Johnstone, William (Prof.) MA BD	1963	2001	(University of Aberdeen)	9/5 Mount Alvernia, Edinburgh EH16 6AW	0131-664 3140
Kerr, Hugh F. MA BD	1968	2006	(Aberdeen: Ruthrieston South)	134C Great Western Road, Aberdeen AB10 6QE	01224 58009
Lundie, Ann V. DCS			(Deaconess)	20 Langdykes Drive, Cove, Aberdeen AB12 3HW [E-mail: ann.lundie@btopenworld.com]	01224 898416
McCallum, Moyra (Miss) MA BD DCS			(Deaconess)	176 Hilton Drive, Aberdeen AB24 4LT [E-mail: moymac@aol.com]	01224 486240
Maciver, Norman MA BD DMin	1976	2006	(Newhills)	4 Mundi Crescent, Newmachar, Aberdeen AB21 0LY [E-mail: norirene@aol.com]	01651 869434
Main, Alan (Prof.) TD MA BD STM PhD DD	1963	2001	(University of Aberdeen)	Kirkfield, Barthol Chapel, Inverurie AB51 8TD [E-mail: amain@talktalk.net]	01651 806773
Montgomerie, Jean B. (Miss) MA BD	1973	2005	(Forfar: St Margaret's)	12 St Ronan's Place, Peterculter, Aberdeen AB14 0QX [E-mail: revjeanb@tiscali.co.uk]	01224 732350
Phillippo, Michael MTh BSc BVetMed MRCVS	2003		(Auxiliary Minister)	25 Deeside Crescent, Aberdeen AB15 7PT [E-mail: phillippo@btinternet.com]	01224 318317
Richardson, Thomas C. LTh ThB	1971	2004	(Cults: West)	19 Kinkell Road, Aberdeen AB15 8HR [E-mail: thomas.richardson7@btinternet.com]	01224 315328

Rodgers, D. Mark BA BD MTh	1987	2003	Hospital Chaplain	152D Gray Street, Aberdeen AB10 6JW	01224 210810
Sefton, Henry R. MA BD STM PhD	1957	1992	(University of Aberdeen)	25 Albury Place, Aberdeen AB11 6TQ	01224 572305
Sheret, Brian S. MA BD DPhil	1982	2000	(Glasgow: Drumchapel Drumry St Mary's)	59 Airyhall Crescent, Aberdeen AB15 7QS	01224 323032
Stewart, James C. MA BD STM	1960	2000	(Aberdeen: Kirk of St Nicholas)	54 Murray Terrace, Aberdeen AB11 7SB	01224 587071
Swinton, John (Prof.) BD PhD	1999		University of Aberdeen	51 Newburgh Circle, Bridge of Don, Aberdeen AB22 8XA	01224 825637
				[E-mail: j.swinton@abdn.ac.uk]	
Torrance, Iain R. (Prof.) TD DPhil DD DTheol LHD FRSE	1982	2012	(President: Princeton Theological Seminary)	17 St Bernard's Crescent, Edinburgh EH4 1NR [E-mail: irt@ptsem.edu]	0131-315 3746
Watson, John M. LTh	1989	2009	(Aberdeen: St Mark's)	20 Greystone Place, Newtonhill, Stonehaven AB39 3UL [E-mail: watson-john18@sky.com]	01569 730604 (Mbl) 07733 334380
Wilkie, William E. LTh	1978	2001	(Aberdeen: St Nicholas Kincorth, South of)	32 Broomfield Park, Portlethen, Aberdeen AB12 4XT	01224 782052
Wilson, Thomas F. BD	1984	1996	Education	55 Allison Close, Cove, Aberdeen AB12 3WG	01224 873501

ABERDEEN ADDRESSES

Congregation / Address		
Bridge of Don Oldmachar	Holburn West	Great Western Road

Cove
  Ashwood Park
  Loirston Primary School,
    Loirston Avenue
	Kingswells	Old Skene Road, Kingswells

Craigiebuckler Springfield Road	Mannofield	Great Western Road x Craigton Road
Cults Quarry Road, Cults	Mastrick	Greenfern Road
Dyce Victoria Street, Dyce	Middlefield	Manor Avenue
Ferryhill Fonthill Road x Polmuir Road	Midstocket	Mid Stocket Road
Garthdee Ramsay Gardens	New Stockethill	
Gilcomston South Union Street x Summer Street	Northfield	Byron Crescent
High Hilton Hilton Drive	Peterculter	Craigton Crescent
	Queen Street	Queen Street
	Queen's Cross	Albyn Place
	Rubislaw	Queen's Gardens
	Ruthrieston West	Broomhill Road
	St Columba's	Braehead Way, Bridge of Don

St George's	Hayton Road, Tillydrone
St John's for the Deaf	at St Mark's
St Machar's	The Chanonry
St Mark's	Rosemount Viaduct
St Mary's	King Street
St Nicholas Kincorth, South of	Kincorth Circle
St Nicholas Uniting, Kirk of	
St Stephen's	Union Street
South Holburn	Powis Place
Summerhill	Holburn Street
Torry St Fittick's	Stronsay Drive
Woodside	Walker Road
	Church Street, Woodside

(32) KINCARDINE AND DEESIDE

Meets in various locations as arranged on the first Tuesday of September, October, November, December, March and May, and on the last Tuesday of June at 7pm.

Clerk:	**REV. HUGH CONKEY BSc BD**	39 St Ternans Road, Newtonhill, Stonehaven AB39 3PF [E-mail: kincardinedeeside@cofscotland.org.uk]	01569 739297

Aberluthnott linked with Laurencekirk (H)

Ronald Gall BSc BD	1985	2001	Aberdeen Road, Laurencekirk AB30 1AJ [E-mail: ronniegall@tiscali.co.uk]	01561 378838

Aboyne and Dinnet (H) (01339 886989) linked with Cromar (E-mail: aboynedinnet.cos@virgin.net)
Frank Ribbons MA BD DipEd 1985 2011 49 Charlton Crescent, Aboyne AB34 5GN
[E-mail: frankribs@gmail.com]
01339 887267

Arbuthnott, Bervie and Kinneff
Dennis S. Rose LTh 1996 2010 10 Kirkburn, Inverbervie, Montrose DD10 0RT
[E-mail: dennis2327@aol.co.uk]
01561 362560

Banchory-Devenick and Maryculter/Cookney (01224 735983) (E-mail: thechurchoffice@tiscali.co.uk)
Vacant The Manse, Kirkton of Maryculter, Aberdeen AB12 5FS
01224 730150

Banchory-Ternan: East (H) (01330 820380) (E-mail: banchoryeastchurchoffice@btconnect.com)
Vacant

Banchory-Ternan: West (H)
Antony Stephen MA BD 2001 2011 The Manse, 2 Wilson Road, Banchory AB31 5UY
[E-mail: tony@banchorywestchurch.com]
01330 822811

Birse and Feughside
Anita van der Wal 2008 2013 The Manse, Finzean, Banchory AB31 6PB
[E-mail: vanderwal@btinternet.com]
01330 850776

Braemar and Crathie
Kenneth I. Mackenzie BD CPS 1990 2005 The Manse, Crathie, Ballater AB35 5UL
[E-mail: crathiemanse@tiscali.co.uk]
01339 742208

Cromar See Aboyne and Dinnet

Drumoak (H)-Durris (H)
Dolly Purnell BD 2003 2012 26 Sunnyside Drive, Drumoak, Banchory AB31 3EW
[E-mail: revdollypurnell@btinternet.com]
01330 811031

Glenmuick (Ballater) (H)
Anthony Watts BD DipTechEd JP 1999 The Manse, Craigendarroch Walk, Ballater AB35 5ZB
[E-mail: tony.watts6@btinternet.com]
01339 754014

Laurencekirk See Aberluthnott

Mearns Coastal
Colin J. Dempster BD CertMin 1990 2010 The Manse, Kirkton, St Cyrus, Montrose DD10 0BW
[E-mail: coldcoast@btinternet.com] 01674 850880

Mid Deeside
Alexander C. Wark MA BD STM 1982 2012 The Manse, Torphins, Banchory AB31 4GQ
[E-mail: alecwark@yahoo.co.uk] 01339 882276

Newtonhill
Hugh Conkey BSc BD 1987 2001 39 St Ternans Road, Newtonhill, Stonehaven AB39 3PF
[E-mail: hugh@conkey.plus.com] 01569 730143

Portlethen (H) (01224 782883)
Flora J. Munro (Mrs) BD DMin 1993 2004 18 Rowanbank Road, Portlethen, Aberdeen AB12 4NX
[E-mail: floramunro@aol.co.uk] 01224 780211

Stonehaven: Dunnottar (H) linked with Stonehaven: South (H)
Rosslyn P. Duncan BD MTh 2007 Dunnottar Manse, Stonehaven AB39 3XL
[E-mail: rpduncan@btinternet.com] 01569 762166

Stonehaven: Fetteresso (H) (01569 767689) (E-mail: fetteresso.office@btinternet.com)
Fyfe Blair BA BD DMin 1989 2009 11 South Lodge Drive, Stonehaven AB39 2PN
[E-mail: fyfeblair@talktalk.net] 01569 762876

Stonehaven: South See Stonehaven: Dunnottar

West Mearns
Catherine A. Hepburn (Miss) BA BD 1982 2000 West Mearns Parish Church Manse, Fettercairn,
Laurencekirk AB30 1UE
[E-mail: cahepburn@btinternet.com] 01561 340203

Brown, J.W.S. BTh	1960	1995	(Cromar)	10 Forestside Road, Banchory AB31 5ZH [E-mail: iainisobel@aol.com] 01330 824353
Cameron, Ann J. (Mrs) CertCS DCE TEFL		2005	Auxiliary Minister	Currently resident in Qatar [E-mail: anncameron2@googlemail.com]
Christie, Andrew C. LTh	1975	2000	(Banchory-Devenick and Maryculter/Cookney)	17 Broadstraik Close, Elrick, Aberdeen AB32 6JP 01224 746888
Forbes, John W.A. BD	1973	1999	(Edzell Lethnot with Fern, Careston and Menmuir with Glenesk)	Little Ennochie Steading, Finzean, Banchory AB31 6LX [E-mail: jrbbbb@icloud.com] 01330 850785

Kinniburgh, Elizabeth B.F. (Miss) MA BD 1970 1986 (Birse with Finzean with Strachan) 21 Glen Tanar, Allachburn, Low Road, Aboyne AB34 5GW   01339 886757

Lamb, A. Douglas MA   1964 2002 (Dalry: St Margaret's) 9 Luther Drive, Laurencekirk AB30 1FE   01561 376816
[E-mail: lamb.edzell@talk21.com]

Smith, Albert E. BD   1983 2006 (Methlick) 42 Haulkerton Crescent, Laurencekirk AB30 1FB   01561 376111
[E-mail: aesmith42@googlemail.com]

Taylor, Peter R. JP BD   1977 2001 (Torphins) 42 Beltie Road, Torphins, Banchory AB31 4JT   01339 882780
[E-mail: ptaylor850@btinternet.com]

Tierney, John P. MA   1945 1985 (Peterhead West: Associate) 3 Queenshill Drive, Aboyne AB34 5DG   01339 886741

Wallace, William F. BDS BD   1968 2008 (Wick: Pulteneytown and Thrumster) Lachan Cottage, 29 Station Road, Banchory AB31 5XX   01330 822259
[E-mail: williamwallace39@talktalk.net]

Watt, William D. LTh   1978 1996 (Aboyne – Dinnet) 2 West Toll Crescent, Aboyne AB34 5GB   01339 886943
[E-mail: wdwatt22@tiscali.co.uk]

Wilson, Andrew G.N. MA BD DMin   1977 2012 (Aberdeen: Rubislaw) Auchintarph, Coull, Tarland, Aboyne AB34 4TT   01339 880918
[E-mail: agn.wilson@gmail.com]

(33) GORDON

Meets at various locations on the first Tuesday of February, March, April, May, September, October, November and December, and on the last Tuesday of June.

Clerk: REV. G. EUAN D. GLEN BSc BD   The Manse, 26 St Ninians, Monymusk, Inverurie AB51 7HF   01467 651470
[E-mail: gordon@cofscotland.org.uk]

Barthol Chapel linked with Tarves
Isabel C. Buchan (Mrs) BSc BD RE(PgCE)   1975   2006   8 Murray Avenue, Tarves, Ellon AB41 7LZ   01651 851250
[E-mail: buchan.123@btinternet.com]

Belhelvie (H)
Paul McKeown BSc PhD BD   2000   2005   Belhelvie Manse, Balmedie, Aberdeen AB23 8YR   01358 742227
[E-mail: pmckeown1@btconnect.com]

Blairdaff and Chapel of Garioch
D. Brian Dobby MA BA   1999   2008   The Manse, Chapel of Garioch, Inverurie AB51 5HE   01467 681619
[E-mail: briandobby@googlemail.com]

Cluny (H) linked with Monymusk (H)
G. Euan D. Glen BSc BD   1992   The Manse, 26 St Ninians, Monymusk, Inverurie AB51 7HF   01467 651470
[E-mail: euan.glen_1@btinternet.com]

Charge / Minister		Address	Telephone
Culsalmond and Rayne linked with Daviot (H) Mary M. Cranfield (Miss) MA BD DMin	1989	The Manse, Daviot, Inverurie AB51 0HY [E-mail: marymc@ukgateway.net]	01467 671241
Cushnie and Tough (T) (H) Rosemary Legge (Mrs) BSc BD MTh	1992 2010	The Manse, Muir of Fowlis, Alford AB33 8JU [E-mail: cushnietough@aol.com]	01975 581239
Daviot See Culsalmond and Rayne			
Echt linked with Midmar (H) Alan Murray BSc BD PhD	2003	The Manse, Echt, Westhill AB32 7AB [E-mail: ladecottage@btinternet.com]	01330 860004
Ellon James M. Davies BSc BD (Interim Minister)	1982 2013	27 Buchan Drive, Newmachar, Aberdeen AB21 0NR [E-mail: daviesjim@btinternet.com]	01651 862281 07921 023144 (Mbl)
Fintray Kinellar Keithhall Ellen Larson Davidson BA MDiv	2007	20 Kinmohr Rise, Blackburn, Aberdeen AB21 0LJ [E-mail: larsondavidson@gmail.com]	01224 791350
Foveran Vacant		The Manse, Foveran, Ellon AB41 6AP	01358 789288
Howe Trinity John A. Cook MA BD	1986 2000	The Manse, 110 Main Street, Alford AB33 8AD [E-mail: john.cook2@homecall.co.uk]	01975 562282
Huntly Cairnie Glass Thomas R. Calder LLB BD WS	1994	The Manse, Queen Street, Huntly AB54 8EB [E-mail: cairniechurch@aol.com]	01466 792630
Insch-Leslie-Premnay-Oyne (H) Vacant		22 Western Road, Insch AB52 6JR	01464 820914

Inverurie: St Andrew's (Website: standrewschurchinverurie.org.uk)

T. Graeme Longmuir OSJ MA BEd FASC	1976	2001	St Andrew's Manse, 1 Ury Dale, Inverurie AB51 3XW [E-mail: standrews@btinternet.com]	01467 620468
Inverurie: West				
Ian B. Groves BD CPS	1989		West Manse, 1 Westburn Place, Inverurie AB51 5QS [E-mail: i.groves@inveruriewestchurch.org]	01467 620285
Kemnay				
John P. Renton BA LTh	1976	1990	Kemnay, Inverurie AB51 9ND [E-mail: johnrenton@btinternet.com]	01467 642219 (Tel/Fax)
Kintore (H) Vacant			28 Oakhill Road, Kintore, Inverurie AB51 0FH	01467 632219
Meldrum and Bourtie				
Alison Jaffrey (Mrs) MA BD FSAScot	1990	2010	The Manse, Urquhart Road, Oldmeldrum, Inverurie AB51 0EX [E-mail: alison@revjaffrey.com]	01651 872250
Methlick Vacant			The Manse, Manse Road, Methlick, Ellon AB41 7DG	01651 806215
Midmar (H) See Echt				
Monymusk See Cluny				
New Machar				
Douglas G. McNab BA BD	1999	2010	The New Manse, Newmachar, Aberdeen AB21 0RD [E-mail: dougie.mcnab@btinternet.com]	01651 862278
Noth				
Regine U. Cheyne (Mrs) MA BSc BD	1988	2010	Manse of Noth, Kennethmont, Huntly AB54 4NP	01464 831690
Skene (H)				
Stella Campbell MA BD	2012		The Manse, Manse Road, Kirkton of Skene, Westhill AB32 6LX [E-mail: minister.skeneparish@mail.com]	01224 745955
Marion G. Stewart (Miss) DCS			Kirk Cottage, Kirkton of Skene, Westhill AB32 6XE	01224 743407

Strathbogie Drumblade
Neil I.M. MacGregor BD — 1995 — 49 Deveron Park, Huntly AB54 8UZ — 01466 792702

Tarves See Barthol Chapel

Udny and Pitmedden
Gillean P. Maclean (Mrs) BD — 1994 2013 — The Manse, Manse Road, Udny Green, Ellon AB41 7RS [E-mail: minister@uppc-org.uk] — 01651 843794

Upper Donside (H) (E-mail: upperdonsideparishchurch@btinternet.com)
Vacant — The Manse, Lumsden, Huntly AB54 4GQ — 01464 861757

Andrew, John MA BD DipRE DipEd	1961	1995	(Teacher: Religious Education)	Cartar's Croft, Midmar, Inverurie AB51 7NJ	01330 833208
Buchan, Alexander MA BD PGCE	1975	1992	(North Ronaldsay with Sanday)	8 Murray Avenue, Tarves, Ellon AB41 7LZ [E-mail: revabuchan@bluebucket.org]	01651 851250
Craggs, Sheila (Mrs)	2001	2008	(Auxiliary Minister)	7 Morar Court, Ellon AB41 9GG	01358 723055
Craig, Anthony J.D. BD	1987	2009	(Glasgow: Maryhill)	4 Hightown, Collieston, Ellon AB41 8RS [E-mail: craig.glasgow@gmx.net]	01358 751247
Dryden, Ian MA DipEd	1988	2001	(New Machar)	16 Glenhome Gardens, Dyce, Aberdeen AB21 7FG [E-mail: ian@idryden.freeserve.co.uk]	01224 722820
Hawthorn, Daniel MA BD DMin	1965	2004	(Belhelvie)	7 Crimond Drive, Ellon AB41 8BT [E-mail: donhawthorn@compuserve.com]	01358 723981
Jones, Robert A. LTh CA	1966	1997	(Marnoch)	13 Gordon Terrace, Inverurie AB51 4GT	01467 622691
Lyon, Andrew LTh	1971	2007	(Fraserburgh West with Rathen West)	Barmekyn, Keig, Alford AB33 8BH [E-mail: andrew@lyon60.orangehome.co.uk]	01975 562768
Macalister, Eleanor	1994	2006	(Ellon)	2 Crimond Drive, Ellon AB41 8BT [E-mail: macal.ster@aol.com]	01358 722711
Mack, John C. JP	1985	2008	(Auxiliary Minister)	The Willows, Auchleven, Insch AB52 6QB	01464 820387
McKay, Margaret MA BD MTh	1991	2003	(Auchaber United with Auchterless)	The Smithy, Knowes of Elrick, Aberchirder, Huntly AB54 7PN [E-mail: elricksmithy@yahoo.co.uk]	(Tel) 01466 780208 (Fax) 01466 780015
McLeish, Robert S.	1970	2000	(Insch-Leslie-Premnay-Oyne)	19 Western Road, Insch AB52 6JR	01464 820749
Pryde, W. Kenneth DA BD	1994	2012	(Foveran)	15 Laurel Gardens, Bridge of Don, Aberdeen AB22 8YY [E-mail: wkpryde@hotmail.com]	
Rodger, Matthew A. BD	1978	1999	(Ellon)	15 Meadowlands Drive, Westhill AB32 6EJ	01224 743184
Scott, Allan D. BD	1977	1989	(Culsalmond with Daviot with Rayne)	20 Barclay Road, Inverurie AB51 3QP	01467 625161
Stewart, George C. MA	1952	1995	(Drumblade with Huntly Strathbogie)	104 Scott Drive, Huntly AB54 8PF	01466 792503
Stoddart, A. Grainger	1975	2001	(Meldrum and Bourtie)	6 Mayfield Gardens, Insch AB52 6XL	01464 821124
Taylor, Jane C. (Miss) BD DipMin	1990	2013	(Insch-Leslie-Premnay-Oyne)	22 Western Road, Insch AB52 6JR [E-mail: jane.c.taylor@btinternet.com]	01464 820914
Thomson, Iain U. MA BD	1970	2011	(Skene)	4 Keithill Gardens, Westhill AB32 6AZ [E-mail: iainuthomson@googlemail.com]	01224 746743

(34) BUCHAN

Meets at St Kane's Centre, New Deer, Turriff on the first Tuesday of February, March, May, September, October, November and December, and on the third Tuesday of June.

Clerk:	MR GEORGE W. BERSTAN	Faithlie, Victoria Terrace, Turriff AB53 4EE [E-mail: buchan@cofscotland.org.uk]	01888 562392

Aberdour linked with Pitsligo
Vacant

The Manse, 49 Pitsligo Street, Rosehearty, Fraserburgh AB43 7JL

Auchaber United linked with Auchterless
Stephen J. Potts BA   2012

The Manse, Auchterless, Turriff AB53 8BA   01888 511058
[E-mail: stevejpotts@hotmail.co.uk]

Auchterless See Auchaber United

Banff linked with King Edward (E-mail: banffkirk@btconnect.com)
David I.W. Locke MA MSc BD   2000   2012

7 Colleonard Road, Banff AB45 1DZ   01261 812107
[E-mail: davidlockerev@yahoo.co.uk]   07776 448301 (Mbl)

Crimond linked with Lonmay
Vacant

The Manse, Crimond, Fraserburgh AB43 8QJ   01346 532431

Cruden (H)
Rodger Neilson BSc BD   1972   1974

The Manse, Hatton, Peterhead AB42 0QQ   01779 841229
[E-mail: minister@crudenchurch.org.uk]

Deer (H)
Sheila M. Kirk BA LLB BD   2007   2010

The Manse, Old Deer, Peterhead AB42 5JB   01771 623582
[E-mail: sheilamkirk@googlemail.com]

Fordyce
Norman Nicoll BD   2003   2010

The Manse, 4 Seafield Terrace, Portsoy, Banff AB45 2QB   01261 842272
[E-mail: fordycechurch@btinternet.com]

Fraserburgh: Old
Peter B. Park BD MCIBS   1997   2007   4 Robbies Road, Fraserburgh AB43 7AF [E-mail: peterpark9@btinternet.com]   01346 515332

Fraserburgh: South (H) linked with Inverallochy and Rathen: East
Ronald F. Yule   1982   15 Victoria Street, Fraserburgh AB43 9PJ   01346 518244

Fraserburgh: West (H) linked with Rathen: West
Carol Anne Parker (Mrs) BEd BD   2009   4 Kirkton Gardens, Fraserburgh AB43 8TU [E-mail: ca.parker76@btinternet.com]   01346 513303

Fyvie linked with Rothienorman
Robert J. Thorburn BD   1978   2004   The Manse, Fyvie, Turriff AB53 8RD [E-mail: rjthorburn@aol.com]   01651 891230

Gardenstown
Donald N. Martin BD   1996   The Manse, Fernie Brae, Gardenstown, Banff AB45 3YL [E-mail: ferniebrae@gmail.com]   01261 851256

Inverallochy and Rathen: East See Fraserburgh: South
King Edward See Banff

Longside
Robert A. Fowlie BD   2007   9 Anderson Drive, Longside, Peterhead AB42 4XG [E-mail: bob.fowlie@googlemail.com]   01779 821224

Lonmay See Crimond

Macduff
Calum Stark LLB BD   2011   10 Ross Street, Macduff AB44 1NS [E-mail: calumstark@yahoo.co.uk]   01261 832316

Marnoch
Alan Macgregor BA BD PhD   1992   2013   Marnoch Manse, 53 South Street, Aberchirder, Huntly AB54 7TS [E-mail: marnochkirk@btconnect.com]   01466 781143

Maud and Savoch linked with New Deer: St Kane's
Paul R. Read BSc MA(Th) 2000 2010 The Manse, New Deer, Turriff AB53 6TD 01771 644216
[E-mail: prr747@aol.com]

Monquhitter and New Byth linked with Turriff: St Andrew's
James Cook MA MDiv 1999 2002 St Andrew's Manse, Balmellie Road, Turriff AB53 4SP 01888 560304
[E-mail: jmscook9@aol.com]

New Deer: St Kane's See Maud and Savoch

New Pitsligo linked with Strichen and Tyrie
Andrew Fothergill BA 2012 Kingsville, Strichen, Fraserburgh AB43 6SQ 01771 637635
[E-mail: andrewfothergill@btinternet.com]

Ordiquhill and Cornhill (H) linked with Whitehills
W. Myburgh Verster BA BTh LTh MTh 1981 2011 6 Craigneen Place, Whitehills, Banff AB45 2NE 01261 861317
[E-mail: wverster8910@btinternet.com]

Peterhead: Old
Vacant 1 Hawthorn Road, Peterhead AB42 2DW

Peterhead: St Andrew's (H)
Abi T. Ngunga GTh LTh MDiv MTh PhD 2001 2011 1 Landale Road, Peterhead AB42 1QN 01779 238200
[E-mail: abi.t.ngunga@gmail.com]

Peterhead: Trinity
Vacant 18 Landale Road, Peterhead AB42 1QP

Pitsligo See Aberdour
Rathen: West See Fraserburgh: West
Rothienorman See Fyvie

St Fergus
Jeffrey Tippner BA MDiv MCS 1991 2012 26 Newton Road, St Fergus, Peterhead AB42 3DD 01779 838287
[E-mail: revjeff@btconnect.com]

Sandhaven
Vacant

Strichen and Tyrie See New Pitsligo
Turriff: St Andrew's See Monquhitter and New Byth

Turriff: St Ninian's and Forglen
Kevin R. Gruer BSc BA   2011   4 Deveronside Drive, Turriff AB53 4SP   01888 563850
[E-mail: minister@stniniansandforglen.org.uk]

Whitehills See Ordiquhill and Cornhill

Blaikie, James BD	1972 1997	(Berwick-on-Tweed: St Andrew's Wallace Green and Lowick)	57 Glenugie View, Peterhead AB42 2BW	01779 490625
Coutts, Fred MA BD	1973 1989	(Hospital Chaplain)	Ladebank, 1 Manse Place, Hatton, Peterhead AB42 0UQ [E-mail: fred.coutts@btinternet.com]	01779 841320
Fawkes, G.M. Allan BA BSc JP	1979 2000	(Lonmay with Rathen: West)	3 Northfield Gardens, Hatton, Peterhead AB42 0SW [E-mail: afawkes@aol.com]	01779 841814
McMillan, William J. CA LTh BD	1969 2004	(Sandsting and Aithsting with Walls and Sandness)	7 Ardinn Drive, Turriff AB53 4PR [E-mail: revbillymcmillan@aol.com]	01888 560727
Macnee, Iain LTh BD MA PhD	1975 2011	(New Pitsligo with Strichen and Tyrie)	Wardend Cottage, Alvah, Banff AB45 3TR [E-mail: macneeiain4@googlemail.com]	01261 815647
Noble, George S. DipTh	1972 2000	(Carfin with Newarthill)	Craigowan, 3 Main Street, Inverallochy, Fraserburgh AB43 8XX	01346 582749
Ross, David S. MSc PhD BD	1978 2013	(Prison Chaplain Service)	3–5 Abbey Street, Old Deer, Peterhead AB42 5LN [E-mail: padsross@btinternet.com]	01771 623994
van Sittert, Paul BA BD	1997 2011	Chaplain: Army	1 Bn The Royal Regiment of Scotland, Dreghorn Barracks, Edinburgh EH13 9QW [E-mail: vansittert@btinternet.com]	

(35) MORAY

Meets at St Andrew's-Lhanbryd and Urquhart on the first Tuesday of February, March, May, September, October, November and December, and at the Moderator's church on the fourth Tuesday of June.

Clerk: **REV. ROBERT J.M. ANDERSON BD FInstLM**   **The Manse, Rothes, Aberlour AB38 7AF**   **01340 831381**
[E-mail: moray@cofscotland.org.uk]

Aberlour (H)
Shuna M. Dicks BSc BD   2010   The Manse, Mary Avenue, Aberlour AB38 9QU   01340 871687
[E-mail: revshuna@btinternet.com]

Alves and Burghead linked with Kinloss and Findhorn
Vacant — The Manse, 4 Manse Road, Kinloss, Forres IV36 3GH — 01309 690931

Bellie linked with Speymouth
Alison C. Mehigan BD DPS — 2003 — 11 The Square, Fochabers IV32 7DG [E-mail: alison@mehigan.org] — 01343 820256

Birnie and Pluscarden linked with Elgin: High
Vacant — Daisy Bank, 5 Forteath Avenue, Elgin IV30 1TQ — 01343 542449

Buckie: North (H) linked with Rathven
Vacant — 14 St Peter's Road, Buckie AB56 1DL — 01542 831328

Buckie: South and West (H) linked with Enzie
Vacant — Craigendarroch, 14 Cliff Terrace, Buckie AB56 1LX — 01542 833775

Cullen and Deskford (Website: www.cullen-deskford-church.org.uk)
Douglas F. Stevenson BD DipMin — 1991 — 2010 — 3 Seafield Place, Cullen, Buckie AB56 4UU [E-mail: dstevenson655@btinternet.com] — 01542 841963

Dallas linked with Forres: St Leonard's (H) linked with Rafford
Donald K. Prentice BSc BD — 1989 — 2010 — St Leonard's Manse, Nelson Road, Forres IV36 1DR [E-mail: donald.prentice@tesco.net] — 01309 672380
Anne Attenburrow BSc MB ChB (Aux) — 2006 — 2013 — 4 Jock Inksons Brae, Elgin IV30 1QE [E-mail: AAttenburrow@aol.com] — 01343 552330
John Morrison BSc BA PGCE (Ordained Local Minister) — 2013 — 35 Kirkton Place, Elgin IV30 6JR [E-mail: shalla57@aol.com] — 01343 550199

Duffus, Spynie and Hopeman (H) (Website: www.duffusparish.co.uk)
Jennifer Adams BEng BD — 2013 — The Manse, Duffus, Elgin IV30 5QP [E-mail: jennyadamsbd@gmail.com] — 01343 830276

Dyke linked with Edinkillie
John Macgregor BD — 2001 — 2011 — Manse of Dyke, Brodie, Forres IV36 2TD [E-mail: john_macg@hotmail.com] — 01309 641239

Edinkillie See Dyke
Elgin: High See Birnie and Pluscarden

Elgin: St Giles' (H) and St Columba's South (01343 551501) (Office: Williamson Hall, Duff Avenue, Elgin IV30 1QS)
Steven Thomson BSc BD   2001   2013   18 Reidhaven Street, Elgin IV30 1QH   01343 545729
[E-mail: stevie.thomson284@btinternet.com]   07841 368797 (Mbl)

Enzie See Buckie: South and West

Findochty linked with Portknockie
Vacant   20 Netherton Terrace, Findochty, Buckie AB56 4QD   01542 833484

Forres: St Laurence (H)
Barry J. Boyd LTh DPS   1993   12 Mackenzie Drive, Forres IV36 2JP   01309 672260
[E-mail: barryj.boydstlaurence@btinternet.com]   07778 731018 (Mbl)

Forres: St Leonard's See Dallas

Keith: North, Newmill, Boharm and Rothiemay (H) (01542 886390)
Vacant   North Manse, Church Road, Keith AB55 5BR   01542 882559

Keith: St Rufus, Botriphnie and Grange (H)
Ranald S.R. Gauld MA LLB BD   1991   1995   Church Road, Keith AB55 5BR   01542 882799
[E-mail: rev_gauld@btinternet.com]
Kay Gauld (Mrs) BD STM PhD (Assoc)   1999   Church Road, Keith AB55 5BR   01542 882799
[E-mail: kay_gauld@btinternet.com]

Kinloss and Findhorn See Alves and Burghead

Knockando, Elchies and Archiestown (H) linked with Rothes (Website: www.moraykirk.co.uk)
Robert J.M. Anderson BD FInstLM   1993   2000   The Manse, Rothes, Aberlour AB38 7AF   01340 831381
[E-mail: robert@carmanse.freeserve.co.uk]

Lossiemouth: St Gerardine's High (H)
Vacant   The Manse, St Gerardine's Road, Lossiemouth IV31 6RA   01343 813146

Lossiemouth: St James'
Graham W. Crawford BSc BD STM   1991   2003   The Manse, Prospect Terrace, Lossiemouth IV31 6JS   01343 810676
[E-mail: pictishreiver@aol.com]

Mortlach and Cabrach (H)
Vacant   Mortlach Manse, Dufftown, Keith AB55 4AR   01340 820380

Portknockie See Findochty
Rafford See Dallas
Rathven See Buckie: North
Rothes See Knockando, Elchies and Archiestown

St Andrew's-Lhanbryd (H) and Urquhart
Andrew J. Robertson BD   2008 2010   39 St Andrews Road, Lhanbryde, Elgin IV30 8PU   01343 843765
[E-mail: ajr247@btinternet.com]

Speymouth See Bellie

Name			Role	Address	Phone
Bain, Brian LTh	1980	2007	(Gask with Methven and Logiealmond)	Bayview, 13 Stewart Street, Portgordon, Buckie AB56 5QT [E-mail: brian.bain4@btinternet.com]	01542 831215
Connolly, Daniel BD DipTheol DipMin	1983	2012	Chaplain: Army	9 Burnside, Kinloss, Forres IV36 3XL	01309 690666
Davidson, A.A.B. MA BD	1960	1997	(Grange with Rothiemay)	11 Sutors Rise, Nairn IV12 5BU	
King, Margaret MA DCS	2002	2012	(Deacon in Presbytery)	56 Murrayfield, Fochabers IV32 7EZ	01343 820937
Mathew, J. Gordon MA BD	1973	2011	(Buckie: North)	2 Mallard Drive, Montrose DD10 9ND	01674 671310
Morton, Alasdair J. MA BD DipEd FEIS	1960	2000	(Bowden with Newtown)	16 St Leonard's Road, Forres IV36 1DW [E-mail: alasgilmor@hotmail.co.uk]	01309 671719
Morton, Gillian M. (Mrs) MA BD PGCE	1983	1996	(Hospital Chaplain)	16 St Leonard's Road, Forres IV36 1DW [E-mail: alasgilmor@hotmail.co.uk]	01309 671719
Munro, Sheila BD	1995	2003	Chaplain: RAF	RAF Lossiemouth, Elgin IV31 6SD [E-mail: sheila.munro781@halton.raf.mod.uk]	
Poole, Ann McColl (Mrs) DipEd ACE LTh	1983	2003	(Dyke with Edinkillie)	Kirkside Cottage, Dyke, Forres IV36 2TF	01309 641046
Rollo, George B. BD	1974	2010	(Elgin: St Giles' and St Columba's South)	'Struan', 13 Meadow View, Hopeman, Elgin IV30 5PL [E-mail: rollos@gmail.com]	01343 835226
Scotland, Ronald J. BD	1993	2003	(Birnie with Pluscarden)	7A Rose Avenue, Elgin IV30 1NX	01343 543086
Shaw, Duncan LTh CPS	1984	2011	(Alves and Burghead with Kinloss and Findhorn)	73 Woodside Drive, Forres IV36 0UF	
Smith, Hugh M.C. LTh	1973	2013	(Mortlach and Cabrach)	6 Concraig Walk, Kingswells, Aberdeen AB15 8DU	01224 745275
Thomson, James M. BA	1952	2000	(Elgin: St Giles' and St Columba's South: Associate)	48 Mayne Road, Elgin IV30 1PD	
Whittaker, Mary	2011		Auxiliary Minister	11 Templand Road, Lhanbryde, Elgin IV30 8BR	01343 547664

Whyte, David LTh   1993 2011   (Boat of Garten, Duthil and Kincardine)   1 Lemanfield Crescent, Garmouth, Fochabers IV32 7LS   01343 870667
[E-mail: whytedj@btinternet.com]
Wright, David L. MA BD   1957 1998   (Stornoway: St Columba)   84 Wyvis Drive, Nairn IV12 4TP   01667 451613

(36) ABERNETHY

Meets at Boat of Garten on the first Tuesday of February, March, May, September, October, November and December, and on the last Tuesday of June.

Clerk: REV. CATHERINE A. BUCHAN MA MDiv   The Manse, Fort William Road, Newtonmore PH20 1DG   01540 673238
[E-mail: abernethy@cofscotland.org.uk]

Abernethy (H) linked with Boat of Garten (H), Duthil (H) and Kincardine
Donald K. Walker BD   1979   2013   The Manse, Deshar Road, Boat of Garten PH24 3BN   01479 831252
[E-mail: donaldandjudithwalker@gmail.com]

Alvie and Insh (T) (H) linked with Rothiemurchus and Aviemore (H)
Vacant   The Manse, 8 Dalfaber Park, Aviemore PH22 1QF   01479 810280

Boat of Garten, Duthil and Kincardine See Abernethy

Cromdale (H) and Advie linked with Dulnain Bridge (H) linked with Grantown-on-Spey (H)
Morris Smith BD   1988   The Manse, Golf Course Road, Grantown-on-Spey PH26 3HY   01479 872084
[E-mail: mosmith.themanse@btinternet.com]

Dulnain Bridge See Cromdale and Advie
Grantown-on-Spey See Cromdale and Advie

Kingussie (H)
Alison H. Burnside (Mrs) MA BD   1991   2013   The Manse, 18 Hillside Avenue, Kingussie PH21 1PA   01540 662327
[E-mail: alisonskyona@btinternet.com]

Laggan (H) linked with Newtonmore: St Bride's (H)
Catherine A. Buchan (Mrs) MA MDiv   2002   2009   The Manse, Fort William Road, Newtonmore PH20 1DG   01540 673238
[E-mail: catherinebuchan567@btinternet.com]

Newtonmore: St Bride's See Laggan
Rothiemurchus and Aviemore (H) See Alvie and Insh

Tomintoul (H), Glenlivet and Inveraven
Vacant

The Manse, Tomintoul, Ballindalloch AB37 9HA   01807 580254

Bjarnason, Sven S. CandTheol	1975 2011	(Tomintoul, Glenlivet and Inveraven)	14 Edward Street, Dunfermline KY12 0JW [E-mail: sven@bjarnason.org.uk] 01383 724625
Burnside, William A.M. MA BD PGCE	1990 2013	(Stromness)	The Manse, 18 Hillside Avenue, Kingussie PH21 1PA [E-mail: bburnside@btinternet.com] 01540 662327
Duncanson, Mary (Ms)	2013	Ordained Local Minister: Presbytery Pastoral Support	3 Balmenach Road, Cromdale, Grantown-on-Spey PH26 3LJ [E-mail: mary1105@hotmail.co.uk] 01479 872165
MacEwan, James A.I. MA BD	1973 2012	(Abernethy with Cromdale and Advie)	59 Achilles Road, Engadine, NSW 2233, Australia [E-mail: wurrus@hotmail.co.uk]
Pickering, John M. BSc BD DipEd	1997 2010	(Dundee: Mains)	Oriole House, Ardbroilach Road, Kingussie PH21 1JY [E-mail: wurrus@hotmail.co.uk] 01479 873419
Ritchie, Christine A.Y. (Mrs) BD DipMin	2002 2012	(Braes of Rannoch with Foss and Rannoch)	25 Beachen Court, Grantown-on-Spey PH26 3JD [E-mail: cayritchie@btinternet.com]
Wallace, Sheila (Mrs) DCS BA BD		Deacon	Beannach Cottage, Spey Avenue, Boat of Garten PH24 3BE [E-mail: sheilad.wallace53@gmail.com] 01479 831548
Whyte, Ron C. BD CPS	1990 2013	(Alvie and Insh with Rothiemurchus and Aviemore)	13 Hillside Avenue, Kingussie PH21 1PA [E-mail: ron4xst@btinternet.com] 01540 661101 (Mbl) 07979 026973

(37) INVERNESS

Meets at Inverness, in Inverness: Trinity, on the first Tuesday of February, March, April, May, September, October, November and December, and at the Moderator's church on the fourth Tuesday of June.

Clerk: REV. REGINALD F. CAMPBELL BD BSc DipChEd   The Manse, Daviot, Inverness IV2 5XL   01463 772242
[E-mail: inverness@cofscotland.org.uk]

Ardersier (H) linked with Petty
Vacant

The Manse, Ardersier, Inverness IV2 7SX   01667 462224

Auldearn and Dalmore linked with Nairn: St Ninian's
Richard Reid BSc BD MTh   1991   2005   The Manse, Auldearn, Nairn IV12 5SX   01667 451675
[E-mail: reidricky8@aol.com]

Cawdor (H) linked with Croy and Dalcross (H)
Janet S. Mathieson MA BD   2003   The Manse, Croy, Inverness IV2 5PH   01667 493217
[E-mail: mathieson173@btinternet.com]

Croy and Dalcross See Cawdor

Culloden: The Barn (H)				
James H. Robertson BSc BD	1975	1994	45 Oakdene Court, Culloden IV2 7XL [E-mail: jim.robertson@barnchurch.org.uk]	01463 790504 07595 465838 (Mbl)
Daviot and Dunlichity linked with Moy, Dalarossie and Tomatin				
Reginald F. Campbell BD BSc DipChEd	1979	2003	The Manse, Daviot, Inverness IV2 5XL [E-mail: campbell578@talktalk.net]	01463 772242
Dores and Boleskine				
Vacant				
Inverness: Crown (H) (01463 238929)				
Peter H. Donald MA PhD BD	1991	1998	39 Southside Road, Inverness IV2 4XA [E-mail: peter.donald7@btinternet.com]	01463 230537
Inverness: Dalneigh and Bona (GD) (H)				
Andrew A. McMillan BD	2012		9 St Mungo Road, Inverness IV3 5AS [E-mail: siberiantiger13@hotmail.com]	01463 232239
Inverness: East (H)				
Andrew T.B. McGowan (Prof.) BD STM PhD	1979	2009	2 Victoria Drive, Inverness IV2 3QD [E-mail: atbmcgowan@invernesseast.com]	01463 238770
Inverness: Hilton				
Duncan MacPherson LLB BD	1994		66 Culduthel Mains Crescent, Inverness IV2 6RG [E-mail: duncan@hiltonchurch.org.uk]	01463 231417
Inverness: Inshes (H)				
David S. Scott MA BD	1987	2013	48 Redwood Crescent, Milton of Leys, Inverness IV2 6HB [E-mail: david@insheschurch.org]	01463 772402
Inverness: Kinmylies (H)				
Andrew Barrie BD	2013		2 Balnafettack Place, Inverness IV3 8TQ [E-mail: andrewabarrie@hotmail.co.uk]	01463 224307
Inverness: Ness Bank (T) (H)				
Fiona E. Smith (Mrs) LLB BD	2010		15 Ballifeary Road, Inverness IV3 5PJ [E-mail: fiona.denhead@btopenworld.com]	01463 234653

Inverness: Old High St Stephen's
Peter W. Nimmo BD ThM | 1996 | 2004 | 24 Damfield Road, Inverness IV2 3HU [E-mail: peter.nimmo7@btinternet.com] | 01463 250802

Inverness: St Columba (New Charge) (H)
Scott A. McRoberts BD MTh | | 2012 | 20 Bramble Close, Inverness IV2 6BS [E-mail: scottmcroberts@stcolumbainverness.org] | 01463 230308 / 07535 290092 (Mbl)

Inverness: Trinity (H)
Alistair Murray BD | 1984 | 2004 | 60 Kenneth Street, Inverness IV3 5PZ [E-mail: a.murray111@btinternet.com] | 01463 234756

Kilmorack and Erchless
Vacant | 'Roselynn', Croyard Road, Beauly IV4 7DJ | 01463 782260

Kiltarlity linked with Kirkhill
Vacant | Wardlaw Manse, Wardlaw Road, Kirkhill, Inverness IV5 7NZ | 01463 831662

Kirkhill See Kiltarlity
Moy, Dalarossie and Tomatin See Daviot and Dunlichity

Nairn: Old (H)
Vacant

Nairn: St Ninian's (H) See Auldearn and Dalmore
Petty See Ardersier

Urquhart and Glenmoriston (H)
Hugh F. Watt BD DPS DMin | 1986 | 1996 | Blairbeg, Drumnadrochit, Inverness IV3 6UG [E-mail: hugh.watt2@btinternet.com] | 01456 450231

Black, Archibald T. BSc | 1964 | 1997 | (Inverness: Ness Bank) | 16 Elm Park, Inverness IV2 4WN | 01463 230588
Brown, Derek G. BD DipMin DMin | 1989 | 1994 | Chaplain: NHS Highland | Cathedral Manse, Croc-an-Lobht, Dornoch IV25 3HN [E-mail: revsbrown@aol.com] | 01862 810296
Buell, F. Bart BA MDiv | 1980 | 1995 | (Urquhart and Glenmoriston) | 6 Towerhill Place, Cradlehall, Inverness IV2 5FN [E-mail: bartbuell@talktalk.net] | 01463 794634
Chisholm, Archibald F. MA | 1957 | 1997 | (Braes of Rannoch with Foss and Rannoch) | 32 Seabank Road, Nairn IV12 4EU | 01667 452001

Name			Position	Address	Phone
Christie, James LTh	1993	2003	(Dores and Boleskine)	20 Wester Inshes Crescent, Inverness IV2 5HL	01463 710534
Duncan, John C. BD MPhil	1987	2001	Chaplain: Army	3 Bn The Black Watch, The Royal Regiment of Scotland, Fort George, Ardersier, Inverness IV1 2TD [E-mail: john.duncan831@mod.uk]	(Mbl) 07825 119227
Fraser, Jonathan MA(Div) MTh ThM	2012		Associate: Inverness: Hilton	20 Moy Terrace, Inverness IV2 4EL [E-mail: jonathan@hiltonchurch.org.uk]	(Home) 01463 711609 (Work) 01463 233310
Frizzell, R. Stewart BD	1961	2000	(Wick: Old)	98 Boswell Road, Inverness IV2 3EW	01463 231907
Hunt, Trevor G. BA BD	1986	2011	(Evie with Firth with Rendall)	7 Woodville Court, Culduthel Avenue, Inverness IV2 6BX [E-mail: trevorhunt@gmail.com]	01463 250355 (Mbl) 07753 423333
Jeffrey, Stewart D. BSc BD	1962	1997	(Banff with King Edward)	10 Grigor Drive, Inverness IV2 4LP [E-mail: stewart.jeffrey@talktalk.net]	01463 230085
Livesley, Anthony LTh	1979	1997	(Kiltearn)	87 Beech Avenue, Nairn IV12 4ST [E-mail: tonylivesley@googlemail.com]	01667 455126
Logan, Robert J.V. MA BD	1962	2001	(Abdie and Dunbog with Newburgh)	Lindores, 1 Murray Place, Smithton, Inverness IV2 7PX [E-mail: rjvlogan@btinternet.com]	01463 790226
Mackenzie, Seoras L. BD	1996	1998	Chaplain: Army	Carver Barracks, Wimbish, Saffron Walden, Essex CB10 2YA	01463 235204
Macritchie, Iain A.M. BSc BD STM PhD	1987	1998	Chaplain: Inverness Hospitals	7 Merlin Crescent, Inverness IV2 3TE	01808 521285
Mitchell, Joyce (Mrs) DCS	1994		(Deacon)	Sunnybank, Farr, Inverness IV2 6XG [E-mail: joyce@mitchell71.freeserve.co.uk]	
Morrison, Hector BSc BD MTh	1981	1994	Principal: Highland Theological College	24 Oak Avenue, Inverness IV2 4NX	01463 238561
Rettie, James A. BTh	1981	1999	(Melness and Eriboll with Tongue)	2 Trantham Drive, Westhill, Inverness IV2 5QT	01463 798896
Robb, Rodney P.T.	1995	2004	(Stirling: St Mark's)	2A Mayfield Road, Inverness IV2 4AE	01463 230831
Robertson, Fergus A. MA BD	1971	2010	(Inverness: Dalneigh and Bona)	16 Druid Temple Way, Inverness IV2 6UQ [E-mail: faavrobertson@yahoo.co.uk]	01463 718462
Stirling, G. Alan S. MA	1960	1999	(Leochel Cushnie and Lynturk with Tough)	97 Lochlann Road, Culloden, Inverness IV2 7HJ	01463 798313
Turner, Fraser K. LTh	1994	2007	(Kiltarlity with Kirkhill)	20 Caulfield Avenue, Inverness IV2 5GA [E-mail: fraseratq@yahoo.co.uk]	01463 794004
Waugh, John L. LTh	1973	2002	(Ardclach with Auldearn and Dalmore)	58 Wyvis Drive, Nairn IV12 4TP [E-mail: jwaugh334@btinternet.com]	(Tel/Fax) 01667 456397
Whiteford, Alexander LTh	1996	2013	(Ardersier with Petty)	17 Netherham Gardens, Houston, Johnstone PA6 7NG [E-mail: alex.whiteford@hotmail.co.uk]	01505 229611
Younger, Alastair S. BScEcon ASCC	1969	2008	(Inverness: St Columba High)	33 Duke's View, Slackbuie, Inverness IV2 6BB [E-mail: younger873@btinternet.com]	01463 242873

INVERNESS ADDRESSES

Inverness

Crown	Kingsmills Road x Midmills Road
Dalneigh and Bona	St Mary's Avenue
East	Academy Street x Margaret Street
Hilton	Druid Road x Tomatin Road
Inshes	Inshes Retail Park
Kinmylies	Kinmylies Way
Ness Bank	Ness Bank x Castle Road
St Stephen's	Old Edinburgh Road x Southside Road
The Old High	Church Street x Church Lane
Trinity	Huntly Place x Upper Kessock Street

Nairn

Old	Academy Street x Seabank Road
St Ninian's	High Street x Queen Street

(38) LOCHABER

Meets at Caol, Fort William, in Kilmallie Church Hall at 6pm, on the first Tuesday of September and December, on the last Tuesday of October and on the fourth Tuesday of March. The June meeting is held at 6pm on the first Tuesday in the church of the incoming Moderator.

Clerk:	MRS ELLA GILL	5 Camus Inas, Acharacle PH36 4JQ
		[E-mail: lochaber@cofscotland.org.uk]
Treasurer:	MR ERIC WALKER	Tigh a' Chlann, Inverroy, Roy Bridge PH31 4AQ
		[E-mail: line15@btinternet.com]

Clerk: **01967 431834**

Treasurer: **01397 712028**

Acharacle (H) linked with Ardnamurchan
Fiona Ogg (Mrs) BA BD   2012   The Manse, Acharacle PH36 4JU   01967 431638
[E-mail: fionaogg@gmail.com]

Ardgour and Kingairloch linked with Morvern linked with Strontian
Donald G.B. McCorkindale BD DipMin   1992   2011   The Manse, 2 The Meadows, Strontian, Acharacle PH36 4HZ   01967 402234
[E-mail: donald.mccorkindale@sky.com]
[E-mail: donald@aksm.org.uk]

Ardnamurchan See Acharacle

Duror (H) linked with Glencoe: St Munda's (H) (T)
Vacant   St Munda's Manse, Brecklet, Ballachulish PH49 4JG   01855 811878

Fort Augustus linked with Glengarry
Tabea Baader   2012   The Manse, Fort Augustus PH32 4BH   01320 366210
[E-mail: tabeabaader@gmx.de]

Fort William: Duncansburgh MacIntosh (H) linked with Kilmonivaig
Vacant   The Manse of Duncansburgh, The Parade, Fort William PH33 6BA   01397 702297

Glencoe: St Munda's See Duror
Glengarry See Fort Augustus

Kilmallie
Richard T. Corbett BSc MSc PhD BD   1992   2005   Kilmallie Manse, Corpach, Fort William PH33 7JS   01397 772736
[E-mail: richard.t.corbett@btinternet.com]

Kilmonivaig See Fort William: Duncansburgh MacIntosh

Kinlochleven (H) linked with Nether Lochaber (H)
Malcolm A. Kinnear MA BD PhD   2010   The Manse, Lochaber Road, Kinlochleven PH50 4QW   01855 831227
[E-mail: malcolm.kinnear563@btinternet.com]

Morvern See Ardgour
Nether Lochaber See Kinlochleven

North West Lochaber
Edgar J. Ogston BSc BD   1976 2013   Church of Scotland Manse, Annie's Brae, Mallaig PH41 4RG   01687 460042
[E-mail: edgar.ogston@macfish.com]

Strontian See Ardgour

Anderson, David M. MSc FCOptom	1984	2012	(Ordained Local Minister)	'Mirlos', 1 Dumfries Place, Fort William PH33 6UQ [E-mail: david@mirlos.co.uk]	01397 702091
Herkes, Moira BD	1985	2007	(Brechin: Gardner Memorial)	St Munda's Manse, Brecklet, Ballachulish PH49 4JG [E-mail: mossherkes@btinternet.com]	01855 811878
Lamb, Alan H.W. BA MTh	1959	2005	(Associate Minister)	Smiddy House, Arisaig PH39 4NH [E-mail: h.a.lamb@handalamb.plus.com]	01687 450227
MacQuarrie, Donald A. BSc BD	1979	2012	(Fort William: Duncansburgh MacIntosh with Kilmonivaig)	Parkfield, 7 Glasdrum Grove, Fort William PH33 6DE [E-mail: pdmacq@ukgateway.net]	01397 698265
Muirhead, Morag (Mrs)	2013		Ordained Local Minister	6 Dumbarton Road, Fort William PH33 6UU [E-mail: mowgli49@aol.com]	01397 703643
Perkins, Mairi	2012		Ordained Local Minister	Ashlea, Cuil Road, Duror, Appin PA38 4DA [E-mail: m.perkins53@btinternet.com]	01631 740313
Rae, Peter C. BSc BD	1968	2000	(Beath and Cowdenbeath: North)	8 Wether Road, Great Cambourne, Cambridgeshire CB23 5DT [E-mail: rae.fairview@btinternet.com]	01954 710079
Varwell, Adrian P.J. BA BD PhD	1983	2011	(Fort Augustus with Glengarry)	19 Enrick Crescent, Kilmore, Drumnadrochit, Inverness IV63 6TP [E-mail: adrian.varwell@btinternet.com]	01456 459352
Winning, A. Ann MA DipEd BD	1984	2006	(Morvern)	'Westering', 13C Carnoch, Glencoe, Ballachulish PH49 4HQ [E-mail: awinning009@btinternet.com]	01855 811929

LOCHABER Communion Sundays Please consult the Presbytery website: www.cofslochaber.co.uk

(39) ROSS

Meets on the first Tuesday of September in the church of the incoming Moderator, and in Dingwall: Castle Street Church on the first Tuesday of October, November, December, February, March and May, and on the last Tuesday of June.

Clerk: MR RONALD W. GUNSTONE BSc   20 Belfield Road, North Kessock, Inverness IV1 3XU   01463 731337
[E-mail: ross@cofscotland.org.uk]

Alness Vacant		27 Darroch Brae, Alness IV17 0SD	01349 882238
Avoch linked with Fortrose and Rosemarkie Alan T. McKean BD CertMin	1982	2010	5 Nessway, Fortrose IV10 8SS [E-mail: a.mckean2345@btinternet.com]	01381 621433
Contin (H) linked with Fodderty and Strathpeffer (H) Fanus Erasmus MA LTh MTh ThD	1978	2013	The Manse, Contin, Strathpeffer IV14 9ES [E-mail: fanuserasmus@yahoo.com]	01997 423296
Cromarty linked with Resolis and Urquhart Vacant		The Manse, Culbokie, Dingwall IV7 8JN	01349 877452
Dingwall: Castle Street (H) Bruce Ritchie BSc BD PhD	1977	2006	16 Achany Road, Dingwall IV15 9JB [E-mail: brucezomba@hotmail.com]	01349 867315
Dingwall: St Clement's (H) Vacant		8 Castlehill Road, Dingwall IV15 9PB	
Fearn Abbey and Nigg linked with Tarbat David V. Scott BTh	1994	2006	Church of Scotland Manse, Fearn, Tain IV20 1TN	01862 832626 (Tel/Fax)
Ferintosh Andrew F. Graham BTh DPS	2001	2006	Ferintosh Manse, Leanaig Road, Conon Bridge, Dingwall IV7 8BE [E-mail: afg1960@tiscali.co.uk]	01349 861275

Fodderty and Strathpeffer (H) See Contin
Fortrose and Rosemarkie See Avoch

Invergordon
Kenneth Donald Macleod BD CPS 1989 2000 The Manse, Cromlet Drive, Invergordon IV18 0BA
[E-mail: kd-macleod@tiscali.co.uk] 01349 852273

Killearnan (H) linked with Knockbain (H)
Vacant The Church of Scotland Manse, Coldwell Road, Artafallie, North Kessock, Inverness IV1 3ZE 01463 731333

Kilmuir and Logie Easter
Fraser M.C. Stewart BSc BD 1980 2011 Delny, Invergordon IV18 0NW
[E-mail: fraserstewart1955@hotmail.com] 01862 842280

Kiltearn (H)
Donald A. MacSween BD 1991 1998 The Manse, Swordale Road, Evanton, Dingwall IV16 9UZ
[E-mail: donaldmacsween@hotmail.com] 01349 830472

Knockbain See Killearnan

Lochbroom and Ullapool (GD)
Vacant The Manse, Garve Road, Ullapool IV26 2SX 01854 612050

Resolis and Urquhart See Cromarty

Rosskeen
Robert Jones BSc BD 1990 Rosskeen Manse, Perrins Road, Alness IV17 0XG
[E-mail: rob2jones@btinternet.com] 01349 882265

Tain
Vacant 14 Kingsway Avenue, Tain IV19 1NJ 01862 894140

Tarbat See Fearn Abbey and Nigg

Urray and Kilchrist
Scott Polworth LLB BD 2009 The Manse, Corrie Road, Muir of Ord IV6 7TL
[E-mail: scottpolworth@btinternet.com] 01463 870259

Name			Charge	Address	Tel
Archer, Nicholas D.C. BA BD	1971	1992	(Dores and Boleskine)	2 Aldie Cottages, Tain IV19 1LZ	01862 821494
Dupar, Kenneth W. BA BD PhD	1965	1993	(Christ's College, Aberdeen)	The Old Manse, The Causeway, Cromarty IV11 8XJ	01381 600428
Forsyth, James LTh	1970	2000	(Fearn Abbey with Nigg Chapelhill)	Rhives Lodge, Golspie, Sutherland KW10 6DD	
Glass, Alexander OBE MA	1998	2009	(Auxiliary Minister)	Craigton, Tulloch Avenue, Dingwall IV15 9TU	01349 863258
Horne, Douglas A. BD	1977	2009	(Tain)	151 Holm Farm Road, Culduthel, Inverness IV2 6BF [E-mail: douglas.horne@talktalk.net]	01463 712677
Liddell, Margaret (Miss) BD DipTh	1987	1997	(Contin)	20 Wyvis Crescent, Conon Bridge, Dingwall IV7 8BZ [E-mail: margaretliddell@talktalk.net]	01349 865997
Mackinnon, R.M. LTh	1968	1995	(Kilmuir and Logie Easter)	27 Riverford Crescent, Conon Bridge, Dingwall IV7 8HL	01349 866293
McLean, Gordon LTh	1972	2008	(Contin)	Beinn Dhorain, Kinnettas Square, Strathpeffer IV14 9BD [E-mail: gmaclean@hotmail.co.uk]	01997 421380
MacLennan, Alasdair J. BD DCE	1978	2001	(Resolis and Urquhart)	Airdale, Seaforth Road, Muir of Ord IV6 7TA	01463 870704
Macleod, John MA	1959	1993	(Resolis and Urquhart)	'Benview', 19 Balvaird, Muir of Ord IV6 7RG [E-mail: sheilaandjohn@yahoo.co.uk]	01463 871286
McWilliam, Thomas M. MA BD	1964	2003	(Contin)	Flat 3, 13 Culduthel Road, Inverness IV2 4AG [E-mail: tommcwilliam@bconnect.com]	01463 718981
Munro, James A. BA BD DMS	1979	2013	(Port Glasgow: Hamilton Bardrainney)	1 Wyvis Crescent, Conon Bridge, Dingwall IV7 8BZ [E-mail: james781munro@btinternet.com]	01349 865752
Niven, William W. BTh	1982	1995	(Alness)	4 Obsdale Park, Alness IV17 0TP	01349 882427
Ramsden, Iain BTh	1999	2013	(Killearnan with Knockbain)	19 Balvaird Terrace, Muir of Ord IV6 7TR [E-mail: s4rev@sky.com]	01463 870453
Rutherford, Ellen B. (Miss) MBE DCS	1994	2013	(Deaconess)	41 Duncanston, Conon Bridge, Dingwall IV7 8JB	01349 877439
Smith, Russel BD			(Dingwall: St Clement's)	1 School Road, Conon Bridge, Dingwall IV7 8AE [E-mail: russanntwo@btinternet.com]	01349 861011
Tallach, John MA MLitt	1970	2010	(Cromarty)	29 Firthview Drive, Inverness IV3 8NS [E-mail: j.tallach@tiscali.co.uk]	01463 418721

(40) SUTHERLAND

Meets at Lairg on the first Tuesday of March, May, September, November and December, and on the first Tuesday of June at the Moderator's church.

Clerk:	REV. MARY J. STOBO	**Druim-an-Sgairnich, Ardgay IV24 3BG** [E-mail: sutherland@cofscotland.org.uk]	**01863 766868**

Altnaharra and Farr
Vacant   The Manse, Bettyhill, Thurso KW14 7SS   01641 521208

Assynt and Stoer
Guardianship of the Presbytery   Canisp Road, Lochinver, Lairg IV27 4LH   01571 844342

Clyne (H) linked with Kildonan and Loth Helmsdale (H)
Vacant — Golf Road, Brora KW9 6QS — 01408 621239
Michael Macdonald (Aux) 2004 2012 — 73 Firhill, Alness IV17 0RT — 01349 884268
[E-mail: mike_mary@hotmail.co.uk]

Creich See Kincardine Croick and Edderton

Dornoch Cathedral (H)
Susan M. Brown (Mrs) BD DipMin 1985 1998 — Cathedral Manse, Cnoc-an-Lobht, Dornoch IV25 3HN — 01862 810296
[E-mail: revsbrown@aol.com]

Durness and Kinlochbervie
John T. Mann BSc BD 1990 1998 — Manse Road, Kinlochbervie, Lairg IV27 4RG — 01971 521287
[E-mail: jimklb@aol.com]

Eddrachillis
John MacPherson BSc BD 1993 — Church of Scotland Manse, Scourie, Lairg IV27 4TQ — 01971 502431

Golspie
John B. Sterrett BA BD PhD 2007 — The Manse, Fountain Road, Golspie KW10 6TH — 01408 633295 (Tel/Fax)
[E-mail: johnbsterrett@yahoo.co.uk]

Kildonan and Loth Helmsdale (H) See Clyne

Kincardine Croick and Edderton linked with Creich linked with Rosehall
Anthony M. Jones 1994 2010 — The Manse, Ardgay IV24 3BG — 01863 766285
  BD DPS DipTheol CertMin FRSA
[E-mail: revanthonymjones@amserve.com]
Hilary Gardner (Miss) (Aux) 2010 2012 — Cayman Lodge, Kincardine Hill, Ardgay IV24 3DJ — 01863 766107
[E-mail: gardnerhilary@hotmail.com]

Lairg (H) linked with Rogart (H)
Vacant — The Manse, Lairg IV27 4EH — 01549 402373

Melness and Tongue (H)
Stewart Goudie BSc BD 2010 — St Andrew's Manse, Tongue, Lairg IV27 4XL — 01847 611230 (Tel/Fax)
07957 237757 (Mbl)
[E-mail: stewart@goudie.me.uk]

Rogart See Lairg
Rosehall See Kincardine Croick and Edderton

Chambers, John OBE BSc	1972 2009	(Inverness: Ness Bank)	Barnlagan Lodge, 4 Earls Cross Gardens, Dornoch IV25 3NR [E-mail: chambersdornoch@btinternet.com]	01862 811520
Goskirk, J.L. LTh	1968 2010	(Lairg with Rogart)	Rathvilly, Lairgmuir, Lairg IV27 4ED [E-mail: leslie_goskirk@sky.com]	01549 402569
McCree, Ian W. BD	1971 2011	(Clyne with Kildonan and Loth Helmsdale)	Tigh Ardachu, Mosshill, Brora KW9 6NG [E-mail: ian@mccree.f9.co.uk]	01408 621185
Muckart, Graeme W.M. MTh MSc FSAScot	1983 2009	(Kincardine Croick and Edderton)	Kildale, Clashmore, Dornoch IV25 3RG [E-mail: avqt18@dsl.pipex.com]	
Stobo, Mary J. (Mrs)	2013	Ordained Local Minister; Community Healthcare Chaplain	Druim-an-Sgairnich, Ardgay IV24 3BG [E-mail: sutherland@cofscotland.org.uk]	01863 766868

(41) CAITHNESS

Meets alternately at Wick and Thurso on the first Tuesday of February, March, May, September, November and December, and the third Tuesday of June.

| Clerk: | REV. RONALD JOHNSTONE BD | 2 Comlifoot Drive, Halkirk KW12 6ZA [E-mail: caithness@cofscotland.org.uk] | 01847 839033 |

Bower linked with Halkirk Westerdale linked with Watten

| Alastair H. Gray MA BD | 1978 2005 | The Manse, Station Road, Watten, Wick KW1 5YN [E-mail: alastair.h.gray@btinternet.com] | 01955 621220 |

Canisbay linked with Dunnet linked with Keiss

| Vacant | The Manse, Canisbay, Wick KW1 4YH | 01955 611756 |

Dunnet See Canisbay
Halkirk Westerdale See Bower
Keiss See Canisbay

Olrig linked with Thurso: St Peter's and St Andrew's (H)

| Vacant | The Manse, 40 Rose Street, Thurso KW14 8RF [E-mail: spacosminister@btinternet.com] | 01847 895186 |

The North Coast Parish

| Vacant | Church of Scotland Manse, Reay, Thurso KW14 7RE | 01847 811441 |

The Parish of Latheron
Gordon Oliver BD | 1979 2010 | Central Manse, Main Street, Lybster KW3 6BJ | 01593 721706
[E-mail: parish-of-latheron@btconnect.com]

Thurso: St Peter's and St Andrew's See Olrig

Thurso: West (H)
Vacant | Thorkel Road, Thurso KW14 7LW | 01847 892663

Watten See Bower

Wick: Pulteneytown (H) and Thrumster
Stuart Farmes | 2011 | The Manse, Coronation Street, Wick KW1 5LS | 01955 603166
[E-mail: thefarmesfamily@tiscali.co.uk]

Wick: St Fergus
John Nugent | 1999 2011 | Mansefield, Miller Avenue, Wick KW1 4DF | 01955 602167
[E-mail: johnnugentis@mail2web.com]

Craw, John DCS	1998 2009	(Deacon)	Liabost, 8 Proudfoot Road, Wick KW1 4PQ [E-mail: johncraw607@btinternet.com]	01955 603805 (Mbl) 07544 761653
Duncan, Esme (Miss)	2013	Ordained Local Minister	Avalon, Upper Warse, Canisbay, Wick KW1 4YD [E-mail: esmeduncan@btinternet.com]	01955 611455
Johnstone, Ronald BD	1977 2011	(Thurso: West)	2 Comlifoot Drive, Halkirk KW12 6ZA [E-mail: ronaldjohnstone@btinternet.com]	01847 839033
Nicol, Robert	2013	Ordained Local Minister	3 Castlegreen Road, Thurso KW14 7DN [E-mail: robert.nicol1@btinternet.com]	
Rennie, Lyall	2013	Ordained Local Minister	Ruachmarra, Lower Warse, Canisbay, Wick KW1 4YB [E-mail: lyall.rennie@btinternet.com]	01955 611756
Stewart, Heather (Mrs)	2013	Ordained Local Minister	Burnthill, Thrumster, Wick KW1 5AX [E-mail: heatherburnthill@btopenworld.com]	01955 651717 (Work) 01955 603333
Warner, Kenneth BD	1981 2008	(Halkirk and Westerdale)	Kilearnan, Clayock, Halkirk KW12 6UZ [E-mail: wmrkenn@btinternet.com]	01847 831825

CAITHNESS Communion Sundays

Bower	1st Jul, Dec	Keiss	1st May, 3rd Nov	West	4th Mar, Jun, Nov
Canisbay	1st Jun, Nov	Latheron	Apr, Jul, Sep, Dec	Watten	1st Jul, Dec
Dunnet	last May, Nov	North Coast	Mar, Easter, Jun, Sep, Dec	Wick: Pulteneytown and Thrumster	1st Mar, Jun, Sep, Dec
Halkirk Westerdale	Apr, Jul, Oct	Olrig	last May, Nov	St Fergus	Apr, Oct
		Thurso: St Peter's and St Andrew's	Mar, Jun, Sep, Dec		

(42) LOCHCARRON – SKYE

Meets in Kyle on the first Tuesday of each month, except January, May, July and August.

| Clerk: | REV. ALLAN I. MACARTHUR BD | High Barn, Croft Road, Lochcarron, Strathcarron IV54 8YA
[E-mail: lochcarronskye@cofscotland.org.uk]
[E-mail: a.macarthur@btinternet.com] | 01520 722278 (Tel)
01520 722674 (Fax) |

Applecross, Lochcarron and Torridon (GD)

| David Macleod | 2008 | The Manse, Colonel's Road, Lochcarron, Strathcarron IV54 8YG
[E-mail: david.macleod@me.com] | 01520 722829 |

Bracadale and Duirinish (GD)

| Geoffrey D. McKee BA | 1997 | 2009 | Duirinish Manse, Dunvegan, Isle of Skye IV55 8WQ
[E-mail: geoff.mckee@btinternet.com] | 01470 521457 |

Gairloch and Dundonnell

| Vacant | | | Church of Scotland Manse, The Glebe, Gairloch IV21 2BT | 01445 712053 (Tel/Fax) |

Glenelg and Kintail

| Roderick N. MacRae BTh | 2001 | 2004 | Church of Scotland Manse, Inverinate, Kyle IV40 8HE
[E-mail: barvalous@msn.com] | 01599 511245 |

Kilmuir and Stenscholl (GD)

| Vacant | | | Staffin, Portree, Isle of Skye IV51 9JX | 01470 562759 (Tel/Fax) |

Lochalsh

| Vacant | | | The Manse, Main Street, Kyle IV40 8DA | 01599 534294 |

Portree (GD)

| Sandor Fazakas BD MTh | 1976 | 2007 | Viewfield Road, Portree, Isle of Skye IV51 9ES
[E-mail: fazakass52@yahoo.com] | 01478 611868 |

Snizort (H) (GD)

| Vacant | | | The Manse, Kensaleyre, Snizort, Portree, Isle of Skye IV51 9XE | 01470 532453 |

Strath and Sleat (GD)

Vacant

John D. Urquhart BA BD
(Part-Time: Gaelic Services)

The Manse, 6 Upper Breakish, Isle of Skye IV42 8PY   01471 820063
The Manse, The Glebe, Kilmore, Teangue, Isle of Skye
IV44 8RG   01471 844469
[E-mail: ministear@hotmail.co.uk]

Name	Ord	Ind	Role	Address	Tel
Anderson, Janet (Miss) DCS	1998	2003	(Deaconess)	Creagard, 31 Lower Breakish, Isle of Skye IV42 8QA [E-mail: jaskye@hotmail.co.uk]	01471 822403
Beaton, Donald MA BD MTh	1961	2002	(Glenelg and Kintail)	Kilmaluag Croft, North Duntulm, Isle of Skye IV51 9UF	01470 552296
Calhoun, Robert L. BBA MDiv DMin	1974	2012	(Snizort)	145 Lamont, San Antonio, TX 78209, USA [E-mail: drre0911@yahoo.com]	
Kellas, David J. MA BD	1966	2004	(Kilfinan with Kyles)	Buarblach, Glenelg, Kyle IV40 8LA [E-mail: davidkellas@btinternet.com]	01599 522257 (Mbl) 07909 577764
Macarthur, Allan I. BD	1973	1998	(Applecross, Lochcarron and Torridon)	High Barn, Croft Road, Lochcarron, Strathcarron IV54 8YA [E-mail: a.macarthur@btinternet.com]	(Tel) 01520 722278 (Fax) 01520 722674
McCulloch, Alen J.R. MA BD	1990	2012	(Chaplain: Royal Navy)	Aros, 6 Gifford Terrace Road, Plymouth PL3 4JE [E-mail: avijoen90@hotmail.com]	01752 657290
Mackenzie, Hector M.	2008		Chaplain: Army	3 Bn The Parachute Regiment, Merville Barracks, Colchester CO2 7UT [E-mail: mackenziehector@hotmail.com]	
Macleod, Donald LTh	1988	2000	(Snizort)	Burnside, Upper Galder, Glenelg, Kyle IV40 8JZ [E-mail: donaldpmacleod_7@btinternet.com]	01599 522265
Martin, George M. MA BD	1987	2005	(Applecross, Lochcarron and Torridon)	8(1) Buckingham Terrace, Edinburgh EH4 3AA	0131-343 3937
Morrison, Derek	1995	2013	(Gairloch and Dundonnell)	2 Cliffton Place, Poolewe, Achnasheen IV22 2JU [E-mail: derekmorrison1@aol.com]	01445 781333
Murray, John W.	2003		Auxiliary Minister	1 Totescore, Kilmuir, Portree, Isle of Skye IV51 9YN [E-mail: jwn7@hotmail.co.uk]	01470 542297

LOCHCARRON – SKYE Communion Sundays

Applecross	1st Sep	Glenshiel	1st Jul
Arnisort	3rd Mar, Sep	Kilmuir	1st Mar, Sep
Bracadale	Last Feb	Kintail	3rd Apr, Jul
Broadford	3rd Jan, Easter, 3rd Sep	Kyleakin	Last Sep
Duirinish	4th Jun	Lochalsh and Stromeferry	4th Jan, Jun, Sep, Christmas, Easter
Dundonnell	1st Aug	Lochcarron and Shieldaig	Easter; communion held on a revolving basis when there is a fifth Sunday in the month
Elgol	3rd Jun, Nov		
Gairloch	2nd Jun, Nov		
Glenelg			

Plockton and Kyle			
Portree	2nd May, 1st Oct	Easter, Pentecost, Christmas,	2nd Mar, Aug, 1st Nov
Sleat	Last May		
Snizort	1st Jan, 4th Mar		
Stenscholl	1st Jun, Dec		
Strath	4th Jan		
Torridon and Kinlochewe			

In the Parish of Strath and Sleat, Easter communion is held on a revolving basis.

(43) UIST

Meets on the first Tuesday of February, March, September and November in Lochmaddy; and on the third Tuesday of June in Leverburgh.

Clerk: MR WILSON McKINLAY   Heatherburn Cottage, Rhughasnish, Isle of South Uist   01870 610393
HS8 5PE
[E-mail: uist@cofscotland.org.uk]

Benbecula (GD) (H)
Vacant
Church of Scotland Manse, Griminish, Isle of Benbecula HS7 5QA   01870 602180

Berneray and Lochmaddy (GD) (H)
Donald Campbell MA BD DipTh   1997   2004
Church of Scotland Manse, Lochmaddy, Isle of North Uist HS6 5AA   01876 500414
[E-mail: dc@hebrides.net]

Carinish (GD) (H)
Vacant
Church of Scotland Manse, Clachan, Locheport, Lochmaddy,   01876 580219
Isle of North Uist HS6 5HD

Kilmuir and Paible (GE)
Vacant
Paible, Isle of North Uist HS6 5ED   01876 510310

Manish-Scarista (GD) (H)
Vacant
Scarista, Isle of Harris HS3 3HX   01859 550200

Tarbert (GD) (H)
Vacant
The Manse, Manse Road, Tarbert, Isle of Harris HS3 3DF   01859 502231

MacDonald, Angus J. BSc BD	1995 2001	(Lochmaddy and Trumisgarry)	7 Memorial Avenue, Stornoway, Isle of Lewis HS1 2QR	01851 706634
Macdonald, Ishabel	2011	Ordained Local Minister	18 Carinish, Isle of North Uist HS6 5HN	
MacInnes, David MA BD	1966 1999	(Kilmuir and Paible)	9 Golf View Road, Kinmylies, Inverness IV3 8SZ	01463 717377
MacIver, Norman BD	1976 2011	(Tarbert)	57 Boswell Road, Wester Inshes, Inverness IV2 3EW	
			[E-mail: norman@n-cmaciver.freeserve.co.uk]	
Macpherson, Kenneth J. BD	1988 2002	(Benbecula)	70 Baile na Cille, Balivanich, Isle of Benbecula HS7 5ND	01870 602751
Morrison, Donald John	2001	Auxiliary Minister	22 Kyles, Tarbert, Isle of Harris HS3 3BS	01859 502341

Petrie, Jackie G.	1989	2011	(South Uist)	7B Malacleit, Sollas, Isle of North Uist HS6 5BX [E-mail: jackiegpetrie@yahoo.com] 01878 700265
Smith, John M.	1956	1992	(Lochmaddy)	Hamersay, Clachan, Locheport, Lochmaddy, Isle of North Uist HS6 5HD
Smith, Murdo MA BD	1988	2011	(Manish-Scarista)	Aisgeir, 15A Upper Shader, Isle of Lewis HS3 3MX 01876 580332

UIST Communion Sundays

Benbecula	2nd Mar, Sep	Carinish	4th Mar, Aug
Berneray and Lochmaddy	4th Jun, last Oct	Kilmuir and Paible	1st Jun, 3rd Nov
		Manish-Scarista	3rd Apr, 1st Oct
		Tarbert	2nd Mar, 3rd Sep

(44) LEWIS

Meets at Stornoway, in St Columba's Church Hall, on the second Tuesday of February, March, September and November. It also meets if required in April, June and December on dates to be decided.

Clerk: REV. THOMAS S. SINCLAIR MA LTh BD   An Caladh, East Tarbert,
Tarbert, Isle of Harris HS3 3DB   01859 502849
07816 455820 (Mbl)
[E-mail: lewis@cofscotland.org.uk]
[E-mail: lewispresbytery@gmail.com]

Barvas (GD) (H)
Paul Amed LTh DPS   1992   2008   Barvas, Isle of Lewis HS2 0QY   01851 840218
[E-mail: paulamed@hebrides.net]

Carloway (GD) (H) (Office: 01851 643211)
Vacant   Church of Scotland Manse, Knock, Carloway, Isle of Lewis HS2 9AU   01851 643255

Cross Ness (GE) (H)
Ian Murdo M. Macdonald DPA BD   2001   Cross Manse, Swainbost, Ness, Isle of Lewis HS2 0TB   01851 810375
[E-mail: crosschurch@me.com]

Kinloch (GE) (H)
Iain M. Campbell BD   2004   2008   Laxay, Lochs, Isle of Lewis HS2 9LA   01851 830218
[E-mail: i455@btinternet.com]

Knock (GE) (H)
Vacant
Knock Manse, Garrabost, Point, Isle of Lewis HS2 0PW   01851 870368

Lochs-Crossbost (GD) (H)
Vacant
Leurbost, Lochs, Isle of Lewis HS2 9NS   01851 860243

Lochs-in-Bernera (GD) (H) linked with Uig (GE) (H)
Hugh Maurice Stewart DPA BD   2008
4 Seaview, Knock, Point, Isle of Lewis HS2 0PD   01851 870379
(Temporary Manse)
[E-mail: berneralwuig@btinternet.com]

Stornoway: High (GD) (H)
Vacant
1 Goathill Road, Stornoway, Isle of Lewis HS1 2NJ   01851 703106

Stornoway: Martin's Memorial (H) (Church office: 01851 700820)
Thomas MacNeil MA BD   2002   2006
Matheson Road, Stornoway, Isle of Lewis HS1 2LR   01851 704238
[E-mail: tommymacneil@hotmail.com]
Stephen Macdonald BD MTh (Assoc)   2008   2012
39B Newmarket, Stornoway, Isle of Lewis HS2 0DY   07570 804193 (Mbl)
[E-mail: sm.2@hotmail.co.uk]

Stornoway: St Columba (GD) (H) (Church office: 01851 701546)
William J. Heenan BA MTh   2012
St Columba's Manse, Lewis Street, Stornoway, Isle of Lewis HS1 2JF   01851 705933
[E-mail: wmheenan@hotmail.co.uk]   07837 770589 (Mbl)

Uig (GE) (H) See Lochs-in-Bernera

Name				Address	Phone
Jamieson, Esther M.M. (Mrs) BD	1984	2002	(Glasgow: Penilee St Andrew)	1 Redburn, Bayview, Stornoway, Isle of Lewis HS1 2UU [E-mail: iandejamieson@btinternet.com]	01851 704789
Johnstone, Ben MA BD DMin	1973	2013	(Strath and Sleat)	Loch Alainn, 5 Breaclete, Great Bernera, Isle of Lewis HS2 9LT [E-mail: benonbernera@gmail.com]	(Mbl) 07867 602963 / 01851 612445
Macdonald, James LTh CPS	1984	2001	(Knock)	Elim, 8A Lower Bayble, Point, Isle of Lewis HS2 0QA [E-mail: elim8a@hotmail.co.uk]	01851 870173
Maciver, Iain BD	2007	2012	(Carinish)	5 MacLeod Road, Stornoway, Isle of Lewis HS1 2HJ [E-mail: iain.maciver@hebrides.net]	
Maclean, Donald A. DCS			(Deacon)	8 Upper Barvas, Isle of Lewis HS2 0QX	01851 840454
MacLennan, Donald Angus	1975	2006	(Kinloch)	4 Kestrel Place, Inverness IV2 3YH [E-mail: maclennankinloch@btinternet.com]	01463 243750 / (Mbl) 07799 668270

Macleod, William	1957 2006	(Uig)	54 Lower Barvas, Isle of Lewis HS2 0QY
Shadakshari, T.K. BTh BD MTh	1998 2006	Healthcare Chaplain	23D Benside, Newmarket, Stornoway, Isle of Lewis HS2 0DZ (Home) 01851 840217
			[E-mail: tk.shadakshari@nhs.net] (Office) 01851 701727
			[E-mail: shadaks2@yahoo.com] (Mbl) 01851 704704 / 07403 697138
Sinclair, Thomas Suter MA LTh BD	1966 2004	(Stornoway: Martin's Memorial)	An Caladh, East Tarbert, Tarbert, Isle of Harris HS3 3DB 01859 502849
			[E-mail: lewis@cofscotland.org.uk] (Mbl) 07816 455820
			[E-mail: thomas@sinclair0438.freeserve.co.uk]

LEWIS Communion Sundays

Barvas	3rd Mar, Sep	Stornoway: High	3rd Apr, 1st Nov	3rd Feb, last Aug
Carloway	1st Mar, last Sep	Martin's Memorial	4th Mar, Sep	3rd Feb, last Aug. 1st Dec, Easter
Cross Ness	2nd Mar, Oct	Stornoway: St Columba	1st Apr, 2nd Sep	3rd Feb, last Aug
Kinloch	3rd Mar, 2nd Jun, 2nd Sep	Uig		3rd Jun, 4th Oct
Knock				
Lochs-Crossbost				
Lochs-in-Bernera				

(45) ORKNEY

Normally meets at Kirkwall, in the East Church King Street Halls, on the second Tuesday of September and February, and on the last Tuesday of November. The Presbytery meets in conference on the first Tuesday in May. One meeting is usually held outwith the King Street Halls.

Clerk:	REV. JAMES WISHART BD		Upper Westshore, Burray, Orkney KW17 2TE	01856 731672
			[E-mail: orkney@cofscotland.org.uk]	
			[E-mail (personal): jwishart06@btinternet.com]	

Birsay, Harray and Sandwick

Andrea E. Price (Mrs)	1997	2001	The Manse, North Biggings Road, Dounby, Orkney KW17 2HZ	01856 771803
			[E-mail: andrea@andreaneil.plus.com]	

East Mainland

Vacant	West Manse, Holm, Orkney KW17 2SB	01856 781422

Eday linked with Stronsay: Moncur Memorial (H)

Vacant	Manse, Stronsay, Orkney KW17 2AF	01857 616311

Evie (H) linked with Firth (H) linked with Rendall linked with Rousay

Vacant	Manse, Finstown, Orkney KW17 2EG	01856 761328

Firth (H) (01856 761117) See Evie

Flotta linked with Hoy and Walls linked with Orphir and Stenness
Vacant — Stenness Manse, Stenness, Stromness, Orkney KW16 3HH

Hoy and Walls See Flotta

Kirkwall: East (H) linked with Shapinsay
Vacant — East Church Manse, Thoms Street, Kirkwall, Orkney KW15 1PF — 01856 874789

Kirkwall: St Magnus Cathedral (H)
G. Fraser H. Macnaughton MA BD — 1982 — Berstane Road, Kirkwall, Orkney KW15 1NA
[E-mail: macnaughton187@btinternet.com] — 01856 873312

North Ronaldsay linked with Sanday (H)
John L. McNab MA BD — 1997 — The Manse, Sanday, Orkney KW17 2BW — 01857 600429

Orphir (H) and Stenness (H) See Flotta

Papa Westray linked with Westray
Iain D. MacDonald BD — 1993 — The Manse, Hilldavale, Westray, Orkney KW17 2DW
[E-mail: idmacdonald@btinternet.com] — 01857 677357 (Tel/Fax) 07710 443780 (Mbl)

Rendall See Evie
Rousay (Church centre: 01856 821271) See Evie
Sanday See North Ronaldsay
Shapinsay See Kirkwall: East

South Ronaldsay and Burray
Stephen Manners MA BD (Assoc) — 1989 — St Margaret's Manse, Church Road, St Margaret's Hope,
Orkney KW17 2SR
[E-mail: sk.manners@me.com] — 01856 831670 / 07747 821458 (Mbl)

Stromness (H)
Magdaléna Trgalová — 2013 — 5 Manse Lane, Stromness, Orkney KW16 3AP — 01856 851487

Stronsay: Moncur Memorial See Eday
Westray See Papa Westray

Brown, R. Graeme BA BD	1961 1998	(Birsay with Rousay)	Bring Deeps, Orphir, Orkney KW17 2LX [E-mail: graeme_sibyl@btinternet.com]	(Tel/Fax) 01856 811707
Clark, Thomas L. BD	1985 2008	(Orphir with Stenness)	7 Headland Rise, Burghead, Elgin IV30 5HA [E-mail: toml.clark@btinternet.com]	01343 830144
Fidler, David G.	2013	Ordained Local Minister	34 Guardhouse Park, Stromness, Orkney KW16 3DP [E-mail: dvdfid@yahoo.co.uk]	01856 850575 (Mbl) 07900 386473
Prentice, Martin	2013	Ordained Local Minister	Cot of Howe, Cairston, Stromness, Orkney KW16 3JU [E-mail: mwm.prentice@virgin.net]	01856 851139 (Mbl) 07795 817213
Tait, Alexander	1967 1995	(Glasgow: St Enoch's Hogganfield)	Ingermas, Evie, Orkney KW17 2PH [E-mail: jen1957@hotmail.co.uk]	01856 751477
Wishart, James BD	1986 2009	(Deer)	Upper Westshore, Burray, Orkney KW17 2TE [E-mail: jwishart06@btinternet.com]	01856 731672

(46) SHETLAND

Meets at Lerwick on the first Tuesday of February, April, June, September, November and December.

Clerk:	**REV. CHARLES H.M. GREIG MA BD**		**6 Hayhoull Place, Bigton, Shetland ZE2 9GA** [E-mail: shetland@cofscotland.org.uk]	**01950 422468**

Burra Isle linked with Tingwall

Wilma A. Johnston MTheol MTh	2006	2008	The Manse, 25 Hogalee, East Voe, Scalloway, Shetland ZE1 0UU [E-mail: rev.wilmajohnston@btinternet.com]	01595 881157

Delting linked with Northmavine

Vacant			The Manse, Grindwell, Brae, Shetland ZE2 9QJ	01806 522219
Robert M. MacGregor	2004		Olna Cottage, Brae, Shetland ZE2 9QS [E-mail: revbobdelting@mypostoffice.co.uk]	01806 522604
CMIOSH DipOSH RSP (Aux)				
Grace Russon (Mrs) (Aux)	2011		Marelda, Park Road, Sandwick, Shetland ZE2 9HP [E-mail: gracerusson@live.co.uk]	01950 431207

Dunrossness and St Ninian's inc. Fair Isle linked with Sandwick, Cunningsburgh and Quarff

Charles H.M. Greig MA BD   1976 1997   6 Hayhoull Place, Bigton, Shetland ZE2 9GA   01950 422468
[E-mail: chm.greig@btopenworld.com]

Fetlar linked with Unst linked with Yell

David Cooper BA MPhil   1975 2008   North Isles Manse, Gutcher, Yell, Shetland ZE2 9DF   01957 744258
(David Cooper is a minister of the Methodist Church)   [E-mail: reverenddavidcooper@googlemail.com]

Lerwick and Bressay

Caroline R. Lockerbie BA MDiv DMin   2007 2013   The Manse, 82 St Olaf Street, Lerwick, Shetland ZE1 0ES   01595 692125
(Transition Minister)   [E-mail: caroline.lockerbie@btinternet.com]

Nesting and Lunnasting linked with Whalsay and Skerries

Irene A. Charlton (Mrs) BTh   1994 1997   The Manse, Marrister, Symbister, Whalsay, Shetland ZE2 9AE   01806 566767
[E-mail: irene.charlton@btinternet.com]
Richard M. Charlton (Aux)   2001   The Manse, Marrister, Symbister, Whalsay, Shetland ZE2 9AE   01806 566767
[E-mail: revrm.charlton@btinternet.com]

Northmavine See Delting

Sandsting and Aithsting linked with Walls and Sandness

Vacant   The Manse, Happyhansel, Walls, Shetland ZE2 9PB   01595 809709

Sandwick, Cunningsburgh and Quarff See Dunrossness and St Ninian's
Tingwall See Burra Isle
Unst See Fetlar
Walls and Sandness See Sandsting and Aithsting
Whalsay and Skerries See Nesting and Lunnasting
Yell See Fetlar

Kirkpatrick, Alice H. (Miss)   1987 2000   (Northmavine)   1 Daisy Park, Baltasound, Unst, Shetland ZE2 9EA
  MA BD FSAScot
Knox, R. Alan MA LTh AInstAM   1965 2004   (Fetlar with Unst with Yell)   27 Killyvalley Road, Garvagh, Co. Londonderry, Northern Ireland BT51 5LX   0829 558925
Macintyre, Thomas MA BD   1972 2011   (Sandsting and Aithsting with Walls and Sandness)   Lappideks, South Voxter, Cunningsburgh, Shetland ZE2 9HF   01950 477549
  [E-mail: the2macs.macintyre@btinternet.com]
Smith, Catherine (Mrs) DCS   1964 2003   (Presbytery Assistant)   21 Lingaro, Bixter, Shetland ZE2 9NN   01595 810207
Williamson, Magnus J.C.   1982 1999   (Fetlar with Yell)   Creekhaven, Houl Road, Scalloway, Shetland ZE1 0XA   01595 880023

(47) ENGLAND

Meets at London, in Crown Court Church, on the second Tuesday of March and December, and at St Columba's, Pont Street, on the second Tuesday of June and October.

Clerk: REV. ALISTAIR CUMMING MSc CCS FInstLM

64 Prince George's Avenue, London SW20 8BH
[E-mail: england@cofscotland.org.uk]

07534 943986 (Mbl)

Corby: St Andrew's (H)
Vacant

Corby: St Ninian's (H) (01536 265245)
Kleber Machado   1998

43 Hempland Close, Corby, Northants NN18 8LR

01536 746429

The Manse, 46 Glyndebourne Gardens, Corby, Northants NN18 0PZ   01536 352430
[E-mail: klebermachado@ymail.com]

Guernsey: St Andrew's in the Grange (H)
Graeme W. Beebee BD   1993   2003

The Manse, Le Villocq, Castel, Guernsey GY5 7SB
[E-mail: beehive@cwgsy.net]

01481 257345

Jersey: St Columba's (H)
Vacant

18 Claremont Avenue, St Saviour, Jersey JE2 7SF

01534 730659

Liverpool: St Andrew's
Guardianship of the Presbytery
Session Clerk: Mr Robert Cottle

0151-524 1915

London: Crown Court (H) (020 7836 5643)
Philip L. Majcher BD   1982   2007

53 Sidmouth Street, London WC1H 8JX
[E-mail: minister@crowncourtchurch.org.uk]

020 7278 5022

Timothy E.G. Fletcher BA FCMA (Aux)   1998

37 Harestone Valley Road, Caterham, Surrey CR3 6HN
[E-mail: fletcherts@btinternet.com]

01883 340826

London: St Columba's (H) (020 7584 2321) linked with Newcastle: St Andrew's (H)
C. Angus MacLeod MA BD   1996   2012

29 Hollywood Road, Chelsea, London SW10 9HT
[E-mail: 959macle@armymail.mod.uk]

020 7584 2321

Dorothy Lunn (Aux)   2002   2002

14 Bellerby Drive, Ouston, Co. Durham DH2 1TW
[E-mail: dorothylunn@hotmail.com]

0191-492 0647

Newcastle: St Andrew's See London: St Columba's

Name			Position	Address	Tel
Bowie, A. Glen CBE BA BSc	1954	1984	(Principal Chaplain: RAF)	16 Weir Road, Hemingford Grey, Huntingdon PE18 9EH	01480 381425
Brown, Scott J. QHC BD	1993	1993	Chaplain of the Fleet: Royal Navy	Principal Church of Scotland and Free Churches Chaplain (Naval), and Director Naval Chaplaincy Service (Capability), MP 1.2, (Mbl) Leach Building, Whale Island, Portsmouth PO2 8BY [E-mail: scott.brown943@mod.uk]	02392 625552 07769 847876
Cairns, W. Alexander BD	1978	2006	(Corby: St Andrew's)	Kirkton House, Kirkton of Craig, Montrose DD10 9TB (Mbl) [E-mail: sandy.cairns@btinternet.com]	07808 588045
Cameron, R. Neil	1975	1981	(Chaplain: Community)	[E-mail: neilandminacameron@yahoo.co.uk]	
Cherry, Alastair J. BA BD FPLD	1982	2009	(Glasgow: Penilee St Andrew's)	6 Upper Abbey Road, Belvedere, Kent DA17 5AJ [E-mail: alastair.j.cherry@btinternet.com]	01322 402818
Coulter, David G. QHC BA BD MDA PhD CF	1989	1994	Chaplain: Army	8 Ashdown Terrace, Tidworth, Wilts SP9 7SQ [E-mail: padredgcoulter@yahoo.co.uk]	01980 842175
Cross, Brian F. MA	1961	1998	(Coalburn)	1474 High Road, Whetstone, London N20 9QD	020 8492 9313
Cumming, Alistair MSc CCS FInstLM	2010		Auxiliary Minister: London: St Columba's	64 Prince George's Avenue, London SW20 8BH (Mbl) [E-mail: afcumming@hotmail.com]	020 8540 7365 07534 943986
Dalton, Mark BD DipMin RN	2002		Chaplain: Royal Navy	COMDEVFLOT, Shackleton Building MO56, Morice Yard, HMNB Devonport, Plymouth PL2 3BG [E-mail: mark.dalton242@mod.uk]	
Dowswell, James A.M.	1991	2001	(Lerwick and Bressay)	Mill House, High Street, Staplehurst, Tonbridge, Kent TN12 0AU [E-mail: jdowswell@btinternet.com]	01580 891271
Duncan, Denis M. BD PhD	1944	1986	(Editor: *The British Weekly*)	24 Caburn Court, Station Street, Lewes BN7 2DA [E-mail: denisduncan@dits.org.uk]	
Fields, James MA BD STM	1988	1997	School Chaplain	The Bungalow, The Ridgeway, Mill Hill, London NW7 1QX	020 8201 1397
Frail, Nicola BLE MBA MDiv	2000	2012	Chaplain: Army	9 Regt Army Air Corps, Dishforth Airfield, Thirsk YO7 3EZ [E-mail: nrfscot@hotmail.com]	
Francis, James BD PhD	2002	2009	Chaplain: Army	37 Millburn Road, Coleraine BT52 1QT	02870 353869 01206 563638
Kingston, David V.F. BD DipPTh	1993		Chaplain: Army	The Chaplain's Office, HQ Colchester Garrison, Gryphon House, Merville Barracks, Colchester CO2 7UT (Mbl) [E-mail: d.v.f.k@btinternet.com]	07802 417947
Langlands, Cameron H. BD MTh ThM PhD MInstLM	1995	2009	Pastoral and Spiritual Care Manager: Lancashire Teaching Hospitals NHS Trust	Department of Pastoral and Spiritual Care, Lancashire Teaching Hospitals NHS Foundation Trust, Royal Preston Hospital, Sharoe Green Lane, Fulwood, Preston PR2 9HT [E-mail: cameron.langlands@lthtr.nhs.uk]	01772 522350
Lovett, Mairi F. BSc BA DipPS MTh	2005	2013	Hospital Chaplain	Royal Brompton Hospital, Sydney Street, London SW3 6NP [E-mail: m.lovett@rbht.nhs.uk]	020 7352 8121 ext. 4736
Lugton, George L. MA BD	1955	1997	(Guernsey: St Andrew's in the Grange)	6 Clos de Beauvoir, Rue Cohu, Guernsey GY5 7TE (Tel/Fax)	01481 254285
Macfarlane, Peter T. BA LTh	1970	1994	(Chaplain: Army)	4 rue de Rives, 37160 Abilly, France	
McIndoe, John H. MA BD STM DD	1966	2000	(London: St Columba's with Newcastle: St Andrew's)	5 Dunlin, Westerlands Park, Glasgow G12 0FE [E-mail: johnandeve@mcindoe555.fsnet.co.uk]	0141-579 1366

Name	Dates	Role	Address	Telephone
MacLeod, Rory N. MA BD	1986 1992	Chaplain: Army	39 Regt, Royal Regiment of Artillery, Albemarle Barracks, Harlow Hill, Newcastle-upon-Tyne NE15 0RF	01344 754098
McMahon, John K.S. MA BD	1998 2012	Head of Spiritual and Pastoral Care, West London Mental Health Trust	Broadmoor Hospital, Crowthorne, Berkshire RG45 7EG [E-mail: john.mcmahonrev@wlmht.nhs.uk]	
Mather, James BA DipArch MA MBA	2010	Auxiliary Minister: University Chaplain	24 Ellison Road, Barnes, London SW13 0AD [E-mail: jsm.johnstonmather@btinternet.com]	(Home) 020 8876 6540 (Work) 020 7361 1670 (Mbl) 07836 715655
Middleton, Paul BMus BD ThM PhD	2000	University Lecturer	97B Whipcord Lane, Chester CH1 4DG	
Munro, Alexander W. MA BD	1978	Chaplain and Teacher of Religious Studies	Columba House, 12 Alexandra Road, Southport PR9 0NB [E-mail: awmunro@tiscali.co.uk]	01704 543044
Pickles, Robert G.D.W. BD MPhil ThD	2003 2010	(Orwell and Portmoak)	Chadacres, 49 Rotton Park Road, Birmingham B16 0SG [E-mail: robert.pickles@btopenworld.com]	0121-454 4046
Rennie, Alistair McR. MA BD	1939 1986	(Kincardine Croick and Edderton)	Noble's Yard, St Mary's Gate, Wirksworth, Derbyshire DE4 4DQ [E-mail: alistairrennie@lineone.net]	01629 820289
Shackleton, Scott J.S. QCVS BA BD PhD RN	1993 2010	Chaplain: Royal Navy	HQ 3 Commando Brigade, RMB Stonehouse, Durnford Street, Plymouth PL1 3QS [E-mail: shackletonscott@hotmail.com]	01752 836397
Trevorrow, James A. LTh	1971 2003	(Glasgow: Cranhill)	12 Test Green, Corby, Northants NN17 2HA [E-mail: jimtrevorrow@compuserve.com]	01536 264018
Walker, R. Forbes BSc BD ThM	1987 2000	School Chaplain	2 Holmleigh, Priory Road, Ascot, Berks SL5 8EA [E-mail: revfw@gmail.com]	01344 883272
Wallace, Donald S.	1950 1980	(Chaplain: RAF)	7 Delfield Close, Watford, Herts WD1 3BL	01923 223289
Ward, Michael J. BSc BD PhD MA PGCE	1983 2009	Training and Development Officer: Presbyterian Church of Wales	Apt 6, Bryn Hedd, Conwy Road, Penmaen-mawr, Gwynedd LL34 6BS [E-mail: revmw@btopenworld.com]	(Mbl) 07765 598816
Wood, Peter J. MA BD	1993	(College Lecturer)	97 Broad Street, Cambourne, Cambridgeshire CB23 6DH [E-mail: pejowood@tiscali.co.uk]	01954 715558

ENGLAND – Church Addresses

Corby: St Andrew's　Occupation Road
St Ninian's　Beanfield Avenue

Liverpool: The Western Rooms, Anglican Cathedral

London: Crown Court　Crown Court WC2
St Columba's　Pont Street SW1

Newcastle: Sandyford Road

(48) EUROPE

Clerk: [E-mail: europe@cofscotland.org.uk]

Amsterdam
Vacant
Jan Willem Brouwersstraat 9, NL-1071 LH Amsterdam, The Netherlands
[E-mail: minister@ercadam.nl]
0031 20 672 2288

Brussels (E-mail: secretary@churchofscotland.be)
Andrew Gardner BSc BD PhD   1997   2004
23 Square des Nations, B-1000 Brussels, Belgium
[E-mail: minister@churchofscotland.be]
0032 2 672 40 56

Budapest (Church telephone: 0036 1 373 0725)
Aaron Stevens   2010
H-1143, Stefánia út 32, Budapest, Hungary
[E-mail: revastevens@yahoo.co.uk]
(Mbl) 0036 70 615 5394

Colombo, Sri Lanka: St Andrew's Scots Kirk
Vacant
73 Galle Road, Colpetty, Colombo 3, Sri Lanka
[E-mail: reverend@sltnet.lk]
0094 (11) 2386774

Costa del Sol
Morris M. Dutch BD BA DipBTI   1998   2011
The Manse, Avenida Jesus Santos Rein, 24 Edf. Lindamar 4 – 3Q, Fuengirola, 29640 Malaga. Spain
[E-mail: mmdutch@yahoo.co.uk]
0034 951 260 982

Geneva
Ian A. Manson BA BD   1989   2001
20 Ancienne Route, 1218 Grand Saconnex, Geneva, Switzerland
[E-mail: cofsg@pingnet.ch]
0041 22 798 29 09
(Office) 0041 22 788 08 31

Gibraltar
Ewen MacLean BA BD   1995   2009
St Andrew's Manse, 29 Scud Hill, Gibraltar
[E-mail: scotskirk@gibraltar.gi]
00350 200 77040

Name			Address	Telephone
Lausanne Ian J.M. McDonald MA BD	1984	2010	26 Avenue de Rumine, CH-1005 Lausanne, Switzerland [E-mail: minister@scotskirklausanne.ch]	0041 21 323 98 28
Lisbon Vacant			Rua da Arriaga 13, 1200-625 Lisbon, Portugal [E-mail: cofslx@netcabo.pt]	00351 218 043 410
Malta T. Douglas McRoberts BD CPS FRSA	1975	2009	La Romagnola, 15 Triq is-Seiqia, Misrah Kola, Attard ATD 1713, Malta [E-mail: doug.mcroberts@btinternet.com] Church address: 210 Old Bakery Street, Valletta, Malta [E-mail: minister@saintandrewsmalta.com]	(Tel/Fax) 00356 214 15465
Paris James M. Cowie BD	1977	2011	10 Rue Thimmonier, F-75009 Paris, France [E-mail: jimcowie@europe.com]	0033 1 48 78 47 94
Regensburg (University) Rhona Dunphy (Mrs) BD DPTheol	2005		Liskircherstrasse 9, D-93049 Regensburg, Germany [E-mail: rhona@dunphy.de]	(Mbl) 0049 (0) 176 83 10 69 67
Rome: St Andrew's William B. McCulloch BD	1997	2002	Via XX Settembre 7, 00187 Rome, Italy [E-mail: revwbmcculloch@hotmail.com]	(Tel) 0039 06 482 7627 (Fax) 0039 06 487 4370
Rotterdam (Church telephone: 0031 10 412 4779) Robert A. Calvert BSc BD DMin	1983	1995	Church address: Schiedamse Vest 119–121, NL-2012 BH Rotterdam, The Netherlands Meeuwenstraat 4A, NL-3071 PE Rotterdam, The Netherlands [E-mail: scotsintchurch@cs.com]	0031 10 220 4199
Trinidad Garwell Bacchas			50 Frederick Street, Port of Spain, Trinidad [E-mail: revbacchas@gmail.com]	001 868 627 9312

Turin
Vacant
Via S. Pio V 17, 10125 Torino, Italy
[E-mail: esc.torino@alice.it]
Church address: Via Sant Anselmo 6, 10125 Turin, Italy
0039 011 650 5770
0039 011 650 9467

Warwick, Bermuda: Christ Church
Barry W. Dunsmore MA BD   1982   2009
Mailing address: PO Box PG88, Paget PG BX, Bermuda   (Office) 001 441 236 1882
Church address: Christ Church, Middle Road, Warwick, Bermuda
[E-mail: christchurch@logic.bm; Website: www.christchurch.bm]
Manse address: The Manse, 6 Manse Road, Paget PG 01, Bermuda

David P. Anderson BSc BD   2002
Irene Bom (Ordained Local Minister: 2008   2007
worship resourcing)
SCOTSDG, Wessex Barracks, Fallingbostel, Germany, BFPO 38
Bergpolderstraat 53A, NL-3038 KB Rotterdam, The Netherlands   0031 10 265 1703
[E-mail: ibsalem@xs4all.nl]

James M. Brown MA BD   1982
Neustrasse 15, D-44787 Bochum, Germany   0049 234 133 65
[E-mail: j.brown56@gmx.de]

James S. Dick MA BTh   1988   1997
[E-mail: jim.s.dick@googlemail.com]   0049 9131 52443

Professor A.I.C. Heron MA BD DTheol   1975   1987
Priessnitzstrasse 10, D-91056 Erlangen, Germany
[E-mail: arheron@gmx.de]

Derek G. Lawson LLB BD   1998   2011
2 Rue Joseph Guillemot, F-87210 Oradour St Genest, France   00 33 5 55 68 53 03
[E-mail: derek.lawson@sfr.fr]

Paraic Reamonn BA BD   1982
359B Route de Mandement, CH-1281 Russin, Switzerland   0041 22 776 4834
[E-mail: paraic.reamonn@gmail.com]

James Sharp (Ordained Local Minister: 2005
pastoral training and support)
102 Rue des Eaux-Vives, CH-1207 Geneva, Switzerland   0041 22 786 4847
[E-mail: jimsharp@bluewin.ch]

(Turin)   Alexander B. Cairns MA   1957   2009
Beechwood, Main Street, Sandhead, Stranraer DG9 9JG   01560 486879
(Bermuda)   T. Alan W. Garrity BSc BD MTh   1969   2008
17 Solomon's View, Dunlop, Kilmarnock KA3 4ES
[E-mail: alangarrity@btinternet.com]

(Rome)   David F. Huie MA BD   1962   2001
15 Rosebank Gardens, Largs KA30 8TD   01475 670733
[E-mail: dfh@davidhuie35.plus.com]

(Brussels)   Charles C. McNeill OBE BD   1962   1991
17 All Saints Way, Beachamwell, Swaffham, Norfolk PE37 8BU
(Brussels)   Thomas C. Pitkeathly MA CA BD   1984   2004
1 Lammermuir Court, Gullane EH31 2HU
(Rotterdam)   Joost Pot BSc (Auxiliary Minister)   1992   2004
[E-mail: joostpot@gmail.com]
(Colombo)   John P.S. Purves MBE BSc BD   1978
37 Hollywood, Largs KA30 8SR   01620 843373
(Budapest)   Bertalan Tamas   2013
Pozsonyi út 34, Budapest H-1137, Hungary   0036 1 239 6315
[E-mail: bertalantamas@hotmail.com]   (Mbl) 0036 30 638 6647

(49) JERUSALEM

Clerk:	MR J.G. MAXWELL	Tabeetha School, PO Box 8170, Jaffa 61081, Israel	(Home)	00972 3 657 2003
		[E-mail: jmaxwell@churchofscotland.org.il]	(Mbl)	00972 52 374 0235
		[E-mail: jimmymaxwell27@yahoo.com]		

Jerusalem: St Andrew's				
George C. Shand MA BD	1981	2009	St Andrew's Scots Memorial Church, 1 David Remez Street, PO Box 8619, Jerusalem 91086, Israel [E-mail: stachjer@netvision.net.il]	(Tel) 00972 2 673 2401
Tiberias: St Andrew's				
Colin D. Johnston MA BD	1986	2009	St Andrew's, Galilee, 1 Gdud Barak Street, PO Box 104, Tiberias 14100, Israel [E-mail: revcdj60@gmail.com]	(Tel) 00972 4 671 0759

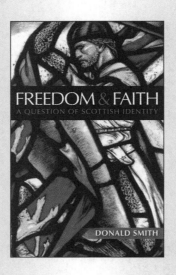

FREEDOM & FAITH

A Question of Scottish Identity

Donald Smith
Introduction by Harry Reid

978-0-86153-813-3 (paperback)

See our website for details of this (out late November 2013)
and other new titles including *Revealing Love: Pray Now Monthly
Devotions & Daily Prayers* and *Looking for Mrs Livingstone.*
www.standrewpress.com

SAINT ANDREW PRESS

SECTION 6

Additional Lists of Personnel

LIST A – ORDAINED LOCAL MINISTERS

NAME	ORD	ADDRESS	TEL	PR
Bom, Irene	2008	Bergpolderstraat 53A, NL-3038 KB Rotterdam, The Netherlands	0031 10 265 1703	48
Breingan, Mhairi	2011	6 Park Road, Inchinnan, Renfrew PA4 4QJ	0141-812 1425	14
Don, Andrew MBA	2006	5 Eskdale Court, Penicuik EH26 8HT	01968 675766	3
Duncan, Esme (Miss)	2013	Avalon, Upper Warse, Canisbay, Wick KW1 4YD	01955 611455	41
Duncanson, Mary (Ms)	2013	3 Balmenach Road, Cromdale, Grantown-on-Spey PH26 3LJ	01479 872165	36
Fidler, David G.	2013	34 Guardhouse Park, Stromness, Orkney KW16 3DP	01856 850575	45
Fulcher, Christine	2012	St Blaan's Manse, Southend, Campbeltown PA28 6RQ	01586 830504	19
Hardman Moore, Susan (Prof.) BA PGCE MA PhD	2013	c/o New College, Mound Place, Edinburgh EH1 2LX	0131-650 8908	1
Harvey, Joyce (Mrs)	2013	4A Allanfield Place, Newton Stewart DG8 6BS	01671 403693	9
Hickman, Mandy R. RGN	2013	Lagnaleon, 4 Wilson Street, Largs KA30 9AQ	01475 675347	12
Hughes, Barry MA	2011	Dunslair, Cardrona Way, Cardrona, Peebles EH45 9LD	01896 831197	4
Johnston, June E. BSc MEd BD	2013	49 Braeside Road South, Gorebridge EH23 4DL	01875 823086	3
McAllister, Anne C. (Mrs)	2013	39 Bowes Rigg, Stewarton, Kilmarnock KA3 5EN	01560 483191	11
Macdonald, Ishabel	2011	18 Carinish, Isle of North Uist HS6 5HN		43
Mack, Lynne (Mrs)	2013	36 Middleton, Menstrie FK11 7HD	01259 761465	23
MacLeod, Iain A.	2012	6 Hallydown Drive, Glasgow G13 1UF (Mbl)	07795 014889	16
Michie, Margaret (Mrs)	2013	3 Loch Leven Court, Wester Balgedie, Kinross KY13 9NE	01592 840602	28
Morrison, John BSc BA PGCE	2013	35 Kirkton Place, Elgin IV30 6JR	01343 550199	35
Muirhead, Morag (Mrs)	2013	6 Dumbarton Road, Fort William PH33 6UU	01397 703643	38
Nicol, Robert	2013	3 Castlegreen Road, Thurso KW14 7DN		41
Perkins, Mairi (Mrs)	2012	Ashlea, Cuil Road, Duror, Appin PA38 3DA (Work)	01631 740313	38
Prentice, Martin	2013	Cott of Howe, Cairston, Stromness, Orkney KW16 3JU	01856 851139	45
Rennie, Lyall	2013	Ruachmarra, Lower Warse, Canisbay, Wick KW1 4YB	01955 611756	41
Sanders, Martyn S. BA CertEd MA	2013	26 Wood Avenue, Annan DG12 6DA (Mbl)	07830 697976	7
Sarle, Andrew BSc BD	2013	114 High Station Road, Falkirk FK1 5LN	01324 621648	22
Sharp, James	2005	102 Rue des Eaux-Vives, CH-1207 Geneva, Switzerland	0041 22 786 4847	48
Stevenson, Stuart	2011	143 Springfield Park, Johnstone PA5 8JT	0141-886 2131	14
Stewart, Heather (Mrs)	2013	Burnthill, Thrunster, Wick KW1 5AX	01955 651717	41
Stobo, Mary J. (Mrs)	2013	Druim-an-Sgairnich, Ardgay IV24 3BG	01863 766868	40
Strachan, Willie MBA DipY&C	2013	Ladywell House, Lucky Slap, Monikie, Dundee DD5 3QG	01382 370286	29
Tweedie, Fiona PhD	2011	44 Campbell Park Crescent, Edinburgh EH13 0HT		1
Wallace, Mhairi (Mrs)	2013	The Manse, Manse Road, Twynholm, Kirkcudbright DG6 4NY	01557 860381	8
Watson, Michael D.	2013	47 Crichton Terrace, Pathhead EH37 5QZ	01875 320043	3

Retired:

Anderson, David M. MSc FCOptom	1984	'Mirlos', 1 Dumfries Place, Fort William PH33 6UQ	01397 702091	38

AUXILIARY MINISTERS

NAME	ORD	ADDRESS	TEL	PR
Attenburrow, Anne BSc MB ChB	2006	4 Jock Inksons Brae, Elgin IV30 1QE	01343 552330	35
Binks, Mike	2007	5 Maxwell Drive, Newton Stewart DG8 6EL	01671 402201	9
Buck, Maxine	2007	Brownlee House, Mauldslie Road, Carluke ML8 5HW	01555 759063	17
Burroughs, Kirsty-Ann (Mrs)				
BA BD CertTheol DRM PhD	2007	Lorne and Lowland Manse, Castlehill, Campbeltown PA28 6AN	01586 552468	19
Cameron, Ann J. (Mrs) CertCS DCE TEFL	2005	Currently resident in Qatar		32
Campbell, Gordon MA BD CDipAF DipHSM				
MCMI MIHM AFRIN ARSGS FRGS FSAScot				
Charlton, Richard M.	2001	2 Falkland Place, Kingoodie, Invergowrie, Dundee DD2 5DY	01382 561383	29
Cumming, Alistair	2001	The Manse, Marrister, Symbister, Whalsay, Shetland ZE2 9AE	01806 566767	46
	2010	64 Prince George's Avenue, London SW20 8BH	020 8540 7365	47
			07534 943986 (Mbl)	
Dick, Roddy S.	2010	27 Easter Crescent, Wishaw ML2 8XB	01698 383453	17
Fletcher, Timothy E.G. BA FCMA	1998	37 Hareston Valley Road, Caterham, Surrey CR3 6HN	01883 340826	47
Forrest, Kenneth P. CBE BSc PhD	2006	5 Carruth Road, Bridge of Weir PA11 3HQ	01505 612651	14
Gardner, Hilary (Miss)	2010	Cayman Lodge, Kincardine Hill, Ardgay IV24 3DJ	01863 766107	40
Griffiths, Ruth I. (Mrs)	2004	Kirkwood, Mathieson Lane, Innellan, Dunoon PA23 7TA	01369 830145	19
Hood, Catriona A.	2006	'Elyside', Dalintober, Campbeltown PA28 6EB	01586 551490	19
Howie, Marion L.K. (Mrs) MA ARCS	1992	51 High Road, Stevenston KA20 3DY	01294 466571	12
Jackson, Nancy	2009	Cygnet House, Holmfarm Road, Catrine, Mauchline KA5 6TA	01290 550511	10
Kemp, Tina MA	2005	12 Oaktree Gardens, Dumbarton G82 1EU	01389 730477	18
Landale, William S.	2005	Green Hope Guest House, Green Hope, Duns TD11 3SG	01361 890242	5
Lunn, Dorothy	2002	14 Bellerby Drive, Ouston, Co. Durham DH2 1TW	0191-492 0647	47
Macdonald, Michael	2004	73 Firhill, Alness IV17 0RT	01349 884268	40
MacDougall, Lorna I. (Miss) MA DipGC	2003	34 Millar Place, Carron, Falkirk FK2 8QB	01324 552739	22
MacGregor, Robert M. CMIOSH DipOSH RSP	2004	Olna Cottage, Brae, Shetland ZE2 9QS	01806 522604	46
Manson, Eileen (Mrs) DipCE	1994	1 Cambridge Avenue, Gourock PA19 1XT	01475 632401	14
Mather, James	2010	24 Ellison Road, Barnes, London SW13 0AD	020 8876 6540 (Home)	47
			020 7361 1670 (Work)	
			07836 715655 (Mbl)	
Moore, Douglas T.	2003	9 Milton Avenue, Prestwick KA9 1PU	01292 671352	10
Morrison, Donald John	2001	22 Kyles, Tarbert, Isle of Harris HS3 3BS	01859 502341	43
Murray, John W.	2003	1 Totescore, Kilmuir, Portree, Isle of Skye IV51 9YN	01470 542297	42
O'Donnell, Barbara	2007	Ashbank, 258 Main Street, Alexandria G83 0NU	01389 752356	18
Paterson, Andrew E. JP	1994	6 The Willows, Kelty KY4 0FQ	01383 830998	24
Perry, Marion (Mrs)	2009	17a Tarbolton Road, Cumbernauld, Glasgow G67 2AJ	01236 898519	22
			07563 180662 (Mbl)	
Ramage, Alastair E. MA BA ADB CertEd	1996	16 Claremont Gardens, Milngavie, Glasgow G62 6PG	0141-956 2897	18

NAME	ORD	ADDRESS	TEL	PR
Riddell, Thomas S. BSc CEng FIChemE	1993	4 The Maltings, Linlithgow EH49 6DS	01506 843251	2
Robson, Brenda (Dr)	2005	2 Baird Road, Ratho, Newbridge EH28 8RA	0131-333 2746	2
Russon, Grace	2011	Marelda, Park Road, Sandwick, Shetland ZE2 9HP	01950 431207	46
Shearer, Anne BA DipEd	2010	10 Colsnaur, Menstrie FK11 7HG	01259 769176	23
Sutherland, David A.	2001	6 Cromarty Drive, Dundee DD2 2UQ	01382 621473	29
Vivers, Katherine A.	2004	Blacket House, Eaglesfield, Lockerbie DG11 3AA	01461 500412	7
Walker, Linda	2008	18 Valeview Terrace, Glasgow G42 9LA	0141-649 1340	16
Wandrum, David	1993	5 Cawder View, Carrickstone Meadows, Cumbernauld, Glasgow G68 0BN	01236 723288	22
Whittaker, Mary	2011	11 Templand Road, Lhanbryde, Elgin IV30 8BR		35
Wilkie, Robert	2011	24 Huntingtower Road, Perth PH1 2JS	01738 628301	28
Zambonini, James LIADip	1997	100 Old Manse Road, Netherton, Wishaw ML2 0EP	01698 350889	17

AUXILIARY MINISTERS (RETIRED)

NAME	ORD	ADDRESS	TEL	PR
Birch, James PgDip FRSA FIOC	2001	1 Kirkhill Grove, Cambuslang, Glasgow G72 8EH	0141-583 1722	16
Brown, Elizabeth (Mrs) JP RGN	1996	8 Viewlands Place, Perth PH1 1BS	01738 552391	28
Cloggie, June (Mrs)	1997	11A Tulipan Crescent, Callander FK17 8AR	01877 331021	23
Craggs, Sheila (Mrs)	2001	7 Morar Court, Ellon AB41 9GG	01358 723055	33
Ferguson, Archibald M. MSc PhD CEng FRINA	1989	The Whins, 2 Barrowfield, Station Road, Cardross, Dumbarton G82 5NL	01389 841517	18
Glass, Alexander OBE MA	1998	Craigton, Tulloch Avenue, Dingwall IV15 9TU	01349 863258	39
Harrison, Cameron	2006	Woodfield House, Priormuir, St Andrews KY16 8LP	01334 478067	26
Jenkinson, John J. JP LTCL ALCM DipEd DipSen	1991	8 Rosehall Terrace, Falkirk FK1 1PY	01324 625498	22
Kay, Elizabeth (Miss) DipYCS	1993	1 Kintail Walk, Inchture, Perth PH14 9RY	01828 686029	29
McAlpine, John BSc	1988	Braeside, 201 Bonkle Road, Newmains, Wishaw ML2 9AA	01698 384610	17
MacDonald, Kenneth MA BA	2001	5 Henderland Road, Bearsden, Glasgow G61 1AH	0141-943 1103	16
MacFadyen, Anne M. (Mrs) BSc BD FSAScot	1995	295 Mearns Road, Glasgow G77 5LT	0141-639 3605	16
Mack, Elizabeth A. (Miss) DipPEd	1994	24 Roberts Crescent, Dumfries DG2 7RS	01387 264847	8
Mack, John C. JP	1985	The Willows, Auchleven, Insch AB52 6QB	01464 820387	33
Mailer, Colin	1996	Innis Chonain, Back Row, Polmont, Falkirk FK2 0RD	01324 712401	22
Munro, Mary (Mrs) BA	1993	14 Auchneel Crescent, Stranraer DG9 0JH	01776 702305	9
Paterson, Maureen (Mrs) BSc	1992	91 Dalmahoy Crescent, Kirkcaldy KY2 6TA	01592 262300	25
Phillippo, Michael MTh BSc BVetMed MRCVS	2003	25 Deeside Crescent, Aberdeen AB15 7PT	01224 318317	31
Pot, Joost BSc	1992	[E-mail: joostpot@gmail.com]		48
Shaw, Catherine A.M. MA	1998	40 Merrygreen Place, Stewarton, Kilmarnock KA3 5EP	01560 483352	11
Thomas, Shirley A. (Mrs) DipSocSci AMIA	2000	14 Kirkgait, Letham, Forfar DD8 2XQ	01307 818084	30
Wilson, Mary D. (Mrs) RGN SCM DTM	1990	Berbice, The Terrace, Bridge of Tilt, Blair Atholl, Pitlochry PH18 5SZ	01796 481619	27

LIST B – CHAPLAINS TO HM FORCES

NAME	ORD	COM	BCH	ADDRESS
Abeledo, Benjamin J.A. BTh DipTh PTh	1991	1999	A	HQ 51 (Scottish) Brigade, Forthside, Stirling FK7 7RR
Aitchison, James W. BD	1993		A	4 Regt RA RHQ, Alanbrooke Barracks, Topcliffe, Thirsk YO7 7EY
Anderson, David P. BSc BD	2002	2007		SCOTSDG, Wessex Barracks, Fallingbostel, Germany, BFPO 38
Berry, Geoff T. BD BSc	2009		OC	4 Bn The Royal Regiment of Scotland, Oerbke-Lager, Fallingbostel, BFPO 38
Blackwood, Keith T. BD DipMin	1997		ACF	Shetland Independent Battery, ACF, TA Centre, Fort Charlotte, Lerwick, Shetland ZE1 0JN
Blakey, Stephen A. BSc BD	1977		TA	6 Bn The Royal Regiment of Scotland, Walcheran Barracks, 122 Hotspur Street, Glasgow G20 8LQ
Blakey, Stephen A. BSc BD	1977		OC	Glasgow Universities Officers' Training Corps
Brown, Scott J. QHC BD	1993		RN	The Chaplain of the Fleet, MP 1.2, Navy Command HQ, Whale Island, Portsmouth, Hants PO2 8BY
Bryson, Thomas M. BD	1997		ACF	2 Bn The Highlanders, ACF, Royal Regiment of Scotland, Cadet Training Centre, Rocksley Drive, Boddam, Peterhead AB42 3BA
Campbell, Karen K. BD MTh DMin	1997		OC	Personnel Recovery Centre, Edinburgh
Campbell, Roderick D.M. OStJ TD BD DMin FSAScot	1975		ACF	Argyll and Sutherland Highlanders Bn, ACF, Royal Regiment of Scotland, Harfield House, Bonhill Road, Dumbarton G82 2DG
Cobain, Alan R. BD	2000		RAF	71 Engineer Regiment, RAF Leuchars, Fife KY16 0JX
Connolly, Daniel BD DipTheol DipMin	1983		A	36 Engr Regt, Kinloss Barracks, Kinloss, Forres IV36 3XL
Coulter, David G. QHC BA BD MDA PhD CF	1989	1994	A	Deputy Chaplain General, MoD Chaplains (Army), HQ Land Forces, 2nd Floor Zone 6, Ramillies Building, Marlborough Lines, Andover, Hants SP11 8HJ
Dalton, Mark BD DipMin RN	2002		RN	Chaplain to the Hydrographic Squadron, COMDEVFLOT, Shackleton Building MO56, Morice Yard, HMNB Devonport, Plymouth PL2 3BG
Davidson, Mark R. MA BD STM RN	2005		RN	The Chaplaincy, HMS *Neptune*, HMNB Clyde, Faslane, Helensburgh G84 8HL
Davidson Kelly, Thomas A. MA BD FSAScot	1975		OC	Army Personnel Centre, Glasgow
Dicks, Shuna M. BSc BD	2010		ACF	2 Bn The Highlanders, ACF, Royal Regiment of Scotland, Cadet Training Centre, Rocksley Drive, Boddam, Peterhead AB42 3BA
Duncan, John C. BD MPhil	1987	2001	A	3 Bn The Black Watch, The Royal Regiment of Scotland, Fort George, Ardersier, Inverness IV1 2TD
Frail, Nicola BLE MBA MDiv	2000		A	9 Regt Army Air Corps, Dishforth Airfield, Thirsk YO7 3EZ
Francis, James BD PhD	2002	2009		School of Signals, Blandford Camp, Blandford, Dorset DT11 8RH
Gardner, Neil N. MA BD	1991		OC	Edinburgh Universities Officers' Training Corps
Goodison, Michael J. BSc BA	2013		A	
Kellock, Chris N. MA BD	1998		A	7 Para RHA, Merville Barracks, Colchester CO2 7UT
Kennon, Stanley BA BD RN	1992	2000	RN	Church of Scotland and Free Churches Chaplain, Britannia Royal Naval College, Dartmouth, Devon TQ6 0HJ
Kingston, David V.F. BD DipPTh	1993		A	HQ Colchester Garrison, Gryphon House, Merville Barracks, Colchester CO2 7UT
Kinsey, Louis BD DipMin TD	1991		TA	205 (Scottish) Field Hospital (V), Graham House, Whitefield Road, Glasgow G51 6JU
Lancaster, Craig MA BD	2004	2011	RAF	Station Chaplain, RAF Leuchars, St Andrews KY16 0JX

Name	Year	Branch	Unit / Address
Logan, David BD MA FRSA	2009	ACF	Black Watch Bn, ACF, Royal Regiment of Scotland, Queen's Barracks, 131 Dunkeld Road, Perth PH1 5BT
McCulloch, Alen J.R. MA BD	1990	ACF	Cornwall ACF. 7 Castle Canyke Road, Bodmin PL31 1DX
MacDonald, Roderick I.T. BD CertMin	1992	ACF	West Lowland Bn, ACF, Royal Regiment of Scotland, Fusilier House, Seaforth Road, Ayr KA8 9HX
MacKay, Stewart A.	2009	A	2 Bn The Parachute Regiment, Merville Barracks, Colchester CO2 7UT
Mackenzie, Cameron BD	2011	ACF	Lothian and Borders Bn, ACF, Royal Regiment of Scotland, Drumshoreland House, Broxburn EH52 5PF
Mackenzie, Hector M.	2008	A	3 Bn The Parachute Regiment, Merville Barracks, Colchester CO2 7UT
Mackenzie, Seoras L. BD	1996	A	Carver Barracks, Wimbish, Saffron Walden CB10 2YA
McLaren, William MA BD	1990	ACF	Angus and Dundee Bn, ACF, Royal Regiment of Scotland, Barry Buddon, Carnoustie DD7 7RY
McLaren, William MA BD	1990	A	225 GS Med Regt
McLay, Neil BA BD	2006	A	QRH, Athlone Barracks, Sennelager, Germany, BFPO 16
MacLean, Marjory A. LLB BD PhD RNR	1991	RNR	HMS *Scotia*, MoD Caledonia, Hilton Road, Rosyth, Dunfermline KY11 2XH
MacLeod, Rory N. MA BD	1986	A	39 Regt, Royal Regiment of Artillery, Albemarle Barracks, Harlow Hill, Newcastle-upon-Tyne NE15 0RF
MacPherson, Duncan J. BSc BD	1993	A	HQ Hereford Garrison, Hereford HR4 7DD
Mathieson, Angus R. MA BD	1988	OC	Edinburgh Garrison
Munro, Sheila BD	1995	RAF	RAF Lossiemouth, Elgin IV31 6SD
Rowe, Christopher J. BA BD	2008	TA	32 (Scottish) Signal Regiment, 21 Jardine Street, Glasgow G20 6JU
Selemani, Ecilo LTh MTh	1993	ACF	Glasgow and Lanark Bn, ACF, Royal Regiment of Scotland, Gilbertfield Road, Cambuslang, Glasgow G72 8YP
Shackleton, Scott J.S. QCVS BA BD PhD RN	1993	RN	HQ 3 Commando Brigade, RMB Stonehouse, Durnford Street, Plymouth PL1 3QS
Stewart, Fraser M.C. BSc BD	1980	ACF	1 Bn The Highlanders, ACF, Royal Regiment of Scotland, Gordonville Road, Inverness IV2 4SU
van Sittert, Paul BA BD	1997	A	1 Bn The Royal Regiment of Scotland, Dreghorn Barracks, Edinburgh EH13 9QW
Whiteford, Alexander LTh	1996	OC	Fort George and Cameron Barracks, Inverness
Wylie, Jonathan		RAF	RAF Honington, Bury St Edmunds, Suffolk IP31 1EE

LIST C – HOSPITAL CHAPLAINS

NHS LOTHIAN

Head of Service, Spiritual Care and Bereavement
Alexander W. Young
Lead Chaplain
Caroline Applegath

Spiritual Care Offices: 0131-242 1990; 0131-537 6516

The Royal Infirmary of Edinburgh
51 Little France Crescent, Edinburgh EH16 4SA (0131-536 1000)
Liberton Hospital
113 Lasswade Road, Edinburgh EH16 6UB (0131-536 7800)
Alexander W. Young	0131-242 1990/1
Anne Mulligan	0131-242 1996
Iain Telfer	0131-242 1997

The Western General Hospital
Crewe Road South, Edinburgh EH4 2XU (0131-537 1000)
Alistair Ridland	0131-537 1400
Liz Markey	0131-537 1401

The Royal Hospital for Sick Children
9 Sciennes Road, Edinburgh EH9 1LF (0131-536 0000)
Caroline Applegath	0131-536 0144

St John's Hospital
Howden Road West, Livingston EH54 6PP (01506 523000)
Georgina Nelson	01506 522188
Joe Gierasik	01506 522187

The Royal Edinburgh Hospital
Morningside Place, Edinburgh EH10 5HF (0131-537 6000)
Lynne MacMurchie	0131-537 6368
Maxwell Reay	0131-537 6366

Edinburgh Community Mental Health (Community Office 0131-220 5159)
Lynne MacMurchie	0131-537 6368
Maxwell Reay	0131-537 6366

Corstorphine
136 Corstorphine Road, Edinburgh EH12 6TT (0131-459 7200)
Rosemary Bayne	0131-537 6516

Seafield Street, Edinburgh EH6 7LN (0131-454 2200)
Trisha Murphy-Black	0131-537 6516

Linlithgow St Michael's
Edinburgh Road, Linlithgow EH49 6QS (01506 842053)
Dr Georgina Nelson	01506 522188

Herdmanflat
Aberlady Road, Haddington EH41 3BU (0131-536 8300)
Rosemary Bayne	0131-537 6516

Roodlands
Hospital Road, Haddington EH41 3PF (0131-536 8300)
Rosemary Bayne	0131-537 6516

Bonnyrigg Community Hospital
70 Eskbank Road, Bonnyrigg EH22 3ND (0131-454 1001)
Trisha Murphy-Black	0131-537 6516

Belhaven
Beveridge Row, Dunbar EH42 1TR (01368 862246)
Laurence H. Twaddle   01368 863098
St Columba's Hospice
Kirklands House, Gogarmuir Road, Gogarbank, Edinburgh EH12 9BZ
Donald Reid   0131-551 1381
Marie Curie Hospice, Edinburgh
Frogston Road West, Edinburgh EH10 7DR
Patrick Ryan   0131-470 2201

For further information and full details of all e-mail/telephone contacts, see www.nhslothian.scot.nhs.uk/Services/A-Z/SpiritualCare

BORDERS

MELROSE –   Rev. Anna Garvie   Chaplaincy Centre, Borders General Hospital,   01896 826564
BORDERS GENERAL HOSPITAL   Mr David Thaw   Melrose TD6 9BS
(These Chaplains also serve the Community Hospitals: Hay Lodge (Peebles), Knoll (Duns), Kelso, Hawick and Eyemouth.)

DUMFRIES AND GALLOWAY

DUMFRIES AND GALLOWAY
ROYAL INFIRMARY
THOMAS HOPE, LANGHOLM
LOCHMABEN
MOFFAT
NEW ANNAN   Rev. Mairi C. Byers   Meadowbank, Plumdon Road, Annan DG12 6SJ   01461 206512
CASTLE DOUGLAS
KIRKCUDBRIGHT   Rev. Douglas R. Irving   6 Bourtree Avenue, Kirkcudbright DG6 4AU   01557 330489
THORNHILL
NEWTON STEWART
STRANRAER: GALLOWAY COMMUNITY

AYRSHIRE AND ARRAN

Chaplaincy Services Manager   Rev. Sheila M. Mitchell   Ailsa Hospital, Ayr KA6 6BQ   01292 513197
AILSA HOSPITAL, AYR   Rev. Sheila M. Mitchell   Ailsa Hospital, Ayr KA6 6BQ   01292 513197
AYR HOSPITAL/BIGGART HOSPITAL   Rev. Paul R. Russell   23 Nursery Wynd, Ayr KA7 3NZ   (Work) 01292 614587

AYRSHIRE CENTRAL	Rev. Alex M. Welsh	8 Greenside Avenue, Prestwick KA9 2HB	(Work)	01563 826128
CROSSHOUSE HOSPITAL, KILMARNOCK	Rev. Alex M. Welsh	8 Greenside Avenue, Prestwick KA9 2HB	(Work)	01563 826128
	Rev. Judith A. Huggett	4 Westmoor Crescent, Kilmarnock KA1 1TX	(Work)	01563 827301
STAFF CARE AND OCCUPATIONAL HEALTH	Rev. Roderick H. McNidder	6 Hollow Park, Alloway, Ayr KA7 4SR		01292 442554
EAST AYRSHIRE	Rev. Judith A. Huggett	4 Westmoor Crescent, Kilmarnock KA1 1TX	(Work)	01563 827301
WAR MEMORIAL, ARRAN	Rev. Elizabeth R.L. Watson	The Manse, Whiting Bay, Brodick, Isle of Arran KA27 8RE		01770 700289
LADY MARGARET, MILLPORT	Rev. Sheila M. Mitchell	Ailsa Hospital, Ayr KA6 6BQ		01292 513197
GIRVAN	Rev. Sheila M. Mitchell	Ailsa Hospital, Ayr KA6 6BQ		01292 513197
ARROLL PARK	Rev. Sheila M. Mitchell	Ailsa Hospital, Ayr KA6 6BQ		01292 513197

LANARKSHIRE

Head of Spiritual Care, NHS Lanarkshire	Rev. Robert P. Devenny	Law House, Airdrie Road, Carluke ML8 5ER	01698 377637
LADY HOME	Rev. Susan G. Cowell	3 Gavel Lane, Regency Gardens, Lanark ML11 9FB	01555 665509
LOCKHART	Rev. Alison A. Meikle	2 Kaimhill Court, Lanark ML11 9HU	01555 662600
CLELAND	Rev. John A. Jackson	The Manse, Bellside Road, Cleland, Motherwell ML1 5NP	01698 860260
KELLO	Rev. Susan G. Cowell	3 Gavel Lane, Regency Gardens, Lanark ML11 9FB	01555 665509
WISHAW GENERAL	Rev. Sharon E.F. Colvin	25 Balblair Road, Airdrie ML6 6GQ	01236 590796
	Rev. Mhorag MacDonald	350 Kirk Road, Wishaw ML2 8LH	01698 381305
	Rev. Kathryn Smith-Anderson	Wishaw General Hospital, 50 Nenthorn Street, Wishaw ML2 0DP	01698 366779
STRATHCLYDE	Rev. David W. Doyle	19 Orchard Street, Motherwell ML1 3JE	01698 263472
HAIRMYRES	Rev. James S.G. Hastie	Hairmyres Hospital, Eaglesham Road, East Kilbride, Glasgow G75 8RG	01355 584301
	Rev. Patricia Johnston	Hairmyres Hospital, Eaglesham Road, East Kilbride, Glasgow G75 8RG	01355 584301
(Mental Health)	Marian McElhinney	Hairmyres Hospital, Eaglesham Road, East Kilbride, Glasgow G75 8RG	01355 584669
STONEHOUSE	Rev. Marjorie Taylor	25 Balblair Road, Airdrie ML6 6GQ	01698 794000
UDSTON	Rev. Sharon E.F. Colvin	Udston Hospital, Farm Road, Burnbank, Hamilton ML3 9LA	01236 590796
NORTH LANARKSHIRE Community Chaplain	Major James Bryden	Airdrie Community Health Clinic, 84–88 Graham Street, Airdrie ML6 6DE	01698 723200
	Rev. David Parker	14 Love Drive, Bellshill ML4 1BY	01236 772269
COATHILL	Rev. James Grier		01698 742545
	Rev. David Parker		01236 772269
MONKLANDS	Rev. Helen Mee	Monklands Hospital, Monkscourt Avenue, Airdrie ML6 0JS	01236 712607
	Rev. Christian Okeke	Monklands Hospital, Monkscourt Avenue, Airdrie ML6 0JS	01236 712607
WESTER MOFFAT	Rev. Helen Mee		01236 712607
	Rev. David Parker		01236 772269
CRAIGHOUSE	Rev. Derek Pope	35 Birrens Road, Motherwell ML1 3NS	01698 266716

GREATER GLASGOW AND CLYDE

Head of Chaplaincy and Spiritual Care

Hospital	Chaplain(s) / Notes	Telephone
GLASGOW ROYAL INFIRMARY (GRI); THE PRINCESS ROYAL MATERNITY HOSPITAL; LIGHTBURN HOSPITAL	Rev. Blair Robertson, Rev. Adam Plenderleith, Rev. Tim Bennison, Mayra Gomez-Sorto	0141-201 2156 0141-211 4661 [E-mail: blair.robertson@ggc.scot.nhs.uk]
BEATSON WEST OF SCOTLAND CANCER CENTRE; GARTNAVEL GENERAL HOSPITAL (GGH) and GLASGOW WESTERN INFIRMARY; BLAWARTHILL HOSPITAL; DRUMCHAPEL HOSPITAL; GLASGOW HOMOEOPATHIC HOSPITAL	Rev. Keith Saunders and Rev. Anne Dougall	Glasgow Western Infirmary Chaplains' Office: 0141-211 2812 Gartnavel General Hospital Chaplains' Office: 0141-211 3026
ROYAL HOSPITAL FOR SICK CHILDREN AT YORKHILL	Rev. Jim Meighan	0141-201 0595
SOUTHERN GENERAL HOSPITAL (SGH)	Rev. Blair Robertson, Rev. Ann Purdie, Mr Andrew Gillies, Rev. Ishaku Bitrus, Imam Mohammed Ishaq (p/t)	0141-201 2156 / 2357
VICTORIA INFIRMARY (VI); MANSIONHOUSE UNIT; MEARNSKIRK HOSPITAL		0141-201 5164
GARTNAVEL ROYAL HOSPITAL (GRH) and Mental Health units in western Glasgow	Rev. Dr Kevin Franz	0141-211 3686
STOBHILL HOSPITAL SITE: THE ORCHARDS; BIRDSTON HOSPITAL; PARKHEAD HOSPITAL; FOURHILLS NURSING HOME; GREENFIELD PARK NURSING HOME	Rev. Jim Meighan	0141-531 5908
LEVERNDALE HOSPITAL and Mental Health units in southern Glasgow	Anne MacDonald DCS	0141-211 6695
RUTHERGLEN ROWANTREE/RODGER PARK NURSING HOME NHS Partnership Beds	Anne MacDonald DCS (Leverndale Hospital Chaplaincy)	0141-211 6695
DARNLEY COURT NURSING HOME	Carmichael and Fleming Wards: contact Leverndale Hospital Chaplaincy Beaton Ward: contact SGH Chaplaincy	
ROYAL ALEXANDRA HOSPITAL, PAISLEY	Rev. Carol Campbell, Rev. Andrew Davis, Rev. Philip Craven	0141-314 9561
INVERCLYDE ROYAL HOSPITAL (IRH) and RAVENSCRAIG HOSPITAL, GREENOCK		01475 504759
VALE OF LEVEN HOSPITAL	Rev. Carol Campbell, Rev. Andrew Davis	0141-314 9561
DYKEBAR HOSPITAL and DUMBARTON JOINT HOSPITAL		0141-314 4211

FORTH VALLEY

Head of Spiritual Care

Role / Unit	Name	Address	Phone
FORTH VALLEY ROYAL	Rev. Margery Collin	Forth Valley Royal Hospital, Larbert FK5 4WR	01324 566072
	Rev. Robert MacLeod	Forth Valley Royal Hospital, Larbert FK5 4WR	01324 566073
	Ms Mary Anne Burgoyne	Forth Valley Royal Hospital, Larbert FK5 4WR	01324 566071
	Rev. Helen Christie	5 Watson Place, Dennyloanhead, Bonnybridge FK4 2BG	01324 813786
MENTAL HEALTH UNITS	Rev. Timothy Njuguna	Forth Valley Royal Hospital, Larbert FK5 4WR	01324 566075
BO'NESS	Mr Frank Hartley	49 Argyll Place, Kilsyth, Glasgow G65 0PY	01236 824135
FALKIRK COMMUNITY	Rev. Helen Christie	5 Watson Place, Dennyloanhead, Bonnybridge FK4 2BG	01324 813786
CLACKMANNAN COUNTY	Rev. Helen Cook	Forth Valley Royal Hospital, Larbert FK5 4WR	01324 566072
STIRLING COMMUNITY	Rev. James Landels	Allan Manse, Bogend Road, Bannockburn, Stirling FK7 8NP	01786 814692

FIFE

Head of Spiritual Care

Role / Unit	Name	Address	Phone
	Mr Mark Evans DCS	Department of Spiritual Care, Queen Margaret Hospital, Whitefield Road, Dunfermline KY12 0SU [E-mail: mark.evans59@nhs.net]	01383 674136
VICTORIA HOSPITAL, KIRKCALDY: Healthcare Chaplains (Acute)	Mr Damian Murray	Victoria Hospital, Hayfield Road, Kirkcaldy KY2 5AH	01592 648158
	Miss Sharon Dick	Victoria Hospital, Hayfield Road, Kirkcaldy KY2 5AH	01592 648158
STRATHEDEN HOSPITAL, CUPAR	Mr Allan Grant	Chaplain's Office, Stratheden Hospital, Stratheden, Cupar KY15 5RR [E-mail: allan.grant@nhs.net]	07795 627697
ADAMSON HOSPITAL, CUPAR: Community Healthcare Chaplain	Rev. Lynn Brady	Adamson Hospital, Bank Street, Cupar KY15 4JG [E-mail: revbrady1963@yahoo.co.uk]	07815 922889
CENTRAL FIFE (CAMERON; GLENROTHES; RANDOLPH WEMYSS): Community Healthcare Chaplain	Miss Lynda Wright DCS	Chaplain's Office, Main Administration Block, Cameron Hospital, Cameron Bridge, Windygates, Leven KY8 5RR [E-mail: lynda.wright1@nhs.net]	07835 303395
ST ANDREWS: Community Healthcare Chaplain	Rev. Dr James Connolly	St Andrews Community Hospital and Health Centre, Largo Road, St Andrews KY16 8AR [E-mail: jamesconnolly@nhs.net]	07711 177655
Community Chaplaincy Listening (Scotland): National Coordinator	Miss Lynda Wright DCS	[E-mail: lynda.wright1@nhs.net]	07835 303395

TAYSIDE

Head of Spiritual Care

Role / Unit	Name	Address	Phone
	Rev. Gillian Munro	Wellbeing Cottage, Royal Victoria Hospital, Dundee DD2 5NF	01382 423116
Staff Support	Mr David Gordon	Wellbeing Cottage, Royal Victoria Hospital, Dundee DD2 5NF	01382 423116
DUNDEE NINEWELLS HOSPITAL	Rev. Anne Findlay	Chaplain's Office, Ninewells Hospital, Dundee DD1 9SY	01382 632755
	Mr Andrew Bennett	Chaplain's Office, Ninewells Hospital, Dundee DD1 9SY	01382 632755
ROXBURGHE HOUSE	Mr Andrew Bennett	Chaplain's Office, Roxburghe House	01382 740804

PERTH ROYAL INFIRMARY	Rev. Anne Findlay	Chaplain's Office, Perth Royal Infirmary	01738 473896
ABERFELDY COMMUNITY	Rev. Anne Brennan		01382 423110
BLAIRGOWRIE COMMUNITY	Rev. Geoff Williams		01382 423110
PITLOCHRY COMMUNITY	Rev. Geoff Williams		01382 423110
CRIEFF COMMUNITY	Rev. James MacDonald		01382 632755
CORNHILL MACMILLAN CENTRE	Rev. Anne Findlay	Chaplain's Office, Ninewells Hospital, Dundee DD1 9SY	01738 473896
ST MARGARET'S COMMUNITY	Rev. Geoff Williams	Chaplain's Office, Perth Royal Infirmary	01382 423110
ARBROATH INFIRMARY	Rev. Alasdair Graham		01382 423110
ANGUS CHAPLAIN	Rev. Rona Phillips	Susan Carnegie Centre, Stracathro Hospital	01382 423110
(Little Cairnie Hospital, Montrose Infirmary, Brechin Infirmary, Stracathro Hospital)			
CARSE VIEW CENTRE	Rev. Alan Gibbon		01382 423110

GRAMPIAN

Co-ordinating Chaplain:
Rev. Mark Rodgers, Chaplains' Office, Aberdeen Royal Infirmary, Foresterhill, Aberdeen AB25 2ZN   01224 553166

1. ACUTE SECTOR
ABERDEEN ROYAL INFIRMARY, ABERDEEN MATERNITY HOSPITAL
Chaplains' Office, Aberdeen Royal Infirmary, Foresterhill, Aberdeen AB25 2ZN

Rev. Mark Rodgers	01224 553316
Rev. James Falconer	01224 554905
Rev. Sylvia Spencer	01224 559214
Mrs Trudy Noble (Assistant Chaplain)	01224 554298

ROYAL ABERDEEN CHILDREN'S HOSPITAL
Chaplain's Office, Royal Aberdeen Children's Hospital, Westburn Drive, Aberdeen AB25 2ZG

Rev. James Falconer	01224 554905

ROXBURGHE HOUSE
Chaplain's Office, Roxburghe House, Ashgrove Road, Aberdeen AB25 2ZH

Rev. Sylvia Spencer	01224 557077

WOODEND HOSPITAL
Chaplain's Office, Woodend Hospital, Eday Road, Aberdeen AB15 6XS

Rev. Alison M. Hutchison	01224 556788
Rev. John Duthie (Assistant Chaplain)	01224 556006
	01224 556007

DR GRAY'S HOSPITAL, ELGIN
Rev. Andrew Willis, Deanshaugh Croft, Mulben, Keith AB55 6YJ   01343 567262
Rev. Norma Milne, 26 Green Road, Huntly AB54 8BE   01542 860240
Rev. David A. Young, 15 Mannachie Rise, Forres IV36 2US   01466 793841
                                                                 01309 672849

THE OAKS, ELGIN
Rev. David A. Young, 15 Mannachie Rise, Forres IV36 2US   01309 672849

2. MENTAL HEALTH
ROYAL CORNHILL HOSPITAL, WOODLANDS
Chaplain's Office, Royal Cornhill Hospital, Cornhill Road, Aberdeen AB25 2ZH
Rev. Jim Simpson   01224 557293
Miss Pamela Adam (Assistant Chaplain)   01224 557484
Mr Donald Meston (Assistant Chaplain)   01224 557231

3. COMMUNITY HOSPITALS

ABOYNE	Rev. John Duthie	Moraine, Inchmarlo, Banchory AB31 4BR	01330 824108
GLEN O' DEE, BANCHORY	Rev. John Duthie	Moraine, Inchmarlo, Banchory AB31 4BR	01330 824108
CHALMERS, BANFF	Mrs Margaret Robb	Chrislouan, Keithhall, Inverurie AB51 0LN	01651 882310
FLEMING, ABERLOUR	Rev. Andrew Willis	Deanshaugh Croft, Mulben, Keith AB55 6YJ	01542 860240
FRASERBURGH	Post vacant		
INVERURIE	Rev. Ian B. Groves	1 Westburn Place, Inverurie AB51 5QS	01467 620285
INSCH	Post vacant		
JUBILEE, HUNTLY	Rev. Norma Milne	26 Green Road, Huntly AB54 8BE	01466 793841
KINCARDINE COMMUNITY, STONEHAVEN	Rev. Margaret Jackson	3 Ramsay Road, Stonehaven AB39 2HJ	07936 366626
LEANCHOIL, FORRES	Rev. David A. Young	15 Mannachie Rise, Forres IV36 2US	01309 672284
MUIRTON	Rev. Andrew Willis	Deanshaugh Croft, Mulben, Keith AB55 6YJ	01542 860240
PETERHEAD COMMUNITY	Rev. David S. Ross	3–5 Abbey Street, Deer, Peterhead AB42 5LN	01771 623994
SEAFIELD, BUCKIE	Rev. Andrew Willis	Deanshaugh Croft, Mulben, Keith AB55 6YJ	01542 860240
STEPHEN, DUFFTOWN			
TURNER, KEITH	Rev. Kay Gauld	The Manse, Church Road, Keith AB55 5BR	01542 882799
TURRIFF	Mrs Margaret Robb	Chrislouan, Keithhall, Inverurie AB51 0LN	01651 882310
UGIE, PETERHEAD	Rev. David S. Ross	3–5 Abbey Street, Deer, Peterhead AB42 5LN	01771 623994

HIGHLAND

Lead Chaplain
THE RAIGMORE HOSPITAL [01463 704000]

Rev. Dr Derek Brown	Raigmore Hospital	01463 704463
Rev. Dr Derek Brown	Cathedral Manse, Cnoc-an-Lobht, Dornoch IV25 3HN	
Mrs Lindsay Rodgers	Raigmore Hospital	01463 704463
Rev. Maureen Wilson	Raigmore Hospital	01463 704463

IAN CHARLES	Rev. Morris Smith	Golf Course Road, Grantown-on-Spey PH26 3HY	01479 872084
ST VINCENT, KINGUSSIE	Janet Davidson		01667 422710 ext. 8811
NEW CRAIGS	Rev. Dr Iain Macritchie		01463 704000
NAIRN TOWN AND COUNTY	Janet Davidson		01667 422710 ext. 8811
BELFORD AND BELHAVEN			01397 702481
GLENCOE			
ROSS MEMORIAL, DINGWALL	Rev. Russel Smith	8 Castlehill Road, Dingwall IV15 9PB	01349 861011
INVERGORDON COUNTY	Rev. Kenneth D. Macleod	The Manse, Cromlet Drive, Invergordon IV18 0BA	01349 852273
LAWSON MEMORIAL	Mr Karl Weidner		01408 664029
MIGDALE	Mr Karl Weidner		01863 766211
CAITHNESS GENERAL	Mr John Craw DCS	Liabost, 8 Proudfoot Road, Wick KW1 4PQ	01955 603805 (Mbl) 07544 761653
DUNBAR	Rev. Alastair H. Gray	The Manse, Station Road, Watten, Wick KW1 5YN	01955 621220
BROADFORD MACKINNON MEMORIAL	Rev. Alastair H. Gray	The Manse, Station Road, Watten, Wick KW1 5YN	01955 621220
PORTREE	Rev. Donald G. MacDonald	Free Church Manse, 3 Sluggans, Portree, Isle of Skye IV51 9LY	01478 613256
CAMPBELTOWN	Mrs Andrea Holden		01586 552224
LOCHGILPHEAD	Mrs Margaret Sinclair	2 Quarry Park, Furnace, Inveraray PA32 8XW	01499 500633
ISLAY			01496 301000
DUNOON			01369 704341
ROTHESAY	Mr Raymond Deans	60 Ardmory Road, Rothesay, Isle of Bute PA20 0PG	01700 504893
LORN AND THE ISLANDS DISTRICT GENERAL	Rev. William Gray	Liogh, Glengallan Road, Oban PA34	01631 567500
Community Healthcare Chaplain (East Sutherland)	Rev. Mary J. Stobo	Druim-an-Sgairnich, Ardgay IV24 3BG	01863 766868

WESTERN ISLES HEALTH BOARD

UIST AND BARRA HOSPITAL WESTERN ISLES, STORNOWAY	Rev. T.K. Shadakshari	23D Benside, Newmarket, Stornoway, Isle of Lewis HS2 0DZ [E-mail: tk.shadakshari@nhs.net] [E-mail: shadaks2@yahoo.com]	(Home) 01851 701727 (Office) 01851 704704 (Mbl) 07403 697138

LIST D – FULL-TIME WORKPLACE CHAPLAINS

NATIONAL DIRECTOR	Rev. Iain McFadzean	iain.mcfadzean@wpcscotland.co.uk	(Mbl) 07969 227696
EDINBURGH AND CENTRAL			
Regional Organiser	Mr Paul Wilson	paul.wilson@wpcscotland.co.uk	(Mbl) 07703 585987
Edinburgh City Centre	Rev. Tony Bryer	tbryer@wpcscotland.co.uk	(Mbl) 07834 748129
Edinburgh West	Rev. Grant MacLaughlan	grant.maclaughlan@wpcscotland.co.uk	(Mbl) 07814 093235
WEST OF SCOTLAND			
Regional Organiser			
EAST OF SCOTLAND			
Regional Organiser	Rev. Chic Lidstone	chiclidstone@blueyonder.co.uk	01738 623022
(Chic Lidstone is not a member of the Church of Scotland but has Corresponding membership of Dundee Presbytery)			
ABERDEEN – City Centre	Mrs Cate Adams	cateadams@wpcscotland.co.uk	(Mbl) 07890 954027
	Rev. Alison Harvey	aharvey@wpcscotland.co.uk	(Mbl) 07508 654423
UK OIL AND GAS INDUSTRY	Rev. Gordon Craig	gordon.craig@ukoilandgaschaplaincy.com	01224 297532

LIST E – PRISON CHAPLAINS

ADVISER TO SCOTTISH PRISON SERVICE (NATIONAL)	Rev. William R. Taylor	SPS HQ, Calton House, 5 Redheughs Rigg, South Gyle, Edinburgh EH12 9DQ [E-mail: bill.taylor@sps.pnn.gov.uk]	0131-244 8640
ABERDEEN	Rev. Louis Kinsey	HM Prison, Aberdeen AB11 8FN	01224 238300
HMP Aberdeen closes on 31 December 2013; HMP Grampian (Peterhead) opens on 1 March 2014.			
ADDIEWELL	Rev. Bob Paterson	HM Prison, Addiewell, West Calder EH55 8QA	01506 874500 ext. 3606
	Rev. Peter Hall		
	Mrs Terry Paterson		

Location	Chaplains	Address	Telephone
CORNTON VALE	Rev. William R. Taylor Ms Deirdre Yellowlees	HM Prison and YOI Cornton Vale, Stirling FK9 5NU	01786 835365
DUMFRIES	Rev. Neil Campbell Rev. Calum Smith	HM Prison, Dumfries DG2 9AX	01387 274214
EDINBURGH: SAUGHTON	Rev. Colin Reid Rev. Prof. Bob Akroyd Rev. Chris Currie Rev. Keith Graham	HM Prison, Edinburgh EH11 3LN	0131-444 3115
GLASGOW: BARLINNIE	Rev. Douglas Clark Rev. Alex Wilson Rev. Jonathan Keefe Rev. Ian McInnes Rev. John Murfin	HM Prison, Barlinnie, Glasgow G33 2QX	0141-770 2059
GLENOCHIL	Rev. Graham Bell Rev. Elizabeth Kenny	HM Prison, Glenochil FK10 3AD	01259 760471 ext. 7211 or 7431
GREENOCK		HM Prison, Gateside, Greenock PA16 9AH	01475 787801 ext. 287
INVERNESS	Rev. Dr Peter Donald Rev. Alexander Shaw Rev. Christopher Smart	HM Prison, Inverness IV2 3HN	01463 229020 ext. 244
KILMARNOCK	Rev. Andrew Black	HMP Kilmarnock, Bowhouse, Mauchline Road, Kilmarnock KA1 5AA	01563 548928
LOW MOSS	Rev. Martin Forrest Mr Craig Bryan Rev. John Craib	HMP Low Moss, Crosshill Road, Bishopbriggs, Glasgow G64 2PZ	0141-762 9727
OPEN ESTATE: CASTLE HUNTLY	Rev. Anne E. Stewart	HMP Open Estate, Castle Huntly, Longforgan, Dundee DD2 5HL	01382 319388
PERTH	Rev. Kenneth G. Russell	Chaplaincy Centre, HM Prison, Perth PH2 7JH	01738 458216

PETERHEAD	Rev. Alison Harvey	HM Prison, Peterhead AB42 6YY	01779 485040

HMP Peterhead closes on 31 December 2013; HMP Grampian (Peterhead) opens on 1 March 2014.

POLMONT	Rev. Donald H. Scott Mr Craig Bryan	Chaplaincy Centre, HMYOI Polmont, Falkirk FK2 0AB	01324 722241
SHOTTS	Ms Dorothy Russell Rev. Murdo Maclean	Chaplaincy Centre, HM Prison, Shotts ML7 4LE	01501 824071

LIST F – UNIVERSITY CHAPLAINS

ABERDEEN	Easter Smart MDiv DMin	01224 488396
ABERTAY, DUNDEE	Leslie M. Barrett BD FRICS	01382 308447
CALEDONIAN		0141-558 7451
CAMBRIDGE	Nigel Uden (U.R.C. and C. of S.)	01223 314586
DUNDEE	Fiona C. Douglas MBE MA BD PhD	01382 384157
EDINBURGH	Richard E. Frazer BA BD DMin (Honorary)	0131-650 2595
GLASGOW	Stuart D. MacQuarrie JP BD BSc	0141-330 5419
HERIOT-WATT	Alistair P. Donald MA PhD BD	0131-451 4508
NAPIER	John R. Smith MA BD (Honorary)	0131-447 8724
OXFORD	Carla Grosch-Miller (U.R.C. and C. of S.)	01865 554358
PAISLEY		0141-571 4059
ROBERT GORDON	Daniel French	01224 262000 (ext. 3506)
ST ANDREWS	Donald G. MacEwan MA BD PhD	01334 462866
STIRLING	Gillian Weighton BD STM (Honorary)	01786 832753
STRATHCLYDE	David T. Young BA BD	0141-553 4144

LIST G – THE DIACONATE

NAME	COM	APP	ADDRESS	TEL	PRES
Beaton, Margaret (Miss) DCS	1989	1988	64 Gardenside Grove, Carmyle, Glasgow G32 8EZ [E-mail: margaret@churchhouse.plus.com]	0141-646 2297 (Mbl) 07796 642382	16
Bell, Sandra (Mrs) DCS	2001	2004	62 Loganswell Road, Thornliebank, Glasgow G46 8AX	0141-638 5884	16
Black, Linda (Miss) BSc DCS	1993	2004	148 Rowan Road, Abronhill, Cumbernauld, Glasgow G67 3DA [E-mail: lnan@blueyonder.co.uk]	01236 786265	22

Name			Address / E-mail	Telephone	No.
Blair, Fiona (Miss) DCS	1994	2010	Mure Church Manse, 9 West Road, Irvine KA12 8RE [E-mail: fiobla12@aol.com]	(Mbl) 07977 235168	11
Buchanan, Marion (Mrs) MA DCS	1983	2006	16 Almond Drive, East Kilbride, Glasgow G74 2HX	01698 292685	16
Burns, Marjory (Mrs) DCS	1997	1998	22 Kirklee Road, Mossend, Bellshill ML4 2QN [E-mail: mburns8070@aol.co.uk]	07792 843922	17
Carson, Christine (Miss) MA DCS	2006		36 Upper Wellhead, Limekilns, Dunfermline KY11 3JQ	01383 873131	24
Cathcart, John Paul (Mr) DCS	2000		9 Glen More, East Kilbride, Glasgow G74 2AP [E-mail: paulcathcart@msn.com]	(Mbl) 07919 137294 01355 243970	16
Corrie, Margaret (Miss) DCS	1989	1998	44 Sunnyside Street, Camelon, Falkirk FK1 4BH	(Mbl) 07708 396074 01324 670656	22
Crawford, Morag (Miss) MSc DCS	1977	1998	118 Wester Drylaw Place, Edinburgh EH4 2TG [E-mail: morag.crawford.dcs@blueyonder.co.uk]	(Tel/Fax) 0131-332 2253 (Mbl) 07970 982563	24
Crocker, Elizabeth (Mrs) DCS DipComEd	1985	2003	77C Craigcrook Road, Edinburgh EH4 3PH	0131-332 0227	1
Cunningham, Ian (Mr) DCS	1994	2002	110 Nelson Terrace, Keith AB55 5FD [E-mail: icunninghamdcs@btinternet.com]		35
Cuthbertson, Valerie (Miss) DipTMus DCS	2003		105 Bellshill Road, Motherwell ML1 3SJ [E-mail: v.cuthbertson333@btinternet.com]	01698 259001	22
Deans, Raymond (Mr) DCS	1994	2003	60 Ardmory Road, Rothesay, Isle of Bute PA20 0PG [E-mail: r.deans93@btinternet.com]	01700 504893	19
Dunnett, Linda (Mrs) BA DCS	1976	2000	5 Fincastle Place, Cowie, Stirling FK7 7DS [E-mail: lindadunnett@sky.com]	01786 818413	23
Evans, Mark (Mr) BSc MSc DCS	1988	2006	13 Easter Drylaw Drive, Edinburgh EH4 2QA [E-mail: mark.evans59@nhs.net]	0131-343 3089 (Office) 01383 674136	1
Gargrave, Mary (Mrs) DCS	1989	2002	The Manse, 90 Mount Annan Drive, Glasgow G44 4RZ [E-mail: mary_gargrave@btinternet.com]	0141-561 4681	16
Getliffe, Dot (Mrs) DCS BA BD DipEd	2006	2013	3 Woodview Terrace, Hamilton ML3 9DP [E-mail: dgetliffe@aol.com]	01698 423504 (Mbl) 07766 910171	16
Gray, Greta (Miss) DCS	1992	1998	67 Crags Avenue, Paisley PA2 6SG [E-mail: greta.gray@ntlworld.com]	0141-884 6178	14
Hamilton, James (Mr) DCS	1997	2000	6 Beckfield Gate, Glasgow G33 1SW [E-mail: j.hamilton111@btinternet.com]	0141-558 3195	16
Hamilton, Karen (Mrs) DCS	1995	2009	6 Beckfield Gate, Glasgow G33 1SW [E-mail: k.hamilton6@btinternet.com]	0141-558 3195 07970 872859	16
Love, Joanna (Ms) BSc DCS	1992	2009	92 Everard Drive, Glasgow G21 1XQ [E-mail: jo@iona.org.uk]	(Mbl) 0141-772 0149	16
Lyall, Ann (Miss) DCS	1980	2011	17 Mercat Loan, Biggar ML12 6DG [E-mail: ann.lyall@btinternet.com]	01899 229443	13
MacDonald, Anne (Miss) BA DCS	1980	2002	502 Castle Gait, Paisley PA1 2PA	0141-840 1875	16
McIntosh, Kay (Mrs) DCS	2008		4 Jacklin Green, Livingston EH54 8PZ [E-mail: kay@backedge.co.uk]	01506 440543	2
McKay, Kenneth D. (Mr) DCS	1996	1998	11F Balgowan Road, Letham, Perth PH1 2IG [E-mail: deakendan@gmail.com]	01738 621169 (Mbl) 07843 883042	28
McPheat, Elspeth (Miss)	1985	2001	11/5 New Orchardfield, Edinburgh EH6 5ET	0131-554 4143	1
Mulligan, Anne MA DCS	1974	1986	27A Craigour Avenue, Edinburgh EH17 7NH [E-mail: mulliganne@aol.com]	0131-664 3426 (Office) 0131-242 1996	1

NAME	COM		ADDRESS	TEL	PRES
Munro, Patricia (Ms) BSc DCS	1986	2012	4 Hewat Place, Perth PH1 2UD [E-mail: pat.munrodcs@gmail.com]	01738 443088 (Mbl) 07814 836314	28
Nicholson, David (Mr) DCS	1994	1993	2D Doonside, Kildrum, Cumbernauld, Glasgow G67 2HX	01236 732260	22
Nicol, Joyce (Mrs) BA DCS	1974	1998	93 Brisbane Street, Greenock PA16 8NY	01475 723235 (Mbl) 07957 642709	14
Ogilvie, Colin (Mr) DCS	1998	2003	32 Upper Bourtree Court, Rutherglen, Glasgow G73 4HT [E-mail: colinogilvie2@gmail.com]	0141-569 2725 (Mbl) 07837 287804	11
Philip, Elizabeth (Mrs) DCS MA BA PGCSE			8 Stratheam Terrace, Crieff PH7 3AQ [E-mail: ephilipstitch@gmail.com]	(Mbl) 07970 767851	24
Porter, Jean (Mrs) HNC BD DCS	2006		3 Cochrie Place, Tullibody, Alloa FK10 2RR [E-mail: jeanjeanniet@aol.com]	(Mbl) 07729 316321	23
Ross, Duncan (Mr) DCS	1996	2006	1 John Neilson Avenue, Paisley PA1 2SX [E-mail: ssornacnud@hotmail.com]	0141-887 2801	14
Rycroft, Pauline (Mrs) DCS	2003	2006	6 Ashville Terrace, Edinburgh EH6 8DD [E-mail: pauline70@rocketmail.com]	0131-554 6564 (Mbl) 07759 436303	1
Stewart, Marion (Miss) DCS	1991	1994	Kirk Cottage, Kirkton of Skene, Westhill, Skene AB32 6XE	01224 743407	33
Thomson, Jacqueline (Mrs) MTh DCS	2004	2004	1 Barron Terrace, Leven KY8 4DL	01333 301115	25
Urquhart, Barbara (Mrs) DCS	1986	2006	9 Standalane, Kilmaurs, Kilmarnock KA3 2NB [E-mail: churchdeacon@blueyonder.co.uk] [E-mail: barbaraurquhart1@gmail.com]	07806 776560 (Mbl) 01563 538289	11
Wallace, Sheila (Mrs) DCS BA BD	2009	2011	Beannach Cottage, Spey Avenue, Boat of Garten PH24 3BE [E-mail: sheilad.wallace53@gmail.com]	01479 831548 (Mbl) 07733 243046	36
Wilson, Glenda (Mrs) DCS	1990	2006	Ardlayne, 23 Bullwood Road, Dunoon PA23 7QJ [E-mail: deacglendamwilson@gmail.com]	01369 700848	19
Wright, Lynda (Miss) BEd DCS	1979	1992	Key Cottage, High Street, Falkland, Cupar KY15 7BU [E-mail: lynda@keyhouse.org]	01337 857705	26

THE DIACONATE (Retired List)

NAME	COM		ADDRESS	TEL	PRES
Allan, Jean (Mrs) DCS	1989		12C Hindmarsh Avenue, Dundee DD3 7LW	01382 827299	29
Anderson, Janet (Miss) DCS	1979	2006	Creagard, 31 Lower Breakish, Isle of Skye IV42 8QA [E-mail: jaskye@hotmail.co.uk]	01471 822403	42
Bayes, Muriel C. (Mrs) DCS	1963		Flat 6, Carleton Court, 10 Fenwick Road, Glasgow G46 4AN	0141-633 0865	16
Buchanan, John (Mr) DCS	2010		19 Gillespie Crescent, Edinburgh EH10 4HZ	0131-229 0794	3
Cameron, Margaret (Mrs) DCS	1961		2 Rowans Gate, Paisley PA2 6RD	0141-840 2479	14
Copland, Agnes M. (Mrs) MBE DCS	1950		Altnacraig House, Lyle Road, Greenock PA16 7XT		14
Craw, John (Mr) DCS	1998		Liabost, 8 Proudfoot Road, Wick KW1 4PQ	01955 603805 (Mbl) 07544 761653	41

Name	Year	Address	Phone	No.
Cunningham, Alison W. (Miss) DCS	1961	23 Strathblane Road, Milngavie, Glasgow G62 8DL	0141-563 9232	18
Drummond, Rhoda (Miss) DCS	1960	Flat K, 23 Grange Loan, Edinburgh EH9 2ER	0131-668 3631	1
Erskine, Morag (Miss) DCS	1979	111 Mains Drive, Park Mains, Erskine PA8 7JJ	0141-812 6096	14
Flockhart, Andrew (Mr) DCS	1988	Flat 0/1, 8 Hardie Avenue, Rutherglen, Glasgow G73 3AS	0141-569 0716	16
Forrest, Janice (Mrs)	1990	38 Lochview Drive, Glasgow G33 1QF	0141-770 9611	16
Gordon, Fiona S. (Mrs) MA DCS	1958	Machrie, 3 Cupar Road, Cuparmuir, Cupar KY15 5RH [E-mail: machrie@madasafish.com]	01334 652341	26
Gordon, Margaret (Mrs) DCS	1998	92 Lanark Road West, Currie EH14 5LA	0131-449 2554	1
Gray, Catherine (Miss) DCS	1969	10C Eastern View, Gourock PA19 1RJ	0475 637479	14
Gray, Christine M. (Mrs) DCS	1969	11 Woodside Avenue, Thornliebank, Glasgow G46 7HR	0141-571 1008-	16
Howden, Margaret (Miss) DCS	1954	38 Munro Street, Kirkcaldy KY1 1PY	01592 205913	25
Hughes, Helen (Miss) DCS	1977	2/2, 43 Burnbank Terrace, Glasgow G20 6UQ	0141-333 9459	16
Hutchison, Alan E.W. (Mr) DCS	1988	132 Lochbridge Road, North Berwick EH39 4DR	01620 894077	3
Johnston, Mary (Miss) DCS	1988	19 Lounsdale Drive, Paisley PA2 9ED	0141-849 1615	14
King, Chris (Mrs) DCS	2002	28 Kilnford, Dundonald, Kilmarnock KA2 9ET [E-mail: chrisking99@tiscali.co.uk]	01563 851197	10
King, Margaret MA DCS	2002	2012 56 Murrayfield, Fochabers IV32 7EZ	01343 820937	35
Lundie, Ann V. (Miss) DCS	1972	20 Langdykes Drive, Cove, Aberdeen AB12 3HW	01224 898416	31
McBain, Margaret (Miss) DCS	1974	33 Quarry Road, Paisley PA2 7RD	0141-884 2920	14
McCallum, Moyra (Miss) MA BD DCS	1965	176 Hilton Drive, Aberdeen AB24 4LT [E-mail: moymac@aol.com]	01224 486240	31
McCully, M. Isobel (Miss) DCS	1974	10 Broadstone Avenue, Port Glasgow PA14 5BB	01475 742240	14
MacKinnon, Ronald (Mr) DCS	1996	12 Mossywood Court, McGregor Avenue, Airdrie ML6 7DY	01236 763389	22
MacLean, Donald A. (Mr) DCS	1988	8 Upper Barvas, Isle of Lewis HS2 0QX	01851 840454	44
McNaughton, Janette (Miss) DCS	1982	4 Dunellan Avenue, Moodiesburn, Glasgow G69 0GB	01236 870180	22
MacPherson, James B. (Mr) DCS	1988	104 Cartside Street, Glasgow G42 9TQ	0141-616 6468	16
MacQuien, Duncan (Mr) DCS	1988	35 Criffel Road, Mount Vernon, Glasgow G32 9JE	0141-575 1137	14
Martin, Janie (Miss) DCS	1979	16 Wentworth Road, Dundee DD2 3SD [E-mail: janimar@aol.com]	01382 813786	29
Merrilees, Ann (Miss) DCS	1994	23 Cuthill Brae, Willow Wood Residential Park, West Calder EH55 8QE [E-mail: ann@merrilees.freeserve.co.uk]	01501 762909	2
Miller, Elsie M. (Miss) DCS	1974	30 Swinton Avenue, Rowanbank, Baillieston, Glasgow G69 6JR	0141-771 0857	22
Mitchell, Joyce (Mrs) DCS	1994	Sunnybank, Farr, Inverness IV2 6XG [E-mail: joyce@mitchell71.freeserve.co.uk]	01808 521285	37
Morrison, Jean (Dr) DCS	1964	45 Corslet Road, Currie EH14 5LZ [E-mail: jean.morrison@blueyonder.co.uk]	0131-449 6859	1
Moyes, Sheila (Miss) DCS	1957	158 Pilton Avenue, Edinburgh EH5 2JZ	0131-551 1731	1
Palmer, Christine (Ms) DCS	2003	Flat 4, Carissima Court, 99 Elmer Road, Elmer, Bognor Regis PO22 6LH	01243 858641	28
Rennie, Agnes M. (Miss) DCS	1974	3/1 Craigmillar Court, Edinburgh EH16 4AD	0131-661 8475	1
Ronald, Norma A. (Miss) MBE DCS	1961	2B Saughton Road North, Edinburgh EH12 7HG	0131-334 8736	1
Rose, Lewis (Mr) DCS	1993	6 Gauldie Crescent, Dundee DD3 0RR [E-mail: scimnorth@uk.uumail.com]	01382 622167 (Mbl) 07899 790446	29
Rutherford, Ellen B. (Miss) MBE DCS	1962	41 Duncanston, Conon Bridge, Dingwall IV7 8JB	01349 877439	39

NAME	ORD	ADDRESS	TEL	PRES
Smith, Catherine (Mrs) DCS	1964	21 Lingaro, Bixter, Shetland ZE2 9NN	01595 810207	46
Steele, Marilynn J. (Mrs) BD DCS	1999	2 Northfield Gardens, Prestonpans EH32 9LQ	01875 811497	1
Steven, Gordon BD DCS	1997	51 Nantwich Drive, Edinburgh EH7 6RB [E-mail: grsteven@btinternet.com]	0131-669 2054 (Mbl) 07904 385256	3
Stuart, Anne (Miss) DCS	1966	1 Murrell Terrace, Aberdour, Burntisland KY3 0XH	01383 860049	24
Tait, Agnes (Mrs) DCS	1995	10 Carnoustie Crescent, Greenhills, East Kilbride, Glasgow G75 8TE	01389 873196	17
Teague, Yvonne (Mrs) DCS	1965	46 Craigcrook Avenue, Edinburgh EH4 3PX	0131-336 3113	1
Thom, Helen (Miss) BA DipEd MA DCS	1959	84 Great King Street, Edinburgh EH3 6QU	0131-556 5687	1
Thomson, Phyllis (Miss) DCS	2003	63 Caroline Park, Mid Calder, Livingston EH53 0SJ	01506 883207	2
Trimble, Robert DCS	1988	5 Templar Rise, Livingston EH54 6PJ	01506 412504	2
Webster, Elspeth H. (Miss) DCS	1950	82 Broomhill Avenue, Burntisland KY3 0BP	01592 873616	25
Wilson, Muriel (Miss) MA BD DCS	1997	28 Bellevue Crescent, Ayr KA7 2DR [E-mail: muriel.wilson4@btinternet.com]	01292 264939	10
Wishart, William (Mr) DCS	1994 2004	10 Stanely Drive, Paisley PA2 6HE	0141-884 4177 (Mbl) 07846 555654	14

THE DIACONATE (Supplementary List)

NAME	ORD	ADDRESS	TEL
Gilroy, Lorraine (Mrs) DCS	1988	5 Bluebell Drive, Cheverel Court, Bedward CO12 0GE	02476 366031
Guthrie, Jennifer M. (Miss) DCS		14 Eskview Terrace, Ferryden, Montrose DD10 9RD	01674 674413
Harris, Judith (Mrs) DCS	1993	243 Western Avenue, Sandfields, Port Talbot, West Glamorgan SA12 7NF	01639 884855
Hood, Katrina (Mrs) DCS	1988	67C Farquhar Road, Edgbaston, Birmingham B18 2QP	
Hudson, Sandra (Mrs) DCS	1982	10 Albany Drive, Rutherglen, Glasgow G73 3QN	
Muir, Alison M. (Mrs) DCS	1969	77 Arthur Street, Dunfermline KY12 0JJ	
Ramsden, Christine (Miss) DCS	1978	2 Wykeham Close, Bassett, Southampton SO16 7LZ	
Walker, Wikje (Mrs) DCS	1970	24 Brodie's Yard, Queen Street, Coupar Angus PH13 9RA	01828 628251
Wallace, Catherine (Mrs) DCS		5 Strathearn Terrace, Perth PH2 0LS	01738 621709

LIST H – MINISTERS HAVING RESIGNED MEMBERSHIP OF PRESBYTERY (in terms of Act III 1992)

(Resignation of Presbytery membership does not imply the lack of a practising certificate. Some of those listed do have practising certificates; others do not.)

NAME	ORD	ADDRESS	TEL	PRES
Adamson, Hugh M. BD	1976	38F Maybole Road, Ayr KA7 4SF [E-mail: hmadamson768@btinternet.com]	01292 440958	11
Anderson, Kenneth G. MA BD	1967	8 School Road, Arbroath DD11 2LT	01241 874825	30

Name	Ord.	Address	Tel	No.
Barbour, Robin A.S. (Prof.) KCVO MC MA BD STM DD	1954	Old Fincastle, Pitlochry PH16 5RJ	01796 473209	27
Bardgett, Frank D. MA BD PhD	1987	Tigh an Iasgair, Street of Kincardine, Boat of Garten PH24 3BY [E-mail: tigh@bardgett.plus.com]	01479 831751	36
Bartholomew, Julia (Mrs) BSc BD	2002	Kippenhill, Dunning, Perth PH2 0RA	01764 684929	28
Beck, John C. BD	1975	31 The Woodlands, Stirling FK8 2LB		35
Birrell, Isobel (Mrs) BD	1994	'Hiddlehame', 5 Hewat Place, Perth PH1 2UD [E-mail: isobel@ibmail.org.uk]	(Mbl) 07540 797945	17
Black, W. Graham MA BD	1983	72 Linksview, Linksfield Road, Aberdeen AB24 5RG [E-mail: graham.black@virgin.net]	01224 492491	31
Blane, Quintin A. BSc BD MSc	1979	18D Kirkhill Road, Penicuik EH26 8HZ [E-mail: quintin@qab.org.uk]	01968 670017	3
Bradley, Andrew W. BD	1975	Flat 1/1, 38 Cairnhill View, Bearsden, Glasgow G61 1RP	0141-931 5344	16
Breakey, Judith (Ms) LizTheol MTh DipEd	2010	[E-mail: judith.breakey@gmail.com]		16
Brown, Alastair BD	1986	52 Henderson Drive, Kintore, Inverurie AB51 0FB	01467 632787	32
Brown, Joseph MA	1954	The Orchard, Hermitage Lane, Shedden Park Road, Kelso TD5 7AN	01573 223481	6
Caie, Albert LTh	1983	34 Ringwell Gardens, Stonehouse, Larkhall ML9 3QW	01698 792187	32
Campbell, J. Ewen R. MA BD	1967	20 St Margaret's Road, North Berwick EH39 4PJ	01620 893814	25
Campbell, Richard S. LTh	1993	3 River Wynd, Strathallan Park, Stirling FK9 5GN [E-mail: revrichards@btinternet.com]	01786 469622	23
Cooper, George MA BD	1943	8 Leighton Square, Alyth, Blairgowrie PH11 8AQ	01828 633746	1
Cowieson, Roy J. BD	1979	The Tides Condominiums 25, 110 20th Street, Courtney, BC V9N 8B1, Canada		13
Craig, Eric MA BD BA	1959	5 West Relugas Road, Edinburgh EH9 2PW	0131-667 8210	1
Craig, Gordon W. MBE MA BD	1972	1 Beley Bridge, Dunino, St Andrews KY16 8LT	0131-334 880285	26
Crawford, S.G. Victor	1980	Crofton, 65 Main Road, East Wemyss, Kirkcaldy KY1 4RL	01592 712325	25
Cumming, David P.L. MA	1957	Shillong, Tarbat Ness Road, Portmahomack, Tain IV20 1YA	01862 871794	19
Currie, Gordon C.M. MA BD	1975	43 Deanburn Park, Linlithgow EH49 6HA	01506 842759	2
Davidson, John F. BSc DipEdTech	1970	49 Craigmill Gardens, Carnoustie DD7 6HX [E-mail: davidson900@btinternet.com]	01241 854566	30
Davies, Gareth W. BA BD	1979	Pitadro House, Fordell Gardens, Dunfermline KY11 7EY	01383 417634	24
Donaldson, Colin V.	1982	3A Playfair Terrace, St Andrews KY16 9HX	01334 472889	3
Drake, Wendy F. (Mrs) BD	1978	21 William Black Place, South Queensferry EH30 9QR [E-mail: revwdrake@hotmail.co.uk]	0131-331 1520	1
Dutton, David W. BA	1973	13 Acredales, Haddington EH41 4NT [E-mail: dutton_sr@yahoo.co.uk]		9
Ellis, David W. GIMechE GIProdE	1962	4 Wester Tarsappie, Rhynd Road, Perth PH2 8PT	01738 449618	16
Emery, Stephen BD DPS	2006	Nook Cottage, 2 Thornyhall, Dalkeith EH22 2ND [E-mail: stephen.emery2@btinternet.com]		33
Ferguson, Ronald MA BD ThM DUniv	1972	Vinbreck, Orphir, Orkney KW17 2RE [E-mail: ronbluebrazil@aol.com]	01856 811353	45
Finlay, Quintin BA BD	1975	Ivy Cottage, Greenlees Farm, Kelso TD5 8BT	(Mbl) 07901 981171	6
Flockhart, D. Ross OBE BA BD DUniv	1955	Longwood, Humbie EH36 5PN [E-mail: rossflock@ednet.co.uk]	01875 833208	3
Gardner, Bruce K. MA BD PhD	1988	21 Hopetoun Crescent, Bucksburn, Aberdeen AB21 9QY [E-mail: drbrucekgardner@aol.com]		31

Name	Date	Address	Tel	No.
Gehrke, Robert B. BSc BD CEng MIEE	1994	2 Hareburn Avenue, Avonbridge, Falkirk FK1 2NR [E-mail: bob.gehrke@gmail.com]	01324 861632	2
Grainger, Alison J. BD	1995	[E-mail: revajgrainger@btinternet.com]		2
Greig, James C.G. MA BD STM	1955	Block 2, Flat 2, Station Lofts, Strathblane, Glasgow G63 9BD [E-mail: james.greig12@btinternet.com]	01360 771915	16
Grubb, George D.W. BA BD BPhil DMin	1962	10 Wellhead Close, South Queensferry EH30 9WA	0131-331 2072	1
Hamilton, David S.M. MA BD STM	1958	49 Paddocks Lane, Cheltenham GL50 4NU	01242 254917	47
Harper, Anne J.M. (Miss) BD STM MTh CertSocPsych	1979	122 Greenock Road, Bishopton PA7 5AS	01505 862466	16
Haslett, Howard J. BA BD	1972	26 The Maltings, Haddington EH41 4EF [E-mail: howard.haslett@btinternet.com]	01620 820292	3
Hosie, James MA BD MTh	1959	Hilbre, Baycrofts, Strachur, Cairndow, Argyll PA27 8BY	01369 860634	19
Howie, William MA BD STM	1964	26 Morgan Road, Aberdeen AB16 5JY	01224 483669	31
Hurst, Frederick R. MA	1965	Flat 6, 21 Bulldale Place, Glasgow G14 0NE	0141-959 2604	40
Lambie, Andrew E. BD	1957	1 Mercat Loan, Biggar ML12 6DG	01899 221352	13
Lindsay, W. Douglas BD CPS	1978	3 Drummond Place, Calderwood, East Kilbride, Glasgow G74 3AD	01355 234169	16
Logan, Thomas M. LTh	1971	3 Duncan Court, Kilmarnock KA3 7TF	01563 524398	11
McAdam, David J. BSc BD (Assoc)	1990	12 Dunellan Crescent, Moodiesburn, Glasgow G69 0GA [E-mail: dmca29@hotmail.co.uk]	01236 870472	16
Macaskill, Donald MA BD PhD	1994	4 Glendale Gardens, Randalstown, Co. Antrim BT41 3EJ	02894 478545	16
McClenaghan, L. Paul BA	1973	23 Willoughby Place, Callander PH17 8DG [E-mail: paul.mcclenaghan@gmail.com]	01877 330785	34
McCreadie, David W.	1961	7 Blacket Place, Edinburgh EH9 1RN	0131-667 2100	23
McDonald, William J.G. DD	1953	Flat 12, Homeburn House, 177 Fenwick Road, Giffnock, Glasgow G46 6JD	0141-620 3235	1
Macfarlane, Alwyn J.C. MA	1951	Westfell, Monreith, Newton Stewart DG8 9LT	01988 700449	1
McGill, Thomas W.	1972	36 Larchfield Neuk, Balerno EH14 7NL		9
McGillivray, A. Gordon MA BD STM	1951	15 Montgomerie Avenue, Fairlie, Largs KA29 0EE	01475 568802	1
McKay, Johnston R. MA BA PhD	1969	[E-mail: johnston.mckay@btopenworld.com]		16
Mackenzie, J.A.R. MA	1947	7 Chattan Drive, Nairn IV12 4QR	01667 452827	26
McKenzie, Mary O. (Miss)	1976	4 Dunellan Avenue, Moodiesburn, Glasgow G69 0GB	01236 870180	16
Mackie, John F. BD	1979	1A Halls Close, Weldon, Corby, Northants NN17 3HH		40
Mackinnon, Thomas J.R. LTh DipMin	1996	4 Flashadder, Arnisort, Portree, Isle of Skye IV51 9PT	01470 582377	39
McLean, John MA BD	1967	16 Eastside Drive, Westhill AB32 6QN	01224 747701	33
Mair, John BSc	1965	21 Kenilworth Avenue, Helensburgh G84 7JR	01436 671744	18
Melville, David D. BD	1989	28 Porterfield, Comrie, Dunfermline KY12 9HJ	01383 850075	24
Millar, John L. MA BD	1981	Flat 0/1, 12 Chesterfield Gardens, Glasgow G12 0BF	0141-339 4098	38
Miller, Irene B. (Mrs) MA BD	1984	5 Braeside Park, Aberfeldy PH15 2DT	01887 829396	27
Morton, Andrew Q. MA BSc BD FRSE	1949	Sunnyside, 4A Manse Street, Aberdour, Burntisland KY3 0TY		18
Murray, Douglas R. MA BD	1965	32 Forth Park, Bridge of Allan, Stirling FK9 5NT [E-mail: d-smurray@supanet.com]	01786 831081	23
Newlands, George M. (Prof.) MA BD PhD DLitt FRSA FRSE	1970	12 Jamaica Street North Lane, Edinburgh EH3 6HQ		16
O'Leary, Thomas BD	1983	1 Carter's Place, Irvine KA12 0BU	01294 313274	11

Name		Address	Tel	
Osbeck, John R. BD	1979	15 Deeside Crescent, Aberdeen AB15 7PT	01224 315595	31
Park, Christopher BSc BD	1977	65 Moubray Road, Dalgety Bay, Dunfermline KY11 9JP [E-mail: chrispark8649@hotmail.com]	01383 821111	24
Paterson, Andrew E. JP	1994	6 The Willows, Kelty KY4 0FQ	01383 830998	24
Paterson, James BSc BD	2003	c/o 9 Oakview, Balmedie, Aberdeen AB23 8SR		1
Peacock, Heather M. BSc PhD BD	2009	9 Frankscroft, Peebles EH45 9DX [E-mail: hmpeacock@btinternet.com]		32
Pryce, Stuart F.A.	1963	36 Forth Park, Bridge of Allan, Stirling FK9 5NT	01786 831026	23
Ramsay, Alan MA	1967	12 Riverside Grove, Lochyside, Fort William PH33 7RD	01397 702054	38
Reid, Janette G. (Miss) BD	1991	c/o Glasgow Presbytery Office, 260 Bath Street, Glasgow G2 4JP		16
Reid, William M. MA BD	1966	10 Rue Rossini, F-75009 Paris, France		48
Ritchie, Garden W.M.	1961	23 Croft Road, Kelso TD5 7EP	01573 224419	6
Roy, Alistair A. MA BD	1955	1 Broaddykes Close, Kingswells, Aberdeen AB15 8UF	01224 743310	31
Scouller, Hugh BSc BD	1985	11 Kirk View, Haddington EH41 4AN [E-mail: h.scouller@btinternet.com]		3
Duncan Shaw of Chapelverna Bundesverdienstkreuz PhD ThDr Drhc	1951	4 Sydney Terrace, Edinburgh EH7 6SL		19
Shaw, D.W.D. BA BD LLB WS DD	1960	4/13 Succoth Court, Edinburgh EH12 6BZ	0131-337 2130	26
Smith, Ralph C.P. MA STM	1960	2A Waverley Road, Eskbank, Dalkeith EH22 3DJ	0131-663 1234	1
Spowart, Mary G. (Mrs) BD	1978	Aldersyde, St Abbs Road, Coldingham, Eyemouth TD14 5NR [E-mail: rcpsmith@waitrose.com]	01890 771697	26
Strachan, Ian M. MA BD	1959	'Cardenwell', Glen Drive, Dyce, Aberdeen AB21 7EN	01224 772028	31
Sutcliffe, Clare B. BSc BD	2000	4 Dalmailing Avenue, Dreghorn, Irvine KA11 4HX		11
Taylor, David J. MA BD	1982	32 Croft an Righ, Inverkeithing KY11 1PF	01383 413227	24
Thomas, W. Colville ChLJ BTh BPhil DPS DSc	1964	11 Muirfield Crescent, Gullane EH31 2HN	01620 842415	3
Thomson, Gilbert L. BA	1965	3 Fortharfield, Freuchie, Cupar KY15 7JJ	01337 857431	25
Turnbull, Julian S. BSc BD MSc CEng MBCS	1980	25 Hamilton Road, Gullane EH31 2HP [E-mail: jules-turnbull@zetnet.co.uk]	01620 842958	3
Weatherhead, James L. CBE MA LLB DD	1960	59 Brechin Road, Kirriemuir DD8 4DE	01575 572237	30
Webster, Brian G. BSc BD CEng MIET	1998	3/1 Cloch Court, 57 Albert Road, Gourock PA19 1NJ [E-mail: revwebby@aol.com]	01475 638332	23
Webster, John G. BSc	1964	Plane Tree, King's Cross, Brodick, Isle of Arran KA27 8RG	01770 700747	16
Wedderburn, A.J.M. (Prof.) MA BA PhD	1975	Therese-Danner-Platz 3, D-80636 Munich, Germany [E-mail: ajmw42@gmx.de]	0049 89 1200 3726	
Westmarland, Colin A.	1971	PO Box 5, Cospicua, CSPOI, Malta	00356 216 923552	48
Wilkie, George D. OBE BL	1948	2/37 Barnton Avenue West, Edinburgh EH4 6EB	0131-339 3973	1

LIST I – MINISTERS HOLDING PRACTISING CERTIFICATES (under Act II, as amended by Act VIII 2000)

Not all Presbyteries have stated whether or not some of those listed have taken a seat in Presbytery. There is still some variation in practice.

NAME	ORD	ADDRESS	TEL	PRES
Adamson, Hugh M. BD	1976	38F Maybole Road, Ayr KA7 4SF [E-mail: hmadamson768@btinternet.com]	01292 440958	11
Alexander, William M. BD	1971	110 Fairview Circle, Danestone, Aberdeen AB22 8YR	01224 703752	31
Anderson, David MA BD	1975	Rowan Cottage, Aberlour Gardens, Aberlour AB38 9LD	01340 871906	35
Anderson, Kenneth G. MA BD	1967	8 School Road, Arbroath DD11 2LT	01241 874825	30
Arbuthnott, Joan E. (Mrs) MA BD	1993	139/1 New Street, Musselburgh EH21 6DH	0131-665 6736	3
Barbour, Robin A.S. (Prof.) KCVO MC MA BD STM DD	1954	Old Fincastle, Pitlochry PH16 5RJ	01796 473209	27
Barclay, Neil W. BSc BEd BD	1986	4 Gibsongray Street, Falkirk FK2 7LN	01324 874681	22
Bardgett, Frank D. MA BD PhD	1987	Tigh an Iasgair, Street of Kincardine, Boat of Garten PH24 3BY [E-mail: tigh@bardgett.plus.com]	01479 831751	36
Bartholomew, Julia (Mrs) BSc BD	2002	Kippenhill, Dunning, Perth PH2 0RA	01764 684929	28
Beattie, Warren R. BSc BD MSc PhD	1991	Director for Mission Research, OMF International, 2 Cluny Road, Singapore 259570 [E-mail: beattiewarren@omf.net]	0065 6319 4550	1
Bell, Ruth	2009	Flat 2/2, 22 Caledonia Street, Clydebank G81 4ER		18
Biddle, Lindsay (Ms)	1991	30 Ralston Avenue, Glasgow G52 3NA [E-mail: lindsaybiddle@hotmail.com]	0141-883 7405	
Birrell, John M. MA LLB BD	1974	'Hiddlehame', 5 Hewat Place, Perth PH1 2UD [E-mail: john.birrell@nhs.net]	01738 443335	28
Black, James S. BD DPS	1976	7 Breck Terrace, Penicuik EH26 0RJ [E-mail: jsb.black@btopenworld.com]	01968 677559	3
Bonar, Sandy F. LTh	1988	7 Westbank Court, Westbank Terrace, Macmerry, Tranent EH33 1QS [E-mail: sandy.bonar@btinternet.com]	01875 615165	3
Boyd, Ian R. MA BD PhD	1989	33 Castleton Drive, Newton Mearns, Glasgow G77 3LE	0141-931 5344	16
Bradley, Andrew W. BD	1975	Flat 1/1, 38 Cairnhill View, Bearsden, Glasgow G61 1RP	01224 491451	31
Brown, Robert F. MA BD ThM	1971	55 Hilton Drive, Aberdeen AB24 4NJ [E-mail: Bjacob546@aol.com]		
Caie, Albert LTh	1983	34 Ringwell Gardens, Stonehouse, Larkhall ML9 3QW	01698 792187	17
Carvalho, Jose R. BD	2002	c/o The Ministries Council, 121 George Street, Edinburgh EH2 4YN (Mr Carvalho is currently living in Brazil)	0131-225 5722	28
Coogan, J. Melvyn LTh	1992	19 Glen Grove, Largs KA30 8QQ		12
Cowieson, Roy J. BD	1979	The Tides Condominiums 25, 110 20th Street, Courtney, BC V9N 8B1, Canada		13
Davidson, John F. BSc DipEdTech	1970	49 Craigmill Gardens, Carnoustie DD7 6HX [E-mail: davidson900@btinternet.com]	01241 854566	30
Davidson, Mark R. MA BD STM RN	2005	20 Kinmohr Rise, Blackburn, Aberdeen AB21 0LJ [E-mail: mark.davidson122@mod.uk]	01224 791350	33

Dickson, Graham T. MA BD	1985	19/4 Stead's Place, Edinburgh EH6 5DY [E-mail: gtd22@blueyonder.co.uk]	0131-476 0187	1
Donaldson, Colin V.	1982	3A Playfair Terrace, St Andrews KY16 9HX	01334 472889	3
Drake, Wendy F. (Mrs) BD	1978	21 William Black Place, South Queensferry EH30 9QR [E-mail: revwdrake@hotmail.co.uk]	0131-331 1520	1
Drummond, Norman W. (Prof.) MA BD FRSE DUniv	1976	c/o Columba 1400 Ltd, Staffin, Isle of Skye IV51 9JY	01478 611400	42
Ellis, David W. GIMechE GIProdE	1962	4 Wester Tarsappie, Rhynd Road, Perth PH2 8PT	01738 449618	16
Ferguson, Ronald MA BD ThM DUniv	1972	Vinbreck, Orphir, Orkney KW17 2RE [E-mail: ronbluebrazil@aol.com]	01856 811353	45
Fowler, Richard C.A. BSc MSc BD	1978	4 Gardentown, Whalsay, Shetland ZE2 9AB	01806 566538	46
Fraser, Ian M. MA BD PhD	1946	Ferndale, Gargunnock, Stirling FK8 3BW	01786 860612	23
Frew, John M. MA BD	1946	17 The Furrows, Walton-on-Thames KT12 3JQ		16
Gow, Neil BSc MEd BD	1996	Hillhead Lodge, Portknockie, Buckie AB56 4PB	01542 840625	35
Groenewald, Jonanda BA BD MTh DD	1999	8 Manse Court, East Calder, Livingston EH53 0HF [E-mail: jonandagroenewald@yahoo.com]	01506 884585	2
Grubb, George D.W. BA BD BPhil DMin	1962	10 Wellhead Close, South Queensferry EH30 9WA	0131-331 2072	1
Harper, Anne J.M. (Miss) BD STM MTh CertSocPsych	1979	122 Greenock Road, Bishopton PA7 5AS	01505 862466	16
Hendrie, Yvonne (Mrs) MA BD	1995	The Manse, 16 McAdam Way, Maybole KA19 8FD	01655 883710	10
Hibbert, Frederick W. BD	1986	4 Cemydd Terrace, Senghenydd, Caerphilly, Mid Glamorgan CF83 4HL	02920 831653	47
Homewood, Ivor Maxwell MSc BD	1997	An der Fließwiese 26, D-14052 Berlin, Germany [E-mail: maxhomewood@me.com]	0049 30 3048722	48
Hosie, James MA BD MTh	1959	Hilbre, Baycrofts, Strachur, Cairndow PA27 8BY	01369 860634	19
Jenkinson, John J. JP LTCL ALCM DipEd DipSen (Aux)	1991	8 Rosehall Terrace, Falkirk FK1 1PY	01324 625498	22
Johnstone, Donald B.	1969	22 Glenhove Road, Cumbernauld, Glasgow G67 2IZ	01236 612479	22
Kenny, Celia G. BA MTh	1995	37 Grosvenor Road, Rathgar, Dublin 6, Ireland		5
Lawrie, Robert M. BD MSc DipMin LLCM(TD) MCMI	1994	18/1 John's Place, Edinburgh EH6 7EN [E-mail: robert.lawrie@ed.ac.uk]	0131-554 9765	1
Liddiard, F.G.B. MA	1957	34 Trinity Fields Crescent, Brechin DD9 6YF	01356 622966	30
Lindsay, W. Douglas BD CPS	1978	3 Drummond Place, Calderwood, East Kilbride, Glasgow G74 3AD	01355 234169	16
Logan, Thomas M. LTh	1971	3 Duncan Court, Kilmarnock KA3 7TF	01563 524398	11
Lyall, David BSc BD STM PhD	1965	16 Brian Crescent, Tunbridge Wells, Kent TN4 0AP [E-mail: lyall3@gmail.com]	01892 670323	47
McAdam, David J. BSc BD (Assoc)	1990	12 Dunellan Crescent, Moodiesburn, Glasgow G69 0GA [E-mail: dmca29@hotmail.co.uk]	01236 870472	16
McDonald, Ross J. BA BD ThM RNR	1998	HMS *Dalriada*, Navy Buildings, Eldon Street, Greenock PA16 7SL [E-mail: rossjmcdonald@tiscali.co.uk]	0141-883 7545 (Mbl) 07952 558767	16
McFadyen, Gavin BEng BD	2006	20 Tennyson Avenue, Bridlington YO15 2EP [E-mail: mcfadyen.gavin@gmail.com]	01262 608659 (Mbl) 07503 971068	18
McGillivray, A. Gordon MA BD STM	1951	36 Larchfield Neuk, Balerno EH14 7NL		1
McKay, Johnston R. MA BA PhD	1969	15 Montgomerie Avenue, Fairlie, Largs KA29 0EE [E-mail: johnston.mckay@btopenworld.com]	01475 568802	16
McKean, Martin I. BD DipMin	1984	56 Kingsknowe Drive, Edinburgh EH14 2JY	0131 466 1157	

Name	Year	Address	Telephone	No.
MacPherson, Gordon C.	1963	203 Capelrig Road, Patterton, Newton Mearns, Glasgow G77 6ND	0141-616 2107	16
McPherson, William M BD DipEd	1993	83 Laburnum Avenue, Port Seton, Prestonpans EH32 0UD	01875 812252	22
Mailer, Colin (Aux)	1996	Innis Chonain, Back Row, Polmont, Falkirk FK2 0RD	01324 712401	22
Main, Arthur W.A. BD	1954	13/3 Eildon Terrace, Edinburgh EH3 5NL	0131-556 1344	16
Masson, John D. M. MA BD PhD BSc	1984	2 Beechgrove, Craw Hall, Brampton CA8 1TS	ex-directory	7
		[E-mail: jmasson96@btinternet.com]		
Melville, David D. BD	1989	28 Porterfield, Comrie, Dunfermline KY12 9HJ	01383 850075	24
Millar, Peter W. MA BD PhD	1971	6/5 Ettrickdale Place, Edinburgh EH3 5JN	0131-557 0517	1
		[E-mail: ionacottage@hotmail.com]		
Miller, Irene B. (Mrs) MA BD	1984	5 Braeside Park, Aberfeldy PH15 2DT	01887 829396	27
Moodie, Alastair R. MA BD	1978	4 Burnbrae Road, Auchinloch, Glasgow G66 5DQ		16
Morton, Andrew Q. MA BSc BD FRSE	1949	Sunnyside, 4A Manse Street, Aberdour, Burntisland KY3 0TY		18
Muir, Margaret A. (Miss) MA LLB BD	1989	59/4 South Beechwood, Edinburgh EH12 5YS	0131-313 3240	13
Newell, Alison M. (Mrs) BD	1986	1A Inverleith Terrace, Edinburgh EH3 5NS	0131-556 3505	1
		[E-mail: alinewell@aol.com]		
Newell, J. Philip MA BD PhD DLitt FRSA FRSE	1982	1A Inverleith Terrace, Edinburgh EH3 5NS	0131-556 3505	1
Newlands, George M. (Prof.)	1970	12 Jamaica Street North Lane, Edinburgh EH3 6HQ		16
Nicolson, John Murdo	1997	731 16th Street North, Lethbridge, Alberta, Canada T1H 3B3		42
Notman, John R. BSc BD	1990	5 Dovecote Road, Bronsgrove, Worcs B61 7BN		47
Ostler, John H. MA LTh	1975	5 Osborne Terrace, Port Seton, Prestonpans EH32 0BZ	01875 814358	3
Owen, Catherine W. MTh	1984	10 Waverley Park, Kirkintilloch, Glasgow G66 2BP	0141-776 0407	16
Paterson, Andrew E. JP	1994	6 The Willows, Kelty KY4 0FQ	01383 830998	24
Penman, Iain D. BD	1977	33/5 Cambee Avenue, Edinburgh EH16 6GA	0131-664 0673	1
		[E-mail: iainpenmanklm@aol.com]	(Mbl) 07931 993427	
Provan, Iain W. MA BA PhD	1991	Regent College, 5800 University Boulevard, Vancouver BC V6T 2E4, Canada	001 604 224 3245	1
Roy, Alistair A. MA BD	1955	1 Broaddykes Close, Kingswells, Aberdeen AB15 8UF	01224 743310	31
Sawers, Hugh BA	1968	2 Rosemount Meadows, Castlepark, Bothwell, Glasgow G71 8EL	01698 853960	17
Scouller, Hugh BSc BD	1985	11 Kirk View, Haddington EH41 4AN		3
		[E-mail: h.scouller@btinternet.com]		
Shaw, D.W.D. BA BD LLB WS DD	1960	4/13 Succoth Court, Edinburgh EH12 6BZ	0131-337 2130	26
Stewart, Margaret L. (Mrs) BSc MB ChB BD	1985	28 Inch Crescent, Bathgate EH48 1EU	01506 653428	2
Storrar, William F. (Prof.) MA BD PhD	1984	Director, Center of Theological Inquiry, 50 Stockton Street, Princeton, NJ 08540, USA		1
Strachan, David G. BD DPS	1978	1 Deeside Park, Aberdeen AB15 7PQ	01224 324101	31
Strachan, Ian M. MA BD	1959	'Cardenwell', Glen Drive, Dyce, Aberdeen AB21 7EN	01224 772028	31
Thomas, W. Colville ChLJ BTh BPhil DPS DSc	1964	11 Muirfield Crescent, Gullane EH31 2HN	01620 842415	3
Tollick, Frank BSc DipEd	1958	3 Bellhouse Road, Aberdour, Burntisland KY3 0TL	01383 860559	24
Turnbull, Julian S.	1980	25 Hamilton Road, Gullane EH31 2HP	01620 842958	3
		[E-mail: jules-turnbull@zetnet.co.uk]		
Weatherhead, James L. CBE MA LLB DD	1960	59 Brechin Road, Kirriemuir DD8 4DE	01575 572237	30

Webster, Brian G. BSc BD CEng MIET	1998	3/1 Cloch Court, 57 Albert Road, Gourock PA19 1NJ [E-mail: revwebby@aol.com]		01475 638332	23
Weir, Mary K. (Mrs) BD PhD	1968	1249 Millar Road RR1, SITEH-46, BC V0N 1G0, Canada		001 604 947 0636	1
Whitton, John P.	1977	115 Sycamore Road, Farnborough, Hants GU14 6RE		01252 674488	47
Wood, James L.K.	1967	1 Glen Drive, Dyce, Aberdeen AB21 7EN		01224 722543	31

LIST J – MINISTRIES DEVELOPMENT STAFF

Associate Ministers and Deacons employed by the Ministries Council and placed in charges appear under the name of the charge.

It has not proved easy to compile a fully comprehensive and accurate list of these valued workers. We offer apologies where there are errors or omissions. Where a year is given, this indicates when the appointment referred to was made.

NAME	APP	ADDRESS	APPOINTMENT	TEL
Adam, Pamela BD	2009	Basement Left Flat, 409 Holburn Street, Aberdeen AB10 7GS [E-mail: thekirk@btinternet.com]	Gordon: Ellon	01358 725690 (Work) 07712 674614 (Mbl)
Anderson, Christopher	2008	14 Edmonstone Drive, Danderhall, Dalkeith EH22 1QQ	Newton and Loanhead	0131-663 0819
Baker, Paula (Mrs)	2007	Kernow, 18 Main Street, Buckpool, Buckie AB56 1XQ [E-mail: mikepaulabaker@aol.com]	Birnie and Pluscarden linked with Elgin: High: Parish Assistant	01542 832662
Barrowcliffe, Donna		[E-mail: donna@ruchazie.eclipse.co.uk]		
Beautyman, Paul H. (Rev.) MA BD	2009	59 Alexander Street, Dunoon PA23 7BB [E-mail: paul.beautyman@argyll-bute.gov.uk]	Argyll Presbytery: Team Leader: Youth Education Ministries	07596 164112 (Mbl)
Blackwood, Katrina BD	2009	Torry St Fittick's Church, 39 Walker Road, Torry, Aberdeen AB11 8DL [E-mail: beanie.blackwood@btinternet.com]	Aberdeen: Torry St Fittick's: Ministry Assistant (p/t)	01224 315748 07853 053579 (Mbl)
Bruce, Nicola (Mrs) BD MTh	2009	11 South Chesters Lane, Bonnyrigg EH19 3GL [E-mail: overhills@hotmail.com]	Lothian Presbytery: Tranent Cluster: Family and Youth Development Worker	0131-663 5252 07711 223100 (Mbl)
Bruce, Stuart	2009	1 Craighill Drive, Clarkston, Glasgow G76 7TG [E-mail: stuart.bruce7@ntl.world.com]	Glasgow: Govanhill Trinity: Parish Assistant	07850 039593 (Mbl)
Campbell, Alasdair BA	2000	3 Gellatly Road, Dunfermline KY11 4BH [E-mail: adcam@talktalk.net]	Dunfermline Presbytery: Dalgety/Forth Churches Group: Parish Assistant	01383 726238
Campbell, Neil MA	2010	36 Clovis Duveau Drive, Dundee DD2 5JB [E-mail: neilcampbel198@btinternet.com]	Dundee: Craigiebank with Douglas and Mid Craigie: Youth and Young Adult Development Worker	01382 561171 (Home) 01382 731173 (Work) 07999 349587 (Mbl)

Name	Year	Address	Charge	Tel
Chaba, Sumtende MSc PgDipCE	2008	61 Anderson Avenue, Aberdeen AB24 4LR [E-mail: astiras@yahoo.com]	Aberdeen	
Cowie, Marjorie (Miss) MA BA	2002	35 Balbirnie Avenue, Markinch, Glenrothes KY7 6BS [E-mail: marjorieh@mhcowiestm.plus.com]	Glenrothes: St Margaret's: Parish Assistant	01592 758402
Crossan, Morag BA	2010	1A Church Hill, Dalmellington, Ayr KA6 7QP [E-mail: morag.crossan@gmail.com]	Dalmellington with Patna Waterside: Youth and Children's Worker	01292 550984 07861 736071 (Mbl)
Crumlin, Melodie (Mrs) BA PGMgt DipBusMgt	2000	Abercromby Business Centre, Suite 2, 279 Abercromby Street, Glasgow G40 2DD [E-mail: projectmanager@peekproject.co.uk]	PEEK (Possibilities for East End Kids): Project Development Manager	0141-558 2589 (Home) 0141-554 3068 (Work) 07904 672891 (Mbl)
Dale-Pimentil, Sheila (Mrs) MA BD	1999/2007	3 Golf Road, Lundin Links, Leven KY8 6BB [E-mail: sdale.pimentil@btinternet.com]	Kennoway, Windygates and Balgonie: St Kenneth's: Parish Assistant	01333 329618 (Home) 01333 351372 (Work)
Dyer, Eildon BSc MSc RGN DNCert	2008	Ruchazie Parish Church, 4 Elibank Street, Glasgow G33 3QN [E-mail: eildon@ruchazie.eclipse.co.uk]	Glasgow: Ruchazie Parish Church: Interim Project Manager	0141-774 2759 07776 201270 (Mbl)
Finch, John BA	2007	231 Kirkintilloch Road, Bishopbriggs, Glasgow G64 2JB [E-mail: johnfinch75@hotmail.com]	Gorbals Parish Church: Community Development Worker	07715 119263 (Mbl)
Finegan, Sarah (Mrs) BA	2007	261 Main Street, East Calder, Livingston EH53 0ED		01506 882628
Gray, Ian	2011	The Mallards, 15 Rossie Island Road, Montrose DD10 9NH [E-mail: iancelia15@aol.com]	Esk Parish Grouping – Angus Presbytery: Pastoral Assistant	01674 677126 (Home) 07757 888233 (Mbl)
Guy, Helen (Miss)		24D Cattofield Place, Aberdeen AB25 3QL [E-mail: helenjguy@googlemail.com]	Aberdeen: St Columba's Bridge of Don	01224 488686 07923 177392 (Mbl)
Haringman, Paul MSc	2010	11 Tower Gardens, Westhill, Inverness IV2 5DQ [E-mail: paul.haringman@barnchurch.org.uk]	Inverness: Culloden: The Barn: Community Worker	01463 798946 (Home) 01463 795428 (Work) 07837 903277 (Mbl)
Harper, Kirsty (Mrs) BA	2009	32/6 Craigmillar Castle Road, Edinburgh EH16 4AR [E-mail: kirsty@granton.org.uk]	Edinburgh: Granton	0131-258 5162 (Home)
Harvey, Stuart		Howard Centre, 5 Portland Road, Kilmarnock KA1 2BT [E-mail: stuart@howardcentre.org]	Ministry Development Coordinator, Howard Centre	01563 541337 (Office) 07851 450742 (Mbl)
Hunter, Jean (Mrs)	2006	Manse, Shiskine, Isle of Arran KA27 8EP [E-mail: j.hunter744@btinternet.com]	Brodick with Corrie with Lochranza: Parish Assistant	01770 860380
Hutchison, John BA	2001	30/4 West Pilton Gardens, Edinburgh EH4 4EG	Edinburgh: The Old Kirk: Parish Assistant	0131-258 5162
Johnstone, Christine	2009	4 Ramsay Avenue, Johnstone PA5 0EU [E-mail: ceejae51@yahoo.co.uk]	East Kilbride: Claremont and South Parishes: Parish Assistant	07974 632112 (Mbl)
Jones, Helen M. (Miss) BA	2007	Further Ministries Team, Canonbie Church Centre, Canonbie DG14 0RA [E-mail: helen.jones@furtherministriesteam.com]	Annandale and Eskdale Further Ministries Team: Youth Worker	01387 371037 (Office) 07789 631822 (Mbl)
Keenan, Deborah	2009	St George's and St Peter's Church, 40 Boyndie Street, Easterhouse, Glasgow G34 9JE [E-mail: debbiedkeenan@gmail.com]	Glasgow: Easterhouse St George's and St Peter's	0141-771 8810 (Work) 07928 116142 (Mbl)

Name	Year	Address / Email	Position	Tel
MacChoille, Stiubhart MA	2009	61 Don Street, Aberdeen AB24 2RX [E-mail: stiumac@outlook.com]	Aberdeen: Craigiebuckler	01224 481359 (Home) 01224 315649 (Work) 07951 846262 (Mbl)
McEwen, Craig	2010	c/o Church Office, Dumfries Northwest Church, Lochside Road, Dumfries DG2 0DZ [E-mail: craigmcewen@dumfriesnorthwest.org.uk]	Dumfries: Northwest: Parish Assistant	01387 249964 (Mbl)
McIlreavy, Gillian (Mrs)		16 Craigiehall Place, Kinning Park, Glasgow G51 1TN	Glasgow: Govan and Linthouse	0141-445 2010 07811 332632 (Mbl)
McIver, Ian LLB DipLP NP	2009	68 York Street, Peterhead AB42 1SP [E-mail: ianmci@hotmail.co.uk]	Aberdeen City Centre Parish Grouping: Community Outreach Worker	01779 479162 (Home) 01224 566451 (Office) 07890 932677 (Mbl)
McKay, Angus Mackenzie, Lynn		35 East Campbell Street, Glasgow G1 5DT 1990 Maryhill Road, Glasgow G20 0EF [E-mail: l.mackenzie@gmopbuzz.org]	Lodging House Mission Greater Maryhill Outreach Project	0141-552 0285 0141-946 3512
Mackenzie, Norman	2009	41 Kilmailing Road, Glasgow G44 5UH [E-mail: mackenzie799@btinternet.com]	Larkhall: Chalmers	0141-637 5958
MacRae, Christopher LLB	2009	Presbytery of Glasgow, 260 Bath Street, Glasgow G2 4JP [E-mail: strategy@presbyteryofglasgow.org.uk]	Presbytery of Glasgow Strategy Officer	0141-332 6606 (Office)
Montgomery, Rilza (Ms)	2009	71 Glendinning Crescent, Edinburgh EH16 6DN	Edinburgh: Muirhouse St Andrew's	0131-440 4442
Naismith, Kenneth BD	2010	1/1, 29 Napier Drive, Govan, Glasgow G51 2LP [E-mail: kencaitheast@btinternet.com]	Glasgow: Govan and Linthouse: Parish Assistant	07789 764105 (Mbl)
Orr, Gillian BA	2009	'Zippity Do Da', Loch Alvie, Aviemore PH22 1QB [E-mail: gillianorr.cosyouth@googlemail.com]	Presbytery of Abernethy: Youth Worker	01479 811699 07969 457191 (Mbl)
Philip, Darren BSc	2009	72 Pinebank, Ladywell, Livingston EH54 6EX [E-mail: darren@lepyouth.com]	Livingston Ecumenical Parish: Youth and Children's Worker	01506 797712
Ramsay, Sheila BA JD	2008	18 Morrison Quadrant, Clydebank G81 2SZ [E-mail: sheila.maryhill@yahoo.co.uk]	Glasgow: Maryhill	07794 508544 (Mbl)
Reford, Susan (Miss) DipHE (Theol)	2001	32 Jedburgh Street, Blantyre, Glasgow G72 0SU [E-mail: susan.reford@btopenworld.com]	Cumbernauld: Abronhill	01698 820122
Reynolds, Jessica (Mrs)		12 Queen Street, Portnahaven, Isle of Islay PA47 7SJ [E-mail: jessica_reynolds@btinternet.com]	Youth and Children's Worker, Argyll	07445 491132 (Mbl)
Robertson, Douglas	2009	Robroyston Parish Church, 34 Saughs Drive, Glasgow G33 1HG [E-mail: dougie.robroyston@hotmail.co.uk]	Robroyston NCD: Church Development Worker	
Ross, Duncan DCS	2009	1 John Neilson Avenue, Paisley PA1 2SX [E-mail: ssornacnud@hotmail.com]	Greenock: Lyle Kirk and Paisley: St Columba Foxbar	0141-887 2801

Ross, Keith W. (Rev.) MA BD	2007	Easter Bavelaw House, Pentland Hills Regional Park, Balerno EH14 7JS [E-mail: keithross.hamiltonpresbytery@googlemail.com]	Hamilton Presbytery: Congregational Development Officer	07855 163449 (Mbl)
Smith, David	2003	66 Hendry Road, Kirkcaldy KY2 5DB [E-mail: dave@stserfschurch.org.uk]	Lochgelly and Benarty: Children's and Young People's Development Worker	01592 641823 / 07587 765602 (Mbl)
Stark, Jennifer MA MATheol	2010	South Leith Parish Halls, 6 Henderson Street, Edinburgh EH6 6BS [E-mail: outreach@leithchurchestogether.org.uk]	Edinburgh: Leith Churches Outreach Project: Leader	0131-554 2578
Stewart, Peter	2009	5 Craigievar Crescent, Glasgow G33 5DN [E-mail: pete@clanstewart.co.uk]	Glasgow: Barlanark Greyfriars	07855 424633 (Mbl)
Stirling, Diane (Miss) BSc DipCPC	2009	28 Kaims Court, Livingston Village EH54 7DB [E-mail: parish.assistant@yahoo.co.uk]	Polbeth Harwood with West Kirk of Calder: Parish Assistant	01506 426887 / 07855 866396 (Mbl)
Taylor, Valerie AssocCIPD PgDip	2010	372 Victoria Road, Torry, Aberdeen AB11 9PA [E-mail: vtaylor.torrystfitticks@gmail.com]	Aberdeen: Torry St Fittick's: MDS	07723 778788 (Mbl)
Thomas, Jason	2009	4 Dairsie Court, Glasgow G44 3JF [E-mail: jasonthomas21@hotmail.com]	Glasgow: St James' Pollok	07512 748011 (Mbl)
Thomson, Andrew (Rev.)	2010	3 Laurel Wynd, Cambuslang, Glasgow G72 7BH	Glasgow: Govan and Linthouse: Pastoral Assistant	0141-641 2936
Wellstood, Keith PGDip MICG	2009	47 Carrington Terrace, Crieff PH7 4DZ [E-mail: keithw2011@btinternet.com]	Perth: Riverside: Community Worker	01764 655678 (Home) / 01738 622341 (Office) / 07963 76782 (Mbl)
Willis, Mags	2008	Chalmers Ardler Church, Turnberry Avenue, Dundee DD2 3TP [E-mail: magswillis@hotmail.com]	Dundee: Chalmers Ardler	01382 858283 / 07513 415835 (Mbl)
Wyllie, John	2007	51 Seafar Drive, Kelty KY4 0JX	Cowdenbeath: Trinity: Pastoral Assistant	01383 839200
Young, Neil James	2001	31 Craigendmuir Street, Blackhill, Glasgow G33 1LG [E-mail: neil@boltfm.co.uk]	Glasgow: St Paul's: Youth Worker	0141-770 8559 / 07748 808488 (Mbl)

LIST K – OVERSEAS LOCATIONS

PRESBYTERY OF EUROPE

AMSTERDAM   The English Reformed Church, The Begijnhof (off the Spui). Service each Sunday at 10:30am. [Website: www.ercadam.nl]

BERMUDA	Christ Church Warwick, Middle Road, Warwick. Sunday services: 8:00am and 11:00am. [Website: www.christchurch.bm]
BOCHUM	English-speaking Christian congregation – ECC Bochum: Pauluskirche, Grabenstraße 9, D-44787 Bochum. Service each Sunday at 12:30pm. [Website: www.ecc-bochum.de]
BRUSSELS	St Andrew's Church, Chaussée de Vleurgat 181 (off Ave. Louise). Service each Sunday at 11:00am. [Website: www.churchofscotland.be]
BUDAPEST	St Columba's Scottish Mission, Vörösmarty utca 51, H-1064 Budapest. (Church Tel) 0036 1 373 0725 Service in English and Sunday School each Sunday at 11:00am. [Website: www.scotskirkhungary.com]
COLOMBO	St Andrew's Scots Kirk, 73 Galle Road, Colombo 3, Sri Lanka. Service each Sunday at 9:30am. (Tel/Fax) 0036 1 460 0708 [Website: www.internationalchurchcolombo.info]
COSTA DEL SOL	Services at Lux Mundi Ecumenical Centre, Calle Nueva 7, Fuengirola, Malaga. (Tel) 0034 952 474840 Service each Sunday at 10:30am. [Website: www.churchofscotlandcostadelsol.eu]
GENEVA	The Calvin Auditoire, Place de la Taconnerie (beside Cathedral of St Pierre). Service each Sunday at 11:00am. [Website: www.churchofscotlandgeneva.com]
GIBRALTAR	St Andrew's Church, Governor's Parade. Service each Sunday at 10:30am. [Website: www.scotskirkgibraltar.com]
LAUSANNE	26 Avenue de Rumine, CH-1005 Lausanne. Service each Sunday at 10:30am. [Website: www.scotskirklausanne.ch]
LISBON	St Andrew's Church, Rua da Arriaga 13–15, Lisbon. Service each Sunday at 11:00am. [Website: www.saintandrewslisbon.com]
MALTA	St Andrew's Church, 210 Old Bakery Street, Valletta. Service each Sunday at 10:30am. [Website: www.saintandrewsmalta.com]
PARIS	The Scots Kirk, 17 Rue Bayard, F-75008 Paris (Metro: Roosevelt). Service each Sunday at 11:00am. [Website: www.scotskirkparis.com]
REGENSBURG	English-language congregation: Alumneum, Am Olberg 2, D-93047 Regensburg. Sunday service: second Sunday 10:30am; fourth Sunday 6:00pm. [Website: www.esg-regensburg.de]
ROME	Via XX Settembre 7, 00187 Rome. Service each Sunday at 11:00am. [Website: www.presbyterianchurchrome.org]

ROTTERDAM	The Scots Kirk, Schiedamsevest 121, Rotterdam. Service each Sunday at 10:30am. Informal service at 9:15am. [Website: www.scotsintchurch.com]	(Tel) 001 868 627 9312
TRINIDAD	Church of Scotland Greyfriars St Ann's, 50 Frederick Street, Port of Spain, Trinidad	
TURIN	English-speaking congregation of the Waldensian Church in co-operation with the Church of Scotland. Via Principe Tommaso 1, 10125 Torino. Service each Sunday at 10:30am. [Website: www.torinovaldese.org]	

AFRICA

MALAWI	**Church of Central Africa Presbyterian**	
	Synod of Blantyre	
	Dr Ruth Shakespeare (2011)	Mulanje Mission Hospital, PO Box 45, Mulanje, Malawi [E-mail: shakespeareruth@gmail.com]	(Tel) 00265 9922 61569 (Fax) 00265 1 467 022
	Synod of Livingstonia	
	Miss Helen Scott (2000, held previous appointment)	CCAP Girls' Secondary School, PO Box 2, Ekwendeni, Malawi [E-mail: helenms1960@yahoo.co.uk]	(Tel) 00265 1929 1932
	Synod of Nkhoma	
	Dr David Morton (2009)	Nkhoma Hospital, PO Box 48, Nkhoma, Malawi [E-mail: kuluva2@gmail.com]	(Tel) 00265 9940 74022
	Mr Rob Jones (2010)	Nkhoma Hospital, PO Box 48, Nkhoma, Malawi [E-mail: robert@thejonesfamily.org.uk]	(Tel) 00265 9918 65705
ZAMBIA	**United Church of Zambia**	
	Mr Keith and Mrs Ida Waddell (Ecum) (2008)	Mwandi UCZ Mission, PO Box 60693, Livingstonia, Zambia [E-mail: keith_ida2002@yahoo.co.uk]	(Tel) 00260 977 328 767
	Ms Jenny Featherstone (Ecum) (2007)	c/o Chodort Training Centre, PO Box 630451, Choma, Zambia [E-mail: jenny.featherstone@googlemail.com]	(Tel) 00260 979 703 130
	Mr Glen Lund (2010)	UCZ Theological College, PO Box 20429, Kitwe, Zambia [E-mail: redhair.community@googlemail.com]	(Tel) 00260 978 363 400

ASIA

BANGLADESH	**Church of Bangladesh**	
	Miss Pat Jamieson (Ecum) (2010)	c/o St Thomas' Church, 54 Johnston Road, Dhaka 1100, Bangladesh	

NEPAL

Mr Joel Githinji (2010)

c/o United Mission to Nepal, PO Box 126, Kathmandu, Nepal
(Tel: 00 977 1 4228 118)
[E-mail: joel.githinji@umn.org.np]

Rev. Malcolm and Mrs Cati Ramsay (Ecum) (2011)

c/o United Mission to Nepal, PO Box 126, Kathmandu, Nepal
(Tel: 00 977 1 4228 118)
[E-mail: malcolm.ramsay@umn.org.np]

MIDDLE EAST

ISRAEL AND
OCCUPIED
PALESTINIAN
TERRITORY

[NOTE: Church Services are held in St Andrew's Scots Memorial Church, Jerusalem, each Sunday at 10:00am, and at St Andrew's, Galilee each Sunday at 6:00pm]

Jerusalem
Rev. George and Mrs Margaret Shand (2009)

St Andrew's, Jerusalem, 1 David Remez Street, PO Box 8619, Jerusalem 91086,
Israel
(Tel: 00 972 2 673 2401; Fax: 00 972 2 673 1711)
[E-mail: stachjer@netvision.net.il]
[Website: www.scotsguesthouse.com]

Mr Kenny and Mrs Alison Roger (2013)

St Andrew's, Jerusalem, 1 David Remez Street, PO Box 8619, Jerusalem 91086,
Israel
(Tel: 00 972 2 673 2401; Fax: 00 972 2 673 1711; Mobile: 00 972 50 542 2262)
[E-mail: kroger@churchofscotland.org.uk]
[Website: www.scotsguesthouse.com]

Tiberias
Rev. Colin D. Johnston (2009)

St Andrew's, Galilee, 1 Gdud Barak Street, PO Box 104, Tiberias 14100, Israel
(Tel: 00 972 4 671 0759; Fax: 00 972 4 672 5282)
[E-mail: revcdj60@gmail.com]
[Website: www.scotshotels.co.il]

Jaffa
Mr Anthony and Mrs Darya Short (2006)

Tabeetha School, 21 Yefet Street, PO Box 8170, Jaffa 61081, Israel
(Tel: 00 972 3 682 1581; Fax: 00 972 3 681 9357; Mobile: 00 972 54 757 2104)
[E-mail: principal@tabeethaschool.org]
[Website: www.tabeethaschool.org]

Mr James Maxwell (2009)

Tabeetha School, 21 Yefet Street, PO Box 8170, Jaffa 61081, Israel
(Tel: 00 972 3 682 1581; Fax: 00 972 3 681 9357)
[E-mail: jmaxwell@churchofscotland.org.il]
[Website: www.tabeethaschool.org]

LIST L – OVERSEAS RESIGNED AND RETIRED MISSION PARTNERS (ten or more years' service)

NAME	APP	RET	AREA	ADDRESS
Anderson, Karen (Mrs)	1992	2006	Israel	23 Allanpark Street, Largs KA30 9AG
Anderson, Kathleen (Mrs)	1955	1968	Pakistan	1A Elms Avenue, Great Shelford, Cambridge CB2 5LN
Archibald, Mary L. (Miss)	1964	1982	Nigeria/Ghana	490 Low Main Street, Wishaw ML2 7PL
Baxter, Mrs Ray	1954	1969	Malawi	91/17 Morningside Road, Edinburgh EH10 4AY
Berkeley, Dr John and Dr Muriel	1967	1977	Bhutan	Drumbeg, Coylumbridge, Aviemore PH22 1QU
Bone, Mr David and Mrs Isobel	1995	1998	Yemen	315 Blackness Road, Dundee DD2 1SH
Bone, Elizabeth (Mrs)	1977	1988	Malawi	2A Elm Street, Dundee DD2 2AY
Boyle, Lexa (Miss)	1950	1964	Malawi	7 Maxwell Grove, Glasgow G41 5JP
Brodie, Rev. Jim	1980	1984	Malawi	25A Keptie Road, Arbroath DD11 3ED
Brown, Janet H. (Miss)	1959	1992	Aden/Yemen/Sudan	6 Baxter Park Terrace, Dundee DD4 6NL
Burnett, Dr Fiona	1955	1974	North India	The Glenholm Centre, Broughton, Biggar ML12 6JF
Burnett, Dr Robin and Mrs Storm	1996 / 1967	1998 / 1980	Nepal / Pakistan	79 Bank Street, Irvine KA12 0LL
Burt, M.R.C. (Miss)	1988	1998	Zambia	22 The Loaning, Chirnside, Duns TD11 3YE
Byers, Rev. Alan and Rev. Mairi	1964	1967	Nigeria	Meadowbank, Plumdon Road, Annan DG12 6SJ
Campbell, George H.	1968	1977	South Africa	20 Woodlands Grove, Kilmarnock KA3 1TZ
Coltart, Rev. Ian O.	1940	1975	Kenya	25 Bothwell Gardens, Dunbar EH42 1PZ
Conacher, Marion (Miss)	1960	1971	Ghana	41 Magdalene Drive, Edinburgh EH15 3BG
Cooper, Rev. George	1957	1971	Livingstonia	8 Leighton Square, Alyth, Blairgowrie PH11 8AQ
Crosbie, Ann R. (Miss)	1967	1985	North India	21 Fieldhead Square, Glasgow G43 1HL
Dawson, Miss Anne	1963	1993	India	31 Colville Gardens, Alloa FK10 1DU
Dodman, Rev. Roy and Mrs Jane	1966 / 1955	1986 / 1967	Kenya / Nigeria	78 Barbican Road, Kingston 6, Jamaica
Drever, Dr Bryan	1976	2000	Malawi	188 Addison Road, King's Head, Birmingham
Duncan, Mr David and Mrs Allison	1983 / 1962	2006 / 1982	Jamaica / Aden/Yemen/Pakistan	7 Newhailes Avenue, Musselburgh EH21 6DW
Duncan, Mr Graham and Mrs Sandra	1952 / 1977	1969 / 1987	Nigeria / South Africa	56 Daphne Road, Maroelana, 0081 Pretoria, South Africa
Dunlop, Mr Walter T. and Mrs Jennifer	1998 / 1979	2006 / 1994	Malawi/Israel	50 Oxgangs Road, Edinburgh EH13 9DR
Fauchelle, Mrs Margaret	1991	1999	Zambia, Malawi, Zimbabwe	Flat 3, 22 North Avenue, Devonport, Auckland 1309, New Zealand
Ferguson, Mr John K.P.	1977	1989	Pakistan	15 Ashgrove, Craigshill, Livingston EH54 5JQ
Finlay, Carol (Ms)	1990	2001	Malawi	96 Broomfield Crescent, Edinburgh EH12 7LX

Name	From	To	Country	Address
Fischbacher, Dr Colin M. and Mrs Sally	1986	1998	Malawi	11 Barclay Square, Gosforth, Newcastle-upon-Tyne NE3 2JB
Foster, Joyce (Miss) BSc	1968	1972	Kenya	99 Sixth Street, Newtongrange EH22 4LA
Fowler, Rev. Margaret	1972	1981	Malawi	
Gaston, Dr Andrew and Mrs Felicity	1988	2007	Jamaica	PO Box 3097, Negril, Westmorland, Jamaica
Irvine, Mr Clive and Mrs Su	1997	2008	Malawi	25 Kimberley Drive, Crown Hill, Plymouth, Devon PL6 5WA
Karam, Ishbel (Mrs)	1984	1999	Nepal	McGregor Flat, 92 Blackford Avenue, Edinburgh EH9 3ES
King, Mrs Betty	1968	1985	Pakistan	Hillsgarth, Baltasound, Unst, Shetland ZE2 9DY
Knowles, Dr John K. and Mrs Heather	1955	1971	North India	23 Main Street, Newstead, Melrose TD6 9DX
Laidlay, Mrs Una	1976	1992	Malawi	Trollopes Hill, Monton Combe, Bath BA2 7HX
Liddell, Margaret (Miss)	1961	1968	Yemen	Isles View, 5 Bell's Road, Lerwick, Shetland ZE1 0QB
Logie, Robina (Mrs)	1968	1971	Pakistan	
McCulloch, Lesley (Mrs)	1971	1978	Yemen	
McCutcheon, Agnes W.F. (Miss)	1964	1980	Zambia	20 Wyvis Crescent, Conon Bridge, Dingwall IV7 8BZ
MacDonald, Dr Alistair and Mrs Freda	1950	1960	North India	23 Stonefield Drive, Inverurie AB51 9DZ
	1982	1992	Malawi/Pakistan	316 North Jones Street, Port Angeles, WA 98362-4218, USA
	1957	1989	India	10A Hugh Murray Grove, Cambuslang, Glasgow G72 7NG
McDougall, Rev. John N.	1949	1962	Nigeria	10 Millside, Morpeth, Northumberland NE61 1PN
McGoff, A.W. (Miss)	1935	1960	West Pakistan	Everill Orr Home, Allendale Road, Mount Albert, Auckland 3, New Zealand
MacGregor, Rev. Margaret S.	1954	1974	Kolhapur	6 Mossvale Walk, Craigend, Glasgow G33 5PF
McKenzie, Rev. William M.	1959	1994	India	16 Learmonth Court, Edinburgh EH4 1PB
MacKinnon, E.L. (Miss)	1958	1974	Zambia	41 Kingholm Road, Dumfries DG1 4SR
McMahon, Mrs Jessie	1952	1972	Nigeria	3 Havoc Road, Dumbarton G82 4JN
Malley, Beryl Stevenson (Miss)	1959	1976	North India	7 Ridgepark Drive, Lanark ML11 7PG
Millar, Rev. Margaret R.M.	1982	1992	Malawi	272/2 Craigcrook Road, Edinburgh EH4 7TF
Millar, Rev. Peter W.	1967	1996	Malawi/Zambia	Fearnoch Cottage, Fearnoch, Taynuilt PA35 1JB
Moir, Rev. Ian A. and Mrs Elsie	1976	1989	South Africa	6/5 Ettrickdale Place, Edinburgh EH3 5JN
Morrice, Mrs Margaret	1962	1973	Buenos Aires/Kenya	28/6 Comely Bank Avenue, Edinburgh EH4 1EL
Morton, Rev. Alasdair J. and Mrs Gillian M.	1971	1998	Zambia	104 Baron's Hill Avenue, Linlithgow EH49 7JG
Munro, Harriet (Miss)	1960	1973	Malawi	16 St Leonard's Road, Forres IV36 1DW
Murray, Rev. Douglas R. and Mrs Sheila	1959	1969	Switzerland	26 The Forge, Braidpark Drive, Glasgow G46 6LB
Murray, Mr Ian and Mrs Isabel	1994	2004	Pakistan	32 Forth Park, Bridge of Allan, Stirling FK9 5NT
Musgrave, Rev. Clarence W. and Mrs Joan	2000	2006	Zambia	17 Piershill Terrace, Edinburgh EH8 7EY
	1966	1980	Jerusalem	4 Ravelston Heights, Edinburgh EH4 3LX
Musk, Mrs Lily	1959	1974	Malawi/Zambia	1 Tulloch Place, St Andrews KY16 8XJ

Name	From	To	Country/Field	Address
Nelson, Mrs Anne	1947	1952	Pakistan	7 Manse Road, Roslin EH25 9LF
Nicholson, Rev. Thomas S.	1952	1959	North India	The Manse, Todholes, Greenlaw, Duns TD10 6XD
Nicol, Catherine (Miss)	1970	1973	North India	St Columba Christian Girls' RTC, Barah Patthar, Sialkot 2, Pakistan
Nutter, Margaret (Miss)	1981	1995	Taiwan	Kilmorich, 14 Balloch Road, Balloch, Alexandria G83 8SR
Pacitti, Rev. Stephen A.	1960	2000	Pakistan	157 Nithsdale Road, Glasgow G41 5RD
Pattison, Rev. Kenneth J.	1966	1979	Pakistan	
and Mrs Susan	1977	1996	Taiwan	
Philip, Mrs Margaret	1966	1977	Malawi	2 Castle Way, St Madoes, Glencarse, Perth PH2 7NY
Philpot, Rev. David	1951	1968	Nigeria	Penlan, Holm Farm Road, Catrine, Mauchline KA5 6TA
Reid, Dr Ann	1981	1995	WCC Geneva	2/27 Pentland Drive, Edinburgh EH10 6PX
Reid, Margaret I. (Miss)	1988	1996	Ghana	36 Kingshill Court, Standish, Wigan WN6 0AR
Rennie, Rev. Alistair M.	1964	1982	Malawi	3/1 Coxfield Lane, Edinburgh EH11 2RF
Ritchie, Ishbel M. (Miss)	1939	1976	Malawi	Noble's Yard, St Mary's Gate, Wirksworth, Derbyshire DE4 4DQ
Ritchie, Rev. James M.	1955	1996	Eastern Himalaya	8 Ross Street, Dunfermline KY12 0AN
Ritchie, Mary Scott (Miss)	1974	1977	Yemen	Flat 2/25, Croft-an-Righ, Edinburgh EH8 8EG
Ross, Rev. Prof. Kenneth R. and Mrs Hester	1968	1991	Malawi/Zambia/Israel	Afton Villa, 1 Afton Bridgend, New Cumnock KA18 4AX
Rough, Mary E. (Miss)	1988	1998	Malawi	The Manse, Kilmelford, Oban PA34 4XA
Roy, Rev. Alan J.	1966	1987	Blantyre	6 Glebe Street, Dumfries DG1 2LF
Russell, M.M. (Miss)	1960	1972	Zambia	14 Comerton Place, Drumoig, Leuchars, St Andrews KY16 0NQ
Samuel, Lynda (Mrs)	1946	1969	Nigeria	14 Hozier Street, Carluke ML8 5DW
Shepherd, Dr Clyne	1974	1990	Madras	28 Braehead, Methven Walk, Dundee DD2 3FJ [E-mail: rasam42@onetel.com]
Smith, Mr Harry	1956	1968	Nigeria	10 Kingsknowe Road South, Edinburgh EH14 2JE
and Mrs Margaret	1959	1967	Nigeria	
Sneddon, Mr Sandy and Mrs Marie	1968	1970	Malawi	31 Woodville Crescent, Sunderland SR4 8RE
Steedman, Martha (Mrs) (née Hamilton)	1986	2003	Pakistan	84 Greenend Gardens, Edinburgh EH17 7QH
Stewart, Marion G. (Miss)	1955	1966	North India	Muir of Blebo, Blebo Craigs, Cupar KY15 5TZ
Stone, Rev. W.V. MA BD	1976	1989	Malawi/Israel	Kirk Cottage, Kirkton of Skene, Westhill, Skene AB32 6XX
Tennant, Frances (Miss)	1949	1966	Zambia	36 Woodrow Court, Port Glasgow Road, Kilmacolm PA13 4QA
Wallace, A. Dorothy (Miss)	1965	1977	Pakistan	101 St John's Road, Edinburgh EH12 6NN
Walker, Rev. Donald K.	1953	1991	North India	Amberley, Mill Lane, Nethy Bridge PH25 3DR
and Mrs Judith	1953	1978	Nagpur	
Westmarland, Rev. Colin A.	1981	1994	Zambia	The Manse, Deshar Road, Boat of Garten PH24 3BN
Wilkie, Rev. James L.	1975	2001	Malta	PO Box 5, Cospicua, CSPOL, Malta
Wilkinson, Dr Alison	1959	1976	Zambia	7 Comely Bank Avenue, Edinburgh EH4 1EW
Wilkinson, Rev. John	1992	2007	Kenya	5 Birch Avenue, Stirling FK8 2PL
Wilson, Irene (Ms)	1946	1975	Kenya	70 Craigleith Hill Gardens, Edinburgh EH4 2JH
Wilson, Rev. Mark	1993	2004	Israel	37 Kings Avenue, Longniddry EH32 0QN

LIST M – PARISH ASSISTANTS AND PROJECT WORKERS

Those who in previous years would have been named here are now included in List J – Ministries Development Staff.

LIST N – READERS

1. EDINBURGH

Brown, Ivan	4 St Cuthberts Court, Edinburgh EH13 0LG	0131-441 1245
	[E-mail: j.ivanb@btinternet.com]	(Mbl) 07730 702860
Christie, Gillian L. (Mrs)	32 Allan Park Road, Edinburgh EH14 1LJ	0131-443 4472
Davies, Ruth (Ms) (attached to Liberton)	4 Hawkhead Grove, Edinburgh EH16 6LS	(Mbl) 07914 883354
	[E-mail: ruth@mdavies.me.uk]	0131-664 3608
Farrant, Yvonne (Ms)	Flat 7, 14 Duddingston Mills, Edinburgh EH8 7NF	0131-661 0672
	[E-mail: yvonne.farrant@crossreach.org.uk]	(Mbl) 07747 766405
Farrell, William J.	50 Ulster Crescent, Edinburgh EH8 7JS	0131-661 1026
	[E-mail: w.farrell154@btinternet.com]	
Farrow, Edmund	14 Brunswick Terrace, Edinburgh EH7 5PG	0131-558 8210
	[E-mail: edmundfarrow@blueyonder.co.uk]	
Johnston, Alan	8/19 Constitution Street, Edinburgh EH6 7BT	0131-554 1326
	[E-mail: alanacj@cairnassoc.wanadoo.co.uk]	(Mbl) 07901 510819
Kerrigan, Herbert A. (Prof.) MA LLB QC	Airdene, 20 Edinburgh Road, Dalkeith EH22 1JY	0131-660 3007
	[E-mail: kerrigan@kerriganqc.com]	(Mbl) 07725 953772
McKenzie, Janet (Mrs)	80C Colinton Road, Edinburgh EH14 1DD	0131-444 2054
	[E-mail: jintymck@talktalk.net]	
McPherson, Alistair	77 Bonaly Wester, Edinburgh EH13 0RQ	0131-478 5384
	[E-mail: amjhmcpherson@blueyonder.co.uk]	
Pearce, Martin	4 Corbiehill Avenue, Edinburgh EH4 5DR	0131-336 4864
	[E-mail: martin.j.pearce@blueyonder.co.uk]	(Mbl) 07801 717222
Sherriffs, Irene (Mrs)	22/2 West Mill Bank, Edinburgh EH13 0QT	0131-466 9530
	[E-mail: reenie.sherriffs@blueyonder.co.uk]	
Tew, Helen (Mrs)	318 Lanark Road, Edinburgh EH14 2LJ	0131-478 1268
	[E-mail: helentew9@gmail.com]	(Mbl) 07986 170802
Wyllie, Anne (Miss)	2F3, 46 Jordan Lane, Edinburgh EH10 4QX	0131-447 9035
	[E-mail: anne.wyllie@tiscali.co.uk]	

2. WEST LOTHIAN

Coyle, Charlotte (Mrs)
28 The Avenue, Whitburn EH47 0DA
[E-mail: paulcharlotte@talktalk.net] — 01501 740687

Elliott, Sarah (Miss)
105 Seafield Rows, Seafield, Bathgate EH47 7AW
[E-mail: sarah.elliott6@btopenworld.com] — 01506 654950

Galloway, Brenda (Dr)
Lochend, 58 St Ninians Road, Linlithgow EH49 7BN
[E-mail: bhgallo@yahoo.co.uk] — 01506 842028

Middleton, Alex
36 Fivestanks Place, Broxburn EH52 6BJ
[E-mail: alex.middleton@btinternet.com] — 01506 852645

Salmon, Jeanie (Mrs)
81 Croftfoot Drive, Fauldhouse, Bathgate EH47 9EH
[E-mail: jeaniesalmon@aol.com] — 01501 772468 (Work) 01501 828509

Scoular, Iain W.
15 Bonnyside Road, Bonnybridge FK4 2AD
[E-mail: iain@iwsconsultants.com] — 01324 812395 (Mbl) 07717 131596

Wilkie, David
53 Goschen Place, Broxburn EH52 5JH
[E-mail: david-fmu_09@tiscali.co.uk] — 01506 854777

3. LOTHIAN

Evans, W. John IEng MIIE(Elec)
Waterlily Cottage, 10 Fenton Steading, North Berwick EH39 5AF
[E-mail: jevans7is@hotmail.com] — 01620 842990

Hogg, David MA
82 Eskhill, Penicuik EH26 8DQ
[E-mail: hogg-d2@sky.com] — 01968 676350 (Mbl) 07821 693946

Millan, Mary (Mrs)
33 Polton Vale, Loanhead EH20 9DF
[E-mail: marymillan@fsmail.net] — 0131-440 1624 (Mbl) 07814 466104

Trevor, A. Hugh MA MTh
29A Fidra Road, North Berwick EH39 4NE
[E-mail: htrevor@talktalk.net] — 01620 894924

Yeoman, Edward T.N. FSAScot
75 Newhailes Crescent, Musselburgh EH21 6EF
[E-mail: edwardyeoman6@aol.com] — 0131-653 2291 (Mbl) 07896 517666

4. MELROSE AND PEEBLES

Cashman, Margaret D. (Mrs)
38 Abbotsford Road, Galashiels TD1 3HR
[E-mail: mcashman@tiscali.co.uk] — 01896 752711

Henderson-Howatt, David
Stoneyknowe, West Linton EH46 7BY
[E-mail: stoneyknowe@aol.com] — 01968 660677

Selkirk, Frances (Mrs)
2 The Glebe, Ashkirk, Selkirk TD7 4PJ
[E-mail: f.selkirk@btinternet.com] — 01750 32204

5. DUNS

Landale, Alison (Mrs)
Green Hope Guest House, Ellemford, Duns TD11 3SG
[E-mail: alison@greenhope.co.uk] — 01361 890242

Taylor, Christine (Mrs)
Rowardennan, Main Street, Gavinton, Duns TD11 3QT
[E-mail: christine2751@btinternet.com] — 01361 882994

6. JEDBURGH

Findlay, Elizabeth (Mrs) — 10 Inch Park, Kelso TD5 7EQ
[E-mail: elizabeth@findlay8124.fsworld.co.uk] — 01573 226641

Knox, Dagmar (Mrs) — 3 Stichill Road, Ednam, Kelso TD5 7QQ
[E-mail: dagmar.knox.riding@btinternet.com] — 01573 224883

7. ANNANDALE AND ESKDALE

Boncey, David — Redbrae, Beattock, Moffat DG10 9RF
[E-mail: david.boncey613@btinternet.com] — 01683 300613

Brown, Martin J. — Lochhouse Farm, Beattock, Moffat DG10 9SG
[E-mail: martin@lochhousefarm.com] — 01683 300451

Brown, S. Jeffrey BA — Skara Brae, 8 Ballplay Road, Moffat DG10 9JU
[E-mail: sjbrown@btinternet.com] — 01683 220475

Chisholm, Dennis A.G. MA BSc — Moss-side, Hightae, Lockerbie DG11 1JR
[E-mail: dchis@talktalk.net] — 01387 811803

Dodds, Alan — Trinco, Battlehill, Annan DG12 6SN
[E-mail: alanandjen46@talktalk.net] — 01461 201235

Jackson, Susan (Mrs) — 48 Springbells Road, Annan DG12 6LQ
[E-mail: peter-jackson24@sky.com] — 01461 204159

Morton, Andrew A. BSc — 19 Sherwood Park, Lockerbie DG11 2DX
[E-mail: andrew.a.morton@btinternet.com]
[E-mail: andrew_morton@mac.com] — 01576 203164

Saville, Hilda A. (Mrs) — 32 Crosslaw Burn, Moffat DG10 9LP
[E-mail: saville.c@sky.com] — 01683 222854

8. DUMFRIES AND KIRKCUDBRIGHT

Carroll, J. Scott — 17 Downs Place, Heathhall, Dumfries DG1 3RF
[E-mail: scott.carroll@btinternet.com] — 01387 265350

Corson, Gwen (Mrs) — 7 Sunnybrae, Borgue, Kirkcudbright DG6 4SJ — 01557 870328

Ogilvie, D. Wilson MA FSAScot — Lingerwood, 2 Nelson Street, Dumfries DG2 9AY — 01387 264267

Paterson, Ronald M. (Dr) — Mirkwood, Ringford, Castle Douglas DG7 2AL
[E-mail: mirkwoodtyke@aol.com] — 01557 820202

9. WIGTOWN AND STRANRAER

McQuistan, Robert — Old Schoolhouse, Carsluith, Newton Stewart DG8 7DT
[E-mail: mcquistan@mcquistan.plus.com] — 01671 820327

Williams, Roy — 120 Belmont Road, Stranraer DG9 7BG
[E-mail: roywilliams84@hotmail.com] — 01776 705762

10. AYR

Anderson, James (Dr)
BVMS PhD DVM FRCPath FIBiol MRCVS
67 Henrietta Street, Girvan KA26 9AN
[E-mail: jc.anderson@tesco.net]
01465 710059
(Mbl) 07952 512720

Black, Sandra (Mrs)
5 Doon Place, Troon KA10 7EQ
[E-mail: blacks_troon@hotmail.com]
01292 220075

Gowans, James
2 Cochrane Avenue, Dundonald, Kilmarnock KA2 9EJ
[E-mail: jim@luker42.freeserve.co.uk]
01563 850904
(Mbl) 07985 916814

Jamieson, Ian A.
2 Whinfield Avenue, Prestwick KA9 2BH
[E-mail: ian@jamieson4189.freeserve.co.uk]
01242 476898

Morrison, James
27 Monkton Road, Prestwick KA9 1AP
[E-mail: jim.morrison@talktalk.net]
01292 479313
07773 287852

Murphy, Ian
56 Lamont Crescent, Netherthird, Cumnock KA18 3DU
[E-mail: ianm_cumnock@yahoo.co.uk]
(Mbl) 01290 423675

Riome, Elizabeth (Mrs)
Monkwood Mains, Minishant, Maybole KA19 8EY
[E-mail: aj.riome@btinternet.com]
01292 443440

11. IRVINE AND KILMARNOCK

Bircham, James F.
8 Holmlea Place, Kilmarnock KA1 1UU
01563 532287

Cooper, Fraser
5 Balgray Way, Irvine KA11 1RP
[E-mail: frasercooper@wightcablenorth.net]
01294 211235

Crosbie, Shona (Mrs)
4 Campbell Street, Darvel KA17 0DA
[E-mail: fawltytowersdarvel@yahoo.co.uk]
01560 322229

Dempster, Ann (Mrs)
20 Graham Place, Kilmarnock KA3 7JN
[E-mail: ademp99320@aol.com]
01563 529361
(Work) 01563 534080
07729 152945

Gillespie, Janice (Miss)
12 Jeffrey Avenue, Kilmarnock KA1 4EB
[E-mail: janice.gillespie@tiscali.co.uk]
(Mbl) 01563 540009

Hamilton, Margaret A. (Mrs)
59 South Hamilton Street, Kilmarnock KA1 2DT
[E-mail: tomhmltn@sky.com]
01563 534431

Jamieson, John H. BSc DEP AFBPSS
22 Moorfield Avenue, Kilmarnock KA1 1TS
[E-mail: johnhjamieson@tiscali.co.uk]
01563 534065

McGeever, Gerard
23 Kinloch Avenue, Stewarton, Kilmarnock KA3 3HQ
[E-mail: gerard@gmcgeever.freeserve.co.uk]
01560 484331
0141-847 5717

MacLean, Donald
1 Four Acres Drive, Kilmaurs, Kilmarnock KA3 2ND
[E-mail: donanmac@yahoo.co.uk]
(Work) 01563 538475

Mills, Catherine (Mrs)
59 Crossdene Road, Crosshouse, Kilmarnock KA2 0JU
[E-mail: cfmills5lib@hotmail.com]
01563 535305

Raleigh, Gavin
21 Landsborough Drive, Kilmarnock KA3 1RY
[E-mail: gavin.raleigh@lineone.net]
01563 539377

Robertson, William
1 Archers Avenue, Irvine KA11 2GB
[E-mail: willie.robert@yahoo.co.uk]
01294 203577

Whitelaw, David
9 Kirkhill, Kilwinning KA13 6NB
[E-mail: whitelawfam@talktalk.net]
01294 551695

12. ARDROSSAN

Name	Address	Phone
Barclay, Elizabeth (Mrs)	2 Jacks Road, Saltcoats KA21 5NT [E-mail: mfiz98@dsl.pipex.com]	01294 471855
Clarke, Elizabeth (Mrs)	Swallowbrae, Torbeg, Isle of Arran KA27 8HE [E-mail: lizahclarke@gmail.com]	01770 860219 (Mbl) 07780 574367
Currie, Archie BD	55 Central Avenue, Kilbirnie KA25 6JP [E-mail: archiecurrie@yahoo.co.uk]	01505 681474
Hunter, Jean C.Q. (Mrs) BD	Church of Scotland Manse, Shiskine, Isle of Arran KA27 3EP [E-mail: j.hunter744@btinternet.com]	(Mbl) 07881 452115 01770 860380
McCool, Robert	17 McGregor Avenue, Stevenston KA20 4BA	01294 466548
Mackay, Brenda H. (Mrs)	19 Eglinton Square, Ardrossan KA22 8LN [E-mail: bremac82@aol.com]	01294 464491
Macleod, Sharon (Mrs)	Creag Dhubh, Golf Course Road, Whiting Bay, Isle of Arran KA27 8QT [E-mail: macleodsharon@hotmail.com]	01770 700353
Nimmo, Margaret (Mrs)	12 Muirfield Place, Kilwinning KA13 6NL [E-mail: margtmcmn@aol.com]	(Work) 01294 553718 01292 220336
Ross, Magnus BA MEd	39 Beachway, Largs KA30 8QH [E-mail: m.b.ross@btinternet.com]	01475 689572
Smith, Nicola (Mrs)	5 Kames Street, Millport, Isle of Cumbrae KA28 0BN [E-mail: nsasmith@fsmail.net]	01475 530747

13. LANARK

Grant, Alan	25 Moss-side Avenue, Carluke ML8 5UG [E-mail: amgrant25@aol.com]	01555 771419
Love, William	30 Barmore Avenue, Carluke ML8 4PE [E-mail: janbill30@tiscali.co.uk]	01555 751243

14. GREENOCK AND PAISLEY

Name	Address	Phone
Allan, Douglas		
Banks, Russell	18 Aboyne Drive, Paisley PA2 7SJ [E-mail: margaret.banks2@ntlworld.com]	0141-884 6925
Bird, Mary Jane		
Boag, Jennifer (Miss)	11 Madeira Street, Greenock PA16 7UJ [E-mail: jenniferboag@hotmail.com]	01475 720125
Campbell, Tom BA DipCPC	3 Grahamston Place, Paisley PA2 7BY [E-mail: tomcam38@googlemail.com]	0141-840 2273
Davey, Charles L.	16 Divert Road, Gourock PA19 1DT [E-mail: charles.davey@talktalk.net]	01475 631544
Geddes, Elizabeth (Mrs)	40 Hazelwood Road, Bridge of Weir PA11 3DT [E-mail: geddes_liz@hotmail.com]	01505 612639

Glenny, John C. — 49 Cloch Road, Gourock PA19 1AT
[E-mail: jacklizg@aol.com]   01475 636415

Hood, Eleanor (Mrs) — 12 Clochoderick Avenue, Kilbarchan, Johnstone PA10 2AY
[E-mail: eleanor.hood.kilbarchan@ntlworld.com]   01505 704208

Jackson, Nancy (Mrs) — 100 Old Greenock Road, Bishopton PA7 5BB
[E-mail: nancyj@ntlworld.com]   01505 863506

MacDonald, Christine (Ms) — 33 Collier Street, Johnstone PA5 8AG
[E-mail: christine.macdonald10@ntlworld.com]   01505 355779

McFarlan, Elizabeth (Miss) — 20 Fauldswood Crescent, Paisley PA2 9PA
[E-mail: elizabeth.mcfarlan@ntlworld.com]   01505 358411

McGill, David — 21 Mains Hill, Park Mains, Erskine PA8 7JA
[E-mail: david.mcgill@ntlworld.com]

McHugh, Jack — 'Earlshaugh', Earl Place, Bridge of Weir PA11 3HA
[E-mail: jackmchugh@tiscali.co.uk]   01505 612789

Marshall, Leon M. — 'Glenisla', Gryffe Road, Kilmacolm PA13 4BA
[E-mail: lm@stevenson-kyles.co.uk]   01505 872417

Maxwell, Sandra A. (Mrs) BD — 2 Grants Avenue, Paisley PA2 6AZ
[E-mail: sandra1.maxwell@virgin.net]   0141-884 3710

Munro, Irene (Mrs) — 80 Bardrainney Avenue, Port Glasgow PA14 6HA
[E-mail: irenemunro906@hotmail.com]   01475 701213

Noonan, Pam (Mrs) — 18 Woodburn Place, Houston, Johnstone PA6 7NA
[E-mail: pam.noonan@btinternet.com]   01505 326254

Orry, Geoff — 'Rhu Ellan', 4 Seaforth Crescent, Barrhead, Glasgow G78 1PL
[E-mail: geoff.orry@googlemail.com]   0141-881 9748

Shaw, Ian — The Grove, 8 Commercial Road, Barrhead, Glasgow G78 1AJ   0141-881 2038

16. GLASGOW

Armstrong, John (Reader Emeritus) — 44 Eckford Street, Glasgow G32 7AJ   0141-778 4745

Bremner, David — Greenhill Lodge, 1 Old Humbie Road, Glasgow G77 5DF
[E-mail: david.bremner@tiscali.co.uk]   0141-639 1742

Campbell, Jack T. BD BEd — 40 Kenmure Avenue, Bishopbriggs, Glasgow G64 2DE
[E-mail: jack.campbell@ntlworld.com]   0141-563 5837

Dickson, Hector M.K. — 'Gwito', 61 Whitton Drive, Giffnock, Glasgow G46 6EF
[E-mail: hectordickson@hotmail.com]   0141-637 0080

Fullarton, Andrew — 225 Aros Drive, Glasgow G52 1TJ   0141-883 9518

Grant, George — 44 Brownside Road, Cambuslang, Glasgow G72 8NJ
[E-mail: reader.grant@gmail.com]   0141-560 0059

Grieve, Leslie — 23 Hertford Avenue, Glasgow G12 0LG
[E-mail: leslie.grieve@gmail.com]   0141-576 1376

Horner, David J. — 20 Ledi Road, Glasgow G43 2AJ
[E-mail: djhorner@btinternet.com]   0141-637 7369

Hunt, Roland BSc PhD CertEd — 4 Flora Gardens, Bishopbriggs, Glasgow G64 1DS
[E-mail: roland.hunt@ntlworld.com]   0141-563 3257
(Evenings and weekends)   0141-563 3257

Name	Address	Telephone
Joansson, Tordur	1/2, 18 Eglinton Court, Glasgow G5 9NE [E-mail: to4ljo@yahoo.co.uk]	0141-429 6733
Kilpatrick, Mrs Joan	39 Brent Road, Regent's Park, Glasgow G46 8JG [E-mail: je-kilpatrick@sky.com]	0141-621 1809
McChlery, Stuart	The Manse, Cheapside Street, Eaglesham, Glasgow G76 0NS [E-mail: s.mcchlery@gcu.ac.uk]	01355 303495
McFarlane, Robert	25 Avenel Road, Glasgow G13 2PB [E-mail: robertmcfrln@yahoo.co.uk]	0141-954 5540
McInally, Gordon	10 Melville Gardens, Bishopbriggs, Glasgow G64 3DF [E-mail: gmcinally@sky.com]	0141-563 2685
Mackenzie, Norman	Flat 3/2, 41 Kilmailing Road, Glasgow G44 5UH [E-mail: mackenzie799@btinternet.com]	(Mbl) 07780 733710
McLaughlin, Cathy (Mrs)	8 Lamlash Place, Glasgow G33 3XH [E-mail: chmclaughlin@talktalk.net]	0141-774 2483
MacLeod, John	2 Shuna Place, Newton Mearns, Glasgow G77 6TN [E-mail: jmacleod2@sky.com]	0141-639 6862
Maxwell, David	248 Old Castle Road, Glasgow G44 5EZ [E-mail: david.maxwell7@ntlworld.com]	0141-569 6379
Millar, Kathleen (Mrs)	9 Glenbank Court, Thornliebank, Glasgow G46 7EJ [E-mail: kathleen.millar@tesco.net]	0141-638 6250 (Mbl) 07793 203045
Montgomery, Hamish	13 Avon Avenue, Bearsden, Glasgow G61 2PS	0141-942 3640
Nairne, Elizabeth	229 Southbrae Drive, Glasgow G13 1TT	0141-959 5066
Nicolson, John	2 Lindsaybeg Court, Chryston, Glasgow G69 9DD [E-mail: john.c.nicolson@btinternet.com]	0141-779 2447
Phillips, John B.	2/3, 30 Handel Place, Glasgow G5 0TP [E-mail: johnphillips@fish.co.uk]	0141-429 7716
Rennie, Katherine (Miss)	12 Westside Gardens, 4 Partickhill Road, Glasgow G11 5BL [E-mail: katherinemrennie@btinternet.com]	0141-339 0540
Robertson, Adam	423 Amulree Street, Glasgow G32 7SS	0141-573 6662
Roy, Mrs Shona	81 Busby Road, Clarkston, Glasgow G76 8BD [E-mail: theroyfamily@yahoo.co.uk]	0141-644 3713
Smith, Ann	52 Robslee Road, Thornliebank, Glasgow G46 7BX	0141-621 0638
Stead, Mrs Mary	9A Carrick Drive, Mount Vernon, Glasgow G32 0RW [E-mail: maystead@hotmail.co.uk]	0141-764 1016
Stewart, James	45 Airthrey Avenue, Glasgow G14 9LY [E-mail: jmstewart325@btinternet.com]	0141-959 5814
Stuart, Alex	107 Baldorran Crescent, Cumbernauld, Glasgow G68 9EX [E-mail: alexpstuart@btopenworld.com]	01236 727710
Sturrock, Roger	36 Thomson Drive, Glasgow G61 3PA [E-mail: rogersturrock@mac.com]	0141-942 7412

Tindall, Margaret (Mrs) — 23 Ashcroft Avenue, Lennoxtown, Glasgow G65 7EN [E-mail: margarettindall@aol.com] — 01360 310911

Watson, Alan — 56 Baldorran Crescent, Cumbernauld, Glasgow G68 9BL [E-mail: watsonalan@btinternet.com] — 01236 729095

Webster, James — 65 Fruin Avenue, Newton Mearns, Glasgow G77 6HG [E-mail: j.webster139@btinternet.com] — 0141-639 0035

Williamson, John G. (Reader Emeritus) — 34 King Edward Road, Glasgow G13 1QW — 0141-959 1300

Wilson, George A. — 46 Maxwell Drive, Garrowhill, Baillieston, Glasgow G69 6LS [E-mail: healthandsafety@talk21.com] — 0141-771 3862

17. HAMILTON

Allan, Angus J. — Blackburn Mill, Chapelton, Strathaven ML10 6RR [E-mail: angus.allan@hotmail.com] — 01357 528548

Beattie, Richard — 4 Bent Road, Hamilton ML3 6QB — 01698 420086

Bell, Sheena — 2 Langdale, East Kilbride, Glasgow G74 4RP [E-mail: richardbeattie1958@hotmail.com] — 01355 248217

[E-mail: belljsheena@hotmail.co.uk]

Chirnside, Peter — 141 Kyle Park Drive, Uddingston, Glasgow G71 7DB — 01698 813769

Codona, Joy (Mrs) — Dykehead Farm, 300 Dykehead Road, Airdrie ML6 7SR [E-mail: jcodona772@btinternet.com] — 01236 767063 — 07810 770609 (Mbl)

Cruickshanks, William — 63 Progress Drive, Caldercruix, Airdrie ML6 7PU — 01236 843352

Haggarty, Frank — 46 Glen Road, Caldercruix, Airdrie ML6 7PZ — 01236 842182

Hastings, William Paul — 186 Glen More, East Kilbride, Glasgow G74 2AN [E-mail: wphastings@hotmail.co.uk] — 01355 521228

Hewitt, Samuel — 3 Corrie Court, Earnock, Hamilton ML3 9XE [E-mail: sambetty1@hotmail.com] — 01698 457403

Hislop, Eric — 1 Castlegait, Strathaven ML10 6FF [E-mail: eric.hislop@tiscali.co.uk] — 01357 520003

Jardine, Lynette — 32 Powburn Crescent, Uddingston, Glasgow G71 7SS [E-mail: lpjardine@blueyonder.co.uk] — 01698 812404

Keir, Dickson — 46 Brackenhill Drive, Hamilton ML3 8AY [E-mail: dickson.keir@btinternet.com] — 01698 457351

Leckie, Elizabeth — 41 Church Street, Larkhall ML9 1EZ [E-mail: elizleckie@blueyonder.co.uk] — 01698 308933

McCleary, Isaac — 719 Coatbridge Road, Baillieston, Glasgow G69 7PH — 01236 421073

MacMillan, Georgina — 1 Darngaber Gardens, Quarter, Hamilton ML3 7XX [E-mail: georgiemac@talktalk.net] — 01698 424040

Murphy, Jim — 10 Hillview Crescent, Bellshill ML4 1NX [E-mail: jim.murphy5@btopenworld.com] — 01698 740189

Preston, J. Steven — 24 Glen Prosen, East Kilbride, Glasgow G74 3TA [E-mail: steven.preston1@btinternet.com] — 01355 237359

Robertson, Rowan — 68 Townhead Road, Coatbridge, ML5 2HU — 01236 425703
Stevenson, Thomas — 34 Castle Wynd, Quarter, Hamilton ML3 7XD — 01698 282263
White, Ian T. — 21 Muirhead, Stonehouse, Larkhall ML9 3HG — 01698 792772
[E-mail: iantwhite@aol.com]

18. DUMBARTON

Foster, Peter — The Forge, Colgrain Steading, Colgrain, Cardross, Dumbarton G82 5JL — 01389 849200
[E-mail: peterafoster@btopenworld.com]
Galbraith, Iain B. MA MPhil MTh ThD FTCL — Beechwood, Overton Road, Alexandria G83 0LJ — 01389 753563
Giles, Donald (Dr) — Levern House, Stuckenduff, Shandon, Helensburgh G84 8NW — 01436 820565
[E-mail: don.giles@btopenworld.com]
Harold, Sandy — The Laurels, Risk Street, Clydebank G81 3LW — 0141-952 3673
[E-mail: harold996@btinternet.com]
Hart, R.J.M. BSc — 7 Kidston Drive, Helensburgh G84 8QA — 01436 672039
[E-mail: rjm7k@yahoo.com]
McCutcheon, John — Flat 2/6 Parkview, Milton Brae, Milton, Dumbarton G82 2TT — 01389 739034
[E-mail: JMccutc933@aol.com]
Morgan, Richard — Annandale, School Road, Rhu, Helensburgh G84 8RS — 01436 821269
[E-mail: themorgans@hotmail.co.uk]
Nutter, Margaret (Miss) — 14 Balloch Road, Balloch, Alexandria G83 8SR — 01436 754505
[E-mail: mnutter@blueyonder.co.uk]
Rettie, Sara (Mrs) — 86 Dennistoun Crescent, Helensburgh G84 7JF — 01436 677984
[E-mail: sarajayne.rettie@btinternet.com]
Robertson, Ishbel (Mrs) — 81 Bonhill Road, Dumbarton G82 2DU — 01389 763436
[E-mail: ishbelrobertson@blueyonder.co.uk]

19. ARGYLL

Binner, Aileen (Mrs) — 'Ailand', North Connel, Oban PA37 1QX — 01631 710264
[E-mail: binners@ailand-plus.com]
Challis, John O. — Bay Villa, Strachur, Cairndow PA27 8DE — 01369 860436
[E-mail: strachur@aol.com]
Logue, David — 3 Braeface, Tayvallich, Lochgilphead PA31 8PN — 01546 870647
[E-mail: david@loguenet.co.uk]
McLellan, James A. — West Drimvore, Lochgilphead PA31 8SU — 01546 606403
[E-mail: james.mclellan8@btinternet.com]
Morrison, John L. — Tigh na Barnashaig, Tayvallich, Lochgilphead PA31 8PN — 01546 870637
[E-mail: jolomo@thejolomostudio.com]
Ramsay, Mathew M. — Portnastorm, Carradale, Campbeltown PA28 6SB — 01583 431381
[E-mail: portnastorm@tiscali.co.uk]

Sinclair, Margaret (Mrs) 2 Quarry Place, Furnace, Inveraray PA32 8XW 01499 500633
[E-mail: margaret_sinclair@btinternet.com]

Stather, Angela (Mrs) 9 Gartness Cottages, Ballygrant, Isle of Islay PA45 7QN 01496 840527
[E-mail: angel.stather@virgin.net]

Thornhill, Christopher R. 4 Ardfern Cottages, Ardfern, Lochgilphead PA31 9QN 01852 500674
[E-mail: c.thornhill@btinternet.com]

Waddell, Martin 2 Kilbrandon Cottages, Balvicar, Isle of Seil, Oban PA34 4RA 01852 300395
[E-mail: waddell1715@btinternet.com]

Zielinski, Jennifer C. (Mrs) 26 Cromwell Street, Dunoon PA23 7AX 01369 706136
[E-mail: jczyefo@aol.com]

22. FALKIRK

Brown, Kathryn (Mrs) 1 Callendar Park Walk, Callendar Grange, Falkirk FK1 1TA 01324 617352
[E-mail: kaybrown1cpw@talktalk.net]

Duncan, Lorna M. (Mrs) BA Richmond, 28 Solway Drive, Head of Muir, Denny FK6 5NS 01324 813020
[E-mail: ell.dee@blueyonder.co.uk]

MacDonald, Monica (Mrs) 32 Reilly Gardens, High Bonnybridge, Bonnybridge FK4 2BB 01324 874807
[E-mail: monica.macdonald55@googlemail.com]

Mathers, Sandra (Mrs) 10 Ercall Road, Brightons, Falkirk FK2 0RS 01324 872253
[E-mail: alexena@btinternet.com]

O'Rourke, Edith (Ms) 16 Achray Road, Condorrat, Cumbernauld G67 4JH 01236 732813
[E-mail: o-rourke45@btinternet.com]

Sarle, Andrew BSc BD 114 High Station Road, Falkirk FK1 5LN 01324 621648
[E-mail: andrew@sarle.me.uk]

Stewart, Arthur MA 51 Bonnymuir Crescent, Bonnybridge FK4 1GD 01324 812667
[E-mail: arthur.stewart1@btinternet.com]

Struthers, Ivar B. 7 McVean Place, Bonnybridge FK4 1QZ 01324 841145
[E-mail: ivar.struthers@btinternet.com] (Mbl) 07921 778208

23. STIRLING

Durie, Alastair (Dr) 25 Forth Place, Stirling FK8 1UD 01786 451029
[E-mail: acdurie@btinternet.com]

Grier, Hunter 17 Station Road, Bannockburn, Stirling FK7 8LG 01786 815192
[E-mail: hunter@xaltmail.com]

Tilly, Patricia (Mrs) 25 Meiklejohn Street, Stirling FK9 5HQ 01786 446401
[E-mail: Trishatilly@aol.com] (Mbl) 07428 559554

Weir, Andrew (Dr) 16 The Oaks, Killearn, Glasgow G63 9SF 01360 550779
[E-mail: andrewweir@btinternet.com] (Mbl) 07534 506075

24. DUNFERMLINE

Adams, William — 24 Foulford Street, Cowdenbeath KY4 0EQ [E-mail: william.adams94@yahoo.co.uk] — 01383 510540

Arnott, Robert G.K. — 25 Sealstrand, Dalgety Bay, Dunfermline KY11 9NG [E-mail: robin.arnott@nibor.org.uk] — 01383 822293

Blane, David — 10 Ordnance Road, Crombie, Dunfermline KY12 8JZ [E-mail: davidblane@virgin.net] — 01383 873002 / 07866 543049 (Mbl) / 01577 840248

Brown, Gordon — Nowell, Fossoway, Kinross KY13 0UW [E-mail: brown.nowell@hotmail.co.uk]

Conway, Bernard — 4 Centre Street, Kelty KY4 0EQ — 01383 830442

Grant, Allan — 6 Normandy Place, Rosyth KY11 2HJ [E-mail: allan75@btinternet.com] — 01383 428760

McCafferty, Joyce (Mrs) — 53 Foulford Street, Cowdenbeath KY4 9AS — 01383 515775

McDonald, Elizabeth (Mrs) — Parleyhill, Culross, Dunfermline KY12 8JD — 01383 880231

Meiklejohn, Barry — 40 Lilac Grove, Dunfermline KY11 8AP [E-mail: barry.meiklejohn@btinternet.com] — 01383 731550

Mitchell, Ian G. QC — 17 Carlingnose Point, North Queensferry, Inverkeithing KY11 1ER [E-mail: igmitchell@easynet.co.uk] — 01383 416240

25. KIRKCALDY

Allardice, Michael — 20 Parbroath Road, Glenrothes KY7 4TH [E-mail: m.allardice@dundee.ac.uk] — 01592 772280 / 07936 203465 (Mbl)

Biernat, Ian — 2 Formonthills Road, Glenrothes KY6 3EF [E-mail: ian.biernat@btinternet.com] — 01592 655565

26. ST ANDREWS

Elder, Morag Anne (Ms) — 5 Provost Road, Tayport DD6 9JE [E-mail: benuardin@tiscali.co.uk] — 01382 552218

King, C.M. (Mrs) — 8 Bankwell Road, Anstruther KY10 3DA — 01333 310017

Kinnis, W.K.B. (Dr) (Reader Emeritus) — 45 Argyle Court, St Andrews KY16 9BW [E-mail: mail@bkinnis.fsnet.co.uk] — 01334 476959

Smith, Elspeth (Mrs) — Whinstead, Dalgairn, Cupar KY15 4PH [E-mail: elspeth.smith@btopenworld.com] — 01334 653269

27. DUNKELD AND MEIGLE

Howat, David — Lilybank Cottage, Newton Street, Blairgowrie PH10 6HZ [E-mail: david@thehowats.net] — 01250 874715

Steele, Grace (Ms)
12A Farragon Drive, Aberfeldy PH15 2BQ
[E-mail: gmfsteele@tiscali.co.uk]
01887 820025

Templeton, Elizabeth (Mrs)
Milton of Pitgur Farmhouse, Dalcapon, Pitlochry PH9 0ND
[E-mail: templeton.e@btinternet.com]
01796 472360

Theaker, Phillip
5 Altamount Road, Blairgowrie PH10 6QL
[E-mail: ptheaker@talktalk.net]
01250 871162

28. PERTH

Archibald, Michael
Wychwood, Culdeesland Road, Methven, Perth PH1 3QE
[E-mail: michael.archibald@gmail.com]
01738 840995

Begg, James
8 Park Village, Turretbank Road, Crieff PH7 4JN
[E-mail: Bjimmy37@aol.com]
01764 655907

Benneworth, Michael
7 Hamilton Place, Perth PH1 1BB
[E-mail: mbenneworth@hotmail.com]
01738 203371

Davidson, Andrew
95 Needless Road, Perth PH2 0LD
[E-mail: andrew_r_davidson@yahoo.co.uk]
01738 620839

Laing, John
10 Graybank Road, Perth PH2 0GZ
[E-mail: johnandmarylaing@hotmail.co.uk]
01738 623888

Livingstone, Alan
Meadowside, Lawmuir, Methven, Perth PH1 3SZ
[E-mail: livingstone24@btinternet.com]
01738 638866
(Mbl) 07860 930154

Ogilvie, Brian
67 Whitecraigs, Kinnesswood, Kinross KY13 9JN
[E-mail: brianj.ogilvie1@btopenworld.com]
01592 840823
(Mbl) 07815 759864

Thorburn, Susan (Mrs) MTh
3 Daleally Cottages, St Madoes Road, Errol, Perth PH2 7TJ
[E-mail: s.thor@yahoo.com]
01821 642681

Yellowlees, Deirdre (Mrs)
Ringmill House, Gannochy Farm, Perth PH2 7JH
[E-mail: d.yellowlees@btinternet.com]
01738 633773
(Mbl) 07920 805399

29. DUNDEE

Brown, Isobel (Mrs)
10 School Wynd, Muirhead, Dundee DD2 5LW
[E-mail: isobel73@btinternet.com]
01382 580545

Brown, Janet (Miss)
G2, 6 Baxter Park Terrace, Dundee DD4 6NL
[E-mail: j.herries.brown@blueyonder.co.uk]
01382 453066

Webster, Charles A.
16C Bath Street, Broughty Ferry, Dundee DD5 2BY
[E-mail: charliewebster@talktalk.net]
01382 739520
(Mbl) 07905 141269

Woodley, Alan G. (Dr)
67 Marlee Road, Broughty Ferry, Dundee DD5 3EU
[E-mail: awoodley@btinternet.com]
01382 739820

Xenophontos-Hellen, Tim
Aspro Spiti, 23 Ancrum Drive, Dundee DD2 2JG
[E-mail: tim.xsf@btinternet.com]
01382 630355
(Work) 01382 567756

30. ANGUS

Beedie, Alexander W.
62 Newton Crescent, Arbroath DD11 3JZ
[E-mail: bill.beedie@hotmail.co.uk]
01241 875001

Davidson, Peter I.
24 Kinnaird Place, Brechin DD9 7HF
[E-mail: mail@idavidson.co.uk]   01241 852666

Edwards, Dougal
25 Mackenzie Street, Carnoustie DD7 6HD
[E-mail: dougal.edwards@blueyonder.co.uk]   01674 677126

Gray, Ian
'The Mallards', 15 Rossie Island Road, Montrose DD10 9NH
[E-mail: iancelia15@aol.com]   01307 464039

Gray, Linda (Mrs)
8 Inchgarth Street, Forfar DD8 3LY
[E-mail: lindamgray@sky.com]

Nicoll, Douglas
16 New Road, Forfar DD8 2AE   01307 463264
Stevens, Peter J. BSc BA
7 Union Street, Montrose DD10 8PZ
[E-mail: peter280stevens@btinternet.com]   01674 673710

Wheat, Michael A.
16A South Esk Street, Montrose DD10 8BJ   01674 676083

31. ABERDEEN
Gray, Peter (Prof.)
165 Countesswells Road, Aberdeen AB15 7RA
[E-mail: pmdgray165@btinternet.com]   01224 318172

32. KINCARDINE AND DEESIDE
Bell, Robert
27 Mearns Drive, Stonehaven AB39 2DZ
[E-mail: r.bell282@btinternet.com]   01569 767173
(Mbl)   07733 014826

Broere, Teresa (Mrs)
3 Balnastraid Cottages, Dinnet, Aboyne AB34 5NE
[E-mail: broere@btinternet.com]   01339 880058

Coles, Stephen
43 Mearns Walk, Laurencekirk AB30 1FA
[E-mail: steve@sbcco.com]   01561 378400

McCafferty, W. John
Lynwood, Cammachmore, Stonehaven AB39 3NR
[E-mail: wjmccafferty@yahoo.co.uk]   01569 730281

McLuckie, John
7 Monaltrie Close, Ballater AB35 5PT
[E-mail: johnemcluckie@btinternet.com]   01339 755489

Middleton, Robin B. (Capt.)
7 St Ternan's Road, Newtonhill, Stonehaven AB39 3PF
[E-mail: randjmiddleton@tiscali.co.uk]   01569 730852

Platt, David
2 St Michael's Road, Newtonhill, Stonehaven AB39 3RW
[E-mail: daveplatt01@btinternet.com]   01569 730465

Simpson, Elizabeth (Mrs)
Connemara, 33 Golf Road, Ballater AB35 5RS
[E-mail: connemara33@yahoo.com]   01339 755597

33. GORDON

Bichard, Susanna (Mrs)	Beechlee, Haddo Lane, Tarves, Ellon AB41 7JZ	01651 851343
	[E-mail: smbichard@aol.com]	
Doak, Alan B.	17 Chievres Place, Ellon AB41 9WH	01358 721819
	[E-mail: alanbdoak@aol.com]	
Findlay, Patricia (Mrs)	Douglas View, Tullynessle, Alford AB33 8QR	01975 562379
	[E-mail: p.a.findlay@btopenworld.com]	
Mitchell, Jean (Mrs)	6 Cowgate, Oldmeldrum, Inverurie AB51 0EN	01651 872745
	[E-mail: j.g.mitchell@btinternet.com]	
Robb, Margaret (Mrs)	Chrislouan, Keithhall, Inverurie AB51 0LN	01651 882310
	[E-mail: Robbminister1@aol.com]	
Robertson, James Y. MA	1 Nicol Road, Kintore, Inverurie AB51 0QA	01467 633001
	[E-mail: j.robertson833@btinternet.com]	

34. BUCHAN

Armitage, Rosaline (Mrs)	Whitecairn, Blackhills, Peterhead AB42 3LR		01779 477267
	[E-mail: r.r.armitage@btinternet.com]		
Barker, Tim	South Silverford Croft, Longmanhill, Banff AB45 3SB		01261 851839
	[E-mail: tbarker05@aol.com]		
Brown, Lillian (Mrs)	45 Main Street, Aberchirder, Huntly AB54 7ST		01466 780330
Davidson, James C.	19 Great Stuart Street, Peterhead AB42 1JX		01779 470242
	[E-mail: jim@jcdavidson.com]		
Forsyth, Alicia (Mrs)	Rothie Inn Farm, Forgue Road, Rothienorman, Inverurie AB51 8YH		01651 821359
	[E-mail: a.forsyth@btinternet.com]		
Givan, James	Zimra, Longmanhill, Banff AB45 3RP		01261 833318
	[E-mail: jim.givan@btinternet.com]	(Mbl)	07753 458664
Higgins, Scott	St Ninian's, Manse Terrace, Turriff AB53 4BA		01888 569103
	[E-mail: mhairiandscott@btinternet.com]		
Lumsden, Vera (Mrs)	8 Queen's Crescent, Portsoy, Banff AB45 2PX		01261 842712
McColl, John	East Cairnchina, Lonmay, Fraserburgh AB43 8RH		01346 532558
	[E-mail: ivsd@lumsden77.freeserve.co.uk]	(Mbl)	07757 303195
MacLeod, Ali (Ms)	11 Pitfour Crescent, Fetterangus, Peterhead AB42 4EL		01771 622992
	[E-mail: solfolly11@gmail.com]	(Mbl)	07821 670705
Macnee, Anthea (Mrs)	Wardend Cottage, Alvah, Banff AB45 3TR		01261 815647
	[E-mail: aliowl@hotmail.com]		
Mair, Dorothy L.T. (Miss)	Flat F, 15 The Quay, Newburgh, Ellon AB41 6DA		
	[E-mail: macneeiain4@googlemail.com]	(Mbl)	07505 051305
Michie, William D.	34 Seafield Street, Whitehills, Banff AB45 2NR		01261 861439
	[E-mail: dorothymair2@aol.com]		
Noble, John M.	44 Henderson Park, Peterhead AB42 2WR		01779 472522
	[E-mail: b.michie@talktalk.net]		
Ogston, Norman	Rowandale, 6 Rectory Road, Turriff AB53 4SU		01888 560342
	[E-mail: john_m_noble@hotmail.co.uk]		
	[E-mail: norman.ogston@gmail.com]		

Simpson, Andrew C. 10 Wood Street, Banff AB45 1JX 01261 812538
[E-mail: andy.louise1@btinternet.com]

Smith, Jenny (Mrs) 5 Seatown Place, Cairnbulg, Fraserburgh AB43 8WP 01346 582364
[E-mail: jennyfsmith@hotmail.com]

Sneddon, Richard 100 West Road, Peterhead AB42 2AQ 01779 480803
[E-mail: richard.sneddon@btinternet.com]

Stewart, William Denend, Strichen, Fraserburgh AB43 6RN 01771 637256
[E-mail: billandjunes@live.co.uk]

Taylor, Elaine (Mrs) 101 Cairntrodlie, Peterhead AB42 2AY 01779 472978
[E-mail: elaine.taylor60@btinternet.com]

Williams, Paul 20 Soy Burn Gardens, Portsoy, Banff AB45 2QG 01261 842338
[E-mail: paul.williams447@virgin.net]

35. MORAY

Benson, F. Stewart 8 Springfield Court, Forres IV36 3WY 01309 671525
[E-mail: janetwbenson@hotmail.com]

Forbes, Jean (Mrs) Greenmoss, Drybridge, Buckie AB56 2JB 01542 831646
[E-mail: dancingfeet@tinyworld.co.uk] (Mbl) 07974 760337

36. ABERNETHY

Bardgett, Alison (Mrs) Tigh an Iasgair, Street of Kincardine, Boat of Garten PH24 3BY 01479 831751
[E-mail: tigh@bardgett.plus.com]

Berkeley, John (Dr) Drumbeg, Coylumbridge, Aviemore PH22 1QU 01479 811055
[E-mail: john@berkeley.freeserve.co.uk]

Thomson, Mary (Mrs) Riverside Flat, Gynack Street, Kingussie PH21 1EL 01540 661772
[E-mail: marythomson835@btinternet.com]

37. INVERNESS

Archer, Morven (Mrs) 42 Firthview Drive, Inverness IV3 8QE 01463 237840
[E-mail: morvarch@btinternet.com]

Cazaly, Leonard 9 Moray Park Gardens, Culloden, Inverness IV2 7FY 01463 794469
[E-mail: len_cazaly@lineone.net]

Cook, Arnett D. 66 Millerton Avenue, Inverness IV3 8RY 01463 224795
[E-mail: arnett.cook@btinternet.com]

Dennis, Barry 50 Holm Park, Inverness IV2 4XU (Work) 01463 225883
[E-mail: barry.dennis@tiscali.co.uk] 01463 663448 01463 230321

MacInnes, Ailsa (Mrs) Kilmartin, 17 Southside Road, Inverness IV2 3BG (Mbl) 07704 485055
[E-mail: ailsa.macinnes@btopenworld.com]

Robertson, Hendry — Park House, 51 Glenurquhart Road, Inverness IV3 5PB — 01463 231858 (Mbl) 07929 766102
[E-mail: hendry.robertson@connectfree.co.uk]

Robertson, Stewart J.H. — 21 Towerhill Drive, Cradlehall, Inverness IV2 5FD — 01463 793144

Roden, Vivian (Mrs) — 15 Old Mill Road, Tomatin, Inverness IV13 7YW — 01808 511355
[E-mail: vroden@btinternet.com]

Todd, Iain — 9 Leanach Gardens, Inverness IV2 5DD — 01887 704915 (Mbl) 01463 791161
[E-mail: itoddyo@aol.com]

38. LOCHABER

Chalkley, Andrew BSc — 2 Telford Place, Claggan, Fort William PH33 6QG — 01397 700271
[E-mail: andrewjoan@googlemail.com]

Ogston, Jean (Mrs) — Church of Scotland Manse, Annie's Brae, Mallaig PH41 4RG — 01687 460042
[E-mail: jeanogston@googlemail.com]

Walker, Eric — Tigh a' Chlann, Inverroy, Roy Bridge PH31 4AQ — 01397 712028
[E-mail: line15@btinternet.com]

Walker, Pat (Mrs) — Tigh a' Chlann, Inverroy, Roy Bridge PH31 4AQ — 01397 712028
[E-mail: pat.line15@btinternet.com]

39. ROSS

Finlayson, Michael R. — Amberlea, Glenskiach, Evanton, Dingwall IV16 9UU — 01349 830598
[E-mail: finlayson935@btinternet.com]

Greer, Kathleen (Mrs) MEd — 17 Duthac Wynd, Tain IV19 1LP — 01862 892065
[E-mail: greer2@talktalk.net]

Gunstone, Ronald W. — 20 Bellfield Road, North Kessock, Inverness IV1 3XU — 01463 731337 (Mbl) 07974 443948
[E-mail: ronald.gunstone@virgin.net]

Jamieson, Patricia A. (Mrs) — 9 Craig Avenue, Tain IV19 1JP — 01862 893154
[E-mail: hapijam179@yahoo.co.uk]

McAlpine, James — 5 Cromlet Park, Invergordon IV18 0RN — 01349 852801
[E-mail: jmca1@tinyworld.co.uk]

McCreadie, Frederick — Inchbroom, Highfield Park, Conon Bridge, Dingwall IV7 8AP — 01349 862171
[E-mail: fredmccreadie@tesco.net]

Munro, Irene (Mrs) — 1 Wyvis Crescent, Conon Bridge, Dingwall IV7 8BZ — 01349 865752
[E-mail: irenemunro@rocketmail.com]

Riddell, Keith — 2 Station Cottages, Fearn, Tain IV20 1RR — 01862 832867 (Mbl) 07719 645995
[E-mail: keithriddell@hotmail.co.uk]

40. SUTHERLAND

Baxter, A. Rosie (Dr) — Creich Old Manse, Bonar Bridge, Ardgay IV24 3AB — 01863 766257
[E-mail: drrosiereid@yahoo.co.uk]

Bruce, Dorothy (Mrs) (Reader Emeritus) — Eastwood, Altass, Rosehall, by Lairg IV27 4EU — 01748 761694 (Mbl) 01549 441285
[E-mail: dorothymbruce@aol.com]

Innes, Derek — Hill Cottage, 24 Lairg Muir, Lairg IV27 4ED
[E-mail: dereklinnes@btinternet.com] — 01549 402215 (Mbl) 07791 125954

Roberts, Irene (Mrs) — Flat 4, Harbour Buildings, Main Street, Portmahomack, Tain IV20 1YG
[E-mail: ireneroberts43@hotmail.com] — 01862 871166 (Mbl) 07854 436854

Weidner, Karl — 6 St Vincent Road, Tain IV19 1JR
[E-mail: kweidner@btinternet.com] — 01862 894202

41. CAITHNESS

42. LOCHCARRON – SKYE
Lamont, John H. BD — 6 Tigh na Filine, Aultbea, Achnasheen IV22 2JE
[E-mail: jhlamont@btinternet.com] — (Mbl) 07714 720753

MacRae, Donald E. — Nethania, 52 Strath, Gairloch IV21 2DB
[E-mail: Dmgair@aol.com] — 01445 712235

Murray, John W. — 1 Totescore, Kilmuir, Portree, Isle of Skye IV51 9YW — 01470 542297
Ross, R. Ian — St Conal's, Inverinate, Kyle IV40 8HB — 01599 511371

43. UIST
Browning, Margaret (Miss) — 1 Middlequarter, Sollas, Lochmaddy, Isle of North Uist HS6 5BU
[E-mail: margaretckb@tiscali.co.uk] — 01876 560392

Lines, Charles M.D. — Flat 1/02, 8 Queen Margaret Road, Glasgow G20 6DP
MacAulay, John — Fernhaven, 1 Flodabay, Isle of Harris HS3 3HA — 01859 530340
MacNab, Ann (Mrs) — Druim Skiivat, Scolpaig, Lochmaddy, Isle of North Uist HS6 5DH
[E-mail: annabhan@hotmail.com] — 01876 510701

44. LEWIS
Macleod, Donald — 14 Balmerino Drive, Stornoway, Isle of Lewis HS1 2TD
[E-mail: donaldmacleod25@btinternet.com] — 01851 704516

Macmillan, Iain — 34 Scotland Street, Stornoway, Isle of Lewis HS1 2JR
[E-mail: macmillan@brocair.fsnet.co.uk] — 01851 704826 (Mbl) 07775 027987

Murray, Angus — 4 Ceann Chilleagraidh, Stornoway, Isle of Lewis HS1 2UJ — 01851 703550

45. ORKNEY
Dicken, Marion (Mrs) — 6 Claymore Brae, Kirkwall, Orkney KW15 1UQ
[E-mail: mj44@hotmail.co.uk] — 01856 879509

Robertson, Johan (Mrs) — Old Manse, Eday, Orkney KW17 2AA — 01857 622251

46. SHETLAND

Christie, William C. (Reader Emeritus)
11 Fullaburn, Bressay, Shetland ZE2 9ET
[E-mail: william.christie2@homecall.co.uk]
01595 820244

Greig, Diane (Mrs) MA
6 Hayhoull Place, Bigton, Shetland ZE2 9GA
[E-mail: mrschm.greig@btinternet.com]
01950 422468

Harrison, Christine (Mrs) BA
Gerdavatn, Baltasound, Unst, Shetland ZE2 9DY
[E-mail: chris4242@btinternet.com]
01957 711578

Smith, M. Beryl (Mrs) DCE MSc
Vakterlee, Cumliewick, Sandwick, Shetland ZE2 9HH
[E-mail: beryl@brooniestaing.co.uk]
01950 431280

47. ENGLAND

Houghton, Mark (Dr)
Kentcliffe, Charney Road, Grange-over-Sands, Cumbria LA11 6BP
[E-mail: mark@chaplain.me.uk]
01539 525048

Mackay, Donald (Reader Emeritus)
90 Hallgarth Street, Elvet, Durham DH1 3AS
(Work) 01629 813505
0191-383 2110

Menzies, Rena (Mrs)
49 Elizabeth Avenue, St Brelade's, Jersey JE3 8GR
[E-mail: menzfamily@jerseymail.co.uk]
01534 741095

Milligan, Elaine (Mrs)
16 Surrey Close, Corby, Northants NN17 2TG
[E-mail: elainemilligan@ntlworld.com]
01536 205259

Munro, William
35 Stour Road, Corby, Northants NN17 2HX
01536 504864

48. EUROPE

Ross, David
Urb. El Campanario, EDF Granada, Esc. 14, Baja B, Ctra Cadiz N-340,
Km 168, 29680 Estepona, Malaga, Spain
[E-mail: rosselcampanario@yahoo.co.uk]
(Tel/Fax) 0034 952 88 26 34

49. JERUSALEM

Oakley-Levstein, Joanna

ASSOCIATE (Ireland)

Binnie, Jean (Miss)
2 Ailesbury Lawn, Dundrum, Dublin 16, Ireland
[E-mail: jeanbinnie@eircom.net]
00353 1 298 7229

LIST O – REPRESENTATIVES ON COUNCIL EDUCATION COMMITTEES

COUNCIL	NAME	ADDRESS	TEL
ABERDEEN	Rev. Eddie McKenna	The Manse, Kincorth Circle, Aberdeen AB12 5NX [E-mail: eddiemckenna@uwclub.net]	01224 872820
ABERDEENSHIRE	Dr Eleanor Anderson	Drumblair Cottage, Forgue, Huntly AB54 6DE [E-mail: edrumblair@hotmail.com]	01464 871329
ANGUS	Mr David Adams	Glebe House, Farnell, by Brechin DD9 6UH [E-mail: david.adams81@btinternet.com]	01674 820227
ARGYLL and BUTE	Mr William Crossan	Gowanbank, Kilkerran Road, Campbeltown PA26 6JL	01259 213872
CLACKMANNAN	Rev. Sang Y. Cha	37A Claremont, Alloa FK10 2DG [E-mail: syc@cantab.net]	
DUMFRIES and GALLOWAY	Mr Robert McQuistan	Old Schoolhouse, Carsluith, Newton Stewart DG8 7DT [E-mail: mcquistan@mcquistan.plus.com]	01671 820327
DUNDEE	Miss Kathleen Mands	27 Noran Avenue, Dundee DD4 7LE [E-mail: kathmands@blueyonder.co.uk]	01382 451140
EAST AYRSHIRE	Mr Ian Rennie	46 Colonsay Place, Wardneuk, Kilmarnock KA3 2JU [E-mail: i.rennie@btinternet.com]	
EAST DUNBARTONSHIRE	Mrs Barbara Jarvie	18 Cannerton Crescent, Milton of Campsie, Glasgow G66 8DR [E-mail: bj@bjarvie.fsnet.co.uk]	01360 319729
EAST LOTHIAN	Mrs Marjorie K. Goldsmith	20 St Lawrence, Haddington EH41 3RL	01620 823249
EAST RENFREWSHIRE	Ms Mary McIntyre	5 Buchanan Drive, Glasgow G77 6HT [E-mail: mmmcintyre@ntlworld.com]	
EDINBURGH CITY	Mr A. Craig Duncan	2 East Barnton Gardens, Edinburgh EH4 6AR [E-mail: acraigduncan@btinternet.com]	0131-336 4432
FALKIRK	Mrs Margaret Coutts	34 Pirleyhill Gardens, Falkirk FK1 5NB [E-mail: margaret.coutts03@btinternet.com]	01324 628732
FIFE			
GLASGOW	Rev. Graham R.G. Cartlidge	54 Mansewood Road, Eastwood, Glasgow G43 1TL [E-mail: cartlidge262@btinternet.com]	0141-649 0463
GLASGOW 2nd rep	Rev. David A. Keddie	21 Ilay Road, Bearsden, Glasgow G61 1QG [E-mail: revkeddie@gmail.com]	0141-942 5173
HIGHLAND	Mr Gordon Smith	Glenwood, Altour Road, Spean Bridge PH34 4EZ [E-mail: gordonsmith934@btinternet.com]	01397 712375
INVERCLYDE	Rev. Andrew T. MacLean	St Andrew's Manse, Barr's Brae, Port Glasgow PA14 5QA [E-mail: standrews.pg@me.com]	01475 741486

MIDLOTHIAN	Mr Paul Hayes	Kingsway Management Services Ltd, 127 Deanburn, Penicuik EH26 0JA [E-mail: paul.hayes@basilicon.com]	01968 673968
MORAY	Rev. Shuna M. Dicks	The Manse, Mary Avenue, Aberlour AB38 9QU [E-mail: revshuna@btinternet.com]	01340 871687
NORTH AYRSHIRE	Mrs Elizabeth Higton	Gorsebraehead, Darvel KA17 0LT [E-mail: elizabethhigton@aol.com]	01560 321180
NORTH LANARKSHIRE	Mr John William Maddock	137 Manse Road, Motherwell ML1 2PS [E-mail: john@maddockfamily.plus.com]	01698 251137
ORKNEY			
PERTH and KINROSS	Mrs Pat Giles	190 Oakbank Road, Perth PH1 1EG [E-mail: patgiles190@yahoo.co.uk]	01738 625805
RENFREWSHIRE	Mr Ian Keith	5 Langside Drive, Kilbarchan PA10 2EL [E-mail: james.keith@fsmail.net]	
SCOTTISH BORDERS	Mr Graeme Donald	1 Upper Loan Park, Lauder TD2 6TR [E-mail: graeme.donald@btopenworld.com]	01578 722422
SHETLAND	Rev. Tom Macintyre	Lappideks, South Voxter, Cunningsburgh, Shetland ZE2 9HF [E-mail: the2macs.macintyre@btinternet.com]	01950 477549
SOUTH AYRSHIRE	Rev. David R. Gemmell	58 Monument Road, Ayr KA7 2UB [E-mail: drgemmell@hotmail.com]	01292 262580
SOUTH LANARKSHIRE	Rev. Sarah L. Ross	22 Lea Rig, Forth, Lanark ML11 8EA [E-mail: rev_sross@btinternet.com]	01555 812832
STIRLING			
WEST DUNBARTONSHIRE	Miss Sheila Rennie	128 Dumbuie Avenue, Dumbarton G82 2JW [E-mail: sheilarennie@tiscali.co.uk]	01389 763246
WEST LOTHIAN	Mrs Lynne McEwen	6 Fernlea, Uphall, Broxburn EH52 6DF [E-mail: lynnemcewen@hotmail.co.uk]	01506 855513
WESTERN ISLES	Dr Neil R. Galbraith	Four Winds, 1 Churchill Drive, Stornoway, Isle of Lewis HS1 2NP [E-mail: n.galbraith@tiscali.co.uk]	01851 702209

LIST P – RETIRED LAY AGENTS

Falconer, Alexander J.   84 Bridge Street, Dollar FK14 7DQ
[E-mail: falconer@falconer59.freeserve.co.uk]
Forrester, Arthur A.   158 Lee Crescent North, Bridge of Don, Aberdeen AB22 8FR
Scott, John W.   15 Manor Court, Forfar DD8 1BR

LIST Q – MINISTERS ORDAINED FOR SIXTY YEARS AND UPWARDS

Until 1992, the *Year Book* contained each year a list of those ministers who had been ordained 'for fifty years and upwards'. Such a list was reinstated in the edition for 2002, including the names of those ordained for sixty years and upwards. With ministers, no less than the rest of society, living longer, it was felt reasonable to proceed on that basis. Correspondence made it clear that this list was welcomed, and it has been included in an appropriately revised form each year since then. Again this year, an updated version is offered following the best enquiries that could be made. The date of ordination is given in full where it is known.

1939	22 December	Alistair McRae Rennie (Kincardine Croick and Edderton)
1941	3 July	Donald William MacKenzie (Auchterarder: The Barony)
1942	24 December	James Bews (Dundee: Craigiebank)
1943	3 September	George Cooper (Delting with Nesting and Lunnasting)
1944	21 June	Denis Macdonald Duncan (Editor: *The British Weekly*)
1945	4 February	James Shirra (St Martins with Scone: New)
	4 September	John Paul Tierney (Peterhead West: Associate)
1946	11 April	James Martin (Glasgow: High Carntyne)
	19 May	John McClymont Frew (Glasgow: Dennistoun)
	23 June	Ian Masson Fraser (Selly Oak Colleges)
	18 September	John Wilkinson (Kikuyu)
	3 October	John Henry Whyte (Gourock: Ashton)
	13 November	Ian Bruce Doyle (Department of National Mission)
1947	22 June	James Alexander Robertson Mackenzie (Largo: St David's)
	27 November	William Duncan Crombie (Glasgow: Calton New with Glasgow: St Andrew's)
1948	31 March	Gilbert Mollison Mowat (Dundee: Albany-Butterburn)
	20 April	Andrew Kerr (Kilbarchan: West)

	6 July	Alexander Chestnut (Greenock: St Mark's Greenbank)
	8 September	David Stuart Forsyth (Belhelvie)
	6 October	George Davidson Wilkie (Kirkcaldy: Viewforth)
1949	5 January	Andrew Queen Morton (Culross and Torryburn)
	14 February	Hamish Norman Mackenzie McIntosh (Fintry)
	17 July	Walter Vernon Stone (Langbank)
	1 September	John Anderson Macnaughton (Glasgow: Hyndland)
	18 December	James McMichael Orr (Aberfoyle with Port of Menteith)
1950	9 July	Alexander Craib Barr (Glasgow: St Nicholas' Cardonald)
	10 July	Kenneth MacVicar (Kenmore with Lawers with Fortingall and Glenlyon)
	26 July	Alexander Hamilton Lawson (Clydebank: Kilbowie)
	5 September	James McLaren Ritchie (Coalsnaughton)
	28 December	Donald Stewart Wallace (Chaplain: RAF)
1951	28 January	William Henry Greenway Bristow (Chaplain: Army)
	12 June	Donald John Barker McAlister (North Berwick: Blackadder)
	26 July	Duncan Shaw (Edinburgh: Craigentinny St Christopher's)
	9 September	Alwyn James Cecil Macfarlane (Glasgow: Newlands South)
	1 October	William James Morris (Glasgow: Cathedral)
	6 November	Alexander Gordon McGillivray (Edinburgh: Presbytery Clerk)
	15 November	Andrew Whittingham Rae (Annan: St Andrew's Greenknowe Erskine)
	20 November	Donald Iain McMillan (Bearsden: South)
	28 November	James Pringle Fraser (Strathaven: Avendale Old and Drumclog)
1952	April	William Frederick Laing (Selkirk: St Mary's West)
	18 May	Campbell Milne Saunders (Ayr: St Leonard's)
	11 June	Archibald Lamont (Kilcalmonell with Skipness)
	2 July	George Compton Stewart (Drumblade with Huntly Strathbogie)
	4 July	Charles Malcolm Henderson (Campbeltown: Highland)
	16 July	James Mercer Thomson (Elgin: St Giles' and St Columba's South: Associate)
	27 August	George Richmond Naismith Rendall Knight Smith (World Alliance of Reformed Churches)
	24 September	George Levack Edington (Tayport)
1953	15 March	John Murrie (Kirkliston)
	4 June	George Dymock Goldie (Aberdeen: Greyfriars)
	21 June	Duncan Cameron McPhee (Department of National Mission)
	28 June	Ian Cameron (Kilbrandon and Kilchattan)
	12 July	John Donald Henderson (Cluny with Monymusk)

19 August	Robert Bell Donaldson (Kilchoman with Portnahaven)
3 September	David Courser Gordon (Gigha and Cara)
30 September	David Peacock Munro (Bearsden: North)
1 October	William James Gilmour McDonald (Edinburgh: Mayfield)
7 October	Peter Brown (Holm)
7 October	George Ivory Lithgow McCaskill (Religious Education)
21 October	Donald Maciver Ross (Industrial Mission Organiser)
25 October	George Mackenzie Philip (Glasgow: Sandyford Henderson Memorial)
6 December	Mark Wilson

LIST R – DECEASED MINISTERS

The Editor has been made aware of the following ministers who have died since the publication of the previous volume of the *Year Book*.

Bennett, George Alestair Alison	(Strathkinness)
Blackley, Jean Ramage Mitchell	(Banton with Twechar)
Blair, Douglas Black	(Grangemouth: Dundas)
Bowman, Norman McGathan	(Edinburgh: St Mary's)
Buchan, John	(Fodderty and Strathpeffer)
Cameron, James Kerr	(University of St Andrews)
Campbell, Andrew McGill	(Motherwell: St Margaret's)
Clarkson, Robert Govan	(Dundee: Strathmartine)
Davidson, Robert	(University of Glasgow)
Doherty, Arthur James	(Fintry)
Douglas, Christina Anne Macdonald	(Inveraven and Glenlivet)
Douglas, Iain Mackechnie	(Farnell with Montrose: St Andrew's)
Downie, Alexander Sellars	(Ardrossan: Park)
Drummond, Robert Hugh	(Balmaclellan and Kells)
Dykes, Alastair Norman	(Galashiels: St Columba's)
Easton, Iain Arthur Girdwood	(Lecturer)
Evans, John Walter	(Elgin: High)
Finlayson, Duncan	(Morvern)
Gilfillan, James	(East Kilbride: Old)
Haughton, Frank	(Kirkintilloch: St Mary's)
Henry, Malcolm Nicholson	(Perth: Craigie)
Holroyd, Gordon	(Dingwall: St Clement's)
Johnstone, Robert	(Aberluthnott with Laurencekirk)
Kant, Everard William	(Kinghorn)

Lacey, Eric Ralph	(Creich with Rosehall)
Lewis, Edward Macbean Haldane	(Glasgow: Drumchapel St Andrew's)
Macallan, Gerald Brian	(Kintore)
MacMillan, Donald Iain	(Bearsden: South)
Milroy, Thomas	(Monifieth: St Rule's)
Morrison, Ranald	Alness
Morton, Thomas	(Rutherglen: Stonelaw)
Nicol, John Chalmers	(Bridge of Allan: Holy Trinity)
Paul, Iain	(Wishaw: Craigneuk and Belhaven)
Peat, Stanley William	(Edinburgh: Leith St Serf's)
Pollock, William	(Isle of Mull Parishes)
Purves, Ian	(Prestwick: Kingcase)
Scott, John Alexander Miller	(Jerusalem)
Sloan, James	(Auchinleck with Catrine)
Slorach, Alexander	(Kirk of Lammermuir with Langton and Polwarth)
Stevenson, Andrew Lockhart	(Balmerino with Wormit)
Stewart, John Masson	(Johnstone with Kirkpatrick Juxta)
Tait, Henry Alexander Gardner	(Crieff: South and Monzievaird)
Taylor, Howard George	(Chaplain: Heriot-Watt University)
Thomson, James Guthrie	(Stranraer: Old)
Tyre, Robert	(Aberdeen: St Ninian's with Aberdeen: Stockethill)
Vincent, Charles Raymond	(Stonehouse)
Watson, Jean Stewart	(Auxiliary Minister)
Wilson, Ian Munro	(Cawdor with Croy and Dalcross)
Wyatt, Glenn Franklin	(Kilmun (St Mun's) with Strone and Ardentinny)
Young, George Stuart	(Blairgowrie: St Andrew's)

SECTION 7

Legal Names and Scottish Charity Numbers for Individual Congregations

(All congregations in Scotland, and congregations furth of Scotland which are registered with OSCR, the Office of the Scottish Charity Regulator)

EXPLANATORY NOTE:
All documents, as defined in the Charities References in Documents (Scotland) Regulations 2007, must specify the Charity Number, Legal Name of the congregation, any other name by which the congregation is commonly known and the fact that it is a Charity.

For more information, please refer to the Law Department circular on the Regulations on the Church of Scotland website.

SCOTTISH CHARITY NUMBER 1.	NEW LEGAL NAME Presbytery of Edinburgh
SC018012	Balerno Church of Scotland
SC001554	Edinburgh Currie Kirk (Church of Scotland)
SC010971	Dalmeny Parish Church of Scotland
SC018321	Albany Deaf Church, Edinburgh (Church of Scotland)
SC014757	Edinburgh Barclay Viewforth Church of Scotland
SC008756	Blackhall St Columba's Church of Scotland, Edinburgh
SC011625	Bristo Memorial Church of Scotland, Craigmillar, Edinburgh
SC012642	Edinburgh: Broughton St Mary's Parish Church (Church of Scotland)
SC015251	Canongate Parish Church of Scotland, Edinburgh
SC004783	Carrick Knowe Parish Church of Scotland, Edinburgh
SC010313	Colinton Parish Church of Scotland, Edinburgh
SC015982	Colinton Mains Parish Church of Scotland, Edinburgh
SC014719	Edinburgh: Corstorphine Craigsbank Parish Church (Church of Scotland)
SC016009	Corstorphine Old Parish Church, Church of Scotland, Edinburgh
SC006300	Edinburgh: Corstorphine St Anne's Parish Church (Church of Scotland)
SC016557	Edinburgh: Corstorphine St Ninian's Parish Church (Church of Scotland)
SC003466	Edinburgh: Craigentinny St Christopher's Parish Church of Scotland
SC010545	Craiglockhart Parish Church, Edinburgh (Church of Scotland)
SC017061	Craigmillar Park Church of Scotland, Edinburgh
SC003430	Cramond Kirk, Edinburgh (Church of Scotland)
SC009470	Davidsons Mains Parish Church of Scotland, Edinburgh
SC001692	Dean Parish Church, Edinburgh – The Church of Scotland
SC005744	Drylaw Parish Church of Scotland, Edinburgh
SC016610	Duddingston Kirk (Church of Scotland), Edinburgh
SC015967	Fairmilehead Parish Church of Scotland, Edinburgh
SC009146	Edinburgh: Gorgie Dalry Church of Scotland
SC011985	Granton Parish Church of Scotland, Edinburgh
SC011325	Edinburgh Greenbank Parish Church of Scotland
SC009749	Edinburgh Greenside Church of Scotland
SC003761	Edinburgh: Greyfriars Tolbooth and Highland Kirk (Church of Scotland)
SC003565	St Giles' Cathedral, Edinburgh (Church of Scotland)
SC012562	Holy Trinity Church of Scotland, Edinburgh
SC000052	Holyrood Abbey Parish Church of Scotland, Edinburgh
SC015442	Edinburgh Inverleith St Serf's Church of Scotland
SC005197	Edinburgh Juniper Green Parish Church of Scotland
SC004950	Kaimes: Lockhart Memorial Church of Scotland, Edinburgh
SC014430	Kirk o' Field Parish Church, Edinburgh (Church of Scotland)
SC004932	Edinburgh Leith North Parish Church of Scotland
SC004695	South Leith Parish Church of Scotland, Edinburgh
SC012680	Leith St Andrew's Church of Scotland, Edinburgh
SC008710	Wardie Parish Church of Scotland, Edinburgh
SC011602	Edinburgh: Liberton Kirk (Church of Scotland)
SC008891	Liberton Northfield Parish Church of Scotland, Edinburgh
SC000896	London Road Church of Scotland, Edinburgh
SC009338	Marchmont St Giles Parish Church of Scotland, Edinburgh
SC000785	Mayfield Salisbury Parish (Edinburgh) Church of Scotland
SC034396	Morningside Parish Church of Scotland, Edinburgh
SC015552	Edinburgh: Morningside United Church
SC000871	Muirhouse Parish Church of Scotland, Edinburgh
SC005198	Edinburgh Murrayfield Parish Church of Scotland
SC000963	New Restalrig Church of Scotland, Edinburgh
SC019117	Newhaven Church of Scotland, Edinburgh
SC006457	The Old Kirk of Edinburgh (Church of Scotland)
SC004291	Edinburgh: Palmerston Place Church of Scotland
SC007277	Edinburgh: Pilrig St Paul's Church of Scotland
SC004183	Polwarth Parish Church, Edinburgh (Church of Scotland)
SC002328	Edinburgh: Portobello Old Parish Church of Scotland
SC007372	Edinburgh: Portobello St James' Parish Church of Scotland
SC011728	St Philip's Church of Scotland: Edinburgh
SC014499	Priestfield Parish Church of Scotland, Edinburgh
SC014027	Church of Scotland, Reid Memorial Church, Edinburgh
SC009035	Richmond Craigmillar Parish Church of Scotland, Edinburgh
SC030896	Slateford Longstone Parish Church of Scotland, Edinburgh
SC002748	Edinburgh: St Andrew's Clermiston Church of Scotland
SC009379	St Catherine's Argyle Parish Church of Scotland Edinburgh
SC010592	St Cuthberts Parish Church of Scotland, Edinburgh
SC004746	St Davids Broomhouse Church of Scotland, Edinburgh
SC008990	St Andrew's and St George's West Church of Scotland, Edinburgh
SC030819	St John's Oxgangs Church of Scotland: Edinburgh
SC004779	St Margaret's Church of Scotland: Edinburgh
SC013918	St Martins Church of Scotland, Portobello, Edinburgh
SC009038	St Michaels Parish Church of Scotland, Edinburgh
SC007068	Edinburgh: St Nicholas' Sighthill Parish Church of Scotland
SC004487	St Stephen's Comely Bank Church of Scotland, Edinburgh
SC010004	Stenhouse St Aidan's Parish Church of Scotland: Edinburgh
SC002499	Stockbridge Parish Church of Scotland, Edinburgh
SC009274	Tron Kirk (Gilmerton and Moredun), Edinburgh, Church of Scotland
SC013924	Kirkliston Parish Church of Scotland

SC002329   Queensferry Parish Church of Scotland
SC001169   Ratho Church of Scotland

2.   Presbytery of West Lothian
SC013100   Abercorn Parish Church of Scotland
SC000791   Armadale Parish Church of Scotland
SC007454   Avonbridge Parish Church of Scotland
SC001881   Boghall Parish Church of Scotland, Bathgate
SC007418   Bathgate High Parish Church of Scotland
SC016755   St John's Parish Church of Scotland, Bathgate
SC024154   Blackburn and Seafield Parish Church of
            Scotland
SC006811   Blackridge Parish Church of Scotland
SC000800   Breich Valley Parish Church of Scotland
SC017180   Broxburn Parish Church of Scotland
SC016313   Fauldhouse St Andrews Parish Church of
            Scotland
SC007601   Harthill St Andrew's Parish Church of
            Scotland
SC013461   Kirk of Calder Parish (Church of Scotland)
SC006973   Kirknewton & East Calder Parish Church of
            Scotland
SC016185   St Michaels Parish Church of Scotland:
            Linlithgow
SC011348   St Ninians Craigmailen Parish Church of
            Scotland, Linlithgow
SC011826   Livingston Old Parish Church of Scotland
SC026230   Pardovan, Kingscavil and Winchburgh Parish
            Church of Scotland
SC017373   Polbeth Harwood Parish Church of Scotland
SC006336   Strathbrock Parish Church of Scotland, Uphall
SC021516   Torphichen Parish Church of Scotland
SC024255   Uphall South Parish Church of Scotland
SC004703   West Kirk of Calder (Church of Scotland)
SC003362   Brucefield Parish Church of Scotland,
            Whitburn
SC001053   Whitburn South Parish Church of Scotland

3.   Presbytery of Lothian
SC004580   Aberlady Parish Church (Church of Scotland)
SC009401   Athelstaneford Parish Church (Church of
            Scotland)
SC007231   Belhaven Parish Church (Church of
            Scotland)
SC032180   Bilston Parish Church (Church of Scotland)
SC003230   Bolton and Saltoun Parish Church (Church of
            Scotland)
SC003482   Bonnyrigg Parish Church (Church of Scotland)
SC004630   Cockenzie and Port Seton: Chalmers Memorial
            Parish Church (Church of Scotland)
SC007052   Cockenzie and Port Seton: Old Parish Church
            (Church of Scotland)
SC013139   Cockpen and Carrington Parish Church
            (Church of Scotland)
SC006926   Tyne Valley Parish (Church of Scotland)
SC008958   Dalkeith: St John's and King's Park Parish
            Church (Church of Scotland)
SC014158   Dalkeith: St Nicholas Buccleuch Parish
            Church (Church of Scotland)
SC004533   Dirleton Parish Church (Church of Scotland)
SC000455   Dunbar Parish Church (Church of Scotland)
SC014299   Dunglass Parish Church (Church of Scotland)
SC014972   Garvald and Morham Parish Church (Church
            of Scotland)
SC005996   Gladsmuir Parish Church (Church of Scotland)
SC030433   Glencorse Parish Church (Church of Scotland)
SC004673   Gorebridge Parish Church (Church of
            Scotland)
SC005237   Gullane Parish Church (Church of Scotland)
SC010614   Haddington: St Mary's Parish Church (Church
            of Scotland)

SC022183   Haddington: West Parish Church (Church of
            Scotland)
SC014364   Howgate Parish Church (Church of Scotland)
SC016765   Humbie Parish Church (Church of Scotland)
SC015878   Lasswade and Rosewell Parish Church
            (Church of Scotland)
SC014420   Loanhead Parish Church (Church of Scotland)
SC016556   Longniddry Parish Church (Church of
            Scotland)
SC004722   Musselburgh: Northesk Parish Church (Church
            of Scotland)
SC000129   Musselburgh: St Andrew's High Parish Church
            (Church of Scotland)
SC001726   Musselburgh: St Clement's and St Ninian's
            Parish Church (Church of Scotland)
SC013559   Musselburgh: St Michael's Inveresk Parish
            Church (Church of Scotland)
SC035087   Newbattle Parish Church (Church of Scotland)
SC030879   Newton Parish Church (Church of Scotland)
SC004761   Abbey Church, North Berwick, Church of
            Scotland
SC006421   St Andrew Blackadder, Church of Scotland,
            North Berwick
SC014810   Ormiston Parish Church (Church of
            Scotland)
SC004871   Pencaitland Parish Church (Church of
            Scotland)
SC010902   Penicuik: North Parish Church (Church of
            Scotland)
SC005838   Penicuik: St Mungo's Parish Church (Church
            of Scotland)
SC011871   Penicuik: South Parish Church (Church of
            Scotland)
SC031191   Prestonpans: Prestongrange Parish Church
            (Church of Scotland)
SC005457   Roslin Parish Church (Church of Scotland)
SC008667   Spott Parish Church (Church of Scotland)
SC017423   Tranent Parish Church (Church of Scotland)
SC012277   Traprain Parish Church (Church of Scotland)
SC000494   Whitekirk and Tyninghame Parish Church
            (Church of Scotland)
SC015414   Yester Parish Church (Church of Scotland)

4.   Presbytery of Melrose and Peebles
SC010768   Ashkirk Parish Church of Scotland
SC006480   Bowden and Melrose Church of Scotland
SC030062   Broughton, Glenholm and Kilbucho Church of
            Scotland
SC016990   Caddonfoot Parish Church of Scotland
SC001340   Carlops Parish Church of Scotland
SC009892   Channelkirk and Lauder Church of Scotland
SC003895   Earlston Parish Church of Scotland
SC010081   Eddleston Parish Church of Scotland
SC010389   Old Parish and St Paul's Church of Scotland:
            Galashiels
SC001386   Galashiels Trinity Church of Scotland
SC034662   Ettrick and Yarrow Parish (Church of
            Scotland)
SC000281   St John's Church of Scotland: Galashiels
SC001100   Innerleithen, Traquair and Walkerburn Parish
            Church of Scotland
SC021456   Lyne & Manor Church of Scotland
SC013481   Maxton and Mertoun Parish Church of
            Scotland
SC000575   Newtown Church of Scotland
SC013316   Peebles Old Parish Church of Scotland
SC009159   Church of Scotland St Andrews Leckie Parish:
            Peebles
SC010210   St Boswells Parish Church of Scotland
SC000228   Stow St Mary of Wedale & Heriot Church of
            Scotland

SC004728	Skirling Church of Scotland
SC001866	Stobo and Drumelzier Church of Scotland
SC013564	Tweedsmuir Kirk Church of Scotland
SC003938	St Andrews Parish Church of Scotland: West Linton
SC018087	Kirkurd and Newlands Parish Church of Scotland
SC014883	Selkirk Parish Church of Scotland

5.   Presbytery of Duns

SC001208	Church of Scotland: Ayton and Burnmouth Parish Church
SC000867	St Andrew's Wallace Green and Lowick Church of Scotland, Berwick-upon-Tweed
SC000246	Bonkyl & Preston Church of Scotland
SC006722	Chirnside Church of Scotland
SC009185	The Church of Scotland, Coldingham Priory
SC001456	Coldstream Parish Church of Scotland
SC005161	Duns Parish Church of Scotland
SC000031	Eccles Parish Church of Scotland
SC007567	Edrom & Allanton Church of Scotland
SC006499	The Church of Scotland, Eyemouth Parish Church
SC002789	Fogo & Swinton Church of Scotland
SC024535	Church of Scotland: Foulden and Mordington Parish Church
SC022349	Gordon St Michael's Church of Scotland
SC016400	Church of Scotland: Grantshouse, Houndwood and Reston Parish Church
SC013136	Greenlaw Parish, Church of Scotland
SC002216	Hutton, Fishwick and Paxton Church of Scotland
SC010680	Langton and Lammermuir Kirk, Church of Scotland
SC009995	Ladykirk and Whitsome Church of Scotland
SC004582	Legerwood Parish, Church of Scotland
SC005115	Leitholm Parish Church (Church of Scotland)
SC004903	Westruther Parish, Church of Scotland

6.   Presbytery of Jedburgh

SC016457	Ale & Teviot United Church of Scotland
SC004550	Cavers and Kirkton Parish Church (Church of Scotland)
SC004517	Hawick Burnfoot Church of Scotland
SC005574	St Mary's & Old Parish Church of Scotland, Hawick
SC005191	Teviot and Roberton Church of Scotland
SC013892	Trinity Parish Church, Hawick (Church of Scotland)
SC017381	Wilton Parish Church of Scotland
SC012830	Hobkirk & Southdean Parish Church of Scotland
SC004530	Jedburgh Old and Trinity Parish Church of Scotland
SC000958	Kelso Country Churches (Church of Scotland)
SC014039	Kelso North and Ednam Parish Church of Scotland
SC010009	Kelso Old & Sprouston Parish Church of Scotland
SC003023	Linton, Morebattle, Hownam and Yetholm Parish Church of Scotland
SC010593	Oxnam Parish Church of Scotland
SC034629	Ruberslaw Parish Church of Scotland
SC006917	Teviothead Parish Church of Scotland

7.   Presbytery of Annandale and Eskdale

SC010555	Annan Old Parish Church of Scotland
SC010891	St Andrews Parish Church of Scotland, Annan
SC013947	Applegarth, Sibbaldbie & Johnstone Church of Scotland
SC012516	Brydekirk Parish Church of Scotland

SC000717	Canonbie Parish Church of Scotland
SC006344	Dalton Parish Church of Scotland
SC004542	Dornock Parish Church of Scotland
SC016747	Gretna Old, Gretna St Andrew's, Half Morton and Kirkpatrick Fleming Parish Church of Scotland
SC022170	Hightae Parish Church of Scotland
SC005701	Kirkpatrick Juxta Church of Scotland
SC011946	Langholm, Eskdalemuir, Ewes and Westerkirk Church of Scotland
SC006519	Liddesdale Parish Church of Scotland
SC004644	Lochmaben Church of Scotland
SC007116	Lockerbie Dryfesdale, Hutton and Corrie Church of Scotland
SC000722	Hoddom, Kirtle-Eaglesfield and Middlebie Church of Scotland
SC012236	St Andrews Church of Scotland, Moffat
SC001060	St Mungo Parish Church of Scotland, Lockerbie
SC043454	The Border Kirk (Church of Scotland)
SC013190	Tundergarth Church of Scotland
SC007536	Wamphray Church of Scotland

8.   Presbytery of Dumfries and Kirkcudbright

SC016850	Auchencairn & Rerrick Church of Scotland
SC016053	Balmaclellan & Kells Church of Scotland
SC000498	Balmaghie Church of Scotland
SC004450	Borgue Parish Church of Scotland
SC003844	Buittle & Kelton Church of Scotland
SC008648	Caerlaverock Parish Church of Scotland
SC015242	Carsphairn Church of Scotland
SC011037	Castle Douglas Parish Church of Scotland
SC005624	Closeburn Parish Church of Scotland
SC009384	Colvend Southwick & Kirkbean Church of Scotland
SC007152	Corsock & Kirkpatrick Durham Church of Scotland
SC014901	Crossmichael & Parton Church of Scotland
SC002443	Dalbeattie Parish Church of Scotland
SC013121	Dalry Kirkcudbrightshire Church of Scotland
SC010748	Dumfries Northwest Church of Scotland
SC006404	St George's Church of Scotland, Dumfries
SC009432	St Mary's-Greyfriars' Parish Church, Dumfries (Church of Scotland)
SC016201	St Michael's & South Church of Scotland, Dumfries
SC000973	Troqueer Parish Church of Scotland, Dumfries
SC016060	Dunscore Parish Church of Scotland
SC014783	Durisdeer Church of Scotland
SC000961	Gatehouse of Fleet Parish Church of Scotland
SC014663	Glencairn & Moniaive Parish Church of Scotland
SC033058	Irongray Lochrutton & Terregles Parish Church of Scotland
SC014150	Kirkconnel Parish Church of Scotland
SC005883	Kirkcudbright Parish Church of Scotland
SC022286	Kirkgunzeon Church of Scotland
SC010508	Kirkmahoe Parish Church of Scotland
SC030785	Kirkmichael Tinwald & Torthorwald Church of Scotland
SC014590	Lochend and New Abbey Church of Scotland
SC015925	Maxwelltown West Church of Scotland, Dumfries
SC015087	Penpont Keir & Tynron Church of Scotland
SC015399	Cummertrees, Mouswald and Ruthwell Church of Scotland
SC000845	St Bride's Parish Church of Scotland: Sanquhar
SC004475	Tarff & Twynholm Church of Scotland
SC012722	Thornhill Parish Church of Scotland
SC014465	Urr Parish Church of Scotland

9.	**Presbytery of Wigtown and Stranraer**
SC003122	Ervie-Kirkcolm Church of Scotland
SC001705	Glasserton and the Isle of Whithorn Church of Scotland
SC007375	Inch Church of Scotland
SC007136	Kirkcowan Parish Church (Church of Scotland)
SC001946	Kirkinner Church of Scotland
SC010150	Kirkmabreck Church of Scotland
SC007708	Kirkmaiden Parish Church (Church of Scotland)
SC009412	Leswalt Parish Church (Church of Scotland)
SC003300	Mochrum Church of Scotland
SC006014	Monigaff Church of Scotland
SC006316	New Luce Church of Scotland
SC005302	Old Luce Church of Scotland
SC031847	Parish of Penninghame (Church of Scotland)
SC015452	Portpatrick Parish Church (Church of Scotland)
SC010621	Sorbie Parish Church of Scotland
SC007346	Stoneykirk Parish Church (Church of Scotland)
SC017312	High Kirk of Stranraer (Church of Scotland)
SC002247	Stranraer: St Ninian's Parish Church (Church of Scotland)
SC009905	Town Kirk of Stranraer (Church of Scotland)
SC016881	Whithorn: St Ninian's Priory Church of Scotland
SC014552	Wigtown Parish Church (Church of Scotland)
10.	**Presbytery of Ayr**
SC012456	Alloway Parish Church of Scotland
SC013225	Annbank Parish Church of Scotland
SC008536	Ballantrae Parish Church of Scotland
SC006707	Auchinleck Parish Church of Scotland
SC001792	Castlehill Parish Church of Scotland: Ayr
SC031474	Dalmellington Parish Church of Scotland
SC001994	Ayr: Newton Wallacetown Church of Scotland
SC001757	St Andrew's Parish Church of Scotland: Ayr
SC009336	St James' Parish Church of Scotland: Ayr
SC016860	St Leonard's Parish Church of Scotland: Ayr
SC015366	Barr Parish Church of Scotland
SC013689	Catrine Parish Church of Scotland
SC005283	Coylton Parish Church (Church of Scotland)
SC002633	Craigie Parish Church of Scotland: Kilmarnock
SC017520	Crosshill Parish Church (Church of Scotland)
SC012591	Dailly Parish Church of Scotland
SC013503	Dalrymple Parish Church (Church of Scotland)
SC008482	Dundonald Church of Scotland
SC008226	Fisherton Church of Scotland
SC007347	Girvan: North Parish Church of Scotland
SC010381	Girvan South Parish Church of Scotland
SC031952	Kirkmichael Parish Church of Scotland: Maybole
SC000213	Kirkoswald Parish Church of Scotland
SC007714	Mauchline Parish Church of Scotland
SC014055	Lugar Parish Church of Scotland
SC004906	St Quivox Parish Church: Ayr (Church of Scotland)
SC014794	New Cumnock Parish Church (Church of Scotland)
SC010606	Muirkirk Parish Church of Scotland
SC003164	Maybole Parish Church of Scotland
SC034504	Church of Scotland Cumnock Trinity Church
SC000130	Ochiltree Parish Church of Scotland
SC006025	Old Cumnock Old Church of Scotland
SC001940	Kingcase Parish Church of Scotland: Prestwick
SC011750	St Nicholas Parish Church of Scotland: Prestwick

SC007403	Prestwick South Church of Scotland
SC004271	Monkton & Prestwick North Parish Church of Scotland
SC014381	St Colmon (Arnsheen Barrhill and Colmonell) Church of Scotland
SC015899	Sorn Parish Church of Scotland
SC035601	Stair Parish Church (Church of Scotland)
SC013366	Straiton (St Cuthbert's) Parish Church of Scotland: Maybole
SC014767	Tarbolton Parish Church of Scotland
SC030714	Drongan: The Schaw Kirk (Church of Scotland)
SC007246	Troon Old Parish Church of Scotland
SC003477	Portland Parish Church of Scotland: Troon
SC015019	Troon St Meddan's Parish Church of Scotland
SC016648	The Auld Kirk of Ayr Church of Scotland
SC008562	Patna Waterside Parish Church of Scotland
SC002144	Symington Parish Church of Scotland
SC014338	Ayr St Columba Church of Scotland
11.	**Presbytery of Irvine and Kilmarnock**
SC011414	Crosshouse Parish Church (Church of Scotland)
SC012014	Darvel Parish Church of Scotland
SC008684	Dreghorn & Springside Parish Church of Scotland
SC000447	Dunlop Church of Scotland
SC010062	Fenwick Parish Church (Church of Scotland)
SC010370	Galston Parish Church of Scotland
SC001084	Hurlford Church of Scotland
SC005491	Girdle Toll Church of Scotland, Irvine New Town
SC008725	Fullarton Parish Church (Church of Scotland), Irvine
SC002299	Mure Parish Church of Scotland, Irvine
SC008345	Irvine Old Parish Church of Scotland
SC002469	Relief Church of Scotland, Irvine
SC010167	St Andrews Church of Scotland: Irvine
SC008154	Kilmarnock: Kay Park Parish Church of Scotland
SC031334	Kilmarnock: New Laigh Kirk (Church of Scotland)
SC006040	Kilmarnock Riccarton Church of Scotland
SC006345	St Andrew's and St Marnock's Parish Church of Scotland, Kilmarnock
SC033107	St Johns Parish Church of Scotland – Onthank: Kilmarnock
SC001324	St Kentigern's Parish Church of Scotland: Kilmarnock
SC012430	Kilmarnock South Parish Church of Scotland
SC009036	St Maurs Glencairn Church of Scotland, Kilmaurs
SC013880	Loudoun Church of Scotland, Newmilns
SC015890	John Knox Parish Church of Scotland, Stewarton
SC013595	St Columba's Parish Church of Scotland, Stewarton
12.	**Presbytery of Ardrossan**
SC004736	Ardrossan Park Parish Church of Scotland
SC002350	Ardrossan Barony St John's Church of Scotland
SC004660	Beith Parish Church of Scotland
SC012017	Brodick Church of Scotland
SC005030	Corrie Parish Church of Scotland
SC004919	Cumbrae Parish Church of Scotland
SC013170	Dalry St Margaret's Parish Church of Scotland
SC006882	Dalry Trinity Church of Scotland
SC017304	Fairlie Parish Church of Scotland
SC016024	Kilbirnie Auld Kirk (Church of Scotland)
SC013750	St Columbas Parish Church of Scotland: Kilbirnie

SC023602	Kilmory Parish Church of Scotland
SC016499	Kilwinning Mansefield Trinity Church of Scotland
SC001856	Kilwinning Old Parish Church of Scotland
SC015072	Lamlash Church of Scotland
SC002782	Largs Clark Memorial Church of Scotland
SC002294	The Church of Scotland, Largs: St Columba's Parish Church
SC009048	Largs St John's Church of Scotland
SC009377	Lochranza & Pirnmill Church of Scotland
SC023003	Saltcoats New Trinity Parish Church of Scotland
SC003299	Saltcoats North Parish Church of Scotland
SC002905	Saltcoats St Cuthberts Parish Church of Scotland
SC005323	Shiskine Church of Scotland
SC015397	Stevenston Ardeer Parish Church of Scotland
SC009848	Stevenston High Church of Scotland
SC000452	Stevenston Livingstone Parish Church of Scotland
SC013464	West Kilbride Parish Church of Scotland
SC014005	Whiting Bay & Kildonan Church of Scotland

13.	**Presbytery of Lanark**
SC000333	Biggar Parish Church of Scotland
SC000603	Blackmount Parish Church (Church of Scotland)
SC017001	Cairngryffe Parish Church (Church of Scotland)
SC026539	Kirkton Parish Church, Carluke (Church of Scotland)
SC013968	St Andrews Parish Church of Scotland: Carluke
SC004066	St Johns Church of Scotland: Carluke
SC016360	Carnwath Parish Church of Scotland
SC028124	Carstairs & Carstairs Junction Church of Scotland
SC016493	Coalburn Parish Church (Church of Scotland)
SC014659	Crossford Church of Scotland
SC003080	Forth St Paul's Parish Church (Church of Scotland)
SC017506	The Upper Clyde Church of Scotland
SC011211	Kirkfieldbank Parish Church (Church of Scotland)
SC014451	Kirkmuirhill Parish Church (Church of Scotland)
SC016504	Greyfriars Parish Church, Lanark (Church of Scotland)
SC011368	St Nicholas Parish Church, Lanark (Church of Scotland)
SC013217	Law Parish Church (Church of Scotland)
SC006516	Lesmahagow Abbeygreen (Church of Scotland)
SC017014	Lesmahagow Old Parish Church (Church of Scotland)
SC016304	Libberton & Quothquan Parish Church (Church of Scotland)
SC009095	Symington Parish Church (Church of Scotland)
SC001718	The Douglas Valley Church (Church of Scotland)

14.	**Presbytery of Greenock and Paisley**
SC015730	Arthurlie Parish Church of Scotland Barrhead
SC016467	Barrhead Bourock Parish Church of Scotland
SC007776	Barrhead South and Levern Church of Scotland

SC006109	Bishopton Parish Church (Church of Scotland)
SC002293	Freeland Church of Scotland, Bridge of Weir
SC003766	Church of Scotland, St Machar's Ranfurly Church, Bridge of Weir
SC008214	Caldwell Parish Church of Scotland
SC015701	Elderslie Kirk (Church of Scotland)
SC017177	Erskine Parish Church of Scotland
SC007324	Old Gourock and Ashton Parish Church of Scotland
SC006412	St Johns Church of Scotland: Gourock
SC010818	Greenock: Lyle Kirk (Church of Scotland)
SC037023	Greenock East End Parish Church of Scotland
SC008357	Greenock The Mount Kirk (Church of Scotland)
SC004855	Old West Kirk, Greenock (Church of Scotland)
SC016711	St Margarets Church of Scotland: Greenock
SC008059	St Ninians Parish Church of Scotland: Greenock
SC001043	Wellpark Mid Kirk of Greenock (Church of Scotland)
SC005106	Greenock Westburn Church of Scotland
SC012822	Houston and Killellan Kirk (Church of Scotland)
SC003487	Howwood Parish Church of Scotland
SC011778	Inchinnan Parish Church (Church of Scotland)
SC001079	Inverkip Church of Scotland
SC009588	Johnstone High Parish Church of Scotland
SC011696	St Andrews Trinity Parish Church of Scotland Johnstone
SC011747	St Pauls Church of Scotland: Johnstone
SC012123	Kilbarchan East Church of Scotland
SC017140	Kilbarchan West Church of Scotland
SC009291	Kilmacolm Old Kirk (Church of Scotland)
SC007992	St Columba Church of Scotland Kilmacolm
SC015085	Langbank Church of Scotland
SC020972	Linwood Parish Church of Scotland
SC014518	Lochwinnoch Parish Church of Scotland
SC035155	Neilston Parish Church of Scotland
SC007633	Paisley Abbey (Church of Scotland)
SC006718	Paisley: Glenburn Parish Church of Scotland
SC006437	Paisley: Stow Brae Kirk (Church of Scotland)
SC012648	Lylesland Parish Church of Scotland, Paisley
SC011798	Paisley: Martyrs Sandyford Church of Scotland
SC005362	Oakshaw Trinity Church, Paisley
SC007484	Sherwood Greenlaw Parish Church of Scotland, Paisley
SC005770	St Columba Foxbar Church of Scotland, Paisley
SC000949	St James's Paisley (Church of Scotland)
SC000558	St Luke's Church of Scotland: Paisley
SC011210	St Marks Church of Scotland (Oldhall): Paisley
SC004753	St Ninians Church of Scotland: Paisley
SC012650	Paisley Wallneuk North Church of Scotland
SC005421	Church of Scotland Port Glasgow: Hamilton Bardrainney Church
SC009018	Port Glasgow: St Andrew's Church of Scotland
SC002410	St Martins Church of Scotland: Port Glasgow
SC006605	Renfrew North Parish Church of Scotland
SC003785	Renfrew Trinity (Church of Scotland)
SC003309	Skelmorlie and Wemyss Bay Parish Church of Scotland

16.	**Presbytery of Glasgow**
SC017638	Banton Parish Church of Scotland
SC012329	Kenmure Parish Church of Scotland
SC005642	Springfield Cambridge Church of Scotland, Bishopbriggs

SC003290	Broom Parish Church of Scotland
SC006633	Burnside Blairbeth Church of Scotland
SC016612	Busby Parish Church of Scotland
SC015193	Cadder Parish Church of Scotland
SC006638	Flemington Hallside Parish Church of Scotland
SC000061	Cambuslang Parish Church of Scotland
SC023596	St Andrews Parish Church of Scotland Cambuslang: Glasgow
SC011456	Trinity St Pauls Church of Scotland, Cambuslang
SC000835	Campsie Parish Church of Scotland
SC006752	Chryston Church of Scotland
SC006377	Eaglesham Parish Church of Scotland
SC001077	Fernhill & Cathkin Church of Scotland
SC007541	Gartcosh Parish Church of Scotland
SC009774	Orchardhill Parish Church of Scotland, Giffnock
SC007807	Giffnock South Parish Church of Scotland
SC002965	Giffnock Park Church of Scotland
SC014631	Anderston Kelvingrove Church of Scotland, Glasgow
SC002220	Glasgow: Mure Memorial Church of Scotland
SC005625	Baillieston St Andrews Church of Scotland, Glasgow
SC000885	Balshagray Victoria Park Parish Church of Scotland, Glasgow
SC025730	Barlanark Greyfriars Parish Church of Scotland, Glasgow
SC006410	Blawarthill Parish Church of Scotland, Glasgow
SC012535	Bridgeton St Francis in the East Church of Scotland, Glasgow
SC007820	Broomhill Church of Scotland, Glasgow
SC006958	Calton Parkhead Parish Church of Scotland, Glasgow
SC010265	Cardonald Parish Church of Scotland, Glasgow
SC011224	Carmunnock Parish Church of Scotland, Glasgow
SC000532	Carmyle Church of Scotland, Glasgow
SC030150	Carnwadric Church of Scotland, Glasgow
SC015309	Glasgow: Castlemilk Parish Church of Scotland
SC002727	Cathcart Old Parish Church of Scotland, Glasgow
SC033802	Cathcart Trinity Church of Scotland, Glasgow
SC013966	Glasgow Cathedral (St Mungo's or High), Church of Scotland
SC012939	Colston Milton Parish Church of Scotland, Glasgow
SC005709	Colston Wellpark Parish Church of Scotland, Glasgow
SC009874	Cranhill Parish Church of Scotland, Glasgow
SC009761	Croftfoot Parish Church of Scotland, Glasgow
SC008824	Glasgow Dennistoun New Parish Church of Scotland
SC022128	Drumchapel St Andrews Parish Church of Scotland, Glasgow
SC008954	St Marks Parish Church of Scotland, Glasgow
SC004642	Glasgow Shettleston New Church of Scotland
SC003021	St Georges & St Peters Parish Church of Scotland: Easterhouse, Glasgow
SC000277	Eastwood Parish Church of Scotland, Glasgow
SC030168	Gairbraid Parish Church of Scotland, Glasgow
SC016862	Garthamlock & Craigend East Parish Church of Scotland, Glasgow
SC002214	Gorbals Parish Church of Scotland, Glasgow
SC004153	Glasgow Govan and Linthouse Parish Church of Scotland
SC012752	Govanhill Trinity Parish Church of Scotland, Glasgow
SC006729	High Carntyne Church of Scotland, Glasgow
SC002614	Hillington Park Church of Scotland, Glasgow
SC007798	St Christophers Church of Scotland: Glasgow
SC002398	Hyndland Parish Church of Scotland, Glasgow
SC009841	Ibrox Parish Church of Scotland, Glasgow
SC027651	John Ross Memorial Church for Deaf People, Glasgow (Church of Scotland)
SC015683	Jordanhill Parish Church of Scotland, Glasgow
SC014414	Kelvin – Stevenson Memorial Parish Church of Scotland, Glasgow
SC006629	Kelvinside Hillhead Parish Church of Scotland, Glasgow
SC008980	Kenmuir Mount Vernon Church of Scotland, Glasgow
SC017040	Kings Park Church of Scotland, Glasgow
SC014895	Kinning Park Parish Church of Scotland, Glasgow
SC007757	Knightswood St Margarets Parish Church of Scotland, Glasgow
SC007055	Langside Parish Church of Scotland, Glasgow
SC015778	Lansdowne Church of Scotland, Glasgow
SC002161	Lochwood Parish Church of Scotland, Glasgow
SC002102	Maryhill Parish Church of Scotland, Glasgow
SC004016	Merrylea Parish Church of Scotland Newlands, Glasgow
SC013281	Mosspark Church of Scotland, Glasgow
SC010138	Glasgow: Clincarthill Church of Scotland
SC000042	Newlands South Church of Scotland, Glasgow
SC008315	Partick South Church of Scotland, Glasgow
SC007632	Partick Trinity Church of Scotland, Glasgow
SC022874	Penilee St Andrew Church of Scotland, Glasgow
SC006683	Pollokshaws Parish Church of Scotland, Glasgow
SC013690	Pollokshields Church of Scotland, Glasgow
SC003241	Possilpark Parish Church of Scotland, Glasgow
SC015858	Priesthill & Nitshill Church of Scotland, Glasgow
SC001575	Queens Park Parish Church of Scotland, Glasgow
SC011423	Renfield St Stephens Parish Church of Scotland, Glasgow
SC032401	Robroyston Church of Scotland, Glasgow
SC003149	Ruchazie Parish Church of Scotland, Glasgow
SC014538	Glasgow: Ruchill Kelvinside Parish Church of Scotland
SC002155	Sandyford Henderson Memorial Church of Scotland, Glasgow
SC009460	Sandyhills Church of Scotland, Glasgow
SC030418	Scotstoun Parish Church of Scotland, Glasgow
SC012969	Shawlands Parish Church of Scotland, Glasgow
SC015155	Sherbrooke St Gilberts Church of Scotland, Glasgow
SC004642	Glasgow Shettleston New Church of Scotland
SC001070	Shettleston Old Parish Church of Scotland, Glasgow
SC010899	South Carntyne Church of Scotland, Glasgow
SC005196	South Shawlands Church of Scotland, Glasgow
SC004397	Springburn Parish Church of Scotland, Glasgow
SC009600	St Andrews East Parish Church, Glasgow (Church of Scotland)
SC006342	St Columbas Gaelic Church of Scotland, Glasgow
SC017297	St Davids Parish Church of Scotland: Glasgow
SC004918	St Enoch's – Hogganfield Parish Church of Scotland, Glasgow
SC004931	St Georges Tron Church of Scotland, Glasgow

SC013313	St James Pollok Parish Church of Scotland: Glasgow
SC012920	St Johns Renfield Church of Scotland, Glasgow
SC032738	Gallowgate Parish Church of Scotland, Glasgow
SC005764	St Margarets Tollcross Church of Scotland: Glasgow
SC011527	St Nicholas Parish Church of Scotland, Cardonald, Glasgow
SC016306	St Pauls Church of Scotland: Provanmill, Glasgow
SC015459	St Rollox Church of Scotland: Glasgow
SC015579	Temple Anniesland Parish Church of Scotland, Glasgow
SC009399	Toryglen Church of Scotland, Glasgow
SC009578	Trinity Possil & Henry Drummond Church of Scotland, Glasgow
SC017015	Tron St Marys Parish Church of Scotland, Glasgow
SC004821	Victoria Tollcross Church of Scotland, Glasgow
SC008840	Glasgow Wallacewell Church of Scotland New Charge
SC000289	Wellington Church of Scotland, Glasgow
SC030362	Whiteinch Church of Scotland, Glasgow
SC017408	Yoker Parish Church of Scotland, Glasgow
SC002834	Glenboig Parish Church of Scotland
SC011453	Greenbank Parish Church of Scotland
SC009866	Kilsyth Anderson Church of Scotland
SC009912	Kilsyth Burns & Old Parish Church of Scotland
SC002424	Kirkintilloch Hillhead Church of Scotland
SC008735	St Columba Parish Church of Scotland, Kirkintilloch
SC007427	St Davids Memorial Park Church of Scotland, Kirkintilloch
SC007260	St Marys Parish Church of Scotland, Kirkintilloch
SC008935	Lenzie Old Parish Church of Scotland
SC015287	Lenzie Union Church of Scotland
SC017317	Maxwell Mearns Church of Scotland
SC007125	Mearns Kirk (Church of Scotland)
SC014735	Milton of Campsie Parish Church of Scotland
SC015303	Netherlee Church of Scotland
SC004219	Newton Mearns Parish Church of Scotland
SC006856	Rutherglen Old Parish Church of Scotland
SC013558	Stonelaw Parish Church of Scotland, Rutherglen
SC007585	Rutherglen West and Wardlawhill Parish Church of Scotland
SC003155	Stamperland Parish Church of Scotland, Clarkston
SC014212	Stepps Parish Church of Scotland, Stepps
SC008426	Thornliebank Parish Church of Scotland
SC016058	Torrance Parish Church of Scotland
SC011672	Twechar Church of Scotland
SC009939	Williamwood Parish Church of Scotland

17.   Presbytery of Hamilton

SC016464	Airdrie Broomknoll Parish Church of Scotland
SC011239	Airdrie Clarkston Parish Church of Scotland
SC014555	Airdrie Flowerhill Parish Church of Scotland
SC024357	Airdrie High Parish Church of Scotland
SC004083	Airdrie Jackson Parish Church of Scotland
SC011674	Airdrie New Monkland Parish Church of Scotland
SC002900	Airdrie St Columbas Parish Church of Scotland
SC004209	Bargeddie Parish Church of Scotland
SC012556	Bellshill Macdonald Memorial Parish Church of Scotland

SC006007	Bellshill Orbiston Parish Church of Scotland
SC008340	Bellshill West Parish Church of Scotland
SC005955	Blantyre St Andrew's Parish Church of Scotland
SC004084	Blantyre Livingstone Memorial Parish Church of Scotland
SC018492	Blantyre Old Parish Church of Scotland
SC012944	The New Wellwynd Parish Church of Scotland Airdrie
SC009819	Bothwell Parish Church of Scotland
SC015831	Calderbank Parish Church of Scotland
SC030492	Caldercruix and Longriggend Parish Church of Scotland
SC008486	Chapelhall Parish Church of Scotland
SC011817	Chapelton Parish Church of Scotland
SC017084	Cleland Parish Church of Scotland
SC009704	Coatbridge Blairhill Dundyvan Parish Church of Scotland
SC006854	Coatbridge Calder Parish Church of Scotland
SC016362	Coatbridge Middle Parish Church of Scotland
SC013521	Coatbridge New St Andrew's Parish Church of Scotland
SC010236	Coatbridge Old Monkland Parish Church of Scotland
SC008809	Coatbridge Townhead Parish Church of Scotland
SC016156	Dalserf Parish Church of Scotland
SC007396	East Kilbride Claremont Parish Church of Scotland
SC030300	East Kilbride Greenhills Parish Church of Scotland
SC016751	East Kilbride Moncreiff Parish Church of Scotland
SC000609	East Kilbride Old Parish Church of Scotland
SC008332	East Kilbride South Parish Church of Scotland
SC000250	East Kilbride West Kirk Church of Scotland
SC001857	East Kilbride Westwood Parish Church of Scotland
SC014716	Glassford Parish Church of Scotland
SC012692	East Kilbride Mossneuk Parish Church of Scotland
SC018154	Greengairs Parish Church of Scotland
SC006611	Cadzow Parish Church of Scotland, Hamilton
SC011571	Hamilton Gilmour & Whitehill Parish Church of Scotland
SC005376	Hamilton Hillhouse Parish Church of Scotland
SC010855	Hamilton Old Parish Church of Scotland
SC007145	Hamilton St Andrew's Parish Church of Scotland
SC008779	Hamilton St John's Parish Church of Scotland
SC022166	Hamilton South Parish Church of Scotland
SC007051	Hamilton Trinity Parish Church of Scotland
SC008451	Hamilton West Parish Church of Scotland
SC012888	Holytown Parish Church of Scotland
SC013309	Chalmers Parish Church of Scotland Larkhall
SC002870	St Machan's Parish Church of Scotland Larkhall
SC008611	Trinity Parish Church of Scotland, Larkhall
SC034242	Church of Scotland Stewartfield New Charge Development East Kilbride
SC008810	Motherwell Crosshill Parish Church of Scotland
SC016821	Motherwell North Parish Church of Scotland
SC008601	Motherwell South Parish Church of Scotland
SC010924	Motherwell St Margaret's Parish Church of Scotland
SC012233	Motherwell St Marys Parish Church of Scotland
SC005427	Newarthill and Carfin Parish Church of Scotland
SC006540	Bonkle Parish Church of Scotland

SC001381	Newmains Coltness Memorial Parish Church of Scotland	SC011630	Old Kilpatrick Bowling Parish Church of Scotland
SC004688	New Stevenston Wrangholm Parish Church of Scotland	SC014833	Renton Trinity Parish Church of Scotland
SC007360	Overtown Parish Church of Scotland	SC010086	Rhu and Shandon Parish Church of Scotland
SC009689	Quarter Parish Church of Scotland	SC001510	Rosneath St Modans Church of Scotland
SC015503	Motherwell Dalziel St Andrew's Parish Church of Scotland	**19.**	**Presbytery of Argyll**
SC013269	Kirk o' Shotts Parish Church of Scotland	SC015795	Appin Parish Church (Church of Scotland)
SC003239	Stonehouse St Ninian's Parish Church of Scotland	SC000680	Ardchattan (Church of Scotland)
		SC010713	Ardrishaig Parish Church (Church of Scotland)
SC001956	Strathaven Avendale Old and Drumclog Memorial Parish Church of Scotland	SC003980	Barra Church of Scotland
		SC002493	Campbeltown: Highland Parish Church of Scotland
SC015591	Strathaven East Parish Church of Scotland	SC011686	Campbeltown: Lorne and Lowland Church of Scotland
SC001020	Strathaven Rankin Parish Church of Scotland		
SC010039	Uddingston Burnhead Parish Church of Scotland	SC035582	Coll Parish Church (Church of Scotland)
		SC031271	Colonsay & Oronsay Church of Scotland
SC006538	Shotts Calderhead – Erskine Parish Church of Scotland	SC006738	Connel Parish Church of Scotland
		SC003718	Craignish Parish Church of Scotland
SC009991	Uddingston Viewpark Parish Church of Scotland	SC016097	Cumlodden, Lochfyneside and Lochgair (Church of Scotland)
SC013037	Wishaw: Cambusnethan North Parish Church of Scotland	SC003216	Dunoon: St John's Church (Church of Scotland)
SC011532	Wishaw Cambusnethan Old and Morningside Parish Church of Scotland	SC017524	Dunoon: The High Kirk (Church of Scotland)
		SC002567	Gigha & Cara Church (Church of Scotland)
SC013841	Wishaw Craigneuk and Belhaven Church of Scotland	SC002121	Glassary, Kilmartin & Ford Parish Church of Scotland
SC011253	Wishaw Old Parish Church of Scotland	SC016665	Glenaray & Inveraray Parish Church (Church of Scotland)
SC012529	Wishaw St Marks Parish Church of Scotland		
SC016893	Uddingston Old Parish Church of Scotland	SC003179	Glenorchy & Innishael Church of Scotland
SC010775	South Wishaw Parish Church of Scotland	SC013247	Innellan Church (Church of Scotland)
		SC036399	Iona Parish Church (Church of Scotland)
18.	**Presbytery of Dumbarton**	SC002925	Jura Parish Church of Scotland
SC001268	Alexandria Parish Church of Scotland	SC009853	Kilarrow Parish Church of Scotland
SC008929	Arrochar Parish Church of Scotland	SC017005	Kilbrandon & Kilchattan Parish Church (Church of Scotland)
SC006355	Baldernock Parish Church of Scotland		
SC037739	Bearsden: Baljaffray Parish Church of Scotland	SC006948	Kilcalmonell Parish Church (Church of Scotland)
SC009748	Killermont Parish Church (Church of Scotland) Bearsden	SC013203	Kilchoman Parish Church (Church of Scotland)
SC012997	New Kilpatrick Parish Church of Scotland	SC009417	Kilchrenan & Dalavich Parish Church (Church of Scotland)
SC009082	The Church of Scotland Bearsden Cross Church	SC006032	Kildalton & Oa Parish Church (Church of Scotland)
SC004489	Westerton Fairlie Memorial Parish Church of Scotland, Bearsden	SC003483	Kilfinan Parish Church (Church of Scotland)
SC000886	Bonhill Church of Scotland	SC013473	Kilfinichen & Kilvickeon & the Ross of Mull Church of Scotland
SC003494	Cardross Parish Church of Scotland		
SC004596	Abbotsford, Church of Scotland, Clydebank	SC016020	Killean & Kilchenzie Parish Church (Church of Scotland)
SC005108	Faifley Parish Church of Scotland, Clydebank	SC015317	Kilmeny Parish Church of Scotland
SC015005	Kilbowie St Andrews Church of Scotland, Clydebank	SC021449	Kilmodan & Colintraive Parish Church of Scotland
SC013242	Radnor Park Church of Scotland, Clydebank	SC011171	Kilmore & Oban Church of Scotland
SC003077	St Cuthberts Parish Church of Scotland: Clydebank	SC001694	Kilmun: St Munn's Church (Church of Scotland)
SC001725	Craigrownie Parish Church of Scotland	SC025506	Kilninian & Kilmore Church of Scotland
SC013599	Dalmuir Barclay Church of Scotland	SC002458	Kilninver & Kilmelford Parish Church of Scotland
SC002937	Riverside Parish Church of Scotland, Dumbarton		
		SC001976	Kirn Parish Church (Church of Scotland)
SC006235	St Andrews Church of Scotland: Dumbarton	SC014928	Kyles Parish Church (Church of Scotland)
SC010474	West Kirk, Dumbarton (Church of Scotland)	SC030972	Lismore Parish Church (Church of Scotland)
SC008854	Duntocher Trinity Parish Church of Scotland	SC016311	Lochgilphead Church of Scotland
SC016699	Garelochhead Parish Church of Scotland	SC006458	Lochgoilhead & Kilmorich Church (Church of Scotland)
SC007801	Park Church of Scotland, Helensburgh		
SC012053	The Church of Scotland: Helensburgh: St Andrew's Kirk	SC013377	Muckairn Parish Church (Church of Scotland)
		SC001002	North Knapdale Parish Church of Scotland
SC012346	Jamestown Parish Church of Scotland	SC004086	Portnahaven Parish Church of Scotland
SC002145	Kilmaronock Gartocharn Church of Scotland	SC006420	Rothesay: Trinity Church (Church of Scotland)
SC017192	Luss Parish Church of Scotland	SC002609	Saddell & Carradale Church (Church of Scotland)
SC009913	Cairns Church of Scotland, Milngavie		
SC003870	St Lukes Church of Scotland: Milngavie		
SC002737	St Pauls Parish Church of Scotland: Milngavie	SC026099	Salen and Ulva Church of Scotland

SC006657	Sandbank Church (Church of Scotland)
SC004280	Skipness: St Brendan's Church (Church of Scotland)
SC005484	Southend Parish Church (Church of Scotland)
SC010782	South Knapdale Parish Church (Church of Scotland)
SC031790	South Uist Church of Scotland
SC001767	Strachur & Strathlachlan Church (Church of Scotland)
SC004088	Strathfillan Parish Church of Scotland
SC003410	Strone & Ardentinny Church (Church of Scotland)
SC002622	Tarbert, Loch Fyne and Kilberry (Church of Scotland)
SC030563	The United Church of Bute (Church of Scotland)
SC000878	Tiree Parish Church of Scotland
SC002878	Tobermory Parish Church of Scotland
SC003909	Torosay & Kinlochspelvie Church of Scotland
SC015531	Toward Church (Church of Scotland)

22.	**Presbytery of Falkirk**
SC029326	Cumbernauld Abronhill Church of Scotland
SC011038	Airth Parish Church of Scotland
SC008191	Bo'ness Old Kirk (Church of Scotland)
SC015225	Bonnybridge St Helen's Parish Church of Scotland
SC001385	Brightons Parish Church of Scotland
SC014816	Camelon Parish Church, Church of Scotland
SC011839	Cumbernauld: Condorrat Parish Church of Scotland
SC000877	Cumbernauld Old Parish Church of Scotland
SC016255	Denny Old Parish Church of Scotland
SC007072	Denny Westpark Church of Scotland
SC002943	Dunipace Parish Church of Scotland
SC000652	Falkirk Old & St Modan's Parish Church of Scotland
SC000775	Grangemouth Abbotsgrange Church of Scotland
SC014536	Haggs Parish Church of Scotland
SC004564	Cumbernauld Kildrum Parish Church of Scotland
SC001603	Grangemouth, Kirk of the Holy Rood, Church of Scotland
SC006456	Larbert East Church of Scotland
SC000445	Larbert Old Church of Scotland
SC012251	Larbert West Parish Church of Scotland
SC007383	Laurieston Parish Church of Scotland
SC003421	Polmont Old Parish Church of Scotland
SC008787	Redding & Westquarter Church of Scotland
SC013602	Slamannan Parish Church of Scotland
SC005066	St Andrews West Church of Scotland, Falkirk
SC002263	Stenhouse & Carron Parish Church of Scotland: Stenhousemuir
SC013114	Grangemouth Zetland Parish Church of Scotland
SC036366	St Mungo's Church of Scotland, Cumbernauld
SC007546	The Church of Scotland Falkirk Erskine Parish Church
SC002512	Blackbraes & Shieldhill Parish Church of Scotland
SC007665	St James Church of Scotland, Falkirk
SC016991	Grahamston United Church
SC011448	St Andrew's Church of Scotland, Bo'ness
SC007571	Muiravonside Parish Church of Scotland
SC009754	Bothkennar & Carronshore Parish Church (Church of Scotland)
SC007811	Carriden Parish Church of Scotland
SC004142	Bainsford Parish Church of Scotland, Falkirk

23.	**Presbytery of Stirling**
SC001308	Aberfoyle Parish Church of Scotland
SC007821	St Mungo's Parish Church of Scotland, Alloa
SC007605	Alloa Ludgate Church of Scotland
SC000006	Alva Parish Church of Scotland
SC005335	Balfron Church of Scotland
SC012316	Balquhidder Parish Church of Scotland
SC002953	Allan Church of Scotland, Bannockburn
SC011345	Bannockburn Ladywell Church of Scotland
SC015171	Bridge of Allan Parish Church of Scotland
SC012927	Buchanan Parish Church of Scotland
SC000833	Buchlyvie Church of Scotland
SC000396	Callander Kirk Church of Scotland
SC019113	Cambusbarron Parish Church of Scotland Bruce Memorial
SC002324	Clackmannan Parish Church of Scotland
SC016296	Cowie and Plean Church of Scotland
SC009713	Dollar Parish Church of Scotland
SC004824	Drymen Church of Scotland
SC004454	Dunblane Cathedral Church of Scotland
SC005185	Dunblane: St Blane's Church of Scotland
SC028465	Fallin Parish Church of Scotland
SC012537	Fintry Church of Scotland
SC012154	Gargunnock Parish Church of Scotland
SC009788	Gartmore Parish Church of Scotland
SC003028	Glendevon Parish Church of Scotland
SC012140	Killearn Kirk (Church of Scotland)
SC010198	Killin & Ardeonaig Parish Church of Scotland
SC012031	Kilmadock Parish Church of Scotland, Doune
SC000802	Kincardine in Menteith Church of Scotland, Blair Drummond
SC004286	Kippen Parish Church of Scotland
SC014031	Lecropt Kirk Parish Church of Scotland
SC001298	Logie Kirk Stirling (Church of Scotland)
SC004778	Menstrie Parish Church of Scotland
SC009418	Muckhart Parish Church of Scotland
SC028719	Norrieston Parish Church of Scotland
SC001864	Port of Menteith Church of Scotland
SC018155	Sauchie and Coalsnaughton Parish Church of Scotland
SC001414	Allan Park South Church of Scotland, Stirling
SC011473	Church of the Holy Rude, Stirling (Church of Scotland)
SC011795	Stirling North Parish Church of Scotland
SC013444	St Columba's Church of Scotland Stirling
SC005432	St Marks Parish Church of Scotland: Stirling
SC016320	St Ninians Old Parish Church of Scotland, Stirling
SC007533	Viewfield Erskine Church of Scotland, Stirling
SC007261	Strathblane Parish Church of Scotland
SC016570	Tillicoultry Parish Church of Scotland
SC005918	St Serfs Church of Scotland, Tullibody

24.	**Presbytery of Dunfermline**
SC005851	St Fillans Church of Scotland: Aberdour
SC031695	Beath and Cowdenbeath North Church of Scotland
SC012892	Cairneyhill Parish Church of Scotland
SC010676	Carnock and Oakley Church of Scotland
SC003799	Cowdenbeath Trinity Church of Scotland
SC015149	Culross & Torryburn Church of Scotland
SC020926	Dalgety Parish Church of Scotland
SC016883	The Abbey Church of Dunfermline (Church of Scotland)
SC035690	Dunfermline East Church of Scotland
SC011659	Dunfermline Gillespie Memorial Church of Scotland
SC013226	Dunfermline North Parish Church of Scotland
SC007302	St Andrew's Erskine Church of Scotland, Dunfermline

SC007799	Dunfermline St Leonard's Parish Church of Scotland
SC007080	Dunfermline St Margaret's Parish Church of Scotland
SC007453	St Ninians Church of Scotland: Dunfermline
SC008085	Dunfermline Townhill & Kingseat Parish Church of Scotland
SC000968	Inverkeithing Parish Church of Scotland
SC011004	Kelty Church of Scotland
SC002435	Limekilns Church of Scotland
SC032353	Lochgelly and Benarty St Serf's Parish Church of Scotland
SC007414	North Queensferry Church of Scotland
SC013620	Rosyth Parish Church of Scotland
SC013688	Saline & Blairingone Parish Church of Scotland
SC002951	Tulliallan & Kincardine Parish Church of Scotland

25.	**Presbytery of Kirkcaldy**
SC031143	Auchterderran St Fothads Parish Church of Scotland
SC025310	Auchtertool Kirk (Church of Scotland)
SC009495	Buckhaven and Wemyss Parish Church of Scotland
SC016418	Burntisland Parish Church of Scotland
SC008991	Dysart St Clair Church of Scotland
SC007397	Glenrothes Christ's Kirk (Church of Scotland)
SC016386	St Columba's Parish Church of Scotland, Glenrothes
SC009845	St Margaret's Parish Church of Scotland: Glenrothes
SC002472	St Ninian's Parish Church of Scotland: Glenrothes
SC016733	Kennoway, Windygates and Balgonie: St Kenneth's Church of Scotland
SC007848	Kinghorn Parish Church of Scotland
SC012030	Kinglassie Parish Church of Scotland
SC002586	Abbotshall Parish Church of Scotland, Kirkcaldy
SC012039	Linktown Church of Scotland, Kirkcaldy
SC002858	Pathhead Parish Church of Scotland, Kirkcaldy
SC031064	St Bryce Kirk, Church of Scotland, Kirkcaldy
SC005628	Bennochy Parish Church of Scotland, Kirkcaldy
SC012756	Templehall Parish Church of Scotland, Kirkcaldy
SC015807	Torbain Parish Church of Scotland, Kirkcaldy
SC014025	Trinity Church of Scotland, Leslie
SC031969	Leven Parish Church of Scotland
SC005820	Markinch Parish Church of Scotland
SC009581	Wellesley Parish Church of Scotland, Methil
SC007949	Methilhill and Denbeath Parish Church of Scotland
SC003417	Thornton Parish Church of Scotland

26.	**Presbytery of St Andrews**
SC004848	Abdie & Dunbog Parish Church of Scotland
SC012986	Anstruther Parish Church of Scotland
SC005402	Auchtermuchty Parish Church of Scotland
SC002542	Balmerino Parish Church of Scotland
SC001108	Boarhills and Dunino Parish Church of Scotland
SC005565	Cameron Parish Church (Church of Scotland)
SC016744	Carnbee Church of Scotland
SC000181	Cellardyke Parish Church of Scotland
SC017442	Ceres, Kemback & Springfield Church of Scotland
SC001601	Crail Parish Church of Scotland
SC001907	Creich, Flisk and Kilmany Church of Scotland

SC013123	Cupar Old & St Michael of Tarvit Parish Church (of Scotland)
SC015721	Cupar St John's and Dairsie United Parish Church of Scotland
SC015226	Edenshead and Strathmiglo Church of Scotland
SC003163	Elie, Kilconquhar and Colinsburgh Church of Scotland
SC012247	Falkland Parish Church of Scotland
SC016622	Freuchie Parish Church of Scotland
SC005381	Howe of Fife Parish Church (Church of Scotland)
SC002653	Kilrenny Parish Church of Scotland
SC012192	Kingsbarns Parish Church of Scotland
SC003465	Largo & Newburn Parish Church of Scotland
SC013075	Largo St David's Church of Scotland
SC009474	Largoward Church of Scotland
SC015677	Leuchars: St Athernase Church of Scotland
SC015182	Monimail Parish (Church of Scotland)
SC004607	Newburgh Parish Church of Scotland
SC006758	Newport-on-Tay Church of Scotland
SC015271	Pittenweem Church of Scotland
SC017173	The Parish Church of the Holy Trinity, St Andrews (Church of Scotland)
SC014934	Hope Park and Martyrs' Parish Church St Andrews (Church of Scotland)
SC013586	St Andrews: St Leonard's Parish Church of Scotland Congregation
SC005556	St Monans Church of Scotland
SC014710	Strathkinness Parish Church of Scotland
SC008659	Tayport Parish Church of Scotland
SC006447	Wormit Parish Church of Scotland

27.	**Presbytery of Dunkeld and Meigle**
SC007899	Aberfeldy Parish Church of Scotland
SC028023	Amulree and Strathbraan Parish Church of Scotland
SC001465	Dull and Weem Parish Church of Scotland
SC000540	Alyth Parish Church of Scotland
SC000098	Ardler Kettins & Meigle Parish Church of Scotland
SC004358	Bendochy Parish Church of Scotland
SC014438	Coupar Angus Abbey Church of Scotland
SC013516	Blair Atholl and Struan Church of Scotland
SC001984	Tenandry Parish Church of Scotland
SC033757	Blairgowrie Parish Church of Scotland
SC011351	Braes of Rannoch Church of Scotland
SC006570	Foss and Rannoch Church of Scotland
SC001957	Caputh and Clunie Church of Scotland
SC009251	Kinclaven Church of Scotland
SC009867	Dunkeld Parish Church of Scotland
SC003310	Fortingall & Glenlyon Church of Scotland
SC006260	Kenmore and Lawers Church of Scotland
SC004275	Grantully Logierait & Strathtay Church of Scotland
SC008021	Kirkmichael Straloch & Glenshee Church of Scotland
SC000323	Rattray Parish Church of Scotland
SC008361	Pitlochry Church of Scotland

28.	**Presbytery of Perth**
SC000586	Abernethy and Dron and Arngask Church of Scotland
SC005203	Almondbank Tibbermore Parish Church of Scotland
SC000139	Ardoch Parish Church of Scotland
SC001688	Auchterarder Parish Church of Scotland
SC010247	Auchtergaven and Moneydie Parish Church of Scotland
SC005594	Blackford Parish Church of Scotland
SC007283	Cargill Burrelton Parish Church of Scotland

SC003168	Cleish Parish Church of Scotland	SC004496	Dundee: Menzieshill Parish Church of Scotland
SC009031	Collace Church of Scotland		
SC001878	Comrie Parish Church of Scotland	SC012137	Monikie & Newbigging and Murroes & Tealing Church of Scotland
SC004304	Crieff Parish Church of Scotland		
SC009638	Dunbarney and Forgandenny Parish Church (Church of Scotland)	SC011775	Dundee: St Andrew's Parish Church of Scotland
SC010311	St Fillans Dundurn Parish Church of Scotland	SC000723	St David's High Kirk Dundee (Church of Scotland)
SC015895	Errol Parish Church of Scotland	SC005210	St James Church of Scotland: Broughty Ferry
SC013157	Fossoway St Serf's & Devonside Parish Church of Scotland	SC000088	St Luke's and Queen Street Church of Scotland: Broughty Ferry
SC002209	Fowlis Wester, Madderty and Monzie Parish Church of Scotland	SC011017	Barnhill St Margaret's Parish Church of Scotland
SC009632	Gask Parish Church of Scotland	SC002198	Dundee Parish Church (St Mary's) Church of Scotland
SC010838	Kilspindie & Rait Parish Church of Scotland		
SC012555	Kinross Parish Church of Scotland	SC003714	St Stephen's & West Parish Church of Scotland: Broughty Ferry
SC010807	Methven and Logiealmond Church of Scotland		
SC004984	Muthill Parish Church of Scotland	SC000384	Stobswell Parish Church of Scotland: Dundee
SC015523	Orwell and Portmoak Parish Church of Scotland	SC018015	Strathmartine Church of Scotland: Dundee
		SC011021	Dundee: Trinity Parish Church of Scotland
SC001330	Perth: Craigie and Moncreiffe Church of Scotland	SC000316	Dundee: Whitfield Parish Church of Scotland
SC007509	Kinnoull Parish Church of Scotland, Perth	SC014314	The Steeple Church: Dundee (Church of Scotland)
SC002467	Perth: Letham St Mark's Church of Scotland	SC008965	Monifieth Parish Church of Scotland
SC013014	Perth North, Church of Scotland	**30.**	**Presbytery of Angus**
SC011113	Perth Riverside Church of Scotland	SC018944	Aberlemno Parish Church of Scotland
SC017132	St John's Kirk of Perth (Church of Scotland)	SC002545	Barry Parish Church of Scotland
SC002919	Perth St Leonard's-in-the-Fields Church of Scotland	SC008630	Brechin Gardner Memorial Church of Scotland
SC016829	Perth: St Matthew's Church of Scotland	SC015146	Carnoustie Church of Scotland
SC010629	Redgorton and Stanley Parish Church – Church of Scotland	SC001293	Colliston Church of Scotland
		SC007997	Farnell Parish Church of Scotland
SC007094	Scone and St Martins Parish Church of Scotland	SC000572	Dun and Hillside Church of Scotland
		SC013105	Edzell Lethnot Glenesk Church of Scotland
SC014964	St Madoes and Kinfauns Church of Scotland, Glencarse	SC009017	Inchbrayock Parish Church of Scotland
		SC031461	The Isla Parishes Church of Scotland
SC030799	The Church of Scotland: The Stewartry of Strathearn	SC013352	Eassie, Nevay and Newtyle Church of Scotland
SC000004	Trinity Gask and Kinkell Church (Church of Scotland)	SC017413	Arbirlot Parish Church of Scotland
		SC006482	Arbroath West Kirk Church of Scotland
		SC011361	Arbroath Knox's Parish Church of Scotland
29.	**Presbytery of Dundee**	SC005478	Arbroath: St Andrew's Church of Scotland
SC007847	Abernyte Parish Church of Scotland	SC017424	Carmyllie Parish Church of Scotland
SC016717	Auchterhouse Parish Church of Scotland	SC004594	Carnoustie Panbride Church of Scotland
SC017449	Dundee: Balgay Parish Church of Scotland	SC003833	Dunnichen, Letham and Kirkden Church of Scotland
SC007031	Broughty Ferry New Kirk (Church of Scotland)	SC004921	Forfar East and Old Parish Church of Scotland
SC003677	Dundee: Camperdown Parish Church of Scotland	SC002417	Forfar Lowson Memorial Parish Church of Scotland
SC021763	Chalmers-Ardler Parish Church of Scotland, Dundee	SC010332	Brechin Cathedral Church of Scotland
SC012089	Dundee: Coldside Parish Church of Scotland	SC005085	Friockheim and Kinnell Parish Church of Scotland
SC016701	Dundee: Craigiebank Parish Church of Scotland	SC017785	Inverkeilor and Lunan Church of Scotland
SC005707	Dundee: Downfield Mains Church of Scotland	SC004395	Kirriemuir St Andrew's Parish Church of Scotland
SC010030	Dundee Douglas and Mid Craigie Church of Scotland	SC015123	The Glens and Kirriemuir Old Parish Church of Scotland
SC033313	Dundee Lochee Parish Church of Scotland		
SC017136	Dundee: West Church of Scotland	SC009016	Montrose Melville South Church of Scotland
SC002792	Fowlis & Liff Parish Church of Scotland	SC009934	Montrose: Old and St Andrew's Church of Scotland
SC009839	Inchture & Kinnaird Parish Church of Scotland		
SC009454	Invergowrie Parish Church of Scotland	SC003049	Arbroath St Vigeans Church of Scotland
SC009115	Dundee: Logie & St John's (Cross) Church of Scotland	SC006317	Oathlaw Tannadice Church of Scotland
		SC001506	Forfar St Margaret's Church of Scotland
SC012230	Longforgan Parish Church of Scotland	SC013052	Arbroath Old and Abbey Church of Scotland
SC001085	Lundie and Muirhead Parish Church of Scotland	SC011205	Glamis, Inverarity and Kinnettles Parish Church of Scotland
SC020742	Fintry Parish Church of Scotland, Dundee	SC017327	Guthrie and Rescobie Church of Scotland
SC013162	Dundee: Meadowside St Paul's Church of Scotland	SC003236	Fern, Careston and Menmuir Church of Scotland

31.	**Presbytery of Aberdeen**
SC025324	Aberdeen Bridge of Don Oldmachar Church of Scotland
SC032413	Cove Church of Scotland, Aberdeen
SC017158	Craigiebuckler Church of Scotland, Aberdeen
SC010756	Aberdeen Ferryhill Parish Church of Scotland
SC022497	Garthdee Parish Church of Scotland, Aberdeen
SC013916	Gilcomston South Church of Scotland, Aberdeen
SC003789	High Hilton Church of Scotland, Aberdeen
SC013318	Holburn West Church of Scotland, Aberdeen
SC001680	Mannofield Church of Scotland, Aberdeen
SC013459	Mastrick Parish Church of Scotland, Aberdeen
SC010643	Midstocket Parish Church of Scotland, Aberdeen
SC034441	Northfield Parish Church of Scotland, Aberdeen
SC014117	Queen Street Church of Scotland Aberdeen
SC002019	Queens Cross Church of Scotland Aberdeen
SC015841	Rubislaw Parish Church of Scotland, Aberdeen
SC013020	Ruthrieston West Church of Scotland, Aberdeen
SC017516	Aberdeen South Holburn Church of Scotland
SC027440	Aberdeen Bridge of Don St Columba's Church of Scotland
SC015451	Aberdeen St Marks Church of Scotland
SC018173	St Mary's Church of Scotland: Aberdeen
SC016043	South St Nicholas & Kincorth Church of Scotland, Aberdeen
SC014120	The Church of Scotland – Aberdeen: St Stephens Church
SC030587	New Stockethill Church of Scotland, Aberdeen
SC007076	Summerhill Parish Church of Scotland, Aberdeen
SC001966	Woodside Parish Church of Scotland, Aberdeen
SC017404	Bucksburn Stoneywood Parish Church of Scotland
SC017517	Cults Parish Church of Scotland
SC011204	Newhills Parish Church of Scotland
SC001452	Peterculter Parish Church of Scotland
SC009020	Torry St Fitticks Parish Church of Scotland, Aberdeen
SC006865	Kingswells Church of Scotland
SC031403	Middlefield Parish Church of Scotland, Aberdeen
SC016950	Dyce Parish Church of Scotland
SC024795	St Georges Tillydrone Church of Scotland, Aberdeen
SC008157	St Machar's Cathedral, Aberdeen, Church of Scotland
SC021283	St John's Church for Deaf People in the North of Scotland, Church of Scotland
SC008689	Kirk of St Nicholas Uniting
32.	**Presbytery of Kincardine and Deeside**
SC016449	Aberluthnott Church of Scotland
SC014112	Aboyne-Dinnet Parish Church of Scotland
SC009239	Arbuthnott, Bervie and Kinneff (Church of Scotland)
SC011251	Banchory-Ternan East Church of Scotland
SC003306	Banchory-Ternan West Parish Church of Scotland
SC013648	Banchory Devenick & Maryculter-Cookney Parish Church of Scotland
SC018517	Birse & Feughside Church of Scotland
SC012075	Braemar and Crathie Parish, The Church of Scotland
SC015856	Parish of Cromar Church of Scotland

SC033779	Drumoak-Durris Church of Scotland
SC005522	Glenmuick (Ballater) Parish Church of Scotland
SC007436	Kinneff Church of Scotland
SC014830	Laurencekirk Church of Scotland
SC011997	Mearns Coastal Parish Church of Scotland
SC012967	Mid Deeside Parish, Church of Scotland
SC005679	Newtonhill Parish Church (Church of Scotland)
SC007420	Portlethen Parish Church of Scotland
SC013165	Stonehaven Dunnottar Church of Scotland
SC011191	Stonehaven Fetteresso Church of Scotland
SC016565	Stonehaven South Church of Scotland
SC016193	West Mearns Parish Church of Scotland
33.	**Presbytery of Gordon**
SC010960	Barthol Chapel Church of Scotland
SC016387	Belhelvie Church of Scotland
SC000935	Insch-Leslie-Premnay-Oyne Church of Scotland
SC004050	Blairdaff and Chapel of Garioch Church of Scotland
SC003429	Cluny Church of Scotland
SC010911	Culsalmond and Rayne Church of Scotland
SC030817	Cushnie and Tough Parish Church of Scotland
SC003254	Daviot Parish Church of Scotland
SC003215	Echt Parish Church of Scotland
SC008819	Ellon Parish Church of Scotland
SC003115	Fintray Kinellar Keithhall Church of Scotland
SC011701	Foveran Church of Scotland
SC007979	Howe Trinity Parish Church of Scotland
SC001405	Huntly Cairnie Glass Church of Scotland
SC008791	St Andrews Parish Church of Scotland Inverurie
SC016907	Inverurie West Church of Scotland
SC014790	Kemnay Parish Church of Scotland
SC001406	Kintore Parish Church of Scotland
SC015960	Meldrum & Bourtie Parish Church of Scotland
SC016542	Methlick Parish Church of Scotland
SC009556	Midmar Parish Church of Scotland
SC004525	Monymusk Parish Church of Scotland
SC024017	Newmachar Parish Church of Scotland
SC007582	Parish of Noth Church of Scotland
SC009462	Skene Parish Church of Scotland
SC017161	Tarves Parish Church of Scotland
SC006056	Udny & Pitmedden Church of Scotland
SC014679	Upper Donside Parish Church of Scotland
SC000534	Strathbogie Drumblade Church of Scotland Huntly
34.	**Presbytery of Buchan**
SC007197	Aberdour Church of Scotland
SC017101	Auchaber United Parish Church of Scotland
SC009168	Auchterless Parish Church of Scotland
SC015501	Banff Parish Church of Scotland
SC006889	Crimond Parish Church of Scotland
SC006408	Cruden Parish Church of Scotland
SC012985	Deer Parish Church of Scotland
SC000522	Fordyce Parish Church of Scotland
SC013119	Fraserburgh Old Church of Scotland
SC005714	Fraserburgh South Church of Scotland
SC016334	Fraserburgh West Parish Church of Scotland
SC001475	Fyvie Church of Scotland
SC012282	Gardenstown Church of Scotland
SC000375	Inverallochy & Rathen East Parish Church of Scotland
SC015077	King Edward Parish Church of Scotland
SC008873	Longside Parish Church of Scotland
SC008813	Lonmay Parish Church of Scotland
SC015786	Macduff Parish Church of Scotland
SC009773	Maud & Savoch Church of Scotland

SC010291	Monquhitter & New Byth Parish Church of Scotland
SC007917	New Deer St Kane's Church of Scotland
SC001107	Marnoch Church of Scotland
SC014620	New Pitsligo Parish Church of Scotland
SC001971	Ordiquhill & Cornhill Church of Scotland
SC011147	Peterhead Old Parish Church of Scotland
SC010841	Peterhead St Andrews Church of Scotland
SC009990	Peterhead Trinity Parish Church of Scotland
SC005498	Pitsligo Parish Church of Scotland
SC015604	Rathen West Parish Church of Scotland
SC032016	Rothienorman Parish Church of Scotland
SC000710	St Fergus Parish Church of Scotland
SC024874	Sandhaven Parish Church of Scotland
SC007273	Strichen and Tyrie Parish Church of Scotland
SC015620	St Andrews Parish Church of Scotland, Turriff
SC007470	Turriff St Ninians and Forglen Parish Church of Scotland
SC002085	Whitehills Parish Church of Scotland

35.   Presbytery of Moray

SC001336	Aberlour Parish Church of Scotland
SC010330	Alves & Burghead Parish Church of Scotland
SC005310	Bellie Parish Church of Scotland
SC016720	Birnie and Pluscarden Church of Scotland
SC001235	Buckie North Church of Scotland
SC005608	Buckie South & West Church of Scotland
SC011231	Cullen & Deskford Church of Scotland
SC015881	St Michael's Parish Church of Scotland, Dallas
SC004853	Duffus Spynie & Hopeman Church of Scotland
SC000585	Dyke Parish Church of Scotland
SC009986	Edinkillie Church of Scotland
SC005240	Elgin High Church of Scotland
SC015164	St Giles & St Columbas Church of Scotland, Elgin
SC015093	Enzie Parish Church of Scotland
SC010045	Findochty Parish Church of Scotland
SC000711	St Laurence Parish Church of Scotland, Forres
SC005094	St Leonard's Church of Scotland, Forres
SC033804	Keith North Newmill Boharm & Rothiemay Church of Scotland
SC031791	Kirk of Keith: St Rufus, Botriphnie and Grange (Church of Scotland)
SC014557	Kinloss & Findhorn Parish Church of Scotland
SC014428	Knockando Elchies & Archiestown Parish Church of Scotland
SC009793	St Gerardine's High Church of Scotland, Lossiemouth
SC000880	St James Church of Scotland: Lossiemouth
SC010193	Mortlach and Cabrach Church of Scotland
SC014485	Portknockie Parish Church of Scotland
SC022567	Rafford Parish Church of Scotland
SC015906	Rathven Parish Church of Scotland
SC016116	Rothes Parish Church of Scotland
SC007113	Speymouth Parish Church of Scotland
SC008850	St Andrews Lhanbryd & Urquhart Parish Church of Scotland, Elgin

36.   Presbytery of Abernethy

SC003652	Abernethy Church of Scotland
SC002884	Cromdale & Advie Church of Scotland
SC010001	Grantown-on-Spey Church of Scotland
SC014015	Dulnain Bridge Church of Scotland
SC021546	Kingussie Church of Scotland
SC003282	Rothiemurchus & Aviemore Church of Scotland
SC001802	Tomintoul, Glenlivet and Inveravon Church of Scotland

SC000043	Alvie and Insh Church of Scotland
SC008346	Boat of Garten, Duthil and Kincardine Church of Scotland
SC008016	Laggan Church of Scotland
SC005490	Newtonmore Church of Scotland

37.   Presbytery of Inverness

SC015446	Ardersier Parish Church of Scotland
SC026653	Auldearn & Dalmore Parish Church of Scotland
SC001695	Cawdor Parish Church (Church of Scotland)
SC013601	Croy & Dalcross Parish Church (Church of Scotland)
SC000662	The Barn, Church of Scotland, Culloden
SC003301	Daviot & Dunlichity Church of Scotland
SC013579	Dores & Boleskine Church of Scotland
SC018159	Crown Church, Inverness (Church of Scotland)
SC011773	Dalneigh & Bona Parish Church of Scotland, Inverness
SC016866	East Church of Scotland Inverness
SC016775	Hilton Parish Church of Scotland, Inverness
SC005553	Inshes Church of Scotland, Inverness
SC010870	Ness Bank Church of Scotland, Inverness
SC035073	Old High St Stephen's Church of Scotland, Inverness
SC008109	Inverness: St Columba Church of Scotland New Charge
SC015432	Inverness Trinity Church of Scotland
SC008121	Kilmorack & Erchless Church of Scotland
SC014918	Kiltarlity Church of Scotland
SC020888	Kinmylies Church of Scotland, Inverness
SC003866	Kirkhill Church of Scotland
SC015653	Moy Dalarossie & Tomatin Church of Scotland
SC000947	Nairn Old Parish Church of Scotland
SC015361	St Ninians Church of Scotland, Nairn
SC004952	Petty Church of Scotland
SC016627	Urquhart & Glenmoriston Church of Scotland

38.   Presbytery of Lochaber

SC002916	Acharacle Parish Church of Scotland
SC008222	Ardgour and Kingairloch Parish Church of Scotland
SC030394	Ardnamurchan Parish Church of Scotland
SC021584	North West Lochaber Church of Scotland
SC018259	Duror Parish Church of Scotland
SC022635	Fort Augustus Parish Church of Scotland
SC013279	Fort William Duncansburgh MacIntosh Parish Church of Scotland
SC005211	Glencoe St Munda's Parish Church of Scotland
SC023413	Glengarry Parish Church of Scotland
SC005687	Kilmallie Parish Church of Scotland
SC014745	Kilmonivaig Parish Church of Scotland
SC030288	Kinlochleven Parish Church of Scotland
SC015532	Morvern Parish Church of Scotland
SC006700	Nether Lochaber Parish Church of Scotland
SC008982	Strontian Parish Church of Scotland

39.   Presbytery of Ross

SC015227	Alness Parish Church of Scotland
SC003921	Avoch Parish Church of Scotland
SC011897	Contin Parish Church of Scotland
SC006666	Cromarty Parish Church of Scotland
SC001167	Dingwall Castle Street Church of Scotland
SC001056	Dingwall St Clements Parish Church of Scotland
SC009309	Fearn Abbey & Nigg Church of Scotland
SC012675	Ferintosh Parish Church of Scotland
SC003499	Fodderty & Strathpeffer Parish Church of Scotland

SC004472	Fortrose & Rosemarkie Parish Church of Scotland
SC010964	Invergordon Church of Scotland
SC010319	Killearnan Parish Church of Scotland
SC013375	Kilmuir & Logie Easter Church of Scotland
SC009180	Kiltearn Parish Church of Scotland
SC014467	Knockbain Parish Church of Scotland
SC015631	Lochbroom & Ullapool Church of Scotland
SC013643	Resolis & Urquhart Church of Scotland
SC010093	Rosskeen Parish Church of Scotland
SC012425	Tain Parish Church of Scotland
SC021420	Tarbat Parish Church of Scotland
SC009902	Urray & Kilchrist Church of Scotland

40.   Presbytery of Sutherland

SC016038	Altnaharra & Farr Church of Scotland
SC010171	Assynt & Stoer Parish Church of Scotland
SC004973	Clyne Church of Scotland
SC003840	Creich Parish Church of Scotland
SC000315	Dornoch Cathedral (Church of Scotland)
SC005079	Durness & Kinlochbervie Church of Scotland
SC007326	Eddrachillis Parish Church of Scotland
SC004560	Golspie (St Andrews) Church of Scotland
SC004056	Kildonan & Loth Helmsdale Church of Scotland
SC016877	Kincardine Croick & Edderton Church of Scotland
SC020871	Lairg Church of Scotland
SC014066	Melness & Tongue Church of Scotland
SC010035	Rogart Church of Scotland
SC017558	Rosehall Church of Scotland

41.   Presbytery of Caithness

SC001363	Bower Church of Scotland
SC032164	Canisbay Parish Church of Scotland
SC030261	Dunnet Church of Scotland
SC008544	Halkirk & Westerdale Church of Scotland
SC010874	Keiss Parish Church of Scotland
SC034424	The Parish of Latheron Church of Scotland
SC010296	Olrig Church of Scotland
SC001815	North Coast Parish Church of Scotland
SC016691	Thurso St Peter's & St Andrew's Church of Scotland
SC007248	Thurso West Church of Scotland
SC003365	Watten Church of Scotland
SC013840	Wick St Fergus Church of Scotland
SC001291	Pulteneytown & Thrumster Church of Scotland

42.   Presbytery of Lochcarron – Skye

SC032334	Applecross, Lochcarron and Torridon Church of Scotland
SC022592	Bracadale and Duirinish Church of Scotland
SC015448	Gairloch and Dundonnell Church of Scotland
SC017510	Glenelg and Kintail Church of Scotland
SC014072	Kilmuir and Stenscholl Church of Scotland
SC016505	Lochalsh Church of Scotland
SC000416	Portree Church of Scotland
SC030117	Snizort Church of Scotland
SC001285	Strath and Sleat Church of Scotland

43.   Presbytery of Uist

SC002191	Benbecula Church of Scotland
SC016358	Berneray and Lochmaddy Church of Scotland
SC016461	Carinish Church of Scotland
SC030955	Kilmuir and Paible Church of Scotland
SC001770	Manish-Scarista Church of Scotland

SC004787	Tarbert Church of Scotland

44.   Presbytery of Lewis

SC006563	Barvas Church of Scotland
SC032250	Carloway Church of Scotland
SC000991	Cross Ness Church of Scotland
SC008004	Kinloch Church of Scotland
SC014492	Knock Church of Scotland
SC024236	Lochs Crossbost Parish Church of Scotland
SC008746	Lochs-in-Bernera Church of Scotland
SC010164	Stornoway High Church of Scotland
SC000753	Martins Memorial Church of Scotland, Stornoway
SC006777	St Columba Old Parish Church of Scotland, Stornoway
SC007879	Uig Parish Church of Scotland

45.   Presbytery of Orkney

SC035048	Birsay Harray & Sandwick Church of Scotland
SC019770	East Mainland Church of Scotland
SC005404	Eday Church of Scotland
SC005062	Evie Church of Scotland
SC013330	Firth Church of Scotland
SC016203	Flotta Parish Church of Scotland
SC023194	Hoy & Walls Parish Church of Scotland
SC018002	Kirkwall East Church, Church of Scotland
SC005322	Kirkwall St Magnus Cathedral (Church of Scotland)
SC030098	North Ronaldsay Parish Church of Scotland
SC016221	Orphir and Stenness Church of Scotland
SC013661	Papa Westray Church of Scotland
SC016806	Rendall Church of Scotland
SC001078	Rousay Church of Scotland
SC000271	Sanday Church of Scotland
SC006097	Shapinsay Church of Scotland
SC003298	South Ronaldsay & Burray Church of Scotland
SC003099	Stromness Church of Scotland
SC006572	Moncur Memorial Church of Scotland, Stronsay
SC025053	Westray Parish Church of Scotland

46.   Presbytery of Shetland

SC030483	Burra Church of Scotland
SC029873	Delting Parish Church (Church of Scotland)
SC015253	Dunrossness and St Ninian's Parish Church (incl. Fair Isle) (Church of Scotland)
SC038365	Fetlar Church of Scotland
SC017535	Lerwick and Bressay Parish Church (Church of Scotland)
SC031996	Nesting and Lunnasting Church of Scotland
SC002341	Northmavine Parish Church of Scotland
SC012345	Sandsting and Aithsting Parish Church of Scotland
SC014545	Sandwick, Cunningsburgh and Quarff Church of Scotland
SC030748	St Paul's Church of Scotland Walls: Shetland
SC032982	Tingwall Parish Church of Scotland
SC007954	Unst Church of Scotland
SC000293	Whalsay and Skerries Parish Church of Scotland
SC020628	Yell Parish Church of Scotland

47.   Presbytery of England

SC043458	Corby: St Andrew's Church of Scotland
SC043757	Corby: St Ninian's Church of Scotland
SC042648	Crown Court Church of Scotland London
SC042854	Liverpool: St Andrew's Church of Scotland

SECTION 8

Church Buildings: Ordnance Survey National Grid References

NOTE:
The placing of symbols denoting churches may vary according to the edition of published maps. The references which follow should be sufficiently accurate to allow church buildings to be located. The correction of any errors will always be welcomed, and appropriate details should be sent to the Editor of the *Year Book*.

The Churches are listed in the order in which they appear in the Presbytery Lists in the *Year Book*.

1. Presbytery of Edinburgh

Albany Deaf Church of Edinburgh, meets at 82 Montrose Terrace
Balerno, NT163664
Barclay Viewforth, NT249726
Blackhall St Columba's, NT219747
Bristo Memorial Craigmillar, NT287716
Broughton St Mary's, NT256748
Canongate, NT265738
Carrick Knowe, NT203721
Colinton, NT216692
Colinton Mains, NT233692
Corstorphine Craigsbank, NT191730
Corstorphine Old, NT201728
Corstorphine St Anne's, NT204730
Corstorphine St Ninian's, NT198730
Craigentinny St Christopher's, NT292748
Craiglockhart, NT224705
Craigmillar Park, NT269714
Cramond, NT190768
Currie, NT183676
Dalmeny, NT144775
Davidson's Mains, NT207752
Dean, NT238742
Drylaw, NT221754
Duddingston, NT284726
Fairmilehead, NT248683
Gorgie Dalry, NT231724
Granton, NT237766
Greenbank, NT243702
Greenside, NT263745
Greyfriars Tolbooth and Highland, NT256734
High (St Giles'), NT257736
Holyrood Abbey, NT274744
Holy Trinity, NT201700
Inverleith St Serf's, NT248761
Juniper Green, NT199687
Kaimes Lockhart Memorial, NT277684
Kirkliston, NT125744
Kirk o' Field, NT263732
Leith North, NT263765
Leith St Andrew's, NT273757
Leith South, NT271761
Leith Wardie, NT246768
Liberton, NT275695
Liberton Northfield, NT280699
London Road, NT268745
Marchmont St Giles', NT256718
Mayfield Salisbury, NT266717
Morningside, NT246707
Morningside United, NT245719
Muirhouse St Andrew's, NT215763
Murrayfield, NT227733
Newhaven, NT254769
New Restalrig, NT284742
Old Kirk, NT220760
Palmerston Place, NT241734
Pilrig St Paul's, NT266752
Polwarth, NT236719
Portobello Old, NT309738
Portobello St James', NT303738
Portobello St Philip's Joppa, NT313736
Priestfield, NT271721
Queensferry, NT130782
Ratho, NT138710
Reid Memorial, NT261710
Richmond Craigmillar, NT296717
St Andrew's and St George's West, NT255741

St Andrew's Clermiston, NT201746
St Catherine's Argyle, NT257721
St Cuthbert's, NT248736
St David's Broomhouse, NT203714
St John's Oxgangs, NT237687
St Margaret's, NT284745
St Martin's, NT305726
St Michael's, NT234722
St Nicholas' Sighthill, NT194707
St Stephen's Comely Bank, NT241748
Slateford Longstone, NT213707
Stenhouse St Aidan's, NT218716
Stockbridge, NT247748
The Tron Kirk (Gilmerton and Moredun):
    Gilmerton, NT293686
    Moredun, NT294697

2. Presbytery of West Lothian

Abercorn, NT082792
Armadale, NS935684
Avonbridge, NS910730
Bathgate: Boghall, NS996686
Bathgate: High, NS976691
Bathgate: St John's, NS977687
Blackburn and Seafield, NS991655
Blackridge, NS897671
Breich Valley, NS968622
Broxburn, NT085723
Fauldhouse: St Andrew's, NS931607
Harthill: St Andrew's, NS896643
Kirknewton and East Calder:
    Kirknewton, NT106670
    East Calder, NT086678
Kirk of Calder, NT074673
Linlithgow: St Michael's, NT002773
Linlithgow: St Ninian's Craigmailen, NS994771
Livingston Ecumenical Parish:
    Carmondean and Knightsridge, NT048693
    Craigshill (St Columba's) and Ladywell (St Paul's), NT054682
    Dedridge and Murieston: Lanthorn Centre, Dedridge, NT060663
Livingston: Old, NT037669
    Deans, NT021686
Pardovan, Kingscavil and Winchburgh:
    Kingscavil, NT030764
    Winchburgh, NT087750
Polbeth Harwood, NT030641
Strathbrock, NT060722
    Ecclesmachan, NT059737
Torphichen, NS969725
Uphall: South, NT061718
West Kirk of Calder, NT014629
Whitburn: Brucefield, NS948650
Whitburn: South, NS947646

3. Presbytery of Lothian

Aberlady, NT462799
Athelstaneford, NT533774
Belhaven, NT668787
Bilston, NT262647
Bolton and Saltoun:
    Bolton, NT507701
    Saltoun, NT474678
Bonnyrigg, NT307654
Cockenzie and Port Seton: Chalmers Memorial, NT403757
Cockenzie and Port Seton: Old, NT401758
Cockpen and Carrington, NT319642
Dalkeith: St John's and King's Park, NT330670
Dalkeith: St Nicholas' Buccleuch, NT333674

Dirleton, NT513842
Dunbar, NT682786
Dunglass:
   Cockburnspath, NT774711
   Innerwick, NT721739
   Oldhamstocks, NT738707
Garvald and Morham:
   Garvald, NT591709
   Morham, NT557726
Gladsmuir, NT457733
Glencorse, NT247627
Gorebridge, NT343619
Gullane, NT483827
Haddington: St Mary's, NT519736
Haddington: West, NT512739
Howgate, NT248580
Humbie, NT461637
Lasswade and Rosewell:
   Lasswade, NT305661
   Rosewell, NT288624
Loanhead, NT278654
Longniddry, NT442763
Musselburgh: Northesk, NT340727
Musselburgh: St Andrew's High, NT345727
Musselburgh: St Clement's and St Ninian's, NT360727
   Wallyford, NT368722
Musselburgh: St Michael's Inveresk, NT344721
   St John's, Whitecraig, NT351701
Newbattle, NT331661:
   Newtongrange, NT334643
   Easthouses, NT348652
Newton, NT315693
North Berwick: Abbey, NT551853
North Berwick: St Andrew Blackadder, NT553853
Ormiston, NT414693
Pencaitland, NT443690
Penicuik: North, NT234603
Penicuik: St Mungo's, NT237599
Penicuik: South, NT236595
Prestonpans: Prestongrange, NT388746
Roslin, NT270631
Spott, NT673755
Tranent, NT403734
Traprain:
   Prestonkirk, NT592778
   Stenton, NT622743
   Whittingehame, NT603737
Tyne Valley Parish:
   Borthwick, NT369596
   Cranston, Crichton and Ford, NT386656
   Fala and Soutra, NT438609
Whitekirk and Tyninghame, NT596815
Yester, NT535681

4. Presbytery of Melrose and Peebles
Ashkirk, NT466220
Bowden and Melrose:
   Bowden, NT554301
   Melrose, NT544344
Broughton, Glenholm and Kilbucho, NT114357
Caddonfoot, NT451348
Carlops, NT161559
Channelkirk and Lauder:
   Channelkirk, NT482545
   Lauder, NT531475
Earlston, NT581388
Eddleston, NT244472
Ettrick and Yarrow:
   Ettrick, NT259145
   Yarrow, NT356278
   Kirkhope, NT390244

Galashiels: Old and St Paul's, NT492358
Galashiels: St John's, NT509357
Galashiels: Trinity, NT491363
Innerleithen, Traquair and Walkerburn:
   Innerleithen, NT332369
   Traquair, NT320335
Kirkurd and Newlands, NT162467
Lyne and Manor:
   Lyne, NT192405
   Manor, NT220380
Maxton and Mertoun:
   Maxton, NT610303
   Mertoun, NT615318
Newtown, NT581316
Peebles: Old, NT250404
Peebles: St Andrew's Leckie, NT253404
St Boswells, NT594310
Selkirk, NT472287
Skirling, NT075390
Stobo and Drumelzier:
   Stobo, NT183377
   Drumelzier, NT135343
Stow: St Mary of Wedale and Heriot:
   Stow: St Mary of Wedale, NT459444
   Heriot, NT390526
Tweedsmuir, NT101245
West Linton: St Andrew's, NT149516

5. Presbytery of Duns
Ayton and Burnmouth:
   Ayton, NT927609
   Burnmouth, NT956610
Berwick-upon-Tweed: St Andrew's Wallace Green
   and Lowick, NT999532
Bonkyl and Preston, NT808596
Chirnside, NT869561
Coldingham and St Abbs, NT904659
Coldstream, NT843398
Duns, NT786539
Eccles, NT764413
Edrom Allanton, NT826558
Eyemouth, NT943640
Fogo and Swinton:
   Fogo, NT773492
   Swinton, NT838477
Foulden and Mordington, NT931558
Gordon: St Michael's, NT645432
Grantshouse and Houndwood and Reston:
   Reston, NT878621
   Grantshouse congregation meets in village hall
Greenlaw, NT712462
Hutton and Fishwick and Paxton:
   Hutton and Fishwick, NT907540
   Paxton, NT934532
Ladykirk and Whitsome:
   Ladykirk, NT889477
   Whitsome, NT861504
Langton and Lammermuir:
   Cranshaws, NT692619
   Langton, NT767523
Legerwood, NT594434
Leitholm, NT791441
Westruther, NT633500

6. Presbytery of Jedburgh
Ale and Teviot United:
   Ancrum, NT627246
   Crailing, NT682250
   Lilliesleaf, NT539253
Cavers and Kirkton:
   Cavers, NT538159

Kirkton, NT541140
Hawick: Burnfoot, NT510162
Hawick: St Mary's and Old, NT502143
Hawick: Teviot and Roberton:
  Hawick: Teviot, NT501144
  Roberton, NT432142
Hawick: Trinity, NT505147
Hawick: Wilton, NT502153
Hobkirk and Southdean:
  Hobkirk, NT587109
  Southdean, NT624109
Jedburgh: Old and Trinity, NT651203
Kelso Country Churches:
  Makerstoun, NT669331
  Roxburgh, NT700307
  Smailholm, NT649364
  Stichill, NT711383
Kelso: North and Ednam:
  Kelso: North, NT725343
  Ednam, NT737372
Kelso: Old and Sprouston:
  Kelso: Old, NT725343
  Sprouston, NT757353
Linton, Morebattle, Hownam and Yetholm:
  Linton, NT773262
  Hoselaw, NT802318
  Morebattle, NT772250
  Hownam, NT778193
  Yetholm, NT826281
Oxnam, NT701190
Ruberslaw:
  Bedrule, NT599179
  Denholm, NT569186
  Minto, NT567201
Teviothead, NT403052

7. Presbytery of Annandale and Eskdale
Annan: Old, NY197666
Annan: St Andrew's, NY193665
Applegarth, Sibbaldbie and Johnstone, NY104843
Brydekirk, NY183705
Canonbie United, NY395763
Dalton, NY114740
Dornock, NY231660
Gretna: Old, Gretna: St Andrew's, Half Morton and
  Kirkpatrick Fleming:
 · Gretna: Old, NY319680
  Gretna: St Andrew's, NY317670
  Kirkpatrick Fleming, NY277701
Hightae, NY090793
Hoddom, Kirtle-Eaglesfield and Middlebie:
  Eaglesfield, NY233743
  Middlebie, NY214762
Kirkpatrick Juxta, NT083009
Langholm Eskdalemuir Ewes and Westerkirk:
  Langholm, NY362844
  Eskdalemuir, NY253979
  Ewes, NY369908
  Westerkirk, NY312903
Liddesdale:
  Castleton, NY482877
  Saughtree, NY562968
Lochmaben, NY084823
Lockerbie: Dryfesdale, Hutton and Corrie
  Hutton and Corrie, NY171908
  Lockerbie: Dryfesdale, NY135818
Moffat: St Andrew's, NT084051
St Mungo, NY143771
The Border Kirk, NY402561
Tundergarth, NY175808
Wamphray, NY131965

8. Presbytery of Dumfries and Kirkcudbright
Auchencairn and Rerrick, NX799512
Balmaclellan and Kells:
  Balmaclellan, NX651791
  Kells, NX632784
Balmaghie, NX722663
Borgue, NX629483
Buittle and Kelton, NX758603
Caerlaverock, NY025962
Carsphairn, NX563932
Castle Douglas, NX765622
Closeburn, NX904923
Colvend, Southwick and Kirkbean:
  Colvend, NX862541
  Southwick, NX927573
Corsock and Kirkpatrick Durham:
  Corsock, NX762760
  Kirkpatrick Durham, NX786699
Crossmichael and Parton:
  Crossmichael, NX729670
  Parton, NX697699
Cummertrees, Mouswald and Ruthwell, NY101683
Dalbeattie, NX831611
Dalry, NX618813
Dumfries: Maxwelltown West, NX967760
Dumfries: North West, NX958774
Dumfries: St George's, NX971764
Dumfries: St Mary's-Greyfriars', NX975763
Dumfries: St Michael's and South, NX975757
Dumfries: Troqueer, NX975751
Dunscore, NX867843
Durisdeer, NS894038
Gatehouse of Fleet, NX602566
Glencairn and Moniaive:
  Glencairn, NX809904
  Moniaive, NX777910
Irongray, Lochrutton and Terregles:
  Irongray, NX915794
  Terregles, NX931771
Kirkconnel, NS728123
Kirkcudbright, NX683509
Kirkgunzeon, NX866667
Kirkmahoe, NX974815:
  Dalswinton, NX942850
Kirkmichael, Tinwald and Torthorwald:
  Kirkmichael, NY005884
  Tinwald, NY003816
  Torthorwald, NY035783
Lochend and New Abbey, NX965660
Penpont, Keir and Tynron, NX849944
Sanquhar: St Bride's, NS779102
Tarff and Twynholm, NX664542
Thornhill, NX883957
Urr, NX817658

9. Presbytery of Wigtown and Stranraer
Ervie Kirkcolm, NX026687
Glasserton and Isle of Whithorn:
  Glasserton, NX421381
  Isle of Whithorn, NX478363
Inch, NX101603
Kirkcowan, NX327610
Kirkinner, NX423514
Kirkmabreck, NX477585
Kirkmaiden, NX125369:
  Drummore, NX135366
Leswalt, NX020638
Mochrum, NX347463
Monigaff, NX410666
New Luce, NX175645
Old Luce, NX197574

Penninghame, NX410654
Portpatrick, NX002544
Sorbie, NX468463
Stoneykirk:
    Sandhead, NX097500
    Ardwell, NX101457
Stranraer: High Kirk, NX057609
Stranraer: Trinity, NX064606
Whithorn: St Ninian's Priory, NX444403
Wigtown, NX436555

10. Presbytery of Ayr
Alloway, NS332180
Annbank, NS407243
Auchinleck, NS552216
Ayr: Auld Kirk of Ayr, NS339219
Ayr: Castlehill, NS347203
Ayr: Newton Wallacetown, NS339224
Ayr: St Andrew's, NS338213
Ayr: St Columba, NS337209
Ayr: St James', NS342232
Ayr: St Leonard's, NS338204
Ayr: St Quivox:
    Auchincruive, NS375241
    Dalmilling, NS363229
Ballantrae, NX083825:
    Glenapp, NX075746
Barr, NX275941
Catrine, NS528260
Coylton, NS422198
Craigie, NS427323
Crosshill, NS327068
Dailly, NS271016
Dalmellington, NS481061:
    Bellsbank, NS480046
Dalrymple, NS358144
Drongan: The Schaw Kirk, NS441185
Dundonald, NS366343
Fisherton, NS275175
Girvan: North (Old and St Andrew's), NX187982
Girvan: South, NX183977
Kirkmichael, NS345090
Kirkoswald, NS240073
Lugar, NS591213
Mauchline, NS498272
Maybole, NS299101
Monkton and Prestwick: North, NS353263
Muirkirk, NS701278
New Cumnock, NS617135
Ochiltree, NS504212
Old Cumnock: Old, NS568202
Old Cumnock: Trinity, NS567200:
    Netherthird, NS578187
Patna Waterside, NS412106
Prestwick: Kingcase, NS348243
Prestwick: St Nicholas', NS351256
Prestwick: South, NS351259
St Colmon (Arnsheen Barrhill and Colmonell):
    Colmonell, NX144857
    Barrhill congregation meets in community centre
Sorn, NS550268
Stair, NS439236
Straiton: St Cuthbert's, NS381049
Symington, NS384314
Tarbolton, NS430272
Troon: Old, NS321309
Troon: Portland, NS323308
Troon: St Meddan's, NS323309

11. Presbytery of Irvine and Kilmarnock
Caldwell, NS435552

Crosshouse, NS395384
Darvel, NS563375
Dreghorn and Springside, NS352383
Dunlop, NS405494
Fenwick, NS465435
Galston, NS500367
Hurlford, NS454372
Irvine: Fullarton, NS316389
Irvine: Girdle Toll, NS341409
Irvine: Mure, NS319390
Irvine: Old, NS322387
Irvine: Relief Bourtreehill, NS344392
Irvine: St Andrew's, NS325399
Kilmarnock: Kay Park, NS431380
Kilmarnock: New Laigh, NS428379
Kilmarnock: Riccarton, NS428364
Kilmarnock: St Andrew's and St Marnock's, NS427377
Kilmarnock: St John's Onthank, NS433399
Kilmarnock: St Kentigern's, NS442388
Kilmarnock: South, NS435359
Kilmaurs: St Maur's Glencairn, NS415408
Newmilns: Loudoun, NS537373
Stewarton: John Knox, NS421460
Stewarton: St Columba's, NS419457
Ayrshire Mission to the Deaf, Kilmarnock, NS430377

12. Presbytery of Ardrossan
Ardrossan: Barony St John's, NS231420
Ardrossan: Park, NS233436
Beith: NS350539
Brodick, NS012359
Corrie, NS024437
Cumbrae, NS160550
Dalry: St Margaret's, NS291496
Dalry: Trinity, NS292494
Fairlie, NS209556
Kilbirnie: Auld Kirk, NS315536
Kilbirnie: St Columba's, NS314546
Kilmory, NR963218
Kilwinning: Mansefield Trinity, NS290432
Kilwinning: Old, NS303433
Lamlash, NS026309
Largs: Clark Memorial, NS202593
Largs: St Columba's, NS203596
Largs: St John's, NS201593
Lochranza and Pirnmill:
    Lochranza, NR937503
    Pirnmill, NR874447
Saltcoats: New Trinity, NS246414
Saltcoats: North, NS252423
Saltcoats: St Cuthbert's, NS244418
Shiskine, NR910295
Stevenston: Ardeer, NS269411
Stevenston: High, NS266422
Stevenston: Livingston, NS268416
West Kilbride, NS207484
Whiting Bay and Kildonan, NS047273

13. Presbytery of Lanark
Biggar, NT040379
Black Mount, NT101464
Cairngryffe, NS923384
Carluke: Kirkton, NS844503
Carluke: St Andrew's, NS844508
Carluke: St John's, NS847503
Carnwath, NS976465
Carstairs and Carstairs Junction, The United Church of:
    Carstairs, NS938461
    Carstairs Junction, NS954450
Coalburn, NS813345
Crossford, NS827466

Culter, NT027342
Forth: St Paul's, NS942538
Kirkfieldbank, NS866438
Kirkmuirhill, NS799429
Lanark: Greyfriars, NS880437
Lanark: St Nicholas', NS881437
Law, NS821527
Lesmahagow: Abbeygreen, NS813402
Lesmahagow: Old, NS814399
Libberton and Quothquan, NS992428
Symington, NS999352
The Douglas Valley Church:
    Douglas, NS835310
    Douglas Water and Rigside, NS873347
Upper Clyde, NS930234

14. Presbytery of Greenock and Paisley
Barrhead: Bourock, NS499589
Barrhead: St Andrew's, NS501588
Bishopton, NS445721
Bridge of Weir: Freeland, NS387656
Bridge of Weir: St Machar's Ranfurly, NS392653
Elderslie Kirk, NS441631
Erskine, NS466707
Gourock: Old Gourock and Ashton, NS243775
Gourock: St John's, NS241778
Greenock: East End, meets at Crawfurdsburn Community
    Centre
Greenock: Lyle Kirk:
    Greenock: Ardgowan, NS271768
    Greenock: Finnart St Paul's, NS265774
    Greenock: Old West Kirk, NS273772
Greenock: Mount Kirk, NS271759
Greenock: St Margaret's, NS255764
Greenock: St Ninian's, NS242755
Greenock: Wellpark Mid Kirk, NS279762
Greenock: Westburn, NS273763
Houston and Killellan, NS410671
Howwood, NS396603
Inchinnan, NS479689
Inverkip, NS207720
Johnstone: High, NS426630
Johnstone: St Andrew's Trinity, NS434623
Johnstone: St Paul's, NS424626
Kilbarchan: East, NS403633
Kilbarchan: West, NS401632
Kilmacolm: Old, NS358700
Kilmacolm: St Columba, NS358697
Langbank, NS380734
Linwood, NS432645
Lochwinnoch, NS353587
Neilston, NS480574
Paisley: Abbey, NS486640
Paisley: Glenburn, NS473617
Paisley: Lylesland, NS488626
Paisley: Martyrs' Sandyford:
    Martyrs', NS474639
    Sandyford, NS493657
Paisley: Oakshaw Trinity, NS480641
Paisley: St Columba Foxbar, NS458622
Paisley: St James', NS477644
Paisley: St Luke's, NS482632
Paisley: St Mark's Oldhall, NS511640
Paisley: St Ninian's Ferguslie, NS464644
Paisley: Sherwood Greenlaw, NS492642
Paisley: Stow Brae Kirk, NS483634
Paisley: Wallneuk North, NS486643
Port Glasgow: Hamilton Bardrainney, NS337733
Port Glasgow: St Andrew's, NS319745
Port Glasgow: St Martin's, NS306747
Renfrew: North, NS508678

Renfrew: Old, NS509676
Renfrew: Trinity, NS505674
Skelmorlie and Wemyss Bay, NS192681

16. Presbytery of Glasgow
Banton, NS752788
Bishopbriggs: Kenmure, NS604698
Bishopbriggs: Springfield, NS615702
Broom, NS554563
Burnside Blairbeth:
    Burnside, NS622601
    Blairbeth, NS616603
Busby, NS577563
Cadder, NS616723
Cambuslang: Flemington Hallside, NS663595
Cambuslang Parish Church, NS645605
Campsie, NS629777
Chryston, NS688702:
    Moodiesburn, NS699708
Eaglesham, NS574519
Fernhill and Cathkin, NS624594
Gartcosh, NS698682
Giffnock: Orchardhill, NS563587
Giffnock: South, NS559582
Giffnock: The Park, NS559593
Glenboig, NS723687
Greenbank, NS574568
Kilsyth: Anderson, NS717782
Kilsyth: Burns and Old, NS716778
Kirkintilloch: Hillhead, NS663730
Kirkintilloch: St Columba's, NS664733
Kirkintilloch: St David's Memorial Park, NS653736
Kirkintilloch: St Mary's, NS654739
Lenzie: Old, NS655720
Lenzie: Union, NS654722
Maxwell Mearns Castle, NS553553
Mearns, NS543551
Milton of Campsie, NS652768
Netherlee, NS577590
Newton Mearns, NS537557
Rutherglen: Old, NS613617
Rutherglen: Stonelaw, NS617612
Rutherglen: West and Wardlawhill, NS609618
Stamperland, NS576581
Stepps, NS657686
Thornliebank, NS546588
Torrance, NS620744
Twechar, NS700753
Williamwood, NS566576
Glasgow: Anderston Kelvingrove, NS577655
Glasgow: Baillieston Mure Memorial, NS673643
Glasgow: Baillieston St Andrew's, NS681639
Glasgow: Balshagray Victoria Park, NS549671
Glasgow: Barlanark Greyfriars, NS667649
Glasgow: Blawarthill, NS522683
Glasgow: Bridgeton St Francis in the East, NS611639
Glasgow: Broomhill, NS549674
Glasgow: Calton Parkhead, NS624638
Glasgow: Cardonald, NS526639
Glasgow: Carmunnock, NS599575
Glasgow: Carmyle, NS649618
Glasgow: Carnwadric, NS544599
Glasgow: Castlemilk, NS596594
Glasgow: Cathcart Old, NS587606
Glasgow: Cathcart Trinity, NS582604
Glasgow: Cathedral (High or St Mungo's), NS603656
Glasgow: Clincarthill, NS586613
Glasgow: Colston Milton, NS592697
Glasgow: Colston Wellpark, NS606692
Glasgow: Cranhill, NS643658
Glasgow: Croftfoot, NS603602

Glasgow: Dennistoun New, NS613652
Glasgow: Drumchapel St Andrew's, NS523707
Glasgow: Drumchapel St Mark's, NS521719
Glasgow: Easterhouse St George's and St Peter's, NS678657
Glasgow: Eastwood, NS558607
Glasgow: Gairbraid, NS568688
Glasgow: Gallowgate, NS614646
Glasgow: Garthamlock and Craigend East, NS658667
Glasgow: Gorbals, NS593638
Glasgow: Govan and Linthouse, NS555658
Glasgow: Govanhill Trinity, NS587627
Glasgow: High Carntyne, NS636653
Glasgow: Hillington Park, NS534639
Glasgow: Hyndland, NS559675
Glasgow: Ibrox, NS560642
Glasgow: John Ross Memorial Church for Deaf People, NS588644
Glasgow: Jordanhill, NS544682
Glasgow: Kelvin Stevenson Memorial, NS576673
Glasgow: Kelvinside Hillhead, NS567673
Glasgow: Kenmuir Mount Vernon, NS655626
Glasgow: King's Park, NS601608
Glasgow: Kinning Park, NS570648
Glasgow: Knightswood St Margaret's, NS536694
Glasgow: Langside, NS582614
Glasgow: Lansdowne, NS576669
Glasgow: Lochwood, NS685663
Glasgow: Maryhill, NS563695
Glasgow: Merrylea, NS575603
Glasgow: Mosspark, NS544633
Glasgow: Newlands South, NS573611
Glasgow: Partick South, NS559665
Glasgow: Partick Trinity, NS563668
Glasgow: Penilee St Andrew, NS518647
Glasgow: Pollokshaws, NS561612
Glasgow: Pollokshields, NS577635
Glasgow: Possilpark, NS592677
Glasgow: Queen's Park, NS579625
Glasgow: Renfield St Stephen's, NS582659
Glasgow: Robroyston, NS638688
Glasgow: Ruchazie, NS643662
Glasgow: Ruchill Kelvinside, NS573683
Glasgow: St Andrew's East, NS619656
Glasgow: St Christopher's Priesthill and Nitshill:
  Nitshill, NS522603
  Priesthill, NS531607
  St Christopher's, NS534616
Glasgow: St Columba, NS583657
Glasgow: St David's Knightswood, NS528689
Glasgow: St Enoch's Hogganfield, NS629660
Glasgow: St George's Tron, NS590655
Glasgow: St James' (Pollok), NS530626
Glasgow: St John's Renfield, NS558683
Glasgow: St Margaret's Tollcross Park, NS637631
Glasgow: St Nicholas' Cardonald, NS524646
Glasgow: St Paul's, NS631671
Glasgow: St Rollox, NS603668
Glasgow: Sandyford Henderson Memorial, NS570659
Glasgow: Sandyhills, NS658638
Glasgow: Scotstoun, NS533676
Glasgow: Shawlands, NS572621
Glasgow: Sherbrooke St Gilbert's, NS561636
Glasgow: Shettleston New, NS647642
Glasgow: Shettleston Old, NS649639
Glasgow: South Carntyne, NS630652
Glasgow: South Shawlands, NS569615
Glasgow: Springburn, NS607677
Glasgow: Temple Anniesland, NS547689
Glasgow: Toryglen, NS602615
Glasgow: Trinity Possil and Henry Drummond, NS593687

Glasgow: Tron St Mary's, NS618676
Glasgow: Victoria Tollcross, NS642632
Glasgow: Wallacewell, NS621690
Glasgow: Wellington, NS570667
Glasgow: Whiteinch, NS540668
Glasgow: Yoker, NS511689

17. Presbytery of Hamilton
Airdrie: Broomknoll, NS761653
Airdrie: Clarkston, NS783661
Airdrie: Flowerhill, NS765655
Airdrie: High, NS760658
Airdrie: Jackson, NS782647
Airdrie: New Monkland, NS753678
Airdrie: St Columba's, NS766665
Airdrie: The New Wellwynd, NS759654
Bargeddie, NS692648
Bellshill: Macdonald Memorial, NS738602
Bellshill: Orbiston, NS729593
Bellshill: West, NS727603
Blantyre: Livingstone Memorial, NS687577
Blantyre: Old, NS679565
Blantyre: St Andrew's, NS693573
Bothwell, NS705586
Calderbank, NS770631
Caldercruix and Longriggend, NS819677
Chapelhall, NS783627
Chapelton, NS685485
Cleland, NS805583
Coatbridge: Blairhill Dundyvan, NS726650
Coatbridge: Calder, NS738639
Coatbridge: Middle, NS723646
Coatbridge: Old Monkland, NS718633
Coatbridge: New St Andrew's, NS733653
Coatbridge: Townhead, NS718664
Dalserf, NS800507:
  Ashgill, NS783503
East Kilbride: Claremont, NS653543
East Kilbride: Greenhills, NS616525
East Kilbride: Moncreiff, NS647555
East Kilbride: Mossneuk, NS607532
East Kilbride: Old, NS635545
East Kilbride: South, NS633537
East Kilbride: Stewartfield, meets in a community centre at NS643561
East Kilbride: West, NS634547
East Kilbride: Westwood, NS618537
Glasford, NS726470
Greengairs, NS783705
Hamilton: Cadzow, NS723550
Hamilton: Gilmour and Whitehill, NS704563
Hamilton: Hillhouse, NS696554
Hamilton: Old, NS723555
Hamilton: St Andrew's, NS723551
Hamilton: St John's, NS724553
Hamilton: South, NS717538
Hamilton: Trinity, NS711543
Hamilton: West, NS712558
Holytown, NS773608
Kirk o' Shotts, NS843629
Larkhall: Chalmers, NS763499
Larkhall: St Machan's, NS763511
Larkhall: Trinity, NS762513
Motherwell: Crosshill, NS756566
Motherwell: Dalziel St Andrew's, NS752571
Motherwell: North, NS741577
Motherwell: St Margaret's, NS769549
Motherwell: St Mary's, NS750566
Motherwell: South, NS757560
Newarthill and Carfin, NS781597
Newmains: Bonkle, NS837571

Newmains: Coltness Memorial, NS819557
New Stevenston: Wrangholm Kirk, NS760596
Overtown, NS801527
Quarter, NS722512
Shotts: Calderhead Erskine, NS877600:
   Allanton, NS850578
Stonehouse: St Ninian's, NS752467
Strathaven: Avendale Old and Drumclog:
   Avendale Old, NS701443
   Drumclog, NS640389
Strathaven: East, NS702446
Strathaven: Rankin, NS701446
Uddingston: Burnhead, NS717614
Uddingston: Old, NS696603
Uddingston: Viewpark, NS702616
Wishaw: Cambusnethan North, NS808554
Wishaw: Cambusnethan Old, NS806553
Wishaw: Craigneuk and Belhaven, NS773561
Wishaw: Old, NS796552
Wishaw: St Mark's, NS801566
Wishaw: South Wishaw, NS797548

18. Presbytery of Dumbarton
Alexandria, NS387817
Arrochar, NM296037
Baldernock, NS577751
Bearsden: Baljaffray, NS534736
Bearsden: Cross, NS543719
Bearsden: Killermont, NS557713
Bearsden: New Kilpatrick, NS543723
Bearsden: Westerton Fairlie Memorial, NS543706
Bonhill, NS395796
Cardross, NS345775
Clydebank: Abbotsford, NS498703
Clydebank: Faifley, NS502732
Clydebank: Kilbowie St Andrew's, NS499712
Clydebank: Radnor Park, NS495713
Clydebank: St Cuthbert's, NS511704
Craigrownie, NS224811
Dalmuir: Barclay, NS479715
Dumbarton: Riverside, NS398752
Dumbarton: St Andrew's, NS407764
Dumbarton: West Kirk, NS390755
Duntocher, NS494727
Garelochhead, NS239912
Helensburgh: Park, NS300823
Helensburgh: St Andrew's Kirk, NS295825
Jamestown, NS397813
Kilmaronock Gartocharn, NS452875
Luss, NS361929
Milngavie: Cairns, NS556748
Milngavie: St Luke's, NS543747
Milngavie: St Paul's, NS557745
Old Kilpatrick Bowling, NS463731
Renton: Trinity, NS390780
Rhu and Shandon, NS267841
Rosneath: St Modan's, NS255832

19. Presbytery of Argyll
Appin, NM938459
Ardchattan, NM944360:
   Benderloch, NM905384
Ardrishaig, NR854852
Barra, NF670034
Campbeltown: Highland, NR720201
Campbeltown: Lorne and Lowland, NR718206
Coll, NM223573
Colonsay and Oronsay, NR390941
Connel, NM914343
Craignish, NM805042
Cumlodden, Lochfyneside and Lochgair:

Cumlodden, NS015997
Lochfyneside, NR979962
Lochgair, NR922905
Dunoon: St John's, NS172769
Dunoon: The High Kirk, NS174765
Gigha and Cara, NR648489
Glassary, Kilmartin and Ford:
   Glassary, NR859935
   Kilmartin, NR834988
   Ford, NM869037
Glenaray and Inveraray, NN095085
Glenorchy and Innishael, NN168275
Innellan, NS151707
Iona, NM285243
Jura, NR527677
Kilarrow, NR312596
Kilbrandon and Kilchattan:
   Kilbrandon, NM758155
   Kilchattan, NM743104
Kilcalmonell, NR763561
Kilchoman, NR257596
Kilchrenan and Dalavich:
   Kilchrenan, NN037229
   Dalavich, NM968124
Kildalton and Oa, NR368450
Kilfinan, NR934789
Kilfinichen and Kilvickeon and the Ross of Mull:
   Kilfinichen and Kilvickeon, NM383218
   The Ross of Mull, NM316232
Killean and Kilchenzie, NR681418
Kilmeny, NR390657
Kilmodan and Colintraive:
   Kilmodan, NR995842
   Colintraive, NS045735
Kilmore and Oban:
   Kilmore, NM872258
   Oban: Old, NM861296
   Corran Esplanade, NM856306
Kilmun (St Munn's), NS166821
Kilninian and Kilmore, NM432517
Kilninver and Kilmelford:
   Kilninver, NM825217
   Kilmelford, NM849130
Kirn, NS184783
Kyles, NR973713
Lismore, NM861435
Lochgilphead, NR863882
Lochgoilhead and Kilmorich:
   Lochgoilhead, NN198015
   Kilmorich, NN181108
Muckairn, NN005310
North Knapdale:
   Kilmichael Inverlussa, NR776859
   Bellanoch, NR797923
   Tayvallich, NR742871
Portnahaven, NR168523
Rothesay: Trinity, NS089645
Saddell and Carradale, NR796376
Salen and Ulva, NM573431
Sandbank, NS163803
Skipness, NR902579
Southend, NR698094
South Knapdale, NR781775
South Uist:
   Daliburgh, NF754214
   Howmore, NF758364
Strachur and Strathlachlan:
   Strachur, NN096014
   Strathlachlan, NS022958
Strathfillan:
   Crianlarich, NN387252

Bridge of Orchy, NN297395
Strone and Ardentinny:
  Strone, NS193806
  Ardentinny, NS188876
Tarbert (Loch Fyne) and Kilberry:
  Kilberry, NR741620
  Tarbert, NR863686
The United Church of Bute, NS086637
Tiree:
  Heylipol, NL964432
  Kirkapol, NM041468
Tobermory, NM504554
Torosay and Kinlochspelvie, NM721367
Toward, NS135679

22. Presbytery of Falkirk
Airth, NS898878
Blackbraes and Shieldhill, NS899769
Bo'ness: Old, NS994813
Bo'ness: St Andrew's, NT007813
Bonnybridge: St Helen's, NS821804
Bothkennar and Carronshore, NS903834
Brightons, NS928778
Carriden, NT019812:
  Blackness, NT053798
Cumbernauld: Abronhill, NS781758
Cumbernauld: Condorrat, NS732730
Cumbernauld: Kildrum, NS767747
Cumbernauld: Old, NS764760
Cumbernauld: St Mungo's, NS757745
Denny: Old, NS812828
Denny: Westpark, NS809828
Dunipace, NS807833
Falkirk: Bainsford, NS887814
Falkirk: Camelon, NS873804
Falkirk: Erskine, NS884798
Falkirk: Grahamston United, NS889807
Falkirk: Laurieston, NS913794
Falkirk: Old and St Modan's, NS887800
Falkirk: St Andrew's West, NS887801
Falkirk: St James', NS893806
Grangemouth: Abbotsgrange, NS928817
Grangemouth: Kirk of the Holy Rood, NS931805
Grangemouth: Zetland, NS931818
Haggs, NS791793
Larbert: East, NS871829
Larbert: Old, NS856822
Larbert: West, NS863827
Muiravonside, NS956770
Polmont: Old, NS937793
Redding and Westquarter, NS921786
Slamannan, NS856734
Stenhouse and Carron, NS876831

23. Presbytery of Stirling
Aberfoyle, NN514013
Alloa: Ludgate, NS884927
Alloa: St Mungo's, NS883926
Alva, NS882970
Balfron, NS547893
Balquhidder, NN536209
Bannockburn: Allan, NS810903
Bannockburn: Ladywell, NS803907
Bridge of Allan, NS791974
Buchanan, NS443903
Buchlyvie, NS577939
Callander, NN629077:
  Trossachs, NN515066
Cambusbarron: The Bruce Memorial, NS778924
Clackmannan, NS910918
Cowie and Plean:

Cowie, NS837892
  Plean, NS836867
Dollar, NS964980
Drymen, NS474881
Dunblane: Cathedral, NN782014
Dunblane: St Blane's, NN783014
Fallin, NS844913
Fintry, NS627862
Gargunnock, NS707943
Gartmore, NS521971
Glendevon, NN979051
Killearn, NS523861
Killin and Ardeonaig, NN573332:
  Morenish, NN607356
Kilmadock, NN727016
Kincardine-in-Menteith, NS719988
Kippen, NS650948
Lecropt, NS781979
Logie, NS818968
Menstrie, NS849969
Muckhart, NO001010
Norrieston, NN670001
Port of Menteith, NN583012
Sauchie and Coalsnaughton, NS897945
Stirling: Allan Park South, NS795933
Stirling: Church of the Holy Rude, NS792937
Stirling: North, NS802920
Stirling: St Columba's, NS796930
Stirling: St Mark's, NS791948
Stirling: St Ninian's Old, NS795916
Stirling: Viewfield, NS795938
Strathblane, NS557797
Tillicoultry, NS923968
Tullibody: St Serf's, NS860954

24. Presbytery of Dunfermline
Aberdour: St Fillan's, NT193855
Beath and Cowdenbeath: North, NT166925
Cairneyhill, NT052863
Carnock and Oakley:
  Carnock, NT043890
  Oakley, NT025890
Cowdenbeath: Trinity:
  Cowdenbeath, NT157908
  Crossgates, NT145893
Culross and Torryburn:
  Culross, NS989863
  Torryburn, NT027861
  Valleyfield, NT003866
Dalgety, NT155836
Dunfermline: Abbey, NT090873
Dunfermline: East, NT127864
Dunfermline: Gillespie Memorial, NT090876
Dunfermline: North, NT086879
Dunfermline: St Andrew's Erskine, NT107884
Dunfermline: St Leonard's, NT096869
Dunfermline: St Margaret's, NT114878
Dunfermline: St Ninian's, NT113868
Dunfermline: Townhill and Kingseat:
  Townhill, NT106894
  Kingseat, NT126904
Inverkeithing, NT131830
Kelty, NT144942
Limekilns, NT078833
Lochgelly and Benarty: St Serf's:
  Lochgelly, NT186933
  Ballingry, NT173977
North Queensferry, NT132808
Rosyth, NT114839
Saline and Blairingone, NT023924
Tulliallan and Kincardine, NS933879

25. Presbytery of Kirkcaldy

Auchterderran: St Fothad's, NT214960
Auchtertool, NT207902
Buckhaven and Wemyss:
Buckhaven, NT358981
Wemyss, NT336968
West Wemyss, NT328949
Burntisland, NT234857
Dysart: St Clair:
Dysart, NT302931
Kirkcaldy: Viewforth, NT294936
Glenrothes: Christ's Kirk, NO275023
Glenrothes: St Columba's, NO270009
Glenrothes: St Margaret's, NO285002
Glenrothes: St Ninian's, NO257007
Kennoway, Windygates and Balgonie: St Kenneth's:
Kennoway, NO350027
Windygates, NO345006
Kinghorn, NT272869
Kinglassie, NT227985
Kirkcaldy: Abbotshall, NT274913
Kirkcaldy: Bennochy, NT275925
Kirkcaldy: Linktown, NT278910
Kirkcaldy: Pathhead, NT291928
Kirkcaldy: St Bryce Kirk, NT279917
Kirkcaldy: Templehall, NT265934
Kirkcaldy: Torbain, NT259939
Leslie: Trinity, NO247015
Leven, NO383009
Markinch, NO297019
Methil: Wellesley, NT370994
Methilhill and Denbeath, NT357999
Thornton, NT289976

26. Presbytery of St Andrews

Abdie and Dunbog, NO257167
Anstruther, NO567037
Auchtermuchty, NO238117
Balmerino, NO368245:
Gauldry, NO379239
Boarhills and Dunino:
Boarhills, NO562137
Dunino, NO541109
Cameron, NO484116
Carnbee, NO532065
Cellardyke, NO574037
Ceres, Kemback and Springfield:
Ceres, NO399117
Kemback, NO419151
Springfield, NO342119
Crail, NO613080
Creich, Flisk and Kilmany:
Creich, NO328200
Kilmany, NO388217
Cupar: Old and St Michael of Tarvit, NO373143
Cupar: St John's and Dairsie United:
Cupar: St John's, NO373147
Dairsie, NO413173
Edenshead and Strathmiglo, NO217103
Elie, Kilconquhar and Colinsburgh:
Elie, NO491001
Kilconquhar, NO485020
Colinsburgh, NO475034
Falkland, NO252074
Freuchie, NO283067
Howe of Fife:
Collessie, NO287133
Cults, NO347099
Kettle, NO310083
Ladybank, NO302102
Kilrenny, NO575049

Kingsbarns, NO593121
Largo and Newburn, NO423035
Largo: St David's, NO419026
Largoward, NO469077
Leuchars: St Athernase, NO455214
Monimail, NO303142
Newburgh, NO240183
Newport-on-Tay, NO422280
Pittenweem, NO549026
St Andrews: Holy Trinity, NO509167
St Andrews: Hope Park and Martyrs', NO505167
St Andrews: St Leonard's, NO502164
St Monans, NO523014
Strathkinness, NO460163
Tayport, NO458286
Wormit, NO403267

27. Presbytery of Dunkeld and Meigle

Aberfeldy, NN854491
Alyth, NO243488
Amulree and Strathbraan, NN899366
Ardler, Kettins and Meigle:
Kettins, NO238390
Meigle, NO287446
Bendochy, NO218415
Blair Atholl, NN874654:
Struan, NN808654
Blairgowrie, NO177454
Braes of Rannoch, NN507566
Caputh and Clunie:
Caputh, NO088401
Clunie, NO109440
Coupar Angus: Abbey, NO223398
Dull and Weem, NN844497
Dunkeld: Cathedral, NO024426:
Little Dunkeld, NO028423
Dowally, NO001480
Fortingall and Glenlyon:
Fortingall, NN742471
Glenlyon, NN588475
Foss and Rannoch:
Foss, NN790581
Rannoch, NN663585
Grantully, Logierait and Strathtay:
Logierait, NN967520
Strathtay, NN908532
Kenmore and Lawers, NN772454
Kinclaven, NO151385
Kirkmichael, Straloch and Glenshee:
Kirkmichael, NO081601
Glenshee, NO109702
Pitlochry, NO940582
Rattray, NO190457
Tenandry, NN911615

28. Presbytery of Perth

Abernethy and Dron and Arngask:
Abernethy, NO190164
Arngask (Glenfarg), NO133104
Almondbank and Tibbermore, NO065264
Ardoch, NO839098
Auchterarder, NN948129
Auchtergaven and Moneydie, NO061347
Blackford, NN899092
Cargill Burrelton, NO202377
Cleish, NT095981
Collace, NO197320
Comrie, NN770221
Crieff, NN867219
Dunbarney and Forgandenny:
Dunbarney, NO130185

Forgandenny, NO087183
Dundurn, NN697241
Errol, NO253230
Fossoway: St Serf's and Devonside, NO033001
Fowlis Wester, Madderty and Monzie:
  Fowlis Wester, NN928241
  Madderty, NN947217
  Monzie, NN879250
Gask, NO003203
Kilspindie and Rait, NO220258
Kinross, NO118023
Methven and Logiealmond, NO026260
Muthill, NN868171
Orwell and Portmoak:
  Orwell, NO121051
  Portmoak, NO183019
Perth: Craigie and Moncreiffe:
  Craigie, NO110228
  Moncreiffe, NO113218
Perth: Kinnoull, NO123235
Perth: Letham St Mark's, NO095243
Perth: North, NO116237
Perth: Riverside, NO110256
Perth: St John's Kirk of Perth, NO119235
Perth: St Leonard's-in-the-Fields, NO117232
Perth: St Matthew's, NO121235
Redgorton and Stanley, NO110329
St Madoes and Kinfauns, NO197212
Scone and St Martins:
  Scone, NO136262
  St David's Stormontfield, NO108298
  St Martins, NO154304
The Stewartry of Strathearn:
  Aberdalgie and Dupplin, NO079203
  Aberuthven, NN979155
  Forteviot, NO052175
  Dunning, NO020147
Trinity Gask and Kinkell, NN963183

29. Presbytery of Dundee
Abernyte, NO267311
Auchterhouse, NO342381
Dundee: Balgay, NO385309
Dundee: Barnhill St Margaret's, NO478316
Dundee: Broughty Ferry New Kirk, NO464309
Dundee: Broughty Ferry St James', NO460307
Dundee: Broughty Ferry St Luke's and Queen Street,
  NO457312
Dundee: Broughty Ferry St Stephen's and West,
  NO458309
Dundee: Camperdown, NO363320
Dundee: Chalmers Ardler, NO377333
Dundee: Coldside, NO403316
Dundee: Craigiebank, NO429315
Dundee: Douglas and Mid Craigie, NO444322
Dundee: Downfield Mains, NO389336
Dundee: Dundee (St Mary's), NO401301
Dundee: Fintry, NO423334
Dundee: Lochee, NO377318
Dundee: Logie and St John's Cross, NO386299
Dundee: Meadowside St Paul's, NO402300
Dundee: Menzieshill, NO362312
Dundee: St Andrew's, NO404307
Dundee: St David's High Kirk:
  St David's North, NO391318
  High Kirk, NO394313
Dundee: Steeple, NO402301
Dundee: Stobswell, NO411315
Dundee: Strathmartine, NO384343
Dundee: Trinity, NO410310
Dundee: West, NO395297

Dundee: Whitfield, NO435334
Fowlis and Liff:
  Fowlis, NO322334
  Liff, NO333328
Inchture and Kinnaird:
  Inchture, NO281288
  Kinnaird, NO243287
Invergowrie, NO346304
Longforgan, NO309300
Lundie and Muirhead:
  Lundie, NO291366
  Muirhead, NO342345
Monifieth:
  Panmure, NO500327
  St Rule's, NO495323
  South, NO493324
Monikie and Newbigging and Murroes and Tealing:
  Monikie, NO518388
  Murroes, NO461351

30. Presbytery of Angus
Aberlemno, NO523555
Arbirlot, NO602406
Arbroath: Knox's, NO638414
Arbroath: Old and Abbey, NO644413
Arbroath: St Andrew's, NO643414
Arbroath: St Vigeans, NO638429
Arbroath: West Kirk, NO636410
Barry, NO541346
Brechin: Cathedral, NO595601:
  Stracathro, NO617657
Brechin: Gardner Memorial, NO601602
Carmyllie, NO549426
Carnoustie, NO559346
Carnoustie: Panbride, NO570347:
  Panbride, NO572358
Colliston, NO604453
Dun and Hillside:
  Dun, NO664600
  Hillside, NO709609
Dunnichen, Letham and Kirkden, NO528488
Eassie, Nevay and Newtyle, NO296413
Edzell Lethnot Glenesk:
  Edzell Lethnot, NO599693
  Glenesk, NO497795
Farnell, NO627554
Fern Careston Menmuir:
  Fern, NO484616
  Careston, NO528603
Forfar: East and Old, NO457506
Forfar: Lowson Memorial, NO465509
Forfar: St Margaret's, NO454505
Friockheim Kinnell, NO592497
Glamis, Inverarity and Kinnettles:
  Glamis, NO386469
  Inverarity, NO453443
Guthrie and Rescobie:
  Guthrie, NO568505
  Rescobie, NO509521
Inchbrayock, NO714567
Inverkeilor and Lunan, NO664496
Kirriemuir: St Andrew's, NO386535
Montrose: Melville South, NO713575
Montrose: Old and St Andrew's, NO715578
Oathlaw Tannadice, NO475581
The Glens and Kirriemuir: Old:
  Kirriemuir: Old, NO386539
  Cortachy, NO396597
  Glen Prosen, NO328657
  Memus, NO427590
The Isla Parishes:

Airlie, NO313515
Glenisla, NO215604
Kilry, NO246538

31. Presbytery of Aberdeen
Aberdeen: Bridge of Don Oldmachar, NJ928121
Aberdeen: Cove, meets in Loirston Primary School
Aberdeen: Craigiebuckler, NJ907053
Aberdeen: Ferryhill, NJ937051
Aberdeen: Garthdee, NJ918034
Aberdeen: Gilcomston South, meets in Aberdeen: South
    Holburn
Aberdeen: High Hilton, NJ923078
Aberdeen: Holburn West, NJ926052
Aberdeen: Mannofield, NJ917045
Aberdeen: Mastrick, NJ902073
Aberdeen: Middlefield, NJ911088
Aberdeen: Midstocket, NJ919066
Aberdeen: Northfield, NJ903085
Aberdeen: Queen Street, NJ943064
Aberdeen: Queen's Cross, NJ925058
Aberdeen: Rubislaw, NJ924058
Aberdeen: Ruthrieston West, NJ924042
Aberdeen: St Columba's Bridge of Don, NJ935104
Aberdeen: St George's Tillydrone, NJ931090
Aberdeen: St John's Church for Deaf People, meets in
    Aberdeen: St Mark's
Aberdeen: St Machar's Cathedral, NJ939088
Aberdeen: St Mark's, NJ937063
Aberdeen: St Mary's, NJ943081
Aberdeen: St Nicholas Kincorth, South of, NJ934033
Aberdeen: St Nicholas Uniting, Kirk of, NJ941063
Aberdeen: St Stephen's, NJ936074
Aberdeen: South Holburn, NJ930042
Aberdeen: Stockethill, meets in community centre
Aberdeen: Summerhill, NJ904063
Aberdeen: Torry St Fittick's, NJ947050
Aberdeen: Woodside, NJ924088
Bucksburn Stoneywood, NJ897096
Cults, NJ886026
Dyce, NJ887130
Kingswells, NJ869063
Newhills, NJ876095
Peterculter, NJ841007

32. Presbytery of Kincardine and Deeside
Aberluthnott, NO687656:
    Luthermuir, NO655685
Aboyne and Dinnet, NO525983
Arbuthnott, Bervie and Kinneff:
    Arbuthnott, NO801746
    Bervie, NO830727
Banchory-Devenick and Maryculter/Cookney, NO857993
Banchory-Ternan: East, NO707958
Banchory-Ternan: West, NO693957
Birse and Feughside, NO605925
Braemar and Crathie:
    Braemar, NO150913
    Crathie, NO265949
Cromar:
    Coull, NJ512024
    Tarland, NJ485047
Drumoak-Durris:
    Drumoak, NO792993
    Durris, NO772965
Glenmuick (Ballater), NO369957
    Glengairn, NJ300012
Laurencekirk, NO718717
Mearns Coastal:
    Johnshaven, NO798672
    St Cyrus, NO750648

Mid Deeside, NJ626021
Newtonhill, NO911934
Portlethen, NO924966
Stonehaven: Dunnottar, NO863853
Stonehaven: Fetteresso, NO869864
Stonehaven: South, NO872857
West Mearns:
    Fettercairn, NO651735
    Fordoun, NO726784
    Glenbervie, NO766807

33. Presbytery of Gordon
Barthol Chapel, NJ814339
Belhelvie, NJ957184
Blairdaff and Chapel of Garioch:
    Blairdaff, NJ704173
    Chapel of Garioch, NJ716242
Cluny, NJ685124
Culsalmond and Rayne, NJ698302
Cushnie and Tough:
    Cushnie, NJ530108
    Tough, NJ616129
Daviot, NJ750283
Echt, NJ739057
Ellon, NJ959304:
    Slains, NK042290
Fintray Kinellar Keithhall:
    Fintray, NJ841166
    Keithhall, NJ803210
Foveran, NJ999253
Howe Trinity, NJ582157
Huntly Cairnie Glass, NJ530398
Insch-Leslie-Premnay-Oyne,
    NJ631283
Inverurie: St Andrew's, NJ777211
Inverurie: West, NJ774215
Kemnay, NJ737162
Kintore, NJ793163
Meldrum and Bourtie:
    Meldrum, NJ813273
    Bourtie, NJ804248
Methlick, NJ858372
Midmar, NJ699065
Monymusk, NJ684152
New Machar, NJ887194
Noth, NJ497272
Skene, NJ803077:
    Westhill, NJ833072
Strathbogie Drumblade:
    Strathbogie, NJ531399
    Drumblade, NJ588402
Tarves, NJ868312
Udny and Pitmedden:
    Udny, NJ880264
    Pitmedden, NJ893274
Upper Donside:
    Strathdon, NJ355127
    Towie, NJ440129
    Lumsden, NJ475220

34. Presbytery of Buchan
Aberdour, NJ885634
Auchaber United, NJ632411
Auchterless, NJ713415
Banff, NJ689638
Crimond, NK054568
Cruden, NK071366
Deer, NJ979477:
    Fetterangus, NJ987508
Fordyce, NJ587659
Fraserburgh: Old, NJ998671

Fraserburgh: South, NJ998666
Fraserburgh: West, NJ994667
Fyvie, NJ768377
Gardenstown, NJ801648
Inverallochy and Rathen: East, NK043651
King Edward, NJ716579
Longside, NK037473
Lonmay, NK038602
Macduff, NJ701643
Marnoch, NJ628527
Maud and Savoch, NJ927478
Monquhitter and New Byth, NJ803506
New Deer: St Kane's, NJ886469
New Pitsligo, NJ880562
Ordiquhill and Cornhill, NJ587583
Peterhead: Old, NK131462
Peterhead: St Andrew's, NK131465
Peterhead: Trinity, NK132463:
    Boddam, NK133423
Pitsligo, NJ929673
Rathen: West, NK000609
Rothienorman, NJ723357
St Fergus, NK093519
Sandhaven, NJ963675
Strichen and Tyrie:
    Strichen, NJ945554
    Tyrie, NJ930631
Turriff: St Andrew's, NJ729497
Turriff: St Ninian's and Forglen,
    NJ723500
Whitehills, NJ655653

35. Presbytery of Moray
Aberlour, NJ264428:
    Craigellachie, NJ290451
Alves and Burghead:
    Alves, NJ125616
    Burghead, NJ114688
Bellie, NJ345588
Birnie and Pluscarden:
    Birnie, NJ207587
    Pluscarden, NJ149573
Buckie: North, NJ427657
Buckie: South and West, NJ426654
Cullen and Deskford, NJ507664
Dallas, NJ122518
Duffus, Spynie and Hopeman:
    Duffus, NJ168687
    Spynie, NJ183642
    Hopeman, NJ144693
Dyke, NH990584
Edinkillie, NJ020466
Elgin: High, NJ215627
Elgin: St Giles' and St Columba's South:
    St Giles', NJ217628
    St Columba's South, NJ219623
Enzie, NJ397643
Findochty, NJ464682
Forres: St Laurence, NJ035588
Forres: St Leonard's, NJ038591
Keith: North, Newmill, Boharm and
    Rothiemay:
    Keith: North, NJ433507
    Newmill, NJ439527
    Boharm, NJ355505
    Rothiemay, NJ547483
Keith: St Rufus, Botriphnie and Grange:
    Keith: St Rufus, NJ430508
    Botriphnie, NJ375441
    Grange, NJ481515
Kinloss and Findhorn:

Kinloss, NJ063617
    Findhorn, NJ042642
Knockando, Elchies and Archiestown, NJ186429
Lossiemouth: St Gerardine's High, NJ233706
Lossiemouth: St James', NJ235707
Mortlach and Cabrach:
    Mortlach, NJ324393
    Lower Cabrach, NJ382313
Portknockie, NJ488684
Rafford, NJ061564
Rathven, NJ444657
Rothes, NJ278492
St Andrew's-Lhanbryd and Urquhart, NJ256622
Speymouth, NJ337607

36. Presbytery of Abernethy
Abernethy, NJ007218:
    Nethy Bridge, NJ003203
Alvie and Insh:
    Alvie, NH864093
    Insh, NH837053
Boat of Garten, Duthil and Kincardine:
    Boat of Garten, NH941190
    Duthil, NH908225
    Kincardine, NH938155
Cromdale and Advie, NJ067289
Dulnain Bridge, NH998249
Grantown-on-Spey, NJ032281
Kingussie, NH761007
Laggan, NN615943
Newtonmore: St Bride's, NN715993
Rothiemurchus and Aviemore:
    Rothiemurchus, NH903108
    Aviemore, NH896130
Tomintoul, Glenlivet and Inveraven:
    Tomintoul, NJ169185
    Inveraven, NJ183376

37. Presbytery of Inverness
Ardersier, NH781553
Auldearn and Dalmore, NH919556
Cawdor, NH844499
Croy and Dalcross, NH797498
Culloden: The Barn, NH719461
Daviot and Dunlichity:
    Daviot, NH722394
    Dunlichity, NH660330
Dores and Boleskine:
    Dores, NH601350
    Boleskine, NH507183
Inverness: Crown, NH671452
Inverness: Dalneigh and Bona:
    Dalneigh, NH655450
    Bona, NH595377
Inverness: East, NH666455
Inverness: Hilton, NH674436
Inverness: Inshes, NH688441
Inverness: Kinmylies, NH646446
Inverness: Ness Bank, NH665448
Inverness: Old High St Stephen's:
    Old High, NH665455
    St Stephen's, NH670447
Inverness: St Columba
Inverness: Trinity, NH661458
Kilmorack and Erchless:
    Beauly, NH525465
    Struy, NH402402
    Cannich, NH336318
Kiltarlity, NH513413
Kirkhill, NH553454
Moy, Dalarossie and Tomatin:

Dalarossie, NH767242
Tomatin, NH803290
Nairn: Old, NH879564
Nairn: St Ninian's, NH883563
Petty, NH767502
Urquhart and Glenmoriston,
NH509294

38. Presbytery of Lochaber
Acharacle, NM674683
Ardgour and Kingairloch:
Ardgour, NN011642
Kingairloch, NM862526
Ardnamurchan, NM488638
Duror, NM993553
Fort Augustus, NH377090
Fort William: Duncansburgh MacIntosh,
NN104741
Glencoe: St Munda's, NN083578
Glengarry, NH304012:
Tomdoun, NH154011
Kilmallie:
Achnacarry, NN181873
Caol, NN106762
Corpach, NN092770
Kilmonivaig, NN212819
Kinlochleven, NN187621
Morvern, NM672452
Nether Lochaber, NN031614
North West Lochaber:
Arisaig, NM661866
Canna, NG277054
Eigg, NM481855
Mallaig: St Columba, NM676967
Strontian, NM817617

39. Presbytery of Ross
Alness, NH647693
Avoch, NH701552
Contin, NH457557:
Kinlochluichart, NH317622
Cromarty, NH786674
Dingwall: Castle Street, NH552588
Dingwall: St Clement's, NH548589
Fearn Abbey and Nigg:
Fearn Abbey, NH837773
Nigg, NH825736
Ferintosh, NH543556
Fodderty and Strathpeffer, NH482580
Fortrose and Rosemarkie:
Fortrose, NH728568
Rosemarkie, NH737576
Invergordon, NH707687
Killearnan, NH577494
Kilmuir and Logie Easter:
Kilmuir, NH758732
Logie Easter, NH779757
Kiltearn, NH607662
Knockbain, NH647530:
Kessock, NH655479
Lochbroom and Ullapool:
Lochbroom, NH177848
Ullapool, NH130942
Resolis and Urquhart, NH608596
Rosskeen, NH658697
Tain, NH780820
Tarbat, NH917846
Urray and Kilchrist:
Urray, NH509524
Muir of Ord, NH528507

40. Presbytery of Sutherland
Altnaharra and Farr:
Altnaharra, NC568355
Farr, NC708622
Strathnaver, NC694439
Assynt and Stoer, NC093225
Clyne, NC905044
Creich, NH611917
Dornoch Cathedral, NH797897
Durness and Kinlochbervie:
Durness, NC404669
Kinlochbervie, NC221564
Eddrachillis, NC151443
Golspie, NC837003
Kildonan and Loth Helmsdale, ND025154
Kincardine Croick and Edderton:
Ardgay, NH595910
Croick, NH457915
Edderton, NH710847
Lairg, NC583065
Melness and Tongue:
Melness, NC586634
Tongue, NC591570
Rogart, Pitfure, NC715038:
St Callan's, NC739035
Rosehall, NC484013

41. Presbytery of Caithness
Bower, ND238622
Canisbay, ND343728
Dunnet, ND220712
Halkirk Westerdale, ND131594
Keiss, ND348611
Olrig, ND191682
The North Coast Parish:
Halladale, NC893558
Reay, NC967648
Strathy, NC843653
The Parish of Latheron:
Lybster, ND248361
Dunbeath, ND157295
Thurso: St Peter's and St Andrew's, ND115683
Thurso: West, ND114681
Watten, ND243547
Wick: Pulteneytown and Thrumster:
Pulteneytown, ND365504
Thrumster, ND333447
Wick: St Fergus, ND362512

42. Presbytery of Lochcarron – Skye
Applecross, Lochcarron and Torridon:
Applecross, NG711417
Lochcarron, NG893391
Shieldaig, NG816542
Torridon, NG864572
Bracadale and Duirinish:
Bracadale, NG369331
Duirinish, NG251479
Gairloch and Dundonnell:
Gairloch, NG807756
Aultbea, NG875886
Dundonnell, NH019919
Glenelg and Kintail:
Glenelg, NG813193
Kintail, NG930213
Kilmuir and Stenscholl:
Kilmuir, NG389694
Stenscholl, NG489673
Lochalsh:
Kirkton, NG829272
Kyle of Lochalsh, NG761277

Plockton, NG801331
Stromeferry, NG863346
Portree, NG482436
Snizort:
  Arnisort, NG348532
  Kensaleyre, NG420517
  Uig, NG398642
Strath and Sleat:
  Broadford, NG642235
  Elgol, NG523143
  Kilmore, NG657069
  Kyleakin, NG751263

43. Presbytery of Uist
Benbecula, NF800519
Berneray and Lochmaddy:
  Berneray, NF920819
  Lochmaddy, NF918684
Carinish, NF811637
Kilmuir and Paible:
  Kilmuir, NF727703
  Sollas, NF802744
Manish-Scarista:
  Manish, NG102892
  Scaristabeg, NG007927
  Leverburgh, NG020868
Tarbert, NG159998

44. Presbytery of Lewis
Barvas, NB360494
Carloway, NB206424
Cross Ness, NB506619
Kinloch:
  Laxay, NB323220
  Lemreway, NB380118
Knock, NB522336
Lochs-Crossbost, NB382255
Lochs-in-Bernera, NB159366
Stornoway: High, NB427330
Stornoway: Martin's Memorial, NB424327
Stornoway: St Columba, NB426330
Uig, NB087347

45. Presbytery of Orkney
Birsay, Harray and Sandwick, HY296206
East Mainland, HY503019
Eday, HY562328
Evie, HY368255
Firth, HY359138
Flotta, ND366931
Hoy and Walls, ND312908
Kirkwall: East, HY451110
Kirkwall: St Magnus Cathedral, HY296206
North Ronaldsay, congregation meets in community
  school, HY758532
Orphir and Stenness:
  Orphir, HY343059
  Stenness, HY311125
Papa Westray, HY496516

Rendall, HY393206
Rousay, HY442278
Sanday, HY659408
Shapinsay, HY497173
South Ronaldsay and Burray:
  St Margaret's Hope, ND449934
  St Peter's Eastside, ND472908
Stromness, HY254090
Stronsay: Moncur Memorial, HY654252
Westray, HY457462

46. Presbytery of Shetland
Burra Isle, HU371330
Delting:
  Brae, HU359673
  Togon, HU404637
  Mossbank, HU451753
  Muckle Roe, HU342647
Dunrossness and St Ninian's:
  Bigton, HU384213
  Boddam, HU391151
  Fair Isle, HZ206706
Fetlar, HU607905
Lerwick and Bressay:
  Lerwick, HU478411
  Gulberwick, HU443389
  Bressay, HU493410
Nesting and Lunnasting:
  Nesting, HU487578
  Lunna, HU486690
Northmavine:
  Hillswick, HU282771
  North Roe, HU365895
  Ollaberry, HU366806
Sandsting and Aithsting, HU345556
Sandwick, Cunningsburgh and Quarff:
  Sandwick, HU432237
  Cunningsburgh, HU430293
  Quarff, HU429358
Tingwall:
  Scalloway, HU401395
  Veensgarth, HU419437
  Weisdale, HU394526
Unst:
  Baltasound, HP614088
  Uyeasound, HP601011
Walls and Sandness:
  Walls, HU240493
  Mid Walls, HU220502
  Sandness, HU195571
  Papa Stour, HU177600
  Foula, HT969378
Whalsay and Skerries:
  Whalsay, HU555654
  Skerries, HU680717
Yell:
  Cullivoe, HP544021
  Hamnavoe, HU494804
  Mid Yell, HU515907

SECTION 9

Discontinued Parish
and Congregational Names

The following list updates and corrects the 'Index of Discontinued Parish and Congregational Names' printed in the previous edition of the *Year Book*. As before, it lists the parishes of the Church of Scotland and the congregations of the United Presbyterian Church (and its constituent denominations), the Free Church (1843–1900) and the United Free Church (1900–29) whose names have completely disappeared, largely as a consequence of union.

It should be noted, as has been stressed in previous years, that this list is *not* intended to be 'a comprehensive guide to readjustment in the Church of Scotland'; that would require a considerably larger number of pages. Despite the annual reiteration of this statement, the Editor's attention continues to be drawn to the omission from the list of this or that now-vanished congregation whose name does not in fact fall within the criteria for inclusion given below.

The specific purpose of this list is to assist those who are trying to identify the present-day successor of some former parish or congregation whose name is now wholly out of use and which can therefore no longer be easily traced. Where the former name has not disappeared completely, and the whereabouts of the former parish or congregation may therefore be easily established by reference to the name of some existing parish, the former name has not been included in this list. Present-day names, in the right-hand column of this list, may be found in the 'Index of Parishes and Places' near the end of this book.

The following examples will illustrate some of the criteria used to determine whether a name should be included or not:

- Where all the former congregations in a town have been united into one, as in the case of Melrose or Selkirk, the names of these former congregations have not been included; but in the case of towns with more than one congregation, such as Galashiels or Hawick, the names of the various constituent congregations are listed.

- The same principle applies in the case of discrete areas of cities. For example, as Dundee: Lochee and Glasgow: Dennistoun New are now the only congregations in Lochee and Dennistoun respectively, there is no need to list Dundee: Lochee St Ninian's, Glasgow: Dennistoun South or any other congregations which had Lochee or Dennistoun in their names.

- Where a prefix such as North, Old, Little, Mid or the like has been lost but the substantive part of the name has been retained, the former name has not been included: it is assumed that someone searching for Little Dalton or Mid Yell will have no difficulty in connecting these with Dalton or Yell.

- Where the present name of a united congregation includes the names of some or all of its constituent parts, these former names do not appear in the list: thus, neither Glasgow: Anderston nor Glasgow: Kelvingrove appears, since both names are easily traceable to Glasgow: Anderston Kelvingrove.

Two other criteria for inclusion or exclusion may also be mentioned:

- Some parishes and congregations have disappeared, and their names have been lost, as a consequence of suppression, dissolution or secession. The names of rural parishes in this category have been included, together with the names of their Presbyteries to assist with identification, but those in towns and cities have not been included, as there will clearly be no difficulty in establishing the general location of the parish or congregation in question.

- Since 1929, a small number of rural parishes have adopted a new name (for example, Whitehills, formerly Boyndie). The former names of these parishes have been included, but it would have been too unwieldy to include either the vast numbers of such changes of name in towns and cities, especially those which occurred at the time of the 1900 and 1929 unions, or the very many older names of pre-Reformation parishes which were abandoned in earlier centuries (however fascinating a list of such long-vanished names as Fothmuref, Kinbathock and Toskertoun might have been).

In this list, the following abbreviations have been used:

C of S	Church of Scotland
FC	Free Church
R	Relief Church
RP	Reformed Presbyterian Church
UF	United Free Church
UP	United Presbyterian Church
US	United Secession Church

Name no longer used	Present name of parish
Abbey St Bathans	Langton and Lammermuir Kirk
Abbotrule	charge suppressed: Presbytery of Jedburgh
Aberargie	charge dissolved: Presbytery of Perth
Aberchirder	Marnoch
Aberdalgie	The Stewartry of Strathearn
Aberdeen: Beechgrove	Aberdeen: Midstocket
Aberdeen: Belmont Street	Aberdeen: St Mark's
Aberdeen: Carden Place	Aberdeen: Queen's Cross
Aberdeen: Causewayend	Aberdeen: St Stephen's
Aberdeen: East	Aberdeen: St Mark's
Aberdeen: Gallowgate	Aberdeen: St Mary's
Aberdeen: Greyfriars	Aberdeen: Queen Street
Aberdeen: Hilton	Aberdeen: Woodside
Aberdeen: Holburn Central	Aberdeen: South Holburn
Aberdeen: John Knox Gerrard Street	Aberdeen: Queen Street
Aberdeen: John Knox's (Mounthooly)	Aberdeen: Queen Street
Aberdeen: King Street	Aberdeen: Queen Street
Aberdeen: Melville	Aberdeen: Queen's Cross
Aberdeen: Nelson Street	Aberdeen: Queen Street
Aberdeen: North	Aberdeen: Queen Street
Aberdeen: North of St Andrew	Aberdeen: Queen Street
Aberdeen: Pittodrie	Aberdeen: St Mary's
Aberdeen: Powis	Aberdeen: St Stephen's
Aberdeen: Ruthrieston (C of S)	Aberdeen: South Holburn
Aberdeen: Ruthrieston (FC)	Aberdeen: Ruthrieston West
Aberdeen: South (C of S)	Aberdeen: South of St Nicholas, Kincorth
Aberdeen: South (FC)	Aberdeen: St Mark's
Aberdeen: St Andrew's	Aberdeen: Queen Street
Aberdeen: St Columba's	Aberdeen: High Hilton
Aberdeen: St Mary's	Aberdeen: St Machar's Cathedral
Aberdeen: St Ninian's	Aberdeen: Midstocket
Aberdeen: Trinity (C of S)	Aberdeen: Kirk of St Nicholas Uniting
Aberdeen: Trinity (FC)	Aberdeen: St Mark's
Aberuthven	The Stewartry of Strathearn
Abington	Upper Clyde
Addiewell	Breich Valley
Afton	New Cumnock
Airdrie: West	Airdrie: New Wellwynd
Airlie	The Isla Parishes
Aldbar	Aberlemno
Aldcambus	Dunglass
Alford	Howe Trinity
Alloa: Chalmers	Alloa: Ludgate
Alloa: Melville	Alloa: Ludgate
Alloa: North	Alloa: Ludgate
Alloa: St Andrew's	Alloa: Ludgate
Alloa: West	Alloa: Ludgate
Altries	charge dissolved: Presbytery of Kincardine and Deeside
Altyre	Rafford
Alvah	Banff
Ancrum	Ale and Teviot United
Annan: Erskine	Annan: St Andrew's
Annan: Greenknowe	Annan: St Andrew's
Anwoth	Gatehouse of Fleet
Arbroath: East	Arbroath: St Andrew's
Arbroath: Erskine	Arbroath: West Kirk
Arbroath: High Street	Arbroath: St Andrew's
Arbroath: Hopemount	Arbroath: St Andrew's

Name no longer used	Present name of parish
Arbroath: Ladyloan	Arbroath: West Kirk
Arbroath: Princes Street	Arbroath: West Kirk
Arbroath: St Columba's	Arbroath: West Kirk
Arbroath: St Margaret's	Arbroath: West Kirk
Arbroath: St Ninian's	Arbroath: St Andrew's
Arbroath: St Paul's	Arbroath: St Andrew's
Ardallie	Deer
Ardclach	charge dissolved: Presbytery of Inverness
Ardwell	Stoneykirk
Arisaig	North West Lochaber
Ascog	The United Church of Bute
Auchindoir	Upper Donside
Auchmithie	Arbroath: St Vigeans
Auldcathie	Dalmeny
Aultbea	Gairloch and Dundonnell
Ayr: Cathcart	Ayr: St Columba
Ayr: Darlington New	Ayr: Auld Kirk of Ayr
Ayr: Darlington Place	Ayr: Auld Kirk of Ayr
Ayr: Lochside	Ayr: St Quivox
Ayr: Martyrs'	Ayr: Auld Kirk of Ayr
Ayr: Sandgate	Ayr: St Columba
Ayr: St John's	Ayr: Auld Kirk of Ayr
Ayr: Trinity	Ayr: St Columba
Ayr: Wallacetown North	Ayr: Newton Wallacetown
Ayr: Wallacetown South	Ayr: Auld Kirk of Ayr
Back	charge dissolved: Presbytery of Lewis
Badcall	Eddrachillis
Balbeggie	Collace
Balfour	charge dissolved: Presbytery of Dundee
Balgedie	Orwell and Portmoak
Baliasta	Unst
Ballachulish	Nether Lochaber
Ballingry	Lochgelly and Benarty: St Serf's
Balmacolm	Howe of Fife
Balmullo	charge dissolved: Presbytery of St Andrews
Balnacross	Tarff and Twynholm
Baltasound	Unst
Banchory-Ternan: North	Banchory-Ternan: West
Banchory-Ternan: South	Banchory-Ternan: West
Bandry	Luss
Bara	Garvald and Morham
Bargrennan	Penninghame
Barnweil	Tarbolton
Barrhead: Arthurlie	Barrhead: St Andrew's
Barrhead: South	Barrhead: St Andrew's
Barrhead: Westbourne	Barrhead: St Andrew's
Barrock	Dunnet
Bearsden: North	Bearsden: Cross
Bearsden: South	Bearsden: Cross
Bedrule	Ruberslaw
Belkirk	Liddesdale
Benholm	Mearns Coastal
Benvie	Fowlis and Liff
Berriedale	The Parish of Latheron
Binny	Linlithgow: St Michael's
Blackburn	Fintray Kinellar Keithhall
Blackhill	Longside

Name no longer used	Present name of parish
Blairlogie	congregation seceded: Presbytery of Stirling
Blanefield	Strathblane
Blantyre: Anderson	Blantyre: St Andrew's
Blantyre: Burleigh Memorial	Blantyre: St Andrew's
Blantyre: Stonefield	Blantyre: St Andrew's
Blyth Bridge	Kirkurd and Newlands
Boddam	Peterhead: Trinity
Bonhill: North	Alexandria
Borthwick	Tyne Valley Parish
Bothwell: Park	Uddingston: Viewpark
Bourtreebush	Newtonhill
Bowmore	Kilarrow
Bow of Fife	Monimail
Boyndie	Whitehills
Brachollie	Petty
Braco	Ardoch
Braehead	Forth
Brechin: East	Brechin: Gardner Memorial
Brechin: Maison Dieu	Brechin: Cathedral
Brechin: St Columba's	Brechin: Gardner Memorial
Brechin: West	Brechin: Gardner Memorial
Breich	Breich Valley
Bridge of Teith	Kilmadock
Brora	Clyne
Bruan	The Parish of Latheron
Buccleuch	Ettrick and Yarrow
Burnhead	Penpont, Keir and Tynron
Cairnryan	charge dissolved: Presbytery of Wigtown and Stranraer
Cambuslang: Old	Cambuslang
Cambuslang: Rosebank	Cambuslang
Cambuslang: St Andrew's	Cambuslang
Cambuslang: St Paul's	Cambuslang
Cambuslang: Trinity	Cambuslang
Cambuslang: West	Cambuslang
Cambusmichael	Scone and St Martins
Campbeltown: Longrow	Campbeltown: Lorne and Lowland
Campsail	Rosneath: St Modan's
Canna	North West Lochaber
Carbuddo	Guthrie and Rescobie
Cardenden	Auchterderran St Fothad's
Carlisle	The Border Kirk
Carmichael	Cairngryffe
Carnoch	Contin
Carnousie	Turriff: St Ninian's and Forglen
Carnoustie: St Stephen's	Carnoustie
Carrbridge	Boat of Garten, Duthil and Kincardine
Carruthers	Hoddom, Kirtle-Eaglesfield and Middlebie
Castle Kennedy	Inch
Castleton	Liddesdale
Caterline	Arbuthnott, Bervie and Kinneff
Chapelknowe	congregation seceded: Presbytery of Annandale and Eskdale
Clatt	Noth
Clayshant	Stoneykirk
Climpy	charge dissolved: Presbytery of Lanark
Clola	Deer
Clousta	Sandsting and Aithsting
Clova	The Glens and Kirriemuir: Old
Clydebank: Bank Street	Clydebank: St Cuthbert's

Name no longer used	Present name of parish
Clydebank: Boquhanran	Clydebank: Kilbowie St Andrew's
Clydebank: Hamilton Memorial	Clydebank: St Cuthbert's
Clydebank: Linnvale	Clydebank: St Cuthbert's
Clydebank: St James'	Clydebank: Abbotsford
Clydebank: Union	Clydebank: Kilbowie St Andrew's
Clydebank: West	Clydebank: Abbotsford
Coatbridge: Clifton	Coatbridge: New St Andrew's
Coatbridge: Cliftonhill	Coatbridge: New St Andrew's
Coatbridge: Coatdyke	Coatbridge: New St Andrew's
Coatbridge: Coats	Coatbridge: New St Andrew's
Coatbridge: Dunbeth	Coatbridge: New St Andrew's
Coatbridge: Gartsherrie	Coatbridge: New St Andrew's
Coatbridge: Garturk	Coatbridge: Calder
Coatbridge: Maxwell	Coatbridge: New St Andrew's
Coatbridge: Trinity	Coatbridge: New St Andrew's
Coatbridge: Whifflet	Coatbridge: Calder
Cobbinshaw	charge dissolved: Presbytery of West Lothian
Cockburnspath	Dunglass
Coigach	charge dissolved: Presbytery of Lochcarron – Skye
Coldstone	Cromar
Collessie	Howe of Fife
Corgarff	Upper Donside
Cortachy	The Glens and Kirriemuir: Old
Coull	Cromar
Covington	Cairngryffe
Cowdenbeath: Cairns	Cowdenbeath: Trinity
Cowdenbeath: Guthrie Memorial	Beath and Cowdenbeath: North
Cowdenbeath: West	Cowdenbeath: Trinity
Craggan	Tomintoul, Glenlivet and Inveraven
Craig	Inchbrayock
Craigdam	Tarves
Craigend	Perth: Craigie and Moncreiffe
Crailing	Ale and Teviot United
Cranshaws	Langton and Lammermuir Kirk
Cranstoun	Tyne Valley Parish
Crawford	Upper Clyde
Crawfordjohn	Upper Clyde
Cray	Kirkmichael, Straloch and Glenshee
Creetown	Kirkmabreck
Crichton	Tyne Valley Parish
Crofthead	Fauldhouse: St Andrew's
Crombie	Culross and Torryburn
Crossgates	Cowdenbeath: Trinity
Cruggleton	Sorbie
Cuikston	Farnell
Culbin	Dyke
Cullicudden	Resolis and Urquhart
Culter	charge dissolved: Presbytery of Lanark
Cults	Howe of Fife
Cumbernauld: Baird	Cumbernauld: Old
Cumbernauld: Bridgend	Cumbernauld: Old
Cumbernauld: St Andrew's	Cumbernauld: Old
Dalgarno	Closeburn
Dalguise	Dunkeld
Daliburgh	South Uist
Dalkeith: Buccleuch Street	Dalkeith: St Nicholas Buccleuch
Dalkeith: West (C of S)	Dalkeith: St Nicholas Buccleuch
Dalkeith: West (UP)	Dalkeith: St John's and King's Park

Name no longer used	Present name of parish
Dalmeath	Huntly Cairnie Glass
Dalreoch	charge dissolved: Presbytery of Perth
Dalry: Courthill	Dalry: Trinity
Dalry: St Andrew's	Dalry: Trinity
Dalry: West	Dalry: Trinity
Deerness	East Mainland
Denholm	Ruberslaw
Denny: Broompark	Denny: Westpark
Denny: West	Denny: Westpark
Dennyloanhead	charge dissolved: Presbytery of Falkirk
Dolphinton	Black Mount
Douglas	The Douglas Valley Church
Douglas Water	The Douglas Valley Church
Dowally	Dunkeld
Drainie	Lossiemouth: St Gerardine's High
Drumdelgie	Huntly Cairnie Glass
Dumbarrow	charge dissolved: Presbytery of Angus
Dumbarton: Bridgend	Dumbarton: West
Dumbarton: Dalreoch	Dumbarton: West
Dumbarton: High	Dumbarton: Riverside
Dumbarton: Knoxland	Dumbarton: Riverside
Dumbarton: North	Dumbarton: Riverside
Dumbarton: Old	Dumbarton: Riverside
Dumfries: Lincluden	Dumfries: Northwest
Dumfries: Lochside	Dumfries: Northwest
Dumfries: Maxwelltown Laurieknowe	Dumfries: Troqueer
Dumfries: Townhead	Dumfries: St Michael's and South
Dunbeath	The Parish of Latheron
Dunblane: East	Dunblane: St Blane's
Dunblane: Leighton	Dunblane: St Blane's
Dundee: Albert Square	Dundee: Meadowside St Paul's
Dundee: Baxter Park	Dundee: Trinity
Dundee: Broughty Ferry East	Dundee: Broughty Ferry New Kirk
Dundee: Broughty Ferry St Aidan's	Dundee: Broughty Ferry New Kirk
Dundee: Broughty Ferry Union	Dundee: Broughty Ferry St Stephen's and West
Dundee: Chapelshade (FC)	Dundee: Meadowside St Paul's
Dundee: Clepington	Dundee: Coldside
Dundee: Douglas and Angus	Dundee: Douglas and Mid Craigie
Dundee: Downfield North	Dundee: Strathmartine
Dundee: Downfield South	Dundee: Downfield Mains
Dundee: Fairmuir	Dundee: Coldside
Dundee: Hawkhill	Dundee: Meadowside St Paul's
Dundee: Martyrs'	Dundee: Balgay
Dundee: Maryfield	Dundee: Stobswell
Dundee: McCheyne Memorial	Dundee: West
Dundee: Ogilvie	Dundee: Stobswell
Dundee: Park	Dundee: Stobswell
Dundee: Roseangle	Dundee: West
Dundee: Ryehill	Dundee: West
Dundee: St Andrew's (FC)	Dundee: Meadowside St Paul's
Dundee: St Clement's Steeple	Dundee: Steeple
Dundee: St David's (C of S)	Dundee: Steeple
Dundee: St Enoch's	Dundee: Steeple
Dundee: St George's	Dundee: Meadowside St Paul's
Dundee: St John's	Dundee: West
Dundee: St Mark's	Dundee: West
Dundee: St Matthew's	Dundee: Trinity
Dundee: St Paul's	Dundee: Steeple
Dundee: St Peter's	Dundee: West

Name no longer used	Present name of parish
Dundee: Tay Square	Dundee: Meadowside St Paul's
Dundee: Victoria Street	Dundee: Stobswell
Dundee: Wallacetown	Dundee: Trinity
Dundee: Wishart Memorial	Dundee: Steeple
Dundurcas	charge suppressed: Presbytery of Moray
Duneaton	Upper Clyde
Dunfermline: Chalmers Street	Dunfermline: St Andrew's Erskine
Dunfermline: Maygate	Dunfermline: Gillespie Memorial
Dunfermline: Queen Anne Street	Dunfermline: St Andrew's Erskine
Dungree	Kirkpatrick Juxta
Duninald	Inchbrayock
Dunlappie	Brechin: Cathedral
Dunning	The Stewartry of Strathearn
Dunoon: Gaelic	Dunoon: St John's
Dunoon: Old	Dunoon: The High Kirk
Dunoon: St Cuthbert's	Dunoon: The High Kirk
Dunrod	Kirkcudbright
Dunsyre	Black Mount
Dupplin	The Stewartry of Strathearn
Ecclefechan	Hoddom, Kirtle-Eaglesfield and Middlebie
Ecclesjohn	Dun and Hillside
Ecclesmachan	Strathbrock
Ecclesmoghriodan	Abernethy and Dron and Arngask
Eckford	Ale and Teviot United
Edgerston	Jedburgh: Old and Trinity
Edinburgh: Abbey	Edinburgh: Greenside
Edinburgh: Abbeyhill	Edinburgh: Holyrood Abbey
Edinburgh: Arthur Street	Edinburgh: Kirk o' Field
Edinburgh: Barony	Edinburgh: Greenside
Edinburgh: Belford	Edinburgh: Palmerston Place
Edinburgh: Braid	Edinburgh: Morningside
Edinburgh: Bruntsfield	Edinburgh: Barclay Viewforth
Edinburgh: Buccleuch	Edinburgh: Kirk o' Field
Edinburgh: Cairns Memorial	Edinburgh: Gorgie Dalry
Edinburgh: Candlish	Edinburgh: Polwarth
Edinburgh: Canongate (FC, UP)	Edinburgh: Holy Trinity
Edinburgh: Chalmers	Edinburgh: Barclay Viewforth
Edinburgh: Charteris Memorial	Edinburgh: Kirk o' Field
Edinburgh: Cluny	Edinburgh: Morningside
Edinburgh: College	Edinburgh: Muirhouse St Andrew's
Edinburgh: College Street	Edinburgh: Muirhouse St Andrew's
Edinburgh: Cowgate (FC)	Edinburgh: Muirhouse St Andrew's
Edinburgh: Cowgate (R)	Edinburgh: Barclay Viewforth
Edinburgh: Cowgate (US)	Edinburgh: Mayfield Salisbury
Edinburgh: Davidson	Edinburgh: Stockbridge
Edinburgh: Dean (FC)	Edinburgh: Palmerston Place
Edinburgh: Dean Street	Edinburgh: Stockbridge
Edinburgh: Fountainhall Road	Edinburgh: Mayfield Salisbury
Edinburgh: Grange (C of S)	Edinburgh: Marchmont St Giles'
Edinburgh: Grange (FC)	Edinburgh: St Catherine's Argyle
Edinburgh: Guthrie Memorial	Edinburgh: Greenside
Edinburgh: Haymarket	Edinburgh: Gorgie Dalry
Edinburgh: Henderson (C of S)	Edinburgh: Craigmillar Park
Edinburgh: Henderson (UP)	Edinburgh: Richmond Craigmillar
Edinburgh: Hillside	Edinburgh: Greenside
Edinburgh: Holyrood	Edinburgh: Holyrood Abbey
Edinburgh: Hope Park	Edinburgh: Mayfield Salisbury
Edinburgh: Hopetoun	Edinburgh: Greenside

Name no longer used	Present name of parish
Edinburgh: John Ker Memorial	Edinburgh: Polwarth
Edinburgh: Knox's	Edinburgh: Holy Trinity
Edinburgh: Lady Glenorchy's North	Edinburgh: Greenside
Edinburgh: Lady Glenorchy's South	Edinburgh: Holy Trinity
Edinburgh: Lady Yester's	Edinburgh: Greyfriars Tolbooth and Highland
Edinburgh: Lauriston	Edinburgh: Barclay Viewforth
Edinburgh: Lochend	Edinburgh: St Margaret's
Edinburgh: Lothian Road	Edinburgh: Palmerston Place
Edinburgh: Mayfield North	Edinburgh: Mayfield Salisbury
Edinburgh: Mayfield South	Edinburgh: Craigmillar Park
Edinburgh: McCrie	Edinburgh: Kirk o' Field
Edinburgh: McDonald Road	Edinburgh: Broughton St Mary's
Edinburgh: Moray	Edinburgh: Holy Trinity
Edinburgh: Morningside High	Edinburgh: Morningside
Edinburgh: New North (C of S)	Edinburgh: Marchmont St Giles'
Edinburgh: New North (FC)	Edinburgh: Greyfriars Tolbooth and Highland
Edinburgh: Newington East	Edinburgh: Kirk o' Field
Edinburgh: Newington South	Edinburgh: Mayfield Salisbury
Edinburgh: Nicolson Street	Edinburgh: Kirk o' Field
Edinburgh: North Morningside	Edinburgh: Morningside United
Edinburgh: North Richmond Street	Edinburgh: Richmond Craigmillar
Edinburgh: Pleasance (FC)	Edinburgh: Muirhouse St Andrew's
Edinburgh: Pleasance (UF)	Edinburgh: Kirk o' Field
Edinburgh: Prestonfield	Edinburgh: Priestfield
Edinburgh: Queen Street (FC)	Edinburgh: St Andrew's and St George's West
Edinburgh: Queen Street (UP)	Edinburgh: Stockbridge
Edinburgh: Restalrig (C of S)	Edinburgh: St Margaret's
Edinburgh: Restalrig (FC)	Edinburgh: New Restalrig
Edinburgh: Rosehall	Edinburgh: Priestfield
Edinburgh: Roxburgh	Edinburgh: Kirk o' Field
Edinburgh: Roxburgh Terrace	Edinburgh: Kirk o' Field
Edinburgh: South Morningside	Edinburgh: Morningside
Edinburgh: St Bernard's	Edinburgh: Stockbridge
Edinburgh: St Bride's	Edinburgh: Gorgie Dalry
Edinburgh: St Colm's	Edinburgh: Gorgie Dalry
Edinburgh: St Columba's	Edinburgh: Greyfriars Tolbooth and Highland
Edinburgh: St David's (C of S)	Edinburgh: Barclay Viewforth
Edinburgh: St David's (FC)	Edinburgh: St David's Broomhouse
Edinburgh: St James' (C of S)	Edinburgh: Greenside
Edinburgh: St James' (FC)	Edinburgh: Inverleith St Serf's
Edinburgh: St James' Place	Edinburgh: Greenside
Edinburgh: St John's	Edinburgh: Greyfriars Tolbooth and Highland
Edinburgh: St Luke's	Edinburgh: St Andrew's and St George's West
Edinburgh: St Matthew's	Edinburgh: Morningside
Edinburgh: St Oran's	Edinburgh: Greyfriars Tolbooth and Highland
Edinburgh: St Oswald's	Edinburgh: Barclay Viewforth
Edinburgh: St Paul's	Edinburgh: Kirk o' Field
Edinburgh: St Stephen's (C of S)	Edinburgh: Stockbridge
Edinburgh: St Stephen's (FC)	Edinburgh: St Stephen's Comely Bank
Edinburgh: Tolbooth (C of S)	Edinburgh: Greyfriars Tolbooth and Highland
Edinburgh: Tolbooth (FC)	Edinburgh: St Andrew's and St George's West
Edinburgh: Trinity College	Edinburgh: Holy Trinity
Edinburgh: Tynecastle	Edinburgh: Gorgie Dalry
Edinburgh: Warrender	Edinburgh: Marchmont St Giles'
Edinburgh: West St Giles	Edinburgh: Marchmont St Giles'
Eigg	North West Lochaber
Eilean Finain	Ardnamurchan
Elgin: Moss Street	Elgin: St Giles' and St Columba's South

Name no longer used	Present name of parish
Elgin: South Street	Elgin: St Giles' and St Columba's South
Ellem	Langton and Lammermuir Kirk
Elsrickle	Black Mount
Eshaness	Northmavine
Essie	Noth
Essil	Speymouth
Ethie	Inverkeilor and Lunan
Ettiltoun	Liddesdale
Ewes Durris	Langholm Eskdalemuir Ewes and Westerkirk
Fala	Tyne Valley Parish
Falkirk: Graham's Road	Falkirk: Grahamston United
Farnua	Kirkhill
Fergushill	Kilwinning: Mansefield Trinity
Ferryden	Inchbrayock
Fetterangus	Deer
Fettercairn	West Mearns
Fetternear	Blairdaff and Chapel of Garioch
Finzean	Birse and Feughside
Fochabers	Bellie
Forbes	Howe Trinity
Ford	Tyne Valley Parish
Fordoun	West Mearns
Forfar: South	Forfar: St Margaret's
Forfar: St James'	Forfar: St Margaret's
Forfar: West	Forfar: St Margaret's
Forgan	Newport-on-Tay
Forgue	Auchaber United
Forres: Castlehill	Forres: St Leonard's
Forres: High	Forres: St Leonard's
Forteviot	The Stewartry of Strathearn
Forvie	Ellon
Foula	Walls and Sandness
Galashiels: East	Galashiels: Trinity
Galashiels: Ladhope	Galashiels: Trinity
Galashiels: South	Galashiels: Trinity
Galashiels: St Aidan's	Galashiels: Trinity
Galashiels: St Andrew's	Galashiels: Trinity
Galashiels: St Columba's	Galashiels: Trinity
Galashiels: St Cuthbert's	Galashiels: Trinity
Galashiels: St Mark's	Galashiels: Trinity
Galashiels: St Ninian's	Galashiels: Trinity
Galtway	Kirkcudbright
Gamrie	charge dissolved: Presbytery of Buchan
Garmouth	Speymouth
Gartly	Noth
Garvell	Kirkmichael, Tinwald and Torthorwald
Garvock	Mearns Coastal
Gauldry	Balmerino
Gelston	Buittle and Kelton
Giffnock: Orchard Park	Giffnock: The Park
Girthon	Gatehouse of Fleet
Girvan: Chalmers	Girvan: North (Old and St Andrew's)
Girvan: Trinity	Girvan: North (Old and St Andrew's)
Glasgow: Abbotsford	Glasgow: Gorbals
Glasgow: Albert Drive	Glasgow: Pollokshields
Glasgow: Auldfield	Glasgow: Pollokshaws
Glasgow: Baillieston Old	Glasgow: Baillieston St Andrew's
Glasgow: Baillieston Rhinsdale	Glasgow: Baillieston St Andrew's

Name no longer used	Present name of parish
Glasgow: Balornock North	Glasgow: Wallacewell
Glasgow: Barmulloch	Glasgow: Wallacewell
Glasgow: Barrowfield (C of S)	Glasgow: Bridgeton St Francis in the East
Glasgow: Barrowfield (RP)	Glasgow: Gallowgate
Glasgow: Bath Street	Glasgow: Renfield St Stephen's
Glasgow: Battlefield East	Glasgow: Clincarthill
Glasgow: Battlefield West	Glasgow: Langside
Glasgow: Bellahouston	Glasgow: Ibrox
Glasgow: Bellgrove	Glasgow: Dennistoun New
Glasgow: Belmont	Glasgow: Kelvinside Hillhead
Glasgow: Berkeley Street	Glasgow: Renfield St Stephen's
Glasgow: Blackfriars	Glasgow: Dennistoun New
Glasgow: Bluevale	Glasgow: Dennistoun New
Glasgow: Blythswood	Glasgow: Renfield St Stephen's
Glasgow: Bridgeton East	Glasgow: Bridgeton St Francis in the East
Glasgow: Bridgeton West	Glasgow: Gallowgate
Glasgow: Buccleuch	Glasgow: Renfield St Stephen's
Glasgow: Burnbank	Glasgow: Lansdowne
Glasgow: Calton New	Glasgow: Gallowgate
Glasgow: Calton Old	Glasgow: Calton Parkhead
Glasgow: Calton Relief	Glasgow: Gallowgate
Glasgow: Cambridge Street	Bishopbriggs: Springfield Cambridge
Glasgow: Candlish Memorial	Glasgow: Govanhill Trinity
Glasgow: Carntyne Old	Glasgow: Shettleston New
Glasgow: Cathcart South	Glasgow: Cathcart Trinity
Glasgow: Central	Glasgow: Gallowgate
Glasgow: Cessnock	Glasgow: Kinning Park
Glasgow: Chalmers (C of S)	Glasgow: Gallowgate
Glasgow: Chalmers (FC)	Glasgow: Gorbals
Glasgow: Claremont	Glasgow: Anderston Kelvingrove
Glasgow: College	Glasgow: Anderston Kelvingrove
Glasgow: Copland Road	Glasgow: Govan and Linthouse
Glasgow: Cowcaddens	Glasgow: Renfield St Stephen's
Glasgow: Cowlairs	Glasgow: Springburn
Glasgow: Crosshill	Glasgow: Queen's Park
Glasgow: Dalmarnock (C of S)	Glasgow: Calton Parkhead
Glasgow: Dalmarnock (UF)	Rutherglen: Old
Glasgow: Dean Park	Glasgow: Govan and Linthouse
Glasgow: Dowanhill	Glasgow: Partick Trinity
Glasgow: Dowanvale	Glasgow: Partick South
Glasgow: Drumchapel Old	Glasgow: Drumchapel St Andrew's
Glasgow: East Campbell Street	Glasgow: Dennistoun New
Glasgow: East Park	Glasgow: Kelvin Stevenson Memorial
Glasgow: Eastbank	Glasgow: Shettleston New
Glasgow: Edgar Memorial	Glasgow: Gallowgate
Glasgow: Eglinton Street	Glasgow: Govanhill Trinity
Glasgow: Elder Park	Glasgow: Govan and Linthouse
Glasgow: Elgin Street	Glasgow: Govanhill Trinity
Glasgow: Erskine	Glasgow: Langside
Glasgow: Fairbairn	Rutherglen: Old
Glasgow: Fairfield	Glasgow: Govan and Linthouse
Glasgow: Finnieston	Glasgow: Anderston Kelvingrove
Glasgow: Garnethill	Glasgow: Renfield St Stephen's
Glasgow: Garscube Netherton	Glasgow: Knightswood St Margaret's
Glasgow: Gillespie	Glasgow: Gallowgate
Glasgow: Gordon Park	Glasgow: Whiteinch
Glasgow: Grant Street	Glasgow: Renfield St Stephen's
Glasgow: Greenhead	Glasgow: Gallowgate

Name no longer used	Present name of parish
Glasgow: Hall Memorial	Rutherglen: Old
Glasgow: Hamilton Crescent	Glasgow: Partick South
Glasgow: Highlanders' Memorial	Glasgow: Knightswood St Margaret's
Glasgow: Househillwood St Christopher's	Glasgow: St Christopher's Priesthill and Nitshill
Glasgow: Hyndland (UF)	Glasgow: St John's Renfield
Glasgow: John Knox's	Glasgow: Gorbals
Glasgow: Johnston	Glasgow: Springburn
Glasgow: Jordanvale	Glasgow: Whiteinch
Glasgow: Kelvinhaugh	Glasgow: Anderston Kelvingrove
Glasgow: Kelvinside Botanic Gardens	Glasgow: Kelvinside Hillhead
Glasgow: Kelvinside Old	Glasgow: Kelvin Stevenson Memorial
Glasgow: Kingston	Glasgow: Carnwadric
Glasgow: Lancefield	Glasgow: Anderston Kelvingrove
Glasgow: Langside Avenue	Glasgow: Shawlands
Glasgow: Langside Hill	Glasgow: Clincarthill
Glasgow: Langside Old	Glasgow: Langside
Glasgow: Laurieston (C of S)	Glasgow: Gorbals
Glasgow: Laurieston (FC)	Glasgow: Carnwadric
Glasgow: London Road	Glasgow: Bridgeton St Francis in the East
Glasgow: Lyon Street	Glasgow: Renfield St Stephen's
Glasgow: Macgregor Memorial	Glasgow: Govan and Linthouse
Glasgow: Macmillan	Glasgow: Gallowgate
Glasgow: Martyrs' East	Glasgow: Cathedral
Glasgow: Martyrs' West	Glasgow: Cathedral
Glasgow: Milton	Glasgow: Renfield St Stephen's
Glasgow: Mount Florida	Glasgow: Clincarthill
Glasgow: Netherton St Matthew's	Glasgow: Knightswood St Margaret's
Glasgow: New Cathcart	Glasgow: Cathcart Trinity
Glasgow: Newhall	Glasgow: Bridgeton St Francis in the East
Glasgow: Newton Place	Glasgow: Partick South
Glasgow: Nithsdale	Glasgow: Queen's Park
Glasgow: North Kelvinside	Glasgow: Ruchill Kelvinside
Glasgow: Old Partick	Glasgow: Partick Trinity
Glasgow: Paisley Road	Glasgow: Kinning Park
Glasgow: Partick Anderson	Glasgow: Partick South
Glasgow: Partick East	Glasgow: Partick Trinity
Glasgow: Partick High	Glasgow: Partick South
Glasgow: Phoenix Park	Glasgow: Springburn
Glasgow: Plantation	Glasgow: Kinning Park
Glasgow: Pollok St Aidan's	Glasgow: St James' Pollok
Glasgow: Pollok Street	Glasgow: Kinning Park
Glasgow: Polmadie	Glasgow: Govanhill Trinity
Glasgow: Queen's Cross	Glasgow: Ruchill Kelvinside
Glasgow: Renfield (C of S)	Glasgow: Renfield St Stephen's
Glasgow: Renfield (FC)	Glasgow: St John's Renfield
Glasgow: Renfield Street	Glasgow: Renfield St Stephen's
Glasgow: Renwick	Glasgow: Gorbals
Glasgow: Robertson Memorial	Glasgow: Cathedral
Glasgow: Rockcliffe	Rutherglen: Old
Glasgow: Rockvilla	Glasgow: Possilpark
Glasgow: Rose Street	Glasgow: Langside
Glasgow: Rutherford	Glasgow: Dennistoun New
Glasgow: Shamrock Street	Glasgow: Renfield St Stephen's
Glasgow: Shawholm	Glasgow: Pollokshaws
Glasgow: Shawlands Cross	Glasgow: Shawlands
Glasgow: Shawlands Old	Glasgow: Shawlands
Glasgow: Sighthill	Glasgow: Springburn
Glasgow: Somerville	Glasgow: Springburn

Name no longer used	Present name of parish
Glasgow: Springbank	Glasgow: Lansdowne
Glasgow: St Andrew's (C of S)	Glasgow: Gallowgate
Glasgow: St Andrew's (FC)	Glasgow: St Andrew's East
Glasgow: St Clement's	Glasgow: Bridgeton St Francis in the East
Glasgow: St Columba Gaelic	Glasgow: Govan and Linthouse
Glasgow: St Cuthbert's	Glasgow: Ruchill Kelvinside
Glasgow: St Enoch's (C of S)	Glasgow: St Enoch's Hogganfield
Glasgow: St Enoch's (FC)	Glasgow: Anderston Kelvingrove
Glasgow: St George's (C of S)	Glasgow: St George's Tron
Glasgow: St George's (FC)	Glasgow: Anderston Kelvingrove
Glasgow: St George's Road	Glasgow: Renfield St Stephen's
Glasgow: St James' (C of S)	Glasgow: St James' Pollok
Glasgow: St James' (FC)	Glasgow: Gallowgate
Glasgow: St John's (C of S)	Glasgow: Gallowgate
Glasgow: St John's (FC)	Glasgow: St John's Renfield
Glasgow: St Kenneth's	Glasgow: Govan and Linthouse
Glasgow: St Kiaran's	Glasgow: Govan and Linthouse
Glasgow: St Luke's	Glasgow: Gallowgate
Glasgow: St Mark's	Glasgow: Anderston Kelvingrove
Glasgow: St Mary's Partick	Glasgow: Partick South
Glasgow: St Matthew's (C of S)	Glasgow: Renfield St Stephen's
Glasgow: St Matthew's (FC)	Glasgow: Knightswood St Margaret's
Glasgow: St Ninian's	Glasgow: Gorbals
Glasgow: St Peter's	Glasgow: Anderston Kelvingrove
Glasgow: St Thomas'	Glasgow: Gallowgate
Glasgow: Steven Memorial	Glasgow: Ibrox
Glasgow: Strathbungo	Glasgow: Queen's Park
Glasgow: Summerfield	Rutherglen: Old
Glasgow: Summertown	Glasgow: Govan and Linthouse
Glasgow: Sydney Place	Glasgow: Dennistoun New
Glasgow: The Martyrs'	Glasgow: Cathedral
Glasgow: The Park	Giffnock: The Park
Glasgow: Titwood	Glasgow: Pollokshields
Glasgow: Tradeston	Glasgow: Gorbals
Glasgow: Trinity	Glasgow: Gallowgate
Glasgow: Trinity Duke Street	Glasgow: Dennistoun New
Glasgow: Tron St Anne's	Glasgow: St George's Tron
Glasgow: Union	Glasgow: Carnwadric
Glasgow: Victoria	Glasgow: Queen's Park
Glasgow: Wellfield	Glasgow: Springburn
Glasgow: Wellpark	Glasgow: Dennistoun New
Glasgow: West Scotland Street	Glasgow: Kinning Park
Glasgow: White Memorial	Glasgow: Kinning Park
Glasgow: Whitehill	Glasgow: Dennistoun New
Glasgow: Whitevale (FC)	Glasgow: Gallowgate
Glasgow: Whitevale (UP)	Glasgow: Dennistoun New
Glasgow: Wilton	Glasgow: Kelvin Stevenson Memorial
Glasgow: Woodlands	Glasgow: Wellington
Glasgow: Woodside	Glasgow: Lansdowne
Glasgow: Wynd (C of S)	Glasgow: Gallowgate
Glasgow: Wynd (FC)	Glasgow: Gorbals
Glasgow: Young Street	Glasgow: Dennistoun New
Glenapp	Ballantrae
Glenbervie	West Mearns
Glenbuchat	Upper Donside
Glenbuck	Muirkirk
Glencaple (Dumfries and Kirkcudbright)	Caerlaverock
Glencaple (Lanark)	Upper Clyde

Name no longer used	Present name of parish
Glen Convinth	Kiltarlity
Glendoick	St Madoes and Kinfauns
Glenfarg	Abernethy and Dron and Arngask
Glengairn	Glenmuick (Ballater)
Glengarnock	Kilbirnie: Auld Kirk
Glenisla	The Isla Parishes
Glenluce	Old Luce
Glenmoriston (FC)	Fort Augustus
Glenprosen	The Glens and Kirriemuir: Old
Glenrinnes	Mortlach and Cabrach
Glenshiel	Glenelg and Kintail
Glentanar	Aboyne and Dinnet
Glen Ussie	Fodderty and Strathpeffer
Gogar	Edinburgh: Corstorphine Old
Gordon	Monquhitter and New Byth
Graemsay	Stromness
Grangemouth: Dundas	Grangemouth: Abbotsgrange
Grangemouth: Grange	Grangemouth: Zetland
Grangemouth: Kerse	Grangemouth: Abbotsgrange
Grangemouth: Old	Grangemouth: Zetland
Greenloaning	Ardoch
Greenock: Ardgowan	Greenock: Lyle Kirk
Greenock: Augustine	Greenock: East End
Greenock: Cartsburn	Greenock: East End
Greenock: Cartsdyke	Greenock: East End
Greenock: Crawfordsburn	Greenock: East End
Greenock: Finnart	Greenock: Lyle Kirk
Greenock: Gaelic	Greenock: Westburn
Greenock: Greenbank	Greenock: Westburn
Greenock: Martyrs'	Greenock: Westburn
Greenock: Middle	Greenock: Westburn
Greenock: Mount Park	Greenock: Mount Kirk
Greenock: Mount Pleasant	Greenock: Mount Kirk
Greenock: North (C of S)	Greenock: Lyle Kirk
Greenock: North (FC)	Greenock: Westburn
Greenock: Old West	Greenock: Lyle Kirk
Greenock: Sir Michael Street	Greenock: Lyle Kirk
Greenock: South	Greenock: Mount Kirk
Greenock: South Park	Greenock: Mount Kirk
Greenock: St Andrew's	Greenock: Lyle Kirk
Greenock: St Columba's Gaelic	Greenock: Lyle Kirk
Greenock: St George's	Greenock: Westburn
Greenock: St Luke's	Greenock: Westburn
Greenock: St Mark's	Greenock: Westburn
Greenock: St Paul's	Greenock: Lyle Kirk
Greenock: St Thomas'	Greenock: Westburn
Greenock: The Old Kirk	Greenock: Westburn
Greenock: The Union Church	Greenock: Lyle Kirk
Greenock: Trinity	Greenock: Lyle Kirk
Greenock: Union Street	Greenock: Lyle Kirk
Greenock: West	Greenock: Westburn
Gress	Stornoway: St Columba
Guardbridge	Leuchars: St Athernase
Haddington: St John's	Haddington: West
Hamilton: Auchingramont North	Hamilton: Old
Hamilton: Avon Street	Hamilton: St Andrew's
Hamilton: Brandon	Hamilton: St Andrew's
Hamilton: Burnbank	Hamilton: Gilmour and Whitehill

Name no longer used	Present name of parish
Hamilton: North	Hamilton: Old
Hamilton: Saffronhall Assoc. Anti-Burgher	Hamilton: Old
Hardgate	Urr
Hassendean	Ruberslaw
Hawick: East Bank	Hawick: Trinity
Hawick: Orrock	Hawick: St Mary's and Old
Hawick: St Andrew's	Hawick: Trinity
Hawick: St George's	Hawick: Teviot
Hawick: St George's West	Hawick: Teviot
Hawick: St John's	Hawick: Trinity
Hawick: St Margaret's	Hawick: Teviot
Hawick: West Port	Hawick: Teviot
Hawick: Wilton South	Hawick: Teviot
Haywood	Forth
Helensburgh: Old	Helensburgh: St Andrew's Kirk
Helensburgh: St Bride's	Helensburgh: St Andrew's Kirk
Helensburgh: St Columba	Helensburgh: St Andrew's Kirk
Helensburgh: The West Kirk	Helensburgh: St Andrew's Kirk
Heylipol	Tiree
Hillside	Unst
Hillswick	Northmavine
Hilton	Ladykirk and Whitsome
Holm	East Mainland
Holywell	The Border Kirk
Holywood	Dumfries: Northwest
Hope Kailzie	charge suppressed: Presbytery of Melrose and Peebles
Horndean	Ladykirk and Whitsome
Howford	charge dissolved: Presbytery of Inverness
Howmore	South Uist
Hume	Kelso Country Churches
Huntly: Princes Street	Strathbogie Drumblade
Inchkenneth	Kilfinichen and Kilvickeon and the Ross of Mull
Inchmartin	Errol
Innerleven: East	Methil: Wellesley
Innerwick	Dunglass
Inverallan	Grantown-on-Spey
Inverchaolain	Toward
Inverkeithny	Auchaber United
Inverness: Merkinch St Mark's	Inverness: Trinity
Inverness: Queen Street	Inverness: Trinity
Inverness: St Mary's	Inverness: Dalneigh and Bona
Inverness: West	Inverness: Inshes
Irving	Gretna, Half Morton and Kirkpatrick Fleming
Johnshaven	Mearns Coastal
Johnstone: East	Johnstone: St Paul's
Johnstone: West	Johnstone: St Paul's
Kames	Kyles
Kearn	Upper Donside
Keig	Howe Trinity
Keith Marischal	Humbie
Keith: South	Keith: North, Newmill, Boharm and Rothiemay
Kelso: East	Kelso: North and Ednam
Kelso: Edenside	Kelso: North and Ednam
Kelso: St John's	Kelso: North and Ednam
Kelso: Trinity	Kelso: North and Ednam
Kennethmont	Noth
Kettle	Howe of Fife
Kilbirnie: Barony	Kilbirnie: Auld Kirk

Name no longer used	Present name of parish
Kilbirnie: East	Kilbirnie: St Columba's
Kilbirnie: West	Kilbirnie: St Columba's
Kilblaan	Southend
Kilblane	Kirkmahoe
Kilbride (Cowal)	Kyles
Kilbride (Dumfries and Kirkcudbright)	Sanquhar
Kilbride (Lorn)	Kilmore and Oban
Kilbride (Stirling)	Dunblane: Cathedral
Kilchattan Bay	The United Church of Bute
Kilchousland	Campbeltown: Highland
Kilcolmkill (Kintyre)	Southend
Kilcolmkill (Lochaber)	Morvern
Kildrummy	Upper Donside
Kilkerran	Campbeltown: Highland
Kilkivan	Campbeltown: Highland
Killintag	Morvern
Kilmacolm: St James'	Kilmacolm: St Columba
Kilmahew	Cardross
Kilmahog	Callander
Kilmarnock: Grange	Kilmarnock: New Laigh Kirk
Kilmarnock: Henderson	Kilmarnock: Kay Park
Kilmarnock: High (C of S)	Kilmarnock: Kay Park
Kilmarnock: High (FC)	Kilmarnock: New Laigh Kirk
Kilmarnock: Howard	Kilmarnock: St Andrew's and St Marnock's
Kilmarnock: King Street	Kilmarnock: St Andrew's and St Marnock's
Kilmarnock: Old High	Kilmarnock: Kay Park
Kilmarnock: Portland Road	Kilmarnock: St Andrew's and St Marnock's
Kilmarnock: St Ninian's Bellfield	Kilmarnock: South
Kilmarnock: Shortlees	Kilmarnock: South
Kilmarrow	Killean and Kilchenzie
Kilmichael (Inverness)	Urquhart and Glenmoriston
Kilmichael (Kintyre)	Campbeltown: Highland
Kilmoir	Brechin: Cathedral
Kilmore	Urquhart and Glenmoriston
Kilmoveonaig	Blair Atholl and Struan
Kilmun: St Andrew's	Strone and Ardentinny
Kilpheder	South Uist
Kilry	The Isla Parishes
Kilwinning: Abbey	Kilwinning: Old
Kilwinning: Erskine	Kilwinning: Old
Kinairney	Midmar
Kincardine O'Neil	Mid Deeside
Kincraig	Alvie and Insh
Kinedar	Lossiemouth: St Gerardine's High
Kingarth	The United Church of Bute
Kingoldrum	The Isla Parishes
Kininmonth	charge dissolved: Presbytery of Buchan
Kinkell	Fintray Kinellar Keithhall
Kinloch	Caputh and Clunie
Kinlochewe	Applecross, Lochcarron and Torridon
Kinlochluichart	Contin
Kinlochrannoch	Foss and Rannoch
Kinneil	Bo'ness: Old
Kinnettas	Fodderty and Strathpeffer
Kinnoir	Huntly Cairnie Glass
Kinrossie	Collace
Kirkandrews	Borgue
Kirkapol	Tiree

Name no longer used	Present name of parish
Kirkcaldy: Abbotsrood	Kirkcaldy: Bennochy
Kirkcaldy: Bethelfield	Kirkcaldy: Linktown
Kirkcaldy: Dunnikier	Kirkcaldy: Bennochy
Kirkcaldy: Gallatown	Dysart: St Clair
Kirkcaldy: Invertiel	Kirkcaldy: Linktown
Kirkcaldy: Old	Kirkcaldy: St Bryce Kirk
Kirkcaldy: Raith	Kirkcaldy: Abbotshall
Kirkcaldy: Sinclairtown	Dysart: St Clair
Kirkcaldy: St Andrew's	Kirkcaldy: Bennochy
Kirkcaldy: St Brycedale	Kirkcaldy: St Bryce Kirk
Kirkcaldy: St John's	Kirkcaldy: Bennochy
Kirkcaldy: Victoria Road	Kirkcaldy: Bennochy
Kirkcaldy: Viewforth	Dysart: St Clair
Kirkchrist	Tarff and Twynholm
Kirkconnel	Gretna, Half Morton and Kirkpatrick Fleming
Kirkcormick	Buittle and Kelton
Kirkdale	Kirkmabreck
Kirkforthar	Markinch
Kirkhope	Ettrick and Yarrow
Kirkintilloch: St Andrew's	Kirkintilloch: St Columba's
Kirkintilloch: St David's	Kirkintilloch: St Columba's
Kirkmadrine (Machars)	Sorbie
Kirkmadrine (Rhinns)	Stoneykirk
Kirkmaiden	Glasserton and Isle of Whithorn
Kirkmichael	Tomintoul, Glenlivet and Inveraven
Kirkpottie	Abernethy and Dron and Arngask
Kirkwall: King Street	Kirkwall: East
Kirkwall: Paterson	Kirkwall: East
Kirriemuir: Bank Street	The Glens and Kirriemuir: Old
Kirriemuir: Barony	The Glens and Kirriemuir: Old
Kirriemuir: Livingstone	Kirriemuir: St Andrew's
Kirriemuir: South	Kirriemuir: St Andrew's
Kirriemuir: St Ninian's	The Glens and Kirriemuir: Old
Kirriemuir: West	The Glens and Kirriemuir: Old
Knoydart	North West Lochaber
Ladybank	Howe of Fife
Lagganallochie	Dunkeld
Lamberton	Foulden and Mordington
Lamington	Upper Clyde
Lanark: Broomgate	Lanark: Greyfriars
Lanark: Cairns	Lanark: Greyfriars
Lanark: St Kentigern's	Lanark: Greyfriars
Lanark: St Leonard's	Lanark: St Nicholas'
Largieside	Killean and Kilchenzie
Lassodie	Dunfermline: Townhill and Kingseat
Lathones	Largoward
Laurieston	Balmaghie
Laxavoe	Delting
Leadhills	Upper Clyde
Leith: Bonnington	Edinburgh: Leith North
Leith: Claremont	Edinburgh: Leith St Andrew's
Leith: Dalmeny Street	Edinburgh: Pilrig St Paul's
Leith: Elder Memorial	Edinburgh: St John's Oxgangs
Leith: Harper Memorial	Edinburgh: Leith North
Leith: Junction Road	Edinburgh: Leith St Andrew's
Leith: Kirkgate	Edinburgh: Leith South
Leith: South (FC)	Edinburgh: Leith St Andrew's
Leith: St Andrew's Place	Edinburgh: Leith St Andrew's

Name no longer used	Present name of parish
Leith: St John's	Edinburgh: St John's Oxgangs
Leith: St Nicholas	Edinburgh: Leith North
Leith: St Ninian's	Edinburgh: Leith North
Leith: St Thomas'	Edinburgh: Leith St Andrew's
Lemlair	Kiltearn
Lempitlaw	Kelso: Old and Sprouston
Leny	Callander
Leochel	Cushnie and Tough
Lesmahagow: Cordiner	Lesmahagow: Abbey Green
Lethendy	Caputh and Clunie
Levern	Barrhead: St Andrew's
Lilliesleaf	Ale and Teviot United
Lindowan	Craigrownie
Linlithgow: East	Linlithgow: St Ninian's Craigmailen
Linlithgow: Trinity	Linlithgow: St Ninian's Craigmailen
Lintrathen	The Isla Parishes
Livingston: Tulloch	Livingston: Old
Livingston: West	Livingston: Old
Lochaline	Morvern
Lochcraig	Lochgelly and Benarty: St Serf's
Lochdonhead	Torosay and Kinlochspelvie
Lochearnhead	Balquhidder
Lochlee	Edzell Lethnot Glenesk
Lochryan	Inch
Logie (Dundee)	Fowlis and Liff
Logie (St Andrews)	charge dissolved: Presbytery of St Andrews
Logiebride	Auchtergaven and Moneydie
Logie Buchan	Ellon
Logie Mar	Cromar
Logie Pert	charge dissolved: Presbytery of Angus
Logie Wester	Ferintosh
Longcastle	Kirkinner
Longformacus	Langton and Lammermuir Kirk
Longnewton	Ale and Teviot United
Longridge	Breich Valley
Longtown	The Border Kirk
Lowther	Upper Clyde
Luce	Hoddom, Kirtle-Eaglesfield and Middlebie
Lude	Blair Atholl and Struan
Lumphanan	Mid Deeside
Lumphinnans	Beath and Cowdenbeath: North
Lumsden	Upper Donside
Luncarty	Redgorton and Stanley
Lund	Unst
Lybster	The Parish of Latheron
Lynturk	Cushnie and Tough
Mailor	The Stewartry of Strathearn
Mainsriddle	Colvend, Southwick and Kirkbean
Makerstoun	Kelso Country Churches
Mallaig	North West Lochaber
Maryburgh	Ferintosh
Marykirk	Aberluthnott
Maryton	Inchbrayock
Meadowfield	Caldercruix and Longriggend
Meathie	Glamis, Inverarity and Kinnettles
Megget	Ettrick and Yarrow
Melville	charge suppressed: Presbytery of Lothian
Memus	The Glens and Kirriemuir: Old

Name no longer used	Present name of parish
Mid Calder: Bridgend	Kirk of Calder
Mid Calder: St John's	Kirk of Calder
Midholm	congregation seceded: Presbytery of Jedburgh
Migvie	Cromar
Millbrex	Fyvie
Millerston	charge dissolved: Presbytery of Glasgow
Millport	Cumbrae
Milnathort	Orwell and Portmoak
Minto	Ruberslaw
Monecht	charge dissolved: Presbytery of Gordon
Monifieth: North	Monikie and Newbigging and Murroes and Tealing
Montrose: Knox's	Montrose: Melville South
Montrose: St George's	Montrose: Old and St Andrew's
Montrose: St John's	Montrose: Old and St Andrew's
Montrose: St Luke's	Montrose: Old and St Andrew's
Montrose: St Paul's	Montrose: Melville South
Montrose: Trinity	Montrose: Old and St Andrew's
Monzievaird	Crieff
Moonzie	charge dissolved: Presbytery of St Andrews
Morton	Thornhill
Mossbank	Delting
Mossgreen	Cowdenbeath: Trinity
Motherwell: Brandon	Motherwell: Crosshill
Motherwell: Cairns	Motherwell: Crosshill
Motherwell: Manse Road	Motherwell: South
Motherwell: South Dalziel	Motherwell: South
Moulin	Pitlochry
Mount Kedar	Cummertrees, Mouswald and Ruthwell
Mow	Linton, Morebattle, Hownam and Yetholm
Moy	Dyke
Moyness	charge dissolved: Presbytery of Moray
Muckersie	The Stewartry of Strathearn
Muirton	Aberluthnott
Murthly	Caputh and Clunie
Musselburgh: Bridge Street	Musselburgh: St Andrew's High
Musselburgh: Millhill	Musselburgh: St Andrew's High
Nairn: High	Nairn: St Ninian's
Nairn: Rosebank	Nairn: St Ninian's
Navar	Edzell Lethnot Glenesk
Nenthorn	Kelso Country Churches
New Leeds	charge dissolved: Presbytery of Buchan
New Liston	Edinburgh: Kirkliston
Newcastleton	Liddesdale
Newdosk	Edzell Lethnot Glenesk
Newmills	Culross and Torryburn
Newseat	Rothienorman
Newtongrange	Newbattle
Newton Stewart	Penninghame
Nigg	charge dissolved: Presbytery of Aberdeen
Nisbet	Ale and Teviot United
North Bute	The United Church of Bute
Norwick	Unst
Ogston	Lossiemouth: St Gerardine's High
Old Cumnock: Crichton Memorial	Old Cumnock: Trinity
Old Cumnock: St Ninian's	Old Cumnock: Trinity
Old Cumnock: West	Old Cumnock: Trinity
Oldhamstocks	Dunglass
Old Kilpatrick: Barclay	Dalmuir: Barclay

Name no longer used	Present name of parish
Ollaberry	Northmavine
Olnafirth	Delting
Ord	Ordiquhill and Cornhill
Paisley: Canal Street	Paisley: Stow Brae Kirk
Paisley: Castlehead	Paisley: Stow Brae Kirk
Paisley: George Street	Paisley: Glenburn
Paisley: High	Paisley: Oakshaw Trinity
Paisley: Laigh Kirk	Paisley: Stow Brae Kirk
Paisley: Merksworth	Paisley: Wallneuk North
Paisley: Middle	Paisley: Stow Brae Kirk
Paisley: Mossvale	Paisley: Wallneuk North
Paisley: New Street	Paisley: Glenburn
Paisley: North	Paisley: Wallneuk North
Paisley: Oakshaw West	Paisley: St Luke's
Paisley: Orr Square	Paisley: Oakshaw Trinity
Paisley: South	Paisley: St Luke's
Paisley: St Andrew's	Paisley: Stow Brae Kirk
Paisley: St George's	Paisley: Stow Brae Kirk
Paisley: St John's	Paisley: Oakshaw Trinity
Paisley: Thread Street	Paisley: Martyrs' Sandyford
Papa Stour	Walls and Sandness
Park	Kinloch
Pathhead	Ormiston
Pathstruie	The Stewartry of Strathearn
Pearston	Dreghorn and Springside
Peebles: West	Peebles: St Andrew's Leckie
Pennersaughs	Hoddom, Kirtle-Eaglesfield and Middlebie
Pentland	Lasswade and Rosewell
Persie	Kirkmichael, Straloch and Glenshee
Perth: Bridgend	Perth: St Matthew's
Perth: East	Perth: St Leonard's-in-the-Fields
Perth: Knox's	Perth: St Leonard's-in-the-Fields
Perth: Middle	Perth: St Matthew's
Perth: St Andrew's	Perth: Riverside
Perth: St Columba's	Perth: North
Perth: St Leonard's	Perth: North
Perth: St Stephen's	Perth: Riverside
Perth: West	Perth: St Matthew's
Perth: Wilson	Perth: St Matthew's
Perth: York Place	Perth: St Leonard's-in-the-Fields
Peterhead: Charlotte Street	Peterhead: Trinity
Peterhead: East	Peterhead: St Andrew's
Peterhead: South	Peterhead: St Andrew's
Peterhead: St Peter's	Peterhead: Trinity
Peterhead: West Associate	Peterhead: Trinity
Pettinain	Cairngryffe
Pitcairn (C of S)	Redgorton and Stanley
Pitcairn (UF)	Almondbank Tibbermore
Pitlessie	Howe of Fife
Pitroddie	St Madoes and Kinfauns
Plockton	Lochalsh
Polmont South	Brightons
Polwarth	Langton and Lammermuir Kirk
Poolewe	Gairloch and Dundonnell
Port Bannatyne	The United Church of Bute
Port Ellen	Kildalton and Oa
Port Glasgow: Clune Park	Port Glasgow: St Andrew's
Port Glasgow: Newark	Port Glasgow: St Andrew's

Name no longer used	Present name of parish
Port Glasgow: Old	Port Glasgow: St Andrew's
Port Glasgow: Princes Street	Port Glasgow: St Andrew's
Port Glasgow: West	Port Glasgow: St Andrew's
Portobello: Regent Street	Edinburgh: Portobello Old
Portobello: Windsor Place	Edinburgh: Portobello Old
Portsonachan	Glenorchy and Innishael
Portsoy	Fordyce
Port William	Mochrum
Prestonkirk	Traprain
Prinlaws	Leslie: Trinity
Quarrier's Mount Zion	Kilmacolm: St Columba
Raasay	Portree
Rathillet	Creich, Flisk and Kilmany
Rathmuriel	Noth
Reay	The North Coast Parish
Redcastle	Killearnan
Restenneth	Forfar: East and Old
Rhynd	Perth: Craigie and Moncreiffe
Rhynie	Noth
Rickarton	charge dissolved: Presbytery of Kincardine and Deeside
Rigg	Gretna, Half Morton and Kirkpatrick Fleming
Rigside	The Douglas Valley Church
Rinpatrick	Gretna, Half Morton and Kirkpatrick Fleming
Roberton	Upper Clyde
Rosehearty	Pitsligo
Rossie	Inchture and Kinnaird
Rothesay: Bridgend	The United Church of Bute
Rothesay: Craigmore High	Rothesay: Trinity
Rothesay: Craigmore St Brendan's	The United Church of Bute
Rothesay: High	The United Church of Bute
Rothesay: New	The United Church of Bute
Rothesay: St James'	Rothesay: Trinity
Rothesay: St John's	The United Church of Bute
Rothesay: West	Rothesay: Trinity
Roxburgh	Kelso Country Churches
Rutherglen: East	Rutherglen: Old
Rutherglen: Greenhill	Rutherglen: Old
Rutherglen: Munro	Rutherglen: West and Wardlawhill
Ruthven (Angus)	The Isla Parishes
Ruthven (Gordon)	Huntly Cairnie Glass
St Andrew's (Orkney)	East Mainland
St Cyrus	Mearns Coastal
St Ola	Kirkwall: St Magnus Cathedral
Saltcoats: Erskine	Saltcoats: New Trinity
Saltcoats: Landsborough	Saltcoats: New Trinity
Saltcoats: Middle	Saltcoats: New Trinity
Saltcoats: South Beach	Saltcoats: St Cuthbert's
Saltcoats: Trinity	Saltcoats: New Trinity
Saltcoats: West	Saltcoats: New Trinity
Sandhead	Stoneykirk
Saughtree	Liddesdale
Saulseat	Inch
Scalloway	Tingwall
Scatsta	Delting
Sclattie	Blairdaff and Chapel of Garioch
Scoonie	Leven
Scourie	Eddrachillis
Seafield	Portknockie

Name no longer used	Present name of parish
Sennick	Borgue
Seton	Tranent
Shawbost	Carloway
Shebster	The North Coast Parish
Sheuchan	Stranraer: High
Shieldaig	Applecross, Lochcarron and Torridon
Shiels	Belhelvie
Shottsburn	Kirk o' Shotts
Shurrery	The North Coast Parish
Simprin	Fogo and Swinton
Skerrols	Kilarrow
Skinnet	Halkirk Westerdale
Slains	Ellon
Smailholm	Kelso Country Churches
Small Isles	North West Lochaber
South Ballachulish	charge dissolved: Presbytery of Lochaber
Soutra	Tyne Valley Parish
Spittal (Caithness)	Halkirk Westerdale
Spittal (Duns)	charge dissolved: Presbytery of Duns
Springfield	Gretna, Half Morton and Kirkpatrick Fleming
Stenton	Traprain
Stewartfield	Deer
Stewarton: Cairns	Stewarton: St Columba's
Stewarton: Laigh	Stewarton: St Columba's
Stichill	Kelso Country Churches
Stirling: Craigs	Stirling: St Columba's
Stirling: North (FC)	Stirling: St Columba's
Stobhill	Gorebridge
Stockbridge	Dunglass
Stonehaven: North	Stonehaven: South
Stoneyburn	Breich Valley
Stornoway: James Street	Stornoway: Martin's Memorial
Stracathro	Brechin: Cathedral
Strachan	Birse and Feughside
Stranraer: Bellevilla	Stranraer: Trinity
Stranraer: Bridge Street	Stranraer: Trinity
Stranraer: Ivy Place	Stranraer: Trinity
Stranraer: Old	Stranraer: Trinity
Stranraer: St Andrew's	Stranraer: Trinity
Stranraer: St Margaret's	Stranraer: High
Stranraer: St Mark's	Stranraer: Trinity
Stranraer: St Ninian's	Stranraer: Trinity
Stranraer: Town Kirk	Stranraer: Trinity
Strathaven: West	Strathaven: Avendale Old and Drumclog
Strathconon	Contin
Strathdeveron	Mortlach and Cabrach
Strathdon	Upper Donside
Stratherrick	Dores and Boleskine
Strathgarve	Contin
Strathglass	Kilmorack and Erchless
Strathmartine (C of S)	Dundee: Downfield Mains
Strathy	The North Coast Parish
Strowan	Comrie
Suddie	Knockbain
Tarfside	Edzell Lethnot Glenesk
Tarland	Cromar
Tarvit	Cupar: Old and St Michael of Tarvit
Temple	Gorebridge

Name no longer used	Present name of parish
Thankerton	Cairngryffe
The Bass	North Berwick: St Andrew Blackadder
Tighnabruaich	Kyles
Tongland	Tarff and Twynholm
Torphins	Mid Deeside
Torrance	East Kilbride: Old
Towie	Upper Donside
Trailflat	Kirkmichael, Tinwald and Torthorwald
Trailtrow	Cummertrees, Mouswald and Ruthwell
Trefontaine	Langton and Lammermuir Kirk
Trossachs	Callander
Trumisgarry	Berneray and Lochmaddy
Tullibole	Fossoway: St Serf's and Devonside
Tullich	Glenmuick (Ballater)
Tullichetil	Comrie
Tullynessle	Howe Trinity
Tummel	Foss and Rannoch
Tushielaw	Ettrick and Yarrow
Uddingston: Aitkenhead	Uddingston: Viewpark
Uddingston: Chalmers	Uddingston: Old
Uddingston: Trinity	Uddingston: Old
Uig	Snizort
Uphall: North	Strathbrock
Uyeasound	Unst
Walston	Black Mount
Wandel	Upper Clyde
Wanlockhead	Upper Clyde
Waterbeck	charge dissolved: Presbytery of Annandale and Eskdale
Waternish	Bracadale and Duirinish
Wauchope	Langholm Eskdalemuir Ewes and Westerkirk
Waulkmill	Insch-Leslie-Premnay-Oyne
Weisdale	Tingwall
Wheelkirk	Liddesdale
Whitehill	New Pitsligo
Whiteness	Tingwall
Whittingehame	Traprain
Wick: Bridge Street	Wick: St Fergus
Wick: Central	Wick: Pulteneytown and Thrumster
Wick: Martyrs'	Wick: Pulteneytown and Thrumster
Wick: Old	Wick: St Fergus
Wick: St Andrew's	Wick: Pulteneytown and Thrumster
Wilkieston	Edinburgh: Ratho
Wilsontown	Forth
Wishaw: Chalmers	Wishaw: South Wishaw
Wishaw: Thornlie	Wishaw: South Wishaw
Wiston	Upper Clyde
Wolfhill	Cargill Burrelton
Wolflee	Hobkirk and Southdean
Woomet	Newton
Ythan Wells	Auchaber United

SECTION 10

Congregational
Statistics
2012

CHURCH OF SCOTLAND
Comparative Statistics: 1972–2012

	2012	*2002*	*1992*	*1982*	*1972*
Communicants	415,705*	571,698	752,719	918,991	1,110,187
Elders	34,138	42,992	46,238	47,679	49,716

* adjusted from figure of 413,488 reported to General Assembly of 2013. In addition, statistics were not to hand for two congregations which in 2011 had 1,447 members.

NOTES ON CONGREGATIONAL STATISTICS

Com   Number of communicants at 31 December 2012.

Eld   Number of elders at 31 December 2012.

G   Membership of the Guild including Young Woman's Group and others as recorded on the 2012 annual return submitted to the Guild Office.

In 12   Ordinary General Income for 2012. Ordinary General Income consists of members' offerings, contributions from congregational organisations, regular fund-raising events, income from investments, deposits and so on. This figure does not include extraordinary or special income, or income from special collections and fund-raising for other charities.

M&M   Final amount allocated to congregations after allowing for Presbytery-approved amendments up to 31 December 2012, but before deducting stipend endowments and normal allowances given for stipend purposes in a vacancy.

–18   This figure shows 'the number of children and young people aged 17 years and under who are involved in the life of the congregation'.

(NB: Figures may not be available for new charges created or for congregations which have entered into readjustment late in 2012 or during 2013. Figures might also not be available for congregations which failed to submit the appropriate schedule.)

Congregation	Com	Eld	G	In 12	M&M	–18
1. Edinburgh						
Albany Deaf Church of Edinburgh	115	–	–	–	–	–
Balerno	714	72	37	131,331	73,629	69
Barclay Viewforth	324	34	–	163,161	108,989	45
Blackhall St Columba's	937	77	26	181,205	102,345	57
Bristo Memorial Craigmillar	92	5	–	55,387	22,730	56
Broughton St Mary's	223	29	–	70,873	46,197	81
Canongate	375	49	–	114,448	62,897	12
Carrick Knowe	426	50	73	61,170	38,241	274
Colinton	920	71	–	199,080	124,475	95
Colinton Mains	176	15	–	49,386	32,289	54
Corstorphine Craigsbank	526	28	–	96,476	58,091	69
Corstorphine Old	471	53	53	90,819	68,019	56
Corstorphine St Anne's	374	51	76	108,719	63,593	42
Corstorphine St Ninian's	766	79	45	156,962	97,402	55
Craigentinny St Christopher's	93	12	–	26,427	17,856	15
Craiglockhart	467	55	29	171,953	97,357	65
Craigmillar Park	221	19	24	72,076	50,830	8
Cramond	1,071	92	–	218,557	155,711	68
Currie	592	41	89	180,056	88,742	64
Dalmeny	108	13	–	20,664	20,301	9
Queensferry	674	47	60	112,563	56,555	118
Davidson's Mains	648	14	39	243,283	108,141	80
Dean	199	21	–	67,290	37,966	15
Drylaw	118	12	–	19,760	12,523	6
Duddingston	565	52	44	116,612	69,729	271
Fairmilehead	671	61	39	84,385	65,645	66
Gorgie Dalry	264	28	–	83,348	80,250	60
Granton	208	18	–	–	29,480	35
Greenbank	814	87	41	259,321	137,081	81
Greenside	156	30	–	–	36,915	95
Greyfriars Tolbooth and Highland Kirk	358	45	–	131,306	79,374	25
High (St Giles')	516	36	–	305,313	158,712	6
Holyrood Abbey	212	30	–	136,103	89,077	85
Holy Trinity	217	24	–	189,791	69,443	64
Inverleith St Serf's	407	46	22	103,639	90,598	22
Juniper Green	343	24	–	101,002	64,991	40
Kaimes Lockhart Memorial	44	6	–	–	2,866	12
Liberton	748	81	50	210,479	110,145	100
Kirkliston	277	31	49	99,479	56,055	22
Kirk o' Field	145	20	–	30,527	31,764	1
Leith North	314	34	–	82,194	53,304	104
Leith St Andrew's	281	33	–	79,684	61,751	168
Leith South	417	64	–	116,908	71,186	92
Leith Wardie	541	66	33	159,302	82,573	146
Liberton Northfield	252	8	25	50,776	31,301	23
London Road	205	30	25	66,050	32,962	11
Marchmont St Giles'	242	35	29	107,638	58,066	29
Mayfield Salisbury	561	54	–	233,972	147,488	50

Congregation	Com	Eld	G	In 12	M&M	–18
Morningside	607	92	23	174,312	118,442	140
Morningside United	229	44	–	120,740	11,980	19
Muirhouse St Andrew's	51	7	–	16,023	378	80
Murrayfield	536	61	–	187,014	92,197	59
Newhaven	178	18	42	–	52,560	68
New Restalrig	150	14	16	–	72,758	34
Old Kirk	107	12	–	17,907	13,370	8
Palmerston Place	415	41	–	–	97,815	99
Pilrig St Paul's	250	16	26	43,166	35,533	41
Polwarth	213	26	17	67,855	58,093	28
Portobello Old	296	43	36	65,442	50,640	–
Portobello St James'	326	38	–	42,598	30,010	12
Portobello St Philip's Joppa	551	49	62	184,042	97,651	232
Priestfield	176	19	19	60,901	46,125	16
Ratho	201	18	–	44,868	25,068	15
Reid Memorial	314	20	–	94,774	65,583	20
Richmond Craigmillar	94	12	–	–	2,273	11
St Andrew's and St George's West	338	52	–	–	149,462	27
St Andrew's Clermiston	236	15	–	52,555	29,564	91
St Catherine's Argyle	294	26	–	164,501	84,545	200
St Cuthbert's	342	49	–	140,055	101,373	14
St David's Broomhouse	154	11	–	31,326	17,674	70
St John's Oxgangs	203	10	–	16,413	17,223	–
St Margaret's	366	38	20	48,885	35,206	50
St Martin's	100	10	–	17,494	1,277	22
St Michael's	362	26	25	73,258	37,485	14
St Nicholas' Sighthill	363	29	16	44,147	29,282	14
St Stephen's Comely Bank	250	18	–	141,882	71,312	105
Slateford Longstone	240	15	43	49,368	30,584	26
Stenhouse St Aidan's	84	10	–	22,852	17,009	4
Stockbridge	227	27	–	68,963	63,713	27
Tron Kirk (Gilmerton and Moredun)	99	14	–	–	3,742	85
2. West Lothian						
Abercorn	74	9	–	13,334	11,814	–
Pardovan, Kingscavil and Winchburgh	275	29	16	71,055	33,338	93
Armadale	555	45	28	73,380	43,469	215
Avonbridge	77	8	–	12,404	6,770	5
Torphichen	244	18	–	57,738	25,196	80
Bathgate: Boghall	252	30	27	74,807	41,296	65
Bathgate: High	531	39	32	97,558	61,591	67
Bathgate: St John's	359	24	35	54,345	37,304	90
Blackburn and Seafield	422	31	–	67,591	40,641	105
Blackridge	77	5	–	29,762	11,682	–
Harthill: St Andrew's	201	11	30	56,758	40,193	62
Breich Valley	199	12	22	26,649	23,590	8
Broxburn	401	41	44	74,700	48,278	165
Fauldhouse: St Andrew's	212	17	–	47,477	31,746	12
Kirknewton and East Calder	338	36	29	108,645	62,634	107
Kirk of Calder	575	44	26	77,075	47,557	50

Congregation	Com	Eld	G	In 12	M&M	-18
Linlithgow: St Michael's	1,401	101	58	323,570	167,054	300
Linlithgow: St Ninian's Craigmailen	446	44	59	76,498	41,538	82
Livingston Ecumenical Parish	530	45	–	–	69,993	229
Livingston: Old	376	39	20	76,051	58,162	47
Polbeth Harwood	181	26	–	27,500	19,549	4
West Kirk of Calder	263	18	18	52,819	37,294	14
Strathbrock	323	32	19	102,195	70,927	80
Uphall: South	207	24	–	–	37,489	62
Whitburn: Brucefield	254	26	18	79,534	49,819	160
Whitburn: South	377	24	30	66,584	47,663	114
3. Lothian						
Aberlady	243	24	–	36,030	21,343	20
Gullane	383	31	25	–	39,802	73
Athelstaneford	206	12	–	26,843	12,835	16
Whitekirk and Tyninghame	143	14	–	–	20,386	14
Belhaven	675	39	62	73,548	44,480	30
Spott	112	7	–	12,659	7,145	6
Bilston	98	5	14	11,796	3,281	–
Glencorse	308	14	–	27,433	16,477	–
Roslin	247	9	–	28,554	20,321	32
Bolton and Saltoun	137	18	–	33,052	16,251	11
Humbie	76	9	–	18,874	11,866	10
Yester	186	16	18	24,192	15,567	12
Bonnyrigg	707	60	42	97,221	64,160	25
Cockenzie and Port Seton: Chalmers Memorial	210	30	35	–	49,515	15
Cockenzie and Port Seton: Old	391	21	18	–	22,585	27
Cockpen and Carrington	234	24	44	26,201	17,350	39
Lasswade and Rosewell	348	23	–	31,545	19,475	8
Dalkeith: St John's and King's Park	515	41	25	98,605	52,873	60
Dalkeith: St Nicholas' Buccleuch	397	22	–	71,142	31,911	9
Dirleton	239	15	–	–	34,771	10
North Berwick: Abbey	306	30	52	–	43,192	22
Dunbar	422	18	39	105,752	59,741	90
Dunglass	310	14	14	26,769	19,343	–
Garvald and Morham	47	10	–	10,748	5,128	17
Haddington: West	477	29	35	66,159	41,483	31
Gladsmuir	188	15	–	–	16,822	36
Longniddry	391	46	39	73,307	49,016	12
Gorebridge	402	15	–	99,992	55,493	50
Haddington: St Mary's	554	40	–	–	78,040	49
Howgate	42	6	–	19,547	8,015	10
Penicuik: South	126	16	–	–	48,437	27
Loanhead	325	24	31	58,517	38,291	35
Musselburgh: Northesk	348	28	45	65,647	40,034	97
Musselburgh: St Andrew's High	342	31	24	70,882	33,523	12
Musselburgh: St Clement's and St Ninian's	214	12	–	21,633	21,457	1
Musselburgh: St Michael's Inveresk	423	39	–	75,871	41,587	25
Newbattle	491	32	25	86,604	38,873	168
Newton	135	9	13	13,087	10,651	25

Congregation	Com	Eld	G	In 12	M&M	–18
North Berwick: St Andrew Blackadder	627	41	30	131,852	74,678	95
Ormiston	181	11	24	35,578	22,645	20
Pencaitland	256	10	–	45,811	32,220	32
Penicuik: North	554	34	–	94,353	55,799	79
Penicuik: St Mungo's	382	23	27	69,174	40,645	13
Prestonpans: Prestongrange	339	30	23	55,110	33,727	35
Tranent	240	14	30	49,811	32,696	15
Traprain	459	32	28	71,576	47,169	63
Tyne Valley Parish	361	31	–	71,397	54,373	34

4. Melrose and Peebles

Congregation	Com	Eld	G	In 12	M&M	–18
Ashkirk	61	10	–	9,953	3,782	1
Selkirk	507	23	–	71,355	42,756	20
Bowden and Melrose	908	72	37	117,354	82,607	42
Broughton, Glenholm and Kilbucho	151	10	27	18,950	10,652	–
Skirling	75	6	–	8,901	5,252	4
Stobo and Drumelzier	91	–	–	–	10,162	–
Tweedsmuir	36	–	–	10,361	3,843	–
Caddonfoot	205	15	–	16,739	7,977	13
Galashiels: Trinity	495	46	45	64,534	47,937	7
Carlops	63	–	–	20,279	6,914	–
Kirkurd and Newlands	107	–	17	33,206	12,378	–
West Linton: St Andrew's	228	–	–	49,121	20,725	–
Channelkirk and Lauder	430	25	28	64,052	33,886	25
Earlston	420	21	12	45,212	32,666	21
Eddleston	111	8	10	16,168	6,608	23
Peebles: Old	519	46	–	110,013	59,517	46
Ettrick and Yarrow	197	18	–	40,614	25,966	9
Galashiels: Old and St Paul's	281	21	29	66,009	42,744	36
Galashiels: St John's	218	14	–	47,682	31,353	82
Innerleithen, Traquair and Walkerburn	403	31	38	55,987	41,966	83
Lyne and Manor	107	7	–	24,476	18,428	–
Peebles: St Andrew's Leckie	621	33	–	97,530	58,742	85
Maxton and Mertoun	131	9	–	13,754	13,275	12
Newtown	149	–	–	18,939	7,366	1
St Boswells	210	23	27	35,261	27,054	33
Stow: St Mary of Wedale and Heriot	187	13	–	–	23,481	15

5. Duns

Congregation	Com	Eld	G	In 12	M&M	–18
Ayton and Burnmouth	169	12	–	18,823	11,019	–
Foulden and Mordington	78	6	–	4,246	5,837	–
Grantshouse and Houndwood and Reston	98	8	16	9,583	11,206	3
Berwick-upon-Tweed: St Andrew's Wallace Green and Lowick	389	24	29	55,970	43,483	15
Bonkyl and Preston	66	7	–	7,937	5,882	–
Chirnside	160	9	15	21,630	15,400	–
Edrom Allanton	68	5	–	5,159	5,612	5
Coldingham and St Abbs	84	9	–	36,376	23,703	8
Eyemouth	188	25	26	37,527	26,223	2
Coldstream	380	26	–	44,367	28,247	34

Congregation	Com	Eld	G	In 12	M&M	–18
Eccles	76	12	17	9,910	6,776	8
Duns	517	27	36	52,259	29,678	25
Fogo and Swinton	114	4	–	7,409	9,616	3
Ladykirk	23	6	–	8,645	7,555	–
Leitholm	74	7	–	–	5,320	1
Whitsome	36	3	–	2,077	3,226	–
Gordon: St Michael's	68	7	–	6,967	6,831	9
Greenlaw	104	7	14	21,435	12,022	–
Legerwood	65	7	–	8,443	4,425	8
Westruther	45	8	16	5,852	3,999	44
Hutton and Fishwick and Paxton	70	8	13	19,720	8,063	–
Langton and Lammermuir Kirk	148	15	23	41,499	33,359	2

6. Jedburgh

Ale and Teviot United	431	30	15	35,657	46,268	7
Cavers and Kirkton	133	9	–	10,678	9,613	–
Hawick: Trinity	769	30	49	46,555	28,819	73
Hawick: Burnfoot	108	12	11	32,082	17,602	98
Hawick: St Mary's and Old	468	23	24	42,605	29,324	105
Hawick: Teviot and Roberton	311	9	13	52,286	35,798	22
Hawick: Wilton	376	26	–	48,595	31,507	70
Teviothead	74	4	6	5,354	4,329	1
Hobkirk and Southdean	170	14	21	16,295	16,590	15
Ruberslaw	263	22	13	29,304	22,486	20
Jedburgh: Old and Trinity	705	18	34	–	50,482	–
Kelso Country Churches	213	17	18	30,053	31,647	23
Kelso: Old and Sprouston	542	32	–	50,546	33,909	8
Kelso: North and Ednam	1,195	73	42	157,285	72,853	53
Linton, Morebattle, Hownam and Yetholm	397	22	38	66,930	44,338	50
Oxnam	125	11	–	14,943	4,758	7

7. Annandale and Eskdale

Annan: Old	395	43	44	69,814	48,051	25
Dornock	147	12	–	–	6,864	14
Annan: St Andrew's	662	44	56	–	38,616	90
Brydekirk	56	6	–	7,544	3,443	2
Applegarth, Sibbaldbie and Johnstone	174	9	8	9,070	11,109	–
Lochmaben	438	25	40	54,281	35,086	8
Canonbie United	103	15	–	33,518	19,174	10
Liddesdale	132	9	22	–	25,696	16
Dalton	106	9	–	15,043	6,837	2
Hightae	82	4	12	10,052	5,323	16
St Mungo	87	12	14	14,000	8,176	6
Gretna: Old, Gretna: St Andrew's Half Morton and Kirkpatrick Fleming	361	33	27	–	27,659	59
Hoddom, Kirtle-Eaglesfield and Middlebie	211	21	27	17,562	17,837	12
Kirkpatrick Juxta	153	8	–	13,889	9,625	–
Moffat: St Andrew's	417	42	27	67,746	45,110	60
Wamphray	53	6	–	8,347	2,894	–
Langholm Eskdalemuir Ewes and Westerkirk	480	42	16	57,070	36,251	20

Congregation	Com	Eld	G	In 12	M&M	–18
Lockerbie: Dryfesdale, Hutton and Corrie	803	48	34	59,594	42,213	26
The Border Kirk	334	45	39	66,435	34,103	48
Tundergarth	51	8	–	10,400	3,555	–

8. Dumfries and Kirkcudbright

Auchencairn and Rerrick	69	7	–	9,853	7,261	–
Buittle and Kelton	161	16	–	18,284	17,430	–
Balmaclellan and Kells	74	7	17	17,034	16,465	11
Carsphairn	95	12	–	10,020	5,166	8
Dalry	152	13	17	18,458	8,127	10
Balmaghie	83	6	6	12,191	8,139	–
Tarff and Twynholm	163	14	25	24,289	18,568	8
Borgue	48	4	–	3,700	4,572	3
Gatehouse of Fleet	268	17	19	–	30,581	10
Caerlaverock	109	7	–	12,350	6,752	4
Dumfries: St Mary's-Greyfriars'	477	34	36	72,486	48,650	8
Castle Douglas	402	28	14	80,051	37,197	14
Closeburn	223	13	–	–	18,324	12
Colvend, Southwick and Kirkbean	239	20	19	81,558	53,363	8
Corsock and Kirkpatrick Durham	93	15	21	21,743	15,432	16
Crossmichael and Parton	167	10	15	22,294	13,118	12
Cummertrees, Mouswald and Ruthwell	201	19	14	–	20,876	–
Dalbeattie	560	35	45	54,326	32,600	40
Urr	188	11	–	–	12,440	18
Dumfries: Maxwelltown West	631	48	47	98,293	55,727	125
Dumfries: Northwest	407	16	20	44,393	29,166	30
Dumfries: St George's	534	51	36	129,246	61,597	28
Dumfries: St Michael's and South	843	41	34	90,811	59,939	125
Dumfries: Troqueer	283	29	34	95,833	61,125	78
Dunscore	235	23	9	31,003	23,405	18
Glencairn and Moniaive	180	24	–	45,780	20,649	13
Durisdeer	152	6	–	20,157	13,627	8
Penpont, Keir and Tynron	169	9	–	20,758	22,217	30
Thornhill	171	11	16	26,463	20,870	–
Irongray, Lochrutton and Terregles	215	25	16	–	24,860	–
Kirkconnel	279	10	–	–	25,404	13
Kirkcudbright	558	30	–	95,920	57,384	36
Kirkgunzeon	54	6	–	6,422	3,278	–
Lochend and New Abbey	207	18	13	24,160	16,942	9
Kirkmahoe	323	16	17	23,837	18,673	10
Kirkmichael, Tinwald and Torthorwald	462	40	35	48,128	41,774	11
Sanquhar: St Bride's	427	24	17	47,760	25,522	33

9. Wigtown and Stranraer

Ervie Kirkcolm	209	15	–	26,817	14,889	25
Leswalt	299	15	–	27,221	17,752	12
Glasserton and Isle of Whithorn	107	7	–	12,652	11,084	–
Whithorn: St Ninian's Priory	322	9	20	47,631	21,083	30
Inch	224	12	10	16,161	13,350	40
Stranraer: Town Kirk	527	46	–	71,037	55,170	51

Congregation	Com	Eld	G	In 12	M&M	–18
Kirkcowan	119	9	–	31,866	20,669	6
Wigtown	182	14	15	35,931	22,454	30
Kirkinner	150	8	14	16,920	9,953	–
Sorbie	138	8	–	13,713	11,031	10
Kirkmabreck	148	12	20	18,013	11,708	–
Monigaff	325	21	–	27,717	26,753	20
Kirkmaiden	218	19	10	24,002	17,895	10
Stoneykirk	325	25	15	40,897	22,652	–
Mochrum	282	–	21	34,436	17,927	–
New Luce	91	7	–	10,100	8,111	5
Old Luce	146	19	28	38,351	25,971	29
Penninghame	443	22	22	67,810	45,262	21
Portpatrick	223	9	25	25,351	14,438	–
Stranraer: St Ninian's	258	17	–	43,662	28,038	15
Stranraer: High Kirk	577	–	25	70,756	48,588	–

10. Ayr

Alloway	1,167	98	–	210,769	121,632	170
Annbank	280	18	22	37,817	24,514	10
Tarbolton	458	30	22	51,965	32,231	12
Auchinleck	334	21	30	–	30,610	22
Catrine	125	12	23	25,819	15,553	2
Ayr: Auld Kirk of Ayr	530	60	37	79,189	56,184	–
Ayr: Castlehill	646	50	47	93,972	66,282	210
Ayr: Newton Wallacetown	423	55	58	126,310	76,012	427
Ayr: St Andrew's	320	27	9	68,188	47,381	105
Ayr: St Columba	1,327	118	74	257,265	124,611	125
Ayr: St James'	432	44	51	68,450	41,847	167
Ayr: St Leonard's	530	52	29	73,592	45,193	16
Dalrymple	251	–	–	26,961	15,844	–
Ayr: St Quivox	261	25	15	56,083	31,684	10
Ballantrae	239	19	32	31,700	26,596	19
St Colmon (Arnsheen Barrhill and Colmonell)	239	11	–	24,555	19,044	6
Barr	66	3	–	3,746	3,920	5
Dailly	150	13	12	16,454	12,097	5
Girvan: South	312	22	30	32,587	21,531	14
Coylton	317	–	–	43,605	19,714	–
Drongan: The Schaw Kirk	193	19	15	35,793	16,519	132
Craigie	119	9	–	12,147	7,960	12
Symington	338	20	19	46,452	35,044	4
Crosshill	180	13	18	12,781	12,031	–
Maybole	370	31	34	62,621	34,105	17
Dalmellington	237	21	39	–	29,837	70
Patna Waterside	134	12	–	–	17,445	12
Dundonald	478	44	57	–	54,118	98
Fisherton	116	9	10	10,726	10,471	–
Kirkoswald	223	14	10	26,367	19,021	8
Girvan: North (Old and St Andrew's)	717	50	–	–	53,626	78
Kirkmichael	214	17	24	22,980	13,951	8
Straiton: St Cuthbert's	173	10	14	–	13,755	10

Congregation	Com	Eld	G	In 12	M&M	–18
Lugar	162	11	14	16,079	8,614	21
Old Cumnock: Old	371	19	33	62,528	43,906	40
Mauchline	440	24	55	80,327	54,594	31
Sorn	150	13	15	21,022	13,839	16
Monkton and Prestwick: North	356	37	47	–	64,286	30
Muirkirk	184	13	–	25,571	17,567	7
Old Cumnock: Trinity	372	21	35	60,287	38,518	17
New Cumnock	498	34	32	76,954	42,186	135
Ochiltree	252	21	18	34,207	23,023	21
Stair	216	16	15	34,215	19,751	42
Prestwick: Kingcase	683	81	72	132,290	86,583	228
Prestwick: St Nicholas'	647	74	71	112,477	69,975	191
Prestwick: South	308	39	36	100,584	53,678	85
Troon: Old	966	64	–	122,753	84,849	100
Troon: Portland	551	53	32	119,539	75,752	32
Troon: St Meddan's	894	100	43	171,659	105,239	24

11. Irvine and Kilmarnock

Caldwell	233	16	–	71,643	42,339	28
Dunlop	403	42	30	63,605	41,218	40
Crosshouse	302	33	17	61,143	30,505	87
Darvel	379	29	41	47,387	26,371	33
Dreghorn and Springside	510	45	31	70,194	49,257	45
Fenwick	332	23	35	62,082	47,649	25
Galston	672	62	67	100,216	71,718	68
Hurlford	386	27	33	–	39,436	15
Irvine: Fullarton	403	43	47	101,163	63,836	168
Irvine: Girdle Toll	163	13	19	–	20,385	83
Irvine: Mure	353	25	25	64,050	46,603	66
Irvine: Old	416	23	20	75,515	56,238	25
Irvine: Relief Bourtreehill	244	23	30	43,979	29,556	12
Irvine: St Andrew's	275	15	32	–	41,873	25
Kilmarnock: Kay Park	596	82	40	–	97,607	20
Kilmarnock: New Laigh Kirk	921	79	70	200,443	131,232	185
Kilmarnock: Riccarton	274	31	21	65,220	43,979	52
Kilmarnock: St Andrew's and St Marnock's	899	106	45	180,662	101,930	496
Kilmarnock: St John's Onthank	266	23	21	50,277	28,817	110
Kilmarnock: St Kentigern's	284	29	–	62,771	34,061	92
Kilmarnock: South	288	21	25	45,721	35,804	45
Kilmaurs: St Maur's Glencairn	305	16	25	47,506	31,669	17
Newmilns: Loudoun	292	9	–	–	44,506	24
Stewarton: John Knox	276	32	20	87,163	46,595	40
Stewarton: St Columba's	458	37	46	66,625	50,476	129

12. Ardrossan

Ardrossan: Barony St John's	231	23	27	47,592	27,720	9
Ardrossan: Park	416	40	48	64,065	42,799	39
Beith	844	60	30	100,020	79,008	36
Brodick	143	18	–	53,629	29,743	75
Corrie	48	–	–	19,374	9,969	–

Congregation	Com	Eld	G	In 12	M&M	–18
Lochranza and Pirnmill	68	12	12	20,671	8,788	3
Shiskine	70	10	15	31,370	12,473	17
Cumbrae	263	23	63	53,582	35,803	72
Dalry: St Margaret's	678	52	31	147,633	73,354	127
Dalry: Trinity	216	18	38	83,079	51,382	32
Fairlie	247	32	45	–	42,276	25
Kilbirnie: Auld Kirk	361	32	–	64,721	25,767	8
Kilbirnie: St Columba's	560	34	20	60,758	34,101	85
Kilmory	42	7	–	10,428	5,491	6
Lamlash	110	16	28	30,605	22,847	15
Kilwinning: Mansefield Trinity	246	16	27	49,315	24,619	20
Kilwinning: Old	609	51	60	109,988	63,461	25
Largs: Clark Memorial	827	103	63	165,462	87,696	41
Largs: St Columba's	415	47	61	104,727	53,504	30
Largs: St John's	775	43	81	128,856	96,140	42
Saltcoats: New Trinity	253	40	20	52,474	36,675	–
Saltcoats: North	316	21	30	47,438	36,413	75
Saltcoats: St Cuthbert's	294	36	11	78,743	54,991	130
Stevenston: Ardeer	284	27	30	36,118	30,302	166
Stevenston: Livingstone	320	31	24	51,679	32,247	11
Stevenston: High	255	23	–	83,370	57,028	28
West Kilbride	435	47	41	119,744	81,705	54
Whiting Bay and Kildonan	97	8	–	42,963	29,457	12

13. Lanark

Congregation	Com	Eld	G	In 12	M&M	–18
Biggar	574	32	40	–	52,809	15
Black Mount	66	8	13	12,252	9,637	2
Culter	–	–	–	–	5,788	–
Libberton and Quothquan	84	11	–	14,884	5,149	12
Cairngryffe	170	13	15	23,806	20,174	10
Symington	200	20	22	–	20,636	9
Carluke: Kirkton	815	46	21	98,961	67,445	365
Carluke: St Andrew's	271	13	21	55,635	33,238	35
Carluke: St John's	734	43	43	93,566	56,070	33
Carnwath	265	17	18	26,276	28,554	–
Carstairs and Carstairs Junction	225	24	25	–	28,563	50
Coalburn	135	9	20	18,681	9,785	12
Lesmahagow: Old	438	24	22	70,941	46,265	–
Crossford	180	7	–	27,565	20,337	19
Kirkfieldbank	86	8	20	20,096	10,620	–
Forth: St Paul's	362	24	46	59,677	38,598	45
Glencaple	183	12	20	20,359	17,715	8
Lowther	35	4	–	–	2,803	3
Kirkmuirhill	293	20	45	97,543	71,697	–
Lanark: Greyfriars	585	41	36	97,730	55,213	196
Lanark: St Nicholas'	525	56	32	–	65,834	102
Law	192	16	34	–	23,261	129
Lesmahagow: Abbeygreen	231	16	–	109,890	52,549	200
The Douglas Valley Church	345	27	41	55,258	32,041	8

Congregation	Com	Eld	G	In 12	M&M	–18
14. Greenock and Paisley						
Barrhead: Arthurlie	250	30	24	71,767	54,875	95
Barrhead: Bourock	445	40	47	90,145	56,241	248
Barrhead: South and Levern	394	27	–	62,602	49,056	150
Bishopton	673	49	–	89,974	61,494	77
Bridge of Weir: Freeland	404	59	–	129,162	66,881	54
Bridge of Weir: St Machar's Ranfurly	433	–	39	99,570	57,253	–
Elderslie Kirk	511	54	53	116,380	70,250	195
Erskine	324	31	67	89,134	62,073	283
Gourock: Old Gourock and Ashton	–	–	37	–	78,272	–
Gourock: St John's	589	66	16	121,847	63,079	334
Greenock: East End	–	–	–	13,860	3,000	–
Greenock: Lyle Kirk	867	89	30	–	127,291	291
Greenock: Mount Kirk	324	35	–	59,044	44,793	160
Greenock: St Margaret's	158	21	–	35,233	12,986	16
Greenock: St Ninian's	220	19	–	30,830	15,698	141
Greenock: Wellpark Mid Kirk	565	42	18	–	60,314	89
Greenock: Westburn	810	95	41	125,091	83,468	140
Houston and Killellan	674	59	72	149,390	93,333	235
Howwood	195	11	19	48,263	30,130	61
Inchinnan	363	33	28	–	41,027	130
Inverkip	382	29	27	42,036	34,173	19
Skelmorlie and Wemyss Bay	332	41	–	85,498	47,620	12
Johnstone: High	240	31	45	102,188	54,981	106
Johnstone: St Andrew's Trinity	234	29	23	44,484	34,253	109
Johnstone: St Paul's	433	68	–	74,177	51,273	166
Kilbarchan: East	354	41	31	78,311	46,725	70
Kilbarchan: West	414	51	30	91,140	64,460	38
Kilmacolm: Old	492	44	–	121,507	72,822	20
Kilmacolm: St Columba	194	31	–	94,661	62,880	103
Langbank	145	12	–	–	20,980	8
Port Glasgow: St Andrew's	547	62	35	81,708	47,857	396
Linwood	336	23	20	–	41,200	12
Lochwinnoch	147	15	–	33,629	26,606	141
Neilston	513	38	23	126,472	59,638	104
Paisley: Abbey	727	47	–	159,219	96,862	101
Paisley: Glenburn	243	22	–	49,811	29,111	20
Paisley: Lylesland	358	47	27	94,013	52,936	27
Paisley: Martyrs' Sandyford	587	71	20	126,069	61,503	154
Paisley: Oakshaw Trinity	524	68	41	151,096	69,152	41
Paisley: St Columba Foxbar	179	21	21	30,679	21,268	127
Paisley: St James'	210	31	–	57,005	37,095	7
Paisley: St Luke's	235	28	–	–	35,932	7
Paisley: St Mark's Oldhall	503	60	79	110,533	66,546	27
Paisley: St Ninian's Ferguslie	56	–	–	–	3,000	20
Paisley: Sherwood Greenlaw	631	82	40	114,614	77,520	190
Paisley: Stow Brae Kirk	487	71	73	95,269	74,702	83
Paisley: Wallneuk North	415	–	–	–	48,380	–
Port Glasgow: Hamilton Bardrainney	196	18	20	45,964	26,308	27
Port Glasgow: St Martin's	173	16	–	–	12,204	22

Congregation	Com	Eld	G	In 12	M&M	–18
Renfrew: North	691	67	29	102,458	70,241	192
Renfrew: Old	–	–	–	56,923	46,705	–
Renfrew: Trinity	301	29	38	86,910	55,381	248

16. Glasgow

Banton	72	12	–	14,637	8,703	10
Twechar	69	13	–	19,835	8,421	12
Bishopbriggs: Kenmure	284	27	55	86,198	58,025	146
Bishopbriggs: Springfield Cambridge	668	47	94	120,132	66,915	170
Broom	598	55	35	133,734	90,468	350
Burnside Blairbeth	639	49	96	272,562	151,216	204
Busby	253	37	30	81,232	43,324	83
Cadder	794	89	54	150,117	89,345	177
Cambuslang: Flemington Hallside	309	13	14	61,542	26,497	80
Cambuslang Parish Church	747	59	48	135,221	96,157	277
Campsie	158	16	15	39,944	34,317	68
Chryston	638	33	18	–	109,948	108
Eaglesham	570	45	67	152,182	74,439	200
Fernhill and Cathkin	271	24	36	55,486	33,070	91
Gartcosh	138	10	–	21,425	9,396	–
Glenboig	114	10	12	–	7,894	15
Giffnock: Orchardhill	445	47	21	141,791	88,833	310
Giffnock: South	728	88	57	185,733	106,340	–
Giffnock: The Park	277	28	–	74,016	40,411	100
Greenbank	918	78	47	213,474	122,987	230
Kilsyth: Anderson	329	19	52	70,913	54,178	115
Kilsyth: Burns and Old	410	29	50	63,961	50,077	89
Kirkintilloch: Hillhead	112	8	14	15,797	8,341	31
Kirkintilloch: St Columba's	463	38	40	90,368	55,805	11
Kirkintilloch: St David's Memorial Park	627	46	33	–	84,977	138
Kirkintilloch: St Mary's	735	46	50	127,211	83,414	–
Lenzie: Old	459	44	–	115,594	69,796	22
Lenzie: Union	680	68	80	181,150	99,904	258
Maxwell Mearns Castle	302	29	–	166,868	92,651	67
Mearns	859	52	–	–	121,258	33
Milton of Campsie	349	38	55	67,678	44,880	121
Netherlee	721	67	30	208,926	115,123	320
Newton Mearns	456	50	20	120,766	74,462	120
Rutherglen: Old	324	29	–	69,009	37,120	29
Rutherglen: Stonelaw	351	38	32	142,910	78,545	38
Rutherglen: West and Wardlawhill	487	54	52	88,923	66,169	29
Stamperland	368	29	24	70,317	41,668	199
Stepps	333	27	–	–	31,989	150
Thornliebank	113	8	39	41,415	32,407	5
Torrance	311	14	–	91,873	51,585	152
Williamwood	433	67	37	115,814	78,874	602
Glasgow: Anderston Kelvingrove	60	9	14	–	18,745	6
Glasgow: Baillieston Mure Memorial	461	27	86	90,184	51,333	176
Glasgow: Baillieston St Andrew's	280	17	40	–	39,059	142
Glasgow: Balshagray Victoria Park	203	36	23	94,878	62,932	48

Congregation	Com	Eld	G	In 12	M&M	–18
Glasgow: Barlanark Greyfriars	93	23	15	47,507	25,800	253
Glasgow: Blawarthill	178	30	27	28,130	17,533	103
Glasgow: Bridgeton St Francis in the East	85	16	11	36,561	22,980	3
Glasgow: Broomhill	444	59	56	–	84,256	212
Glasgow: Calton Parkhead	87	12	–	18,805	10,558	85
Glasgow: Cardonald	398	38	71	114,325	75,642	231
Glasgow: Carmunnock	311	27	28	49,911	35,883	13
Glasgow: Carmyle	96	5	16	22,527	15,691	21
Glasgow: Kenmuir Mount Vernon	133	11	24	49,517	34,117	68
Glasgow: Carnwadric	148	16	–	40,106	20,636	39
Glasgow: Castlemilk	214	26	7	39,230	27,888	18
Glasgow: Cathcart Old	272	51	44	102,344	61,361	424
Glasgow: Cathcart Trinity	461	52	56	–	111,516	127
Glasgow: Cathedral (High or St Mungo's)	404	54	–	97,068	65,143	10
Glasgow: Clincarthill	275	35	45	106,856	75,062	128
Glasgow: Colston Milton	66	8	–	31,086	16,853	14
Glasgow: Colston Wellpark	107	14	–	–	20,957	69
Glasgow: Cranhill	45	8	–	–	3,903	56
Glasgow: Croftfoot	274	44	43	79,483	45,792	70
Glasgow: Dennistoun New	299	37	26	82,511	61,613	90
Glasgow: Drumchapel St Andrew's	200	43	–	43,690	41,474	17
Glasgow: Drumchapel St Mark's	69	7	–	15,431	1,977	30
Glasgow: Easterhouse St George's and St Peter's	57	9	–	8,042	1,200	40
Glasgow: Eastwood	238	49	40	88,897	54,405	73
Glasgow: Gairbraid	135	14	17	37,462	21,673	11
Glasgow: Gallowgate	71	17	–	31,552	8,260	7
Glasgow: Gardner Street	–	–	–	–	–	–
Glasgow: Garthamlock and Craigend East	88	14	–	–	3,332	85
Glasgow: Gorbals	90	12	–	30,802	16,492	26
Glasgow: Govan and Linthouse	229	48	43	–	39,104	200
Glasgow: Govanhill Trinity	84	19	–	27,478	18,633	6
Glasgow: High Carntyne	288	24	56	56,799	42,158	131
Glasgow: Hillington Park	291	34	35	72,029	41,221	128
Glasgow: Househillwood St Christopher's	120	10	–	11,824	7,536	35
Glasgow: Hyndland	244	34	27	93,129	55,170	28
Glasgow: Ibrox	136	21	23	53,762	33,908	94
Glasgow: John Ross Memorial (for Deaf People)	57	4	–	–	–	–
Glasgow: Jordanhill	413	68	28	187,900	106,062	160
Glasgow: Kelvin Stevenson Memorial	140	23	15	35,608	31,612	95
Glasgow: Kelvinside Hillhead	162	29	–	–	48,419	98
Glasgow: King's Park	661	80	50	152,464	90,210	105
Glasgow: Kinning Park	138	13	–	34,487	20,041	9
Glasgow: Knightswood St Margaret's	236	29	34	–	34,759	17
Glasgow: Langside	207	43	19	84,933	48,661	170
Glasgow: Lansdowne	84	14	–	9,614	7,216	5
Glasgow: Lochwood	68	2	7	–	7,165	109
Glasgow: Maryhill	173	15	15	42,777	23,493	123
Glasgow: Merrylea	324	65	35	78,506	52,239	120
Glasgow: Mosspark	135	27	39	55,362	34,085	60
Glasgow: Newlands South	514	68	24	159,007	98,017	22

Congregation	Com	Eld	G	In 12	M&M	–18
Glasgow: Partick South	147	25	–	57,036	35,685	35
Glasgow: Partick Trinity	171	23	–	86,446	40,910	–
Glasgow: Penilee St Andrew's	120	21	–	–	25,161	125
Glasgow: Pollokshaws	126	21	–	40,498	29,619	28
Glasgow: Pollokshields	199	32	36	90,690	65,242	24
Glasgow: Possilpark	160	25	15	29,701	16,890	20
Glasgow: Priesthill and Nitshill	115	16	–	33,995	19,954	17
Glasgow: Queen's Park	196	27	33	104,908	53,159	18
Glasgow: Renfield St Stephen's	146	22	32	–	47,585	16
Glasgow: Robroyston	39	–	–	32,839	1,300	7
Glasgow: Ruchazie	28	6	–	6,208	4,737	141
Glasgow: Ruchill Kelvinside	89	18	–	53,975	56,414	15
Glasgow: St Andrew's East	72	15	22	38,285	20,564	44
Glasgow: St Columba	135	14	13	50,312	16,356	12
Glasgow: St David's Knightswood	315	29	49	88,134	57,492	25
Glasgow: St Enoch's Hogganfield	152	16	30	40,169	20,491	6
Glasgow: St George's Tron	380	–	–	–	102,824	–
Glasgow: St James' (Pollok)	152	25	21	48,706	35,680	86
Glasgow: St John's Renfield	350	44	–	145,961	95,230	167
Glasgow: St Margaret's Tollcross Park	132	5	–	–	13,808	12
Glasgow: St Nicholas' Cardonald	281	27	12	53,756	37,387	356
Glasgow: St Paul's	62	6	–	–	4,819	157
Glasgow: St Rollox	76	11	–	39,917	19,480	28
Glasgow: Sandyford Henderson Memorial	247	26	16	186,528	91,125	20
Glasgow: Sandyhills	310	29	50	–	44,417	43
Glasgow: Scotstoun	184	8	–	60,113	42,784	25
Glasgow: Shawlands	269	20	35	85,026	59,320	67
Glasgow: Sherbrooke St Gilbert's	248	44	–	141,235	78,302	137
Glasgow: Shettleston New	241	35	30	79,399	48,893	93
Glasgow: Shettleston Old	226	31	18	56,201	28,107	93
Glasgow: South Carntyne	59	7	–	–	19,261	41
Glasgow: South Shawlands	173	27	–	67,459	46,622	127
Glasgow: Springburn	222	33	29	55,562	45,495	125
Glasgow: Temple Anniesland	312	28	70	96,551	57,290	94
Glasgow: Toryglen	96	12	–	17,510	13,327	4
Glasgow: Trinity Possil and Henry Drummond	76	8	–	–	36,210	4
Glasgow: Tron St Mary's	120	18	–	45,714	28,240	70
Glasgow: Victoria Tollcross	124	–	23	–	16,430	–
Glasgow: Wallacewell	126	–	–	–	–	–
Glasgow: Wellington	233	24	–	81,337	63,749	20
Glasgow: Whiteinch	58	5	–	45,140	30,000	99
Glasgow: Yoker	97	10	–	23,749	17,581	8

17. Hamilton

Airdrie: Broomknoll	248	32	29	67,260	31,357	100
Calderbank	116	9	18	23,291	13,435	4
Airdrie: Clarkston	364	36	25	67,997	35,295	98
Airdrie: Flowerhill	592	37	20	119,923	78,178	132
Airdrie: High	322	34	–	67,197	40,851	160
Airdrie: Jackson	334	51	20	84,630	42,753	203

Congregation	Com	Eld	G	In 12	M&M	–18
Airdrie: New Monkland	296	30	18	57,805	29,691	137
Greengairs	132	9	–	23,547	14,736	12
Airdrie: St Columba's	236	6	–	–	10,287	53
Airdrie: The New Wellwynd	723	79	–	142,511	75,436	69
Bargeddie	110	8	–	–	37,996	12
Bellshill: Macdonald Memorial	249	20	20	47,713	26,723	10
Bellshill: Orbiston	190	18	12	12,364	8,654	7
Bellshill: West	535	49	29	81,074	44,666	27
Blantyre: Livingstone Memorial	247	24	20	50,960	35,151	160
Blantyre: Old	270	19	–	53,984	37,479	20
Blantyre: St Andrew's	237	23	26	58,502	38,301	50
Bothwell	484	50	43	–	66,592	147
Caldercruix and Longriggend	217	12	–	51,971	29,573	67
Chapelhall	234	25	43	43,139	30,125	110
Chapelton	170	17	22	32,890	11,178	25
Strathaven: Rankin	548	62	32	82,401	50,223	145
Cleland	186	18	–	33,003	16,984	–
Coatbridge: Blairhill Dundyvan	282	24	22	58,955	40,172	146
Coatbridge: Calder	341	–	36	–	36,312	–
Coatbridge: Old Monkland	294	24	21	–	34,148	75
Coatbridge: Middle	355	38	38	66,239	31,282	192
Coatbridge: New St Andrew's	763	75	24	110,317	77,379	242
Coatbridge: Townhead	160	15	30	46,346	29,630	119
Dalserf	223	22	30	–	56,197	82
East Kilbride: Claremont	612	60	–	–	63,946	308
East Kilbride: Greenhills	172	15	35	28,528	18,620	18
East Kilbride: Moncreiff	684	72	55	114,052	70,720	245
East Kilbride: Mossneuk	263	17	–	31,229	25,332	180
East Kilbride: Old	710	66	41	–	64,387	123
East Kilbride: South	319	37	30	79,268	54,766	15
East Kilbride: Stewartfield	–	–	–	15,393	3,000	–
East Kilbride: West	402	34	53	63,546	43,922	150
East Kilbride: Westwood	560	43	–	79,717	50,496	214
Glasford	128	8	21	20,487	12,858	–
Strathaven: East	307	36	39	65,383	31,187	38
Hamilton: Burnbank	74	9	–	24,444	16,669	8
Hamilton: North	75	29	–	34,424	23,203	7
Hamilton: Cadzow	468	62	56	123,816	71,005	165
Hamilton: Gilmour and Whitehill	136	26	–	39,148	21,750	116
Hamilton: Hillhouse	376	49	31	89,709	43,906	45
Hamilton: Old	461	60	21	–	76,753	78
Hamilton: St Andrew's	193	31	–	56,791	38,496	131
Hamilton: St John's	512	55	56	111,196	72,372	250
Hamilton: South	229	29	26	60,402	33,686	25
Quarter	106	16	18	24,125	15,021	19
Hamilton: Trinity	299	25	–	55,425	28,251	115
Hamilton: West	276	28	–	68,417	47,985	21
Holytown	185	20	28	47,143	28,063	73
New Stevenston: Wrangholm Kirk	102	10	19	34,867	25,130	43
Kirk o' Shotts	169	11	9	28,682	21,279	20

Congregation	Com	Eld	G	In 12	M&M	–18
Larkhall: Chalmers	116	14	30	33,356	18,105	10
Larkhall: St Machan's	452	49	42	100,067	64,789	105
Larkhall: Trinity	187	22	28	47,882	27,812	167
Motherwell: Crosshill	442	59	61	87,308	51,158	87
Motherwell: St Margaret's	359	19	20	40,348	25,421	230
Motherwell: Dalziel St Andrew's	528	73	41	131,531	80,848	200
Motherwell: North	205	21	–	46,293	34,408	135
Motherwell: St Mary's	822	97	66	133,264	72,256	239
Motherwell: South	422	57	97	111,135	66,746	305
Newarthill and Carfin	426	27	21	57,230	42,179	–
Newmains: Bonkle	146	–	–	35,598	24,266	–
Newmains: Coltness Memorial	211	26	18	–	42,865	79
Overtown	278	32	52	46,741	30,110	160
Shotts: Calderhead Erskine	471	34	28	86,154	51,585	28
Stonehouse: St Ninian's	355	38	38	85,852	47,592	40
Strathaven: Avendale Old and Drumclog	766	66	55	114,242	79,867	50
Uddingston: Burnhead	259	21	10	48,254	22,388	92
Uddingston: Old	603	70	50	117,070	76,766	36
Uddingston: Viewpark	445	54	38	94,197	56,256	250
Wishaw: Cambusnethan North	477	32	–	72,946	51,433	130
Wishaw: Cambusnethan Old and Morningside	443	37	25	80,023	44,721	214
Wishaw: Craigneuk and Belhaven	159	28	26	53,673	31,167	25
Wishaw: Old	232	29	–	43,651	31,205	70
Wishaw: St Mark's	345	34	46	70,782	49,607	115
Wishaw: South Wishaw	481	37	38	88,048	60,097	118

18. Dumbarton

Congregation	Com	Eld	G	In 12	M&M	–18
Alexandria	306	37	23	78,077	47,411	36
Arrochar	66	10	17	23,897	11,600	52
Luss	107	15	18	50,929	35,669	32
Baldernock	185	19	–	39,865	24,666	9
Bearsden: Baljaffray	364	31	60	80,159	40,616	80
Bearsden: Cross	855	107	38	192,379	116,379	72
Bearsden: Killermont	646	60	68	153,944	90,370	215
Bearsden: New Kilpatrick	1,533	128	129	292,798	160,348	168
Bearsden: Westerton Fairlie Memorial	389	46	38	98,520	49,902	52
Bonhill	836	67	–	77,057	47,312	82
Renton: Trinity	255	19	–	33,289	19,263	2
Cardross	403	36	27	105,299	56,623	15
Clydebank: Abbotsford	283	16	–	44,218	35,069	43
Dalmuir: Barclay	214	16	18	47,472	28,102	16
Clydebank: Faifley	188	16	34	45,623	23,333	30
Clydebank: Kilbowie St Andrew's	275	27	18	50,958	31,029	105
Clydebank: Radnor Park	173	23	35	46,822	33,161	–
Clydebank: St Cuthbert's	120	13	23	–	13,350	6
Duntocher	245	32	36	39,889	33,228	2
Craigrownie	188	18	28	38,126	28,798	16
Rosneath: St Modan's	135	11	28	25,643	16,831	1
Dumbarton: Riverside	526	62	62	126,193	62,798	256
Dumbarton: St Andrew's	121	22	–	36,104	20,007	2

Congregation	Com	Eld	G	In 12	M&M	–18
Old Kilpatrick Bowling	251	28	22	52,785	37,057	98
Dumbarton: West Kirk	291	37	38	–	27,830	6
Garelochhead	174	14	–	67,134	36,665	47
Helensburgh: Park	369	35	13	66,851	48,952	5
Helensburgh: St Andrew's Kirk	988	111	46	240,661	129,203	29
Jamestown	352	23	21	–	32,396	6
Kilmaronock Gartocharn	215	12	–	29,678	17,518	8
Milngavie: Cairns	501	40	–	129,256	80,118	14
Milngavie: St Luke's	385	39	28	81,981	43,494	42
Milngavie: St Paul's	968	–	84	220,279	119,326	–
Rhu and Shandon	274	22	34	67,983	49,662	15

19. Argyll

Appin	99	14	21	18,381	10,366	12
Lismore	53	–	15	13,887	6,767	–
Ardchattan	121	–	9	23,326	12,775	–
Ardrishaig	148	22	27	34,524	22,645	14
South Knapdale	34	6	–	9,444	3,121	1
Campbeltown: Highland	415	37	21	57,031	38,261	9
Campbeltown: Lorne and Lowland	838	60	38	98,094	54,374	129
Coll	15	3	–	3,679	809	–
Connel	126	22	10	49,720	27,583	5
Colonsay and Oronsay	14	2	–	–	4,588	–
Craignish	50	5	–	–	4,626	–
Kilbrandon and Kilchattan	98	16	–	–	13,838	19
Kilninver and Kilmelford	63	7	–	13,902	5,741	12
Cumlodden, Lochfyneside and Lochgair	94	–	16	22,546	12,146	–
Dunoon: St John's	184	21	45	42,705	32,788	9
Kirn	294	30	–	58,419	48,193	25
Sandbank	114	10	–	11,225	12,407	3
Dunoon: The High Kirk	347	–	43	–	37,414	–
Innellan	86	12	–	21,519	14,129	11
Toward	96	11	–	18,759	11,691	14
Gigha and Cara	33	6	–	9,048	4,963	10
Glassary, Kilmartin and Ford	99	13	–	18,837	16,818	14
North Knapdale	52	6	–	26,420	24,969	1
Glenaray and Inveraray	108	20	–	24,315	15,902	6
Glenorchy and Innishael	67	–	–	16,354	3,933	–
Strathfillan	43	–	–	13,152	4,386	–
Iona	17	7	–	4,973	883	3
Kilfinichen and Kilvickeon and the Ross of Mull	30	6	–	7,217	4,851	15
Jura	28	6	–	9,202	6,140	–
Kilarrow	50	14	–	31,458	22,442	6
Kildalton and Oa	110	–	–	42,904	21,841	–
Kilcalmonell	49	–	14	10,085	3,509	–
Killean and Kilchenzie	156	14	21	18,771	18,324	14
Kilchoman	88	–	–	14,305	17,662	–
Kilmeny	32	5	–	–	4,871	–
Portnahaven	24	–	11	–	2,118	–
Kilchrenan and Dalavich	25	–	7	11,295	8,179	–

Congregation	Com	Eld	G	In 12	M&M	–18
Muckairn	144	19	10	34,649	14,092	12
Kilfinan	29	4	–	6,598	2,121	–
Kilmodan and Colintraive	83	10	–	19,139	11,408	10
Kyles	116	18	24	29,387	16,978	10
Kilmore and Oban	558	–	41	–	59,302	–
Kilmun (St Munn's)	86	8	21	19,000	10,166	–
Strone and Ardentinny	115	10	16	30,076	19,077	5
Kilninian and Kilmore	27	4	–	10,837	6,547	–
Salen and Ulva	35	5	–	12,766	5,336	31
Tobermory	60	11	–	35,667	11,643	–
Torosay and Kinlochspelvie	24	4	–	7,554	2,520	1
Lochgilphead	215	19	21	34,545	18,568	25
Lochgoilhead and Kilmorich	64	10	–	21,365	20,981	2
Strachur and Strachlachlan	95	16	20	29,105	26,561	8
Rothesay: Trinity	396	37	28	69,865	40,773	72
Saddell and Carradale	196	14	23	35,028	19,576	10
Southend	239	12	16	30,975	20,328	7
Skipness	25	3	–	6,075	3,398	–
Tarbert, Loch Fyne and Kilberry	150	19	18	–	22,775	4
The United Church of Bute	562	78	50	69,587	45,519	43
Tiree	87	13	20	25,616	13,996	4
22. Falkirk						
Airth	155	6	18	–	26,577	30
Blackbraes and Shieldhill	171	17	17	30,393	16,926	14
Muiravonside	198	26	–	–	25,487	7
Bo'ness: Old	404	–	13	60,194	42,364	–
Bo'ness: St Andrew's	515	–	–	88,252	52,654	–
Bonnybridge: St Helen's	349	17	–	63,875	35,738	20
Bothkennar and Carronshore	233	25	–	29,960	21,110	14
Brightons	659	38	57	–	84,402	230
Carriden	463	41	23	52,640	32,657	19
Cumbernauld: Abronhill	232	26	37	62,168	43,990	130
Cumbernauld: Condorrat	417	31	37	71,562	46,632	104
Cumbernauld: Kildrum	305	41	–	57,610	36,679	197
Cumbernauld: Old	364	43	–	60,299	54,267	107
Cumbernauld: St Mungo's	244	35	–	41,820	30,240	26
Denny: Old	385	47	30	–	46,285	100
Denny: Westpark	523	33	40	102,204	58,388	120
Dunipace	372	32	14	–	38,976	66
Falkirk: Bainsford	206	12	–	40,629	22,852	80
Falkirk: Camelon	336	–	25	–	56,666	–
Falkirk: Erskine	364	43	–	75,618	48,412	35
Falkirk: Grahamston United	366	–	38	58,930	41,720	–
Falkirk: Laurieston	222	21	29	40,618	24,184	20
Redding and Westquarter	161	13	23	30,248	17,766	9
Falkirk: Old and St Modan's	497	56	7	116,078	65,972	90
Falkirk: St Andrew's West	472	31	–	85,838	69,073	58
Falkirk: St James'	241	25	–	34,964	21,786	55
Grangemouth: Abbotsgrange	516	50	27	67,786	42,445	98

Congregation	Com	Eld	G	In 12	M&M	–18
Grangemouth: Kirk of the Holy Rood	471	–	–	60,502	42,412	–
Grangemouth: Zetland	791	72	70	113,189	74,256	197
Haggs	267	28	15	39,414	24,495	72
Larbert: East	664	51	50	114,411	67,003	267
Larbert: Old	467	–	–	100,523	59,855	–
Larbert: West	408	41	37	77,188	50,862	115
Polmont: Old	402	–	50	–	56,840	–
Slamannan	220	–	–	23,909	22,022	–
Stenhouse and Carron	395	36	20	–	49,058	15

23. Stirling

Congregation	Com	Eld	G	In 12	M&M	–18
Aberfoyle	112	10	20	22,183	15,641	11
Port of Menteith	57	8	–	16,268	6,124	1
Alloa: Ludgate	320	23	25	76,612	55,368	12
Alloa: St Mungo's	382	45	56	79,675	43,903	18
Alva	522	56	28	79,613	45,356	60
Balfron	146	19	22	–	34,791	20
Fintry	122	10	18	18,747	13,651	9
Balquhidder	71	2	–	13,831	14,575	4
Killin and Ardeonaig	110	6	9	19,826	15,583	10
Bannockburn: Allan	398	33	–	58,638	38,949	25
Bannockburn: Ladywell	410	22	–	–	17,797	10
Bridge of Allan	751	56	46	131,688	81,891	80
Buchanan	95	8	–	28,018	13,516	9
Drymen	266	21	–	70,547	35,373	42
Buchlyvie	216	14	15	32,829	18,980	6
Gartmore	65	11	–	17,708	13,925	–
Callander	589	28	40	116,620	75,308	40
Cambusbarron: The Bruce Memorial	333	17	–	56,106	28,554	65
Clackmannan	425	31	40	–	45,554	32
Cowie and Plean	198	10	6	23,390	14,504	–
Fallin	243	8	–	–	19,187	65
Dollar	408	33	57	98,873	57,492	14
Glendevon	44	3	–	5,736	2,751	–
Muckhart	116	8	–	23,078	10,366	14
Dunblane: Cathedral	881	80	58	219,688	124,769	360
Dunblane: St Blane's	356	40	37	104,463	59,465	35
Gargunnock	153	14	–	21,142	17,757	19
Kilmadock	98	10	–	12,414	8,827	4
Kincardine-in-Menteith	81	7	–	17,406	8,385	14
Killearn	417	28	40	90,996	58,697	121
Kippen	234	18	21	31,660	24,434	–
Norrieston	119	11	13	19,522	13,868	1
Lecropt	172	16	–	47,941	28,293	28
Logie	543	57	34	92,371	58,338	34
Menstrie	385	22	25	–	42,165	12
Sauchie and Coalsnaughton	633	30	10	58,144	39,774	–
Stirling: Allan Park South	190	29	–	43,522	29,518	38
Stirling: Church of the Holy Rude	188	24	–	–	31,583	8
Stirling: Viewfield Erskine	330	21	30	42,022	31,563	16

Congregation	Com	Eld	G	In 12	M&M	–18
Stirling: North	372	32	24	93,949	46,585	72
Stirling: St Columba's	509	68	–	114,220	61,172	12
Stirling: St Mark's	207	8	–	32,439	19,842	77
Stirling: St Ninian's Old	741	61	–	92,384	49,159	51
Strathblane	198	18	43	77,407	49,818	34
Tillicoultry	716	62	39	90,509	59,610	101
Tullibody: St Serf's	402	17	24	–	37,686	60
24. Dunfermline						
Aberdour: St Fillan's	401	24	–	69,758	50,462	67
Beath and Cowdenbeath: North	222	21	15	52,986	33,010	47
Cairneyhill	117	21	–	28,305	14,592	12
Limekilns	278	50	–	–	44,136	14
Carnock and Oakley	191	18	20	58,358	33,288	39
Cowdenbeath: Trinity	343	27	20	63,950	39,684	60
Culross and Torryburn	235	18	–	53,889	31,087	24
Dalgety	541	36	25	109,390	70,942	85
Dunfermline: Abbey	690	73	–	135,452	83,186	160
Dunfermline: Gillespie Memorial	273	64	21	84,000	63,506	33
Dunfermline: North	186	12	–	41,463	23,581	7
Dunfermline: St Andrew's Erskine	197	26	18	50,023	29,774	24
Dunfermline: St Leonard's	353	28	30	63,397	44,177	32
Dunfermline: St Margaret's	256	51	19	71,792	37,745	57
Dunfermline: St Ninian's	201	26	31	–	24,691	86
Dunfermline: St Paul's East	–	–	–	21,003	2,000	60
Dunfermline: Townhill and Kingseat	349	28	30	66,395	41,121	24
Inverkeithing	330	35	–	58,702	40,797	103
North Queensferry	62	7	–	18,437	10,573	16
Kelty	296	25	41	58,768	49,410	14
Lochgelly and Benarty: St Serf's	429	46	–	60,199	42,972	32
Rosyth	253	31	–	40,394	20,687	20
Saline and Blairingone	157	13	15	40,612	28,981	28
Tulliallan and Kincardine	433	21	38	53,503	33,904	8
25. Kirkcaldy						
Auchterderran St Fothad's	255	20	11	38,949	30,284	19
Kinglassie	155	13	–	–	13,356	9
Auchtertool	70	7	–	9,647	4,375	5
Kirkcaldy: Linktown	275	34	37	57,095	39,400	24
Buckhaven and Wemyss	269	33	26	52,342	31,130	8
Burntisland	333	35	18	56,937	44,070	14
Dysart: St Clair	525	34	16	75,052	52,413	16
Glenrothes: Christ's Kirk	230	19	41	48,432	30,907	12
Glenrothes: St Columba's	496	32	7	57,775	36,184	27
Glenrothes: St Margaret's	314	31	37	63,075	39,442	66
Glenrothes: St Ninian's	263	40	13	68,451	41,530	22
Kennoway, Windygates and Balgonie: St Kenneth's	662	45	67	–	53,873	32
Kinghorn	377	19	–	70,568	49,022	55
Kirkcaldy: Abbotshall	529	45	–	75,187	50,821	8
Kirkcaldy: Bennochy	502	48	59	93,020	71,672	6

Congregation	Com	Eld	G	In 12	M&M	–18
Kirkcaldy: Pathhead	368	35	37	71,114	53,716	115
Kirkcaldy: St Bryce Kirk	430	27	37	87,586	69,044	66
Kirkcaldy: Templehall	198	22	17	37,831	29,108	11
Kirkcaldy: Torbain	235	29	16	44,520	25,787	94
Thornton	155	8	–	17,418	13,119	7
Leslie: Trinity	209	20	19	32,469	22,378	5
Leven	525	37	33	109,874	68,064	10
Markinch	520	40	23	68,604	54,573	49
Methil: Wellesley	337	25	35	53,061	34,769	127
Methilhill and Denbeath	209	19	36	28,071	21,810	14

26. St Andrews

	Com	Eld	G	In 12	M&M	–18
Abdie and Dunbog	164	18	–	24,699	14,340	21
Newburgh	236	14	–	20,462	14,718	31
Anstruther	220	21	–	44,797	28,832	6
Cellardyke	264	22	41	51,930	29,008	9
Kilrenny	121	14	18	28,680	19,332	16
Auchtermuchty	275	21	20	41,927	20,633	–
Edenshead and Strathmiglo	171	12	–	–	17,246	6
Balmerino	133	14	17	–	16,789	5
Wormit	262	20	34	40,416	20,912	11
Boarhills and Dunino	143	9	–	21,378	14,443	–
Cameron	91	13	13	18,385	12,202	14
St Andrews: St Leonard's	588	46	32	121,478	75,607	38
Carnbee	104	15	19	15,029	12,919	5
Pittenweem	258	16	16	22,102	22,631	14
Ceres, Kemback and Springfield	423	37	26	56,952	73,390	10
Crail	391	34	35	42,835	43,044	51
Kingsbarns	79	8	–	–	11,866	–
Creich, Flisk and Kilmany	112	13	16	20,398	14,165	6
Monimail	104	15	–	24,755	15,188	7
Cupar: Old and St Michael of Tarvit	619	40	29	–	69,643	65
Cupar: St John's and Dairsie United	760	51	42	92,555	65,520	20
Elie Kilconquhar and Colinsburgh	535	42	68	79,600	65,247	14
Falkland	254	17	–	34,753	23,725	7
Freuchie	204	14	12	30,124	15,148	12
Howe of Fife	503	30	–	51,746	37,690	39
Largo and Newburn	268	20	–	54,793	28,713	10
Largo: St David's	148	18	33	32,964	20,924	2
Largoward	81	6	–	10,274	4,961	10
St Monans	278	13	46	–	39,021	–
Leuchars: St Athernase	344	29	36	57,790	41,077	15
Newport-on-Tay	389	43	–	70,981	46,686	64
St Andrews: Holy Trinity	485	39	54	133,816	65,161	53
St Andrews: Hope Park and Martyrs'	670	59	40	129,715	83,210	–
Strathkinness	101	11	–	20,562	11,988	–
Tayport	375	28	27	51,956	33,087	9

27. Dunkeld and Meigle

	Com	Eld	G	In 12	M&M	–18
Aberfeldy	204	14	15	–	29,781	238

Congregation	Com	Eld	G	In 12	M&M	–18
Amulree and Strathbraan	21	3	–	–	2,805	–
Dull and Weem	104	10	18	20,265	14,317	11
Alyth	710	32	26	71,411	47,782	19
Ardler, Kettins and Meigle	413	24	48	46,054	36,736	15
Bendochy	89	12	–	25,020	13,699	2
Coupar Angus: Abbey	298	20	–	43,093	24,586	96
Blair Atholl and Struan	141	15	9	18,910	21,117	–
Tenandry	54	11	–	21,474	14,257	5
Blairgowrie	913	55	42	115,496	67,100	43
Braes of Rannoch	30	6	–	15,344	8,581	–
Foss and Rannoch	92	11	13	18,735	14,258	–
Caputh and Clunie	163	16	18	21,892	18,854	–
Kinclaven	153	15	18	23,854	13,502	–
Dunkeld	386	27	13	–	61,218	40
Fortingall and Glenlyon	49	9	–	15,557	14,407	12
Kenmore and Lawers	81	8	14	31,297	24,013	15
Grantully, Logierait and Strathtay	141	9	10	34,074	28,618	8
Kirkmichael, Straloch and Glenshee	108	5	–	14,740	11,486	7
Rattray	365	16	28	30,995	20,647	2
Pitlochry	409	32	20	82,609	52,214	56
28. Perth						
Abernethy and Dron and Arngask	316	26	–	34,679	40,065	10
Almondbank Tibbermore	289	20	38	–	26,360	8
Methven and Logiealmond	295	20	17	–	21,829	–
Ardoch	172	16	24	23,968	25,162	30
Blackford	109	15	–	25,404	11,644	34
Auchterarder	584	29	39	111,973	53,148	–
Auchtergaven and Moneydie	506	28	35	43,698	30,963	106
Redgorton and Stanley	363	25	33	40,951	29,585	30
Cargill Burrelton	287	11	28	31,319	25,758	4
Collace	117	8	14	14,257	11,922	3
Cleish	225	16	21	49,592	36,594	–
Fossoway: St Serf's and Devonside	248	19	–	47,719	28,063	20
Comrie	439	26	21	138,638	47,705	–
Dundurn	58	9	–	15,388	11,140	–
Crieff	792	46	33	112,225	68,829	100
Dunbarney and Forgandenny	581	33	12	79,005	48,994	20
Errol	289	18	20	38,861	26,359	38
Kilspindie and Rait	66	6	–	9,300	8,645	–
Fowlis Wester, Madderty and Monzie	309	30	12	50,873	29,507	20
Gask	92	10	14	16,872	19,031	2
Kinross	671	38	45	105,124	54,315	159
Muthill	269	24	17	39,088	25,742	15
Trinity Gask and Kinkell	55	4	–	9,202	3,903	–
Orwell and Portmoak	471	36	33	–	46,029	13
Perth: Craigie and Moncrieffe	733	39	33	66,792	48,637	51
Perth: Kinnoull	435	41	23	–	46,543	26
Perth: Letham St Mark's	540	10	24	108,903	57,985	90
Perth: North	1,112	95	25	210,554	107,750	56

Congregation	Com	Eld	G	In 12	M&M	–18
Perth: Riverside	68	5	–	40,139	16,500	18
Perth: St John's Kirk of Perth	505	35	–	96,096	61,534	–
Perth: St Leonard's-in-the-Fields	484	36	–	88,569	61,726	8
Perth: St Matthew's	810	48	22	–	70,331	243
St Madoes and Kinfauns	298	29	24	51,492	25,975	64
St Martins	174	–	25	–	6,069	–
Scone: New	458	–	45	–	39,433	–
Scone: Old	553	–	–	–	41,273	–
The Stewartry of Strathearn	434	30	–	–	54,568	53

29. Dundee

Abernyte	92	10	–	17,451	9,494	14
Inchture and Kinnaird	206	29	–	34,879	17,589	14
Longforgan	190	20	27	–	19,002	12
Auchterhouse	147	15	15	22,892	16,358	16
Monikie and Newbigging and Murroes and Tealing	560	32	22	–	44,342	16
Dundee: Balgay	403	34	21	76,482	52,692	40
Dundee: Barnhill St Margaret's	793	58	58	181,845	81,170	33
Dundee: Broughty Ferry New Kirk	820	60	48	110,023	72,222	26
Dundee: Broughty Ferry St James'	256	9	25	–	36,288	54
Dundee: Broughty Ferry St Luke's and Queen Street	449	50	34	78,927	50,764	29
Dundee: Broughty Ferry St Stephen's and West	333	26	–	49,338	24,335	24
Dundee: Camperdown	149	13	11	–	22,294	10
Dundee: Chalmers Ardler	228	21	38	–	48,712	106
Dundee: Clepington and Fairmuir	351	24	–	57,389	32,397	43
Dundee: Craigiebank	209	12	–	28,377	28,364	110
Dundee: Douglas and Mid Craigie	149	19	16	39,370	19,259	75
Dundee: Downfield Mains	408	34	21	94,658	60,750	29
Dundee: Dundee (St Mary's)	573	53	27	117,007	62,748	14
Dundee: Fintry Parish Church	102	9	–	59,939	32,417	29
Dundee: Lochee	608	34	31	–	45,925	195
Dundee: Logie and St John's Cross	302	16	21	124,083	70,254	46
Dundee: Meadowside St Paul's	515	22	23	69,197	52,469	35
Dundee: Menzieshill	278	15	–	42,365	25,252	130
Dundee: St Andrew's	499	61	30	121,960	56,222	25
Dundee: St David's High Kirk	299	49	33	–	37,217	53
Dundee: Steeple	321	33	–	121,642	77,636	20
Dundee: Stobswell	478	41	–	70,358	48,845	6
Dundee: Strathmartine	297	21	25	52,155	37,256	4
Dundee: Trinity	497	37	35	–	34,095	81
Dundee: West	323	29	28	79,309	50,257	–
Dundee: Whitfield	43	8	–	–	4,662	109
Fowlis and Liff	150	14	15	–	28,966	11
Lundie and Muirhead	317	29	–	46,386	27,176	23
Invergowrie	423	51	47	66,600	40,034	112
Monifieth	1,181	67	47	157,951	82,313	97

30. Angus

Aberlemno	197	10	–	20,260	11,978	15
Guthrie and Rescobie	222	10	12	20,308	13,785	14

Congregation	Com	Eld	G	In 12	M&M	–18
Arbirlot	173	12	–	–	14,990	7
Carmyllie	120	12	5	–	16,778	–
Arbroath: Knox's	319	23	31	43,985	27,841	12
Arbroath: St Vigeans	567	39	28	67,348	44,143	12
Arbroath: Old and Abbey	547	39	33	104,989	69,701	60
Arbroath: St Andrew's	625	64	36	142,886	76,434	120
Arbroath: West Kirk	859	77	44	82,580	57,675	65
Barry	208	13	15	29,404	15,065	4
Carnoustie	392	24	26	72,101	45,089	30
Brechin: Cathedral	759	35	19	–	54,069	40
Brechin: Gardner Memorial	517	23	–	–	36,869	20
Farnell	117	11	–	8,125	9,525	10
Carnoustie: Panbride	714	33	–	67,810	38,281	55
Colliston	182	9	11	20,851	10,409	5
Friockheim Kinnell	153	16	21	18,587	11,131	2
Inverkeilor and Lunan	141	8	22	22,823	16,029	11
Dun and Hillside	429	49	40	63,011	38,970	35
Dunnichen, Letham and Kirkden	293	17	25	37,056	29,343	5
Eassie, Nevay and Newtyle	305	16	20	23,710	22,707	15
Edzell Lethnot Glenesk	340	26	30	47,250	35,315	30
Fern Careston Menmuir	100	7	–	13,958	13,804	5
Forfar: East and Old	862	60	50	91,874	56,155	44
Forfar: Lowson Memorial	927	38	29	84,819	47,165	114
Forfar: St Margaret's	552	29	18	–	49,323	96
Glamis, Inverarity and Kinettles	397	26	–	43,779	37,027	79
Inchbrayock	198	11	–	33,145	30,437	22
Montrose: Melville South	288	18	–	35,885	21,035	6
Kirriemuir: St Andrew's	320	24	40	–	35,387	12
Oathlaw Tannadice	166	9	–	17,726	17,782	12
Montrose: Old and St Andrew's	763	45	34	92,015	61,968	46
The Glens and Kirriemuir: Old	1,042	67	40	–	90,148	83
The Isla Parishes	253	23	9	36,415	26,225	20

31. Aberdeen

Congregation	Com	Eld	G	In 12	M&M	–18
Aberdeen: Bridge of Don Oldmachar	236	–	–	65,938	48,380	–
Aberdeen: Cove	85	7	–	32,459	4,235	31
Aberdeen: Craigiebuckler	790	75	53	–	69,496	130
Aberdeen: Ferryhill	400	53	27	79,804	56,821	40
Aberdeen: Garthdee	230	12	12	–	17,152	9
Aberdeen: Ruthrieston West	363	34	20	76,104	43,275	10
Aberdeen: Gilcomston South	326	27	–	187,510	111,466	60
Aberdeen: High Hilton	380	24	27	48,519	93,623	130
Aberdeen: Holburn West	445	44	25	108,399	64,563	28
Aberdeen: Mannofield	1,220	123	58	–	109,211	192
Aberdeen: Mastrick	292	19	12	46,682	28,755	7
Aberdeen: Middlefield	114	8	–	13,798	1,760	10
Aberdeen: Midstocket	611	53	43	–	73,489	35
Aberdeen: Northfield	251	12	15	24,716	17,544	80
Aberdeen: Queen Street	522	55	44	–	64,463	67
Aberdeen: Queen's Cross	439	48	26	–	88,441	130

Congregation	Com	Eld	G	In 12	M&M	–18
Aberdeen: Rubislaw	503	72	36	146,900	87,529	108
Aberdeen: St Columba's Bridge of Don	272	16	–	–	57,280	75
Aberdeen: St George's Tillydrone	105	11	13	–	8,609	5
Aberdeen: St John's Church for Deaf People	96	–	–	–	–	–
Aberdeen: St Machar's Cathedral	632	46	–	120,713	75,485	15
Aberdeen: St Mark's	387	39	32	97,759	62,298	25
Aberdeen: St Mary's	445	35	–	62,902	39,036	60
Aberdeen: St Nicholas Kincorth, South of	362	29	28	67,518	35,342	55
Aberdeen: St Nicholas Uniting, Kirk of	399	46	15	–	14,791	8
Aberdeen: St Stephen's	178	21	14	–	41,636	55
Aberdeen: South Holburn	629	51	54	94,496	76,598	53
Aberdeen: Stockethill	85	–	–	26,334	4,000	16
Aberdeen: Summerhill	139	20	–	26,088	19,279	9
Aberdeen: Torry St Fittick's	399	22	19	70,215	31,522	–
Aberdeen: Woodside	289	31	26	46,297	29,094	41
Bucksburn Stoneywood	470	20	9	41,559	30,989	10
Cults	789	69	43	154,823	88,664	25
Dyce	1,110	53	34	–	52,182	267
Kingswells	396	30	24	50,263	32,483	12
Newhills	467	44	53	130,729	72,896	20
Peterculter	636	46	–	112,529	60,889	189

32. Kincardine and Deeside

Congregation	Com	Eld	G	In 12	M&M	–18
Aberluthnott	207	7	12	12,623	12,656	3
Laurencekirk	459	11	32	31,288	23,296	10
Aboyne and Dinnet	332	7	27	50,016	37,107	40
Cromar	236	13	–	–	18,182	–
Arbuthnott, Bervie and Kinneff	–	–	35	73,322	51,769	–
Banchory-Devenick and Maryculter/Cookney	181	16	9	33,649	33,870	5
Banchory-Ternan: East	578	43	30	113,474	64,873	50
Banchory-Ternan: West	585	29	34	118,846	67,321	70
Birse and Feughside	236	20	22	32,384	32,045	15
Braemar and Crathie	222	37	18	66,314	46,946	18
Drumoak-Durris	412	30	28	55,203	50,362	58
Glenmuick (Ballater)	294	22	24	44,042	25,173	–
Mearns Coastal	282	15	20	25,251	22,503	12
Mid Deeside	699	36	25	62,614	52,529	30
Newtonhill	360	11	14	27,557	20,479	80
Portlethen	319	14	–	59,042	47,542	155
Stonehaven: Dunnottar	675	32	26	84,965	50,852	16
Stonehaven: South	278	18	–	52,478	27,145	16
Stonehaven: Fetteresso	810	35	30	183,259	100,505	143
West Mearns	512	18	43	47,990	37,022	19

33. Gordon

Congregation	Com	Eld	G	In 12	M&M	–18
Barthol Chapel	92	11	10	–	3,531	16
Tarves	404	18	38	34,918	22,721	4
Belhelvie	385	36	22	–	52,300	43
Blairdaff and Chapel of Garioch	398	36	15	42,296	30,108	44
Cluny	211	11	7	29,980	15,391	17

Congregation	Com	Eld	G	In 12	M&M	–18
Monymusk	114	5	–	20,894	10,582	13
Culsalmond and Rayne	179	7	–	11,309	8,936	19
Daviot	142	9	–	14,850	11,880	16
Cushnie and Tough	279	16	10	30,008	20,895	15
Echt	245	10	–	16,987	16,330	5
Midmar	151	7	–	12,977	10,383	4
Ellon	1,566	93	–	138,603	96,003	166
Fintray Kinellar Keithhall	197	14	14	28,166	26,016	–
Foveran	327	16	–	54,477	23,065	42
Howe Trinity	593	25	30	41,850	35,452	25
Huntly Cairnie Glass	668	13	–	41,009	32,490	4
Insch-Leslie-Premnay-Oyne	344	30	24	–	27,695	18
Inverurie: St Andrew's	1,033	34	31	128,090	65,918	–
Inverurie: West	704	46	31	86,513	58,946	52
Kemnay	530	207	–	64,443	44,863	148
Kintore	729	44	–	–	71,471	130
Meldrum and Bourtie	461	34	37	62,241	47,554	21
Methlick	353	23	20	51,445	35,805	18
New Machar	453	20	22	54,798	47,263	45
Noth	302	13	–	25,377	20,778	8
Skene	1,348	94	59	146,989	84,257	177
Strathbogie Drumblade	548	38	30	70,563	45,464	51
Udny and Pitmedden	276	26	19	78,706	36,562	88
Upper Donside	400	24	–	37,978	33,240	53

34. Buchan

Congregation	Com	Eld	G	In 12	M&M	–18
Aberdour	113	9	12	10,779	6,859	10
Pitsligo	98	10	–	18,503	8,914	–
Auchaber United	155	14	12	13,821	13,275	10
Auchterless	190	18	17	22,930	14,492	10
Banff	630	29	21	64,780	50,151	146
King Edward	152	15	9	–	13,529	12
Crimond	213	11	–	–	11,472	–
Lonmay	108	12	14	13,757	10,176	46
Cruden	428	27	26	60,393	32,383	9
Deer	746	26	24	56,032	45,972	10
Fordyce	425	18	36	40,018	41,043	–
Fraserburgh: Old	608	60	73	–	75,577	217
Fraserburgh: South	288	20	–	–	25,139	9
Inverallochy and Rathen: East	89	11	–	20,716	5,893	7
Fraserburgh: West	547	46	–	62,677	42,403	159
Rathen: West	105	10	–	12,465	4,394	24
Fyvie	279	20	31	35,552	26,094	–
Rothienorman	134	10	13	14,946	7,240	20
Gardenstown	66	9	30	51,564	33,936	47
Longside	512	28	–	55,091	40,695	97
Macduff	676	33	56	93,023	53,050	151
Marnoch	400	14	16	27,299	24,022	2
Maud and Savoch	207	13	–	21,754	17,961	–
New Deer: St Kane's	371	26	17	53,031	35,100	62

Congregation	Com	Eld	G	In 12	M&M	–18
Monquhitter and New Byth	327	19	11	26,140	20,623	12
Turriff: St Andrew's	553	28	15	52,695	29,121	76
New Pitsligo	290	6	–	24,613	17,750	19
Strichen and Tyrie	539	19	30	47,255	28,856	60
Ordiquhill and Cornhill	138	9	11	11,530	8,170	24
Whitehills	289	20	26	48,015	25,469	3
Peterhead: Old	401	26	28	71,241	40,007	44
Peterhead: St Andrew's	485	37	35	62,612	34,248	33
Peterhead: Trinity	302	21	24	108,048	67,049	1
St Fergus	180	12	14	15,505	6,075	10
Sandhaven	72	6	–	7,460	4,017	55
Turriff: St Ninian's and Forglen	805	29	39	73,584	52,169	41

35. Moray

Congregation	Com	Eld	G	In 12	M&M	–18
Aberlour	317	–	24	58,804	29,307	–
Alves and Burghead	155	–	37	32,915	16,642	–
Kinloss and Findhorn	94	–	13	25,034	13,752	–
Bellie	315	–	31	46,130	36,487	–
Speymouth	205	–	15	20,281	12,547	–
Birnie and Pluscarden	288	–	41	–	23,955	–
Elgin: High	595	–	–	68,997	43,329	–
Buckie: North	439	–	59	56,150	37,911	–
Rathven	97	–	23	18,811	13,440	–
Buckie: South and West	305	–	38	41,385	24,966	–
Enzie	91	–	15	15,426	10,710	–
Cullen and Deskford	364	–	23	47,215	33,602	–
Dallas	60	–	10	11,144	8,138	–
Forres: St Leonard's	242	–	42	44,929	34,681	–
Rafford	78	–	–	14,451	6,368	–
Duffus, Spynie and Hopeman	319	–	16	47,212	29,693	–
Dyke	139	–	8	36,379	12,770	–
Edinkillie	91	–	–	13,381	13,174	–
Elgin: St Giles' and St Columba's South	1,109	–	45	131,527	85,086	–
Findochty	49	–	9	16,326	11,513	–
Portknockie	77	–	19	18,716	15,374	–
Forres: St Laurence	437	–	44	79,668	51,433	–
Keith: North, Newmill, Boharm and Rothiemay	632	–	27	60,803	74,488	–
Keith: St Rufus, Botriphnie and Grange	1,034	–	30	82,659	53,939	–
Knockando, Elchies and Archiestown	252	–	13	46,130	22,301	–
Rothes	318	–	12	43,852	23,148	–
Lossiemouth: St Gerardine's High	381	–	28	45,017	35,486	–
Lossiemouth: St James'	339	–	33	51,742	30,843	–
Mortlach and Cabrach	383	–	15	25,353	22,483	–
St Andrew's-Lhanbryd and Urquhart	479	–	31	66,374	44,340	–

36. Abernethy

Congregation	Com	Eld	G	In 12	M&M	–18
Abernethy	147	23	–	39,496	25,880	79
Cromdale and Advie	83	2	–	14,589	14,980	–
Alvie and Insh	66	7	–	29,585	18,212	34
Rothiemurchus and Aviemore	80	–	–	18,872	10,481	–

Congregation	Com	Eld	G	In 12	M&M	–18
Boat of Garten, Duthil and Kincardine	156	16	34	28,652	21,581	–
Dulnain Bridge	35	–	–	11,599	9,685	–
Grantown-on-Spey	222	18	12	45,731	26,144	18
Kingussie	102	–	–	26,726	17,765	–
Laggan	40	–	–	16,846	9,357	–
Newtonmore: St Bride's	83	14	–	32,057	16,324	30
Tomintoul, Glenlivet and Inveraven	149	11	–	–	19,246	6

37. Inverness

Congregation	Com	Eld	G	In 12	M&M	–18
Ardersier	55	11	–	16,883	10,773	14
Petty	69	10	10	18,904	11,066	5
Auldearn and Dalmore	65	3	–	12,856	9,161	–
Nairn: St Ninian's	219	15	27	49,665	29,744	20
Cawdor	154	18	–	32,073	22,084	7
Croy and Dalcross	55	7	10	15,161	8,790	12
Culloden: The Barn	355	–	27	80,387	49,252	–
Daviot and Dunlichity	59	6	–	16,420	11,231	8
Moy, Dalarossie and Tomatin	33	–	11	11,227	8,864	–
Dores and Boleskine	70	8	–	13,440	13,228	–
Inverness: Crown	571	72	44	–	80,207	135
Inverness: Dalneigh and Bona	258	24	20	90,076	59,418	118
Inverness: East	275	33	–	112,053	74,470	150
Inverness: Hilton	267	13	17	91,404	46,859	59
Inverness: Inshes	213	16	–	136,642	72,460	97
Inverness: Kinmylies	98	9	–	34,547	23,226	65
Inverness: Ness Bank	607	70	36	163,022	67,695	179
Inverness: Old High St Stephen's	435	50	–	121,696	73,731	28
Inverness: St Columba	92	3	–	42,076	1,000	18
Inverness: Trinity	240	32	20	76,282	49,542	50
Kilmorack and Erchless	112	10	18	–	28,529	30
Kiltarlity	54	–	8	19,834	13,876	–
Kirkhill	73	12	14	27,855	8,197	8
Nairn: Old	561	50	21	104,809	67,818	31
Urquhart and Glenmoriston	126	7	–	54,825	35,789	40

38. Lochaber

Congregation	Com	Eld	G	In 12	M&M	–18
Acharacle	40	5	–	17,397	12,174	22
Ardnamurchan	18	5	–	9,936	4,005	9
Ardgour	53	6	16	13,226	9,144	1
Morvern	44	6	9	9,288	7,256	9
Strontian	31	5	–	15,806	3,898	20
Duror	36	6	13	11,367	6,524	5
Glencoe: St Munda's	50	10	12	–	9,034	5
Fort Augustus	72	8	6	21,234	14,314	7
Glengarry	27	5	8	–	8,770	15
Fort William: Duncansburgh MacIntosh	398	34	36	90,840	61,316	70
Kilmonivaig	74	7	12	18,537	19,465	14
Kilmallie	125	12	25	35,814	32,521	13
Kinlochleven	59	8	18	24,267	11,483	22
Nether Lochaber	46	7	–	14,319	11,461	2

Congregation	Com	Eld	G	In 12	M&M	–18
North West Lochaber	99	9	16	25,616	25,716	15

39. Ross

Alness	84	7	–	35,794	20,525	33
Avoch	17	4	–	16,824	9,826	12
Fortrose and Rosemarkie	115	15	–	42,939	26,322	10
Contin	54	12	–	15,751	16,958	–
Fodderty and Strathpeffer	113	15	–	30,701	18,689	28
Cromarty	47	6	–	12,605	2,960	6
Resolis and Urquhart	67	7	–	33,911	18,820	12
Dingwall: Castle Street	138	24	26	55,236	30,340	10
Dingwall: St Clement's	220	29	29	58,889	35,579	18
Fearn Abbey and Nigg	85	10	–	–	20,862	1
Tarbat	57	8	–	14,613	9,571	–
Ferintosh	161	23	17	44,543	30,298	35
Invergordon	155	11	–	52,028	30,922	35
Killearnan	123	17	–	34,856	28,920	6
Knockbain	56	10	–	–	14,158	–
Kilmuir and Logie Easter	73	9	26	28,800	20,404	6
Kiltearn	56	6	–	27,768	17,455	19
Lochbroom and Ullapool	40	5	12	29,385	17,565	12
Rosskeen	130	10	20	59,002	32,712	65
Tain	116	7	20	46,872	39,566	6
Urray and Kilchrist	76	14	15	55,613	25,926	110

40. Sutherland

Altnaharra and Farr	22	2	–	–	8,043	4
Assynt and Stoer	9	1	–	12,766	7,184	4
Clyne	64	11	–	27,913	14,513	2
Kildonan and Loth Helmsdale	33	5	–	15,593	5,488	9
Dornoch Cathedral	327	31	60	111,542	74,496	78
Durness and Kinlochbervie	19	2	–	–	13,131	5
Eddrachillis	11	2	–	16,028	7,806	3
Golspie	79	15	15	42,029	22,871	5
Kincardine Croick and Edderton	49	13	16	22,667	16,776	18
Creich	17	7	–	17,150	14,790	1
Rosehall	20	4	–	11,150	4,795	8
Lairg	49	7	21	–	14,997	4
Rogart	17	3	–	11,762	10,876	1
Melness and Tongue	48	7	–	–	12,135	17

41. Caithness

Bower	36	–	12	13,008	6,353	–
Halkirk Westerdale	57	7	11	14,401	11,113	9
Watten	40	4	–	12,608	7,828	13
Canisbay	45	7	16	–	6,604	17
Dunnet	18	3	7	–	3,922	22
Keiss	25	1	10	9,520	4,226	–
Olrig	51	3	10	7,451	5,271	10

Congregation	Com	Eld	G	In 12	M&M	–18
Thurso: St Peter's and St Andrew's	182	16	31	65,611	39,195	5
The North Coast Parish	53	15	26	22,643	14,482	6
The Parish of Latheron	68	16	19	24,685	17,940	36
Thurso: West	208	27	28	53,147	40,640	19
Wick: Pulteneytown and Thrumster	241	12	28	51,120	31,366	30
Wick: St Fergus	259	42	29	69,473	41,723	5

42. Lochcarron – Skye

Applecross, Lochcarron and Torridon	87	–	21	28,035	27,524	–
Bracadale and Duirinish	70	9	20	32,006	19,241	9
Gairloch and Dundonnell	84	–	–	61,186	46,697	–
Glenelg and Kintail	53	–	–	25,876	22,691	–
Kilmuir and Stenscholl	44	6	–	32,879	29,041	12
Lochalsh	48	5	16	28,273	27,202	9
Portree	84	9	–	60,248	34,505	21
Snizort	41	4	–	32,538	25,283	4
Strath and Sleat	172	9	19	92,380	58,638	40

43. Uist

Barra	46	4	–	23,364	7,059	54
Benbecula	68	11	8	31,519	24,593	40
Berneray and Lochmaddy	50	4	14	34,264	21,818	–
Carinish	70	6	15	44,101	31,451	7
Kilmuir and Paible	25	4	–	30,879	21,924	12
Manish-Scarista	35	4	–	43,509	24,282	8
South Uist	54	11	–	18,242	20,285	27
Tarbert	140	12	–	65,547	52,204	55

44. Lewis

Barvas	83	–	–	79,285	48,696	–
Carloway	50	–	–	33,839	16,778	–
Cross Ness	69	–	–	58,003	30,248	–
Kinloch	46	–	–	36,475	20,659	–
Knock	52	–	–	–	25,741	–
Lochs-Crossbost	26	–	–	23,913	13,272	–
Lochs-in-Bernera	24	–	–	17,002	12,344	–
Uig	30	–	–	27,559	17,525	–
Stornoway: High	250	–	–	118,678	78,797	–
Stornoway: Martin's Memorial	270	–	17	155,384	43,488	–
Stornoway: St Columba	124	–	49	87,644	46,869	–

45. Orkney

Birsay, Harray and Sandwick	329	32	32	34,698	28,561	12
East Mainland	238	20	17	–	24,883	10
Eday	10	1	–	4,670	1,264	4
Stronsay: Moncur Memorial	83	7	–	15,980	8,549	16
Evie	29	4	–	5,860	8,340	–
Firth	94	9	–	–	15,395	40
Rendall	48	3	–	12,483	6,858	23

Congregation	Com	Eld	G	In 12	M&M	–18
Rousay	17	2	–	1,498	3,526	–
Flotta	25	7	–	5,179	1,893	–
Hoy and Walls	55	10	14	5,449	2,365	–
Orphir and Stenness	160	12	14	22,281	16,359	10
Kirkwall: East	394	42	31	65,252	48,147	31
Shapinsay	49	7	–	6,199	4,417	9
Kirkwall: St Magnus Cathedral	560	45	27	–	45,017	–
North Ronaldsay	12	–	–	–	1,410	–
Sanday	74	4	8	12,140	7,022	–
Papa Westray	8	4	–	4,784	2,904	5
Westray	77	17	27	21,818	14,839	35
South Ronaldsay and Burray	142	9	13	18,113	11,199	10
Stromness	323	25	23	45,517	31,777	40

46. Shetland

Burra Isle	37	6	20	8,980	3,805	13
Tingwall	139	17	10	29,636	21,212	–
Delting	78	8	13	19,517	9,648	15
Northmavine	67	9	–	–	6,575	10
Dunrossness and St Ninian's	52	13	–	16,545	12,463	46
Sandwick, Cunningsburgh and Quarff	78	10	6	24,227	15,901	21
Fetlar	17	5	–	1,160	904	–
Unst	116	7	18	19,240	12,456	–
Yell	108	13	16	12,372	9,583	–
Lerwick and Bressay	381	27	9	72,249	49,452	48
Nesting and Lunnasting	34	5	16	5,563	7,388	–
Whalsay and Skerries	191	15	15	29,432	14,612	15
Sandsting and Aithsting	44	9	–	6,028	3,208	23
Walls and Sandness	34	10	–	10,564	3,668	2

47. England

Corby: St Andrew's	264	13	37	54,873	25,904	7
Corby: St Ninian's	199	15	–	36,050	28,989	4
Guernsey: St Andrew's in the Grange	200	21	–	71,406	40,859	22
Jersey: St Columba's	123	17	–	66,794	42,326	21
Liverpool: St Andrew's	35	4	–	23,384	10,998	7
London: Crown Court	249	27	8	–	56,260	12
London: St Columba's	999	56	–	–	157,245	31
Newcastle: St Andrew's	99	19	–	–	5,785	26

INDEX OF ADVERTISERS

INDEX OF MINISTERS

NOTE: Ministers who are members of a Presbytery are designated 'A' if holding a parochial appointment in that Presbytery, or 'B' if otherwise qualifying for membership. 'A-1, A-2' etc. indicate the numerical order of congregations in the Presbyteries of Edinburgh, Glasgow and Hamilton.

Also included are:

(1) Ministers who have resigned their seat in Presbytery (List 6-H)

(2) Ministers who hold a Practising Certificate (List 6-I)

(3) Ministers serving overseas (List 6-K)

(4) Auxiliary Ministers (List 6-A)

(5) Ministers ordained for sixty years and upwards (List 6-Q)

(6) Ministers who have died since the publication of the last *Year Book* (List 6-R)

NB *For a list of the Diaconate, see List 6-G.*

INDEX OF PARISHES AND PLACES

NOTE: Numbers on the right of the column refer to the Presbytery in which the district lies. Names in brackets are given for ease of identification. They may refer to the name of the parish, which may be different from that of the district, or they distinguish places with the same name, or they indicate the first named charge in a union.

INDEX OF SUBJECTS